Mike Ashley is a leading authority on horror, fantasy and science fiction. Since 1974 he has written and edited over thirty books, including *Weird Legacies, Souls in Metal, Mrs Gaskell's Tales of Mystery and Horror, Jewels of Wonder, Best of British SF* (2 vols.), *Who's Who in Horror and Fantasy Fiction*, and *The Mammoth Book of Short Horror Novels, Pendragon Chronicles* and *The Camelot Chronicles*.

He has also contributed widely to fantasy magazines and encyclopedias in Britain and America, including *Amazing Stories, Locus* and *Twilight Zone Magazine*.

# THE MAMMOTH BOOK OF
# HISTORICAL WHODUNNITS

# The Mammoth Book of
# HISTORICAL
# WHODUNNITS

Edited by
Mike Ashley

Robinson
London

Robinson Publishing Ltd
7 Kensington Church Court
London W8 4SP

First published by Robinson Publishing Ltd 1993

Introductory material and this arrangement copyright
© Mike Ashley 1993

ISBN 1-85487-229-X

Typeset by
Hewer Text Composition Services, Edinburgh.

Printed and bound in Great Britain by
Caledonian International Book Manufacturing Ltd, Glasgow

12   13   14   15   16   17   18   19   20

# Contents

# PART IV: HOLMES AND BEYOND

# Acknowledgements

There have been a number of people who have helped me in the compilation of this anthology. First and foremost I must thank Miss Edith Pargeter for kindly providing the foreword, and her own words of encouragement on the project. I must also thank Jack Adrian, a most learned expert on mystery and detective fiction, who suggested a number of stories to me, and provided me with copies of the lesser known ones. Likewise Peter Berresford Ellis who brought several other stories to my attention. My thanks to Michael Williams who provided me with his memories of Wallace Nichols. Finally my thanks to Robert Adey and Richard Dalby, both of whom took the great risk of loaning me copies of particularly rare volumes, and which I hope are now safely restored to them.

Acknowledgements are accorded to the following for the rights to reprint the stories in this anthology.

"Captain Nash and the Wroth Inheritance" © 1975 by Ragan Butler. Originally published by Harwood-Smart Publishing, Lewes. Reprinted by permission of the author.

"The Gentleman from Paris" © 1950 by John Dickson Carr. First appeared in *Ellery Queen's Mystery Magazine*, April 1950. Reprinted by permission of the agents for the author's estate, David Higham Associates (UK).

"Murder Lock'd In" © 1980 by Lillian de la Torre. First appeared in *Ellery Queen's Mystery Magazine*, December 1, 1980. Reprinted by permission of the author's agents, David Higham Associates (UK), and in the US by Harold Ober Associates.

"The Case of the Deptford Horror" © 1954 by Adrian Conan Doyle. Originally published in *The Exploits of Sherlock Holmes* (London: John Murray, 1954). Reprinted by permission of Richard Doyle for the author's estate.

"The Witch's Tale" © 1993 by Margaret Frazer. First printing, used by permission of the authors.

"A Sad and Bloody Hour" © 1965 by Joe Gores. First appeared in

*Ellery Queen's Mystery Magazine*, April 1965. Reprinted by permission of the author.

"The Confession of Brother Athelstan" © 1993 by Paul Harding. First printing, used by permission of the author.

"Murder in the Rue Royale" © 1967 by Michael Harrison. Originally published in *Ellery Queen's Mystery Magazine*, January 1968. Unable to trace the author's representative.

"The Golden Nugget Poker Game" © 1986 by Edward D. Hoch. Originally published in *Ellery Queen's Mystery Magazine*, March 1987.

"Five Rings in Reno" © 1976 by Edward D. Hoch [R. L. Stevens]. Originally published in *Ellery Queen's Mystery Magazine*, July 1976. Reprinted by permission of the author.

"Socrates Solves a Murder" © 1954 by Brèni James. Originally published in *Ellery Queen's Mystery Magazine*, October 1954. Unable to trace the author or the author's representative.

"Leonardo Da Vinci, Detective" © 1958 by Theodore Mathieson. Originally published in *Ellery Queen's Mystery Magazine*, January 1959. Reprinted by permission of the author.

"The Treasury Thefts" © 1950 by Wallace Nichols. Originally published as "The Case of the Empress's Jewels" in the *London Mystery Magazine*, April 1950, and as "The Treasury Thefts" in the *London Mystery Magazine*, June 1950. Unable to trace the author's representative.

"The Locked Tomb Mystery" © 1989 by Elizabeth Peters. First published in *Sisters in Crime*, edited by Marilyn Wallace, New York: Berkley Books, 1989. Reprinted by permission of the author's agent, David Grossman Literary Agency.

"Foreword" © 1993 by Ellis Peters. First printing, used by permission of the author.

"The Price of Light" © 1979 by Ellis Peters. Originally published in *Winter's Crimes 11*, edited by George Hardinge (London, Macmillan, 1979), and in the author's collection *A Rare Benedictine* (London, Headline Book Publishing PLC 1988). Reprinted by permission of the author and the author's publisher, Headline Book Publishing PLC.

"Father Hugh and the Deadly Scythe" © 1990 by Mary Monica

Pulver. Originally printed in *Alfred Hitchcock's Mystery Magazine*, 1990. Reprinted by permission of the author.

"The Christmas Masque" © 1976 by S.S. Rafferty. First appeared in *Ellery Queen's Mystery Magazine*, December 1976. Reprinted by permission of the author.

"A Byzantine Mystery" © 1993 by Mary Reed and Eric Mayer. First printing, used by permission of the author.

"Mightier Than the Sword" © 1993 by John Maddox Roberts. First printing, used by permission of the author.

"The High King's Sword" © 1993 by Peter Tremayne. First printing, used by permission of the authors.

"He Came With the Rain" © 1967 by Robert van Gulik. First published in *Judge Dee at Work* (London: William Heinemann, 1967). Reprinted by permission of Dr. Thomas M. van Gulik.

Every effort has been made to trace the owners of copyright material. The Editor would be pleased to hear from anyone if they believe there has been any inadvertent transgression of copyright, and also from anyone who can help trace the representatives of Michael Harrison, Brèni James and Wallace Nicols.

# Introduction
# THE CHRONICLES
# OF CRIME

This anthology is the first of a kind. It's the first to bring together a selection of stories featuring detectives from the entire history of the civilised world.

Stories about historical detectives are relatively new, though they are not as new as some may feel. To many, the historical detective field burst forth fully fledged with the Brother Cadfael novels of Ellis Peters. There is no doubt that Miss Peters's superbly developed works created a little niche of their own with the medieval mystery story, and that world has grown substantially in the last ten years. But the historical detective story has been around a while longer than that, though until Ellis Peters's creation, it lacked an identity.

So, what do I mean by the historical detective story. Quite simply it's the union of two much older literary fields – the historical fiction field with that of the detective story, but the emphasis has to be on the detective element, otherwise it is nothing more than a historical story containing some element of mystery. For the purposes of this anthology, and to give it some structure, I have been rather stringent in my definition of the historical detective story. Strictly speaking any detective story set in a period earlier than its composition would have to be regarded as historical. But I personally believe that any writer who can draw upon his direct personal memories of the past is still, in his own mind, writing a relatively contemporary work. I have thus been very restrictive and decided that a historical detective story should, at the very least, be set at a period before the author's birth, and to all intents and purposes that really means before the twentieth century.

I've made one exception to that self-imposed rule for a special reason that will be obvious when you encounter it. As you will see from the contents page, the stories I have selected range from as far back as 1400 BC, down through the years to the time of Sherlock Holmes. En route they pass through ancient Greece and Rome, the mystic Orient, the Middle Ages and Elizabethan period, to the Regency and Victorian periods. Over three thousand years of historical detection.

As an afterword I have reprinted a piece on the origins of detective work to show how it really developed. I've also assembled a checklist of novels and stories featuring historical detectives for further reading.

It's perhaps a little surprising that the fields of historical fiction and detective fiction didn't come together earlier than they did, but throughout the nineteenth century they kept to their own separate paths.

The detective story was created almost single-handedly by that tragic American genius Edgar Allan Poe, with his gruesome "The Murders in the Rue Morgue", published in *Graham's Magazine* for April 1841. It introduced the first detective in fiction, C. Auguste Dupin. Poe wrote two more stories featuring Dupin, "The Mystery of Marie Rogêt" (1842) and "The Purloined Letter" (1844). Since the settings for these stories were contemporary for Poe they could not qualify for this anthology, even though the stories are most certainly historic if not historical. However, a hundred-and-twenty years later the author Michael Harrison wrote a new series of stories about Dupin, and these of course do qualify. So I'm delighted to be able to include a story featuring the first ever fictional detective.

Dupin was a master of logical or ratiocinative deduction, a skill brought to the ultimate by the doyen of detection, Sherlock Holmes. Indeed, Dupin was one of a number of influences upon Arthur Conan Doyle in creating Holmes. I find it surprising that Doyle did not create a historical detective because Doyle preferred writing historical fiction and, in later years, came to resent the time he felt obliged to spend on creating new Holmes' stories. Quite why he never put the two together I do not know.

In researching for this anthology I tried to find if Doyle had written any story set in the past featuring someone using detective skills. A few of the Brigadier Gerard stories, set in the Napoleonic period, involve mysteries but no detection. With the assistance of Christopher and Barbara Roden of the Arthur Conan Doyle Society, the closest we could get was "The Silver Hatchet". This was written in 1883 but set in 1861 when Doyle was two years old, so it almost qualified. However, although the story does feature a police detective, he does very little detection.

I almost cheated! The Sherlock Holmes stories themselves are often set in periods earlier than their writing, as Watson dusts off another set of papers from his archives and recounts an ancient case. The earliest recorded investigation by Holmes is "The Gloria Scott", published in 1893 but set some twenty years earlier when Holmes was at college. But the story has a contemporary setting with Holmes relating to Watson his first case. It doesn't really qualify. Still, it's a good game working out the gap between the publication of a Holmes story and its setting. There are in fact a number of stories about Holmes by Doyle published well into the twentieth century but set in the 1880s and 90s, and the biggest span of years I could find is with "The Adventure of the Veiled Lodger" set in 1896 but not published until 1927.

However, I decided to remain pure to the cause. There have, in fact, been many stories written about Sherlock Holmes since Conan Doyle laid down his pen, including several by his son, Adrian. These have been unfairly overlooked, and since they are genuine historical detective stories, I have selected one of those for this volume.

The first author to write a story featuring a genuine historical detective was an American lawyer, Melville Davisson Post. In Uncle Abner, Post created a strong, upright, god-fearing man, in the early years of the nineteenth century, who had phenomenal powers of observation and deduction and at times equals Holmes in his perceptiveness. The first Uncle Abner story, "Angel of the Lord", was published in the *Saturday Evening Post* in 1911, and Post wrote another twenty or so over the next few years. "The Doomdorf Mystery", which is reprinted in this volume, remains to my mind the most ingenious.

Some may argue that there was an earlier historical detective in print, none other than the Scarlet Pimpernel, created by Baroness Orczy in 1905. There is no denying the popularity and influence of the character, but Sir Percy Blakeney, who masqueraded as the Pimpernel in the days of the French revolution, was really a secret agent and the purist in me does not regard a secret agent as a genuine detective.

In fact although the occasional short story appeared which could perhaps be shoe-horned into the historical detective *genre*, including some by the great author of swashbucklers, Rafael Sabatini, the Uncle Abner stories remained unique for almost thirty years. Then, in the forties, the American academic and mystery writer Lillian de la Torre, saw the wonderful opportunities presented by the British giant of letters, Dr Samuel Johnson, with his ready-made Watson, James Boswell. Starting in 1943 she began what has become the longest-running series of historical detective stories featuring the investigations of Dr Sam Johnson, Detector.

At about that same time, Agatha Christie became attracted to the possibilities of writing a detective novel set in ancient Egypt. It was in response to an idea suggested by an Egyptologist friend, Professor Stephen Glanville, to whom the book is dedicated. Up until that time no one had written an entire detective novel set in an historical period, let alone one so far back as 2000 BC.

It wasn't long though before another great writer of detective stories started to make the historical detective novel something of his own. John Dickson Carr, the master of the impossible crime, had toyed with historical mysteries for some years as short stories, but in 1950 he completed *The Bride of Newgate*. Set at the end of the Napoleonic era, the story is about Richard Darwent, imprisoned in Newgate and then pardoned for a crime he did not commit, who sets out to identify the real criminal. It is one of Carr's best novels, written when he was at the peak of his power. It was at the same time that he penned the story included in this anthology, "The Gentleman from Paris".

Carr wrote ten historical mystery novels. Some use as a device a modern-day character regressing in time, of which the best is *The Devil in Velvet* (1955), where a professor, following an apparent pact with the devil, has the chance to go back and solve a murder before it happens.

A genuine historical mystery was the subject of *The Daughter of Time* (1951) by Josephine Tey. Voted the favourite novel of all time by the Crime Writers Association, it is not technically an historical detective story. It features Tey's present-day detective, Alan Grant, who while laid up in hospital uses an acquaintance to help him research the deaths of the princes in the Tower. This was the same method used by Colin Dexter in his award-winning Inspector Morse novel, *The Wench is Dead*.

During the 1950s a number of authors turned to the historical detective form. Wallace Nichols, a poet and writer, began a long-running series about Sollius, the Slave Detective, in the *London Mystery Magazine*. His first case is reprinted here.

Robert van Gulik, one-time Dutch ambassador to Japan, had become fascinated by an eighteenth-century Chinese detective novel, *Dee Goong An*, which featured the cases of a real historical character, Dee Goong, a seventh-century Chinese magistrate. While on war duties in the Pacific, van Gulik translated the stories into English as *Dee Goong An: Three Murder Cases of Judge Dee* (1949). By then he had become so fascinated with this character that he continued to write about him for the next twenty years, producing a delightful series of novels and stories, one of which is reprinted here.

In America, Theodore Mathieson struck upon the idea of setting major historical characters difficult crimes to solve. The stories were collected together as *The Great Detectives* (1960), and showed the detective skills of Alexander the Great, Leonardo da Vinci, Captain Cook, even Florence Nightingale. Since several of these stories were set in the Middle Ages one might argue that Mathieson was the first to write a medieval mystery.

By the sixties and seventies there were a number of writers producing novels set in the nineteenth century. Leaving aside the many stories that feature Sherlock Holmes, there were a series of Victorian police procedurals, of which the best are Peter Lovesey's books about Sergeant Cribb, and there were several novels featuring the Bow Street Runners, such as those by Richard Falkirk and Jeremy Sturrock.

So, as we can see, by the time Brother Cadfael first tended his herb garden at Shrewsbury Abbey, the historical detective story had been gathering pace for some years. Yet, the stories had not been sown in especially fertile soil. Ellis Peters, on the other hand, if I may mix my metaphors, had struck a particularly rich vein. Here, for the first time, was an author skilled both in detective fiction and, under her real name of Edith Pargeter, equally skilled at historical fiction. She was thus able to blend the two genres seamlessly, along with immaculate characterisation and an ability to bring the past alive as no other had before.

A further boost came from the publication of *The Name of the Rose* (1980) by Umberto Eco, a superbly gothic detective novel set in a remote Italian monastery where Brother William seeks to solve a series of increasingly bizarre murders. Despite the gothic trappings the novel owes much to Sherlock Holmes. It is a fascinating puzzle and made an equally fascinating film, starring Sean Connery.

With the success of Brother Cadfael and *The Name of the Rose*, others have followed: the Brother Athelstan novels by Paul Harding, the Hugh Corbett books by Paul Doherty, the Matthew Stock stories by Leonard Tourney, the Nicholas Bracewell books by Edward Marston. These and many more are listed in the appendix.

In this anthology I have sought to include new stories by many of today's leading writers of historical whodunnits, as well as reprinting some of the classics of the field. I am also delighted that Ellis Peters has kindly provided a foreword for the collection. Since she opened up a whole new vein in mystery fiction, I can do no better than to hand over to her to declare this anthology open.

Mike Ashley
March 1993

# Foreword
# by Ellis Peters

I was not aware when I began my first novel featuring Brother Cadfael that I was opening or developing a new area of fiction. True, I had encountered hardly any previous historical mysteries, though I can recall reading a few short stories, including one which featured Aristotle as a detective. In general I avoid reading anything that may overlap what I'm working on, in subject or period, to put all influence out of the question.

In 1976 I was between books and passing the time while I thought about the next one, and it happened that I dipped into the massive *History of Shrewsbury* compiled by two nineteenth century clerics, Owen and Blakeway; books I'd had since I was fifteen and knew very well.

The story of the expedition from the Abbey to acquire a saint's relics from Wales was familiar enough, but it suddenly occurred to me that it would make a good plot for a murder mystery, and a novel way of disposing of a body. So, *A Morbid Taste for Bones* was conceived from the beginning as a murder mystery rather than an historical novel. Its locations, Shrewsbury and North Wales, were laid down by historical facts – historical, at least, according to the life of Saint Winifred which Prior Robert Pennant afterwards wrote, concluding it with the account of his own expedition into Wales to find and bring her back. The book, by the way, is in the Bodleian if anyone cares to pursue the study, though I have not seen it myself.

With so much recorded fact, I was not going to meddle too much with the story, though I admit to a major departure from the actual version of the result of the expedition. The whole process of working fiction into fact without playing tricks with history appealed to me strongly. The difficulties arising are half the attraction, like a cryptic crossword puzzle.

I did not intend a series when I began. The first novel was written as a one-off. But about a year later, after I had written another book, I became fascinated by King Stephen's siege of Shrewsbury and as that happened only a short time after the translation of St. Winifred, I could use the same cast of characters. From then on the books took up a rhythm of their own.

Brother Cadfael did not emerge immediately. The cast of the novel was limited to the party of monks from Shrewsbury and the population of Gwytherin, so my protagonist had to be one of the Brothers: one with wider experience of life than an oblatus donated in infancy could have, so in middle life and with half a world behind him. He had to be one who spoke Welsh, a reason for including in the party a Brother of otherwise modest function. And so he started to emerge: elderly, travelled, humanely curious about his fellowmen, and Welsh. I hunted for a name unusual even in Wales, and found only two references to Cadfael in Lloyd's *History of Wales*, so I borrowed that name. And there he was.

All the greater magnates in the novels are real – the abbots, bishops, Welsh princes, even the Dublin Danish adventurers. There was an Abbot Radulfus as there was an Abbot Heribert before him, and Heribert was demoted just as related, by the Legatine Council that appointed Radulfus in his place. Prior Robert was real enough, as he proved by writing his book. Hugh Beringar is my own man. At that time FitzAlan was sheriff, but he fled when Stephen stormed Shrewsbury, and I can find no record of the man Stephen must have appointed in his place. So I was free to fill the vacancy and free to suppose that in time Gilbert Prestcote died and gave place to his equally imaginary deputy, Hugh Beringar.

The steady progression of the books has surprised me, and has led to an emphasis on season, weather and the religious sequence of the year; but as soon as I realized it, I recognised how appropriate it is, since we are concerned with the regular lives of a community. As a result I have been able to focus on the day-to-day detail of community life, and I believe it is that which has made the books so popular.

In the years since I began the Cadfael books I have not read many other historical mysteries, so I am fascinated by the wonderfully mixed bag of stories included in this anthology. I have also read Lindsey Davis's novels set in Vespasian's Rome, told in the colloquial style of a slightly seedy private eye, which I think absolutely first class. She brings Imperial Rome to life from the street angle, laundresses, thuggish trainee gladiators and all, and still presents us with a very likeable young protagonist.

Perhaps that is the secret of the successful historical detective story: the ability to include a human and likeable detective in a background that comes to life and becomes as real to today's readers as it was to the souls living all those centuries ago.

# PART I
# The Ancient World

# THE LOCKED TOMB
# MYSTERY
## Elizabeth Peters

*Elizabeth Peters (b. 1927) is ideally suited to open this anthology. Under her real name of Barbara Mertz she is a noted Egyptologist and has written a number of studies of ancient Egypt, including* Temples, Tombs and Hieroglyphs *(1964), which is the story of Egyptology. Under two pen names – Elizabeth Peters and Barbara Michaels – she has written a long line of mystery and detective novels. These include* The Curse of the Pharaohs *(1981), which introduced the Victorian archeologist, Amelia Peabody and her husband Radcliffe Emerson who, on their trips to Egypt, encounter any amount of bizarre crimes.*

*Elizabeth Peters has the following to say about our first fictional sleuth in the following story. "Amenhotep Sa Hapu was a real person who lived during the fourteenth century* BC. *Later generations worshipped him as a sage and scholar; he seems like a logical candidate for the role of ancient Egyptian detective."*

S enebtisi's funeral was the talk of southern Thebes. Of course, it could not compare with the burials of Great Ones and Pharaohs, whose Houses of Eternity were furnished with gold and fine linen and precious gems, but ours was not a quarter where nobles lived; our people were craftsmen and small merchants, able to afford a chamber-tomb and a coffin and a few spells to ward off the perils of the Western Road – no more than that. We had never seen anything like the burial of the old woman who had been our neighbor for so many years.

The night after the funeral, the customers of Nehi's tavern could talk of nothing else. I remember that evening well. For one thing, I had just won my first appointment as a temple scribe. I was looking forward to boasting a little, and perhaps paying for a round of beer, if my friends displayed proper appreciation of my good fortune. Three of the others were already at the tavern when I arrived, my linen shawl wrapped tight around me. The weather was cold even for winter, with a cruel, dry wind driving sand into every crevice of the body.

"Close the door quickly," said Senu, the carpenter. "What weather! I wonder if the Western journey will be like this – cold enough to freeze a man's bones."

This prompted a ribald comment from Rennefer, the weaver, concerning the effects of freezing on certain of Senebtisi's vital organs. "Not that anyone would notice the difference," he added. "There was never any warmth in the old hag. What sort of mother would take all her possessions to the next world and leave her only son penniless?"

"Is it true, then?" I asked, signaling Nehi to fetch the beer jar. "I have heard stories – "

"All true," said the potter, Baenre. "It is a pity you could not attend the burial, Wadjsen; it was magnificent!"

"You went?" I inquired. "That was good of you, since she ordered none of her funerary equipment from you."

Baenre is a scanty little man with thin hair and sharp bones. It is said that he is a domestic tyrant, and that his wife cowers when he comes roaring home from the tavern, but when he is with us, his voice is almost a whisper. "My rough kitchenware would not be good enough to hold the wine and fine oil she took to the tomb. Wadjsen, you should have seen the boxes and jars and baskets – dozens of them. They say she had a gold mask, like the ones worn by great nobles, and that all her ornaments were of solid gold."

"It is true," said Rennefer. "I know a man who knows one of the servants of Bakenmut, the goldsmith who made the ornaments."

"How is her son taking it?" I asked. I knew Minmose slightly; a shy, serious man, he followed his father's trade of stone carving. His mother had lived with him all his life, greedily scooping up his profits, though she had money of her own, inherited from her parents.

"Why, as you would expect," said Senu, shrugging. "Have you ever heard him speak harshly to anyone, much less his mother? She was an old she-goat who treated him like a boy who has not cut off the side lock; but with him it was always 'Yes, honored mother,' and 'As you say, honored mother.' She would not even allow him to take a wife."

"How will he live?"

"Oh, he has the shop and the business, such as it is. He is a hard worker; he will survive."

In the following months I heard occasional news of Minmose. Gossip said he must be doing well, for he had taken to spending his leisure time at a local house of prostitution – a pleasure he never had dared enjoy while his mother lived. Nefertiry, the loveliest and most expensive of the girls, was the object of his desire, and Rennefer remarked that the maiden must have a kind heart, for she could command higher prices than Minmose was able to pay. However, as time passed, I forgot Minmose and Senebtisi, and her rich burial. It was not until almost a year later that the matter was recalled to my attention.

The rumors began in the marketplace, at the end of the time of inundation, when the floodwater lay on the fields and the farmers were idle. They enjoy this time, but the police of the city do not; for idleness leads to crime, and one of the most popular crimes is tomb robbing. This goes on all the time in a small way, but when the Pharaoh is strong and stern, and the laws are strictly enforced, it is a very risky trade. A man stands to lose more than a hand or an ear if he is caught. He also risks damnation after he has entered his own tomb; but some men simply do not have proper respect for the gods.

The king, Nebmaatre (may he live forever!), was then in his prime, so there had been no tomb robbing for some time – or at least none had been detected. But, the rumors said, three men of west Thebes had been caught trying to sell ornaments such as are buried with the dead. The rumors turned out to be correct, for once. The men were questioned on the soles of their feet and confessed to the robbing of several tombs.

Naturally all those who had kin buried on the west bank – which included most of us – were alarmed by this news, and half the nervous matrons in our neighborhood went rushing across the river to make sure the family tombs were safe. I was not surprised to hear that that dutiful son Minmose had also felt obliged to make sure his mother had not been disturbed.

However, I was surprised at the news that greeted me when I paid my next visit to Nehi's tavern. The moment I entered, the others began to talk at once, each eager to be the first to tell the shocking facts.

"Robbed?" I repeated when I had sorted out the babble of voices. "Do you speak truly?"

"I do not know why you should doubt it," said Rennefer. "The richness of her burial was the talk of the city, was it not? Just what the tomb robbers like! They made a clean sweep of all the gold, and ripped the poor old hag's mummy to shreds."

At that point we were joined by another of the habitués, Merusir. He is a pompous, fat man who considers himself superior to the rest of us because he is Fifth Prophet of Amon. We put up with his patronizing ways because sometimes he knows court gossip. On that particular evening it was apparent that he was bursting with excitement. He listened with a supercilious sneer while we told him the sensational news. "I know, I know," he drawled. "I heard it much earlier – and with it, the other news which is known only to those in the confidence of the Palace."

He paused, ostensibly to empty his cup. Of course, we reacted as he had hoped we would, begging him to share the secret. Finally he condescended to inform us.

"Why, the amazing thing is not the robbery itself, but how it was done. The tomb entrance was untouched, the seals of the necropolis were unbroken. The tomb itself is entirely rock-cut, and there was not the slightest break in the walls or floor or ceiling. Yet when Minmose entered the burial chamber, he found the coffin open, the mummy mutilated, and the gold ornaments gone."

We stared at him, openmouthed.

"It is a most remarkable story," I said.

"Call me a liar if you like," said Merusir, who knows the language of polite insult as well as I do. "There was a witness – two, if you count Minmose himself. The sem-priest Wennefer was with him."

This silenced the critics. Wennefer was known to us all. There was not a man in southern Thebes with a higher reputation. Even Senebtisi had been fond of him, and she was not fond of many people. He had officiated at her funeral.

Pleased at the effect of his announcement, Merusir went on in his most pompous manner. "The king himself has taken an interest in the matter. He has called on Amenhotep Sa Hapu to investigate."

"Amenhotep?" I exclaimed. "But I know him well."

"You do?" Merusir's plump cheeks sagged like bladders punctured by a sharp knife.

Now, at that time Amenhotep's name was not in the mouth of everyone, though he had taken the first steps on that astonishing career that was to make him the intimate friend of Pharaoh. When I first met him, he had been a poor, insignificant priest at a local shrine. I had been sent to fetch him to the house where my master lay dead of a stab wound, presumably murdered. Amenhotep's fame had begun with that matter, for he had discovered the truth and saved an innocent man from execution. Since then he had handled several other cases, with equal success.

My exclamation had taken the wind out of Merusir's sails. He had hoped to impress us by telling us something we did not know. Instead it was I who enlightened the others about Amenhotep's triumphs. But when I finished, Rennefer shook his head.

"If this wise man is all you say, Wadjsen, it will be like inviting a lion to rid the house of mice. He will find there is a simple explanation. No doubt the thieves entered the burial chamber from above or from one side, tunneling through the rock. Minmose and Wennefer were too shocked to observe the hole in the wall, that is all."

We argued the matter for some time, growing more and more heated as the level of the beer in the jar dropped. It was a foolish argument, for none of us knew the facts; and to argue without knowledge is like trying to weave without thread.

This truth did not occur to me until the cool night breeze had cleared my head, when I was halfway home. I decided to pay Amenhotep a visit. The next time I went to the tavern, I would be the one to tell the latest news, and Merusir would be nothing!

Most of the honest householders had retired, but there were lamps burning in the street of the prostitutes, and in a few taverns. There was a light, as well, in one window of the house where Amenhotep lodged. Like the owl he resembled, with his beaky nose and large, close-set eyes, he preferred to work at night.

The window was on the ground floor, so I knocked on the wooden shutter, which of course was closed to keep out night demons. After a few moments the shutter opened, and the familiar nose appeared. I spoke my name, and Amenhotep went to open the door.

"Wadjsen! It has been a long time," he exclaimed. "Should I ask what brings you here, or shall I display my talents as a seer and tell you?"

"I suppose it requires no great talent," I replied. "The matter of Senebtisi's tomb is already the talk of the district."

"So I had assumed." He gestured me to sit down and hospitably indicated the wine jar that stood in the corner. I shook my head.

"I have already taken too much beer, at the tavern. I am sorry to disturb you so late – "

"I am always happy to see you, Wadjsen." His big dark eyes reflected the light of the lamp, so that they seemed to hold stars in their depths. "I have missed my assistant, who helped me to the truth in my first inquiry."

"I was of little help to you then," I said with a smile. "And in this case I am even more ignorant. The thing is a great mystery, known only to the gods."

"No, no!" He clapped his hands together, as was his habit when annoyed with the stupidity of his hearer. "There is no mystery. I know who robbed the tomb of Senebtisi. The only difficulty is to prove how it was done."

\* \* \*

At Amenhotep's suggestion I spent the night at his house so that I could accompany him when he set out next morning to find the proof he needed. I required little urging, for I was afire with curiosity. Though I pressed him, he would say no more, merely remarking piously, "'A man may fall to ruin because of his tongue; if a passing remark is hasty and it is repeated, thou wilt make enemies.'"

I could hardly dispute the wisdom of this adage, but the gleam in Amenhotep's bulging black eyes made me suspect he took a malicious pleasure in my bewilderment.

After our morning bread and beer we went to the temple of Khonsu, where the sem-priest Wennefer worked in the records office. He was copying accounts from pottery ostraca onto a papyrus that was stretched across his lap. All scribes develop bowed shoulders from bending over their writing; Wennefer was folded almost double, his face scant inches from the surface of the papyrus. When Amenhotep cleared his throat, the old man started, smearing the ink. He waved our apologies aside and cleaned the papyrus with a wad of lint.

"No harm was meant, no harm is done," he said in his breathy, chirping voice. "I have heard of you, Amenhotep Sa Hapu; it is an honor to meet you."

"I, too, have looked forward to meeting you, Wennefer. Alas that the occasion should be such a sad one."

Wennefer's smile faded. "Ah, the matter of Senebtisi's tomb. What a tragedy! At least the poor woman can now have a proper reburial. If Minmose had not insisted on opening the tomb, her *ba* would have gone hungry and thirsty through eternity."

"Then the tomb entrance really was sealed and undisturbed?" I asked skeptically.

"I examined it myself," Wennefer said. "Minmose had asked me to meet him after the day's work, and we arrived at the tomb as the sun was setting; but the light was still good. I conducted the funeral service for Senebtisi, you know. I had seen the doorway blocked and mortared and with my own hands had helped to press the seals of the necropolis onto the wet plaster. All was as I had left it that day a year ago."

"Yet Minmose insisted on opening the tomb?" Amenhotep asked.

"Why, we agreed it should be done," the old man said mildly. "As you know, robbers sometimes tunnel in from above or from one side, leaving the entrance undisturbed. Minmose had brought tools. He did most of the work himself, for these old hands of mine are better with a pen than a chisel. When the doorway was clear, Minmose lit a lamp and we entered. We were crossing the hall beyond the entrance corridor when Minmose let out a shriek. 'My mother, my mother,' he cried – oh, it was pitiful to hear! Then I saw it too. The thing – the thing on the floor . . .''

"You speak of the mummy, I presume," said Amenhotep. "The thieves had dragged it from the coffin out into the hall?"

"Where they despoiled it," Wennefer whispered. "The august body was ripped open from throat to groin, through the shroud and the wrappings and the flesh."

"Curious," Amenhotep muttered, as if to himself. "Tell me, Wennefer, what is the plan of the tomb?"

Wennefer rubbed his brush on the ink cake and began to draw on the back surface of one of the ostraca.

"It is a fine tomb, Amenhotep, entirely rock-cut. Beyond the entrance is a flight of stairs and a short corridor, thus leading to a hall broader than it is long, with two pillars. Beyond that, another short corridor; then the burial chamber. The august mummy lay here." And he inked in a neat circle at the beginning of the second corridor.

"Ha," said Amenhotep, studying the plan. "Yes, yes, I see. Go on, Wennefer. What did you do next?"

"I did nothing," the old man said simply. "Minmose's hand shook so violently that he dropped the lamp. Darkness closed in. I felt the presence of the demons who had defiled the dead. My tongue clove to the roof of my mouth and – "

"Dreadful," Amenhotep said. "But you were not far from the tomb entrance; you could find your way out?"

"Yes, yes, it was only a dozen paces; and by Amon, my friend, the sunset light has never appeared so sweet! I went at once to fetch the necropolis guards. When we returned to the tomb, Minmose had rekindled his lamp – "

"I thought you said the lamp was broken."

"Dropped, but fortunately not broken. Minmose had opened one of the jars of oil – Senebtisi had many such in the tomb, all of the finest quality – and had refilled the lamp. He had replaced the mummy in its coffin and was kneeling by it praying. Never was there so pious a son!"

"So then, I suppose, the guards searched the tomb."

"We all searched," Wennefer said. "The tomb chamber was in a dreadful state; boxes and baskets had been broken open and the contents strewn about. Every object of precious metal had been stolen, including the amulets on the body."

"What about the oil, the linen, and the other valuables?" Amenhotep asked.

"The oil and the wine were in large jars, impossible to move easily. About the other things I cannot say; everything was in such confusion – and I do not know what was there to begin with. Even Minmose was not certain; his mother had filled and sealed most of the boxes herself. But I know what was taken from the mummy, for I saw the golden amulets and ornaments placed on it when it was wrapped by the embalmers. I do not like to speak evil of anyone, but you know, Amenhotep, that the embalmers . . ."

"Yes," Amenhotep agreed with a sour face. "I myself watched the wrapping of my father; there is no other way to make certain the ornaments will go on the mummy instead of into the coffers of the embalmers. Minmose did not perform this service for his mother?"

"Of course he did. He asked me to share in the watch, and I was glad to agree. He is the most pious – "

"So I have heard," said Amenhotep. "Tell me again, Wennefer, of the condition of the mummy. You examined it?"

"It was my duty. Oh, Amenhotep, it was a sad sight! The shroud was still tied firmly around the body; the thieves had cut straight through it and through the bandages beneath, baring the body. The arm bones were broken, so roughly had the thieves dragged the heavy gold bracelets from them."

"And the mask?" I asked. "It was said that she had a mask of solid gold."

"It, too, was missing."

"Horrible," Amenhotep said. "Wennefer, we have kept you from your work long enough. Only one more question. How do you think the thieves entered the tomb?"

The old man's eyes fell. "Through me," he whispered.

I gave Amenhotep a startled look. He shook his head warningly.

"It was not your fault," he said, touching Wennefer's bowed shoulder.

"It was. I did my best, but I must have omitted some vital part of the ritual. How else could demons enter the tomb?"

"Oh, I see." Amenhotep stroked his chin. "Demons."

"It could have been nothing else. The seals on the door were intact, the mortar untouched. There was no break of the smallest size in the stone of the walls or ceiling or floor."

"But – " I began.

"And there is this. When the doorway was clear and the light entered, the dust lay undisturbed on the floor. The only marks on it were the strokes of the broom with which Minmose, according to custom, had swept the floor as he left the tomb after the funeral service."

"Amon preserve us," I exclaimed, feeling a chill run through me.

Amenhotep's eyes moved from Wennefer to me, then back to Wennefer. "That is conclusive," he murmured.

"Yes," Wennefer said with a groan. "And I am to blame – I, a priest who failed at his task."

"No," said Amenhotep. "You did not fail. Be of good cheer, my friend. There is another explanation."

Wennefer shook his head despondently. "Minmose said the same, but he was only being kind. Poor man! He was so overcome, he could scarcely walk. The guards had to take him by the arms to lead him from the tomb. I carried his tools. It was the least – "

"The tools," Amenhotep interrupted. "They were in a bag or a sack?"

"Why, no. He had only a chisel and a mallet. I carried them in my hand as he had done."

Amenhotep thanked him again, and we took our leave. As we crossed the courtyard I waited for him to speak, but he remained silent; and after a while I could contain myself no longer.

"Do you still believe you know who robbed the tomb?"

"Yes, yes, it is obvious."

"And it was not demons?"

Amenhotep blinked at me like an owl blinded by sunlight.

"Demons are a last resort."

He had the smug look of a man who thinks he has said something clever; but his remark smacked of heresy to me, and I looked at him doubtfully.

"Come, come," he snapped. "Senebtisi was a selfish, greedy old woman, and if there is justice in the next world, as our faith decrees, her path through the Underworld will not be easy. But why would diabolical powers play tricks with her mummy when they could torment her spirit? Demons have no need of gold."

"Well, but – "

"Your wits used not to be so dull. What do you think happened?"

"If it was not demons – "

"It was not."

"Then someone must have broken in."

"Very clever," said Amenhotep, grinning.

"I mean that there must be an opening, in the walls or the floor, that Wennefer failed to see."

"Wennefer, perhaps. The necropolis guards, no. The chambers of the tomb were cut out of solid rock. It would be impossible to disguise a break in such a surface, even if tomb robbers took the trouble to fill it in – which they never have been known to do."

"Then the thieves entered through the doorway and closed it again. A dishonest craftsman could make a copy of the necropolis seal . . ."

"Good." Amenhotep clapped me on the shoulder. "Now you are beginning to think. It is an ingenious idea, but it is wrong. Tomb robbers work in haste, for fear of the necropolis guards. They would not linger to replace stones and mortar and seals."

"Then I do not know how it was done."

"Ah, Wadjsen, you are dense! There is only one person who could have robbed the tomb."

"I thought of that," I said stiffly, hurt by his raillery. "Minmose was the last to leave the tomb and the first to reenter it. He had good reason to desire the gold his mother should have left to him. But, Amenhotep, he could not have robbed the mummy on either occasion; there was not time. You know the funeral ritual as well as I. When the priests and mourners leave the tomb, they leave together. If Minmose had lingered in the burial chamber, even for a few minutes, his delay would have been noted and remarked upon."

"That is quite true," said Amenhotep.

"Also," I went on, "the gold was heavy as well as bulky. Minmose could not have carried it away without someone noticing."

"Again you speak truly."

"Then unless Wennefer the priest is conspiring with Minmose – "

"That good, simple man? I am surprised at you, Wadjsen. Wennefer is as honest as the Lady of Truth herself."

"Demons – "

Amenhotep interrupted with the hoarse hooting sound that passed for a laugh with him. "Stop babbling of demons. There is one man besides myself who knows how Senebtisi's tomb was violated. Let us go and see him."

He quickened his pace, his sandals slapping in the dust. I followed, trying to think. His taunts were like weights that pulled my mind to its farthest limits. I began to get an inkling of truth, but I could not make sense of it. I said nothing, not even when we turned into the lane south of the temple that led to the house of Minmose.

There was no servant at the door. Minmose himself answered our summons. I greeted him and introduced Amenhotep.

Minmose lifted his hands in surprise. "You honor my house, Amenhotep. Enter and be seated."

Amenhotep shook his head. "I will not stay, Minmose. I came only to tell you who desecrated your mother's tomb."

"What?" Minmose gaped at him. "Already you know? But how? It is a great mystery, beyond – "

"You did it, Minmose."

Minmose turned a shade paler. But that was not out of the way; even the innocent might blanch at such an accusation.

"You are mad," he said. "Forgive me, you are my guest, but – "

"There is no other possible explanation," Amenhotep said. "You stole the gold when you entered the tomb two days ago."

"But, Amenhotep," I exclaimed. "Wennefer was with him, and Wennefer saw the mummy already robbed when – "

"Wennefer did not see the mummy," Amenhotep said. "The tomb was dark; the only light was that of a small lamp, which Minmose promptly dropped. Wennefer has poor sight. Did you not observe how he bent over his writing? He caught only a glimpse of a white shape, the size of a wrapped mummy, before the light went out. When next Wennefer saw the mummy, it was in the coffin, and his view of it then colored his confused memory of the first supposed sighting of it. Few people are good observers. They see what they expect to see."

"Then what did he see?" I demanded. Minmose might not have been there. Amenhotep avoided looking at him.

"A piece of linen in the rough shape of a human form, arranged on the floor by the last person who left the tomb. It would have taken him only a moment to do this before he snatched up the broom and swept himself out."

"So the tomb was sealed and closed," I exclaimed. "For almost a year he waited – "

"Until the next outbreak of tomb robbing. Minmose could assume this would happen sooner or later; it always does. He thought he was being clever by asking Wennefer to accompany him – a witness of irreproachable character who could testify that the tomb entrance was untouched. In fact, he was too careful to avoid being compromised; that would have made me doubt him, even if the logic of the facts had not pointed directly at him. Asking that same virtuous man to share his supervision of the mummy wrapping, lest he be suspected of connivance with the embalmers; feigning weakness so that the necropolis guards would have to support him, and thus be in a position to swear he could not have concealed the gold on his person. Only a guilty man would be so anxious to appear innocent. Yet there was reason for his precautions. Sometime in the near future, when that loving son Minmose discovers a store of gold hidden in the house, overlooked by his mother – the old do forget sometimes – then, since men have evil minds, it might be necessary for Minmose to prove beyond a shadow of a doubt that he could not have laid hands on his mother's burial equipment."

Minmose remained dumb, his eyes fixed on the ground. It was I who responded as he should have, questioning and objecting.

"But how did he remove the gold? The guards and Wennefer searched the tomb, so it was not hidden there, and there was not time for him to bury it outside."

"No, but there was ample time for him to do what had to be done in the burial chamber after Wennefer had tottered off to fetch the guards. He overturned boxes and baskets, opened the coffin, ripped through the mummy wrappings with his chisel, and took the gold. It would not take long, especially for one who knew exactly where each ornament had been placed."

Minmose's haggard face was as good as an admission of guilt. He did not look up or speak, even when Amenhotep put a hand on his shoulder.

"I pity you, Minmose," Amenhotep said gravely. "After years of devotion and self-denial, to see yourself deprived of your inheritance . . . And there was Nefertiry. You had been visiting her in secret, even before your mother died, had you not? Oh, Minmose, you should have remembered the words of the sage: "Do not go in to a woman who is a stranger; it is a great crime, worthy of death." She has brought you to your death, Minmose. You knew she would turn from you if your mother left you nothing."

Minmose's face was gray. "Will you denounce me, then? They will beat me to make me confess."

"Any man will confess when he is beaten," said Amenhotep, with a curl of his lip. "No, Minmose, I will not denounce you. The court of the vizier demands facts, not theories, and you have covered your tracks very neatly. But you will not escape justice. Nefertiry will consume your gold as the desert sands drink water, and then she will cast you off; and all the while Anubis, the Guide of the Dead, and Osiris, the Divine Judge, will be waiting for you. They will eat your heart, Minmose, and your spirit will hunger and thirst through all eternity. I think your punishment has already begun. Do you dream, Minmose? Did you see your mother's face last night, wrinkled and withered, her sunken eyes accusing you, as it looked when you tore the gold mask from it?"

A long shudder ran through Minmose's body. Even his hair seemed to shiver and rise. Amenhotep gestured to me. We went away, leaving Minmose staring after us with a face like death.

After we had gone a short distance, I said, "There is one more thing to tell, Amenhotep."

"There is much to tell." Amenhotep sighed deeply. "Of a good man turned evil; of two women who, in their different ways, drove him to crime; of the narrow line that separates the virtuous man from the sinner . . ."

"I do not speak of that. I do not wish to think of that. It makes me feel strange . . . The gold, Amenhotep – how did Minmose bear away the gold from his mother's burial?"

"He put it in the oil jar," said Amenhotep. "The one he opened to get fresh fuel for his lamp. Who would wonder if, in his agitation, he spilled a quantity of oil on the floor? He has certainly removed it by now. He has had ample opportunity, running back and forth with objects to be repaired or replaced."

"And the piece of linen he had put down to look like the mummy?"

"As you well know," Amenhotep replied, "the amount of linen used to wrap a mummy is prodigious. He could have crumpled that piece and thrown it in among the torn wrappings. But I think he did something else. It was a cool evening, in winter, and Minmose would have worn a linen mantle. He took the cloth out in the same way he had brought it in. Who would notice an extra fold of linen over a man's shoulders?

"I knew immediately that Minmose must be the guilty party, because he was the only one who had the opportunity, but I did not see how he had managed it until Wennefer showed me where the supposed mummy lay. There was no reason for a thief to drag it so far from the coffin and the burial chamber – but Minmose could not afford to have Wennefer catch even a glimpse of that room, which was then undisturbed. I realized then that what the old man had seen was not the mummy at all, but a substitute."

"Then Minmose will go unpunished."

"I said he would be punished. I spoke truly." Again Amenhotep sighed.

"You will not denounce him to Pharaoh?"

"I will tell my lord the truth. But he will not choose to act. There will be no need."

He said no more. But six weeks later Minmose's body was found floating in the river. He had taken to drinking heavily, and people said he drowned by accident. But I knew it was otherwise. Anubis and Osiris had eaten his heart, just as Amenhotep had said.

# THE THIEF VERSUS KING RHAMPSINITUS
## Herodotus

*Although all of the other stories in this volume date from the present century, and many of them are new, this story is over 2,400 years old. And it is a genuine historical mystery.*

*Herodotus, who lived between about 490 and 425 BC, has rightly been called the father of history. Born at Halicarnassus, in Asia Minor, he travelled throughout the Greek and Egyptian world, gathering facts and stories as he went. He settled down around 440 BC and at that time wrote his* History. *Herodotus did not always believe all he was told, but knew a good story when he heard one. He thus recorded for posterity this story of the Egyptian pharaoh Rhampsinitus, who is believed to equate to Rameses III, and who reigned seven hundred years earlier, in the twelfth century BC.*

King Rhampsinitus was possessed, they said, of great riches in silver – indeed to such an amount, that none of the princes, his successors, surpassed or even equaled his wealth. For the better custody of this money, he proposed to build a vast chamber of hewn stone, one side of which was to form a part of the outer wall of his palace. The builder, therefore, having designs upon the treasures, contrived, as he was making the building, to insert in this wall a stone, which could easily be removed from its place by two men, or even one. So the chamber was finished, and the king's money stored away in it.

Time passed, and the builder fell sick; when finding his end approaching, he called for his two sons, and related to them the contrivance he had made in the king's treasure-chamber, telling them it was for their sakes he had done it, so that they might always live in affluence. Then he gave them clear directions concerning the mode of removing the stone, and communicated the measurements, bidding them carefully keep the secret, whereby they would be Comptrollers of the Royal Exchequer so long as they lived.

Then the father died, and the sons were not slow in setting to work; they went by night to the palace, found the stone in the wall of the building, and having removed it with ease, plundered the treasury of a round sum.

When the king next paid a visit to the apartment he was astonished to see that the money was sunk in some of the vessels wherein it was stored away. Whom to accuse, however, he knew not, as the seals were all perfect, and the fastenings of the room secure. Still each time that he repeated his visits, he found that more money was gone. The thieves in truth never stopped, but plundered the treasury ever more and more.

At last the king determined to have some traps made, and set near the vessels which contained his wealth. This was done, and when the thieves came, as usual, to the treasure chamber, and one of them entering through the aperture, made straight for the jars, suddenly he found himself caught in one of the traps. Perceiving that he was lost, he instantly called his brother, and telling him what had happened, entreated him to enter as quickly as possible and cut off his head, that when his body should be discovered it might not be recognized, which would have the effect of bringing ruin upon both. The other thief thought the advice good, and was persuaded to follow it; then, fitting the stone into its place, he went home, taking with him his brother's head.

When day dawned, the king came into the room, and marveled greatly to see the body of the thief in the trap without a head, while the building was still whole, and neither entrance nor exit was to be seen anywhere. In this perplexity he commanded the body of the dead man to be hung up outside the palace wall, and set a guard to watch it, with orders that if any persons were seen weeping or lamenting near the place, they should be seized and brought before him. When the mother heard of this exposure of the corpse of her son, she took it sorely to heart, and spoke to her surviving child, bidding him devise some plan or other to get back the body, and threatening that if he did not exert himself she would go herself to the king and denounce him as the robber.

The son said all he could to persuade her to let the matter rest, but in vain: she still continued to trouble him, until at last he yielded to her importunity, and contrived as follows: Filling some skins with wine, he loaded them on donkeys, which he drove before him till he came to the place where the guards were watching the dead body, when pulling two or three of the skins towards him, he untied some of the necks which dangled by the asses' sides. The wine poured freely out, whereupon he began to beat his head and shout with all his might, seeming not to know which of the donkeys he should turn to first.

When the guards saw the wine running, delighted to profit by the occasion, they rushed one and all into the road, each with some vessel or other, and caught the liquor as it was spilling. The driver pretended anger, and loaded them with abuse; whereon they did their best to pacify him, until at last he appeared to soften, and recover his good humor, drove his asses aside out of the road, and set to work to re-arrange their burthens; meanwhile, as he talked and chatted with the guards, one of them began to rally him, and make him laugh, whereupon he gave them one of the skins as a gift. They now made up their minds to sit down and have a drinking-bout where they were, so they begged him to remain and drink with them. Then the man let himself be persuaded, and stayed.

As the drinking went on, they grew very friendly together, so presently he gave them another skin, upon which they drank so copiously that they were all overcome with liquor, and growing drowsy, lay down, and fell asleep on the spot. The thief waited till it was the dead of the night, and then took down the body of his brother; after which, in mockery, he shaved off the right side of all the soldiers' beards, and so left them. Laying his brother's body upon the asses, he carried it home to his mother, having thus accomplished the thing that she had required of him.

When it came to the king's ears that the thief's body was stolen away, he was sorely vexed. Wishing, therefore, whatever it might cost, to catch the man who had contrived the trick, he had recourse (the priest said) to an expedient which I can scarcely credit. He announced that he would bestow his own daughter upon the man who would narrate to her the best story of the cleverest and wickedest thing done by himself. If anyone in reply told her the story of the thief, she was to lay hold of him, and not allow him to get away.

The daughter did as her father willed, whereon the thief, who was well aware of the king's motive, felt a desire to outdo him in craft and cunning. Accordingly he contrived the following plan: He procured the corpse of a man lately dead, and cutting off one of the arms at the shoulder, put it under his dress, and so went to the king's daughter. When she put the question to him as she had done to all the rest, he replied that the wickedest thing he had ever done was cutting off the head of his brother when he was caught in a trap in the king's treasury, and the cleverest was making the guards drunk and carrying off the body. As he spoke, the princess caught at him, but the thief took advantage of the darkness to hold out to her the hand of the corpse. Imagining it to be his own hand, she seized and held it fast; while the thief, leaving it in her grasp, made his escape by the door.

The king, when word was brought him of this fresh success, amazed at the sagacity and boldness of the man, sent messengers to all the towns in his dominions to proclaim a free pardon for the thief, and to promise him a rich reward, if he came and made himself known. The thief took the king at his word, and came boldly into his presence; whereupon Rhampsinitus, greatly admiring him, and looking on him as the most knowing of men, gave him his daughter in marriage. "The Egyptians," he said, "excelled all the rest of the world in wisdom, and this man excelled all other Egyptians."

# SOCRATES SOLVES A MURDER
# Brèni James

*Socrates was one of the greatest of Athenian philosophers whose religious attitudes found him at odds with the Greek establishment and led ultimately to his death. Ever questioning, ever seeking to banish ignorance, Socrates is an ideal choice as a detective.*

*He was portrayed in this role in two stories written by Brèni James in the 1950s. The one reprinted here was her first story, and won a special award in* Ellery Queen's Mystery Magazine's *annual competition. I am unable to tell you anything about her, other than that her real name was Mrs Brenie Pevehouse, under which name she published a third story in Ellery Queen's.*

Aristodemus was awakened towards daybreak by a crowing of cocks, and when he awoke, the others were either asleep, or had gone away; there remained only Socrates, Aristophanes, and Agathon . . . And first of all Aristophanes dropped off, then, when the day was already dawning, Agathon. Socrates, having laid them to sleep, rose to depart; Aristodemus, as his manner was, following him . . . to the Lyceum. – PLATO: Symposium (Jowett trans.)

Socrates strolled along barefoot, having left his sandals behind at Agathon's. Aristodemus, barefoot as always, ran on short legs to catch up with his friend.

Aristodemus: Here, Socrates; you left your sandals.

Socrates: You seem to be more interested in what I have forgotten, Aristodemus, than in what you ought to have learned.

Aristodemus: Well, it is true my attention wandered a bit, and I missed some of your discourse, but I agreed with your conclusions.

Socrates: My dear friend, your confidence is like that of a man who drinks from a goblet of vinegar because his host has recited a paean in praise of wine.

The philosopher, after this nettling remark, obliged his companion by stopping to put on the sandals; and they resumed their walk through the town, passing out of the two eastern gates. The sun was rising above Mount Pentelicus, and Hymettus glowed before them in shadows as purple as the thyme which bloomed on its slopes.

They were soon climbing the gentle rise which led them to the shrine of Apollo Lyceus. It was a small, graceful temple whose columns and caryatids had been hewn from sugarbright marble.

At the hilltop shrine they saw the fading wisps of smoke rising from its eastern altar. The priestess, her sacrifices completed, was mounting the stairs to enter the golden doors of her sanctuary. She was clothed in the flowing white robes of her office; her hair fell in a tumble of shimmering black coils about her shoulders; and a garland of laurel leaves dipped on her forehead. Her gray eyes were serene, and on her lips played a smile that was not gentle.

Socrates: What omens, Alecto?

Alecto: For some, good. For some, evil. The smoke drifted first to the west; but now, as you see, it hastens to the god.

Indeed, as she spoke, a gentle gust of wind rose from the slope before them and sent the smoke into the shrine.

Alecto withdrew, and the two men proceeded down the short path which led to the Lyceum itself and to their destination, the swimming pool.

It appeared at first that their only companion this morning would be the statue which stood beside the pool, a beautiful Eros that stood on tiptoe as if it were about to ascend on quivering wings over the water that shivered beneath it.

The statue was not large – scarcely five feet high even on its pedestal; but the delicacy of its limbs and the airy seeming-softness of its wings gave an illusion of soaring height. The right arm of the god was extended; in the waxing light it appeared to be traced with fine blue veins. The hand was palm upward; and the face, touched with a smile that was at once roguish and innocent, was also turned to the heavens.

When Socrates and Aristodemus came closer to the edge of the pool, they perceived for the first time a young man, kneeling before the statue in prayer. They could not distinguish his words, but he was apparently supplicating the god of love with urgency.

No sooner had they taken note of this unexpected presence than a concussion of strident voices exploded from the palaestra adjoining the pool, and a party of perhaps a dozen young men bounded into view. All laughing, they raced to the water's edge and leaped in one after another, with much splashing and gurgling.

Socrates led his companion to a marble bench a few yards from the pool, and bade him sit down.

"But," frowned Aristodemus, "I thought we came to swim. Surely you have not become afraid of cold water and morning air?"

"No," replied his friend, tugging at his paunch with laced fingers, "but I consider it prudent to discourse in a crowd, and swim in solitude."

Socrates turned from Aristodemus to watch the sleek young men at their play in the pool, and he listened with an indulgent smile on his satyr's face to their noisy banter.

Suddenly a piercing *Eee-Eee*, *Eee-EEE* screeched at the south end of the pool, where stood Eros and knelt the pious youth.

"A hawk!" Socrates pointed to a shadow that sat on the fragile hand of Eros. The bird, not a large one, seemed a giant thing on so delicate a mount.

Its screams had not attracted the young men in the water. Their laughter was incongruous and horrible as the marble Eros swayed on its pedestal and then crashed to the ground at the pool's edge, sending the evil bird crying into the sun.

The two friends rushed to the assistance of the youth who, with only a glance at the bird, had remained at his prayers. The body of Eros was rubble; but its wings – which had seemed so tremulous, so poised for flight – had swept down like cleavers. One wing had cleanly severed the youth's head.

Socrates knelt beside the broken bodies, marble and flesh, the one glistening in crystalline fragments, the other twitching with the false life of the newly dead. He gently tossed a dark curl from the boy's pale forehead, and he looked into the vacant blue eyes for a long time before he drew down the lids.

Aristodemus, fairly dancing with excitement and fright, shouted, "Socrates, you know him? It is Tydeus, the Pythagorean. What a fool he was to try to bargain with Eros! The god has paid him justly!"

The philosopher rose slowly, murmuring, "Eros dispenses love, not justice." His eyes strayed over the rubble, now becoming tinted with the red of sunlight and the deeper red. A white cluster of fat clung to the shattered marble fingers of the god.

"The sacrifice," said Aristodemus, following his glance. "Tydeus was going to sacrifice that piece of lamb."

By this time the crowd of swimmers, glistening and shivering, had run to see what had happened. They chattered like birds, their voices pitched high by death.

"Someone must run to tell his friend Euchecrates," cried Aristodemus.

At this, the group fell silent. Socrates looked intently on each of the young men. "You are unwilling," he said mildly, "to tell a man of his friend's death?"

At last a youth spoke up: "We were all at dinner together last night, Tydeus and Euchecrates among us. Our symposiarch suggested that we discourse on the theme of Fidelity, for we all knew that Tydeus found it difficult to remain loyal to his friend Euchecrates. The symposiarch thought to twit him about it."

"But," broke in one of the others, "Tydeus immediately took up the topic and spoke as though he, not Euchecrates, were the victim of faithlessness!"

The first boy nodded. "It became a personal argument between them, then, instead of a discussion among friends. They began to rail at each other about gifts of money and gamecocks and I know not what. All manner of fine things, from what Tydeus said."

Socrates: Then these gifts were from our dead friend Tydeus to Euchecrates?

Youth: Yes, Socrates; and Tydeus was angry because Euchecrates had given them all away to someone else.

Socrates: To whom did Euchecrates give the gifts of Tydeus?

Once again silence fell, and the young men exchanged puzzled looks. But a bronzed athlete who had been standing outside the circle blurted out: "Even Tydeus didn't know who it was!"

Socrates: Why do you say that?

Athlete: I came here to the palaestra before any of the others, just at daybreak, and I met Tydeus on his way to the god. I recall that I asked him if he were going to swim, and he said, no, he was about to offer a prayer to Eros for a misdeed. Then I teased him about losing his gifts . . .

Socrates: And asked him who Euchecrates's admirer was?

Athlete: Yes, but Tydeus flew into a rage and began to say things in a distracted fashion about "that person," as he put it, "whoever it may be." I wanted to speculate with him on the identity, but Tydeus said he must hurry to Eros, for he wished to complete his prayer before the sun rose above the horizon.

Socrates: And he said nothing further? Well, then, will you now please go to Euchecrates's house and tell him what has befallen his friend Tydeus, and ask him to meet Socrates at the Shrine of Apollo Lyceus?

The bronzed youth agreed to do so, and Socrates took his companion Aristodemus by the arm, leading him back up the path to the shrine. "I shall return with water," he said, passing through the crowd, "that you who have touched the body may purify yourselves."

When they were out of the hearing of the young men, Aristodemus said in a low voice, "I know, Socrates, that you seek answers by the most devious questions; but I cannot discover what it is you attempt to glean from all that you have asked of those boys."

Socrates: I believe you said that the piece of fat which we saw in the rubble was sacrificial lamb?

Aristodemus: I would say so. And we saw Tydeus sacrificing, did we not?

Socrates: We saw him praying. Do you recall that the bronzed fellow told us that when first he saw Tydeus, he asked Tydeus if he were going to swim?

Aristodemus: Yes, I remember.

Socrates: And would it not be an exceedingly odd question to ask of a man who was carrying a sacrifice?

Aristodemus: That is true, Socrates; but what does it mean?

Socrates: You recall, too, that you spoke of Tydeus as a Pythagorean?

Aristodemus: Yes, I know that he was.

Socrates: Then perhaps you will also remember that, among Pythagoreans, it is a custom never to offer living sacrifice, or to kill any animal that does not harm man?

Aristodemus: I had forgotten, Socrates. And I see now that it could not have been possible that Tydeus intended to sacrifice.

Socrates: Yet we saw a piece of lamb, did we not? How else could we account for it, if it were not brought to be sacrificed?

Aristodemus: It seems unaccountable.

Socrates: Do you remember where you saw it?

Aristodemus: It was on the hand of Eros.

Socrates: And so, also, was the hawk. Does that not suggest another reason for the fat?

Aristodemus: Why, yes! It must have been placed on the hand as bait for the bird!

Socrates: Clearly, that is what was intended. And I think it must have been fastened there in some manner, for the hawk did not pick it up and fly off, but rather balanced himself on the fingertips and pulled at it until the statue was overbalanced.

The two had walked, in their preoccupation, to the very steps of the altar before the Shrine of Apollo Lyceus. The eastern doors of the marble sanctuary were still open, and they could see the god within, gold and ivory, gleaming softly now in the full morning light.

But at that moment they heard shouts from a footpath on their right, and they saw the bronzed athlete running toward them. He pulled up abruptly and panted heavily.

"He's dead, Socrates! Euchecrates is dead! I found him at Tydeus's house, in the doorway. He'd hanged himself from a porch beam!"

Socrates: Are you certain Euchecrates took his own life?

Athlete: Quite certain, Socrates. For he had scrawled a message on the wall, and I recognized his writing.

Socrates: What was his message?

Athlete: "Hide me in a secret place." Does not that mean he was ashamed?

Socrates: That is so.

"Who wishes to be hidden?" asked a woman's voice, and the three men turned to see Alecto, the priestess of the shrine, slowly and gracefully descending the marble steps.

Socrates: Euchecrates, who has killed himself, Alecto.

Alecto: It is indeed a dreadful thing to hear, Socrates.

Aristodemus: Oh, there is more! See where the statue has fallen? Tydeus lies dead beneath it.

Alecto: He must have displeased Eros mightily to have been felled by the god's own image?

Aristodemus: No, I think it fell because Euchecrates contrived that it should.

Alecto: How could it have been contrived, Aristodemus?

Socrates: Alecto, we came to ask you for some water which we will take to the Lyceum, for there are those of us who have not yet purified ourselves.

The priestess nodded and left. She returned in a few moments with a vessel of water.

Socrates: I should have asked also on behalf of this young man, so that he may take some to the place where he found Euchecrates.

Athlete: No, there is not need of that; for there was water there.

Socrates: Indeed? Then, Alecto, who preceded us with such a request?

Alecto: For water? Why, no one.

Socrates: Can purificatory water be simply drawn out of a well, or a pool, or any other ordinary source?

Alecto: No, of course it must be obtained from a priest or a priestess.

Socrates: And there is no other priest or priestess so close to the house of Tydeus, where Euchecrates lies?

Alecto: No, I am the closest.

Socrates: Then can we not assume the water was obtained here? Do you not recall such a request?

Alecto: Only that of Tydeus, several hours ago. I didn't know why he asked for water, but it would now seem to be for that reason.

Socrates: And we know also from this, do we not, Aristodemus, that Euchecrates was already dead when Tydeus went to pray to Eros? Tell me, Alecto, when Tydeus came for water, do you recall that he asked for anything else?

Alecto: I recall nothing else.

Socrates: Tydeus had told this young man that he could not stand and talk with him, since he wished to complete his prayers before the sun's rise. Does that not indicate that Tydeus knew beforehand that his prayers would be of some length?

Alecto: Yes, surely it does.

Socrates: And since he stayed to complete them even though the sun had already risen, and was not even distracted from his intentions by the presence and noise of the bird, what is the likely conclusion?

Aristodemus: I would say that he had a particular prayer to complete.

Socrates: Excellent. That would be my conclusion. Now, Alecto, do you think it likely that a young man still angry from a quarrel – indeed distraught – would sit down and compose a lengthy prayer?

Alecto: He would be more likely to pray spontaneously.

Socrates: But these things seem not to agree. The prayer, we may suppose, was planned beforehand; yet the young man was not prepared to plan the prayer. What may we surmise, then?

Alecto: That someone else composed the prayer for him?

Socrates: I believe so. And who would be likely to have done that?

Alecto: It would be someone expert in such matters, no doubt.

Socrates: Such as a priest or priestess?

Alecto: Yes, it must be so.

Socrates: And since Tydeus called, as you have said, upon yourself, Alecto, does it not seem inevitable that he asked you to compose his prayer?

Alecto: I am compelled to admit he did just that, Socrates.

Socrates: And one last matter: You were sacrificing lamb here at dawn?

Alecto: Yes, lamb and honey.

Socrates: And where is the fat of the lamb which you sacrificed this morning, Alecto? While Tydeus was within memorizing his prayer, did you not go down to the statue of Eros and affix some of the fat to that extended hand?

Alecto: You have a daemon advising you, Socrates!

Aristodemus: Oh, no, Alecto. It is as Cebes has said: Socrates can put a question to a person in such a way that only the true answer comes out! But, Alecto, how did Tydeus dare come to you?

Alecto: He did not know that it was to me his friend Euchecrates had given his gifts. But when Tydeus confessed to me that he had caused my lover's suicide, I could not but avenge the death!

The priestess turned her cold eyes proudly on Socrates. "I was named Alecto for good reason," she said with fierce triumph; "for like that divine Alecto, the Well-Wisher, I too found myself singled out by the gods to wreak vengeance!"

"But remember," cautioned Socrates quietly, "we call the divine Alecto the 'well-wisher' only to placate her. She is still one of the Furies. She still pursues the blood-guilty to death or madness. And think, Alecto: You are only mortal, and you have done murder."

Alecto's eyes widened with the sudden, horrible knowledge of her own fate.

The priestess wept then, and drew the heavy black coils of hair about her face like a shroud.

# MIGHTIER THAN THE SWORD
## John Maddox Roberts

*John Maddox Roberts (b. 1947) is the author of over twenty novels, most of them in the fantasy field, including a number featuring that mighty-thewed hero, Conan the Barbarian, created by Robert E. Howard. But Roberts also has a fascination for and an intense knowledge of the world of ancient Rome, and in a series of historical novels, starting with* SPQR *(1990), he has brought vividly to life the Roman world through the eyes of Decius Caecilius Metellus.*

*Roberts provides some further background:*

*"The advantage of writing about Decius Metellus is that he lived for a long time and had plenty of adventures. He was born around 93–91 BC. The stories are in the form of a memoir, written when he was a very old man, during the reign of Augustus. He has outlived most of his old enemies and rivals and is past caring what Augustus (whom he despises) does to him."*

*The first four novels take place early in Decius's career when he was a young and unimportant official. The present story, which was written specially for this anthology, jumps ahead a few years to 53 BC. The city is in utter turmoil. All three triumvirs are away from Italy and the gangs of Clodius, Milo and other politicians are staging daily riots in the streets. Decius is serving as a plebeian aedile and is trying to stay out of trouble by spending his days in the cellars of Rome – one of the tasks of his office is to inspect for building violations. But Decius can't go long without stumbling over a murder.*

The wonderful thing about being *Aedile* is that you get to spend your days poking through every foul, dangerous, rat-infested, pestilential cellar in Rome. Building inspection is part of the job, and you can spend your whole year just prosecuting violations of the building codes, never mind putting on the Games and inspecting all the whorehouses, also part of the job. And I'd landed the office in a year when a plebeian couldn't be *Curule Aedile*. The *Curule* got to wear a purple border on his toga and sat around the markets all day in a folding chair, attended by a lictor and levying fines for violations of the market laws. No, Marcus Aemilius Lepidus got that job. Well, he never amounted to anything, so there is justice in the world, after all. Mind you, he got to be Triumvir some years later, but considering that the other two were Antony and Octavian, he might as well have been something unpleasant adhering to the heel of Octavian's sandal.

And the worst thing was, you didn't have to serve as *Aedile* to stand for higher office! It was just that you had not a prayer of being elected *Praetor* unless, as *Aedile*, you put on splendid Games as a gift to the people. If you gave them enough chariot races, and plays and pageants and public feasts and Campanian gladiators by the hundred, then, when you stood for higher office, they would remember you kindly. Of course the State only provided a pittance for these Games, so you had to pay for them out of your own pocket, bankrupting yourself and going into debt for years. That was what being *Aedile* meant.

That was why I was in a bad mood when I found the body. It wasn't as if bodies were exactly rare in Rome, especially that year. It was one of the very worst years in the history of the City. The election scandals of the previous year had been so terrible that our two Consuls almost weren't allowed to assume office in January, and the year got worse after that. My good friend, Titus Annius Milo, politician and gang leader, was standing for Consul for the next year, as was the equally disreputable Plautius Hypsaeus. Milo's deadly enemy and mine, Publius Clodius Pulcher, was standing for *Praetor*. Their mobs battled each other in the streets day and night, and bodies were as common as dead pigeons in the Temple of Jupiter.

But that was in the streets. Another plebeian *Aedile*, whose name I no longer recall, had charge of keeping the streets clean. I resented finding them in my nice, peaceful if malodorous cellars. And it wasn't in one of the awful, disgusting tenement cellars, either, uninspected for decades and awash with the filth of poverty and lax enforcement of the hygienic laws.

Instead, it was in the clean, new basement of a town house just built on the Aventine. I was down there inspecting because in Rome honest building contractors are as common as volunteer miners in the Sicilian sulphur pits. My slave Hermes preceded me with a lantern. He was a fine, handsome, strapping young man by this time, and very good at controlling his criminal tendencies. Unlike so many, the basement smelled pleasantly of new-cut timber and the dry, dusty scent of stone fresh from the quarry. There was another, less pleasant smell beneath these, though.

Hermes stopped, a yellow puddle of light around his feet spilling over a shapeless form.

"There's a stiff here, Master."

"Oh, splendid. And I thought this was going to be my only agreeable task all day. I don't suppose it's just some old beggar, come down here to get out of the weather and died of natural causes?"

"Not unless there's beggars in the Senate, these days," Hermes said.

My scalp prickled. There were few things I hated worse than finding a high-ranking corpse. "Well, some of us are poor enough to qualify. Let's see who we have."

I squatted by the body while Hermes held the lantern near the face. Sure enough, the man wore a tunic with a senator's wide, purple stripe. He was middle-aged, bald and beak-nosed, none of which were distinctions of note. And he had had at least one enemy, who had stabbed him neatly through the heart. It was a tiny wound, and only a small amount of blood had emerged to form a palm-sized blot on his tunic, but it had done the job. Three thin streaks of blood made stripes paralleling the one that proclaimed his rank.

"Do you know him?" Hermes asked.

I shook my head. Despite all the exiles and purges by the Censors, there were still more than four hundred Senators, and I couldn't very well know all of them.

"Hermes, run to the Curia and fetch Junius the secretary. He knows every man in the Senate by sight. Then inform the *Praetor* Varus. He's holding court in the Basilica Aemilia today and by this hour he's dying for a break in the routine. Then go find Asklepiodes at the Statilian School."

"But that's across the river!" Hermes protested.

"You need the exercise. Hurry, now. I want Asklepiodes to have a look at him before the *Libitinarii* come to take him to the undertaker's."

He dashed off, leaving the lantern. I continued to study the body but it told me nothing. I sighed and scratched my head, wishing I had thought to bring along a skin of wine. Not yet half over, and it was one of the worst years of my life. And it had started out with such promise, too. The Big Three were out of Rome for a change: Caesar was gloriously slaughtering barbarians in Gaul, Crassus was doing exactly the opposite in Syria, and Pompey was sulking in Spain while his flunkies tried to harangue the Senate into making him Dictator. Their excuse this time was that only a Dictator could straighten out the disorder in the city.

It needed the straightening, although making a Dictator was a little drastic. My life wasn't worth a lead denarius after dark in my own city. The thought made me nervous, all alone with only a corpse for company. I was so deeply in debt from borrowing to support my office that I couldn't even afford a bodyguard. Milo would have lent me some thugs but the family wouldn't hear of it. People would think the Metelli were taking the Milo side in the great Clodius-Milo rivalry. Better to lose a Metellus of marginal value than endanger the family's vaunted neutrality.

After an hour or so Varus appeared, escorted by his lictors. Junius was close behind, his stylus tucked behind his ear, accompanied by a slave carrying a satchel full of wax tablets.

"Good afternoon, *Aedile*," Varus said. "So you've found a murder to brighten my day?"

"You didn't happen to bring any wine along, did you?" I said, without much hope.

"You haven't changed any, Metellus. Who do we have?" His lictors carried enough torches to light the place like noon in the Forum. The smoke started to get heavy, though.

Junius bent forward. "It's Aulus Cosconius. He doesn't attend the Senate more than three or four times a year. Big holdings in the City. This building is one of his, I think. Extensive lands in Tuscia as well." He held out a hand and his slave opened the leaves of a wooden tablet, the depressions on their inner sides filled with the finest beeswax, and slapped it into the waiting palm. Junius took his stylus from behind his ear and used its spatulate end to scrape off the words scratched on the wax lining. It was an elegant instrument of bronze inlaid with silver, befitting so important a scribe, as the high-grade wax befitted Senate business. With a dextrous twirl he reversed it and began to write with the pointed end. "You will wish to make a report to the Senate, *Praetor*?"

Varus shrugged. "What's to report? Another dead Senator. It's not like a visitation from Olympus, is it?"

Yes, the times were like that.

"I've sent for Asklepiodes," I said. "He may be able to tell something from the condition of the body."

"I doubt he'll be able to come up with much this time," Varus said, "but if you want, I'll appoint you to investigate. Make a note of it, Junius."

"Will you lend me a lictor?" I asked. "I'll need to summon people."

Varus pointed to one of his attendants and the man sighed. The days of cushy duty in the basilica were over. I said, "Go and inform the family of the late Senator Auius Cosconius that they have just been bereaved and that they can claim the body here. Junius should be able to tell you where they live. Then go to the contractor who built this place. His name is . . ." I opened one of my own wax tablets. ". . . Manius Varro. He has a lumber yard by the Circus Flaminius, next to the temple of Bellona. Tell him to call on me first thing tomorrow morning, at my office in the Temple of Ceres."

The man handed his torch to a companion and conferred with Junius, then he shouldered his *fasces* and marched importantly away.

Asklepiodes arrived just as Junius and Varus were leaving, trailed by two of his Egyptian slaves, who carried his implements and other impedimenta. Hermes was with him, carrying a wineskin. I had trained him well.

"Ah, Decius," the Greek said. "I can always count upon you to find something interesting for me." He wore a look of bright anticipation. Sometimes I wondered about Asklepiodes.

"Actually, this looks rather squalid, but the man was of some importance and somebody left him in a building I was inspecting. I don't like that sort of thing." Hermes handed me a full cup and I drained it and handed it back.

Asklepiodes took the lantern and ran the pool of light swiftly over the body, then paused to examine the wound. "He died within the last day, I cannot be more precise than that, from the thrust of a very thin-bladed weapon, its blade triangular in cross-section."

"A woman's dagger?" I asked. Prostitutes frequently concealed such weapons in their hair, to protect themselves from violent customers and sometimes to settle disputes with other prostitutes.

"Quite possibly. What's this?" He said something incomprehensible to one of his slaves. The man reached into his voluminous pouch and emerged with a long, bronze probe decorated with little golden acanthus leaves and a stoppered bottle, rather plain. Asklepiodes took the instrument and pried at the wound. It came away with an ugly little glob of something no bigger than a dried pea. This the Greek poked into the little bottle and restoppered it. He handed the probe and the bottle to the slave, who replaced it in his pouch.

"It looks like dried blood to me," I said.

"Only on the surface. I'll take it to my surgery and study it in the morning, when there is light."

"Do you think he was killed somewhere else and dragged down here? That's not much blood for a skewered heart."

"No, with a wound like this most of the bleeding is internal, I believe he died on this spot. His clothing is very little disarranged."

He poked at the feet. "See, the heels of his sandals are not scuffed, as usually happens when a body is dragged."

I was willing to take his word for it. As physician to the gladiators he had seen every possible wound to the human body, hundreds of times over. He left promising to send me a report the next day.

Minutes later the family arrived, along with the *Libitinarii* to perform the lustrations to purify the body. The dead man's son went through the pantomime of catching his last breath and shouted his name loudly, three times. Then the undertaker's men lifted the body and carried it away. The women set up an extravagant caterwauling. It wasn't a patch on the howling the professional mourners would raise at the funeral, but in the closed confines of the cellar it was sufficiently loud.

I approached the young man who had performed the final rites. "I am Decius Caecilius Metellius the Younger, plebeian *Aedile*. I found your father's body and I have been appointed investigator by the *Praetor* Varus. Would you come outside with me?"

"Quintus Cosconius," he said, identifying himself, "only son of Aulus." He was a dark, self-possessed young man. He didn't look terribly put out by the old man's passing: not an uncommon attitude in a man who has just found out that he has come into his inheritance. Something about the name ticked at my memory.

"Quintus Cosconius? Aren't you standing for the tribuneship for next year?"

"I'm not alone in that," he said. Indeed he wasn't. Tribune was the office to have, in those years. They got to introduce the laws that determined who got what in the big game of empire. Since the office was restricted to plebeians, Clodius, a patrician, had gone to the extremity of having himself adopted into a plebeian family just so he could serve as tribune.

"Did your father have enemies? Did any of the feuding demagogues have it in for him?" I was hoping he would implicate Clodius.

"No, in recent years he avoided the Senate. He had no stomach for a faction fight." I detected a faint sneer in his words.

"Who did he support?"

"Crassus, when he supported anyone. They had business dealings together." That made sense. Crassus held the largest properties in Rome. If you dealt in real estate, you probably dealt with Crassus.

"I take it you don't support Crassus yourself?"

He shrugged. "It's no secret. When I am Tribune I shall support Pompey. I've been saying that in the Forum since the start of the year. What has this to do with my father's murder?"

"Oh, politics has everything to do with murder, these days. The streets are littered with the bodies of those who picked the wrong side in the latest rivalries for office. But, since your father was a lukewarm member of the Crassus faction at best, it probably has no bearing upon his death."

"I should think not. What you need to do something about is the unchecked and unpunished violence in the City. It strikes me as ludicrous that our Senatorial authorities can pacify whole provinces but are helpless to make Rome a safe city." He looked as if a new thought had occurred to him. "Decius Caecilius Metellus the Younger? A friend of Milo's are you not?" It wasn't the first time that association had been held against me.

"Yes, but, like your father's political connections, it has no bearing here. If Milo should prove to be responsible, I shall hale him before the *Praetor* like any other malefactor."

"Rome needs a genuine police force!" he said, heatedly. "And laws with teeth!"

I was getting tired of this. "When did you last see your father?"

"Yesterday morning. He spoke to me in the Forum. He had been out of the City, touring his country estates – " I saw that look of satisfaction cross his face. They were *his* estates now. "– but he came back to inspect one of his town properties. This one, I think."

"He certainly seems to have ended up here. What plans did he have for this building?"

He shrugged again. "The usual, I suppose: Let out the ground floor to some well-to-do tenant and the upper floors to the less affluent. He owned many such properties." He smoothed a fold of his exceptionally white toga. "Will there be anything else?"

"Not at present. But I may wish to speak with you again."

"Anything for one on the service of the Senate and People of Rome," he said, none too warmly.

With the crowd gone, I went back to my inspection duties, giving them less than half of my attention. Much as I disliked the man's attitude, Quintus Cosconius had spoken nothing but the truth when he said that Rome needed a police force. Our ancient laws forbade the presence of armed soldiers within the sacred walls, and that extended to any citizen bearing arms in the City. From time to time someone would suggest forming a force of slave-police, on the old Athenian model, but that meant setting slaves in power over citizens, and that was unthinkable.

The trouble was that any force of armed men in the City would quickly become a private army for one of the political criminals who plagued the body politic in those days. In earlier times we had done well enough without police, because Romans were a mostly law-abiding people with a high respect for authority and civic order. Ever since the Gracchi, though, mob action had become the rule in Rome, and every aspiring politician curried favor with a criminal gang, to do his dirty work in return for protection in the courts.

The Republic was very sick and, despite my fondest hopes, there was to be no cure.

"You've been drinking," Julia said when I got home.

"It's been that sort of day." I told her about the dead Senator while we had dinner in the courtyard.

"You have no business investigating while you're in another office," she said. "Varus should appoint a *Iudex.*"

"It may be years before a Court for Assassins is appointed to look into this year's murders. They're happening by the job lot. But this one occurred on my territory."

"You just like to snoop. And you're hoping to get something on Clodius."

"What will one more murder laid at his doorstep mean? No, for once, I doubt that Clodius had anything to do with it." Luckily for me, my Julia was a favourite niece of the great Caius Julius Caesar, darling of the Popular Assemblies. Clodius was Caesar's man and dared not move against me openly, and by this time he considered himself the veritable uncrowned king of Rome, dispensing largesse and commanding his troops in royal fashion. As such, sneaky, covert assassination was supposedly beneath his dignity. Supposedly.

At that time, there were two sorts of men contending for power: The Big Three were all that were left of the lot that had been trying to gain control of the whole Empire for decades. Then there were men like Clodius and Milo, who just wanted to rule the City itself. Since the great conquerors had to be away from the City for years at a time, all of them had men to look after their interests in Rome. Clodius represented Caesar. Milo had acted for Crassus, although he was also closely tied in with Cicero and the star of Crassus was rapidly fading, to wink out that summer, did we but know it at the time. Plautius Hypsaeus was with the Pompeian faction, and so it went.

"Tell me about it," Julia said, separating an orange into sections. She always believed her woman's intuition could greatly improve upon the performance of my plodding reasoning. Sometimes she was right, although I carefully refrained from telling her so.

"So you think a prostitute killed him?" she said when she had heard me out.

"I only said that was in keeping with the weapon. I have never known a man to use such a tool to rid himself of an enemy."

"Oh, yes. Men like sharp edges and lots of blood."

"Exactly. This little skewer bespeaks a finesse I am reluctant to credit to our forthright cutthroats."

"But if the man owned property all over the City, why take his hired companion to the cellar of an unfurnished house?"

"Good question," I allowed. "Of course, in such matters, some men have truly recondite tastes. Why, your own Uncle Caius Julius has been known to enjoy . . ."

"Spare me," she said, very clearly, considering that her teeth were clamped tightly together.

With my fellow *Aediles* I shared the warren of office space beneath the ancient Temple of Ceres. A man was waiting for me when I climbed the steps. "*Aedile* Metellus?" He was a short, bald man and he wore a worried look that furrowed his brow all the way back to the middle of his scalp. "I am Manius Varro, the builder."

"Ah, yes. You recently completed a townhouse property for Aulus Cosconius?"

"I did," he said, still worried. "And I used only the best . . ."

"You will be happy to learn that I found no violations of the code concerning materials or construction."

Relief washed over his face like a wave on a beach. "Oh. It's just about the body, then?" He shook his head ruefully, trying to look concerned. "Poor Aulus Cosconius. I'd done a fair amount of business for him over the years."

"Was there any dispute over your payment?"

He looked surprised that I should ask. "No. He paid in full for that job months ago. He'd been planning to put up a big tenement in the Subura, but he cancelled that a few days ago."

"Did he say why?"

"No, just that he didn't want to start anything big with uncertain times ahead. I thought he meant we might have a Dictator next year. You never can tell what that might mean."

"Very true," I said, my gaze wandering out over one of Rome's most spectacular views, the eye-stunning expanse of the Circus Maximus stretching out below us. To a native son of Rome, that view is immensely satisfying because it combines three of our passions: races, gambling and enormous, vulgar buildings. His gaze followed mine.

"Ah, *Aedile*, I take it you'll be organizing the races next month?"

"To the great distress of my purse, yes."

"Do you know who's driving in the first race?"

"Victor for the Reds, Androcles for the Greens, Philip for the Blues and Paris for the Whites." I could have reeled off the names of all sixteen horses they would be driving as well. I was good at that sort of thing.

"You Caecilians are Reds, aren't you?"

"Since Romulus," I told him, knowing what was coming.

"I support the Blues. Fifty sesterces on Philip in the first race, even money?" He undoubtedly knew the names of all the horses as well.

"The Sparrow has a sore forefoot," I said, naming the Red's near-side trace horse. "Give me three to two."

"Done!" he grinned. We took out the little tablets half the men in Rome carry around to record bets. With our styli we scratched our names and bets in each other's tablets. He walked away whistling and I felt better, too. Victor had assured me personally that the Sparrow's foot would be fine in plenty of time for the race. I flicked the accumulation of wax from the tip of my stylus, my mind going back to the condition of Cosconius's body.

I had dismissed Varro as a suspect in the murder. Building contractors as a class are swindlers rather than murderers and his manner was all wrong. But our little bet had set me on a promising mental trail. My borrowed lictor was sitting on the base of the statue of Proserpina that stood in front of the temple before the restorations commissioned by Maecaenas. He looked bored senseless. I summoned him.

"Let's go to the Forum." At that he brightened. Everything really interesting was happening in the Forum. In the Forum, lictors were respected as symbols of *imperium*. With him preceding me, we went down the hill and across the old Cattle Market and along the Tuscan Street to the Forum.

The place was thronged, as usual. It held an aura of barely-contained menace in that unruly year, but people still respected the symbol of the *fasces* and made way for the lictor. I made a slow circuit of the area, finding out who was there and, more importantly, who was not. To my great relief, neither Clodius nor Milo were around with their crowds of thugs. Among the candidates for the next year's offices I saw the young Quintus Cosconius. Unlike the others standing for the tribuneship in their specially whitened togas he wore a dingy, brown toga and he had not shaved his face nor combed his hair, all in token of mourning.

On the steps of the Basilica Opimia I found Cicero, surrounded as always by clients and friends. Ordinarily I would have waited upon his notice like everyone else, but my office and my lictor allowed me to approach him at once.

"Good morning, *Aedile*," he saluted, always punctilious in matters of office. He raised an eyebrow at sight of my lictor. "Does your office now carry *imperium*? I must have dozed off during the last Senate meeting."

"Good morning, Marcus Tullius, and no, I'm just carrying out an investigation for Varus. I would greatly appreciate your advice."

"Of course." We made that little half-turn that proclaimed that we were now in private conference and the others directed their attention elsewhere. "Is it the murder of Aulus Cosconius? Shocking business."

"Exactly. What were the man's political leanings, if any?"

"He was a dreadfully old-fashioned man, the sort who oppose almost anything unsanctioned by our remote ancestors. Like most of the men involved in City property trade, he supported Crassus. Before he left for Syria, Crassus told them all to fight Pompey's efforts to become Dictator. That's good advice, even coming from Crassus. I've spent months trying to convince the tribunes not to introduce legislation to that effect."

"What about next year's tribunes?" I asked.

"Next year's? I'm having trouble enough with the ones we have now."

"Even if Pompey isn't named Dictator, he's almost sure to be one of next year's Consuls. If the Tribunes for next year are all Pompey's men, he'll have near-dictatorial authority and the proconsular province of his choosing. He'll be able to take Syria from Crassus, or Gaul from Caesar, if he wants."

Cicero nodded. "That has always been Pompey's style – let someone else do all the fighting, then get the Tribunes to give him command in time for the kill." Now he looked sharply at me. "What are you getting at, Decius?"

"Be patient with me, Marcus Tullius. I have . . ." at that moment I saw a slave, one of Asklepiodes's silent Egyptian assistants, making his way toward me, holding a folded piece of papyrus, which he handed to me. I opened up the papyrus, read the single word it held, and grinned. "Marcus Tullius," I said, "if a man were standing for public office and were caught in some offense against the ancient laws – say, he carried arms within the boundaries set by Romulus – would it abnegate his candidacy?" My own solution to the law was to carry a *caestus*. The spiked boxing glove was, technically, sports equipment rather than a proper weapon.

"It's a commonly violated custom in these evil times, but if I were standing for office against that man I would prosecute him and tie him up in litigation so thoroughly that he would never take office."

"That is just what I needed to know. Marcus Tullius, if I might impose upon you further, could you meet with me this afternoon at the *ludus* of Statilius Taurus?"

Now he was thoroughly mystified, something I seldom managed to do to Cicero. "Well, my friend Balbus has been writing me from Africa for months to help him arrange the Games he will be giving when he returns. I could take care of that at the same time."

"Thank you, Marcus Tullius." I started to turn away.

"And, Decius?"

I turned back. "Yes?"

"Do be entertaining. That's a long walk."

"I promise it."

At the bottom of the steps I took the tablet thonged to the slave's belt and wrote on the wax with my stylus. "Take this to your master," I instructed. He nodded wordlessly and left. Asklepiodes's slaves could speak, but only in Egyptian, which in Rome was the same thing as being mute. Then I gave the lictor his orders.

"Go to Quintus Cosconius, the man in mourning dress over there with the candidates, and tell him that he is summoned to confer with me at the Statilian School in" – I glanced up at the angle of the sun – "three hours."

He ran off and I climbed the lower slope of the Capitoline along the Via Sacra to the Archive. I spoke with Calpurnius, the freedman in charge of estate titles, and he brought me a great stack of tablets and scrolls, bulky with thick waxen seals, recording the deeds of the late Aulus Cosconius. The one for the Aventine town house where I had discovered his body was a nice little wooden diptych with bronze hinges. Inside, one leaf bore writing done with a reed pen in black ink. The other had a circular recess that held the wax seal protecting it from damage.

"I'll just take this with me, if you don't mind," I said.

"But I do mind," Calpurnius said. "You have no subpoena from a *Praetor* demanding documents from this office." One always has to deal with such persons, on public duty. After much wrangling and talking with his superiors and swearing of sacred oaths upon the altars of the State, I got away with the wretched document, to be returned the next morning or forfeit my life.

Thus armed, I made my leisurely way toward the river and crossed the Aemilian Bridge into the Trans-Tiber district. There, among the river port facilities of Rome's newest district, was the *ludus* of Statilius

Taurus, where the best gladiators outside of Campania were trained.
I conferred with Statilius for an hour or so, making arrangements for
the Games that had already bankrupted me. Then Cicero arrived to
do the same on behalf of his friend Balbus. He was accompanied by
five or six clients, all men of distinction in their own right.

With our business concluded, we went out to the gallery that
overlooked the training yard. It was an hour when only the fighters
of the first rank were working out, while the tyros watched from the
periphery. These men despised practice weapons, preferring to train
with sharp steel. Their skill was amazing to see. Even Cicero, who
had little liking for the public shows, was impressed.

Asklepiodes arrived as we were thus engaged, holding a folded
garment. "This is the oddest task you have ever asked of me," he
said, "but you always furnish amusement of the highest sort, so I
expect to be amply rewarded." He handed me the thing.

"Excellent!" I said. "I was afraid the undertaker might have
thrown it away."

"*Aedile*," Cicero said a bit testily. "I do hope this is leading
somewhere. My time is not without value."

I saw a man in a dark toga come through the archway leading
to the practice yard. "I promise not to disappoint you. Here's my
man now."

Young Cosconius looked around, then saw me gesturing from
the distinguished group on the gallery. He came up the stair,
very stiff and dignified. He was surprised to see Cicero and his
entourage, but he masked his perplexity with an expression of
*gravitas* befitting one recently bereaved and seeking high office. He
saluted Cicero, ex-Consul and the most important man currently
residing in Rome.

"I am here on a matter of business," Cicero said. "I believe your
business is with the *Aedile*."

"I apologize for summoning you here," I said. "I know that you
must be preoccupied with your late father's obsequies." When I had
last seen him, he had been busy grubbing votes.

"I trust you've made progress in finding my father's murderer,"
he said, coldly.

"I believe I have." I looked out over the men training in the yard
below. "It's a chore, arranging for public Games. You'll find that
out. I suppose you'll be exhibiting funeral games for your father?"

He shrugged. "He specified none in his will, which was read this
morning. But I may do so when I hold the aedileship."

Confident little bastard, I thought. I pointed to a pair of men
who were contending with sword and shield. One carried the big,

oblong legionary shield and *gladius*, the other a small, round shield and curved shortsword.

"That's Celadus with the Thracian weapons," I said, referring to the latter. "Do you support the Big Shields or the Small Shields?"

"The Big Shields," he said.

"I've always liked the Small Shields," I told him. "Celadus fights Petraites from the School of Ampliatus at next month's Games." Petraites was a ranking Big Shield fighter of the time. I saw that special gleam come into his eye.

"Are you proposing a wager?"

"A hundred on Celadus, even money?" This was more than reasonable. Petraites had the greater reputation.

"Done," he said, taking out his tablet and stylus, handing the tablet to me. I gave him mine, then rummaged around in my tunic and toga.

"I've lost my stylus. Would you lend me yours?"

He handed it over. "Now, I believe you called me here concerning my father's murder."

"Oh, yes, I was coming to that, Quintus Cosconius, I charge you with the murder of your father, Senator Aulus Cosconius."

"You are insane!" he said, his dark face going suddenly pale, as well it might. Of the many cruel punishments on our law books, the one for parricide is one of the worst.

"That is a serious charge, *Aedile*," Cicero said. "Worse than poisoning, worse than treason, even worse than arson."

Cosconius pointed a finger at me. "Maybe you aren't mad. You are just covering up for another of your friend Milo's crimes."

"Asklepiodes pronounced that death was the result of a wound inflicted by a thin blade piercing the heart. He found a bit of foreign substance adhering to the wound, which he took to his surgery to study. I thought at first that the weapon was a bodkin such as prostitutes sometimes carry, but this morning it occurred to me that a writing stylus would serve as well, provided it was made of bronze." I held up the piece of paper Asklepiodes had sent me with its one word: "wax."

"This confirms it. Aulus Cosconius was stabbed through the heart with a stylus uncleaned by its owner since its last use. A bit of wax still adhered to its tip and was left on the wound."

Quintus Cosconius snorted. "What of it? Nearly every literate man in Rome carries a stylus!"

"Actually, I didn't really forget my own stylus today." I took it out. "You see, the common styli are round or quadrangular. Mine, for instance, is slightly oval in cross-section." Cicero and his friends drew out their own implements and showed them. All were as I had described. Cicero's was made of ivory, with a silver scraper.

"Yet Asklepiodes's examination indicated that the weapon used to kill Aulus Cosconius was triangular. You will note that young Quintus's implement is of that geometrical form, which is most rare among styli." I handed it to Cicero.

Then I shook out the tunic the dead man had been wearing. "Note the three parallel streaks of blood. That is where he wiped off the sides of the stylus."

"A coward's weapon," snorted one of Cicero's companions.

"But young Cosconius here is standing for office," I pointed out. "He couldn't afford to be caught bearing arms within the *pomerium*. But most Romans pack a stylus around. It isn't much of a weapon, but no one is going to survive having one thrust through his heart."

"Why should I do such a thing?" Cosconius demanded. You could smell the fear coming off him.

"Yesterday," I said, "you told me you didn't know what use your father intended for that town house. Here is the deed from the Archive." I took the diptych from a fold of my toga and opened it. "And here he states plainly that it is 'to serve as a residence for his only surviving son, Lucius.' He didn't bother showing you this deed or getting your seal on it because he was a very old-fashioned man, and by the ancient law of *patria potestas* you were a minor and could not legally own property while your father was alive. He took you to show you your new digs, and that is where you argued and you killed him."

Everyone glared at Cosconius, but by this time he had gained enough wisdom to keep his mouth shut.

"Killed the old man for his inheritance, did he?" Cicero said grimly.

I shook my head. "No, nobody gets killed over money these days. It's always politics. Aulus Cosconius was generous enough with his wealth, else why give his son a whole town house to himself? But he supported Crassus and Quintus here is Pompey's man. Aulus wouldn't stick his neck out for Crassus, but he could keep Pompey from getting another tame Tribune without risk, or so he thought."

I addressed Cosconius directly. "Sometime during the tour of that townhouse he told you that he forbade you to stand for Tribune. As *pater familias* it was his legal right to do so. Or perhaps he had told you before, and you waited until you were together in a lonely spot to kill him. The law admits of no distinction in such a case."

Cosconius started to get hold of himself, but Cicero deflated him instantly. "I shall prosecute personally, unless you wish to, Decius Caecilius."

"I shall be far too busy for the balance of this year."

Cosconius knew then he was a dead man. Cicero was the greatest prosecutor in the history of Roman jurisprudence, which was precisely why I had asked him there in the first place. He took few cases in those days, but a parricide in a senatorial family would be the splashiest trial of the year.

I summoned the owner of the school. "Statilius, lend me a few of your boys to escort this man to the basilica. I don't want him jumping into the river too soon."

Cosconius came out of his stupor. "Gladiators? You can't let scum like that lay hands on a free man!"

"You'll have worse company soon," Cicero promised him. Then, to me: "*Aedile*, do your duty." I nodded to my borrowed lictor. He walked up behind Quintus Cosconius and clapped a hand on his shoulder, intoning the old formula: "Come with me to the *Praetor*."

That's the good part about being *Aedile*: You get to arrest people.

These were the events of two days in the year 703 of the city of Rome, the consulship of Marcus Valerius Messalla Rufus and Cnaeus Domitius Calvinus.

# THE TREASURY THEFTS
## Wallace Nichols

*So far as I know Wallace Nichols (1888–1967) was the first writer to set a genuine detective story in ancient Rome. His stories about Sollius, the Slave detective, became extremely popular in the pages of the* London Mystery Magazine, *where over sixty of them ran between 1950 and 1968.*

*Michael Williams, a Cornish publisher and friend of Nichols for over thirty years called him "the most extraordinary man I have ever known." The author of over sixty books, Nichols was first and last a poet. His first book of poetry was published when he was sixteen. Born in Birmingham, he was for a while on the editorial staff of the* Windsor Magazine *and a reader at Ward Lock's before he moved to Cornwall for health reasons in 1934. In addition to his poetry and his detective stories he wrote historical novels and boys' adventures. He had known Churchill and Elgar, Dylan Thomas and Lawrence of Arabia. He spoke five modern languages and several ancient ones, including Egyptian and Babylonian. He had written his autobiography which sadly was never published and may well now be lost.*

*At least we can still savour the magic of his writing. His first two stories about Sollius are so intricately connected that I have run them together here as one full-length novella. This is the first time they have been reprinted in over forty years.*

## EPISODE I
## THE CASE OF THE EMPRESS'S JEWELS

Titius Sabinus the Senator found the Emperor in a dejected mood. Knowing Marcus Aurelius to be a philosopher, he set this down either to some unsolved problem of thought, or else to some domestic trouble which had broken into his usual calm of mind. He knew that rumour spoke of the Empress Faustina as being a very extravagant woman, and also of their son, the young Commodus, as being a stubborn, difficult youth to control. But Sabinus made a point of listening to rumour, especially to Roman rumour, with great cautiousness.

Gazing now at the Emperor's tired face, he began to wonder, with not a little unease, why he had been summoned so unexpectedly to the huge imperial palace on the Esquiline. As far as he knew, there was no public crisis of any kind upon which his advice might be required, nor, as he could see at a glance, had any other senator been summoned to the same audience. He was still more astonished when the Emperor, taking him aside at once, made a seemingly earnest enquiry about nothing of greater importance than a private occurrence in the Senator's household.

"Yes, sir, the thief was discovered," the Senator answered the Emperor, "and the money," he added, rubbing his hands, "was found also. I lost nothing – except my sleep for a few nights."

"It was, then, quite a large sum, Sabinus?"

"It was, sir. My steward from Sardinia had just come with the money from the sale of my lead mines there. He arrived late, and there was no time to deposit it in the bank before morning, and by morning – it had gone!"

"An unpleasant experience," commented the Emperor. "But you got it back – and found the culprit?"

"Both, sir, by the favour of the gods," replied Sabinus, and a rich man's satisfaction oozed from every syllable.

"Rumour has been busy with the affair," smiled Marcus Aurelius.

"Oh, rumour!" muttered Sabinus, and spread out his hands.

"I hope that for once," the Augustus went on, "rumour is true."

"Sir?"

"It is said that you owe the discovery both of the thief and the money's hiding-place to the cleverness of one of your slaves."

"That is so, Augustus," Sabinus answered, still surprised at the Emperor's apparently deep interest. "It is not the first time, either, that the wits of my good Sollius have served me well in the same way. But never before in so large a matter, but only in cases of petty pilfering at my house here in Rome or at one of my country villas."

"What did you say was his name?" asked Marcus Aurelius.

"Sollius, O Augustus."

"I understand, too," pursued the Emperor, "that he has been useful in uncovering thefts for one or two of your friends."

"I did not know," said Sabinus, unable longer to hide his astonishment at the course of the interview, "that the doings of one of my slaves had interested your august ear. I hope that he has not been meddling in public matters and joining a – conspiracy, sir!"

Marcus Aurelius laughed, and laid his hand familiarly on the other's shoulder.

"I only wanted your report of him," he said. "You see – "

The Emperor hesitated, and laughed again.

"You see," he concluded, "I wish to borrow him from you."

"Augustus!" cried Sabinus, and his mouth remained open.

"Listen, Sabinus," said Marcus Aurelius, and indicating an ivory chair to his guest, he took his seat on a small, gilded Greek couch nearby. "Listen, and I will explain. But what I am about to tell you," he went on in a voice suddenly vibrant with all the might of his august and sacred authority, "must be as secret as one of the old Mysteries until I release you myself from the obligation of silence."

"Why, of course, sir," answered Sabinus obsequiously, not a little flattered by the Emperor's personal confidence, for it was the first time in his life that he had been so honoured.

"It is like this," the Emperor continued. "The Treasury is being robbed."

"The gods forbid!" ejaculated Sabinus. "Who could do such a thing?"

"That is the problem," was the dry answer. "That is why I wish to borrow your cunning slave."

"Certainly, O Augustus, certainly; he is at your service, wholly at your service, of course! If I had known, I would myself have brought him with me – "

"Wait, wait, Sabinus," said Marcus Aurelius. "You go too quickly."

"Your pardon, sir!"

"The investigations of the Treasury officials," the Emperor went on gravely, "have discovered nothing. There are even no suspicions, and where there are no suspicions there can be no evidence. Probably, too, the whole matter touches someone highly placed. I have therefore to go very carefully. I must not make a mistake when I accuse – whomever I shall accuse. The whole affair, politically, could be very dangerous. It must be handled with more than secrecy, more than discretion: it must be handled wisely."

"Most truly spoken, sir!" hastily agreed the Senator.

"I must therefore test this slave of yours, Sabinus, before I permit him to touch an investigation so dangerous."

"You will find him wholly trustworthy."

"He is – a young man?"

"No, sir. He is a man in late middle life."

"So much the better. He is educated, I suppose?"

"He was the favourite slave of my uncle, from whom I inherited him," replied Sabinus. "He was picked out, even as a youth, to be my uncle's reader – and my uncle was a great lover of philosophy and poetry, sir – and he had Sollius educated and well trained for that purpose."

"Excellent!" said the Emperor.

He considered a moment, frowning and stroking his beard, before saying anything further, and Sabinus looked at him expectantly. He thought that the master of the Roman world appeared less philosophical than usual, as if, indeed, he were seriously worried. He was pale, and his heavily lidded eyes lacked their usual lustre. Sabinus was about to venture a remark as to his slave's complete dependability when abruptly the Emperor took up the subject himself.

"These thefts," he said, "from the Treasury – for there have been more than one – are so delicate a matter that I would try your Sollius first, my good Sabinus, in something a little less serious before finally giving him so important and confidential a mission."

"Yes, Augustus, I fully understand," replied Sabinus, nodding.

"It happens that the occasion is unfortunately only too immediate – both in time and for my own peace of mind," went on Marcus Aurelius with a touch of awkwardness. "The Empress has lost some valuable jewels, and again everybody who has been employed to find them, or the stealer of them, has failed. Say nothing to your slave about the more serious matter; tell him merely that he is to help in seeking to discover the whereabouts of the Empress's lost jewels, and send him to me with a serious caution, Sabinus, as to his silence and discretion. I shall give him his instructions myself. Let him come about an hour after noon tomorrow, and ask for Alexias, my Greek freedman."

"You shall be obeyed, O Augustus," answered Titius Sabinus, and fussily took his leave.

Immediately on his return to his own house he sent for the slave named Sollius, and explained to him the great honour that was to be his in serving the Emperor himself, and then at great length, and without the slightest necessity, warned him to be thoroughly prudent and entirely secret.

"You are not to tell even *me* anything," he concluded, as if that was the final height and test of all perfect discretion.

Sollius the slave was a small man, but inclining to corpulency. His scanty hair was thin and greying, and he was more than beginning to go bald. He had a long, slightly fleshy nose with wide nostrils, and very dark, round eyes. He was cleanshaven, and walked with somewhat of a limp, for his left foot had been caught in a wolf-trap when he was a boy. He had a soft voice and a gentle manner. Always intensely neat as to his person, he went about his concerns and household duties with the candid gaze of an overgrown child. His fellow slaves regarded him without special friendliness, but not with enmity or suspicion; that is to say, he was one among them, but not exactly of them, except in the one undeniable fact of their common slavery. That they did not resent his aloofness, or call it the vanity of a favourite with their master, was a tribute to his natural goodness of heart, for he was as kindly a nurse in any case of their sickness as he was skilful as a prober into any matter of mystery.

He had, however, one friend in the son of a slave-girl who had died some years before, a youth now eighteen years old, and named Lucius. It was as though he had taken this youth under his special protection, and some of his fellow slaves would nudge each other when watching the elder man's kindness to the younger, and whisper together that they thought they knew why! Sollius had taught Lucius many scraps of his own knowledge. More than that, he had found him useful, since he had quick wits and a keen pair of eyes, in his various investigations of theft. He was a strong, healthy and athletic young man, and a general favourite in the Senator's household. Sollius had already determined in mind to use him as his assistant should he need help in what the Emperor might be going to ask him to do.

At the time appointed, Sollius had entered the great palace of the Roman Cæsars on the Esquiline Hill, and, evidently expected, was immediately escorted by a centurion of the Prætorians, the imperial bodyguard, into the presence of Alexias, the Emperor's principal and confidential freedman. He was a lean, dark Greek, with a cold, haughty manner, and he subjected the slave to a close, not to say jealous, scrutiny.

"How do you usually begin your enquiries?" he asked at once, as soon as the centurion had left them, and without wasting any words on greeting.

"By understanding the circumstances of the theft," quietly answered Sollius, and the modesty in his tone and manner was already mollifying the freedman's disapprobation of the slave's privileged employment. Alexias had been resolved to give him no unnecessary assistance, but found that his personality was disarming. He coughed, and a slight, involuntary smile touched his lips.

"I am to take you to the Augustus," he said without further preliminary, and at once led the way towards the Emperor's private apartments and into a small chamber filled with innumerable books and scrolls, but otherwise sparsely and most plainly furnished. It looked out on to a small marble portico from which gleaming steps led down into the vast palace gardens.

The Emperor was dictating to Alexander, his Greek secretary, as they entered, and indicating by a gesture that Alexias and Sollius were to stand quietly on the threshold, he continued pacing up and down and wording aloud a despatch to the commander of the Roman army on the Rhine. It was, Sollius soon decided, of no very great importance, and was more an injunction to be watchful rather than active; but the Emperor seemed to be taking unusual pains over the language in which he was clothing his commands. At moments, as he turned in his pacing, he would glance towards the slave of Titius Sabinus, so that by the time that his dictating was concluded he had already made a shrewd assessment of the man's character from the evidences of his features and manner. He was pleased to notice that instead of keeping his eyes respectfully, or timidly, on the ground, the slave had been regarding him with as much open interest as he himself had been regarding the slave.

"Come nearer," he said quietly and suddenly. "You are Sollius?"

"I am Sollius, Augustus."

"You are clever, I am told, in discovering thieves and lost property."

"I have been lucky, sir, and yet – yes! – I have an aptitude for such things."

Marcus Aurelius smiled. He was never one to appreciate the falsely modest when the simple truth could be spoken without vanity.

"The Empress," he said, "has lost a number of her jewels."

"When?" asked Sollius quickly.

The secretary and the freedman both stared. It was not usual for the Emperor to be challenged so abruptly – not even by a senator or a victorious general on leave.

Marcus Aurelius hesitated, and frowned thoughtfully. Sollius looked at him with eyes suddenly bright.

"Three days ago," said the Emperor, closing the slight pause with imperial decisiveness.

Sollius lowered his eyelids for a moment, and then, with an upward glance, he asked:

"Were they taken from her sleeping-chamber?"

"They were last seen in her sleeping-chamber," carefully replied the Emperor.

"Who saw them – last?"

"The Empress herself. She was choosing a ring from the casket containing them. They were there then."

"Was this at morning or at night?"

"It was about sunset. When the Empress retired to rest some hours later, and gave the ring to her attendant to put away, the casket was found empty."

"I should like to see the chamber, the empty casket and the waitingwoman."

"See to that, Alexias – and Sollius is to be admitted to me, without any delay, at all such times as he may wish," ordered the Emperor.

Alexias and Sollius bowed.

"Come," whispered the freedman, and when the Emperor's voice began dictating again they were already in the long, gilded and painted corridor.

"This way," whispered Alexias again. "Follow me."

A guard, another Prætorian, was on duty by a lofty, decorated door. Recognizing Alexias, he let them both pass.

The chamber of the Empress Faustina was spacious, beautifully proportioned and, in the eyes of Sollius at least, unbelievably luxurious. He stood in the doorway, marvelling. But, even while marvelling, he was darting his looks in all directions, and completing in his mind a picture which he knew would remain in his memory with great exactitude.

"This is Marcia," murmured Alexias, and a young, handsome woman came forward from the dressing-table, which she had been engaged in tidying at the moment of their entrance. "You are to answer all the questions which Sollius – this is Sollius, Marcia – will put to you," the freedman went on. "It is the Augustus's own command."

Marcia fixed Sollius with a clear and resentful gaze.

"I suppose you have already decided that I stole them," she burst out. "Not even the Empress thinks that, and I will not take it from a slave!"

"You yourself are a freedwoman?" asked Sollius with a smile.

"You mistake," she answered proudly. "I am the daughter of a freedman and a freedwoman, free on both sides, and I am a dutiful servant to the Roman Augusta."

"I do not doubt it," replied Sollius. "But tell me this: were you here when the Empress took the ring out of the casket? Oh, is that the same casket over there?"

She nodded, and he went across to the ornate, marble dressing-table. Its appointments were of gold, and the casket itself also was of gold. He stood staring down at it without touching it. Then, without turning, he repeated his previous question.

"I was, slave."

"Did you yourself see whether the casket was then filled with its jewels as usual?"

"I did, and it was, slave," said Marcia.

"Was the casket not kept locked?"

"It was always kept locked. It is only unlocked now because it is empty. Look!"

She moved to his side, and opened the casket by the mere insertion of a painted nail under its lid. It was certainly empty.

"Who entered this room between the time that the Empress took the ring out of this casket and the finding that the rest of the jewels had been stolen?" asked Sollius.

"Myself, twice," she answered. "None else, at least, had any right or proper occasion to enter."

Sollius rubbed his chin.

"Not even the Empress herself – and, perhaps, a friend with her?"

Marcia shook her head.

"The Empress was at a dinner party," she said. "Also," she went on, a trifle maliciously, as if she enjoyed making the problem still more difficult for the slave, "a guard, one of the Prætorians, stood in the corridor all the while."

"Was the guard changed during any part of the time?"

"He had but newly taken his post when the Empress left her chamber, and he had not been relieved," replied Marcia, "by the time of her return."

"Do you know this Prætorian personally?" asked Sollius sharply.

"No more," she answered with a faint, scornful smile, "than I know others of the Prætorians who take their turn of guard. He is not, though you seem to suspect so, my lover. I look higher, slave, than a soldier!"

"Is the same guard on duty now?"

"No, it is another man."

Sollius turned to Alexias.

"I should like to see that guard," he said.

"He shall be summoned," the freedman promised.

Sollius fixed his gaze once more upon Marcia, and eyed her for a moment or so in silence, but she did not fidget under his scrutiny, and returned it with the same proud scorn as before.

"Have you no guess, yourself, as to the thief?" he asked, and his voice was neither accusatory nor suspicious, but strangely compelling.

"None, O slave, I know nothing, and equally suspect nothing."

"Thank you," he answered, bowed courteously, and turned to go.

"I must see that guard as soon as possible," he said when he and Alexias were walking away down the corridor. "I should like also a list of the jewels. Judging from the size of the gold box from which they were taken, they were smallish in size and number."

"You shall have the list, Sollius," replied Alexias. "But I can tell you myself that they consisted of rings, ear-rings, bracelets and hair-adornments – but, though small and containable within a single casket, of great value. The Empress would not wear them if they were not," he added with a swift, sharp glance.

"That is true," answered Sollius gravely.

"What else do you wish to see, or do?" asked the freedman.

"I should like," replied Sollius, "to examine that part of the gardens which is outside the chamber that we have just left."

Alexias looked instantly dubious.

"That is a very private part of the gardens," he said. "I should have to obtain the permission of the Empress to take you there. She may be there herself at this hour – and no one may intrude upon her privacy."

"She is not there," answered Sollius confidently. "I saw no sign of her when I looked out over the gardens just now. Besides," he continued, drawing himself up into an attitude very unbecoming, thought Alexias, in a slave, "I have the Emperor's own commands to do as I wish – or have I not? You heard them from his own lips."

"He did not give you permission to intrude upon the privacy of the Augusta," said Alexias stubbornly. "I heard nothing about that. Be reasonable, Sollius."

"I *must* see that part of the gardens," insisted the slave of Sabinus. "Above all things it is important. Shall I go to the Augustus for his permission? He would, I am confident, give it to me."

"Come," answered the freedman brusquely. "I will take the risk!"

He led the other forth by secret passages into the air and the sunlight. Outside Faustina's apartments, below their position and the marble steps leading down from them into the scented luxury of the gardens themselves, Sollius became quickly busy, examining the grass, the shrubs, the nearest flower-beds, the gleaming steps, top to bottom, and, indeed, the whole vicinity. He was almost like a sniffing dog, thought Alexias disgustedly, for he could not see what good was being done by such actions, and he was annoyed, too, over having been forced to bring the slave into the imperial gardens at all. But the Emperor had a use for the fellow . . . he shrugged his shoulders, and stood watching while Sollius continued his investigations below the Empress's apartments.

"Do not be too long," whispered Alexias, staring nervously around. "The Empress could have us whipped for this – even *me*."

"I am ready now," said Sollius. "There is nothing to be seen – which is often as good, my friend, as to see everything! The two sides of a coin make but one piece of money after all, not two."

Alexias wrinkled his brows in the effort to understand such a puzzling remark, but what with his haste to leave the place where they were and his still doubtful opinion of the slave's qualities, he left the matter without comment, and hurried his companion back into the palace.

"What now?" he asked.

"I am going home," answered Sollius, "to think. I shall come again and ask for you early in the morning – and let that Prætorian be with you."

With a pleasant smile he begged the freedman to show him the nearest way out of the palace, for with its hundreds of confusing corridors and passages he felt bewildered, or so he said.

Alexias stared after him as he saw him forth, and wondered what would come of his enquiry. He had a sudden cold feeling about the heart, and turned away to his other duties with a deep sigh.

As soon as Sollius had returned to his master's house he sought out Lucius. He found him carrying in a huge basket of vegetables from the garden towards the kitchen.

"When you have taken those to the cook," he said, "I have need of you."

"But, Sollius, if the cook wants me to do more errands for him – "

"This is more important, far more important," Sollius answered. "It is on – ahem! – our master's business, and you can tell Tuphus the cook that for a little while you are as good as *my* slave."

Lucius looked at him enquiringly, and then suddenly a grin spread over his face.

"Good, Sollius! Oh, good!" he cried, and shouldering his basket once more, he went off into the kitchen. Almost immediately he was back again.

"Come," said Sollius, and he led the way along a dark passage which came out near the chariot-house and the stables.

Behind these lay a walled enclosure containing a round, stone pool filled with carp. It was a place where they could generally count upon being able to talk undisturbed. Standing beside the pool, and looking down among the dark, swimming forms without any expression upon his face, Sollius began to speak. He told his young companion everything. He knew that he could trust him, and that he would have to employ a helper in his new task, and also that there was nobody else, as he had already proved, with the right kind of aptitude for being his assistant.

"I suppose," said Lucius after he had listened carefully, "that either the waiting-woman – did you say she was named Marcia? – or the guard took them."

"I cannot answer about the guard," replied Sollius, "for I have not yet questioned him. But I am sure that Marcia had nothing to do with it, for I think that she is as puzzled as I am. I could see it in her eyes."

"And *are* you puzzled, Sollius?" asked Lucius seriously.

"I am," answered Sollius, and sighed. "The signs are so contradictory. I have even wondered whether there has been any theft at all!"

Lucius gaped at him.

"But would the Emperor himself have employed you to find out about it if – if there had *not* been anything stolen?" he asked.

"It could be possible: he might himself be deceived," said Sollius, musingly, still gazing down into the pool. "There are so many rumours," he muttered under his breath, "about the debts of the young Commodus – and his mother has always spoilt him."

"When you say that the signs are contradictory, what," asked Lucius, "do you mean?"

"I mean," Sollius replied, "that I saw no scratches about the small keyhole of the casket; that I saw no marks beneath the Empress's apartment; that Marcia was more puzzled than afraid, when I should have expected her to be more afraid than puzzled; and that I felt Alexias was, as it were, playing a part, as if he thought that my intrusion into the mystery was unnecessary, but that he dared not tell the Emperor so. All this," he added, spreading out his hands so that they made a shadow fall across the water and disturbed the otherwise sleepy carp, "makes me wonder if I am being – deliberately misled. But, Lucius, I must question that Prætorian who was on guard on the evening of the supposed theft before I make up my mind about that word 'supposed.'"

He sighed, and then was silent for a while, staring down into the pool at his feet. Suddenly he spoke again, and more briskly:

"There is something that I want you to do for me, Lucius."

"What is that, Sollius?" asked Lucius, and his eyes brightened.

"I want you to mingle with the slaves in the money-changers' quarters. Find out from gossip whether any jewels have been pledged for security yesterday or to-day, or sold for any large sum, or – any gossip about a sudden appearance of jewels in unusual places."

"I can do that, Sollius," replied Lucius eagerly.

"Meanwhile I shall see that Prætorian," mused Sollius. "But I doubt – I really doubt – if I shall learn much from him."

He shook his head dubiously, and led the way back to the kitchen quarters.

"Go on your errand at once," he whispered. "I will make it right with Tuphus – or our master will, if I fail. Is not the Emperor behind it?"

Lucius grinned, and sped away.

Early, as promised, Sollius hastened to the palace next morning, and asked for Alexias. He was taken to a small, bare room, somewhat away from the imperial apartments, and lit only by a pale, dusty light that filtered through a grating. It was like a guardroom, except that its appointments were domestic rather than military. He was left there alone for quite a long time, and was beginning to feel impatient, and even a little angry, when Alexias hurried in with a scared face.

"He has disappeared!" he whispered hollowly. "I went for him myself, but he was not in his quarters. He has disappeared," he repeated, "just as if he were a deserter. Nobody can understand it. Nobody!"

"Has the Emperor been told?" asked Sollius, plucking at his lips.

"It is not a nice report to make," answered Alexias, and gestured impotently.

Then his face brightened as he produced a scroll from somewhere about him.

"But I have the list of the missing jewels," he said.

Sollius brushed it aside, and the Emperor's freedman stared.

"But you asked for it?" he stammered.

"I know," said Sollius. "I may need it – or may not. But the disappearance of this Prætorian changes the order of my plans. The sooner he is found, whether alive or dead – "

"Dead?" cried Alexias in horror. "Do you think *that*?"

"I fear it," replied Sollius. "Have you seen the man's centurion?"

"He knows nothing."

"You mean that he *says* he knows nothing," answered Sollius. "Bring him here," he ordered abruptly.

The freedman drew himself up, but meeting Sollius's eye, he shrugged his shoulders.

"As you will," he said stiffly. "We have the Emperor's command to obey you."

He turned quickly, and left the slave once again alone. Sollius stood perfectly still, and closed his eyes. He did not open them until he heard the rustle of metal as the centurion was brought in by Alexias. Then he fixed the man with a deep stare.

"Your name?" he asked.

"Decius," answered the centurion sullenly.

He seemed to have come unwillingly and to resent any interrogation by a slave. He stood rigidly, one hand on the brazen hilt of his short stabbing-sword.

"What is the name of this missing soldier?" pursued Sollius.

"Constans."

"When did you last see him?"

"Last night – in a tavern."

"Was he drunk?"

"Constans had a strong head," answered Decius, and would have laughed if he had not remembered that his questioner was a slave. He stood more rigidly than ever.

"Did you leave him in the tavern, or did he come away with you?"

"I said I saw him last *in* a tavern – not going to it, nor coming from it," replied Decius.

"You did not part from him at the tavern door – in the street?"

"I left him with a girl on his knee," said Decius gruffly.

"Which tavern was it?"

"*The Two Cranes*, in the Subura," answered the centurion without hesitation.

Sollius rubbed his chin while he thought briefly.

"And you have no idea at all what has happened to him?" he asked.

"I know less about it than about the Emperor's philosophy," replied the still sullen centurion, yet with a fugitive touch of contemptuous humour, nevertheless, for he was beginning to thaw a little under the slave's quiet and assured manner.

"Has anybody been sent to that tavern to make enquiries?" asked Sollius.

"The tribune sent," was the answer.

"With no result?"

"With no result!"

"Did nobody there remember his leaving?"

"Nobody," answered Decius. "At least," he added, a little less surlily, "nobody was willing to admit to remembering anything."

"Ah-h!" breathed Sollius. "Has this tavern a good reputation?"

"It is in the Subura," answered the centurion with a meaning shrug.

"Even the worst district of Rome," said the slave, "can have one decent tavern in it!"

"Then your experience is different from mine," replied Decius, and this time he laughed outright.

He had a clear-cut, honest face, thought Sollius, looking at him with a newly probing gaze. Suddenly he made up his mind.

"Come, centurion, we will go there now, you and I, together."

"Softly, slave!" cried Decius. "Who are you to give me orders? I have answered your questions because Alexias told me to answer 'em, and Alexias is the Emperor's own servant. But this is another matter. What'll my tribune say? A soldier – and a Prætorian, mind you! – can only take orders from his own officers."

"That is all right," said Sollius quietly. "Alexias will tell you that in this matter my orders are as good as the Emperor's own."

"What, slave!" burst out Decius.

"Quietly," said Alexias, and touched the centurion's arm. "It is as he says. He has the Emperor's authority for what he is doing. Go with him. I will explain to your tribune."

"Castor and Pollux flay me!" cried Decius. "This is a pretty thing: a centurion of the Prætorians to take orders from a slave!"

Nevertheless, in spite of his bluster, for once it was so, and he and Sollius presently departed on their errand side by side, the upright, marching Prætorian, and the fattish, shuffling slave making a comical enough sight for those who passed by them in the narrow, tortuous and crowded streets.

The thoroughfares of Rome were inordinately dirty and noisy, and those who walked had a bad time of it, being continually pushed to the walls by the litters of the important or the wealthy, borne by running slaves, generally of huge stature, negroes or Cappadocians being the favourites for that kind of work. All Rome was dirty, tortuous, unsavoury and crowded, but no quarter was as bad in all those respects as the infamous Subura, the haunt and kennel of the worst elements of the population. Sollius knew it well, but he never entered it without the utmost distaste. The inns and hovels were little better than thieves' dens, and worse; every kind of rascality and vice was at home; it stank both physically and morally.

The centurion led the way down an evil-smelling byway between high walls that leant crookedly towards one another like two drunken men seeking to hold each other up, yet never managing to make actual contact in their swaying towards one another for support.

Though the day itself was bright, the byway was so dark that Sollius frequently stumbled over the uneven cobbles, slippery with all kinds of nauseous garbage.

The two had uttered no word during their journey. But it would have been difficult to have conversed amid such constant jostling and noise; and now, in that quieter spot, the centurion cleared his throat, spat and spoke:

"We are nearly there, O slave. The open doorway at the end, see?"

It was more like the entrance to a dark cave than the door of a supposedly inviting tavern, and was no advertisement of its pleasures. Indeed, thought Sollius, it needed courage to enter at all. At night it would be even more daunting to a timid man, though, no doubt, there would be a torch in the iron sconce at the side of the entrance.

"I'll see you come to no harm," grunted the centurion through the side of his mouth as if he had read his companion's thoughts.

He plunged into the darkest recesses of the alley with the familiarity of frequent experience, and was about to enter into the black mouth of the doorway when a man, rushing out as in a violent hurry, thrust him against the wall, and was gone before either he or Sollius could catch at him and hold him. They could hear his sandals slapping against the cobbles as he sped away down other thoroughfares, and then the noise was swallowed up in the greater noises round and about.

The centurion grunted angrily, and then entered the tavern without further hindrance. Sollius followed at his heels. It was lighter inside than the slave had expected, for two or three clay lamps were diffusing a pale light in an inner room. But the immediate entrance, a smaller room like a vestibule, was both dark and empty. The whole place smelt of rancid oil, sour wine, stale vegetables and fetid odours of every conceivable variety of dirt and corruption. Sollius sniffed audibly.

"You're too dainty!" muttered Decius as he led the way through towards the inner room.

But Sollius had not been savouring the unpleasant layers of dead air about him, but was trying to remember where he had smelt before the perfume which had come from the garments of the man who had rushed out past them. And then he knew. It had been in the bedchamber of the Empress. His mind suddenly grew wary. They should have stopped that running man!

He gave a swift glance about him as they entered the inner room. It had benches about the walls; winecasks at one end, in a kind of bricked, recessed tunnel, too small to be termed a cellar, yet serving something of the same purpose; and stools, some still lying where they had fallen the previous night, and others disposed about conveniently for those drinking. At the moment, however, only two occupants faced the centurion and Sollius as they entered, the tavern-keeper himself and a flute-boy, the latter very pale, puffed under the eyes, and drowsy. A flight of shallow stone steps led to an upper floor. They were festooned with cobwebs and covered with dust and dirt. The whole place seemed never to have been swept or cleaned since it had been built, perhaps over a hundred years before.

"What d'ye want?" asked the tavern-keeper, glowering through the dim light.

"You're to answer some questions," replied the centurion brusquely, "and mind you tell us no lies."

"I've been badgered with questions for hours," growled the other. "I know nothing. Your comrade strode out o' that doorway as well as he entered through it – or nearly as well," he added with a truculent leer. "I won't say as he wasn't drunk."

"Who helped him out?" asked Sollius.

"And who are *you* to be asking that or any other question?" demanded the tavern-keeper.

"I am his uncle," answered Sollius, lying glibly, "and his mother, my sister, lies dying. He must be fetched home. Cannot you help us at all?"

His voice was pitched just in the right key, neither wheedling nor exacting, but anxiously pleading. The centurion stared sidelong at him with a new appreciation of his parts.

"If I had nothing to tell a Prætorian officer," grunted the tavern-keeper, "am I like to have anything to tell a fat rascal like you who couldn't even pay me for a blind man's wink?"

"Even a blind man's wink," laughed Sollius, "might tell me what he had heard with his ears!"

"I heard nothing; I saw nothing; I know nothing," said the other, and his tone had finality. "D'ye think I'm such a fool as not to be able to sell any kind o' knowledge to a good bidder? Or not to save my skin if I had knowledge when a Prætorian officer came sniffing around with a meddling nose? I heard nothing; I saw nothing; I know nothing," he repeated, and spat without caring where.

"There was no brawl?" went on Sollius doggedly.

"There's always a brawl!" leered the other. "That's life: drink and brawling. Men are men in the Subura."

"There was a girl – " suggested Sollius.

"He had no money," answered the tavern-keeper shortly. "She wasn't on his knee long, I can tell you that. I don't allow it – when there's no money. But why this fuss over a missing soldier?" he asked with lowered brows, suspiciously. "What's he been doing? Threatening the life of the Emperor? Or teaching young Commodus evil manners? But any teacher o' such 'ud soon end by being the pupil o' that young lad, prince as he may be, and dainty brought up! I wonder his father lets him out of his eye. I'd keep him well watched, *I* would – or send him to one o' the frontiers to learn war."

"Peace, rascal!" cried the centurion. "D'ye want a whipping after I've made my report?"

"I'm only saying what everybody is saying," growled the tavern-keeper, and made a lewd gesture. "The Emperor is too good for such dogs. Good men don't see all as they ought to see, and there's a lot in Rome that needs looking at – though I hope it won't be in *my* time," he added with a salacious grin. "I've my living to get!"

Sollius could bear the fetid atmosphere no longer, and he was convinced by now that the tavern-keeper really knew nothing. He turned.

"Come," he said brusquely over his shoulder to the centurion. "There is nothing to learn here."

He stumbled out through the dark outer room and so to the alley outside. As soon as they were a little distance down this, he laid a hand on the centurion's arm, and whispered urgently:

"Go back, and fetch out that fluteboy!"

Decius stared, but seeing the expression on Sollius's face, he bit back the sarcastic retort which he had intended to make, turned smartly on his heel and re-entered the tavern. He was out again with the flute-boy before Sollius had reached the corner where the alley debouched into the crowded and wider way. The fluteboy appeared terrified. The centurion held him firmly by an arm.

"Come with us," said Sollius, and his voice was kindly. "We mean you no harm."

"What do you want?" stammered the boy. "I have done nothing. I'm a good boy. Everybody round here will give me a good name."

"Nobody round here could give anybody a good name!" answered Sollius a little primly. "Don't let go of him, centurion."

"Where are you taking me?" whimpered the boy.

"We can't talk in this noisy bustle," replied the slave, and he led the way, with the centurion still grasping the flute-boy by the arm, at his heels.

He did not lead them to the imperial palace, but to the house of Titius

Sabinus, his master. There he took them to the same walled enclosure behind the chariot-house where he had talked with Lucius.

"We can be private here," he said.

It was certainly very quiet, there by the carp-pool.

"Tell me," Sollius began, "who it was that hurriedly left as we entered the tavern where you play your flute."

The boy was shaking with fear, and could hardly stammer out:

"He had b-been there all n-night."

"You have seen him in the tavern before?"

"Once or twice – lately. What are you w-wanting of me?"

"Only true answers to my questions," replied Sollius softly, "and then you can go back as quickly as you can run. Do you know his name?"

The flute-boy shook his head.

"He is a rich young man," he said, "but no one mentions his name."

"Have you seen him close – under the lamp? Does he wear a great deal of jewellery: rings and gold chains and so on?"

"He wouldn't in the Subura!" muttered the centurion. "Or not for long!"

"Answer me, flute-boy!"

"Not that I have seen. Myrtis says – "

"Who is Myrtis?"

"One of the girls in the house. I play for their dances."

"Go on."

"Myrtis says he is a gladiator. But – "

"Go on."

"I don't suppose she really knows. She is always telling lies."

At that moment Lucius joined them.

"I heard you had returned, Sollius," he said, "and Tuphus said you had come this way."

Sollius took his arm, and they walked to the other side of the carp-pool out of hearing of the others.

"What have you found out?" he asked in a lowered voice.

"Nothing, Sollius. No jewels in any quantity have been sold or pledged just lately."

"Not by – the Empress's son?"

Lucius started, and then looked scared.

"I did hear something about him," he whispered. "He is in great debt and seeking a loan."

Sollius rubbed his chin.

"Then no jewels have been – ahem! – abstracted for *his* benefit," he muttered in a muse, "so everything hangs upon finding that lost

Prætorian. Ah, you won't have heard about that," he added, and gave a brief account of his own researches that morning. "The flute-boy, after all, knows nothing. I am disappointed. I had expected more from him. I think it very likely that the man who brushed past us was a gladiator, as Myrtis says. Even his scentedness is a confirmation."

"A *scented* gladiator?" exclaimed Lucius. "But they are such tough men – they have to be!"

"Many of them," answered Sollius dryly, "are ladies' favourites. But that is a different matter."

He broke off with an impatient gesture, and led the way back to the centurion and the flute-boy.

"You can go," he said to the latter with a smile, and clapped him on the back. "Take him into the kitchen," he directed Lucius, "and wheedle Tuphus into giving him some aniseed cakes."

Lucius took the flute-boy away.

"A further question or two, my friend, and you can go, too," said Sollius to the centurion.

Decius mumbled under his breath, but appeared ready to answer, nevertheless.

"Had this missing Constans relatives in Rome?"

"A mother and an elder brother, a cobbler. Neither has heard of him. I was sent myself to find out."

Sollius frowned, and once more rubbed his chin.

"Had he any special interest in life outside his being a soldier?" he asked after pondering silently for a while.

"Drinking and girls: I know of naught else," answered the centurion bluntly and a little sourly.

"What was his character – as a soldier?"

"As a soldier? He wouldn't be one of *us*," said the centurion of the Prætorians proudly, "if he hadn't a good name and a clean tablet in records."

"Desertion has been hinted," suggested Sollius.

"No Prætorian ever deserts!" roundly asserted the other. "The pickings are too good!"

"I know you are the most privileged troops in the Empire," said Sollius placatingly. "But I am sure that you can tell me something that I ought to know – something that, perhaps, you don't realize that you know yourself. Think for a moment quietly. Look at the carp there as you think; their quiet swimming about will help to compose your mind. I have often found it useful in that way. And then speak the first thing about this Constans which enters your thoughts, no matter how trivial or how silly it may seem – just the first thing that enters your head, centurion."

Decius did as he was told, staring down at the carp in puckered concentration. Suddenly he began to laugh.

"What is it? What have you remembered?" cried Sollius eagerly.

"It was nothing, nothing at all," replied Decius, still laughing, "but it was funny at the time. We all laughed about it. Anyway, he got a gold piece from the Emperor for it, and the promise of a gardener's job when his service days are over. We've nicknamed him 'the gardener,' though I've never seen him dig in our camp garden all the while I've been stationed in Rome, and that is many years now, slave."

"Why did the Emperor give him a gold piece? Go on, go on!" urged Sollius impatiently.

"It was this way," answered the centurion leisurely, and laughing and smiling as he talked. "It was the Empress's birthday, and we were paraded in her honour. We had a rose issued to each of us, and we were ordered in the march past to throw our roses in a heap at her feet, each file in turn. Constans had had a thick night at a tavern, and had come on parade without breaking his fast, but with a bunch of radishes hid in his tunic to chew while standing at ease before the Augusta's arrival. We always have to parade hours before time! Well, somehow, after the roses had been issued to us and fastened in our helmets, Constans had the ill luck to drop his and lose it during a bit o' drill we were put through to fill out the time. It was a real bit of evil luck, for he would be on the outside of his file as it marched past the Emperor and Empress, and it would have been seen that he had nothing to throw on the heap. Had he been on the inside it might have passed unnoticed, though an officer *was* level with the rank behind. However, there it was, and without his rose he was in a fair sweat, I can tell you. When the time came, what else could he do but fling down his bunch o' radishes? Large 'uns, they were, too! Quite like prize ones! With luck, in such a shower o' roses, they'd not have been noticed. But Constans was never a lucky man. We often say he's the victim o' the evil eye! Anyhow, the Empress saw it. Sharp eyes, as well as beautiful ones, has the Empress! And she whispered to the Emperor. After the parade Constans was summoned to the Empress's footstool, and accused o' being disrespectful and unsoldierly. He was like to be whipped, but he always had a tongue in his head, had Constans, and the cheekiness of a British gooseboy. I have served in Britain, and know! Well, he got out of it. Said they were his own growing. Said he thought it more of a real homage to the Empress to give her something of his own, and not a mere flower provided by the Senate! The Emperor laughed, and the Empress – though I don't think that at first she had meant to be kind about it – took a look at the Emperor's face – and fetched up a smile. All was safely over – and then the Emperor made his promise to take Constans on as a gardener when his time of service should be up. And he no gardener at all! Laugh! That night the whole barracks was one roar! Well, that's all – and it can't have anything to do with his disappearance now. It was over a year ago."

"Thank you for telling me," said Sollius quietly. "Thank you, too, for taking me to *The Two Cranes*. I'd not like to go there alone. I think that is all I want of you."

"Then I'll go back to barracks," answered the centurion. "It's been better than drilling, anyway, even if it has been o' no use. If you want to know what *I* think, Constans is in the Tiber with some woman's husband's knife in him. Why there's such a fuss about him is what puzzles *me*."

He nodded, and marched away, whistling.

Lucius found Sollius still standing by the carp-pool.

"The flute-boy has gone," he said.

Sollius did not answer.

"Have you discovered anything?" asked Lucius after a pause.

Sollius sighed.

"I am not sure," he answered, and his face was grave and unhappy. "I do not like being – deceived. And I can see only deception, whichever way I look."

Lucius stared at him.

"I don't understand," he said.

"Neither do I," answered Sollius ruefully. "Is our master within?"

Lucius nodded.

Sollius went indoors, sought out the Senator his master, and put a single question.

"Why, yes," replied Sabinus. "It is about three miles out along the Appian Way. I have had the honour of visiting there myself. How are your investigations getting on?" he asked anxiously. "It was on my recommendation that the Emperor is employing you in this matter, and I should not like you to – fail," he whispered.

He looked at the slave questioningly, but Sollius did not respond in the confidential way that the Senator had expected.

"I have discovered hardly anything," murmured Sollius. "But a swallow can smell spring ahead before he begins flying home from Africa!"

Sabinus dismissed him almost irritably.

"I am going to the Augustus's palace, Lucius," announced Sollius in the early evening of the same day. "I wish to ask Alexias one more question."

The house of Sabinus stood in its own grounds, with extensive gardens, and the way from the house itself to the gates was long, winding and overshadowed by chestnut trees. It was growing dusk, and the sky was already filled with the first stars. Nearer the gates the trees were more crowded and the darkness more complete. Sollius strode on through the shadowy avenue in a deep muse. He was both sure and puzzled.

Something like a large corn-sack was suddenly and swiftly drawn over his head; his legs were knocked from under him; and then his hands were roped behind him, and his ankles were bound together at the same time. Evidently his assailants were two in number. And now, one taking his shoulders and the other his feet, he was carried away, half-smothered in the sack, he knew not whither.

He had not struggled with his captors, for he was not a man of violence. Except for being startled at first, he was not frightened. He was, in fact, intensely curious, eager to know what would happen next, for he knew that his abduction must have some connection with what he was investigating. He felt, too, that if they had been going to kill him they would have done so straightway.

They did not carry him very far, but transferred him to a vehicle of some sort, drawn either, he judged from the sounds, by a pair of horses or mules. Probably, he guessed from the creaking noise of four wooden wheels, it was some kind of a farmcart.

In this he was taken a considerable distance, but in what direction he had no means of telling. The cart was hooded, he judged, for all outside sounds seemed muffled – and by more than the sack over his head – even the voices of the driver and his companion. It was now quite dark, not only within the vehicle, but in the open air and the countryside through which they were passing. It must have been quite late at night when the cart suddenly stopped to the furious barking of watchdogs and the rattling of their chains in the kennels. He recognized the peculiar bark of one of them. It was, surely, a Gallic hound. Sabinus possessed one, which had been the gift of the Emperor himself. He was glad that none of the dogs was loose. To have him torn to pieces might be a good way to dispose of him with all the appearance of accident, and very unpleasant, indeed! But the longer he had thought – and he had had plenty of time for cogitation – the more sure he had become that no real violence was intended.

He was lifted out of the vehicle in the same manner that he had been lifted in, and carried into what seemed to be one of the outhouses of a farm. The corn-sack was taken from his head as he was laid against one of the mud walls, but neither his feet nor his hands were untied. A single clay lamp on the floor in one corner dimly lit the place. A number of spades and other agricultural implements were lying about, and he thought that his guess was probably correct, and that he was in an outbuilding of a farm, or perhaps of a country villa. He looked at the two men who had abducted him, and recognized neither; but he had not expected to recognize them. The dogs were still barking.

"Dost thou know why thou'st been brought here?" asked one of the men in a harsh, truculent voice.

"I think so," quietly answered Sollius, blinking in the light of the lamp which the other man had taken up and was now holding close to the prisoner's eyes. Sollius noticed that this second man was tall, lean and very straight of back.

"Thou'dst be a fool if not!" snarled the first man. "We have orders to tell thee to stop looking for the thief o' – thou knowest what as well as I do."

As he spoke he showed what he was holding in his hand: a short length of thin, knotted strangler's cord.

"Well, thou seest, slave? And understandest?"

The other man straightened himself, and laughed.

"Thou canst not escape," he said, and put down the lamp on a dusty tool-bench nearby.

Sollius looked at him.

"You, of course, are Constans," he said.

"Oho!" laughed the Prætorian, in no way disconcerted. "Thou'rt a sharp one!"

He seemed more good-humoured than his fellow, who was scowling, thought Sollius, in a very horrible manner. How far would they go in torturing him? He wondered if what he had come to guess could really be right! If it was, he could laugh at the proceedings; if not, he was in a most miserable and fearful position – and might never know the truth. To die without knowing all about the affair shook his equanimity in prospect more than the actual danger in which he stood.

It was Constans who finally menaced him with a woodcutter's axe, swinging it above his head, all his outward good-humour gone in a flash as his companion rasped out:

"A dead guesser can't guess – right. But it might save your life – to guess wrong."

"Dost hear, slave?" asked Constans, the axe still poised in air.

"What dost thou know?" demanded the other, fingering the knotted length of cord.

"Answer, slave!" said the Prætorian in a hissing whisper.

"I can tell what I know only to the Emperor," answered Sollius, and hoped that his voice sounded firm.

"Leave the Emperor out of this!" said the man with the strangler's cord.

"It is the Emperor's business," replied Sollius. "How, then, can I leave him out? I shall tell you nothing," he added with as much show of courage as he could imitate, and even then he did not know whether he had cause for his worst fears – or not. Well, he had to test it, the one way or the other. "You can kill me," he said huskily, "but you won't get a word out of me. And you must not be too sure," he added, blinking up at them, "that I have anything to tell."

"Anything or nothing, our orders are the same," said the man with the cord, and glanced at his companion.

Constans lowered the axe, and gave Sollius a nicely calculated blow with a chopping fist, and the slave knew no more.

When he came to himself, he found that he was lying near the gates of his master's house, with Lucius bending anxiously over him, and two others of his fellow slaves standing by. It was still night.

"What happened, Sollius?"

"That," replied Sollius ruefully, "is *my* question, not yours!"

"We heard a cry," said Lucius, "and found you unconscious on the ground here."

"It wasn't *my* cry," muttered Sollius.

"That is all we know."

"It was a signal – to fetch you out," whispered Sollius.

"Who attacked you?" asked one of the others.

"Help me up," murmured Sollius.

They led him into the slaves' quarters of the house, and attended to his bruises. He had more than one. He felt dizzy, and his head, neck and jaw ached most painfully. He was undressed and laid in his bed. Lucius watched over his uneasy slumbers until morning. It was not a long watch.

Sabinus, who had been informed of the "accident" to his favourite slave, came to see him with the first light.

"How did it happen, my good Sollius?" he asked.

Sollius answered with great care:

"I do not remember very much about it, lord. I was – thinking – and walking near the gates, and was suddenly attacked – and

I remember nothing more until I was found by Lucius and the others."

Sabinus rose from the stool on which he had been sitting, tiptoed to the door, and looked along the corridor outside the slaves' dormitory with exaggerated caution. Then he returned, and speaking in a whisper, said:

"You have discovered something, then, my good Sollius? The thief tried to silence you? Excellent! You must tell the Emperor to-day."

"Indeed, lord," replied Sollius weakly, "I had intended to ask for an audience to-day. I have not told you everything – but on second thoughts, lord, I will. I was more than just attacked," he went on, his voice gathering strength as he related the rest. "I was abducted, too."

Sabinus, after he had heard the whole of his slave's adventures, rubbed his hands.

"Excellent, Sollius, excellent!" he cried, beaming. "You are clearly on the right track. I am well pleased with you! I will myself accompany you to the Augustus."

Marcus Aurelius received them again in his small, plainly furnished, private chamber, filled with innumerable books and scrolls and scroll containers. There were just the four of them: the Emperor, Sabinus, Alexias and Sollius.

"You say," said the Emperor, a slight smile on the lips under his beard, "that you have discovered the thief of the Empress's jewels. This is quick work, Sabinus!"

The Senator, in a fluster of pleasure and self-satisfaction, bowed. He might have spoken had the Emperor given him the opportunity, but Marcus Aurelius, used to quelling the loquacity of senators, immediately addressed Sollius again:

"Have you the jewels?"

"No, sir," answered Sollius.

The Emperor frowned.

"But you know the thief?"

Sollius hesitated briefly, and then answered:

"If, O Augustus, I may set out what I take to be the circumstances, I think that you yourself will be able to name – the culprit."

"I shall be interested in every word you say," replied the Emperor. "Let me hear!"

"I have had many suspicions," Sollius began, "chasing one after the other like a dog after many hares. First, I suspected Marcia, the Augusta's waiting-woman, but there were no true signs pointing to her, and both she and Alexias seemed so genuinely puzzled – I had toyed with the idea of both of them being in league. I soon dismissed both from the case; but I had to consider them."

He glanced apologetically at the Emperor's Greek freedman, but received only a glare in response. He sighed, and went on:

"Have I your pardon, Augustus, for aught I may say? You have commanded me to tell you everything, yet if I do – "

He spread out his hands.

"Offence may come!" he whispered.

"I am no Caligula or Nero," replied Marcus Aurelius gravely. "Tell me everything you had in mind."

"Sir, I wondered whether the Empress herself might not have – secretly sold them."

"The Empress – sold them!" exclaimed Marcus Aurelius incredulously.

"For the money," pursued Sollius quietly.

"But the Empress," said Faustina's husband, "has no need of money."

"Perhaps," Sollius suggested in a lower tone, "to pay some debt of Prince Commodus."

The Emperor frowned.

"But I have just this morning paid his debts myself," he said in a voice of half-angry distaste.

"I am only relating my suspicions, O Augustus, in the order of their crossing my mind. I found out that I was certainly wrong in this one."

"Found out? How?" questioned the Emperor, very seriously.

"I had enquiries made in the quarter of the money-changers," the slave answered. "But no jewels had recently been offered for sale, or pledged, and Prince Commodus had been seeking a loan – before this morning, Augustus! – so no jewels had been sold for his benefit. And when the Prætorian was missing I was all the more certain of the Augusta's innocence. It was, in fact, the disappearance of the Prætorian which set me upon the right way. For, sir, a Prætorian does not 'disappear' – discipline in the Guards is too strong. But had he been murdered – because he knew something that it would be fatal to the thief for me to discover? Yet, had he been murdered, his body should have been found, probably near the tavern of *The Two Cranes* in the Subura. But it is clear that he left there, at least, safely. I decided that he had not been killed, but just – removed out of my way. That brought back into my mind the lack of evidence that there was concerning a theft at all."

He paused, and gave the Emperor a direct look.

"The jewels, after all," the Emperor quietly reminded him, "were missing from the Empress's casket."

"Precisely, sir: missing – from the casket. But 'stolen' is another word. I looked over the ground outside the Augusta's chamber, but saw no sign of any intruder. An intruder into that secret part of the imperial gardens would need wings to drop from Heaven: he could not go thither on his feet. It was the print of feet, and any other kind of visible disturbance, that I could not find. I decided against a thief entering from the gardens, O Augustus. And then the Prætorian was missing. At first, I did not understand that, and suspected, indeed, that he had been killed; but when I visited the tavern in the Subura where he had last been seen, I found no sign of anything like murder. I concluded that whatever had happened to him had taken place after he had left the tavern and not in the tavern itself. I saw a scented gladiator there – but suspected other matters, none relative to the missing man. But, sir, a scented gladiator is himself a cause for enquiry."

He gave the Emperor another deep glance, wondering the while how much, or how little, that august personage knew of the fearful rumours concerning his wife. He guessed that any clever woman could outwit that noble character, so philosophical in temper, so simple of heart. But Marcus Aurelius gave no sign of inward disturbance.

"Go on," was all he said.

The three listeners hung on the slave's every word, spellbound by what he was telling: Sabinus, smilingly proud of being his master; Alexias deeply puzzled and beginning to prick with unknown fears; the Emperor enigmatically calm.

"Then," continued Sollius, still fixing the Emperor with his gaze, "I was set upon. I expected to be slain out of hand. But I was not slain; I was abducted; I expected to be tortured to tell all that I knew, but I was not tortured, only threatened. Then I was knocked out skilfully – and returned where I was taken. There seemed no purpose in it unless it was to frighten me. I *was* frightened, of course. I am only an elderly slave, not a man of war or adventure. But when I came to no serious harm, I began to think again over all my scraps of evidence. One of the men who had abducted me was the missing Prætorian. Who could have employed *him*, except one whom he would obey without question? His companion, too, I recognized, though not at first: he is one of a troupe of actors. You, O Augustus, have shown him favour for his playing in Plautus."

"It does sound like a prank of Sicinius Malvus," said the Emperor with a smile.

"Then," pursued Sollius, "I recognized the kind of bark peculiar to a breed of hound among the many barkings at the farm to which they had taken me. It was the bark of a Gallic hound. There are few of them in Rome. My master has one, a gracious present from yourself, Augustus. Previously, as he will bear witness, I asked my master a question. He answered that a certain small, private villa and farm lay off the Appian Way about three miles out. I guessed that it was thither that I had been taken – and where else could the Prætorian have been so well hidden? When I came to myself, safely back at my master's gates, I knew the truth. It is that truth, sir, which I am waiting for you to command me to tell."

"Do you need my 'command' to tell it to me?" asked Marcus Aurelius, stroking his beard.

"I dare not tell it without, O Augustus," answered Sollius.

The Emperor rose, crossed the chamber to a recess containing some marble shelves upon which stood a number of circular, silver containers of scrolls and rolled books. Bringing one back with him, he returned to his former place, and tipped its contents on to a small, round, marble table in front of him. The missing jewels poured out in a glittering cascade of rainbow-coloured beauty.

"I took them with the Empress's permission," he said, smiling, "to make a test of your powers, Sollius, before I employed you in a more serious matter. I seem to have deceived you very ill! I hope that Malvus and Constans were not too rough with you. But I had to test your courage as well as your wits. I am satisfied. Sabinus, will you lend me this clever slave for as long as I need his quick brain?"

"Ah, Augustus," cried Sabinus, bowing and self-important – it might have been he who had unravelled the little mystery and not Sollius! – "all that I have is at your command."

"But I ask only for your Sollius," laughed the Emperor. "I have great need of him. If you will leave him behind you, Sabinus, I will tell him, now, at once, everything that is known about these thefts from the Treasury, and then he can set to work on a real mystery!"

## EPISODE II
## THE TREASURY THEFTS

The vaults under the ancient Temple of Saturn, which housed the imperial treasury at Rome, were vast, dark, and very like those of a prison. Sollius shuddered involuntarily as he was led down into them, though he was there at the Emperor's command to investigate the thefts which had so mysteriously been taking place, and though he was in the company, and under the protection, of Alexias, the Emperor's favourite freedman, and of Decius, a centurion of the Prætorians, who had been assigned as his official bodyguard during his enquiries. He had himself asked for Decius, whom he had met when looking for the supposedly stolen jewels of the Empress Faustina, and to whom he had taken a liking, though he was aware that the man regarded him with a superior and only half-tolerant contempt. Sollius sighed; to the centurion, he knew, he was only an elderly slave. At the moment, however, the Emperor's commission had given him a certain authority to which even the Prætorian would have to bow – and the treasury officials no less.

Gennadius, the chief clerk to the treasury, was accompanying them, a middle-aged, burly man, though somewhat round-shouldered from his avocation. He was of full citizenship, being the son of a freedman, and an official and civil servant of long standing, proud of his position, haughty and pompous to his inferiors, but servile enough where servility might possibly advantage him.

Sollius and he had exchanged searching glances on their introduction by Alexias, and if the chief clerk had made less of the slave than the slave of the chief clerk, that was only because the men possessed different attributes. Each in his sphere was probably equally clever, and that at least was spontaneously recognized by both. Sollius had eyed the other a second time, while Gennadius and Alexias had whispered for a moment or so apart, and he had wondered whether behind the mask of departmental acquiescence in the slave's investigations there had been any touch of personal apprehension. But he had seen nothing in the man's face or manner to suggest it.

Gennadius broke off his brief whispering with Alexias, and turned more graciously to the slave detective than when he had first greeted him.

"I hear much praise of you," he said "But the Emperor, I suppose," he went on smilingly, "would not employ you in this most important task if you were not the right man for it. Come!"

So saying, he had led the way down worn and winding steps into the vast, underground passages. Decius the centurion was carrying a torch, by the flaring light of which their descent was sufficiently illuminated.

"Ask whatever you will," said Gennadius, "and I will answer with truth."

He was still gracious towards the slave, and evidently filled with more curiosity than his habitual pompous pride could easily keep subdued.

They came to an iron grille which sealed off a huge section of the temple's vaults. Its inset gate was both locked and chained. This Gennadius importantly opened, and a stridence of harsh, unoiled metal echoed hollowly about; then, as soon as all had passed through, he relocked and rechained it with the same ceremony.

"We oil the lock and the hinges but rarely," he said, turning to Sollius. "It cannot, as you heard, be opened silently – and therefore not secretly. You approve of my simple precaution?"

Sollius bowed without speaking. His eyes were beginning to be busy. One fact he had already noted: the key to the gate was itself chained to the person of the chief clerk.

"Does the key ever leave your possession?" he asked abruptly. "Who has it when you sleep?"

Gennadius smiled complacently, and answered as though to a child. Many spoke to Sollius as though to a child – and repented of it afterwards.

"No one unlocks this gate but myself," he answered. "I have no deputy. At night the key hangs in my chamber on a nail at the head of my couch. It could not be reached without waking me."

("Unless," thought Sollius, "you were drugged in your drink at supper!")

"And when you go on leave?" he enquired aloud.

"Then I hand it to the Emperor himself, and he appoints a guardian for it. But I have not been on leave during the period of the thefts," replied Gennadius, as if pleased at being able to make the task of Sollius more and more difficult. "This way," he went on, and led them down a passage which dripped with moisture in both roof and walls. But the chamber into which finally they passed was itself dry enough and of considerable extent. It was, thought Sollius, like a great wine-cellar, with deep bins of bronze along three of its sides.

At one corner, within a small niche of dusty marble, stood a tutelary statuette in silver, but stained and tarnished from lack of proper care. It was a delicate work of art, and Sollius, in the lifted light of the torch, stared upon it with appreciation. He recognized it for a figure of the young, dead Verus, once the Emperor's much-loved colleague, though unworthy of his affection.

"It was set yonder a year ago," commented Gennadius, "by the Augustus in person. As a tutelary image," he added, with a slight cough, "it has brought us but little luck!"

"Why set it here?" asked Sollius curiously.

"Verus loved jewels, and came here often to inspect the hoard of centuries. We never left him alone with them," added Gennadius with a dry smile. "It seemed right to the Augustus to make his dead spirit their guardian."

Sollius smiled, and lost interest.

"You can set the torch in the iron ring yonder," Gennadius directed the centurion.

So disposed, the torch illuminated the whole chamber with vivid crimson, and there being no draught, the flame burned with a calm glow.

"It is from here," announced Gennadius, "that the money and jewels are missing. But I must explain. This is not the section of the treasury in which the current money for the business of the State is stored; it is hardly ever entered by way of business, and is really a kind of museum of money, though the value of what is stored here transcends that of the current coin of the Empire. This section holds the tribute of subject peoples for generations; some of it even from the days of the Republic. It is all, of course, negotiable; especially the naked gold and the raw silver. I mean, the thief could sell at a great profit what he has stolen."

"How great," asked Sollius, "do you reckon the loss to the treasury from these thefts?"

Gennadius mentioned a sum so large that Sollius could scarcely believe his ears, but he had no doubt of the truth of the statement. A smaller sum would not so seriously have perturbed the philosophic Emperor, and that Marcus Aurelius was seriously perturbed had been very plain both in the accents of his voice and in the troubled weariness of his heavily lidded eyes when giving Sollius his instructions.

"How many thefts have there been?"

"As far as we know: two."

"How were they discovered?"

"We take a periodic inventory," answered Gennadius. "Each of these bronze containers is filled with either gold, silver or jewels. You can see for yourself at a glance. Some of the jewels are of fabulous value. The third container on the wall to your left, and the seventh on the wall to your right, are empty. The others are full and untouched. When I came down to make the inventory two months ago, I saw at once that a container – that on your left – which had held a most valuable collection of eastern jewellery, some of it said to be part of the spoils brought back to Rome by Pompeius the Great, was empty. That was the first that we knew of any theft, and when it had taken place we had no means of knowing. The lock seemed not to have been forced, nor the chain broken; everything at

the grille was as it should have been. We could none of us understand
it. But the jewels certainly had vanished."

"And the second theft?" asked Sollius. "You said, I think, that
there have been two thefts?"

"That is so," responded the chief clerk. "The very next day, on
descending to superintend the fixing of a new chain and a new lock,
so that if a key had been made to fit the old lock it should be found
useless by the thief, I went again to examine the empty container.
On looking round, I discovered, to my utter consternation, that a
second container – that on your right – was empty, too. It had held
bars of Parthian gold. Not one was left!"

"And the lock and the chain were again apparently undisturbed?"
asked Sollius.

"There was not a sign of the iron grille having been forced in
any way," answered Gennadius, throwing up his hands. "It is an
incredible thing!"

"It is one matter to break through the grille," murmured Sollius
thoughtfully, "and it is another to carry the stuff away. The gold,
at least, would be heavy."

"Very heavy," agreed Gennadius. "But the jewels would be fairly
easily borne off in a sack – at most in two sacks."

"More than one man would seem to be necessary for either
operation," said Sollius, stroking his chin, and Gennadius nodded.

"Yet we have nobody whom we can even suspect," the chief clerk
muttered in accents of despair. "My assistants are picked men; I
would charge none of them. I trust them all."

"Have any been recently appointed?" enquired the slave.

"Not one. All are old and well-tried officials," was the answer.
"Responsibility calls for honest men, and honesty here is the very
condition of service. It must be."

"Are there any outside servants who should be considered more
carefully? Some new doorkeeper, or porter?" Sollius asked.

"All are trusty men – most of them former gladiators," replied
Gennadius, "and each is of long service. It is really a complete
mystery," he sighed. "I have done my best to unravel it. But
when nothing points in any way to a possible culprit, where can
we begin? I do not wish to discourage you – the gods forbid! – but
I have little hope of your succeeding where I, and Alexias here,
have so completely failed. Still, Alexias says that you astonished the
Augustus by your astuteness in another matter, so I shall watch you
with – ahem! – interest, intense and immense interest, Sollius. That
is your name?"

Sollius wasted no time in answering an unnecessary question, but went across to each of the two empty bronze coffers – for such they were – and examined them briefly in turn.

"There is nothing for me here," he said with a sigh. "The cleverest hunter cannot follow a spoor that does not exist."

"You give up – so soon?" asked Gennadius, his mouth agape.

"Not so," replied Sollius, smiling, "but I must begin elsewhere. You all began here – and got nowhere. Had there been a clue in these vaults you would, I am sure, have found it. The clues, therefore, are not to be found where the jewels and gold were stolen, but in some other place. It is that other place which I must find, and then work backwards to establish the means, and forwards to discover the user of the means, the thief. Perhaps I shall travel in a circle, and forwards and backwards will meet."

He turned away, and strode back towards the grille. The centurion took the torch from the ring, and moved behind him like a shadow which itself cast another shadow, and Alexias and Gennadius, after exchanging puzzled and slightly contemptuous glances, followed. Arrived at the grille, Sollius paused while Gennadius began the business of unlocking and unchaining. Suddenly the slave snatched the torch from the Prætorian, and held it high above his head. The roof of the vault sent back wisps of reek and smoke, while the bars of the grille seemed to run drippingly with fiery blood as Sollius slowly waved the torch searchingly about along the grille's iron face. Then, with a grunt, he returned the torch to Decius, and the gate being now open, stepped through into the passage beyond.

"Tell me," he said to Gennadius, who had stepped through before him, "what are the formalities by which a man may reach as far as this grille? To pass beyond has its special difficulty, as I have seen; but how easy is it for one to reach to this side of it, even if not through to the other side?"

The chief clerk gave him a shrewd, approving glance.

"The treasury office is above, in the temple. The only way down to these vaults is by the steps by which we descended and are now returning. They are perpetually guarded by soldiers at the top, as you saw when we passed through their watch. The door to these passages is never left for an instant. It would need a full cohort to force a way down. But – "

He paused, looked about him, took Sollius by the arm, and led him aside.

"It is said – it is but rumour – that there is a secret way down to other vaults from behind the altar of the temple itself," he whispered. "I speak not of my own knowledge. If such a way exists, it will be known only to the priest of Saturn. Peace! – do not interrupt. As I was about to explain: this secret way down would still not lead *behind* the grille. There is no other way in to the vaults of the treasury except through the grille. Every inch of the walls has been most carefully examined."

"Has the priest of Saturn been interrogated?" asked Sollius.

"By the Emperor himself – to no purpose. He knows nothing."

"You mean: he says that he knows nothing."

"I would take whatever he says to be true," answered Gennadius. "He is an elderly and most reputable person, learned, and of high family. I freely admit as much, though I dislike him – for his pride. We are not on speaking terms."

"How many priests are there in the college of Saturn?" enquired Sollius without comment.

"But three," replied the other. "It is a merely perfunctory tradition nowadays, and the sacrifices are few. The temple's function to-day is chiefly that of Rome's treasury. But it is never advisable to break entirely with even the superstition of the past, for who knows what magic truth may still linger in the ancient forms that swayed men's minds for so long? The prevalent Stoicism, however, seems slowly to be killing priesthood, and all augury and divination with it."

"I should like to see this priest of Saturn," said Sollius.

"Alexias shall conduct you to him," agreed Gennadius, "for, as I said, he and I are not on speaking terms. His chamber is behind the hangings at the temple's western end."

"Show me but the way," said Sollius firmly, "and I will intrude upon him unannounced."

The other stared at him. He could not forget that Sollius was a slave. Yet the slave had the Emperor's authority to do as he would! Gennadius shrugged his shoulders, and when they were back again in the temple itself, he pointed to where some rich hangings were draped between two archaic pillars.

"Behind, you will see a small door," he said, and stood and watched the slave pass on down the temple's full length.

"What a strange fellow!" he murmured to Alexias. "Is he really as clever as you say?"

"Not as *I* say," replied Alexias, a little waspishly, "but as the Emperor, my friend, wishes to think."

"But what think *you* of him, O Alexias? That is what I wish to know. I have faith in your judgement of men."

"He is certainly very astute," answered Alexias cautiously, "but he has never before had so difficult a matter to solve, and I hold back my praises, Gennadius, until he has finally deserved them."

"How wise! How philosophic!" murmured the chief clerk with

every accent of admiration, though inwardly condemning the Emperor's freedman for an empty time-server, in which opinion, as he really knew when less irritated, he was unjust.

Decius, meanwhile, had stood like a military statue until relieved of his torch by an attendant. He then strode a few paces in the wake of the man whom he was supposed to protect, and when he saw him disappear behind the hangings he remained there on guard.

The chamber of the priest of Saturn was furnished in the outworn fashion of the days of Augustus. It was bare and austere. The man seated on a folding ivory stool, reading a roll of ancient manuscript, was at least seventy years of age, thin, pale, and aristocratic, with long, compressed lips, a hawklike nose, and piercing dark eyes. Sollius had entered without ceremony, announcing his presence merely by a cough.

"Who are you? What do you want?" demanded the priest of Saturn, looking up in surprise and displeasure.

Sollius explained who he was, and produced his credentials, a small tablet of wax impressed with the private imperial seal.

"I have already been questioned by the Augustus himself," was the haughty answer, "and have nothing to tell you."

"There is, I understand, a secret way from this part of the temple into the vaults below," persisted Sollius.

"That is well and widely rumoured," said the priest with a faint smile of condescension, "but not how to find it. That is passed on from priest to priest, and is known only to them. I cannot divulge it."

Sollius gave him a long glance.

"But there *is* such a way?" he asked finally.

"There is," replied the other. "But it does not lead to that part of the vaults which houses Rome's treasure," he went on. "I can tell you that."

"When did you yourself descend to the vaults last?" pursued Sollius.

"Many years ago," answered the priest of Saturn with a flash of scornful amusement in his eyes. "I am an old man; the steps downward are not easy for the aged; also, there is nothing there except darkness, damp, and empty chambers and passages. In the days of the Republic it was different. The Temple of Saturn had then a more important life. But now – "

He spread out his hands in a gesture of resignation.

"Have you visited the treasury vaults?" he asked.

"I have visited them," replied Sollius precisely.

"Did you find any indication of how they were entered or forced?"

"I can answer only the Augustus as to that," said Sollius.

The priest of Saturn smiled thinly.

"You are quite right; I should not have asked. Did you see the silver statuette of Verus? It is a pity that so lovely a thing is so tarnished. Had *he* been alive, I should know, at least, who *loved* jewels and gold beyond most men – not, I mean, for their value in money, but for their beauty – and you might not have had to seek . . . farther. But, of course, he is dead."

"Yes, he is dead," agreed Sollius dully, and then added with a flash of humour, "I do not really suspect him."

The other laughed, and Sollius bowed, and adroitly withdrew before the conversation could be prolonged, as he felt it would have been, uselessly.

He found the others waiting for him where he had left them, the centurion still as though on guard, and Gennadius and Alexias conversing in whispers. At that end of the temple there was considerable activity of scribes, seated at desks in rows as in some great business of money-changing.

"What more would you see, O Sollius?" asked Gennadius, coming a pace or so forward to meet him. But his smile was false. Alexias, carefully watching so as to be able to report every detail to the Emperor, had taken no personal part whatever as yet in the investigation, and took no part now. He was an observer, not a participant, perhaps too jealous as a freedman to help a slave unnecessarily, yet not jealous enough – for, at bottom, he was a just man – wilfully to hinder, and he was waiting for the answer of Sollius with a certain studied mingling of indifference and curiosity.

"I have seen, I think, all that may be seen here," came the slave's words after a brief hesitation, and Alexias found that he had been holding his breath, but now he expended it in what was almost a sigh of relief. "I may come hither again tomorrow," Sollius went on. "But now I would return home to my master's house to think. Farewell!"

He departed without further courtesy, and left both the chief treasury clerk and the Emperor's freedman slightly outraged by his casual manners. Decius the centurion marched stolidly at his heels, and saw the slave safely to the house of Sabinus the senator, where, at the Emperor's command, he was to be billeted during the course of the investigations, and so be at hand when necessary, whether by day or by night.

"How did it go, Sollius?" asked young Lucius, the slave's usual confidant and sometimes his assistant.

Sollius related his morning's visit to the Temple of Saturn in close detail. The telling served not only to inform Lucius of everything, but likewise to arrange it all neatly within his own mind. They were pacing up and down in their favourite solitude, beside the small carp-pool behind the chariot-house.

"It is indeed a puzzle!" breathed Lucius. "How could anyone pass through that locked and chained grille?"

"Someone did," answered Sollius dryly. "Two, as I guess, were in it."

"Think you, then, that they stole the key? But, since it never leaves the person of this Gennadius, how?"

"The key was not stolen. The grille, Lucius, was never unlocked, nor unchained," said Sollius in a tone of certainty. "I am sure of all that."

Lucius gaped.

"But − " he began.

"I asked myself these two questions," Sollius broke in with a smile. "Was the gate of the grille opened? If it was not opened, is there another entrance? I think that the gate of the grille was *not* unlocked and unchained; but there is another entrance from the temple itself. The priest of Saturn did not deny it. But he did deny going down by the secret way for many years, and I believed him."

"But you said, Sollius," interjected Lucius, "that the secret way down does not come out *behind* the grille."

"That is so," returned Sollius placidly. "But the priest of Saturn made a slip. Did you not notice it, and see the implication?"

Lucius stared at his companion blankly.

"I have told you everything he said," pursued Sollius, and he gave the youth a sly, whimsical glance. "You do not see it?"

Lucius puckered his brows, and then shook his head.

"He asked me," said Sollius, "if I had seen the silver statuette of Verus. This, as I told you, is in the chamber behind the grille, and invisible from the grille because of the winding passages. Yet he had himself told me that he had not been in the vaults for many years − and again I say that I believe him. Moreover, this silver statuette had been placed in its marble niche but a year ago. How did he know that the statuette was − tarnished? Because he had been told so. He could not know it otherwise. Therefore, though he had not been in that treasury chamber himself, he has spoken to someone who *has* been there. It is that person whom I must discover."

"Might he not have heard it from Gennadius?" asked Lucius.

"They are not on speaking terms," replied Sollius. "I told you."

"Did you not ask him how he knew?"

"The time was not ripe. I shall ask him at the right moment, be assured!"

"He made a slip indeed!" said Lucius.

Sollius pursed his lips.

"I am not so sure, after all," he murmured. "Perhaps he was seeking to tell me something – by suggestion, I mean, rather than by statement. He has a very clever face. If I can, I would learn who it was who told him of the tarnished silver statuette by other methods than by direct questioning. I think it would be more – fruitful. Nor, I feel, would direct questioning succeed. His reticence has made that plain – and he was reticent even with the Augustus himself."

"How will you go about it, Sollius?" asked Lucius curiously.

"I shall not go about it," replied Sollius with a sly laugh. "*You* will!"

"I?" exclaimed Lucius, astonished and yet delighted, for he loved helping Sollius in his investigations, partly because of the excitement in doing so, but partly, too, because it took him away from his kitchen duties, for his position as a young slave in the house of Sabinus the senator was ordinarily that of one of the cook's menials, an occupation of much drudgery and little amusement.

"You," repeated Sollius. "Loiter outside the Temple of Saturn, and strike acquaintance with one of the porters. Any gossip about the old priest of Saturn – such as constant, or unusual, visitors to him of late – may kindle a little lamp in my brain. Go, Lucius, at once. I will explain to Tuphus the cook."

Lucius obeyed eagerly, and sped off like a stone from a Dacian sling.

Sollius remained by the carp-pool, pacing round and round in an unbroken muse. He admitted to himself that he was puzzled; the problem was like nothing that he had investigated before, and he did not know whether he was equal to its solution. But though a slave, he was a proud man, and he whipped his mind once more. He knew how entrance through the grille had been effected. He had not admitted that to Lucius, and certainly had not divulged it to either Gennadius or Alexias; he would keep it to himself for a while. He felt it was perhaps a dangerous thing to know, and assuredly a dangerous thing to blurt out until he had the whole matter plain in his mind and ready for laying before the Emperor.

His cogitations were abruptly broken by the running arrival of one of his fellow slaves.

"Our master wants you," the latter gasped out breathlessly. "You are to go to his private chamber at once."

Shaking himself free of his concentration, Sollius followed his summoner indoors, though more sedately than he had been fetched, and then proceeded alone through the cool, dark atrium to the inner chamber of Sabinus, his master and owner.

He paused on the threshold before entering, for he could hear many voices in a continual murmur of conversation. He was surprised and not a little annoyed. Surely Sabinus was not fool enough to waste the time of a man devoted to the Emperor's most secret business by exhibiting him as a curiosity to a pack of his idle friends? He knew only too well how garrulous Sabinus was, and how he was wont to boast over his slave's unusual aptitude for solving mysteries, but now that slave was more the Emperor's servant than his master's, and the senator should have recognized the position. With an impatient click of his tongue, Sollius entered, only to be brought to an amazed standstill as soon as his eye beheld the company whom his master was entertaining.

"Ah, there you are!" cried Sabinus, who obviously had been nervously on the look-out for him. "This is the fellow, Cæsar. Come hither, Sollius!"

A silence had fallen at the slave's appearance in the doorway, and every gaze was now fixed upon him as he moved forward to where his master stood beside a youth, who was dressed in the extreme of fashion, jewelled and scented – a dark, handsome, sullen youth, with lowering brows and a low forehead overhung by a crisply trimmed fringe. His hair, otherwise, was cut close to his head. Though he had not seen this young man before, Sollius knew immediately that it was the Emperor's son, already associated by his doting father in the imperial power, though but little over sixteen years of age and without any particular gifts except for the sports of the amphitheatre.

Sollius and Commodus took stock of one another as the former humbly approached: Commodus with more than a touch of insolence in his bearing, Sollius with a direct and piercing glance, such as the other was clearly unaccustomed to receive, and an unwilling flush suddenly stained the young Cæsar's cheeks. With an inward smile, the slave wondered whether the prince had ever been embarrassed by a human eye before – unless by his father's, and Marcus Aurelius was credited with a parental indulgence which was the very reverse of disciplinary.

"You are the slave Sollius?" asked Commodus in a husky voice that seemed only recently to have broken.

"Yes, Cæsar, this is my Sollius," put in Sabinus before his slave could reply.

"I have heard of you," went on Commodus without taking the

least notice of the senator and, in fact, almost turning his back upon his host. "You were very clever over my mother's jewels. I laughed for a whole hour! I am ready to like a man who has properly amused me."

Sollius bowed low.

"The most honourable Sabinus tells me that he has lent you again to my father," pursued Commodus.

Once more Sollius bowed. He could more easily feign humility in his limbs than in his eyes.

"Has he lost one of his precious philosophical treatises?" the prince asked with a laugh.

"If he has, Cæsar," replied Sollius quietly, "he has not employed *me* to find it."

The amusement died out of both voice and glance of the imperial youth, leaving only a tigerish glare and felinity in its place, as he demanded peremptorily what thing it was for which his father had employed him to look.

"After all, slave, I am half the Augustus," Commodus reminded him, "and I have a legitimate interest in what affects my father. Do you search for some thread of conspiracy against him – or against *me*?"

"No, Cæsar," answered Sollius.

Commodus waited as though in the sure expectation that the slave would say more, but being disappointed, frowned, and asked haughtily:

"What has he lost? Even my mother does not know!"

Sollius, on an impulse, knelt before the young man.

"Lord," he said, "the Augustus has laid secrecy upon me like a yoke upon the neck of a pair of ploughing oxen. I dare not tell you!"

"Not tell, not tell, Sollius," cried Sabinus irritably, "when the lord Commodus commands?"

Commodus himself had said nothing, but was standing motionless, biting his painted finger-nails.

"The Augustus commanded otherwise," said Sollius. "Not even to the lord Commodus can I tell anything."

Sabinus puffed out his cheeks in his annoyance at his promise to the young prince going unfulfilled.

"I like not this in you, Sollius," he muttered. "I might have you whipped for it."

The slave rose slowly to his feet.

"At the moment, master, I am the Emperor's; when I return as *your* slave, I will submit to your punishment," he said with dignity.

"There, there, Sollius," answered Sabinus, a little abashed, "I spoke hastily. The Emperor's commands must come first."

"It is a pity, slave," said one of the young courtiers standing about Commodus and who had accompanied him to the senator's house, "that you do not remember that even emperors are mortal, and that it is wise to anticipate the future. You seem as clever at losing as at finding!" he added with a malicious smile.

But it was not with his eyes that Sollius was really noticing him, but with his nose. He had savoured before the particular scent which hung about the young man's rich garments, and knew very well where: in the bedroom of the Empress Faustina when he had been investigating the supposed loss of her jewels; and, once again, a man so scented had brushed past him and Decius from the doorway of one of the lowest taverns in the Subura during the same investigation. Was he the same man? He had not seen his face then.

"Peace, Gaius," cried Commodus. "The slave has not offended me."

He gave Sollius, nevertheless, a suspicious and venomous look, and then with affected indolence turned away to his host. Sabinus made a curt sign of dismissal, and Sollius was only too glad to escape from the crowded chamber and from the curious eyes of those who had watched every imperial gesture and listened to each imperial word so as to adjust their own attitude to the notorious slave of Sabinus with the right obsequious agreement.

In the corridor Sollius met his master's household overseer, an Apulian freedman, for Sabinus was a widower.

"I did not hear that the Emperor's son had been invited to-day," said the slave, pausing as they passed one another.

"He was not," replied the other, and swore in Greek under his breath. "It has put us out, by Heracles, abominably! The accursed young man invited himself."

They separated, and Sollius went to his own quarters. It had been an interlude which had broken his concentration, and now, with an exasperated sigh, he endeavoured to immerse himself once again in his previous thoughts. Two new facts, moreover, had come teasingly into his mind, and he began trying to fit them into the pattern of his reasoning.

Lucius did not return until dusk. "I fear, Sollius," he reported disconsolately, "that I have only little things to tell you, and none of them, I think, likely to be useful."

"It is the adding up of the little things that makes the large things," said the older slave with a comfortable smile. "Set out your 'little things' in a row like stones on the top of a wall, and let us flick them away, or keep them, one by one."

"First," replied Lucius, "the priest of Saturn hardly ever leaves the temple; he lives like a hermit."

"Hardly ever leaves the temple, and lives like a hermit," repeated Sollius in a meditative echo.

"Then his three assistant priests," went on Lucius, "are, two of them, but so in name, and are present only at the annual sacrifice ordained by the State; each is a kind of relative of the Empress, and their connection with the rites of Saturn are perfunctory and official. Neither has entered the temple these six months."

"Neither has entered the temple these six months," echoed Sollius as before." And the third priest?" he asked.

"The third priest," Lucius replied, "is only a kind of servant who performs the daily offices about the place. It is really a temple no longer, but is given over to the business of the treasury; only the one end is still reserved to the god."

"As I saw," mused Sollius. "And now: what visitors has this priest of Saturn?"

"As few as a real hermit might have," said Lucius. "In fact, if the doorkeeper speaks true – and why should he not? – the only visitor he has had for many a long month is his nephew."

"His – nephew?" repeated Sollius.

"A young man – so said the doorkeeper – who has won some notoriety," Lucius went on, "as a gladiator. One or two of the young sprigs of fashion have ventured into the arena in competition with the professionals."

"Much to the Emperor's disgust," put in Sollius, "for his son is one of them. Did you learn this young man's name?"

"Rutilius Marcianus," said Lucius.

Sollius shook his head disappointedly.

"I do not know the name," he muttered. Then, after a pause, he added abruptly: "Has the lord Commodus ever visited this priest of Saturn?"

"I was not told so," Lucius answered, "and I think it would have been a sufficiently noteworthy occasion to have remained in the mind of that gossiping old doorkeeper!"

"Very like, very like," said Sollius. "Does this nephew of the priest of Saturn visit his uncle constantly, or only at long intervals?"

Lucius suddenly grinned.

"I have this for you," he said. "He has begun visiting his uncle only in the last few months. Until then nobody knew that the old priest had a nephew."

"All this may yet mean nothing," answered Sollius casually. "But I should like to see this young man – without his knowing either that I do see him or that I even wish to see him."

"Perhaps we could go to the arena," suggested Lucius, his eyes sparkling in anticipation. "He might be performing – "

"And might not," smiled Sollius, "and it would then be a waste of time. I must think of a better way."

But it was not through any thought or scheming of his own that the slave met with Rutilius Marcianus, and that in the very near future; in fact, on the next day, or, rather, the next night. He was summoned in the late evening by a messenger from the Temple of Saturn.

This messenger was a gigantic Cappadocian, the kind of man who usually was a litter-bearer. Sollius took him for one of the treasury porters.

"Do you come from Gennadius?" he asked.

The Cappadocian grinned, and nodded. He seemed a very pleasant kind of fellow, thought Sollius.

They set out for the temple at once, with the aroused centurion marching at Sollius's heels, lean, sinewy, upright and watchful, and as stiffly correct as if on parade in the Campus Martius. They reached their destination without delay, and Sollius was surprised and interested – and perhaps a little more interested than surprised – that the Cappadocian led him, not to the great bronze treasury doors themselves, but to a small, secret door in another part of the temple. This was opened at the first knocking upon it, and Sollius was beckoned inside by the man who had answered to the Cappadocian's knuckles. Sollius entered first, followed immediately by his Prætorian bodyguard, for whom the Cappadocian, with an alien politeness, made way. The door was then shut after them with silent precision.

A single lamp was burning in a niche. By its gleam Sollius saw that they were in a descending stone passage of considerable antiquity. But he was given no time for examining his surroundings at all closely.

"Go forward," whispered the Cappadocian.

After a few yards the passage turned abruptly at right angles and went on for some distance, still descending. This passage, too, was lit by a lamp in a niche. At the end was a small, bronze door, embossed with symbolic figures and green with damp and age. As the Cappadocian pushed it open with his huge hand, a metallic sigh seemed to echo along the passage. The door had been recently oiled, decided Sollius, but not quite well enough. Probably, however, the noise of its opening would not be heard in the temple, for clearly they were by now well underground.

The opened door led directly to an upward flight of ancient, worn, and uneven steps. The man who had opened the first door to them caught up the lamp from the niche in the passage, and led the way up. At the top a narrow aperture, hung with a heavy curtain, gave into a small chamber – the same chamber in which Sollius had had his interview with the priest of Saturn. A long, roundabout way, he reflected wryly, to bring him back to it! He was not surprised at finding himself there; he had suspected whither he was being taken; but he was somewhat more than surprised by the scene which immediately presented itself to his gaze, for the chamber was occupied by two men, both of whom he recognized on the instant, and one of them, the priest of Saturn himself, was leaning back in his chair as though asleep. But from more than one visible sign it was plain that it was no true sleep, but a drugged unconsciousness. The other occupant was the same scented young man who had been with the Emperor's son at the house of Sabinus on the previous day, and whom Sollius now certainly believed to be the man he had once encountered in one of the worst alleys of the Subura.

They were three to two, with the unconscious priest of Saturn between them.

"I expected you to bring him alone," said the scented young man to the Cappadocian.

"This fellow has the Emperor's orders to follow him everywhere he goes," was the sullen answer. "Could I order him away?"

"Stand by the door, Balbus!" commanded the scented young man, and he who had let them in moved a pace or so back and posted himself between the centurion and retreat. Decius fixed his eyes upon the slave, and wondered what his charge would do. As for himself, he had no fear. He was a trained soldier and was armed, and would confidently have taken on more than any such three at a time, unskilled men as they probably were. The Cappadocian, however, was of a terrible size ... The centurion fingered the heavy stabbing-sword at his belt: it was just as well for a man to be ready.

The scented young man turned to Sollius.

"You know me?" he asked.

"I recognize you," answered the slave. "You were at my master's yesterday."

"I am Gaius Rutilius Marcianus," the scented young man went on. "I am a practised gladiator," he added, his gaze falling for a moment on the centurion. "The priest of Saturn is my uncle," he continued, turning back to Sollius. "No, he is not poisoned: have no fears. He does but sleep – after a drink of wine containing – no matter what. It will do him no harm. He will wonder a little at his strange, sudden 'illness' – and will find his nephew most assiduous! Well, slave, understand this: you are not the only person able to make enquiries; I, too, have made some, and to-day I know for certain what yesterday was only a guess: that you are thrusting your nose into the thefts from the treasury. You need not, out of duty to the Augustus, deny it," he concluded in a tone of menace.

"I do not deny it."

"You are not so clever as you think, or you would not have let yourself be brought hither," sneered Marcianus.

"Perhaps I wished to be brought – wherever I might be taken," answered the slave, and their glances clashed.

"Shall I kill this scented fellow?" cried out the centurion.

"No, no; oh no!" answered Sollius in a tone of horror. "We wish for no killing here."

"Who wishes for no killing?" asked Marcianus with a laugh. "You, slave? Or is it I? There is little chance of our having the same wishes about that! Silence is what we have brought you hither to have from you, and there is no surer silence than death's."

The centurion drew his sword, but in the same instant the huge Cappadocian twined an arm about the Prætorian's neck and held him in a choking grip, while Balbus kicked his legs from under him, and caught at his falling weapon. The conventionally trained soldier is always at a disadvantage against irregulars who do not play fair, that is to say, not in accordance with professional tactics. Marcianus laughed once more, and then his eyes narrowed with suspicious astonishment.

"You do not, slave, go on your knees for mercy?" he asked.

"Even a slave," replied Sollius, "can face death standing."

"But not here," said Marcianus. "Here your body would be found; but I know of a place where it will never be found."

He moved swiftly and caught Sollius by the arm, and exerted force to drag him towards a kind of apse in the wall to the right. To his surprise, the slave did not resist, but docilely allowed himself to be led whither his captor would.

"Bring the soldier after us," commanded Marcianus over his shoulder, and he touched one of the bricks. The back of the apse swung open, and some stone steps were seen to descend into darkness. So that, thought Sollius, was the secret way down into the vaults known to the priests of Saturn.

Marcianus, with his grasp still upon the slave's arm, paused at the top of the steps, and whistled a few sharp notes. There came an answering whistle from below, and gradually a pale light diffused itself about the bottom of the steps.

"Come," cried Marcianus brusquely, and he led Sollius down.

Behind them came the muffled noise of a sudden struggle, and Marcianus swore under his breath. He was about to turn back to see what was happening, though he could guess very well, when Sollius forestalled him by calling upward:

"Decius! Decius! You are to come quietly. It is my order, and my orders are the Emperor's! You know that. Come down quietly, Decius, and without protest."

In a sullen and contemptuous indignation the centurion allowed himself to be thrust down into the same underground passage of the vaults beneath the temple. The soft, diffused light which had dimly illuminated their descent was now seen to emanate from a lamp held high above the head of one dressed as a gladiator. The helmet, ornate and gleaming like gold in the lamplight, shadowed the face. With its fringe of metal teeth over eyes and nose, it was as good as a mask. The man turned as soon as they drew near, and led the way until they came to the grille.

Marcianus laughed, and struck the gate of the grille with his hand.

"Chained and locked," he said jeeringly. "And yet – someone – passed through. That is a puzzle, slave, for even *your* exalted wits."

"My wits," replied Sollius with a smile, "may not be exalted, but the entrance past this grille, at least, is no puzzle to them."

The other stared, and the lampbearer turned, and stared also.

"Your last boast, slave," mocked Marcianus, "is your most foolish."

Sollius spread out his hands in deprecation.

"It is no boast," he said.

"How, slave? You *know* the way in through this grille?"

"As well as – you," replied Sollius.

The lampbearer audibly caught his breath.

"What do you mean, wretch?" cried the scented but not all-effeminate Marcianus, and he gripped Sollius by the shoulder.

"I mean but this," Sollius answered. "That I know *how* the theft was worked."

"And by *whom*?" demanded Marcianus, and he began to shake the man in his grasp.

"Gently," said the centurion gruffly. "I am still here."

"But unarmed," the Cappadocian reminded him with a grin, and showed the Prætorian's sword which he had taken from Balbus.

"Answer me!" cried Marcianus, and his grip on the slave's shoulder cruelly tightened. "Do you know the *thief*?"

"No," said Sollius simply.

The other loosed him with a harsh laugh.

"I think you know nothing," he jeered. "But you are too cleverly nosy a fellow to be let live. Throttle him, Balbus!" he commanded. "Balbus," he laughed, "is a Samnite wrestler, and knows how to throttle a man, I can tell you!"

Balbus moved forward with a grim leer.

"Wait!" said the man holding the lamp.

Marcianus, Balbus and the Cappadocian stiffened where they stood.

"You have forgotten," went on the man with the lamp petulantly, "that I am here."

Marcianus raised his right arm in graceful salute, and was about to reply, when the other interrupted him:

"Before this fellow is killed – and I shall enjoy watching Balbus's strong thumbs! – I would learn what he knows. Slave, answer me: how is this grille to be passed through and not by its locked and chained door?"

Sollius caught his breath. It was barely perceptible, and he mastered himself at once. He did not think that his involuntary start had been noticed, and he answered as calmly as he could:

"Sir, will you lift your lamp higher – and nearer to the grille?"

The other moved a pace or two, and raised his lamp. Again Sollius caught his breath, but again checked himself, and went on as calmly as before:

"It needed two men. I knew that as soon as I was sure that the gate had not been opened by the – thieves. One man remained on this side of the grille; the other climbed through the upper part, stole what he would, passed it through to his companion, and then, with his help – without his help it would have been too difficult – climbed out again. That was how it was done."

"But that is folly," blustered Balbus. "There is not space enough between any of the bars, upper or lower, for a dog to be pushed through. How could a man, climb he ever so high, squeeze through the bars?"

"I will show you," answered Sollius. "Your – friend – has raised his lamp in *exactly* the right place! Look! Those three bars in the upper part of the grille beyond the crossbar have been sawn through, and replaced by being simply mortared together again. That was clever. They look so right, and so strong, still! I say again, it was clever. If the bars had been sawn in the lower part of the grille, that is to say, below the cross-bar, it might have been found out at any time, even by accident; but, having sawn them asunder in the upper half, there would be no occasion at all for them to be touched, even accidentally, for who, unnecessarily, would *climb* the grille? And who would examine them with any closeness – except an elderly slave who is too easily suspicious? Have I answered you?"

"Has the time come?" asked Balbus the Samnite, extending his hands with their fingers spread open.

"So we, Gaius there and I," pursued the man with the lamp, "are the thieves?"

Sollius nodded.

"Both of you sawed the bars and afterwards replaced them; you, I think – yes, you, certainly, for your lamp picked out the very place without hesitation – climbed in; and your confederate helped you to climb out again, and received the sacks with the jewels and the gold."

"Shall we deal with him?" cried the Cappadocian impatiently.

"Wait," commanded the other, and his voice, though strangely young in its tone, had authority. "What would you tell the Emperor, slave, if you lived to tell him anything?"

"That I had accomplished the task he set me," replied Sollius instantly.

"Could you, then, name the thieves? Though I am honoured, as you showed, by your suspicion," went on the young, authoritative, and now sarcastic voice, "you could not, I think, give *me* a name."

"If I am not to live to tell the Emperor anything," answered Sollius carefully, "does my knowledge matter?"

"That, at least," interjected the Cappadocian, "is a good, sensible remark! Balbus – "

At the sound of his name the Samnite wrestler edged nearer to his intended victim and again thrust out his hands with their fingers spread wide. The Cappadocian, leering in anticipation of a fine sight, and anxious not to miss a single instant of it, had grown careless. Decius saw his opportunity. He twisted aside, and in the same movement deftly wrenched his own sword from the other's grasp.

"Ha!" he cried in a loud voice. "Quick! Get behind me, slave!"

And he sent up a challenging roar as when in some battle in Mesopotamia a Roman legionary should invite a Persian "Immortal" to single combat. Sollius, however, did not accept his counsel to seek shelter behind him; instead, he set his back to the grille, and fixed his eyes on the man with the lamp.

The fight that followed between Decius and Marcianus, the Cappadocian, and the Samnite was as brief as it was savage. The centurion, who was no fool and knew well what he was about, raised as much clamour as he could, shouting, stamping and clashing steel against steel, for both the Samnite and the Cappadocian were armed with long knives. His armour protected him against any but the shrewdest thrust in the right place, and he was too skilled in his trade to lay himself open unwarily. He had not waited for their attack, but had taken the offensive right from the beginning, and very early in the proceedings had reduced his enemies to two – for the man with the lamp took no part in the struggle at all – by wounding the Samnite severely in the right arm. But almost immediately after he had thus lessened the odds, the event which he had expected, and for which his deliberate noisiness had played, came to pass, and the vaults were rushed by the guard which was on watch above at the ordinary entrance to them from the temple.

The fight was over at once, and the four contestants were roughly separated and impartially seized.

"Not *me*, asses!" spluttered Decius. "Do you not recognize me, Tribonius? Bid them take their hands off me!"

"What, you, old comrade!" cried the centurion of the watch. "What is all this about? It sounded as if old Hannibal's elephants were trampling about down here. What has been happening?"

"I am under the Emperor's own orders," replied the released Decius. "I am acting as a bodyguard – *his* bodyguard," he added, pointing to Sollius.

Tribonius stared at the slave fixedly.

"What is he doing at this grille?" he demanded, and his tone was both suspicious and truculent. "It is all very well, Decius, but I am in charge here, and I have a right to know what you are all up to. How did any of you get into these vaults? First tell me that. Not through *us*, anyway! Is there another way down? If so, it should have a sentry posted, and I must see to it."

Decius opened his mouth to reply, but Sollius forestalled him:

"That can wait," he said impatiently. "There is work to be done here in the Emperor's name."

He produced his tablet of authority. Tribonius took and examined it in amazement, stared at Sollius, and from Sollius to Decius.

"I told you," said the latter, who was beginning to enjoy the bewilderment of his fellow centurion and to appreciate his own favoured position beside the investigating slave, "I am his bodyguard, and he is on the Emperor's business. I am under his orders; and now *you* are, too!"

He laughed, and saluted Sollius in a half-mocking fashion, yet Sollius felt that the Prætorian's contempt for him, nevertheless, was rapidly thawing. Decius then summarily took the tablet from the still doubtful Tribonius, and gave it back to the slave with a wink and a flourish.

"It is always good to have a pass!" he said.

Sollius was again staring at the man with the lamp, the light of which was no longer necessary, since one of the soldiers was carrying a torch that blazed over a wide area. The whole grille was illuminated until it seemed like a huge spider's web iridescent with a bloody dew.

The man with the lamp remained still and silent. Suddenly he blew out his lamp, and let it fall. Being of clay, it flew into a dozen pieces on the stone floor, and the oil made a little puddle, redly gleaming in the flame of the torch. It might have been a pool of blood from some murdered man.

"I think that is enough," he said in a raised, overbearing tone, and he took his gladiator's helmet from his head. The two centurions and the soldiers at once gasped, stiffened and saluted. It was the Emperor's son. Sollius remained quietly at the grille, and he was smiling with a kind of sly passiveness.

Commodus took a pace or so forward.

"Take forth these men," he commanded, "and execute them without further delay. I charge them all with complicity in the thefts from Rome's treasure which this slave has been investigating at my father's order. I not only charge them, but myself bear witness against their deeds, and as Cæsar I now judge them."

The centurion of the treasury guard was obviously embarrassed, for there was no legality in the young Cæsar's command, and yet it was already widely known that the wrath of Commodus was more dangerous to awake than a sleeping tiger's. He looked at Decius, but found no help in his fellow centurion's expression; he then looked at Sollius, as if pleading for guidance.

"Did you not hear, centurion?" rasped Commodus.

"Cæsar – " said Sollius.

"What is it, slave?" cried Commodus, turning to him irritably. "I shall tell my father that you unearthed the plot and exposed the chief villain, Gaius Rutilius Marcianus yonder. By other ways I had come to the same conclusion – "

Marcianus started, opened his mouth to speak violently, but meeting the young prince's hard, level gaze, thought better of it and remained silent, and Commodus turned again to Sollius.

"You will not lose by this if you are circumspect," he went on, stressing his words. "What more can you wish? I shall speak well of you to the Augustus. If I did not, your master would be mulcted of a slave, I can tell you that! – but you can die more happily – and much older," he added, his eyes fierce, but his lips smiling.

"Cæsar," persisted Sollius, and he could not prevent his limbs from feeling as though made of water, "the Augustus has put this matter into my hands, and I must report to him before anyone can be condemned for his guilt. Your sacred father will then know how to punish."

Commodus stared at him.

"You address me as 'Cæsar'," he said, "but clearly have no idea what Cæsarship means!"

"Sir," answered Sollius, "under your permission, I am but seeking to obey the Augustus."

Commodus bit his underlip, but if he had flushed, the torchlight was too red for any addition to his cheeks to be noticeable.

"We are to hear," he burst out contemptuously, "a slave's suggestion, ha! Well, give it, give it! Let us hear this impertinent wisdom!"

"Have the three arrested, sir – even as they are already – and let my report be made to the Emperor this night – and in your presence, Cæsar – and everything will then be accomplished with speed and efficiency – except one thing," he added underbreath to himself.

"What is that you are murmuring?" demanded Commodus, frowning and glowering with suspicion.

"That even if we have found the culprits, Cæsar, we have not recovered what they stole," Sollius replied meekly. "But where it is hidden, no doubt, torture will get from them," he added, glancing sideways at Marcianus, who started, and turned impulsively to the Emperor's son, but his movement was immediately checked by the soldier at his side.

"Cæsar!" implored Marcianus. "You will not allow this – you cannot allow it! Why, you yourself, Cæsar – "

"Silence!" Commodus broke in shrilly. "All shall be thoroughly sifted; justice shall be done, Gaius! Centurion," he ordered, "take those two men to the Mamertine. You, Gaius, accompany me! I will be responsible for him," he said in a lower tone to Tribonius, "and will deliver him myself to the Emperor's will. You, slave, do as you suggested: go to my father at once. I shall meet you in his presence. Tell everything that you have seen here – and I will confirm it. Gaius, with *me*! Come!"

Taking Marcianus firmly by the arm, Commodus went up quickly into the temple above, and the commands which he had given to Tribonius were put into action at once and without question.

"We, Decius," said Sollius, "are for the Emperor's palace: let us get there as soon as we can."

Though the hour was considerably after midnight, Marcus Aurelius was reading and meditating still, and was at once accessible. Sollius was admitted to the Emperor's private study by Alexander, the Greek secretary, while Decius posted himself with the other guards in the gilded and painted corridor. Complete silence reigned in the vast palace, and only a single lamp was burning by the Emperor's marble writing-table. Alexias was not present.

"Well, Sollius?" asked the Augustus, turning to him somewhat wearily, and rubbing his tired, heavy eyes. "So you have something to report?"

Sollius was silent for a brief instant before replying. He had so great a veneration for the wise and benevolent Emperor that he hesitated to bring pain to his noble heart, and what he had to tell, he knew, would bring nothing but pain.

"Have no fears and no hesitations," said Marcus Aurelius, as if he had read the slave's doubtful thoughts. "Tell me everything. Should I have employed you if I had not desired the truth, the full truth?"

Carefully and completely the slave related what had taken place as far as the arrival of the treasury guard upon the clamour raised by Decius, but at that point in his narrative he paused, and glanced at the Emperor as though inviting question or comment. Marcus Aurelius had been listening with his head propped upon his hand as he leaned a little forward at the marble table, and when Sollius paused, had given a sigh.

"I know Marcianus," he breathed slowly. "He is a young man of parts and charm, and one of my son's – friends. Alas, that Rome's inner society should be touched in this unsavoury matter! But that is what I had feared, Sollius; yet I had to know and be certain. It was my duty to know and be certain. I can tell you now why I employed *you*. An official, or a courtier, would have been tempted to hide what implicated the man of rank; you, a slave, would have no such inhibition."

The imperial study was an inner chamber beyond a larger chamber, with two entrances, the one – that by which Sollius had been introduced – from the corridor, and the other through an archway from this larger chamber, into which the more private apartment could be thrown open, on occasions of council or reception, by the lifting of the hangings between. These, of a richly woven purple, were now drawn; but though Sollius had heard no sound, he was suddenly conscious that a listener was standing on the other side of these hangings in the large room beyond them, and he thought that he could very easily guess who that listener was.

Abruptly the Emperor asked the question which Sollius had been dreading:

"Who was the man in the gladiator's helmet? Did you see his face? Did you find out?"

Sollius knelt.

"It was the Cæsar!" he answered.

Marcus Aurelius started, and covered his face with his two hands.

"What was he doing beneath the temple?" he muttered. "Was he there to protect his friend from his wrong-doing? It must have been so. Was it, Sollius?" he asked earnestly, lowering his hands, and fixing the slave with a pleading scrutiny.

As Sollius looked up into the Emperor's face, he caught a slight movement in the folds of the purple hangings, as if a hand had been laid on them preparatory to someone's entrance, but as though, nevertheless, the man waiting still hesitated to make his appearance. But it was the Emperor's features which held the kneeling slave's deepest attention, and what he read in them struck him to the heart. That the master of the world, so constant and indefatigable in working for its well-being and happiness, should himself be so unhappy and so apprehensive of shame, and that his noble affections should be in such danger of that most horrible of disillusionments, the knowing his nearest and dearest to be unworthy of trust and even love: all this troubled Sollius in the depths of his soul. He could not add the final words which would reveal truth in its naked hideousness.

He rose, and keeping his eyes steadfastly away from the hangings, answered the Emperor's question with deliberate care.

"As I understood," he said in a clear voice, "the Cæsar had had his own suspicions of his friend, and had been playing a part to trap him. You employed *me*, O Emperor, to solve the mystery, but you owe your son a great deal of the evidence."

"You give me great comfort," sighed Marcus Aurelius.

As he spoke, the hangings were lifted, and Commodus made his entrance.

"My dear father," he said humbly, and went across and kissed the Emperor's cheek.

"My son," murmured Marcus Aurelius, and fleetingly laid a hand on the young man's scented garments with a briefly lingering, pathetic fondness.

"Has this good slave reported on our adventure of to-night?"

asked Commodus, glancing round at Sollius with a faint, satiric smile.

"Fully, as I think," returned his father. "I shall not forget his services."

"Nor I," murmured Commodus, lowering his gaze bashfully as he added: "Services to you and the Roman State are services to me also."

"There will, I am confident," said Sollius quietly, and not daring to glance even flickeringly at the young Cæsar, "be no more thefts from the imperial treasury."

"You have deserved well of Rome," answered Marcus Aurelius, smiling. "I shall tell Sabinus so, and your reward shall turn one slave into a rich man." He smiled again, and went on: "The Cappadocian and the Samnite strangler shall be tried in secret and, if found guilty, executed. What have you done with Marcianus, my son?" he asked. "You took him away with you, I understand, under your personal arrest."

"That is so, father," replied Commodus, and his meekness suddenly put on a mask of sadness and diffident unease. "I grieve to announce unwelcome news, but as I brought him through the streets – we were both cloaked against the common gaze of night-prowlers – he broke into a swerving run to escape. My Gaulish freedman was with me, and thinking that he was doing right, he threw his knife at once at the fugitive – the Gauls are very swift with the knife! – and it took Marcianus between the shoulders. It hurts me that Gaius should be immune from Rome's justice!"

"He is dead?" asked the Emperor.

"He is dead," answered Commodus, and turned and gave Sollius a direct look of arrogant complacency.

"Then I am foiled of magnanimity," said Marcus Aurelius with a sigh. "However, the mystery is cleared up, and the distressing matter closed. I am grateful to the gods. Do you think," he asked abruptly, speaking to his son, "that the stolen jewels and gold will be found at your dead friend's villa?"

"We can search it, father," replied Commodus gravely, "but I have no hopes of finding them. He was a clever man – always too clever for *me*, at any rate," he sighed.

"What say *you*, Sollius?" asked the Emperor.

Sollius gave a swift look at the Cæsar, and then answered:

"I do not think, sir, that any investigation into the whereabouts of the stolen treasure will ever succeed."

"Then you would not undertake it?"

"I would not undertake it with any hope, sir," answered the slave firmly.

"I see," muttered Marcus Aurelius, frowning a little, and then he rubbed his eyes more wearily than ever. "I see," he repeated. "Return to your master's house, Sollius, and tell him that I am well pleased with you. Where are you going, my son? Stay with me while I put away my tablets – "

The slave left the Augustus and the Cæsar together, and dismissing Decius to his barracks, since he no longer needed a bodyguard, he returned alone to the house of his master.

"But who did steal the treasure?" asked Lucius the next day, after Sollius had narrated all that had happened.

"If the lord Commodus had not lifted his lamp at exactly the right place in the grille where the thieves had broken in," answered Sollius, "I should not perhaps have known for a certainty that he himself was one of them, and I should have looked for the true accomplice of Marcianus – oh yes, he was the other of the two – in vain. I did little in this investigation, Lucius; they gave themselves away to me – probably out of the fear that I was really cleverer than I am!"

"Does the Emperor guess, think you?"

"I hope not," sighed Sollius. "Had you only seen his face you would have lied to him as I did."

"And the treasure *is* lost?" asked Lucius.

"Quite lost," said Sollius. "None of it will ever be seen in Rome again. No doubt, however, it will turn up in different thievish hands, dispersed in various parts of the Empire," he concluded, smiling at his own ironic thoughts, "and current coin will have taken its place – we know in whose private coffers. The arena, at least, and the fashionable gambling-houses will receive the final benefit of the criminal daring of a good man's son. It is the way of mankind under the indifference of the gods!"

In most of this Sollius was right, but not in everything. For instance, one portion of the treasure *was* seen again in Rome. For Sollius received a token of approval from the lord Commodus, a valuable and curiously barbaric jewel, which the slave was sure in his own mind had once formed part of the treasure brought as part of the tribute to the Roman people by the great Pompeius after his victorious campaigns against Mithridates of Pontus.

# A BYZANTINE MYSTERY
# Mary Reed and Eric Mayer

*Mary Reed is an ex-patriate Brit (or more appropriately an ex-pat Geordie) who moved to the United States in 1976. She had already made a name for herself in the small circle of British science-fiction fans for her delightful ramblings in the amateur magazines. In America she began to develop her writing in a variety of fields, with a special interest in food and the weather (a predictable British trait).*

*Her first published fiction was a detective story involving food, "Local Cuisine" (1987). Here, in collaboration with her husband Eric Mayer, who helped provide much of the plotline, Mary has written a story specially for this volume set in the volatile days of the Byzantine Empire.*

John the Eunuch, Lord Chamberlain to Emperor Justinian though he be, yet served a higher lord than his temporal ruler. Thus it was that, in the dog watches of a January morning which would normally be as dark as any other in Constantinople, were it not for the lurid glare of the Church of the Holy Wisdom of God burning to the ground, upon receiving an urgent summons to attend the emperor, he first finished the ceremonial meal being served beneath the starred ceiling of the Lord of Truth's underground sanctuary.

When John finally emerged, pulling his cloak closer against the chill of early morning air, he found a dark-robed and visibly shaken underling waiting by the entrance, torch in hand. Its guttering flames revealed a face know to John, although he had never seen it so pallid.

"Anatolius, what ails you?" he asked softly, thinking that to be summoned at this hour by the Emperor's private secretary meant there was more to be dealt with than household accounts or the ongoing riots. He said as much as they hurried along a flagstoned path crossing the grounds of the Great Palace. Out under a clear sky, the noise from the rioting was louder, drifting in huge gulps of incoherent rage over the palace walls as the wind shifted. Clouds of smoke could be seen blotting out patches of stars, and an occasional scream cut through the distant hubbub like a knife through a sacrificial bull. A few sparkling tracers marked the passage of windwhipped embers near the burnt-out gateway to the complex, heavily guarded by the Royal Bodyguard.

"The Emperor was contemplating flight," Anatolius confided, "but the Empress counseled him to stay."

"Well, between her and the guards, what does he want me for?" John was irritated. "Surely he doesn't expect me to wear a sword?"

"By Mithra!" his companion swore. "If he knew you were at a religious service with the city in an uproar, and blood fresh in the gutters . . ."

"Well, no doubt he's been doing a fair bit of praying himself."

"It's true that the Patriarch was here some time." They were approaching the doors of the Throne Room, which was standing open, and John, was surprised to see, unguarded. As they approached, Anatolius lowered his voice. "But then the Church is burning down, and the mob not yet crushed."

"Well, it's not too late to persuade Their Excellencies to leave for their country retreat, I suppose. Perhaps we could disguise them as Greens? Or Blues? Which do you think?"

Anatolius glared at him. Although the Emperor and Empress were commonly linked with the Blue faction, she had been born a Green, but since both factions were equally involved in the rampage of scattered destruction and pillage across the city, blame would be difficult to apportion – but, thought John as he stepped into the half-lit room, so would retribution. Behind him Anatolius' footsteps receded quickly, and, he thought sourly, thankfully into the distance.

Justinian, ever mindful of his position, occupied the great canopied throne, which John approached slowly, bowing his head to his earthly ruler.

The tall dark-haired man with arched brows, hooded eyes and a weak chin, spoke in a whisper. *And an odd thing, that*, John thought, *since they were alone*, as he bent his head respectfully to hear what had summoned him to this strange appointment.

"I have a special commision for you," the Emperor said, "of such delicacy that I cannot reveal it save but to you and the Empress." The chamberlain raised mental enquiring eyebrows while keeping a poker face. "The only other person who knows – as yet – is the Patriarch. But soon enough word will get out, and we must have the matter resolved by then." He paused. "It is a spiritual matter."

*Ah*, thought John. *No wonder the Patriarch is involved*. Like many followers of Mithra, he was amused by the similarities of the new – to them – religion, and his older, more spartan, cult. John found the encrusted palaces of the gentle god little to his taste, and thus the destruction of the Church of the Holy Wisdom, its smoldering ruins not far from where they stood, of little emotional consequence, unlike the deep blow it had been to Justinian, Although he, John, admittedly would have liked to have dealt harshly with the looters whom he had seen carrying out gem-encrusted reliquaries and beautifully painted icons, only to shatter them on the cobbles almost under the horrified nose of the stylite in the square – not so much because of outraged religious feelings, but because it offended his sense of order. What was it to him that an icon supposedly painted by St. Luke was regarded as protecting the city – not to mention the staff of Moses, or any number of other holy relics cared for by the white-togaed priests. Mere superstitious nonsense, in his opinion.

Justinian stood, pushing aside an ornate footstool with an impatient toe. "By God and all his angels, swear never to reveal what you will learn", he said hoarsely, descending from the dais and gripping John's arm tightly. The latter was reminded of King Midas's barber, who was given a secret to keep, but eventually unburdened himself to the reeds which whispered it abroad.

"Of course I swear," John said.

"I will rebuild the Church," Justinian said obliquely, in a distracted way, "and it will outdo Solomon. It will be a worthy home for all the relics which protect us, and of course, the city."

*How like Justinian to mention protection for himself first*, John thought contemptuously, for he did not suppose that the "us" was anything but the imperial us. He inclined his head respectfully as the Emperor spoke quickly and sibilantly in the shadowy hall.

"The Nubian is over six feet tall and has the strength of ten," protested Alexander, head charioteer of the Blue faction, picking his way over the rubble of a small wine shop toward a large barn. "And with all, clever with his hands. A fine carpenter and worker of wood, in fact right now repairing my best chariot, the one that nearly killed me by losing its axle last week." He turned his attention to his old friend John. "But he has the mind of a child. I doubt you'll get anything from him even if he understood you. His Greek is virtually nonexistent." His glance was curious, but he did not enquire in so many words what had brought John to visit, since he had appeared at the walnut door robed in officialdom from the red wool cloak to the golden wand of office.

John smiled thinly. "We'll see, Alexander."

"But what makes you think he can cast light on whatever it is?"

"My dear Alexander, even in a half-light of leaping flames and confusion, a man of his size stands out. He was seen on the spot. He may have . . . information." His tone was neutral but Alexander thanked Apollo *he* wasn't about to be interviewed. They entered the high-ceilinged building. Sitting at a workbench next to a wheel-less chariot, carving one of several pieces of wood with sure hands, was the slave under discussion. He glanced up as they entered, rising quickly to his feet. John looked at the young man before him. Tall and well proportioned, he noted, with symmetrical scars on his chest – tribal marks no doubt – he wore an ornate silver cross, a woodshaving-bedecked kilt and a disturbingly blank look.

"Mahmoud, I wish for you to answer the Lord Chamberlain's questions in all particulars, and truthfully, as a good servant should." The master spoke kindly and carefully as to the child to whom the giant had been compared. The man nodded, his eyes moving slowly to John as he spoke, then back to Alexander as he answered, as if it were the latter who was interrogating him. But he had nothing to tell, and indeed denied even being outside his master's enclosure during the riots, maintaining that he had been cowering in the barn during the entire night. Although he looked progressively more and more uneasy and upset, nothing changed his story, and, in the end, John told him to return to his work, gesturing Alexander to go outside. Sunshine washed the cobbles as they returned the way they had come.

"So," said his friend, "it seems he cannot assist."

"As you say, the mind of a child, although a faithful and certainly a talented one."

"He has given good service," Alexander replied, "and I would certainly be sorry to lose him if you're thinking of making an offer."

But lose him he did, because only four hours later, the body of the child-man was pulled out of the Bosphorus, as the barn burned down, taking with it his former master's best racing chariot.

John the Eunuch knelt long before the image of his lord, praying for divine help. The Emperor had given him but 24 hours to find the culprit, and he was no closer to solving the mystery. He had a feeling he might well find himself in the unenviable role of scapegoat, particularly since the Empress was just as likely to insist a Green such as himself was responsible – and had the power to make the allegation unchallenged truth. No, the prospects were not pleasant. His eye wandered over the sanctuary carvings, seeking inspiration as he formulated fantastic theories as to who the culprit could be. He was tired, and so was his mind, after interviewing several citizens seen, or supposedly seen (Constantinople being a city which thrived on intrigue and counterintrigue) abroad in the riots, pockets of which were still being put down by Imperial troops. How curious it would be if the culprit was not one of the street, but at a higher level of the hierarchy. *Why*, he thought with a thin smile that Alexander would recognize but shudder at, *what if it were the Empress herself*? It was said that she was devoted to Justinian, who upon marrying her had raised her from lowly ranks, but her back-stair intrigues were common enough knowledge, and her ambition endless.

His thoughts flowed on, from the highest to the lowest, or, in other words, the Nubian. How strange that he should have died so suddenly, so soon after he had seen him. Alexander had been angry about the loss of such valued property. John had replied he could only suspect suicide, or an accident, but now his thoughts began to take a different road. A slave might kill himself, although in his experience it was fairly uncommon. Accidents happened, of course, although this one was oddly timed. Yet who would want to kill a man like the Nubian? Unless, of course, he knew something he had not revealed. Or perhaps he thought he had been found guilty *in absentia*, and was terrified of the possibility of being taken away by the "gold stick man's" guards. Pillars of the community had a hard enough time establishing their innocence, particularly if they got on the wrong side of Empress Theodora. The vulgar irony of the thought prodded him into laughter, its chuckling echoes suddenly ceasing as John thought again, *Pillars of the community?* Pausing only to utter a quick prayer of thanks, he hurried out from the small room into late afternoon sunshine.

Riots may come, emperors may go, city buildings might burn all about him like red-tongued flowers from Hell, but the ancient stylite still stood 30 cubits above the Augusteum, wild eyed and half-naked, content to eat whatever was left by charity or a passing bird, standing aloft until his joints locked and his flesh mortified in more ways than one. There on his pillar, he communed with God and himself, always there, never descending, as much a part of the landscape as the Senate House or the statues on Zeuxippus' Baths – not that the stylite likely frequented the latter, John thought, wrinkling his nose a little as he ascended the ladder, to address the saintly occupant of the pillar, who had just received a pious gift of edibles.

"Bless you, my son," said the old man, through a mouthful of fish. John inclined his head in acknowledgement.

"O father," he began in a hoarse whisper, although there was little need to do so with the usual clamor from the street rising up about them, providing a cocoon of babbling sound which effectively masked their conversation. "I am here in the name of the Emperor, and wish to enquire of you certain things."

"Ask on, then, my son," the greybeard said, sunken eyes gentle under tangled brows, eyes much younger than the weatherbeaten face from which they peered. They were eyes, John hoped, which could, and had, seen far – and well.

"Tell me what you saw a night ago," he commanded.

The stylite smiled. "Ah, many things! It was as a vision, of hell on earth, with the flames of torment destroying all before them, and damned souls stalking the streets, crying for salvation, yet finding none." John hoped fervently that his informant would not, at this particular time, be seized with visions to recount. He was beginning to feel ludicrous, not to say precarious, as the wind from the Sea of Marmara plucked at his cloak. Furthermore, his sandals were increasingly insecure on the rungs. His informant bent kindly eyes upon him, fervent words a contrast to the gentleness of his gaze.

"It was as Orpheus must have experienced on his trip to Hades," the old man said. "Even to dark demons with treasures to tempt the faithful, stalking the pious in the shadows." John narrowed his eyes slightly. "Yes?" he prompted, wondering if he was barking up the wrong ladder. *Hell, demons, torment, indeed.* "Demons aside, did you see anything in the vicinity of the Church? It was certainly light enough."

"Yes, my son, I did. I saw the faithful remove all they could from the wicked conflagrations of the Devil blooming all over the city. Surely those pious souls were reserved a place in heaven because of their actions?"

John, noting to himself that while the stylite had excellent eyesight, he could not see too well, in that those whom he had characterized as pious souls saving religious treasures were actually looting the beautiful Church now in ruins to their left. A blindness which he shared, he felt, seeing, but not seeing. And time was growing short, darkness was creeping around the ramparts of the city. It would be another wet and cold night.

His informant wiped sticky fingers on his wild beard. "Yes, they stalk the night," he said, almost reading John's mind. "The demons, the demons . . ."

But more than that he was not prepared to say.

Justinian sat once more on the double throne on the dais below the domed roof, every inch an Emperor. He smiled kindly upon his Lord

Chamberlain, once more standing before him in the straight-backed stance of a man with good tidings.

"The results of your enquiries?" The tone was appropriately imperious.

John bowed. "Success, Excellency. The culprit was a simple-minded slave, now dead, who apparently saw his opportunity in the general unrest and took it. I have been able to recover . . . it."

Justinian beckoned him to the throne. "Bring it here!" he commanded, yet in a trembling voice. John obeyed, mounting gold-cloth covered stairs to three or four below the top, bowing low. Extending a thin, sunburnt hand, he placed into the Emperor's grasp a nondescript, slightly splintered piece of wood. John received it as his salvation, as indeed, John thought, he would consider it.

"This is from the True Cross itself," the Emperor said, eyes ablaze, "our most holy relic. You may go." John tactfully withdrew from the Great Hall, thankful to get away before the Emperor commanded further details of how he had found the relic in the teeming streets of Constantinople without being able to even reveal what he sought. He left the building, walking slowly along the winding path. A hundred yards away a burst of song issued from the Imperial Guard barracks. He smiled briefly. They served the Lord of Light in their own way. And, in his simple fashion, he served Him also.

For what was the Nubian but the dark demon with treasures (seen by the stylite emerging from the shadows) or rather with the gem-encrusted reliquary which had housed the holy relic for centuries? And why? Because he believed it would protect his master's chariot. Doubtless, the blasphemy of it would not enter his calculations, but enquiries from the Lord Chamberlain would certainly terrify him. Not to mention the possibility of retribution from the master he evidently loved. Thus it seemed likely he set the barn on fire and willed himself to destroy both evidence and himself. *A martyr to his religion*, John thought, standing in the shadows of a small pavilion in a garden which in a few months would bloom with all the flowers of the East. He could almost pity the slave, but had expected none from Justinian, if he had failed on his mission. Thus he had accordingly equipped himself with a piece of wood to replace the holy fragment, reasoning few had seen it, buried so long in its priceless reliquary, and those who might have would scarcely dare to contradict the Emperor. For what, after all, was in it but superstition? Still and all, if nothing else, the Blues would have no supernatural advantage now, thought John the Eunuch, servant of Mithra and supporter of the Greens, as he walked slowly home.

# HE CAME WITH
# THE RAIN
# Robert van Gulik

*Robert van Gulik (1910–1967) was a Dutch ambassador to Japan who became fascinated with the traditional tales about a seventh-century Chinese magistrate, Judge Dee. While on war duties, he translated the stories into English as* Dee Goong An: Three Murder Cases of Judge Dee *(1949). He then continued by writing new novels and stories about the character, starting with* The Chinese Bell Murders *(1958) and continuing through to* Poets and Murder *(1968).*

*"He Came With the Rain" is set early in Judge Dee's career, in the first year of his magistracy, and follows on from the events featured in* The Chinese Gold Murders *(1959), his earliest case, and* The Lacquer Screen *(1964).*

"This box won't do either!" Judge Dee's First Lady remarked disgustedly. "Look at the grey mould all along the seam of this blue dress!" She slammed the lid of the red-leather clothes-box shut, then turned to the Second Lady. "I've never known such a hot, damp summer. And the heavy downpour we had last night! I thought the rain would never stop. Give me a hand, will you?"

The judge, seated at the tea-table by the open window of the large bedroom, looked on while his two wives put the clothes-box on the floor, and went on to the third one in the pile. Miss Tsao, his First Lady's friend and companion, was drying robes on the brass brazier in the corner, draping them over the copper-wire cover above the glowing coals. The heat of the brazier, together with the steam curling up from the drying clothes, made the atmosphere of the room nearly unbearable, but the three women seemed unaware of it.

With a sigh he turned round and looked outside. From the bedroom here on the second floor of his residence one usually had a fine view of the curved roofs of the city, but now everything was shrouded in a thick leaden mist that blotted out all contours. The mist seemed to have entered his very blood, pulsating dully in his veins. Now he deeply regretted the unfortunate impulse that, on rising, had made him ask for his grey summer robe. For that request had brought his First Lady to inspect the four clothes-boxes, and finding mould on the garments, she had at once summoned his Second and Miss Tsao. Now the three were completely engrossed in their work, with apparently no thought of morning tea, let alone breakfast. This was their first experience of the dog-days in Peng-lai, for it was just seven months since he had taken up his post of magistrate there. He stretched his legs, for his knees and feet felt swollen and heavy. Miss Tsao stooped and took a white dress from the brazier.

"This one is completely dry," she announced. As she reached up to hang it on the clothes-rack, the judge noticed her slender, shapely body. Suddenly he asked his First Lady sharply: "Can't you leave all that to the maids?"

"Of course," his First replied over her shoulder. "But first I want to see for myself whether there's any real damage. For heaven's sake, take a look at this red robe, dear!" she went on to Miss Tsao. "The mould has absolutely eaten into the fabric! And you always say this dress looks so well on me!"

Judge Dee rose abruptly. The smell of perfume and stale cosmetics mingling with the faint odour of damp clothes gave the hot room an atmosphere of overwhelming femininity that suddenly jarred on his taut nerves. "I'm just going out for a short walk," he said.

"Before you've even had your morning tea?" his First exclaimed. But her eyes were on the discoloured patches on the red dress in her hands.

"I'll be back for breakfast," the judge muttered. "Give me that blue robe over there!" Miss Tsao helped the Second put the robe over his shoulders and asked solicitously: "Isn't that dress a bit too heavy for this hot weather?"

"It's dry at least," he said curtly. At the same time he realized with dismay that Miss Tsao was perfectly right: the thick fabric clung to his moist back like a coat of mail. He mumbled a greeting and went downstairs.

He quickly walked down the semi-dark corridor leading to the small back door of the tribunal compound. He was glad his old friend and adviser Sergeant Hoong had not yet appeared. The sergeant knew him so well that he would sense at once that he was in a bad temper, and he would wonder what it was all about.

The judge opened the back door with his private key and slipped out into the wet, deserted street. What was it all about, really? he asked himself as he walked along through the dripping mist. Well, these seven months on his first independent official post had been disappointing, of course. The first few days had been exciting, and then there had been the murder of Mrs. Ho, and the case at the fort. But thereafter there had been nothing but dreary office routine: forms to be filled out, papers to be filed, licences to be issued . . . In the capital he had also had much paperwork to do, but on important papers. Moreover, this district was not really his. The entire region from the river north was a strategic area, under the jurisdiction of the army. And the Korean quarter outside the East Gate had its own administration. He angrily kicked a stone, then cursed. What had looked like a loose boulder was in fact the top of a cobblestone, and he hurt his toe badly. He must take a decision about Miss Tsao. The night before, in the intimacy of their shared couch, his First Lady had again urged him to take Miss Tsao as his Third. She and his Second were fond of her, she had said, and Miss Tsao herself wanted nothing better. "Besides," his First had added with her customary frankness, "your Second is a fine woman but she hasn't had a higher education, and to have an intelligent, well-read girl like Miss Tsao around would make life much more interesting for all concerned." But what if Miss Tsao's willingness was motivated only by gratitude to him for getting her out of the terrible trouble she had been in? In a way it would be easier if he didn't like her so much. On the other hand, would it then be fair to marry a woman one didn't really like? As a magistrate he was entitled to as many as four wives, but personally he held the view that two wives ought to be sufficient unless both of them proved barren. It was all very difficult and confusing. He pulled his robe closer round him, for it had begun to rain.

He sighed with relief when he saw the broad steps leading up to the Temple of Confucius. The third floor of the west tower had been converted into a small tea-house. He would have his morning tea there, then walk back to the tribunal.

In the low-ceilinged, octagonal room a slovenly-dressed waiter was leaning on the counter, stirring the fire of the small tea-stove with iron tongs. Judge Dee noticed with satisfaction that the youngster didn't recognize him, for he was not in the mood to acknowledge bowing and scraping. He ordered a pot of tea and a dry towel and sat down at the bamboo table in front of the counter.

The waiter handed him a none-too-clean towel in a bamboo basket. "Just one moment please, sir. The water'll be boiling soon." As the judge rubbed his long beard dry with the towel, the waiter went on, "Since you are up and about so early, sir, you'll have heard already about the trouble out there." He pointed with his thumb at the open window, and as the judge shook his head, he continued with relish, "Last night a fellow was hacked to pieces in the old watchtower, out there in the marsh."

Judge Dee quickly put the towel down. "A murder? How do you know?"

"The grocery boy told me, sir. Came up here to deliver his stuff while I was scrubbing the floor. At dawn he had gone to the watchtower to collect duck eggs from that half-witted girl who lives up there, and he saw the mess. The girl was sitting crying in a corner. Rushing back to town, he warned the military police at the blockhouse, and the captain went to the old tower with a few of his men. Look, there they are!"

Judge Dee got up and went to the window. From this vantage-point he could see beyond the crenellated top of the city wall the vast green expanse of the marshlands overgrown with reeds, and further on to the north, in the misty distance, the grey water of the river. A hardened road went from the quay north of the city straight to the lonely tower of weather-beaten bricks in the middle of the marsh. A few soldiers with spiked helmets came marching down the road to the blockhouse halfway between the tower and the quay.

"Was the murdered man a soldier?" the judge asked quickly. Although the area north of the city came under the jurisdiction of the army, any crime involving civilians there had to be referred to the tribunal.

"Could be. That half-witted girl is deaf and dumb, but not too bad-looking. Could be a soldier went up the tower for a private conversation with her, if you get what I mean. Ha, the water is boiling!"

Judge Dee strained his eyes. Now two military policemen were riding from the blockhouse to the city, their horses splashing through the water that had submerged part of the raised road.

"Here's your tea, sir! Be careful, the cup is very hot. I'll put it here on the sill for you. No, come to think of it, the murdered man was no soldier. The grocery boy said he was an old merchant living near the North Gate – he knew him by sight. Well, the military police will catch the murderer soon enough. Plenty tough, they are!" He nudged the judge excitedly. "There you are! Didn't I tell you they're tough? See that fellow in chains they're dragging from the blockhouse? He's wearing a fisherman's brown jacket and trousers. Well, they'll take him to the fort now, and . . ."

"They'll do nothing of the sort!" the judge interrupted angrily. He hastily took a sip from the tea and scalded his mouth. He paid and rushed downstairs. A civilian murdered by another civilian, that was clearly a case for the tribunal! This was a splendid occasion to tell the military exactly where they got off! Once and for all.

All his apathy had dropped away from him. He rented a horse

from the blacksmith on the corner, jumped into the saddle and rode to the North Gate. The guards cast an astonished look at the dishevelled horseman with the wet house-cap sagging on his head. But then they recognized their magistrate and sprang to attention. The judge dismounted and motioned the corporal to follow him into the guardhouse beside the gate. "What is all this commotion out on the marsh?" he asked.

"A man was found murdered in the old tower, sir. The military police have arrested the murderer already; they are questioning him now in the blockhouse. I expect they'll come down to the quay presently."

Judge Dee sat down on the bamboo bench and handed the corporal a few coppers. "Tell one of your men to buy me two oilcakes!"

The oilcakes came fresh from the griddle of a street vendor and had an appetizing smell of garlic and onions, but the judge did not enjoy them, hungry though he was. The hot tea had burnt his tongue, and his mind was concerned with the abuse of power by the army authorities. He reflected ruefully that in the capital one didn't have such annoying problems to cope with: there, detailed rules fixed the exact extent of the authority of every official, high or low. As he was finishing his oilcakes, the corporal came in.

"The military police have now taken the prisoner to their watchpost on the quay, sir."

Judge Dee sprang up. "Follow me with four men!"

On the river quay a slight breeze was dispersing the mist. The judge's robe clung wetly to his shoulders. "Exactly the kind of weather for catching a bad cold," he muttered. A heavily armed sentry ushered him into the bare waiting-room of the watchpost.

In the back a tall man wearing the coat of mail and spiked helmet of the military police was sitting behind a roughly made wooden desk. He was filling out an official form with laborious, slow strokes of his writing-brush.

"I am Magistrate Dee," the judge began. "I demand to know . . ." He suddenly broke off. The captain had looked up. His face was marked by a terrible white scar running along his left cheek and across his mouth. His misshapen lips were half-concealed by a ragged moustache. Before the judge had recovered from this shock, the captain had risen. He saluted smartly and said in a clipped voice:

"Glad you came, sir. I have just finished my report to you." Pointing at the stretcher covered with a blanket on the floor in the corner, he added, "That's the dead body, and the murderer is in the back room there. You want him taken directly to the jail of the tribunal, I suppose?"

"Yes. Certainly," Judge Dee replied, rather lamely.

"Good." The captain folded the sheet he had been writing on and handed it to the judge. "Sit down, sir. If you have a moment to spare, I'd like to tell you myself about the case."

Judge Dee took the seat by the desk and motioned the captain to sit down too. Stroking his long beard, he said to himself that all this was turning out quite differently from what he had expected.

"Well," the captain began, "I know the marshland as well as the palm of my hand. That deaf-mute girl who lives in the tower is a harmless idiot, so when it was reported that a murdered man was lying up in her room, I thought at once of assault and robbery, and sent my men to search the marshland between the tower and the riverbank."

"Why especially that area?" the judge interrupted. "It could just as well have happened on the road, couldn't it? The murderer hiding the dead body later in the tower?"

"No, sir. Our blockhouse is located on the road halfway between the quay here and the old tower. From there my men keep an eye on the road all day long, as per orders. To prevent Korean spies from entering or leaving the city, you see. And they patrol that road at night. That road is the only means of crossing the marsh, by the way. It's tricky country, and anyone trying to cross it would risk getting into a swamp or quicksand and would drown. Now my men found the body was still warm, and we concluded he was killed a few hours before dawn. Since no one passed the blockhouse except the grocery boy, it follows that both the murdered man and the criminal came from the north. A pathway leads through the reeds from the tower to the riverbank, and a fellow familiar with the layout could slip by there without my men in the blockhouse spotting him." The captain stroked his moustache and added, "If he had succeeded in getting by our river patrols, that is."

"And your men caught the murderer by the waterside?"

"Yes, sir. They discovered a young fisherman, Wang San-lang his name is, hiding in his small boat among the rushes, directly north of the tower. He was trying to wash his trousers which were stained with blood. When my men hailed him, he pushed off and tried to paddle his boat into midstream. The archers shot a few string arrows into the hull, and before he knew where he was he was being hauled back to shore, boat and all. He disclaimed all knowledge of any dead man in the tower, maintained he was on his way there to bring the deaf-mute girl a large carp, and that he got the blood on his trousers while cleaning that carp. He was waiting for dawn to visit her. We searched him, and we found this in his belt."

The captain unwrapped a small paper package on his desk and showed the judge three shining silver pieces. "We identified the corpse by the visiting-cards we found on it." He shook the contents of a large envelope out on the table. Besides a package of cards there were two keys, some small change, and a pawn-ticket. Pointing at the ticket, the captain continued, "That scrap of paper was lying on the floor, close to the body. Must have dropped out of his jacket. The murdered man is the pawnbroker Choong, the owner of a large and well-known pawnshop, just inside the North Gate. A wealthy man. His hobby is fishing. My theory is that Choong met Wang somewhere on the quay last night and hired him to take him out in his boat for a night of fishing on the river. When they had got to the deserted area north of the tower, Wang lured the old man there under some pretext or other and killed him. He had planned to hide the body somewhere in the tower – the thing is half in ruins, you know, and the girl uses only the second storey – but she woke up and caught him in the act. So he just took the silver and left. This is only a theory, mind you, for the girl is worthless as a witness. My men tried to get something out of her, but she only scribbled down some incoherent nonsense about rain spirits and black goblins. Then she had a fit, began to laugh and to cry at the same time. A poor, harmless half-wit." He rose, walked over to the stretcher and lifted the blanket. "Here's the dead body."

Judge Dee bent over the lean shape, which was clad in a simple brown robe. The breast showed patches of clotted blood, and the sleeves were covered with dried mud. The face had a peaceful look, but it was very ugly: lantern-shaped, with a beaked nose that was slightly askew, and a thin-lipped, too large mouth. The head with its long, greying hair was bare.

"Not a very handsome gentleman," the captain remarked. "Though I should be the last to pass such a remark!" A spasm contorted his mutilated face. He raised the body's shoulders and showed the judge the large red stain on the back. "Killed by a knife thrust from behind that must have penetrated right into his heart. He was lying on his back on the floor, just inside the door of the girl's room." The captain let the upper part of the body drop. "Nasty fellow, that fisherman. After he had murdered Choong, he began to cut up his breast and belly. I say *after* he had killed him, for as you see those wounds in front haven't bled as much as one would expect. Oh yes, here's my last exhibit! Had nearly forgotten it!" He pulled out a drawer in the desk and unwrapped the oiled paper of an oblong package. Handing the judge a long thin knife, he said, "This was found in Wang's boat, sir. He says he uses it for cleaning his fish. There was no trace of blood on it. Why should there be? There was plenty of water around to wash it clean after he had got back to the boat! Well, that's about all, sir. I expect that Wang'll confess readily enough. I know that type of young hoodlum. They begin by stoutly denying everything, but after a thorough interrogation they break down and then they talk their mouths off. What are your orders, sir?"

"First I must inform the next of kin, and have them formally identify the body. Therefore, I . . ."

"I've attended to that, sir. Choong was a widower, and his two sons are living in the capital. The body was officially identified just now by Mr. Lin, the dead man's partner, who lived together with him."

"You and your men did an excellent job," the judge said. "Tell your men to transfer the prisoner and the dead body to the guards I brought with me." Rising, he added, "I am really most grateful for your swift and efficient action, captain. This being a civilian case, you only needed to report the murder to the tribunal and you could have left it at that. You went out of your way to help me and . . ."

The captain raised his hand in a deprecatory gesture and said in his strange dull voice, "It was a pleasure, sir. I happen to be one of Colonel Meng's men. We shall always do all we can to help you. All of us, always."

The spasm that distorted his misshapen face had to be a smile. Judge Dee walked back to the guardhouse at the North Gate. He had decided to question the prisoner there at once, then go to the scene of the crime. If he transferred the investigation to the tribunal, clues might get stale. It seemed a fairly straightforward case, but one never knew.

He sat down at the only table in the bare guardroom and settled down to a study of the captain's report. It contained little beyond what the captain had already told him. The victim's full name was Choong Fang, age fifty-six; the girl was called Oriole, twenty years of age, and the young fisherman was twenty-two. He took the visiting-cards and the pawn-ticket from his sleeve. The cards stated that Mr. Choong was a native of Shansi Province. The pawn-ticket was a tally, stamped with the large red stamp of Choong's pawnshop; it concerned four brocade robes pawned the day before by a Mrs. Pei for three silver pieces, to be redeemed in three months at a monthly interest of 5 per cent.

The corporal came in, followed by two guards carrying the stretcher.

"Put it down there in the corner," Judge Dee ordered. "Do you know about that deaf-mute girl who lives in the watchtower? The military police gave only her personal name – Oriole."

"Yes, sir, that's what she is called. She's an abandoned child. An old crone who used to sell fruit near the gate here brought her up and taught her to write a few dozen letters and a bit of sign language. When the old woman died two years ago, the girl went to live in the tower because the street urchins were always pestering her. She raises ducks there, and sells the eggs. People called her Oriole to make fun of her being dumb, and the nickname stuck."

"All right. Bring the prisoner before me."

The guards came back flanking a squat, sturdily built youngster. His tousled hair hung down over the corrugated brow of his swarthy, scowling face, and his brown jacket and trousers were clumsily patched in several places. His hands were chained behind his back, an extra loop of the thin chain encircling his thick, bare neck. The guards pressed him down on his knees in front of the judge.

Judge Dee observed the youngster in silence for a while, wondering what would be the best way to start the interrogation. There was only the patter of the rain outside, and the prisoner's heavy breathing. The judge took the three silver pieces from his sleeve.

"Where did you get these?"

The young fisherman muttered something in a broad dialect that the judge didn't quite understand. One of the guards kicked the prisoner and growled: "Speak louder!"

"It's my savings. For buying a real boat."

"When did you first meet Mr. Choong?"

The boy burst out in a string of obscene curses. The guard on his right stopped him by hitting him over his head with the flat of his sword. Wang shook his head, then said dully, "Only knew him by sight because he was often around on the quay." Suddenly he added viciously: "If I'd ever met him, I'd have killed the dirty swine, the crook . . ."

"Did Mr. Choong cheat when you pawned something in his shop?" Judge Dee asked quickly.

"Think I have anything to pawn?"

"Why call him a crook then?"

Wang looked up at the judge who thought he caught a sly glint in his small, bloodshot eyes. The youngster bent his head again and replied in a sullen voice: "Because all pawnbrokers are crooks."

"What did you do last night?"

"I told the soldiers already. Had a bowl of noodles at the stall on the quay, then went up river. After I had caught some good fish, I moored the boat on the bank north of the tower and had a nap. I'd planned to bring some fish to the tower at dawn, for Oriole."

Something in the way the boy pronounced the girl's name caught

Judge Dee's attention. He said slowly, "You deny having murdered the pawnbroker. Since, besides you, there was only the girl about, it follows it was she who killed him."

Suddenly Wang jumped up and went for the judge. He moved so quickly that the two guards only got hold of him just in time. He kicked them but got a blow on his head that made him fall down backwards, his chains clanking on the floorstones.

"You dog-official, you . . ." the youngster burst out, trying to scramble up. The corporal gave him a kick in the face that made his head slam back on the floor with a hard thud. He lay quite still, blood trickling from his torn mouth.

The judge got up and bent over the still figure. He had lost consciousness.

"Don't maltreat a prisoner unless you are ordered to," the judge told the corporal sternly. "Bring him round, and take him to the jail. Later I shall interrogate him formally, during the noon session. You'll take the dead body to the tribunal, corporal. Report to Sergeant Hoong and hand him this statement, drawn up by the captain of the military police. Tell the sergeant that I'll return to the tribunal as soon as I have questioned a few witnesses here." He cast a look at the window. It was still raining. "Get me a piece of oiled cloth!"

Before Judge Dee stepped outside he draped the oiled cloth over his head and shoulders, then jumped into the saddle of his hired horse. He rode along the quay and took the hardened road that led to the marshlands.

The mist had cleared a little and as he rode along he looked curiously at the deserted, green surface on either side of the road. Narrow gullies followed a winding course through the reeds, here and there broadening into large pools that gleamed dully in the grey light. A flight of small water birds suddenly flew up, with piercing cries that resounded eerily over the desolate marsh. He noticed that the water was subsiding after the torrential rain that had fallen in the night; the road was dry now, but the water had left large patches of duck-weed. When he was about to pass the blockhouse the sentry stopped him, but he let him go on as soon as the judge had shown him the identification document he carried in his boot.

The old watchtower was a clumsy, square building of five storeys, standing on a raised base of roughly hewn stone blocks. The shutters of the arched windows had gone and the roof of the top storey had caved in. Two big black crows sat perched on a broken beam.

As he came nearer he heard loud quacking. A few dozen ducks were huddling close together by the side of a muddy pool below the tower's base. When the judge dismounted and fastened the reins to a moss-covered stone pillar, the ducks began to splash around in the water, quacking indignantly.

The ground floor of the tower was just a dark, low vault, empty but for a heap of old broken furniture. A narrow, rickety flight of wooden stairs led up to the floor above. The judge climbed up, seeking support with his left hand from the wet, mould-covered wall, for the bannisters were gone.

When he stepped into the half-dark, bare room, something stirred among the rags piled up on the roughly made plank-bed under the arched window. Some raucous sounds came from under a soiled, patched quilt. A quick look around showed that the room only contained a rustic table with a cracked teapot, and a bamboo bench against the side wall. In the corner was a brick oven carrying a large pan; beside it stood a rattan basket filled to the brim with pieces of charcoal. A musty smell of mould and stale sweat hung in the air.

Suddenly the quilt was thrown to the floor. A half-naked girl with long, tousled hair jumped down from the plank-bed. After one look at the judge, she again made that strange, raucous sound and scuttled to the farthest corner. Then she dropped to her knees, trembling violently.

Judge Dee realized that he didn't present a very reassuring sight. He quickly pulled his identification document from his boot, unfolded it and walked up to the cowering girl, pointing with his forefinger at the large red stamp of the tribunal. Then he pointed at himself.

She apparently understood, for now she scrambled up and stared at him with large eyes that held an animal fear. She wore nothing but a tattered skirt, fastened to her waist with a piece of straw rope. She had a shapely, well-developed body and her skin was surprisingly white. Her round face was smeared with dirt but was not unattractive. Judge Dee pulled the bench up to the table and sat down. Feeling that some familiar gesture was needed to reassure the frightened girl, he took the teapot and drank from the spout, as farmers do.

The girl came up to the table, spat on the dirty top and drew in the spittle with her forefinger a few badly deformed characters. They read: "Wang did not kill him."

The judge nodded. He poured tea on the table-top, and motioned her to wipe it clean. She obediently went to the bed, took a rag and began to polish the table top with feverish haste. Judge Dee walked over to the stove and selected a few pieces of charcoal. Resuming his seat, he wrote with the charcoal on the table-top: "Who killed him?"

She shivered. She took the other piece of charcoal and wrote: "Bad black goblins." She pointed excitedly at the words, then scribbled quickly: "Bad goblins changed the good rain spirit."

"You saw the black goblins?" he wrote.

She shook her tousled head emphatically. She tapped with her forefinger repeatedly on the word "black", then she pointed at her closed eyes and shook her head again. The judge sighed. He wrote: "You know Mr. Choong?"

She looked perplexedly at his writing, her finger in her mouth. He realized that the complicated character indicating the surname Choong was unknown to her. He crossed it out and wrote "old man".

She again shook her head. With an expression of disgust she drew circles round the words "old man" and added: "Too much blood. Good rain spirit won't come any more. No silver for Wang's boat any more." Tears came trickling down her grubby cheeks as she wrote with a shaking hand: "Good rain spirit always sleep with me." She pointed at the plank-bed.

Judge Dee gave her a searching look. He knew that rain spirits played a prominent role in local folklore, so that it was only natural that they figured in the dreams and vagaries of this overdeveloped young girl. On the other hand, she had referred to silver. He wrote: "What does the rain spirit look like?"

Her round face lit up. With a broad smile she wrote in big, clumsy letters: "Tall. Handsome. Kind." She drew a circle round each of the three words, then threw the charcoal on the table and, hugging her bare breasts, began to giggle ecstatically.

The judge averted his gaze. When he turned to look at her again, she had let her hands drop and stood there staring straight ahead with wide eyes. Suddenly her expression changed again. With a quick gesture she pointed at the arched window, and made some strange sounds. He turned round. There was a faint colour in the leaden sky, the trace of a rainbow. She stared at it, in childish delight, her mouth half open. The judge took up the piece of charcoal for one final question: "When does the rain spirit come?"

She stared at the words for a long time, absentmindedly combing her long, greasy locks with her fingers. At last she bent over the table and wrote: "Black night and much rain." She put circles round the words "black" and "rain", then added: "He came with the rain."

All at once she put her hands to her face and began to sob convulsively. The sound mingled with the loud quacking of the ducks from below. Realizing that she couldn't hear the birds, he rose and laid his hand on her bare shoulder. When she looked up he was shocked by the wild, half-crazed gleam in her wide eyes. He quickly drew a duck on the table, and added the word "hunger". She clasped her hand to her mouth and ran to the oven. Judge Dee scrutinized the large flagstones in front of the entrance. He saw there a clean space on the dirty, dust-covered floor. Evidently it was there that the dead man had lain, and the military police had swept up the floor. He remembered ruefully his unkind thoughts about them. Sounds of chopping made him turn round. The girl was cutting up stale rice cakes on a primitive chopping board. The judge watched with a worried frown her deft handling of the large kitchen knife. Suddenly she drove the long, sharp point of the knife in the board, then shook the chopped up rice cakes into the pan on the oven, giving the judge a happy smile over her shoulder. He nodded at her and went down the creaking stairs.

The rain had ceased, a thin mist was gathering over the marsh. While untying the reins, he told the noisy ducks: "Don't worry, your breakfast is under way!"

He made his horse go ahead at a sedate pace. The mist came drifting in from the river. Strangely shaped clouds were floating over the tall reeds, here and there dissolving in long writhing trailers that resembled the tentacles of some monstrous water-animal. He wished he knew more about the hoary, deeply rooted beliefs of the local people. In many places people still venerated a river god or goddess, and farmers and fishermen made sacrificial offerings to these at the waterside. Evidently such things loomed large in the deaf-mute girl's feeble mind, shifting continually from fact to fiction, and unable to control the urges of her fullblown body. He drove his horse to a gallop.

Back at the North Gate, he told the corporal to take him to the pawnbroker's place. When they had arrived at the large, prosperous-looking pawnshop the corporal explained that Choong's private residence was located directly behind the shop and pointed at the narrow alleyway that led to the main entrance. Judge Dee told the corporal he could go back, and knocked on the black-lacquered gate.

A lean man, neatly dressed in a brown gown with black sash and borders, opened it. Bestowing a bewildered look on his wet, bearded visitor, he said: "You want the shop, I suppose. I can take you, I was just going there."

"I am the magistrate," Judge Dee told him impatiently. "I've just come from the marsh. Had a look at the place where your partner was murdered. Let's go inside, I want to hand over to you what was found on the dead body."

Mr. Lin made a very low bow and conducted his distinguished visitor to a small but comfortable side hall, furnished in conventional style with a few pieces of heavy blackwood furniture.

He ceremoniously led the judge to the broad bench at the back. While his host was telling the old manservant to bring tea and cakes, the judge looked curiously at the large aviary of copper wire on the wall table. About a dozen paddy birds were fluttering around inside.

"A hobby of my partner's," Mr. Lin said with an indulgent smile. "He was very fond of birds, always fed them himself."

With his neatly trimmed chin-beard and small, greying moustache Lin seemed at first sight just a typical middle-class shopkeeper. But a closer inspection revealed deep lines around his thin mouth, and large, sombre eyes that suggested a man with a definite personality. The judge set his cup down and formally expressed his sympathy with the firm's loss. Then he took the envelope from his sleeve and shook out the visiting-cards, the small cash, the pawn-ticket and the two keys. "That's all, Mr. Lin. Did your partner as a rule carry large sums of money on him?"

Lin silently looked the small pile over, stroking his chin-beard.

"No, sir. Since he retired from the firm two years ago, there was no need for him to carry much money about. But he certainly had more on him than just these few coppers when he went out last night."

"What time was that?"

"About eight, sir. After we had had dinner together here downstairs. He wanted to take a walk along the quay, so he said."

"Did Mr. Choong often do that?"

"Oh yes, sir! He had always been a man of solitary habits, and after the demise of his wife two years ago, he went out for long walks nearly every other night and always by himself. He always had his meals served in his small library upstairs, although I live here in this same house, in the left wing. Last night, however, there was a matter of business to discuss and therefore he came down to have dinner with me."

"You have no family, Mr. Lin?"

"No, sir. Never had time to establish a household! My partner had the capital, but the actual business of the pawnshop he left largely to me. And after his retirement he hardly set foot in our shop."

"I see. To come back to last night. Did Mr. Choong say when he would be back?"

"No, sir. The servant had standing orders not to wait up for him. My partner was an enthusiastic fisherman, you see. If he thought it looked like good fishing weather on the quay, he would hire a boat and pass the night up river."

Judge Dee nodded slowly. "The military police will have told you that they arrested a young fisherman called Wang San-lang. Did your partner often hire his boat?"

"That I don't know, sir. There are scores of fishermen about on the quay, you see, and most of them are eager to make a few extra coppers. But if my partner rented Wang's boat, it doesn't astonish me that he ran into trouble, for Wang is a violent young ruffian. I know of him, because being a fisherman of sorts myself, I have often heard the others talk about him. Surly, uncompanionable youngster." He sighed. "I'd like to go out fishing as often as my partner did, only I haven't got that much time . . . Well, it's very kind of you to have brought these keys, sir. Lucky that Wang didn't take them and throw them away! The larger one is the key of my late partner's library, the other of the strongbox he has there for keeping important papers." He stretched out his hand to take the keys, but Judge Dee scooped them up and put them in his sleeve.

"Since I am here," he said, "I shall have a look at Mr. Choong's papers right now, Mr. Lin. This is a murder case, and until it is solved, all the victim's papers are temporarily at the disposal of the authorities for possible clues. Take me to the library, please."

"Certainly, sir." Lin took the judge up a broad staircase and pointed at the door at the end of the corridor. The judge unlocked it with the larger key.

"Thanks very much, Mr. Lin. I shall join you downstairs presently."

The judge stepped into the small room, locked the door behind him, then went to push the low, broad window wide open. The roofs of the neighbouring houses gleamed in the grey mist. He turned and sat down in the capacious armchair behind the rosewood writing-desk facing the window. After a casual look at the iron-bound strongbox on the floor beside his chair, he leaned back and pensively took stock of his surroundings. The small library was scrupulously clean and furnished with simple, old-fashioned taste. The spotless whitewashed walls were decorated with two good landscape scrolls, and the solid ebony wall table bore a slender vase of white porcelain, with a few wilting roses. Piles of books in brocade covers were neatly stacked on the shelves of the small bookcase of spotted bamboo.

Folding his arms, the judge wondered what connection there could be between this tastefully arranged library that seemed to belong to an elegant scholar rather than to a pawnbroker, and the bare, dark room in the half-ruined watchtower, breathing decay, sloth and the direst poverty. After a while he shook his head, bent and unlocked the strongbox. Its contents matched the methodical neatness of the room: bundles of documents, each bound up with green ribbon and provided with an inscribed label. He selected the bundles marked "private correspondence" and "accounts and receipts". The former contained a few important letters about capital investment and correspondence from his sons, mainly about their family affairs and asking Mr. Choong's advice and instructions. Leafing through the second bundle, Judge Dee's practised eye saw at once that the deceased had been leading a frugal, nearly austere life. Suddenly he frowned. He had found a pink receipt, bearing the stamp of a house of assignation. It was dated back a year and a half. He quickly went through the bundle and found half a dozen similar receipts, the last dated back six months. Apparently Mr. Choong had, after his wife's demise, hoped to find consolation in venal love, but had soon discovered that such hope was vain. With a sigh he opened the large envelope which he had taken from the bottom of the box. It was marked: "Last Will and Testament". It was dated one year before, and stated that all of Mr. Choong's landed property – which was considerable – was to go to his two sons, together with two-thirds of his capital. The remaining one-third, and the pawnshop, was bequeathed to Mr. Lin "in recognition of his long and loyal service to the firm".

The judge replaced the papers. He rose and went to inspect the bookcase. He discovered that except for two dog-eared dictionaries, all the books were collections of poetry, complete editions of the most representative lyrical poets of former times. He looked through one volume. Every difficult word had been annotated in red ink, in an unformed, rather clumsy hand. Nodding slowly, he replaced the volume. Yes, now he understood. Mr. Choong had been engaged in a trade that forbade all personal feeling, namely that of a pawnbroker. And his pronouncedly ugly face made tender attachments unlikely. Yet at heart he was a romantic, hankering after the higher things of life, but very self-conscious and shy about these yearnings. As a merchant he had of course only received an elementary education, so he tried laboriously to expand his literary knowledge, reading old poetry with a dictionary in this small library which he kept so carefully locked.

Judge Dee sat down again and took his folding fan from his sleeve. Fanning himself, he concentrated his thoughts on this unusual pawnbroker. The only glimpse the outer world got of the sensitive nature of this man was his love of birds, evinced by the paddy birds downstairs. At last the judge got up. About to put his fan back into his sleeve, he suddenly checked himself. He looked at the fan absentmindedly for a while, then laid it on the desk. After a last look at the room he went downstairs.

His host offered him another cup of tea but Judge Dee shook his head. Handing Lin the two keys, he said, "I have to go back to the tribunal now. I found nothing among your partner's papers suggesting that he had any enemies, so I think that this case is exactly what it seems, namely a case of murder for gain. To a poor man, three silver pieces are a fortune. Why are those birds fluttering about?" He went to the cage. "Aha, their water is dirty. You ought to tell the servant to change it, Mr. Lin."

Lin muttered something and clapped his hands. Judge Dee groped in his sleeve. "How careless of me!" he exclaimed. "I left my fan on the desk upstairs. Would you fetch it for me, Mr. Lin?"

Just as Lin was rushing to the staircase, the old manservant came in. When the judge had told him that the water in the reservoir of the birdcage ought to be changed daily, the old man said, shaking his head, "I told Mr. Lin so, but he wouldn't listen. Doesn't care for birds. My master now, he loved them, he . . ."

"Yes, Mr. Lin told me that last night he had an argument with your master about those birds."

"Well yes, sir, both of them got quite excited. What was it about, sir? I only caught a few words about birds when I brought the rice."

"It doesn't matter," the judge said quickly. He had heard Mr. Lin come downstairs. "Well, Mr. Lin, thanks for the tea. Come to the chancery in, say, one hour, with the most important documents relating to your late partner's assets. My senior clerk will help you fill out the official forms, and the registration of Mr. Choong's will."

Mr. Lin thanked the judge profusely and saw him respectfully to the door.

Judge Dee told the guards at the gate of the tribunal to return his rented horse to the blacksmith, and went straight to his private residence at the back of the chancery. The old housemaster informed him that Sergeant Hoong was waiting in his private office. The judge nodded. "Tell the bathroom attendant that I want to take a bath now."

In the black-tiled dressing-room adjoining the bath he quickly stripped off his robe, drenched with sweat and rain. He felt soiled, in body and in mind. The attendant sluiced him with cold water, and vigorously scrubbed his back. But it was only after the judge had been lying in the sunken pool in hot water for some time that he began to feel better. Thereafter he had the attendant massage his shoulders, and when he had been rubbed dry he put on a crisp clean robe of blue cotton, and placed a cap of thin black gauze on his head. In this attire he walked over to his women's quarters.

About to enter the garden room where his ladies usually passed the morning, he halted a moment, touched by the peaceful scene. His two wives, clad in flowered robes of thin silk, were sitting with Miss Tsao at the red-lacquered table in front of the open sliding doors. The walled-in rock garden outside, planted with ferns and tall, rustling bamboos, suggested refreshing coolness. This was his own private world, a clean haven of refuge from the outside world of cruel violence and repulsive decadence he had to deal with in his official life. Then and there he took the firm resolution that he would preserve his harmonious family life intact, always.

His First Lady put her embroidery frame down and quickly came to meet him. "We have been waiting with breakfast for you for nearly an hour!" she told him reproachfully.

"I am sorry. The fact is that there was some trouble at the North Gate and I had to attend to it at once. I must go to the chancery now, but I shall join you for the noon rice." She conducted him to the door. When she was making her bow he told her in a low voice, "By the way, I have decided to follow your advice in the matter we discussed last night. Please make the necessary arrangements."

With a pleased smile she bowed again, and the judge went down the corridor that led to the chancery.

He found Sergeant Hoong sitting in an armchair in the corner of his private office. His old adviser got up and wished him a good morning. Tapping the document in his hand, the sergeant said, "I was relieved when I got this report, Your Honour, for we were getting worried about your prolonged absence! I had the prisoner locked up in jail, and the dead body deposited in the mortuary. After I had viewed it with the coroner, Ma Joong and Chiao Tai, your two lieutenants, rode to the North Gate to see whether you needed any assistance."

Judge Dee had sat down behind his desk. He looked askance at the pile of dossiers. "Is there anything urgent among the incoming documents, Hoong?"

"No, sir. All those files concern routine administrative matters."

"Good. Then we shall devote the noon session to the murder of the pawnbroker Choong."

The sergeant nodded contentedly. "I saw from the captain's report, Your Honour, that it is a fairly simple case. And since we have the murder suspect safely under lock and key . . ."

The judge shook his head. "No, Hoong, I wouldn't call it a simple case, exactly. But thanks to the quick measures of the military police, and thanks to the lucky chance that brought me right into the middle of things, a definite pattern has emerged."

He clapped his hands. When the headman came inside and made

his bow the judge ordered him to bring the prisoner Wang before him. He went on to the sergeant, "I am perfectly aware, Hoong, that a judge is supposed to interrogate an accused only publicly, in court. But this is not a formal hearing. A general talk for my orientation, rather."

Sergeant Hoong looked doubtful, but the judge vouchsafed no further explanation, and began to leaf through the topmost file on his desk. He looked up when the headman brought Wang inside. The chains had been taken off him, but his swarthy face looked as surly as before. The headman pressed him down on his knees, then stood himself behind him, his heavy whip in his hands.

"Your presence is not required, Headman," Judge Dee told him curtly.

The headman cast a worried glance at Sergeant Hoong. "This is a violent ruffian, Your Honour," he began diffidently. "He might . . ."

"You heard me!" the judge snapped.

After the disconcerted headman had left, Judge Dee leaned back in his chair. He asked the young fisherman in a conversational tone, "How long have you been living on the waterfront, Wang?"

"Ever since I can remember," the boy muttered.

"It's a strange land," the judge said slowly to Sergeant Hoong. "When I was riding through the marsh this morning, I saw weirdly shaped clouds drifting about, and shreds of mist that looked like long arms reaching up out of the water, as if . . ."

The youngster had been listening intently. Now he interrupted quickly: "Better not speak of those things!"

"Yes, you know all about those things, Wang. On stormy nights, there must be more going on in the marshlands than we city-dwellers realize."

Wang nodded vigorously. "I've seen many things," he said in a low voice, "with my own eyes. They all come up from the water. Some can harm you, others help drowning people, sometimes. But it's better to keep away from them, anyway."

"Exactly! Yet you made bold to interfere, Wang. And see what has happened to you now! You were arrested, you were kicked and beaten, and now you are a prisoner accused of murder!"

"I told you I didn't kill him!"

"Yes. But did you know who or what killed him? Yet you stabbed him when he was dead. Several times."

"I saw red . . ." Wang muttered. "If I'd known sooner, I'd have cut his throat. For I know him by sight, the rat, the . . ."

"Hold your tongue!" Judge Dee interrupted him sharply. "You cut up a dead man, and that's a mean and cowardly thing to do!"

He continued, calmer, "However, since even in your blind rage you spared Oriole by refraining from an explanation, I am willing to forget what you did. How long have you been going with her?"

"Over a year. She's sweet, and she's clever too. Don't believe she's a half-wit! She can write more than a hundred characters. I can read only a dozen or so."

Judge Dee took the three silver pieces from his sleeve and laid them on the desk. "Take this silver, it belongs rightly to her and to you. Buy your boat and marry her. She needs you, Wang." The youngster snatched the silver and tucked it in his belt. The judge went on, "You'll have to go back to jail for a few hours, for I can't release you until you have been formally cleared of the murder charge. Then you'll be set free. Learn to control your temper, Wang!"

He clapped his hands. The headman came in at once. He had been waiting just outside the door, ready to rush inside at the first sign of trouble.

"Take the prisoner back to his cell, headman. Then fetch Mr. Lin. You'll find him in the chancery."

Sergeant Hoong had been listening with mounting astonishment. Now he asked with a perplexed look, "What were you talking about with that young fellow, Your Honour? I couldn't follow it at all. Are you really intending to let him go?"

Judge Dee rose and went to the window. Looking out at the dreary, wet courtyard, he said, "It's raining again! What was I talking about, Hoong? I was just checking whether Wang really believed all those weird superstitions. One of these days, Hoong, you might try to find in our chancery library a book on local folklore."

"But you don't believe all that nonsense, sir!"

"No, I don't. Not all of it, at least. But I feel I ought to read up on the subject, for it plays a large role in the daily life of the common people of our district. Pour me a cup of tea, will you?"

While the sergeant prepared the tea, Judge Dee resumed his seat and concentrated on the official documents on his desk. After he had drunk a second cup, there was a knock at the door. The headman ushered Mr. Lin inside, then discreetly withdrew.

"Sit down, Mr. Lin!" the judge addressed his guest affably. "I trust my senior clerk gave you the necessary instructions for the documents to be drawn up?"

"Yes, indeed, Your Honour. Right now we were checking the landed property with the register and . . ."

"According to the will drawn up a year ago," the judge cut in, "Mr. Choong bequeathed all the land to his two sons, together with two-thirds of his capital, as you know. One-third of the capital, and the pawnshop, he left to you. Are you planning to continue the business?"

"No, sir," Lin replied with his thin smile. "I have worked in that pawnshop for more than thirty years, from morning till night. I shall sell it, and live off the rent from my capital."

"Precisely. But suppose Mr. Choong had made a new will? Containing a new clause stipulating that you were to get only the shop?" As Lin's face went livid, he went on quickly, "It's a prosperous business, but it would take you four or five years to assemble enough capital to retire. And you are getting on in years, Mr. Lin."

"Impossible! How . . . how could he . . ." Lin stammered. Then he snapped, "Did you find a new will in his strongbox?"

Instead of answering the question, Judge Dee said coldly: "Your partner had a mistress, Mr. Lin. Her love came to mean more to him than anything else."

Lin jumped up. "Do you mean to say that the old fool willed his money to that deaf-mute slut?"

"Yes, you know all about that affair, Mr. Lin. Since last night, when your partner told you. You had a violent quarrel. No, don't try to deny it! Your manservant overheard what you said, and he will testify in court."

Lin sat down again. He wiped his moist face. Then he began, calmer now, "Yes, sir, I admit that I got very angry when my partner informed me last night that he loved that girl. He wanted to take her away to some distant place and marry her. I tried to make him see how utterly foolish that would be, but he told me to mind my own business and ran out of the house in a huff. I had no idea he would go to the tower. It's common knowledge that that young hoodlum Wang is carrying on with the half-wit. Wang surprised the two, and he murdered my partner. I apologize for not having mentioned these facts to you this morning, sir. I couldn't bring myself to compromise my late partner . . . And since you had arrested the murderer, everything would have come out anyway in court . . ." He shook his head. "I am partly to blame, sir. I should have gone after him last night, I should've . . ."

"But you did go after him, Mr. Lin," Judge Dee interrupted curtly. "You are a fisherman too, you know the marsh as well as your partner. Ordinarily one can't cross the marsh, but after a heavy rain the water rises, and an experienced boatman in a shallow skiff could paddle across by way of the swollen gullies and pools."

"Impossible! The road is patrolled by the military police all night!"

"A man crouching in a skiff could take cover behind the tall reeds,

Mr. Lin. Therefore your partner could only visit the tower on nights after a heavy rain. And therefore the poor half-witted girl took the visitor for a supernatural being, a rain spirit. For he came with the rain." He sighed. Suddenly he fixed Lin with his piercing eyes and said sternly, "When Mr. Choong told you about his plans last night, Lin, you saw all your long-cherished hopes of a life in ease and luxury go up into thin air. Therefore you followed Choong, and you murdered him in the tower by thrusting a knife into his back."

Lin raised his hands. "What a fantastic theory, sir! How do you propose to prove this slanderous accusation?"

"By Mrs. Pei's pawn-ticket, among other things. It was found by the military police on the scene of the crime. But Mr. Choong had completely retired from the business, as you told me yourself. Why then would he be carrying a pawn-ticket that had been issued that very day?" As Lin remained silent, Judge Dee went on, "You decided on the spur of the moment to murder Choong, and you rushed after him. It was the hour after the evening rice, so the shopkeepers in your neighbourhood were on the lookout for their evening custom when you passed. Also on the quay, where you took off in your small skiff, there were an unusual number of people about, because it looked like heavy rain was on its way." The glint of sudden panic in Lin's eyes was the last confirmation the judge had been waiting for. He concluded in an even voice, "If you confess now, Mr. Lin, sparing me the trouble of sifting out all the evidence of the eyewitnesses, I am prepared to add a plea for clemency to your death sentence, on the ground that it was unpremeditated murder."

Lin stared ahead with a vacant look. All at once his pale face became distorted by a spasm of rage. "The despicable old lecher!" he spat. "Made me sweat and slave all those years . . . and now he was going to throw all that good money away on a cheap, half-witted slut! The money I made for him . . ." He looked steadily at the judge as he added in a firm voice, "Yes, I killed him. He deserved it."

Judge Dee gave the sergeant a sign. While Hoong went to the door the judge told the pawnbroker, "I shall hear your full confession during the noon session."

They waited in silence till the sergeant came back with the headman and two constables. They put Lin in chains and led him away.

"A sordid case, sir," Sergeant Hoong remarked dejectedly.

The judge took a sip from his teacup and held it up to be refilled. "Pathetic, rather. I would even call Lin pathetic, Hoong, were it not for the fact that he made a determined effort to incriminate Wang."

"What was Wang's role in all this, sir? You didn't even ask him what he did this morning!"

"There was no need to, for what happened is as plain as a pikestaff. Oriole had told Wang that a rain spirit visited her at night and sometimes gave her money. Wang considered it a great honour that she had relations with a rain spirit. Remember that only half a century ago in many of the river districts in our Empire the people immolated every year a young boy or girl as a human sacrifice to the local river god – until the authorities stepped in. When Wang came to the tower this morning to bring Oriole her fish, he found in her room a dead man lying on his face on the floor. The crying Oriole gave him to understand that goblins had killed the rain spirit and changed him into an ugly old man. When Wang turned over the corpse and recognized the old man, he suddenly understood that he and Oriole had been deceived, and in a blind rage pulled his knife and stabbed the dead man. Then he realized that this was a murder case and he would be suspected. So he fled. The military police caught him while trying to wash his trousers which had become stained with Choong's blood."

Sergeant Hoong nodded. "How did you discover all this in only a few hours, sir?"

"At first I thought the captain's theory hit the nail on the head. The only point which worried me a bit was the long interval between the murder and the stabbing of the victim's breast. I didn't worry a bit about the pawn-ticket, for it is perfectly normal for a pawnbroker to carry a ticket about that he has made out that very same day. Then, when questioning Wang, it struck me that he called Choong a crook. That was a slip of the tongue, for Wang was determined to keep both Oriole and himself out of this, so as not to have to divulge that they had let themselves be fooled. While I was interviewing Oriole she stated that the 'goblins' had killed and *changed* her rain spirit. I didn't understand that at all. It was during my visit to Lin that at last I got on the right track. Lin was nervous and therefore garrulous, and told me at length about his partner taking no part at all in the business. I remembered the pawn-ticket found on the murder scene, and began to suspect Lin. But it was only after I had inspected the dead man's library and got a clear impression of his personality that I found the solution. I checked my theory by eliciting from the manservant the fact that Lin and Choong had quarrelled about Oriole the night before. The name Oriole meant of course nothing to the servant, but he told me they had a heated argument about birds. The rest was routine."

The judge put his cup down. "I have learned from this case how important it is to study carefully our ancient handbooks of detection, Hoong. There it is stated again and again that the first step of a murder investigation is to ascertain the character, daily life and habits of the victim. And in this case it was indeed the murdered man's personality that supplied the key."

Sergeant Hoong stroked his grey moustache with a pleased smile. "That girl and her young man were very lucky indeed in having you as the investigating magistrate, sir! For all the evidence pointed straight at Wang, and he would have been convicted and beheaded. For the girl is a deaf-mute, and Wang isn't much of a talker either!"

Judge Dee nodded. Leaning back in his chair, he said with a faint smile:

"That brings me to the main benefit I derived from this case, Hoong. A very personal and very important benefit. I must confess to you that early this morning I was feeling a bit low, and for a moment actually doubted whether this was after all the right career for me. I was a fool. This is a great, a magnificent office, Hoong! If only because it enables us to speak for those who can't speak for themselves."

# THE HIGH KING'S SWORD
## Peter Tremayne

*One of the pleasures of assembling this anthology is seeing the ancient world come alive through the eyes of keen observers of the day – and you can't get keener observers than the detectives featured here. When Peter Tremayne submitted his manuscript for the following story he explained that it was set in March 664. As the previous story was set in the year 663, we can see in the breadth of two stories two vastly differing cultures on opposite sides of the world, united by man's weakness for crime.*

*The following story features a new detective, Sister Fidelma. Tremayne has called her a "Dark Age Irish Perry Mason". Apart from being a religieuse, she is a dálaighe, or an advocate at the Brehon court. The background to the story is historically accurate. The Yellow Plague swept through Europe reaching Britain and Ireland in AD 664. The joint High Kings of Ireland, Blathmac and Diarmuid, died within days of each other in that year, and this provides the starting point for the story.*

*Peter Tremayne (b. 1943) is a well-known writer of fantasy and horror novels and stories and, under his real name of Peter Berresford Ellis, is a noted biographer and Celtic historian. He has already written several more stories about Sister Fidelma, including a full-length novel, so a new character is born.*

"God's curse is upon this land," sighed the Abbot Colmán, spiritual advisor to the Great Assembly of the chieftains of the five kingdoms of Ireland.

Walking at his side through the grounds of the resplendent palace of Tara, the seat of the High Kings of Ireland, was a tall woman, clad in the robes of a *religieuse*, her hands folded demurely before her. Even at a distance one could see that her costume did not seem to suit her for it scarcely hid the attractiveness of her youthful, well-proportioned figure. Rebellious strands of red hair crept from beneath her habit adding to the allure of her pale fresh face and piercing green eyes. Her cheeks dimpled and there was a scarcely concealed humour behind her enforced solemnity which hinted at a joy in living rather than being weighted down by the sombre pensiveness of religious life.

"When man blames God for cursing him, it is often to disguise the fact that he is responsible for his own problems," Sister Fidelma replied softly.

The Abbot, a thick-set and ruddy faced man in his mid-fifties, frowned and glanced at the young woman at his side. Was she rebuking him?

"Man is hardly responsible for the terrible Yellow Plague that has swept through this land," replied Colmán, his voice heavy with irritation. "Why, it is reported that one third of our population has been carried off by its venomousness. It has spared neither abbot, bishop nor lowly priest."

"Nor even High Kings," added Sister Fidelma, pointedly.

The official mourning for the brothers Blathmac and Diarmuid, joint High Kings of Ireland, who had died within days of each other from the terrors of the Yellow Plague, had ended only one week before.

"Surely, then, a curse of God?" repeated the Abbot, his jaw set firmly, waiting for Sister Fidelma to contradict him.

Wisely, she decided to remain silent. The Abbot was obviously in no mood to discuss the semantics of theology.

"It is because of these events that I have asked you to come to Tara," the Abbot went on, as he preceded her into the chapel of the Blessed Patrick, which had been built next to the High King's palace. Sister Fidelma followed the Abbot into the gloomy, incensed-sweetened atmosphere of the chapel, dropping to one knee and genuflecting to the altar before she followed him to the sacristy. He settled his stocky figure into a leather chair and motioned for her to be seated.

She settled herself and waited expectantly.

"I have sent for you, Sister Fidelma, because you are an advocate, a *dálaighe*, of the Brehon courts, and therefore knowledgeable in law."

Sister Fidelma contrived to shrug modestly while holding herself in repose.

"It is true that I have studied eight years with the Brehon Morann, may his soul rest in peace, and I am qualified to the level of *anruth*."

The Abbot pursed his lips. He had not yet recovered from his astonishment at his first meeting with this young woman who was

so highly qualified in law, and held a degree which demanded respect
from the highest in the land. She was only one step below an *ollamh*
who could even sit in the presence of the High King himself. The
Abbot felt awkward as he faced Sister Fidelma of Kildare. While
he was her superior in religious matters, he, too, had to defer to the
social standing and legal authority which she possessed as a *dálaighe*
of the Brehon Court of Ireland.

"I have been told of your qualification and standing, Sister
Fidelma. But, apart from your knowledge and authority, I have also
been told that you possess an unusual talent for solving puzzles."

"Whoever has told you that flatters me. I have helped to clarify
some problems. And what little talent I have in that direction is at
your service."

Sister Fidelma gazed with anticipation at the Abbot as he rubbed
his chin thoughtfully.

"For many years our country has enjoyed prosperity under the
joint High Kingship of Blathmac and Diarmuid. Therefore their
deaths, coming within days of one another, must be viewed as a
tragedy."

Sister Fidelma raised an eyebrow.

"Is there anything suspicious about their deaths? Is that why you
have asked me here?"

The Abbot shook his head hurriedly.

"No. Their deaths were but human submission to the fearsome
Yellow Plague which all dread and none can avoid once it has
marked them. It is God's will."

The Abbot seemed to pause waiting for some comment but, when
Sister Fidelma made none, he continued.

"No, Sister, there is nothing suspicious about the deaths of
Blathmac and Diarmuid. The problem arises with their successor
to the kingship."

Sister Fidelma frowned.

"But I thought that the Great Assembly had decided that
Sechnasach, the son of Blathmac, would become High King?"

"That was the decision of the provincial kings and chieftains of
Ireland," agreed the Abbot. "But Sechnasach has not yet been
inaugurated on the sacred Stone of Destiny." He hesitated. "Do
you know your Law of Kings?"

"In what respect?" Sister Fidelma countered, wondering where
the question was leading.

"That part relating to the seven proofs of a righteous king."

"The Law of the Brehons states that there are seven proofs of
the righteous king," recited Sister Fidelma dutifully. "That he be

approved by the Great Assembly. That he accept the Faith of the One True God. That he hold sacred the symbols of his office and swear fealty on them. That he rule by the Law of the Brehons and his judgement be firm and just and beyond reproach. That he promote the commonwealth of the people. That he must never command his warriors in an unjust war . . ."

The Abbot held up his hand and interrupted.

"Yes, yes. You know the law. The point is that Sechnasach cannot be inaugurated because the great sword of the Uí Néill, the 'Caladchalog', which was said to have been fashioned in the time of the ancient mist by the smith-god Gobhainn, has been stolen."

Sister Fidelma raised her head, lips slightly parted in surprise.

The ancient sword of the Uí Néill was one of the potent symbols of the High Kingship. Legend had it that it had been given by the smith-god to the hero Fergus Mac Roth in the time of the ancient ones, and then passed down to Niall of the Nine Hostages, whose descendants had become the Uí Néill kings of Ireland. For centuries now the High Kings had been chosen from either the sept of the northern Uí Néill or from the southern Uí Néill. The "Caladchalog", "the hard dinter", was a magical, mystical sword, by which the people recognized their righteous ruler. All High Kings had to swear fealty on it at their inauguration and carry it on all state occasions as the visible symbol of their authority and kingship.

The Abbot stuck out his lower lip.

"In these days, when our people go in fear from the ravages of the plague, they need comfort and distraction. If it was known throughout the land that the new High King could not produce his sword of office on which to swear his sacred oath of kingship then apprehension and terror would seize the people. It would be seen as an evil omen at the start of Sechnasach's rule. There would be chaos and panic. Our people cling fiercely to the ancient ways and traditions but, particularly at this time, they need solace and stability."

Sister Fidelma compressed her lips thoughtfully. What the Abbot said was certainly true. The people firmly believed in the symbolism which had been handed down to them from the mists of ancient times.

"If only people relied on their own abilities and not on symbols," the Abbot was continuing. "It is time for reform, both in secular as well as religious matters. We cling to too many of the pagan beliefs of our ancestors from the time before the Light of Our Saviour was brought to these shores."

"I see that you yourself believe in the reforms of Rome," Sister Fidelma observed shrewdly.

The Abbot did not conceal his momentary surprise.

"How so?"

Sister Fidelma smiled.

"I have done nothing clever, Abbot Colmán. It was an elementary observation. You wear the tonsure of St. Peter, the badge of Rome, and not that of St. John from whom our own Church takes its rule."

The corner of the Abbot's mouth drooped.

"I make no secret that I was in Rome for five years and came to respect Rome's reasons for the reforms. I feel it is my duty to advocate the usages of the Church of Rome among our people to replace our old rituals, symbolisms and traditions."

"We have to deal with people as they are and not as we would like them to be," observed Sister Fidelma.

"But we must endeavour to change them as well," replied the Abbot unctuously, "setting their feet on the truth path to God's grace."

"We will not quarrel over the reforms of Rome," replied Sister Fidelma quietly. "I will continue to be guided by the rule of the Holy Brigid of Kildare, where I took my vows. But tell me, for what purpose have I been summoned to Tara?"

The Abbot hesitated, as if wondering whether to pursue his theme of Rome's reforms. Then he sniffed to hide his irritation.

"We must find the missing sword before the High King's inauguration, which is tomorrow, if we wish to avoid civil strife in the five kingdoms of Ireland."

"From where was it stolen?"

"Here, from this very chapel. The sacred sword was placed with the *Lia Fáil*, the Stone of Destiny, under the altar. It was locked in a metal and wood chest. The only key was kept on the altar in full view. No one, so it was thought, would ever dare violate the sanctuary of the altar and chapel to steal its sacred treasures."

"Yet someone did?"

"Indeed they did. We have the culprit locked in a cell."

"And the culprit is . . .?"

"Ailill Flann Esa. He is the son of Donal, who was High King twenty years ago. Ailill sought the High Kingship in rivalry to his cousin, Sechnasach. It is obvious that, out of malice caused by the rejection of the Great Assembly, he seeks to discredit his cousin."

"What witnesses were there to his theft of the sword?"

"Three. He was found in the chapel alone at night by two guards of the royal palace, Congal and Erc. And I, myself, came to the chapel a few moments later."

Sister Fidelma regarded the Abbot with bewilderment.

"If he were found in the chapel in the act of stealing the sword, why was the sword not found with him?"

The Abbot sniffed impatiently.

"He had obviously hidden it just before he was discovered. Maybe he heard the guards coming and hid it."

"Has the chapel been searched?"

"Yes. Nothing has been found."

"So, from what you say, there were no witnesses to see Ailill Flann Esa actually take the sword?"

The Abbot smiled paternally.

"My dear sister, the chapel is secured at night. The deacon made a check last thing and saw everything was in order. The guards passing outside observed that the door was secure just after midnight, but twenty minutes later they passed it again and found it open. They saw the bolt had been smashed. The chapel door is usually bolted on the inside. That was when they saw Ailill at the altar. The altar table had been pushed aside, the chest was open and the sword gone. The facts seem obvious."

"Not yet so obvious, Abbot Colmán," Sister Fidelma replied thoughtfully.

"Obvious enough for Sechnasach to agree with me to have Ailill Flann Esa incarcerated immediately."

"And the motive, you would say, is simply one of malice?"

"Obvious again. Ailill wants to disrupt the inauguration of Sechnasach as High King. Perhaps he even imagines that he can promote civil war in the confusion and chaos, and, using the people's fears, on the production of the sacred sword from the place where he has hidden it, he thinks to overthrow Sechnasach and make himself High King. The people, in their dread of the Yellow Plague, are in the mood to be manipulated by their anxieties."

"If you have your culprit and motive, why send for me?" Sister Fidelma observed, a trace of irony in her voice. "And there are better qualified *dálaighe* and Brehons at the court of Tara, surely?"

"Yet none who have your reputation for solving such conundrums, Sister Fidelma."

"But the sword must still be in the chapel or within its vicinity."

"We have searched and it cannot be found. Time presses. I have been told that you have the talent to solve the mystery of where the sword has been hidden. I have heard how skilful you are in questioning suspects and extracting the truth from them. Ailill has, assuredly, hidden the sword nearby and we must find out where before the High King's inauguration."

Sister Fidelma pursed her lips and then shrugged.

"Show me the where the sword was kept and then I will question Ailill Flann Esa."

Ailill Flann Esa was in his mid-thirties; tall, brown-haired and full-bearded. He carried himself with the pride of the son of a former High King. His father had been Donal Mac Aed of the northern Uí Néill, who had once ruled from Tara twenty years before.

"I did not steal the sacred sword," he replied immediately Sister Fidelma identified her purpose.

"Then explain how you came to be in the chapel at such a time," she said, seating herself on the wooden bench that ran alongside the wall of the tenebrous grey stone cell in which he was imprisoned. Ailill hesitated and then seated himself on a stool before her. The stool, with a wooden bed and a table, comprised the other furnishings of the cell. Sister Fidelma knew that only Ailill's status gave him the luxury of these comforts and alleviated the dankness of the granite jail in which he was confined.

"I was passing the chapel . . ." began Ailill.

"Why?" interrupted Sister Fidelma. "It was after midnight, I believe?"

The man hesitated, frowning. He was apparently not used to people interrupting. Sister Fidelma hid a smile as she saw the struggle on his haughty features. It was clear he wished to respond in annoyance but realized that she was an *anruth* who had the power of the Brehon Court behind her. Yet he hesitated for a moment or two.

"I was on my way somewhere . . . to see someone."

"Where? Who?"

"That I cannot say."

She saw firmness in his pinched mouth, in the compressed lips. He would obviously say nothing further on that matter. She let it pass.

"Continue," she invited after a moment's pause.

"Well, I was passing the chapel, as I said, and I saw the door open. Usually, at that time of night, the door is closed and the bolt in place. I thought this strange, so I went in. Then I noticed that the altar had been pushed aside. I went forward. I could see that the chest, in which the sword of office was kept, had been opened . . ."

He faltered and ended with a shrug.

"And then?" prompted Sister Fidelma.

"That is all. The guards came in at that moment. Then the

Abbot appeared. I found myself accused of stealing the sword. Yet I did not."

"Are you saying that this is all you know about the matter?"

"That is all I know. I am accused but innocent. My only misdemeanour is that I am my father's son and presented a claim before the Great Assembly to succeed Blathmac and Diarmuid as High King. Although Sechnasach won the support of the Great Assembly for his claim, he has never forgiven me for challenging his succession. He is all the more ready to believe my guilt because of his hatred of me."

"And have you forgiven Sechnasach for his success before the Great Assembly?" Sister Fidelma asked sharply.

Ailill grimaced in suppressed annoyance.

"Do you think me a mean person, Sister? I abide by the law. But, in honesty, I will tell you that I think the Great Assembly has made a wrong choice. Sechnasach is a traditionalist at a time when our country needs reforms. We need reforms in our secular law and in our Church."

Sister Fidelma's eyes narrowed.

"You would support the reforms being urged upon us by the Roman Church? To change our dating of Easter, our ritual and manner of land-holding?"

"I would. I have never disguised it. And there are many who would support me. My cousin Cernach, the son of Diarmuid, for example. He is a more vehement advocate of Rome than I am."

"But you would admit that you have a strong motive in attempting to stop Sechnasach's inauguration?"

"Yes. I admit that my policies would be different to those of Sechnasach. But above all things I believe that once the Great Assembly chooses a High King, then all must abide by their decision. Unless the High King fails to abide by the law and fulfil its obligations, he is still High King. No one can challenge the choice of the Great Assembly."

Sister Fidelma gazed directly into Ailill's smouldering brown eyes.

"And did you steal the sword?"

Ailill sought to control the rage which the question apparently aroused.

"By the powers, I did not! I have told you all I know."

The warrior named Erc scuffed at the ground with his heel, and stirred uneasily.

"I am sure I cannot help you, Sister. I am a simple guardsman and there is little to add beyond the fact that I, with my companion Congal, found Ailill Flann Esa in the chapel standing before the chest from which the sacred sword had been stolen. There is nothing further I can add."

Sister Fidelma compressed her lips. She gazed around at the curious faces of the other warriors who shared the dormitory of the High King's bodyguard. The murky chamber, shared by a hundred warriors when they were resting from their guard duties, stank of spirits and body sweat which mixed into a bitter scent.

"Let me be the judge of that." She turned towards the door. "Come, walk with me for a while in the fresh air, Erc. I would have you answer some questions."

Reluctantly the burly warrior laid aside his shield and javelin and followed the *religieuse* from the dormitory, accompanied by a chorus of whispered comments and a few lewd jests from his comrades.

"I am told that you were guarding the chapel on the night the theft occurred," Sister Fidelma said as soon as they were outside, walking in the crystal early morning sunlight. "Is that correct?"

"Congal and I were the guards that night, but our duties were merely to patrol the buildings of which the chapel is part. Usually from midnight until dawn the doors of the chapel of the Blessed Patrick are shut. The chapel contains many treasures and the Abbot has ordered that the door be bolted at night."

"And what time did you arrive at your posts?"

"At midnight exactly, Sister. Our duties took us from the door of the royal stables, fifty yards from the chapel, to the door of the great refectory, a route which passes the chapel door."

"Tell me what happened that night."

"Congal and I took up our positions, as usual. We walked by the chapel door. It seemed shut as usual. We turned at the door of the great refectory from which point we followed a path which circumvents the buildings, so that our patrol follows a circular path."

"How long does it take to circumnavigate the buildings?"

"No more than half-an-hour."

"And how long would you be out of sight of the door of the chapel?"

"Perhaps twenty minutes."

"Go on."

"It was on our second patrol, as I say, a half-hour later, that we passed the door of the chapel. It was Congal who spotted that the door was opened. We moved forward and then I saw that the door had been forced. The wood was splintered around the bolt on the inside of the door. We entered and saw Ailill Flann Esa standing before the altar. The altar had been pushed back from the position where it covered the Stone of Destiny and the chest in which the sacred sword was kept had been opened."

"What was Ailill doing? Did he look flustered or short of breath?"

"No. He was calm enough. Just staring down at the open chest."

"Wasn't it dark in the chapel? How did you see so clearly?"

"Some candles were lit within the chapel and provided light enough."

"And then?"

"He saw our shadows and started, turning to us. At that point the Abbot came up behind us. He saw the sacrilege at once and pointed to the fact that the sword was gone."

"Did he question Ailill?"

"Oh, surely he did. He said the sword had gone and asked what Ailill had to say."

"And what did Ailill say?"

"He said that he had just arrived there."

"And what did you say?"

"I said that was impossible because we were patrolling outside and had the chapel door in sight for at least ten minutes from the royal stable doorway. Ailill must have been inside for that ten minutes at least."

"But it was night time. It must have been dark outside. How could you be sure that Ailill had not just entered the chapel before you, covered by the darkness?"

"Because the torches are lit in the grounds of the royal palace every night. It is the law of Tara. Where there is light, there is no treachery. Ailill must have been in the chapel, as I have said, for at least ten minutes. That is a long time."

"Yet even ten minutes does not seem time enough to open the chest, hide the sword, and repose oneself before you entered."

"Time enough, I'd say. For what else could be done with the sword but hide it?"

"And where is your companion, Congal? I would question him."

Erc looked troubled and genuflected with a degree of haste.

"God between me and evil, Sister. He has fallen sick with the Yellow Plague. He lies close to death now and maybe I will be next to succumb to the scourge."

Sister Fidelma bit her lip, then she shook her head and smiled reassuringly at Erc.

"Not necessarily so, Erc. Go to the apothecary. Ask that you be given an infusion of the leaves and flowers of the *centaurium vulgare*. It has a reputation for keeping the Yellow Plague at bay."

"What is that?" demanded the warrior, frowning at the unfamiliar Latin words.

"*Dréimire buí*," she translated to the Irish name of the herb. "The apothecary will know it. To drink of the mixture is supposedly a good preventative tonic. By drinking each day, you may avoid the scourge. Now go in peace, Erc. I have done with you for the meanwhile."

Sechnasach, lord of Midhe, and High King of Ireland, was a thin man, aged in his mid-thirties, with scowling features and dark hair. He sat slightly hunched forward on his chair, the epitome of gloom.

"Abbot Colmán reports that you have not yet discovered where Ailill has hidden the sword of state, Sister," he greeted brusquely as he gestured for Sister Fidelma to be seated. "May I remind you that the inauguration ceremony commences at noon tomorrow?"

The High King had agreed to meet her, at her own request, in one of the small audience chambers of the palace of Tara. It was a chamber with a high vaulted ceiling and hung with colourful tapestries. There was a crackling log fire in the great hearth at one end before which the High King sat in his ornate carved oak chair. Pieces of exquisite furniture, brought as gifts to the court from many parts of the world, were placed around the chamber with decorative ornaments in gold and silver and semi-precious jewels.

"That presupposes Ailill stole the sword," observed Sister Fidelma calmly as she sat before him. She observed strict protocol. Had she been trained to the degree of *ollamh* she could have sat in the High King's presence without waiting for permission. Indeed, the chief *ollamh* of Ireland, at the court of the High King, was so influential that even the High King was not allowed to speak at the Great Assembly before the chief *ollamh*. Sister Fidelma had never been in the presence of a High King before and her mind raced hastily over the correct rituals to be observed.

Sechnasach drew his brows together at her observation.

"You doubt it? But the facts given by Abbot Colmán are surely plain enough? If Ailill did not steal it, who then?"

Sister Fidelma raised a shoulder and let it fall.

"Before I comment further I would ask you some questions, Sechnasach of Tara."

The High King made a motion of his hand as though to invite her questions.

"Who would gain if you were prevented from assuming the High Kingship?"

Sechnasach grimaced with bitter amusement.

"Ailill, of course. For he stands as *tánaiste* by choice of the Great Assembly."

Whenever the Great Assembly elected a High King, they also elected a *tánaiste* or 'second'; an heir presumptive who would assume office should the High King become indisposed. Should the High King be killed or die suddenly then the Great Assembly would meet to confirm the *tánaiste* as High King but at no time were the five kingdoms left without a supreme potentate. Under the ancient Brehon Law of Ireland, only the most worthy were elected to kingship and there was no such concept of hereditary right by primogeniture such as practised in the lands of the Saxons or Franks.

"And no one else? There are no other claimants?"

"There are many claimants. My uncle Diarmuid's son, Cernach, for example, and Ailill's own brothers, Conall and Colcu. You must know of the conflict between the southern and northern Uí Néill? I am of the southern Uí Néill. Many of the northern Uí Neill would be glad to see me deposed."

"But none but Ailill stand as the obvious choice to gain by your fall?" pressed Sister Fidelma.

"None."

Compressing her lips, Sister Fidelma rose.

"That is all at this time, Sechnasach," she said.

The High King glanced at her in surprise at the abruptness of her questioning.

"You would give me no hope of finding the sacred sword before tomorrow?"

Sister Fidelma detected a pleading tone to his voice.

"There is always hope, Sechnasach. But if I have not solved this mystery by noon tomorrow, at the time of your inauguration, then we will see the resolution in the development of events. Events will solve the puzzle."

"Little hope of averting strife, then?"

"I do not know," Sister Fidelma admitted candidly.

She left the audience chamber and was moving down the corridor when a low soprano voice called to her by name from a darkened doorway. Sister Fidelma paused, turned and gazed at the dark figure of a girl.

"Come inside for a moment, Sister."

Sister Fidelma followed the figure through heavy drapes into a brightly lit chamber.

A young, dark haired girl in an exquisitely sewn gown of blue, bedecked in jewels, ushered her inside and pulled the drape across the door.

"I am Ornait, sister of Sechnasach," the girl said breathlessly.

Sister Fidelma bowed her head to the High King's sister.

"I am at your service, Ornait."

"I was listening behind the tapestries, just now," the girl said, blushing a little. "I heard what you were saying to my brother. You don't believe Ailill stole the sacred sword, do you?"

Sister Fidelma gazed into the girl's eager, pleading eyes, and smiled softly.

"And you do not want to believe it?" she asked with gentle emphasis.

The girl lowered her gaze, the redness of her cheeks, if anything, increasing.

"I know he could not have done this deed. He would not." She seized Sister Fidelma's hand. "I know that if anyone can prove him innocent of this sacrilege it will be you."

"Then you know then that I am an advocate in the Brehon Court?" asked Sister Fidelma, slightly embarrassed at the girl's emphatic belief in her ability.

"I have heard of your reputation from a sister of your order at Kildare."

"And the night Ailill was arrested in the chapel, he was on his way to see you? It was foolish of him not to tell me."

Ornait raised her small chin defiantly.

"We love each other!"

"But keep it a secret, even from your brother?"

"Until after my brother's inauguration as High King, it will remain a secret. When he feels more kindly disposed towards Ailill for standing against him before the Great Assembly, then we shall tell him."

"You do not think Ailill feels any resentment towards your brother, a resentment which might have motivated him to hide the sacred sword to discredit Sechnasach?"

"Ailill may not agree with my brother on many things but he agrees that the decision of the Great Assembly, under the Brehon Law, is sacred and binding," replied Ornait, firmly. "And he is not alone in that. My cousin, Cernach Mac Diarmuid, believes that he has a greater right to the High Kingship than Sechnasach. He dislikes my brother's attitude against any reform suggested by Rome. But Cernach does not come to the 'age of choice' for a while yet when he can legally challenge my brother to the High Kingship. Being too young to challenge for office, Cernach supported Ailill in his claim. It is no crime to be unsuccessful in the challenge for the High Kingship. Once the Great Assembly make the decision, there is an end to it. No, a thousand times – no! Ailill would not do this thing."

"Well, Sister?" The Abbot stared at Sister Fidelma with narrowed eyes.

"I have nothing to report at the moment, just another question to ask."

She had gone to see Abbot Colmán in his study in the abbey building behind the palace of Tara. The Abbot was seated behind a wooden table where he had been examining a colourful illuminated manuscript. He saw her eyes fall on the book and smiled complacently.

"This is the Gospel of John produced by our brothers at Clonmacnoise. A beautiful work which will be sent to our brothers at the Holy Island of Colmcille."

Sister Fidelma glanced briefly at the magnificently wrought handiwork. It was, indeed, beautiful but her thoughts were occupied elsewhere. She paused a moment before asking:

"If there were civil strife in the kingdom, and from it Ailill was made High King, would he depart from the traditional policies propounded by Sechnasach?"

The Abbot was taken off guard, his jaw dropping and his eyes rounding in surprise. Then he frowned and appeared to ponder the question for a moment.

"I would think the answer is in the affirmative," he answered at last.

"Particularly," went on Sister Fidelma, "would Ailill press the abbots and bishops to reform the Church?"

The Abbot scratched an ear.

"It is no secret that Ailill favours a rapprochement with the Church of Rome, believing its reforms to be correct. There are many of the Uí Néill house who do. Cernach Mac Diarmuid, for instance. He is a leading advocate among the laymen for such reforms. A bit of a hothead but influential. A youth who stands near the throne of Tara but doesn't reach the 'age of choice' for a month or so when he may take his place in the assemblies of the five kingdoms."

"But Sechnasach does not believe in reforms and would adhere strongly to the traditional rites and liturgy of our Church?"

"Undoubtedly."

"And, as one of the pro-Roman faction, you would favour Ailill's policies?"

The Abbot flushed with indignation.

"I would. But I make no secret of my position. And I hold

my beliefs under the law. My allegiance is to the High King as designated by that law. And while you have a special privilege as an advocate of the Brehon Court, may I remind you that I am abbot of Tara, father and superior to your order?"

Sister Fidelma made a gesture with her hand as if in apology.

"I am merely seeking facts, Abbot Colmán. And it is as *dálaighe* of the Brehon Court that I ask these questions, not as a Sister of Kildare."

"Then here is a fact. I denounced Ailill Flann Esa. If I had supported what he has done in order to overthrow Sechnasach simply because Ailill would bring the Church in Ireland in agreement with Rome, then I would not have been willing to point so quickly to Ailill's guilt. I could have persuaded the guards that someone else had carried out the deed."

"Indeed," affirmed Sister Fidelma. "If Ailill Flann Esa were guilty of this sacrilege then you would not profit."

"Exactly so," snapped the Abbot. "And Ailill is guilty."

"So it might seem."

Sister Fidelma turned to the door, paused and glanced back.

"One tiny point, to clarify matters. How is it that you came to be in the chapel at that exact time?"

The Abbot drew his brows together.

"I had left my *Psalter* in the sacristy," he replied irritably. "I went to retrieve it."

"Surely it would have been safe until morning? Why go out into the cold of night to the chapel?"

"I needed to look up a reference; besides I did not have to go out into the night . . ."

"No? How then did you get into the chapel?"

The Abbot sighed, in annoyance.

"There is a passage which leads from the abbey here into the chapel sacristy."

Sister Fidelma's eyes widened. She suddenly realized that she had been a fool. The fact had been staring her in the face all the time.

"Please show me this passage."

"I will get one of the brethren to show you. I am busy with the preparations for the inauguration."

Abbot Colmán reached forward and rang a silver bell which stood upon the table.

A moon-faced man clad in the brown robes of the order of the abbey entered almost immediately, arms folded in the copious sleeves of his habit. Even from a distance of a few feet, Sister Fidelma could smell the wild garlic on his breath, a pungent odour which caused her to wrinkle her nose in distaste.

"This is Brother Rogallach," the Abbot motioned with his hand. "Rogallach, I wish you to show Sister Fidelma the passage to the chapel." Then, turning to her, he raised his eyebrows in query. "Unless there is anything else . . .?"

"Nothing else, Colmán," Sister Fidelma replied quietly. "For the time being."

Brother Rogallach took a candle and lit it. He and Sister Fidelma were standing in one of the corridors of the abbey building. Rogallach moved towards a tapestry and drew it aside to reveal an entrance from which stone steps led downwards.

"This is the only entrance to the passage which leads to the chapel?" asked Sister Fidelma, trying to steel her features against his bad breath.

Brother Rogallach nodded. He stood slightly in awe of the young woman for it was already common gossip around the abbey as to her status and role.

"Who knows about it?" she pressed.

"Why, everyone in the abbey. When the weather is intemperate we use this method to attend worship in the chapel." The monk opened his mouth in an ingenuous smile, displaying broken and blackened teeth.

"Would anyone outside the abbey know about it?"

The monk grimaced eloquently.

"It is no secret, Sister. Anyone who has lived at Tara would know of it."

"So Ailill would know of its existence?"

Brother Rogallach gestured as if the answer were obvious.

"Lead on then, Brother Rogallach," Sister Fidelma instructed, thankful to push the monk ahead of her so that she was not bathed by the foul stench of his breathing.

The moon-faced monk turned and preceded her down the steps and through a musty but dry passage whose floor was laid with stone flags. It was a winding passage along which several small alcoves stood, most of them containing items of furniture. Sister Fidelma stopped at the first of them and asked Rogallach to light the alcove with his candle. She repeated this performance at each of the alcoves.

"They are deep enough for a person to hide in let alone to conceal a sword," she mused aloud. "Were they searched for the missing sword?"

The monk nodded eagerly drawing close so that Sister Fidelma took an involuntary step backward. "Of course. I was one of those called to assist in the search. Once the chapel was searched, it was obvious that the next place as a likely hiding place would be this passageway."

Nevertheless, Sister Fidelma caused Rogallach to halt at each alcove until she had examined it thoroughly by the light of his candle. At one alcove she frowned and reached for a piece of frayed cloth caught on a projecting section of wood. It was brightly coloured cloth, certainly not from the cheerless brown robes of a *religieux*, but more like the fragment of a richly woven cloak. It was the sort of cloth that a person in the position of wealth and power would have.

It took a little time to traverse the passage and to come up some steps behind a tapestry into the sacristy. From there Sister Fidelma moved into the chapel and across to the chapel door.

Something had been irritating her for some time about the affair. Now that she realized the existence of the passage, she knew what had been puzzling her.

"The chapel door is always bolted from the inside?" she asked.

"Yes," replied Rogallach.

"So if you wanted to enter the chapel, how would you do it?"

Rogallach smiled, emitting another unseen cloud of bitter scent to engulf her.

"Why, I would merely use the passage."

"Indeed, if you knew it was there," affirmed Sister Fidelma, thoughtfully.

"Well, only a stranger to Tara, such as yourself, would not know that."

"So if someone attempted to break into the chapel from the outside, they would obviously not know of the existence of the passage?"

Rogallach moved his head in an affirmative gesture.

Sister Fidelma stood at the door of the chapel and gazed down at the bolt, especially to where it had splintered from the wood and her eyes narrowed as she examined the scuff marks on the metal where it had obviously been hit with a piece of stone. Abruptly, she smiled broadly as she realized the significance of its breaking. She turned to Rogallach.

"Send the guard Erc to me."

Sechnasach, the High King, stared at Sister Fidelma with suspicion.

"I am told that you have summoned the Abbot Colmán, Aillil

Flann Esa, my sister Ornait and Cernach Mac Diarmuid to appear here. Why is this?"

Sister Fidelma stood, hands demurely folded before her, as she confronted Sechnasach.

"I did so because I have that right as a *dálaighe* of the Brehon courts and with the authority that I can now solve the mystery of the theft of your sword of state."

Sechnasach leaned forward in his chair excitedly. "You have found where Ailill has hidden it?"

"My eyes were blind for I should have seen the answer long ago," Sister Fidelma replied.

"Tell me where the sword is," demanded Sechnasach.

"In good time," Sister Fidelma answered calmly. "I need a further answer from you before I can reveal the answer to this puzzle. I have summoned Cernach, the son of your uncle Diarmuid, who was, with your father, joint High King."

"What has Cernach to do with this matter?"

"It is said that Cernach is a most vehement supporter of the reforms of the Church of Rome."

Sechnasach frowned, slightly puzzled.

"He has often argued with me that I should change my attitudes and support those abbots and bishops of Ireland who would alter our ways and adopt the rituals of Rome. But he is still a youth. Why, he does not achieve the 'age of choice' for a month or so and cannot even sit in council. He has no authority though he has some influence on the young members of our court."

Sister Fidelma nodded reflectively.

"This agrees with what I have heard. But I needed some confirmation. Now let the guards bring in Ailill and the others and I will tell you what has happened."

She stood silently before the High King while Ailill Flann Esa was brought in under guard, followed by the Abbot Colmán. Behind came a worried-looking Ornait, glancing with ill-concealed anxiety at her lover. After her came a puzzled-looking, dark-haired young man who was obviously Cernach Mac Diarmuid.

They stood in a semi-circle before the High King's chair. Sechnasach glanced towards Sister Fidelma, inclining his head to her as indication that she should start.

"We will firstly agree on one thing," began Sister Fidelma. "The sacred sword of the Uí Néill kings of Tara was stolen from the chapel of the Blessed Patrick. We will now also agree on the apparent motive. It was stolen to prevent the inauguration of Sechnasach as High King tomorrow . . . or to discredit him in the eyes of the people, to ferment civil disorder in the five kingdoms which might lead to Sechnasach being overthrown and someone else taking the throne."

She smiled briefly at Sechnasach.

"Are we agreed on that?"

"That much is obvious." It was Abbot Colmán who interrupted in annoyance. "In these dark times, it would only need such an omen as the loss of the sacred sword to create chaos and alarm within the kingdoms of Ireland. I have already said as much."

"And what purpose would this chaos and alarm, with the overthrow of Sechnasach, be put to?" queried Sister Fidelma. Before anyone could reply she went on. "It seems easy to see. Sechnasach is sworn to uphold the traditions of the kingdoms and of our Church. Rome claims authority over all the Churches but this claim has been disputed by the Churches of Ireland, Britain and Armorica as well as the Churches of the East. Rome wishes to change our rituals, our liturgy and the computations whereby we celebrate the *Cáisc* in remembrance of our Lord's death in Jerusalem. And there are some among us, even abbots and bishops, who support Rome and seek the abandoning of our traditions and a union with the Roman Church. So even among us we do not all speak with one voice. Is that not so, Ailill Flann Esa?"

Ailill scowled.

"As I have told you, I have never denied my views."

"Then let us agree entirely on the apparent inner motive for the theft of the sword. Destabilization of the High King and his replacement by someone who would reject the traditionalist ways and throw his support behind the reforms in line with Rome."

There was a silence. She had their full attention.

"Very well," went on Sister Fidelma. "This seems an obvious motive. But let us examine the facts of the theft. Two guards passed the door of the chapel in which the sword was kept shortly after midnight. The door was secured. But when they passed the chapel door twenty minutes later, they saw the door ajar with the bolt having been forced. Entering, they saw Ailill standing at the altar staring at the empty chest where the sword had been kept. Then the Abbot entered. He came into the chapel from the sacristy to which he had gained entrance from the passage which leads there from the abbey. He accused Ailill of stealing the sword and hiding it. The sword was not found in the chapel. If Ailill had stolen the sword, how had he time to hide it so well and cleverly? Even the ten minutes allowed him by the guards was not time enough. This is the first problem that struck my thoughts."

She paused and glanced towards Ornait, the sister of the High King.

"According to Ailill Flann Esa, he was walking by the chapel. He saw the door ajar and the bolt forced. He went inside out of curiosity and perceived the empty chest. That is his version of events."

"We know this is what he claims," snapped Sechnasach. "Have you something new to add?"

"Only to clarify," replied Fidelma unperturbed by the High King's agitation. "Ailill's reason to be passing the chapel at that hour was because he was on his way to meet with Ornait."

Ornait flushed. Sechnasach turned to stare at his sister, mouth slightly open.

"I regret that I cannot keep your secret, Ornait," Sister Fidelma said with a grimace. "But the truth must be told for much is in the balance."

Ornait raised her chin defiantly towards her brother.

"Well, Ornait? Why would Ailill meet with you in dead of night?" demanded the High King.

The girl pushed back her head defiantly.

"I love Ailill and he loves me. We wanted to tell you, but thought we would do so after your inauguration when you might look on us with more charity."

Sister Fidelma held up her hand as Sechnasach opened his mouth to respond in anger.

"Time enough to sort that matter later. Let us continue. If Ailill speaks the truth, then we must consider this. Someone knew of Ailill's appointment with Ornait. That person was waiting inside the chapel. Being a stranger to Tara, I had not realized that the chapel could be entered from within by means of a passageway. In this matter I was stupid. I should have known at once by the fact that the chapel doors bolted from *within*. The fact was staring me in the face. I should have realized that if the chapel was left bolted at night, then there must obviously be another means for the person who secured the bolt to make their exit."

"But everyone at Tara knows about that passage," pointed out Sechnasach.

"Indeed," smiled Sister Fidelma. "And it would be obvious that at some stage I would come to share that knowledge."

"The point is that the bolt on the door was forced," Abbot Colmán pointed out in a testy tone.

"Indeed. But not from the outside," replied Sister Fidelma. "Again my wits were not swift, otherwise I would have seen it immediately. When you force a bolted door, it is the metal on the door jamb, that which secures the bolt, that gets torn from its fixtures. But the bolt itself, on the chapel door, was the section which had been splintered away from its holdings."

She stood looking at their puzzled expressions for a moment.

"What happened was simple enough. The culprit had entered the chapel from the passage within. The culprit had taken the key, pushed back the altar, opened the chest. The sword had been removed and taken to a place of safety. Then the culprit had returned to arrange the scene. Ensuring that the guards were well beyond the door, the perpetrator opened it, took up a stone and smashed at the bolt. Instead of smashing away the metal catch on the door jamb, the bolt on the door was smashed. It was so obvious a clue that I nearly overlooked it. All I saw, at first, was a smashed bolt."

Ornait was smiling through her tears.

"I knew Ailill could not have done this deed. The real perpetrator did this deed for the purpose of making Ailill seem the guilty one. Your reputation as a solver of puzzles is well justified, Sister Fidelma."

Sister Fidelma responded with a slightly wan smile.

"It needed no act of genius to deduce that the evidence could only point to the fact the Ailill Flann Esa could not have stolen the sword in the manner claimed."

Ailill was frowning at Sister Fidelma.

"Then who is the guilty person?"

"Certain things seemed obvious. Who benefited from the deed?" Sister Fidelma continued, ignoring his question. "Abbot Colmán is a fierce adherent of Rome. He might benefit in this cause if Sechnasach was removed. And Abbot Colmán was in the right place at the right time. He had the opportunity to do this deed."

"This is outrageous!" snarled the Abbot. "I am accused unjustly. I am your superior, Fidelma of Kildare. I am the abbot of Tara and . . ."

Sister Fidelma grimaced. "I need not be reminded of your position in the Church, Abbot Colmán," she replied softly. "I also remind you that I speak here as an advocate of the Brehon Court and was invited here to act in this position by yourself."

Colmán, flushed and angry, hesitated and then said slowly:

"I make no secret of my adherence to the Rome order but to suggest that I would be party to such a plot . . ."

Sister Fidelma held up a hand and motioned him to silence.

"This is true enough. After all, Ailill would be Colmán's natural ally. If Colmán stole the sword, why would he attempt to put the blame onto Ailill and perhaps discredit those who advocated the cause of Rome? Surely, he would do his best to support Ailill so that when civil strife arose over the non-production of the sacred sword, Ailill, as *tánaiste*, the heir presumptive, would be in a position to immediately claim the throne of Sechnasach?"

"What are you saying?" asked Sechnasach trying to keep track of Sister Fidelma's reasoning.

Sister Fidelma turned to him, her blue eyes level, her tone unhurried.

"There is another factor in this tale of political intrigue. Cernach Mac Diarmuid. His name was mentioned to me several times as a fierce adherent of Rome."

The young man who had so far stood aloof and frowning, now started, his cheeks reddening. A hand dropped to his side as if seeking a weapon. But no one, save the High King's bodyguard, was allowed to carry a weapon in Tara's halls.

"What do you mean by this?"

"Cernach desired the throne of Tara. As son of one of the joint High Kings, he felt that it was his due. But moreover, he would benefit most if both Sechnasach and Ailill were discredited."

"Why . . .!" Cernach started forward, anger on his face. One of the warriors gripped the young man's arm so tightly that he winced. He turned and tried to shake off the grip but made no further aggressive move.

Sister Fidelma spoke to one of the guards.

"Is the warrior, Erc, outside?"

The guard moved to the door and called.

The burly warrior entered holding something wrapped in cloth. He glanced at Sister Fidelma and nodded briefly.

Sister Fidelma turned back to the High King.

"Sechnasach, I ordered this man, Erc, to search the chamber of Cernach."

Cernach's face was suddenly bloodless. His eyes were bright, staring at the object in Erc's hand.

"What did you find there, Erc?" asked Sister Fidelma quietly.

The warrior moved forward to the High King's seat, unwrapping the cloth as he did so. He held out the uncovered object. In his hands there was revealed a sword of rich gold and silver mountings, encrusted with a colourful display of jewels.

"The 'Caladchalo'!" gasped the High King. "The sword of state!"

"It's a lie! A lie!" cried Cernach, his lips trembling. "It was planted there. She must have planted it there!"

He threw out an accusing finger towards Sister Fidelma. Sister Fidelma simply ignored him.

"Where did you find this, Erc?"

The burly warrior licked his lips. It was clear he felt awkward in the presence of the High King.

"It was lying wrapped in cloth under the bed of Cernach, the son of Diarmuid," he replied, brusquely.

Everyone's eyes had fallen on the trembling young man.

"Was it easy to find, Erc?" asked Sister Fidelma.

The burly warrior managed a smile.

"Almost too easy."

"Almost too easy," repeated Sister Fidelma with a soft emphasis.

"Why did you do this deed, Cernach Mac Diarmuid?" thundered Sechnasach. "How could you behave so treacherously?"

"But Cernach did not do it."

Fidelma's quiet voice caused everyone to turn back to stare at her in astonishment.

"Who then, if not Cernach?" demanded the High King in bewilderment.

"The art of deduction is a science as intricate as any of the mysteries of the ancients," Sister Fidelma commented with a sigh. "In this matter I found myself dealing with a mind as complicated in thinking and as ruthless in its goal as any I have encountered. But then the stake was the High Kingship of Ireland."

She paused and gazed around at the people in the chamber, letting her eyes finally rest on Sechnasach.

"There has been one thing which has been troubling me from the start. Why I was called to Tara to investigate this matter? My poor reputation in law is scarcely known out of the boundaries of Holy Brigid's house at Kildare. In Tara, at the seat of the High Kings, there are many better qualified in law, many more able *dálaighe* of the Brehon Courts, many more renowned Brehons. The Abbot Colmán admitted that someone had told him about me for he did not know me. I have had a growing feeling that I was being somehow used. But why? For what purpose? By whom? It seemed so obvious that Ailill was demonstrably innocent of the crime. Why was it obvious?"

Ailill started, his eyes narrowing as he stared at her. Sister Fidelma continued oblivious of the tension in the chamber.

"Abbot Colmán summoned me hither. He had much to gain from this affair, as we have discussed. He also had the opportunity to carry out the crime."

"That's not true!" cried the Abbot.

Sister Fidelma turned and smiled at the ruddy-faced cleric.

"You are right, Colmán. And I have already conceded that fact. You did not do it."

"But the sword was found in Cernach's chamber," Sechnasach pointed out. "He must surely be guilty."

"Several times I was pointed towards Cernach as a vehement advocate of Roman reforms. A youthful hothead, was one description. Several times I was encouraged to think that the motive lay in replacing Sechnasach, a traditionalist, with someone who would encourage those reforms. And, obligingly, the sword was placed in Cernach's chamber by the real culprit, for us to find. To Cernach my footsteps were carefully pointed . . . But why Cernach? He was not even of the 'age of choice', so what could he gain?"

There was a silence as they waited tensely for her to continue.

"Abbot Colmán told me that Cernach was a supporter of Rome. So did Ailill and so did Ornait. But Ornait was the only one who told me that Cernach desired the throne, even though unable to do so by his age. Ornait also told me that he would be of age within a month."

Sister Fidelma suddenly wheeled round on the girl.

"Ornait was also the only person who knew of my reputation as a solver of mysteries. Ornait told the Abbot and encouraged him to send for me. Is this not so?"

She glanced back to Abbot Colmán who nodded in confusion.

Ornait had gone white, staring at Sister Fidelma.

"Are you saying that I stole the sword?" she whispered with ice in her voice.

"That's ridiculous!" cried Sechnasach. "Ornait is my sister."

"Nevertheless, the guilty ones are Ailill and Ornait," replied Sister Fidelma.

"But you have just demonstrated that Ailill was innocent of the crime," Sechnasach said in total bewilderment.

"No. I demonstrated that evidence was left for me in order that I would believe Ailill was innocent; that he could not have carried out the deed as it was claimed he had. When things are obvious, beware of them."

"But why would Ornait take part in this theft?" demanded the High King.

"Ornait conceived the plan. Its cunning was her own. It was carried out by Ailill and herself and no others."

"Explain."

"Ailill and Ornait entered the chapel that night in the normal way through the passage. They proceeded to carry out the plan. Ornait took the sword while Ailill broke the bolt, making sure of the obvious mistake. They relied on discovery by the two guards and Ailill waited for them. But, as always in such carefully laid plans, there comes the unexpected. As Ornait was proceeding back through the passage she saw the Abbot coming along it. He had left his *Psalter* in the sacristy and needed it. She pressed into an alcove and hid until he had gone by. When she left the alcove she tore her gown on some obstruction."

Sister Fidelma held out the small piece of frayed colourful cloth.

"But the rest of the plan worked perfectly. Ailill was imprisoned. The second part of the plan was now put into place. Ornait had been informed by a sister from my house at Kildare that I was a solver of mysteries. In fact, without undue modesty, I may say that Ornait's entire plan had been built around me. When the sword could not be found, she was able to persuade Abbot Colmán to send for me to investigate its mysterious disappearance. Colmán himself had never heard of me before Ornait dropped my name in his ear. He has just admitted this."

The Abbot was nodding in agreement as he strove to follow her argument.

"When I arrived, the contrived evidence led me immediately to believe Ailill Flann Esa was innocent, as it was supposed to do. It also led me to the chosen scapegoat, Cernach Mac Diarmuid. And in his chamber, scarcely concealed, was the sacred sword. It was all too easy for me. That ease made me suspicious. Both Ailill and Ornait were too free with Cernach's name. Then I saw the frayed cloth in the passage and I began to think."

"But if it was a simple plot to discredit me by the non-production of the sword," observed Sechnasach, "why such an elaborate plot? Why not simply steal the sword and hide it where it could not be so easily recovered?"

"That was the matter which caused the greatest puzzle. However, it became clear to me as I considered it. Ornait and Ailill had to be sure of your downfall. The loss of the sword would create alarm and dissension among the people. But it was not simply chaos that they wanted. They wanted your immediate downfall. They had to ensure that the Great Assembly would come to regret their decision and immediately proclaim for Ailill at the inauguration."

"How could they ensure that?" demanded Abbot Colmán. "The Great Assembly had already made their decision."

"A decision which could be overturned any time before the inauguration. After aspersions had been cast on Sechnasach's judgement, his ability to treat people fairly, the Great Assembly could change its support. By showing the Great Assembly that Sechnasach was capable of unjustly accusing one who had been his rival, this could be done. I am also sure that Sechnasach would be accused of personal enmity because of Ornait's love of Ailill. I was part of Ornait's plan to depose her brother and replace him with Ailill. I was to be invited to Tara for no other purpose but to demonstrate Ailill's innocence and Cernach's guilt. Doubt on Sechnasach's judgement would be a blemish on his ability for the High Kingship. Remember the Law of Kings, the law of the seven proofs of a righteous King? That his judgement be firm and just and beyond reproach. Once Sechnasach's decision to imprison Ailill was shown to have been unjust, Ailill, as *tánaiste*, would be acclaimed in his place with Ornait as his queen."

Sechnasach sat staring at his sister, reading the truth in her scowling features. If the veracity of Sister Fidelma's argument needed support, it could be found in the anger and hate written on the girl's features and that humiliation on Ailill's face.

"And this was done for no other reason than to seize the throne, for no other motive than power?" asked the High King incredulously. "It was not done because they wanted to reform the Church in line with Rome?"

"Not for Rome. Merely for power," Fidelma agreed. "For power most people would do anything."

# PART II
# The Middle Ages

# THE PRICE OF LIGHT
## Ellis Peters

*This anthology would not be complete without Brother Cadfael, the twelfth-century monk whose crime-solving abilities brought the medieval mystery to life.*

*Ellis Peters is the crime-writing persona of Edith Pargeter (b. 1913), in her own right a talented writer of historical novels. Her first book had been a short historical novel set in Roman times,* Hortensius, Friend of Nero *(1936), but the initial poor sales of her historical books caused her to turn to crime fiction. She first introduced her character of Inspector Felse in* Fallen Into the Pit *(1951); a later Felse novel,* Death and the Joyful Woman *(1961) won the Mystery Writers of America Edgar Award as the Year's Best Mystery Novel.*

*Brother Cadfael first appeared in* A Morbid Taste for Bones *and has now featured in nineteen novels and three short stories. The short story reprinted here is his earliest case as a monk. Although "A Light on the Road to Woodstock" is set earlier, Cadfael was still then a man of the world. "The Price of Light" takes place two years before* A Morbid Taste for Bones, *and reintroduces us to many of the familiar characters.*

Hamo FitzHamon of Lidyate held two fat manors in the north-eastern corner of the county, towards the border of Cheshire. Though a gross feeder, a heavy drinker, a self-indulgent lecher, a harsh landlord and a brutal master, he had reached the age of sixty in the best of health, and it came as a salutary shock to him when he was at last taken with a mild seizure, and for the first time in his life saw the next world yawning before him, and woke to the uneasy consciousness that it might see fit to treat him somewhat more austerely than this world had done. Though he repented none of them, he was aware of a whole register of acts in his past which heaven might construe as heavy sins. It began to seem to him a prudent precaution to acquire merit for his soul as quickly as possible. Also as cheaply, for he was a grasping and possessive man. A judicious gift to some holy house should secure the welfare of his soul. There was no need to go so far as endowing an abbey, or a new church of his own. The Benedictine abbey of Shrewsbury could put up a powerful assault of prayers on his behalf in return for a much more modest gift.

The thought of alms to the poor, however ostentatiously bestowed in the first place, did not recommend itself. Whatever was given would be soon consumed and forgotten, and a rag-tag of beggarly blessings from the indigent could carry very little weight, besides failing to confer a lasting lustre upon himself. No, he wanted something that would continue in daily use and daily respectful notice, a permanent reminder of his munificence and piety. He took his time about making his decision, and when he was satisfied of the best value he could get for the least expenditure, he sent his law-man to Shrewsbury to confer with abbot and prior, and conclude with due ceremony and many witnesses the charter that conveyed to the custodian of the altar of St. Mary, within the abbey church, one of his free tenant farmers, the rent to provide light for Our Lady's altar throughout the year. He promised also, for the proper displaying of his charity, the gift of a pair of fine silver candlesticks, which he himself would bring and see installed on the altar at the coming Christmas feast.

Abbot Heribert, who after a long life of repeated disillusionments still contrived to think the best of everybody, was moved to tears by this penitential generosity. Prior Robert, himself an aristocrat, refrained, out of Norman solidarity, from casting doubt upon Hamo's motive, but he elevated his eyebrows, all the same. Brother Cadfael, who knew only the public reputation of the donor, and was sceptical enough to suspend judgement until he encountered the source, said nothing, and waited to observe and decide for himself. Not that he expected much; he had been in the world fifty-five years, and learned to temper all his expectations, bad or good.

It was with mild and detached interest that he observed the arrival of the party from Lidyate, on the morning of Christmas Eve. A hard, cold Christmas it was proving to be, that year of 1135, all bitter black frost and grudging snow, thin and sharp as whips before a withering east wind. The weather had been vicious all the year, and the harvest a disaster. In the villages people shivered and starved, and Brother Oswald the almoner fretted and grieved the more that the alms he had to distribute were not enough to keep all those bodies and souls together. The sight of a cavalcade of three good riding horses, ridden by travellers richly wrapped up from the cold, and followed by two pack-ponies, brought all the wretched petitioners crowding and crying, holding out hands blue with frost. All they got out of it was a single perfunctory handful of small coin, and when they hampered his movements FitzHamon used his whip as a matter of course to clear the way. Rumour, thought Brother Cadfael, pausing on his way to the infirmary with his daily medicines for the sick, had probably not done Hamo FitzHamon any injustice.

Dismounting in the great court, the knight of Lidyate was seen to be a big, over-fleshed, top-heavy man with bushy hair and beard and eyebrows, all grey-streaked from their former black, and stiff and bristling as wire. He might well have been a very handsome man before indulgence purpled his face and pocked his skin and sank his sharp black eyes deep into flabby sacks of flesh. He looked more than his age, but still a man to be reckoned with.

The second horse carried his lady, pillion behind a groom. A small figure she made, even swathed almost to invisibility in her woollens and furs, and she rode snuggled comfortably against the groom's broad back, her arms hugging him round the waist. And a very well-looking young fellow he was, this groom, a strapping lad barely twenty years old, with round, ruddy cheeks and merry, guileless eyes, long in the legs, wide in the shoulders, everything a country youth should be, and attentive to his duties into the bargain, for he was down from the saddle in one lithe leap, and reaching up to take the lady by the waist, every bit as heartily as she had been clasping him a moment before, and lift her lightly down. Small, gloved hands rested on his shoulders a brief moment longer than was necessary. His respectful support of her continued until she was safe on the ground and sure of her footing; perhaps a few seconds more. Hamo FitzHamon was occupied with Prior Robert's ceremonious welcome, and the attentions of the hospitaller, who had made the best rooms of the guest-hall ready for him.

The third horse also carried two people, but the woman on the pillion did not wait for anyone to help her down, but slid quickly to the ground and hurried to help her mistress off with the great outer cloak in which she had travelled. A quiet, submissive young woman, perhaps in her middle twenties, perhaps older, in drab homespun, her hair hidden away under a coarse linen wimple. Her face was thin and pale, her skin dazzlingly fair, and her eyes, reserved and weary, were of a pale, clear blue, a fierce colour that ill suited their humility and resignation.

Lifting the heavy folds from her lady's shoulders, the maid showed a head the taller of the two, but drab indeed beside the bright little bird that emerged from the cloak. Lady FitzHamon came forth graciously smiling on the world in scarlet and brown, like a robin, and just as confidently. She had dark hair braided about a small, shapely head, soft, full cheeks flushed rosy by the chill air, and large dark eyes assured of their charm and power. She could not possibly have been more than thirty, probably not so much. FitzHamon had a grown son somewhere, with children of his own, and waiting some said with little patience, for his inheritance. This girl must be a second or a third wife, a good deal younger than her stepson, and a beauty, at that. Hamo was secure enough and important enough to keep himself supplied with wives as he wore them out. This one must have cost him dear, for she had not the air of a poor but pretty relative sold for a profitable alliance, rather she looked as if she knew her own status very well indeed, and meant to have it acknowledged. She would look well presiding over the high table at Lidyate, certainly, which was probably the main consideration.

The groom behind whom the maid had ridden was an older man, lean and wiry, with a face like the bole of a knotty oak. By the sardonic patience of his eyes he had been in close and relatively favoured attendance on FitzHamon for many years, knew the best and the worst his moods could do, and was sure of his own ability to ride the storms. Without a word he set about unloading the pack-horses, and followed his lord to the guest-hall, while the young man took FitzHamon's bridle, and led the horses away to the stables.

Cadfael watched the two women cross to the doorway, the lady springy as a young hind, with bright eyes taking in everything around her, the tall maid keeping always a pace behind, with long steps curbed to keep her distance. Even thus, frustrated like a mewed hawk, she had a graceful gait. Almost certainly of villein stock, like the two grooms. Cadfael had long practice in distinguishing the free from the unfree. Not that the free had any easy life, often they were worse off than the villeins of their neighbourhood; there were plenty of free men, this Christmas, gaunt and hungry, forced to hold out begging hands among the throng round the gatehouse. Freedom, the first ambition of every man, still could not fill the bellies of wives and children in a bad season.

FitzHamon and his party appeared at Vespers in full glory to see the candlesticks reverently installed upon the altar in the Lady Chapel. Abbot, prior and brothers had no difficulty in sufficiently admiring the gift, for they were indeed things of beauty, two fluted stems ending in the twin cups of flowering lilies. Even the veins of the leaves showed delicate and perfect as in the living plant. Brother Oswald the almoner, himself a skilled silversmith when he had time to exercise his craft, stood gazing at the new embellishments of the altar with a face and mind curiously torn between rapture and regret, and ventured to delay the donor for a moment, as he was being ushered away to sup with Abbot Heribert in his lodging.

"My lord, these are of truly noble workmanship. I have some

knowledge of precious metals, and of the most notable craftsmen in these parts, but I never saw any work so true to the plant as this. A countryman's eye is here, but the hand of a court craftsman. May we know who made them?"

FitzHamon's marred face curdled into deeper purple, as if an unpardonable shadow had been cast upon his hour of self-congratulation. He said brusquely: "I commissioned them from a fellow in my own service. You would not know his name – a villein born, but he had some skill." And with that he swept on, avoiding further question, and wife and men-servants and maid trailed after him. Only the older groom, who seemed less in awe of his lord than anyone, perhaps by reason of having so often presided over the ceremony of carrying him dead drunk to his bed, turned back for a moment to pluck at brother Oswald's sleeve, and advise him in a confidential whisper: "You'll find him short to question on that head. The silversmith – Alard, his name was – cut and ran from his service last Christmas, and for all they hunted him as far as London, where the signs pointed, he's never been found. I'd let that matter lie, if I were you."

And with that he trotted away after his master, and left several thoughtful faces staring after him.

"Not a man to part willingly with any property of his," mused Brother Cadfael, "metal or man, but for a price, and a steep price at that."

"Brother, be ashamed!" reproved Brother Jerome at his elbow. "Has he not parted with these very treasures from pure charity?"

Cadfael refrained from elaborating on the profit FitzHamon expected for his benevolence. It was never worth arguing with Jerome, who in any case knew as well as anyone that the silver lilies and the rent of one farm were no free gift. But Brother Oswald said grievingly: "I wish he had directed his charity better. Surely these are beautiful things, a delight to the eyes, but well sold, they could have provided money enough to buy the means of keeping my poorest petitioners alive through the winter, some of whom will surely die for the want of them."

Brother Jerome was scandalized. "Has he not given them to Our Lady herself?" he lamented indignantly. "Beware of the sin of those apostles who cried out with the same complaint against the women who brought the pot of spikenard, and poured it over the Saviour's feet. Remember Our Lord's reproof to them, that they should let her alone, for she had done well!"

"Our Lord was acknowledging a well-meant impulse of devotion," said Brother Oswald with spirit. "He did not say it was well advised!

'She hath done what she could' is what he said. He never said that with a little thought she might not have done better. What use would it have been to wound the giver, after the thing was done? Spilled oil of spikenard could hardly be recovered."

His eyes dwelt with love and compunction upon the silver lilies, with their tall stems of wax and flame. For these remained, and to divert them to other use was still possible, or would have been possible if the donor had been a more approachable man. He had, after all, a right to dispose as he wished of his own property.

"It is sin," admonished Jerome sanctimoniously, "even to covet for other use, however worthy, that which has been given to Our Lady. The very thought is sin."

"If Our Lady could make her own will known," said Brother Cadfael drily, "we might learn which is the graver sin, and which the more acceptable sacrifice."

"Could any price be too high for the lighting of this holy altar?" demanded Jerome.

It was a good question, Cadfael thought, as they went to supper in the refectory. Ask Brother Jordan, for instance, the value of light. Jordan was old and frail, and gradually going blind. As yet he could distinguish shapes, but like shadows in a dream, though he knew his way about cloisters and precincts so well that his gathering darkness was no hindrance to his freedom of movement. But as every day the twilight closed in on him by a shade, so did his profound love of light grow daily more devoted, until he had forsaken other duties, and taken upon himself to tend all the lamps and candles on both altars, for the sake of being always irradiated by light, and sacred light, at that. As soon as Compline was over, this evening, he would be busy devoutly trimming the wicks of candle and lamp, to have the steady flames smokeless and immaculate for the Matins of Christmas Day. Doubtful if he would go to his bed at all until Matins and Lauds were over. The very old need little sleep, and sleep is itself a kind of darkness. But what Jordan treasured was the flame of light, and not the vessel holding it; and would not those splendid two-pound candles shine upon him just as well from plain wooden sconces?

Cadfael was in the warming-house with the rest of the brothers, about a quarter of an hour before Compline, when a lay brother from the guest-hall came enquiring for him.

"The lady asks if you'll speak with her. She's complaining of a bad head, and that she'll never be able to sleep. Brother Hospitaller recommended her to you for a remedy."

Cadfael went with him without comment, but with some curiosity, for at Vespers the Lady FitzHamon had looked in blooming health and sparkling spirits. Nor did she seem greatly changed when he met her in the hall, though she was still swathed in the cloak she had worn to cross the great court to and from the abbot's house, and had the hood so drawn that it shadowed her face. The silent maid hovered at her shoulder.

"You are Brother Cadfael? They tell me you are expert in herbs and medicines, and can certainly help me. I came early back from the lord abbot's supper, with such a headache, and have told my lord that I shall go early to bed. But I have such disturbed sleep, and with this pain how shall I be able to rest? Can you give me some draught that will ease me? They say you have a perfect apothecarium in your herb garden, and all your own work, growing, gathering, drying, brewing and all. There must be something there that can soothe pain and bring deep sleep."

Well, thought Cadfael, small blame to her if she sometimes sought a means to ward off her old husband's rough attentions for a night, especially for a festival night when he was likely to have drunk heavily. Nor was it Cadfael's business to question whether the petitioner really needed his remedies. A guest might ask for whatever the house afforded.

"I have a syrup of my own making," he said, "which may do you good service. I'll bring you a vial of it from my workshop store."

"May I come with you? I should like to see your workshop." She had forgotten to sound frail and tired, the voice could have been a curious child's. "As I already am cloaked and shod," she said winningly. "We just returned from the lord abbot's table."

"But should you not go in from the cold, madam? Though the snow's swept here in the court, it lies on some of the garden paths."

"A few minutes in the fresh air will help me," she said, "before trying to sleep. And it cannot be far."

It was not far. Once away from the subdued lights of the buildings they were aware of the stars, snapping like sparks from a cold fire, in a clear black sky just engendering a few tattered snow-clouds in the east. In the garden, between the pleached hedges, it seemed almost warm, as though the sleeping trees breathed tempered air as well as cutting off the bleak wind. The silence was profound. The herb garden was walled, and the wooden hut where Cadfael brewed and stored his medicines was sheltered from the worst of the cold. Once inside, and a small lamp kindled, Lady FitzHamon forgot her invalid role in wonder and delight, looking round her with bright, inquisitive eyes. The maid, submissive and still, scarcely turned her head, but her eyes ranged from left to right, and a faint colour touched life into her cheeks. The many faint, sweet scents made her nostrils quiver, and her lips curve just perceptibly with pleasure.

Curious as a cat, the lady probed into every sack and jar and box, peered at mortars and bottles, and asked a hundred questions in a breath.

"And this is necessary, these little dried needles? And in this great sack – is it grain?" She plunged her hands wrist-deep inside the neck of it, and the hut was filled with sweetness. "Lavender? Such a great harvest of it? Do you, then, prepare perfumes for us women?"

"Lavender has other good properties," said Cadfael. He was filling a small vial with a clear syrup he made from eastern poppies, a legacy of his crusading years. "It is helpful for all disorders that trouble the head and spirit, and its scent is calming. I'll give you a little pillow filled with that and other herbs, that shall help to bring you sleep. But this draught will ensure it. You may take all that I give you here, and get no harm, only a good night's rest."

She had been playing inquisitively with a pile of small clay dishes he kept by his work-bench, rough dishes in which the fine seeds sifted from fruiting plants could be spread to dry out; but she came at once to gaze eagerly at the modest vial he presented to her. "Is it enough? It takes much to give me sleep."

"This," he assured her patiently, "would bring sleep to a strong man. But it will not harm even a delicate lady like you."

She took it in her hand with a small, sleek smile of satisfaction. "Then I thank you indeed! I will make a gift – shall I? – to your almoner in requital. Elfgiva, you bring the little pillow. I shall breathe it all night long. It should sweeten dreams."

So her name was Elfgiva. A Norse name. She had Norse eyes, as he had already noted, blue as ice, and pale, fine skin worn finer and whiter by weariness. All this time she had noted everything that passed, motionless, and never said word. Was she older, or younger, than her lady? There was no guessing. The one was so clamant, and the other so still.

He put out his lamp and closed the door, and led them back to the great court just in time to take leave of them and still be prompt for Compline. Clearly the lady had no intention of attending. As for the lord, he was just being helped away from the abbot's lodging, his grooms supporting him one on either side, though as yet he was not gravely drunk. They headed for the guest-hall at an easy roll. No doubt only the hour of Compline had concluded the drawn-out supper, probably to the abbot's considerable relief. He was no drinker, and could have very little in common with Hamo FitzHamon. Apart, of course, from a deep devotion to the altar of St. Mary.

The lady and her maid had already vanished within the guest-hall. The younger groom carried in his free hand a large jug, full, to judge by the way he held it. The young wife could drain her draught and clutch her herbal pillow with confidence; the drinking was not yet at an end, and her sleep would be solitary and untroubled. Brother Cadfael went to Compline mildly sad, and obscurely comforted.

Only when service was ended, and the brothers on the way to their beds, did he remember that he had left his flask of poppy syrup unstoppered. Not that it would come to any harm in the frosty night, but his sense of fitness drove him to go and remedy the omission before he slept.

His sandalled feet, muffled in strips of woollen cloth for warmth and safety on his frozen paths, made his coming quite silent, and he was already reaching out a hand to the latch of the door, but not yet touching, when he was brought up short and still by the murmur of voices within. Soft, whispering, dreamy voices that made sounds less and more than speech, caresses rather than words, though once at least words surfaced for a moment. A man's voice, young, wary, saying: "But how if he *does* . . .?" And a woman's soft, suppressed laughter: "He'll sleep till morning, never fear!" And her words were suddenly hushed with kissing, and her laughter became huge, ecstatic sighs; the young man's breath heaving triumphantly, but still, a moment later, the note of fear again, half-enjoyed: "Still, you know him, he *may* . . ." And she, soothing: "Not for an hour, at least . . . then we'll go . . . it will grow cold here . . ."

That, at any rate, was true; small fear of them wishing to sleep out the night here, even two close-wrapped in one cloak on the bench-bed against the wooden wall. Brother Cadfael withdrew very circumspectly from the herb garden, and made his way back in chastened thought towards the dortoir. Now he knew who had swallowed that draught of his, and it was not the lady. In the pitcher of wine the young groom had been carrying? Enough for a strong man, even if he had not been drunk already. Meantime, no doubt, the body-servant was left to put his lord to bed, somewhere apart from the chamber where the lady lay supposedly nursing her indisposition and sleeping the sleep of the innocent. Ah, well, it was no business of Cadfael's, nor had he any intention of getting involved. He did not feel particularly censorious. Doubtful if she ever had any choice about marrying Hamo; and with this handsome boy for ever about them, to point the contrast . . . A brief experience of genuine passion, echoing old loves, pricked sharply through the years of his vocation. At least he knew what he was condoning. And who could help feeling some admiration for her opportunist daring, the quick wit that had procured the means, the alert eye that had seized on the most remote and adequate shelter available?

Cadfael went to bed, and slept without dreams, and rose at the Matin bell, some minutes before midnight. The procession of the brothers wound its way down the night stairs into the church, and into the soft, full glow of the lights before St. Mary's altar.

Withdrawn reverently some yards from the step of the altar, old Brother Jordan, who should long ago have been in his cell with the rest, knelt upright with clasped hands and ecstatic face, in which the great, veiled eyes stared full into the light he loved. When Prior Robert exclaimed in concern at finding him there on the stones, and laid a hand on his shoulder, he started as if out of a trance, and lifted to them a countenance itself all light.

"Oh, brothers, I have been so blessed! I have lived through a wonder . . . Praise God that ever it was granted to me! But bear with me, for I am forbidden to speak of it to any, for three days. On the third day from today I may speak . . .!"

"Look, brothers!" wailed Jerome suddenly, pointing, "Look at the altar!"

Every man present, except Jordan, who still serenely prayed and smiled, turned to gape where Jerome pointed. The tall candles stood secured by drops of their own wax in two small clay dishes, such as Cadfael used for sorting seeds. The two silver lilies were gone from the place of honour.

Through loss, disorder, consternation and suspicion, Prior Robert would still hold fast to the order of the day. Let Hamo FitzHamon sleep in happy ignorance till morning, still Matins and Lauds must be properly celebrated. Christmas was larger than all the giving and losing of silverware. Grimly he saw the services of the church observed, and despatched the brethren back to their beds until Prime, to sleep or lie wakeful and fearful, as they might. Nor would he allow any pestering of Brother Jerome by others, though possibly he did try in private to extort something more satisfactory from the old man. Clearly the theft, whether he knew anything about it or not, troubled Jordan not at all. To everything he said only: "I am enjoined to silence until midnight of the third day." And when they asked by whom? he smiled seraphically, and was silent.

It was Robert himself who broke the news to Hamo FitzHamon, in the morning, before Mass. The uproar, though vicious, was somewhat tempered by the after-effects of Cadfael's poppy draught, which dulled the edges of energy, if not of malice. His body-servant, the older groom Sweyn, was keeping well back out of reach, even with

Robert still present, and the lady sat somewhat apart, too, as though still frail and possibly a little out of temper. She exclaimed dutifully, and apparently sincerely, at the outrage done to her husband, and echoed his demand that the thief should be hunted down, and the candlesticks recovered. Prior Robert was just as zealous in the matter. No effort should be spared to regain the princely gift, of that they could be sure. He had already made certain of various circumstances which should limit the hunt. There had been a brief fall of snow after Compline, just enough to lay down a clean film of white on the ground. No single footprint had as yet marked this pure layer. He had only to look for himself at the paths leading from both parish doors of the church to see that no one had left by that way. The porter would swear that no one had passed the gatehouse; and on the one side of the abbey grounds not walled, the Meole brook was full and frozen, but the snow on both sides of it was virgin. Within the enclave, of course, tracks and cross-tracks were trodden out everywhere; but no one had left the enclave since Compline, when the candlesticks were still in their place.

"So the miscreant is still within the walls?" said Hamo, glinting vengefully. "So much the better! Then his booty is still here within, too, and if we have to turn all your abode doors out of dortoirs, we'll find it! It, and him!"

"We will search everywhere," agreed Robert, "and question every man. We are as deeply offended as your lordship at this blasphemous crime. You may yourself oversee the search, if you will."

So all that Christmas Day, alongside the solemn rejoicings in the church, an angry hunt raged about the precincts in full cry. It was not difficult for all the monks to account for their time to the last minute, their routine being so ordered that brother inevitably extricated brother from suspicion; and such as had special duties that took them out of the general view, like Cadfael in his visit to the herb garden, had all witnesses to vouch for them. The lay brothers ranged more freely, but tended to work in pairs, at least. The servants and the few guests protested their innocence, and if they had not, all of them, others willing to prove it, neither could Hamo prove the contrary. When it came to his own two grooms, there were several witnesses to testify that Sweyn had returned to his bed in the lofts of the stables as soon as he had put his lord to bed, and certainly empty-handed; and Sweyn, as Cadfael noted with interest, swore unblinkingly that young Madoc, who had come in an hour after him, had none the less returned with him, and spent that hour, at Sweyn's order, tending one of the pack-ponies, which showed signs of a cough, and that otherwise they had been together throughout.

A villein instinctively closing ranks with his kind against his lord? wondered Cadfael. Or does Sweyn know very well where that young man was last night, or at least what he was about, and is he intent on protecting him from a worse vengeance? No wonder Madoc looked a shade less merry and ruddy than usual this morning, though on the whole he kept his countenance very well, and refrained from even looking at the lady, while her tone to him was cool, sharp and distant.

Cadfael left them hard at it again after the miserable meal they made of dinner, and went into the church alone. While they were feverishly searching every corner for the candlesticks he had forborne from taking part, but now they were elsewhere he might find something of interest there. He would not be looking for anything so obvious as two large silver candlesticks. He made obeisance at the altar, and mounted the step to look closely at the burning candles. No one had paid any attention to the modest containers that had been substituted for Hamo's gift, and just as well, in the circumstances, that Cadfael's workshop was very little visited, or these little clay pots might have been recognized as coming from there. He moulded and baked them himself as he wanted them. He had no intention of condoning theft, but neither did he relish the idea of any creature, however sinful, falling into Hamo FitzHamon's mercies.

Something long and fine, a thread of silver-gold, was caught and coiled in the wax at the base of one candle. Carefully he detached candle from holder and unlaced from it a long, pale hair; to make sure of retaining it, he broke off the imprisoning disc of wax with it, and then hoisted and turned the candle to see if anything else was to be found under it. One tiny oval dot showed; with a fingernail he extracted a single seed of lavender. Left in the dish from beforetime? He thought not. The stacked pots were all empty. No, this had been brought here in the fold of a sleeve, most probably, and shaken out while the candle was being transferred.

The lady had plunged both hands with pleasure into the sack of lavender, and moved freely about his workshop investigating everything. It would have been easy to take two of these dishes unseen, and wrap them in a fold of her cloak. Even more plausible, she might have delegated the task to young Madoc, when they crept away from their assignation. Supposing, say, they had reached the desperate point of planning flight together, and needed funds to set them on their way to some safe refuge . . . yes, there were possibilities. In the meantime, the grain of lavender had given Cadfael another idea. And there was, of course, that long, fine hair, pale as flax, but brighter. The boy was fair. But so fair?

He went out through the frozen garden to his herbarium, shut himself securely into his workshop, and opened the sack of lavender, plunging both arms to the elbow and groping through the chill, smooth sweetness that parted and slid like grain. They were there, well down, his fingers traced the shape first of one, then a second. He sat down to consider what must be done.

Finding the lost valuables did not identify the thief. He could produce and restore them at once, but FitzHamon would certainly pursue the hunt vindictively until he found the culprit; and Cadfael had seen enough of him to know that it might cost life and all before this complainant was satisfied. He needed to know more before he would hand over any man to be done to death. Better not leave the things here, however. He doubted if they would ransack his hut, but they might. He rolled the candlesticks in a piece of sacking, and thrust them into the centre of the pleached hedge where it was thickest. The meagre, frozen snow had dropped with the brief sun. His arm went in to the shoulder, and when he withdrew it, the twigs sprang back and covered all, holding the package securely. Whoever had first hidden it would surely come by night to reclaim it, and show a human face at last.

It was well that he had moved it, for the searchers, driven by an increasingly angry Hamo, reached his hut before Vespers, examined everything within it, while he stood by to prevent actual damage to his medicines, and went away satisfied that what they were seeking was not there. They had not, in fact, been very thorough about the sack of lavender; the candlesticks might well have escaped notice even if he had left them there. It did not occur to anyone to tear the hedges apart, luckily. When they were gone, to probe all the fodder and grain in the barns, Cadfael restored the silver to its original place. Let the bait lie safe in the trap until the quarry came to claim it, as he surely would, once relieved of the fear that the hunters might find it first.

Cadfael kept watch that night. He had no difficulty in absenting himself from the dortoir, once everyone was in bed and asleep. His cell was by the night stairs, and the prior slept at the far end of the long room, and slept deeply. And bitter though the night air was, the sheltered hut was barely colder than his cell, and he kept blankets there for swathing some of his jars and bottles against frost. He took his little box with tinder and flint, and hid himself in the corner behind the door. It might be a wasted vigil; the thief, having survived one day, might think it politic to venture yet another before removing his spoils.

But it was not wasted. He reckoned it might be as late as ten o'clock

when he heard a light hand at the door. Two hours before the bell
would sound for Matins, almost two hours since the household had
retired. Even the guest-hall should be silent and asleep by now; the
hour was carefully chosen. Cadfael held his breath, and waited. The
door swung open, a shadow stole past him, light steps felt their way
unerringly to where the sack of lavender was propped against the
wall. Equally silently Cadfael swung the door to again, and set his
back against it. Only then did he strike a spark, and hold the blown
flame to the wick of his little lamp.

She did not start or cry out, or try to rush past him and escape into
the night. The attempt would not have succeeded, and she had had
long practice in enduring what could not be cured. She stood facing
him as the small flame steadied and burned taller, her face shadowed
by the hood of her cloak, the candlesticks clasped possessively to
her breast.

"Elfgiva!" said Brother Cadfael gently. And then: "Are you here for
yourself, or for your mistress?" But he thought he knew the answer
already. That frivolous young wife would never really leave her rich
husband and easy life, however tedious and unpleasant Hamo's
attentions might be, to risk everything with her penniless villein
lover. She would only keep him to enjoy in secret whenever she felt
it safe. Even when the old man died she would submit to marriage
at an overlord's will to another equally distasteful. She was not the
stuff of which heroines and adventurers are made. This was another
kind of woman.

Cadfael went close, and lifted a hand gently to put back the hood
from her head. She was tall, a hand's-breadth taller than he, and
erect as one of the lilies she clasped. The net that had covered her
hair was drawn off with the hood, and a great flood of silver-gold
streamed about her in the dim light, framing the pale face and
startling blue eyes. Norse hair! The Danes had left their seed as far
south as Cheshire, and planted this tall flower among them. She was
no longer plain, tired and resigned. In this dim but loving light she
shone in austere beauty. Just so must Brother Jordan's veiled eyes
have seen her.

"Now I see!" said Cadfael. "You came into the Lady Chapel, and
shone upon our half-blind brother's darkness as you shine here. You
are the visitation that brought him awe and bliss, and enjoined silence
upon him for three days."

The voice he had scarcely heard speak a word until then, a voice
level, low and beautiful, said: "I made no claim to be what I am not.
It was he who mistook me. I did not refuse the gift."

"I understand. You had not thought to find anyone there, he took you by surprise as you took him. He took you for Our Lady herself, disposing as she saw fit of what had been given her. And you made him promise you three days' grace." The lady had plunged her hands into the sacks, yes, but Elfgiva had carried the pillow, and a grain or two had filtered through the muslin to betray her.

"Yes," she said, watching him with unwavering blue eyes.

"So in the end you had nothing against him making known how the candlesticks were stolen." It was not an accusation, he was pursuing his way to understanding.

But at once she said clearly: "I did not steal them. I took them. I will restore them – to their owner."

"Then you don't claim they are yours?"

"No," she said, "they are not mine. But neither are they FitzHamon's."

"Do you tell me," said Cadfael mildly, "that there has been no theft at all?"

"Oh, yes," said Elfgiva, and her pallor burned into a fierce brightness, and her voice vibrated like a harp-string. "Yes, there has been a theft, and a vile, cruel theft, too, but not here, not now. The theft was a year ago, when FitzHamon received these candlesticks from Alard who made them, his villein, like me. Do you know what the promised price was for these? Manumission for Alard, and marriage with me, what we had begged of him three years and more. Even in villeinage we would have married and been thankful. But he promised freedom! Free man makes free wife, and I was promised, too. But when he got the fine works he wanted then he refused the promised price. He laughed! I saw, I heard him! He kicked Alard away from him like a dog. So what was his due, and denied him, Alard took. He ran! On St. Stephen's Day he ran!"

"And left you behind?" said Cadfael gently.

"What chance had he to take me? Or even to bid me farewell? He was thrust out to manual labour on FitzHamon's other manor. When his chance came, he took it and fled. I was not sad! I rejoiced! Whether I live or die, whether he remembers or forgets me, he is free. No, but in two days more he will be free. For a year and a day he will have been working for his living in his own craft, in a charter borough, and after that he cannot be haled back into servitude, even if they find him."

"I do not think," said Brother Cadfael," "that he will have forgotten you! Now I see why our brother may speak after three days. It will be too late then to try to reclaim a runaway serf. And you hold that these exquisite things you are cradling belong by right to Alard who made them?"

"Surely," she said, "seeing he never was paid for them, they are still his."

"And you are setting out tonight to take them to him. Yes! As I heard it, they had some cause to pursue him towards London . . . indeed, into London, though they never found him. Have you had better word of him? *From* him?"

The pale face smiled. "Neither he nor I can read or write. And whom should he trust to carry word until his time is complete, and he is free? No, never any word."

"But Shrewsbury is also a charter borough, where the unfree may work their way to freedom in a year and a day. And sensible boroughs encourage the coming of good craftsmen, and will go far to hide and protect them. I know! So you think he may be here. And the trail towards London a false trail. True, why should he run so far, when there's help so near? But, daughter, what if you do not find him in Shrewsbury?"

"Then I will look for him elsewhere until I do. I can live as a runaway, too, I have skills, I can make my own way until I do get word of him. Shrewsbury can as well make room for a good seamstress as for a man's gifts, and someone in the silversmith's craft will know where to find a brother so talented as Alard. I shall find him!"

"And when you do? Oh, child, have you looked beyond that?"

"To the very end," said Elfgiva firmly. "If I find him and he no longer wants me, no longer thinks of me, if he is married and has put me out of his mind, then I will deliver him these things that belong to him, to do with as he pleases, and go my own way and make my own life as best I may without him. And wish well to him as long as I live."

Oh, no, small fear, she would not be easily forgotten, not in a year, not in many years. "And if he is utterly glad of you, and loves you still?"

"Then," she said, gravely smiling, "if he is of the same mind as I, I have made a vow to Our Lady, who lent me her semblance in the old man's eyes, that we will sell these candlesticks where they may fetch their proper price, and that price shall be delivered to your almoner to feed the hungry. And that will be our gift, Alard's and mine, though no one will ever know it."

"Our Lady will know it," said Cadfael, "and so shall I. Now, how were you planning to get out of this enclave and into Shrewsbury? Both our gates and the town gates are closed until morning."

She lifted eloquent shoulders. "The parish doors are not barred. And even if I leave tracks, will it matter, provided I find a safe hiding-place inside the town?"

"And wait in the cold of the night? You would freeze before morning. No, let me think. We can do better for you than that."

Her lips shaped: "*We?*" in silence, wondering, but quick to understand. She did not question his decisions, as he had not questioned hers. He thought he would long remember the slow, deepening smile, the glow of warmth mantling her cheeks. "You believe me!" she said.

"Every word! Here, give me the candlesticks, let me wrap them, and do you put up your hair again in net and hood. We've had no fresh snow since morning, the path to the parish door is well trodden, no one will know your tracks among the many. And, girl, when you come to the town end of the bridge there's a little house off to the left, under the wall, close to the town gate. Knock there and ask for shelter over the night till the gates open, and say that Brother Cadfael sent you. They know me, I doctored their son when he was sick. They'll give you a warm corner and a place to lie, for kindness' sake, and ask no questions, and answer none from others, either. And likely they'll know where to find the silversmiths of the town, to set you on your way."

She bound up her pale, bright hair and covered her head, wrapping the cloak about her, and was again the maidservant in homespun. She obeyed without question his every word, moved silently at his back round the great court by way of the shadows, halting when he halted, and so he brought her to the church, and let her out by the parish door into the public street, still a good hour before Matins. At the last moment she said, close at his shoulder within the half-open door. "I shall be grateful always, Some day I shall send you word."

"No need for words," said Brother Cadfael, "if you send me the sign I shall be waiting for. Go now, quickly, there's not a soul stirring."

She was gone, lightly and silently, flitting past the abbey gatehouse like a tall shadow, towards the bridge and the town. Cadfael closed the door softly, and went back up the night stairs to the dortoir, too late to sleep, but in good time to rise at the sound of the bell, and return in procession to celebrate Matins.

There was, of course, the resultant uproar to face next morning, and he could not afford to avoid it, there was too much at stake. Lady FitzHamon naturally expected her maid to be in attendance as soon as she opened her eyes, and raised a petulant outcry when there was no submissive shadow waiting to dress her and do her hair. Calling failed to summon and search to find Elfgiva, but it was an hour or more before it dawned on the lady that she had lost her accomplished maid for good. Furiously she made her own toilet, unassisted, and raged out to complain to her husband, who had risen before her, and was waiting for her to accompany him to Mass. At her angry declaration that Elfgiva was nowhere to be found, and must have run away during the night, he first scoffed, for why should a sane girl take herself off into a killing frost when she had warmth and shelter and enough to eat where she was? Then he made the inevitable connection, and let out a roar of rage.

"Gone, is she? And my candlesticks gone with her, I dare swear! So it was *she*! The foul little thief! But I'll have her yet, I'll drag her back, she shall not live to enjoy her ill-gotten gains . . ."

It seemed likely that the lady would heartily endorse all this; her mouth was already open to echo him when Brother Cadfael, brushing her sleeve close as the agitated brothers ringed the pair, contrived to shake a few grains of lavender on to her wrist. Her mouth closed abruptly. She gazed at the tiny things for the briefest instant before she shook them off, she flashed an even briefer glance at Brother Cadfael, caught his eye, and heard in a rapid whisper: "Madam, softly! – proof of the maid's innocence is also proof of the mistress's."

She was by no means a stupid woman. A second quick glance confirmed what she had already grasped, that there was one man here who had a weapon to hold over her at least as deadly as any she could use against Elfgiva. She was also a woman of decision, and wasted no time in bitterness once her course was chosen. The tone in which she addressed her lord was almost as sharp as that in which she had complained of Elfgiva's desertion.

"She your thief, indeed! That's folly, as you should very well know. The girl is an ungrateful fool to leave me, but a thief she never has been, and certainly is not this time. She can't possibly have taken the candlesticks, you know well enough when they vanished, and you know I was not well that night, and went early to bed. She was with me until long after Brother Prior discovered the theft. I asked her to stay with me until you came to bed. *As you never did!*" she ended tartly. "You may remember!"

Hamo probably remembered very little of that night; certainly he was in no position to gainsay what his wife so roundly declared. He took out a little of his ill-temper on her, but she was not so much in awe of him that she dared not reply in kind. Of course she was certain of what she said! *She* had not drunk herself stupid at the lord abbot's table, she had been nursing a bad head of another kind, and even with Brother Cadfael's remedies she had not slept until after midnight, and Elfgiva had then been still beside her. Let him hunt a runaway maidservant, by all means, the thankless hussy, but never call her a thief, for she was none.

Hunt her he did, though with less energy now it seemed clear he would not recapture his property with her. He sent his grooms and half the lay servants off in both directions to enquire if anyone had seen a solitary girl in a hurry; they were kept at it all day, but they returned empty-handed.

The party from Lidyate, less one member, left for home next day. Lady FitzHamon rode demurely behind young Madoc, her cheek against his broad shoulders; she even gave Brother Cadfael the flicker of a conspiratorial smile as the cavalcade rode out of the gates, and detached one arm from round Madoc's waist to wave as they reached the roadway. So Hamo was not present to hear when Brother Jordan, at last released from his vow, told how Our Lady had appeared to him in a vision of light, fair as an angel, and taken away with her the candlesticks that were hers to take and do with as she would, and how she had spoken to him, and enjoined on him his three days of silence. And if there were some among the listeners who wondered whether the fair woman had not been a more corporeal being, no one had the heart to say so to Jordan, whose vision was comfort and consolation for the fading of the light.

That was at Matins, at midnight of the day of St. Stephen's. Among the scattering of alms handed in at the gatehouse next morning for the beggars, there was a little basket that weighed surprisingly heavily. The porter could not remember who had brought it, taking it to be some offerings of food or old clothing, like all the rest; but when it was opened it sent Brother Oswald, almost incoherent with joy and wonder, running to Abbot Heribert to report what seemed to be a miracle. For the basket was full of gold coin, to the value of more than a hundred marks. Well used, it would ease all the worst needs of his poorest petitioners, until the weather relented.

"Surely," said Brother Oswald devoutly, "Our Lady has made her own will known. Is not this the sign we have hoped for?"

Certainly it was for Cadfael, and earlier than he had dared to hope for it. He had the message that needed no words. She had found him, and been welcomed with joy. Since midnight Alard the silversmith had been a free man, and free man makes free wife. Presented with such a woman as Elfgiva, he could give as gladly as she, for what was gold, what was silver, by comparison?

# THE CONFESSION OF BROTHER ATHELSTAN
## Paul Harding

*After Ellis Peters, Paul Harding is the most prolific writer of historical mystery novels. Harding is one of several pen names used by Paul C. Doherty, Headmaster of a school in Essex. As Doherty he has written a series of novels featuring the thirteenth-century clerk in Chancery, Hugh Corbett, who first appeared in* Satan in St. Mary's *(1986). As Michael Clynes he is the author of the Sir Roger Shallot series set at the time of Henry VIII, which started with* The White Rose Murders *(1991). Most recently, under the name C. L. Grace, he has signed a contract with an American publisher for a series about a woman physician/detective in fifteenth-century Canterbury.*

*Brother Athelstan first appeared in* The Nightingale Gallery *(1991), and three novels have followed. This is his first short story, specially written for this volume. Set in the summer of 1376 it features the wine-loving, corpulent Sir John Cranston, Coroner of London, and his amanuensis, Brother Athelstan, a Dominican monk and parish priest of St. Erconwald's in Southwark.*

I was reading Bartholomew the Englishman's *The Nature of Things* in which he describes the planet Saturn as cold as ice, dark as night and malignant as Satan. In an interesting after-thought he claims it governs the murderous intent of men; I wonder if Saturn governs my life. The death of my own brother in battle still plagues my dreams whilst Cranston and I deal with murder every week: men, violent in drink or overtaken by some ill humour, drawing sword, mace or club to hack and slash. Cranston says it's strange work for a priest, I remind him how the first crime mentioned in the Bible was one of murder – Cain plotting to slay his brother Abel and afterwards claiming he knew nothing about it. The first great mystery! Cain was discovered and he bore the mark which, I think, stains in varying hues all our souls. Again, I was reading John's gospel where Christ, arguing with the Pharisees, dismissed Satan as "An assassin from the start". An assassin! Someone who lurks in the shadows plotting violent death. Now most murders we witness are after the blood has been spilt and the body lies dead, but recently Cranston and I saw an evil, well-plotted murder carried out before our very eyes.

Spring had come, snapping winter's vice-like grip. The Thames, frozen from bank to bank, thawed and the waters flowed quickly, full of life. The rains loosened the soil and the sun rose higher and stronger. The crowds poured back into the London streets and, to mark the changing seasons, John of Gaunt, Duke of Lancaster, uncle of the young King and Regent, announced a great tournament to be held at Smithfield. Varlets, squires and men-at-arms poured into London. The streets were packed with men, helmeted and armoured. Great destriers, caparisoned in all the colours and awesome regalia of war, moved majestically along the roads. High in the saddle rode the knights and men of war resplendent in coloured surcoats, their slit-eyed helmets swinging from the saddlebow, their bannered lances carried before them by page or squire. To the crash of grating hooves, hordes of others followed, retainers, gaudy in the livery of great lords and the bright, French silks of the young gallants who swarmed into the city like butterflies returning under the warm sun and blue skies. They thronged the taverns, their coloured garments a sharp contrast to the dirty leather aprons of the blacksmiths and the short jerkins and caps of their apprentices. For days before the tournament London rejoiced. There were miracle plays, fairs, cock fights, dog battles and savage contests between wild hogs and mangy bears. Bonfires were lit in Cheapside and the Great Conduit ran with wine. Cranston and I saw it all, being very busy as men and women, drenched with drink, quarrelled and violently fought each other: a man was hacked to death for stealing ale, a woman, slashed from jaw to groin, was found floating in the Walbrook. Sometimes the assailants were found but usually all we got were blank glances and evasive replies. Cranston's temper, never the best, grew more abrupt.

"Brother," he announced at the end of one tiring day as we both squatted in the coolness of my parish church, sharing a bowl of watered ale. "Brother, we need a respite from this. The day after tomorrow, Thursday, the tournament begins at Smithfield. We should go."

I shook my head.

"No, Sir John, I thank you but I have had enough of war and violent death."

"Not this time," he answered quickly. "The first tournament is a game of great skill, a joust with blunted lances between two court favourites, Oliver Le Marche and Robert Woodville. No deaths there, Brother. They fight for the favour of Lady Isabella Lyons, a distant kinswoman of the King." He nudged me in the ribs and came closer. "My wife will come. You could always bring Benedicta."

I blushed not daring to ask how he knew about the widow woman. Cranston laughed. He was still bellowing when he got up and walked out of the church after making me agree I would think about it.

At early Mass the next morning I saw Benedicta with the other two members of my congregation kneeling at the entrance to the rood screen, her ivory face framed in its veil of black, luxurious curls. After Mass, as usual, she stayed to light a candle before the statue of the Virgin. Benedicta smiled as I approached, asking softly if I was well. I blurted out my invitation, her violet blue eyes rounded in surprise but she smiled and agreed so quickly I wondered if she too felt a kinship with me. God forgive me, I was in my own private heaven, so pleased I did not even bother to study the stars despite the sky being cloud-free and my mind unwilling to rest even for sleep. Instead I tossed and turned, hoping the boy I had sent, Girth the bricklayer's son, had delivered my acceptance at the coroner's house. I rose at dawn, said my Mass, pleased to see Benedicta kneeling there, her hair now braided, hidden under a wimple, a small basket by her side.

After Mass we talked and quietly walked to meet Cranston at the "Golden Pig", a comfortable tavern on the Southwark side of the river. The coroner's wife, small and pert, was cheerful as a little sparrow, accepting Benedicta as a long-lost sister. Cranston, with a flagon of wine down him already, was in good form, nudging me in the ribs and leering lecherously at Benedicta. We took a boat across the Thames not rowed, thank God, by one of my parishioners and made our way up Thames Street to the "Kirtle Tavern" which stands on the edge of Smithfield just under the vast forbidding walls of Newgate prison.

The day proved to be a fine one, the streets were hot and dusty so we welcomed the tavern's coolness. We sat in a corner watching the citizens of every class and station go noisily by, eager to get in a good place to watch the day's events. Merchants sweltering under beaver hats, their fat wives clothed in gaudy gowns, beggars, quacks, story tellers, hordes of apprentices and men from the guilds. I groaned and hid my face as a group of my parishioners, Black Hod, Crispin the carpenter, Ranulf the ratcatcher and Watle son of the dung-collector, passed the tavern door, roaring a filthy song at the tops of their voices. We waited until Cranston finished his refreshment and, with Benedicta so close beside me my heart kept skipping for joy, we walked out into the great area around Smithfield.

Three blackened, crow-pecked corpses still swung from the gibbet but the crowd ignored them. The food sellers were doing a roaring trade in spiced sausages whilst beside them water-sellers, great buckets slung around their necks, sold cooling drinks to soothe the mouths of those who chewed the hot, spicy meat. I watched and turned away, my gorge rising in my throat as I saw Ranulf the ratcatcher sidle up behind one of these water-sellers and quietly piss into one of the buckets.

Smithfield itself had been cleared for the joust; even the dung heaps and piles of ordure had been taken away. A vast open space had been cordoned off for the day. At one side was the royal enclosure with row after row of wooden seats all covered in purple or gold cloth. In the centre a huge canopy shielded the place where the King and his leading nobility would sit. The banners of John of Gaunt, resplendent with the gaudy device of the House of Lancaster, curled and waved lazily in the breeze. Marshals of the royal household resplendent in tabards, their white wands of office held high, stopped and directed us to our reserved seats. All around us the benches were quickly filling, ladies in silk gowns giggling and chattering, clutching velvet cushions to their bosoms as they simpered past the young men who stood eyeing them. These gallants, their hair long and curled, their bodies dripping in pearls and lace, proved to be raucous and strident. Cranston was merry but some of these young men were already far gone in their cups. I ignored the lustful glances directed at Benedicta, trying to curb the sparks of jealousy which flared in my own heart and, once we were seated, studied the tournament area. The field, a great grassy plain, was divided down the centre by a huge tilt barrier covered in a black and white checkered canvas. At each end of this barrier were two pavilions; one gold, the other blue. Already the contestants were preparing for the joust, around each pavilion scuttled pages and squires, armour glinted and dazzled in the sun. I stared at the jousting lances, great 14-foot-long ashpoles, each in its own case on a long wooden rack. I asked Cranston why there were so many.

"Oh, it's simple, Brother," he replied. "Each course run will use up one lance and, as this is a friendly combat, ten or twelve lances may be broken before an outright victory is won."

A bray of trumpets drowned his words, a shrill so angry the birds in the trees around Smithfield rose in noisy protesting flocks. The royal party had now arrived. I noticed John of Gaunt, Earl of Lancaster, a majestic, cruel face under his silver hair, with skin burnt dark brown from his campaigns in Castile; on either side of him, his brothers and a collection of young lords. In the centre with one of Gaunt's hands on his shoulder, stood a young boy, his face white as snow under a mop of gold hair, a silver chaplet on his head. Beside him a young lady, her red hair just visible under a lacey white veil, a real eye-catching beauty in her tawny samite dress. Again the shrill bray of trumpets sounded. Gaunt lifted his hand as if welcoming the plaudits of the crowd. There was some clapping from the claque of young courtiers around us but the London mob was stony silent and I remembered Cranston's mutterings about how the expensive tastes of the court, coupled with the military defeats against the French, had brought Gaunt and his party into disrepute.

"There's the King!" the coroner whispered to his wife though his voice carried for yards around us. "And beside him is Lady Isabella Lyons, the queen of the tournament."

I looked sideways at Benedicta and my heart lurched. She had turned slightly in her seat, staring coolly back at a young, dark-faced gallant, resplendent in red and white silks, who lounged in his seat with eyes for no one but my fair companion. Cranston, sharp enough under his bluff drunken exterior, caught my drift. He leaned over and tapped me on the arm.

"The joust is about to begin, Brother," he said. "Watch carefully, you may learn something."

Another shrill blast from the trumpets, banners were lowered, the noise of the crowd died away as the two contestants emerged and mounted their great destriers. Each donned a war helm, took a lance and rode gently into the middle of the field to stand on either side of the Master Herald. Slowly they advanced before the royal box, an awesome vision of grey steel armour and silken surcoats, all the more ominous for the silence, no sound except for the gentle screech of leather. Both knights had their visors raised; I glimpsed young faces, lined and scarred, eyes impatient for the contest to begin. They lowered their lances and saluted both the King and the object of their desires, who simpered back, hiding her face behind her hands. Then each knight turned away, riding back towards the pavilions, taking up their positions at either end of the tilt barrier. The Master Herald, a great, bald-headed man, dressed in the royal blue and gold tabard, raised himself in the stirrups and in a loud, booming voice announced the tournament, a joust with blunted lances.

"Any knight," he bellowed, glaring fiercely around, "who breaks the rules of the tournament or tarnishes the honour of chivalry, will be stripped of his arms, his shield reversed and covered in dust and he will be dismissed from the field."

"That's Sir Michael Lyons," Cranston whispered, nodding to the Master Herald, "father to our great beauty. They say he thoroughly enjoys his daughter being the object of desire of two redoubtable warriors."

Sir Michael bowed towards the young King who raised his hand as a sign for the joust to commence. The herald turned his horse and lifted his white baton of office. At either end of the field the two knights prepared, visors were lowered as their squires grasped the reins of the horses. Cranston burped, his wife cooed with embarrassment. A crash of trumpets, the crowd burst into loud cheering as both riders started advancing together, first at a walk then a quick trot. There was another short trumpet blast, the audience gave a long sigh which grew into a resounding cheer as both knights charged, shields up, lances lowered, the pennants at either end of the lance snapping up and down like the wings of some beautiful bird. The knights met in the centre with a resounding crash of lances against shields. Then they were past each other, back again to their squires, who brought up fresh lances, making sure they avoided the wicked, sharpened hooves of the now fiery destriers.

Benedicta smiled at me, clutching my arm tightly. I felt happy, free like a bird which whirls under the bluest of skies. Again the trumpets, the sound of hooves drumming on the packed earth, war-like and ominous. I heard the crowd gasp and I looked up. Woodville had begun his charge but he seemed out of control, swaying in the saddle as if he was drunk, his lance fell and his shield arm dropped, his posture was all askew but Le Marche did not stop. He came thundering down, lance lowered. Woodville tried to defend himself but, too late, his opponent hit him full in the chest. Woodville was lifted from the saddle, high in the air and crashed to earth like a bird brought down by sling shot. He lay in a crumpled heap, his splendid armour now defaced by blood and dirt. His gaudy plumage, shorn from the crest of his helmet, drifted like snowflakes on the breeze.

"Brave lance!" someone shouted, then silence.

Le Marche turned, his horse now prancing back as the Master Herald, followed by other marshals and squires, ran up to the fallen knight. They gathered round and the herald turned, hands extended, and shouted.

"He is dead! My Lord Woodville is dead!"

The crowd remained silent before bursting into a loud raucous chorus of boos and jeers. Mud, dirt and other offal were flung in the direction of Le Marche. The herald walked over and looked up at Le Marche.

"Your lance, my Lord, was pointed."

The booing and catcalls increased, a few rocks were thrown. John of Gaunt rose and gestured with his hand. A deafening blast of trumpets brought royal men-at-arms as if from nowhere, to throw a cordon of steel around the crowd. In the near distance, stripped of its armour, the corpse of Sir Robert Woodville was being carried away on a makeshift pallet. Meanwhile the Master Herald was conferring with John of Gaunt. The trumpets blared out again, the herald bellowed that, for this day at least, the tournament was finished. His message was greeted with a chorus of catcalls and jeers but the moment passed; the crowd began to break up and drift away to seek further amusements amongst the booths and stalls of the nearby fair.

I glanced across at the royal enclosure: the young King sat as if carved from wood, looking blankly over at the tournament field, where royal serjeants were now circling Le Marche, gesturing that he dismount and surrender his weapons. The knight shouted his innocence but obeyed their orders. Beside the King the young queen of the tournament sat disconsolate, head in hand. Cranston's wife muttered, "Oh, the pity! Oh, the pity!"

Benedicta clung close to me, her face white and drawn as if Woodville's death had reawakened memories in her own soul. Cranston, however, stood transfixed, rooted to the spot, his mouth open. He just stared across at the confusion around the tilt barrier.

"Sir John Cranston! Sir John Cranston!"

A young page, wearing the surcoat of the royal household, came weaving through the crowd.

"Sir John . . .!"

"Here!" I called.

The boy just dismissed me with a flicker of his girlish eyelashes.

"Here I am!" Cranston bellowed. "What is it, boy?"

"My Lord of Lancaster wishes to have words with you."

"I wonder," Cranston murmured. He glanced slyly at me. "Come on, Brother. Maude," he turned to his wife. "Look after Benedicta."

He waddled off with me in tow, pushing through the guards into the royal enclosure, the page skipping in front like a frisky puppy. Knight bannerets of the King's household stopped him but the pageboy, jumping up and down, screamed his orders so they let Cranston by. I stood outside the protective ring of steel watching Cranston bow at the foot of the steps and fall to one knee. John of Gaunt came down, laughing, tapped him on the shoulder and, raising him up, whispered into his ear, Cranston replied. Gaunt looked up and stared like a hungry cat back at me, his eyes yellow, hard and unblinking. He nodded, muttered something and Cranston backed away. Sir John said nothing until he had taken me further away from the royal enclosure.

"Brother," he muttered, "this is a right midden heap. Woodville was one of Gaunt's principal retainers and now my Lord wants the truth about his death."

Cranston narrowed his eyes and whispered out of the corner of his mouth.

"Gaunt thinks it's murder, Brother. So do I."

Oh, I could have laughed! Here we were on a glorious day, a festival, and murder had appeared as the poet says 'stalking across the green fields like the evil which walks at mid-day'. I now wished we had gone somewhere else – or was it me, was I a Jonah? Did murder and assassination always trail my footsteps? I looked up, clouds were beginning fitfully to block the sun, I gazed back over my shoulder. Cranston's wife was making herself comfortable on a bench whilst the gallant who had been eyeing Benedicta, had now moved down and was talking quietly with her. He was teasing her but Benedicta did not seem to mind. Cranston, however, pushing me by the elbow, hurried me on across to Woodville's tent.

Inside the pavilion retainers were already laying out and dressing the corpse of the dead knight, who would have looked as peaceful and composed as an effigy in a church, except for the awful ragged gash in his chest. Cranston looked around; the retainers he dismissed but went direct as an arrow to Eustace Howard, Woodville's principal squire in the recent deadly joust. Eustace, round-faced, with a scrub of ginger hair, fearful green eyes and a petulant mouth, was loud in condemnation of what had happened. He nervously fingered a rosary as Cranston questioned him. The squire was about to launch into a further litany of protest when Sir Michael Lyons, the Master Herald, swaggered into the tent. He was a magnificent fellow: a broad, rubicund face and a leonine head, his grey hair swept back over his forehead. His martial appearance was made all the more threatening by watery blue eyes and a long drooping moustache. Sir Michael greeted Cranston warmly but dismissed Eustace and myself with a look of disdain.

"Cranston," he rasped. "I know why you are here but I am Master Herald and chief steward of the tournament. Woodville," he nodded at the corpse, "was murdered."

"By whom, Sir Michael?"

"God's teeth, Cranston!" Lyons snarled. "By Le Marche of course. His lance should have been blunted but the pointed steel cap had been replaced. We have found two of his other lances similarly armed. If Woodville had not been killed on the second run course, it would have undoubtedly happened later."

"And does that make Le Marche a murderer?" Cranston asked.

Lyons stared at Cranston so hard his blue eyes seemed to pop out of his rubicund face whilst his white goatee beard bristled with anger.

"I mean," Cranston smiled, "Le Marche should have used a blunted lance but did not. I concede that but I cannot see how that makes him a murderer."

Howard bleated like a sheep whilst Lyons stroked his beard.

"Oh, come, Sir John!"

"Oh, come, Sir Michael!" Cranston mildly interrupted. "We are old soldiers. Let us not charge the first enemy in sight but, as Vegetius maintains in his manual of war, let us be patient. First, why should the noble Le Marche kill Woodville? Secondly, if he did, his method bordered on madness. He used a pointed lance, he must have known this would be discovered and the blame fall on him."

Cranston stared at the Master Herald.

"There is one other perplexing problem. Would you say Le Marche and Woodville were equally matched?"

"Yes," the Master Herald grunted.

"So," Cranston continued, "how did Le Marche, even with his lethal lance, know he would be successful? Remember history, Sir Michael, the great Richard the Lionheart was killed by a man with a broken crossbow and a frying pan to protect himself. Come, Sir Michael," he flattered soothingly, "you are an old warhorse like me, in battle nothing is predictable."

The Master Herald allowed himself a small smirk of self-satisfaction.

"As always, Sir John, you are correct." He took a deep breath and looked round the pavilion. "This morning," he continued, "I thought how fortunate I was, my beautiful Isabella, queen of the tournament, the lady love of the two greatest champions in the kingdom. Now both are gone. Sir Robert lies dead and Sir Oliver is disgraced. I thought one of them, for they were both poor men, would have won the one hundred pounds prize and my daughter's affection."

Cranston whistled.

"So great a prize!" he said.

"God's teeth!" Sir Michael snarled. "Now all is gone!"

He looked scathingly at Eustace, who surprisingly stood his ground.

"Do not blame me, Sir Michael!" he cried.

"Who said he was?" Cranston asked.

"Someone will pay," Sir Michael replied. "Something is rotten here."

He looked at me, for the first time bothering to acknowledge my presence.

"I inspected everything according to the rules of the tournament. Their horses, their armour."

"And their lances?" I added.

"Yes, each knight lays them out on the grass before they are taken and put in the racks." He shook his head. "Sir Oliver must have known the lance was tipped."

"We will see Sir Oliver," Cranston soothingly interrupted. "Come, Brother!"

"Pompous fool!" Cranston muttered after we had left the tent. "He is the reason Gaunt told me to intervene in this matter. A good warrior, Sir Michael," he added, "but a greedy climber. A courtier with great ambitions, without the talent to match. Mind you," he looked sideways at me, "we all have our failures, don't we, Brother?"

The sun had slipped behind a cloud, I felt tired and unable to deal with Sir John's teasing. The tournament field was now empty. All the glory was gone. The banners had lost their gloss and finery. The tilt barrier was damaged, the ground on either side pounded to a dust which whirled in small clouds as a cold breeze blew in. Only the pavilions remained, each ringed by men-at-arms and a few ostlers and grooms looking after the horses. I dare not look across at Benedicta and I cursed myself for being a love-lorn idiot but, I suppose, love makes fools of us all. I trailed along beside Cranston, through the ring of armed men into Le Marche's pavilion. The young knight, his blood-red hair cropped to a stubble, was calm enough in the circumstances. I was surprised how young he was, though his eyes wore that aged look you often see in men steeped in the blood of others. "Men of contrasts" I call these knights with their courtly ways, silken clothes and lust for killing and war. Sir Oliver gazed stonily at both of us before returning to glare at his squire who was polishing his armour with a greasy rag. The squire kept his back to us, head bowed and I gathered there had been harsh words between master and servant before we entered. Cranston waddled across, barking at the lazing men-at-arms to get out.

"You are Sir Oliver Le Marche?"

"Of course," Le Marche replied. "And you, because of your weight and wine-drenched breath, must be Sir John Cranston!"

"King's Coroner!" Cranston tartly retorted.

"Of course," Le Marche replied and swung slightly to one side to look at me. "And, of course, the faithful Brother Athelstan. That," he indicated with his hand towards the squire, "is my ever devoted servant Giles Le Strange." Le Marche stood up. "Now the courtesies are over, let's be blunt. I did not kill Woodville. I did not know my lance was tipped with a metal point. You know, Sir John, how easy it is to slip the metal point onto a blunted lance. Anyone could have done it."

Cranston pursed his lips.

"Yes, I do," he said. "So what did happen?"

Sir Oliver sighed.

"Well, you saw the racks beside my pavilion at the end of the tilt barrier? I ran the first course, the lance was shattered. I returned to my position and my squire gave me a fresh one. I did not know the lance was pointed. I believed all of them were blunted, the metal points taken off." He shrugged. "Anyway, it was not my fault."

"Then whose was it, Sir?" Cranston barked.

Le Marche squared his shoulders.

"I could say, ask Woodville. All I remember is cantering towards him. My horse broke into a gallop, I lowered my lance. Only then did I notice something wrong."

"What?"

"Woodville seemed to sway in his saddle, his shield lowered, his lance askew. I could not have stopped even if I had wanted to." Le Marche bit his lip. "My lance was aimed for his shield; when that dropped, I took him full on the chest."

He looked at me for pity.

"Even then I thought all would be well. Perhaps Woodville would be a little bruised, nothing else. I am as distressed as anyone that he is dead."

"Surely," I queried, "as you lowered your lance, you would have seen the metal point sheathed on the tip?"

Cranston guffawed.

"No, Brother." Le Marche smiled. "Remember, I was helmeted, my visor down and the first rule of a jouster is never to watch your lance but your opponent."

"Did you like Woodville?" I asked.

"No, I did not."

"Why?"

"He belonged to the faction of John of Gaunt, the King's uncle. I am a retainer of Gaunt's younger brother, Thomas of Gloucester. You know, as the whole kingdom does, there is little liking between the brothers and the same goes for their retainers. I am a loyal man. What Lord Thomas dislikes I dislike. He disliked Gaunt. He disliked Woodville and so do I!"

"Was there more?" I asked. "I mean, the lady?"

"Yes, there was more," Le Marche retorted bitterly. "Lady Isabella. I had asked for her hand in marriage but Gaunt refused because she is a royal ward. Woodville, too, had asked. She's a fair lady."

"And owns even fairer lands?" Cranston commented.

Le Marche's eyes snapped up.

"Yes, she owns lands. Woodville was a suitor, a rival for her hand. For that I could have killed him but in fair combat. I did not murder him in the tournament."

"And the prize," I queried, "you wanted that?"

"Of course," Le Marche retorted. "Now, if I am found guilty of foul play, I forfeit that as well as my honour!"

Cranston looked at the squire.

"And you, Giles. Surely you inspected the lances?"

The squire turned, a dour, whey-faced lad, though his eyes were anger-bright. If looks were arrows, Le Marche would have dropped dead on the spot.

"Why should I?" he answered, throwing the rag to the ground. "Yes, I put the lances in the rack but have you ever carried a lance, Sir John? You never think of looking at the tip, fourteen feet high, well over twice your height. The lances are in the rack, your master comes galloping back, you take one, you put it in his hand and the noble knight," his eyes flickered up to his master, "charges on for greater honour and the favour of his lady."

Le Marche smiled sourly at his squire's attempt to be sardonic.

"My squire, Giles," Le Marche interrupted, "does not like me and does not like tournaments. In fact, you've recently quarrelled with me, haven't you, Giles?" Le Marche looked at me. "Do you know, Brother, Giles here wants to be a priest. He wants to leave the military life, believes he is not fitted for it."

"Is that true, Giles?" I asked.

I looked at his thin face and large eyes. For all his bluster, the squire seemed a gentle man, more suited to study and prayer than hacking at his fellow man, be it on the tournament field or in the real, bloody business of war.

"Yes," the squire murmured. "I have a vocation, Brother, but I also have an indenture," he glared at his master, "with Sir Oliver Le Marche; it has another six months to run. When it is finished, so am I. I intend to return to my own village in Northampton, seek an audience with the bishop and ask to be ordained as a priest."

"Some people," I said slowly, "might say that you, Giles, disliked your master so much you were prepared to take your revenge by depicting him as a knight who cheated in a tournament. After all, two men touched those lances. You and your master. Or," I turned, ignoring the squire's look of fury, "they might say, Sir Oliver, that you hated Woodville so much, you thought it was worth killing him to win the hand of the fair Isabella."

"That's a lie!" the knight snapped, his hand falling to his belt where his sword should have been.

"Brother Athelstan," Cranston tactfully interrupted, "is not accusing either of you. He is just repeating what other people might say."

"Some people," I continued, "might even allege that it was a conspiracy between you, Sir Oliver and your squire, to kill Sir Robert Woodville. I am only repeating, Sir Oliver," I concluded, "what other people might say. Woodville was killed by your lance."

"My master is a knight banneret," the squire protested. "Yes, I dislike serving him but would a knight break his honour and would I, called to the priesthood, commit such a dreadful act?"

Cranston made a rude noise with his lips and looked around the tent. I knew what he was searching for. No drink can be hidden from Sir John for long and he'd glimpsed the earthenware jug full of coarse wine on a tray in the corner of the tent. He went across and picked it up. Le Marche sauntered over with a pewter cup he took from a chest.

"Sir John, you are thirsty? Be my guest."

Cranston filled the cup to the brim until it spilt over, the red wine dripping to the ground like drops of blood and, in one great gulp, drank and immediately refilled it. He looked at me and rolled his eyes heavenwards.

"So," he said expansively, "what we have here is one knight, you, Sir Oliver with an intense dislike for your opponent. A dislike which has its roots in the rivalry between both your royal masters as well as rivalry for the fair hand of Lady Isabella. Secondly, we have your squire, Giles, who has little love for you. Thirdly, the tournament is ready, the lances are inspected by Sir Michael earlier in the day though you, Sir Oliver, never touched a lance until you ran the first course."

Le Marche nodded, filled a wine cup and drank greedily from it.

"Yes," he said, smacking his lips as if he hadn't a care in the world. "That's how it was and, if any man believes, alleges or even thinks I am responsible for Woodville's death he should produce the proof before King's Bench or answer to me on the field of combat, and that includes you, Sir John, even though you are the King's Coroner. As for you, Brother," Le Marche grinned across at me, "you can say what you like. I am used to your type." He nodded to his squire. "I have him preaching to me every second of the waking day. However, I repeat, I did not kill Woodville."

"But someone did!"

We all turned as Sir Michael Lyons, the Master Herald, strode into the tent.

"I, too, am concerned, Sir Oliver, by what many people saw: as Woodville charged he lost control of his horse, his lance slipped, his shield went down. Now I have just examined his destrier, there is a cut on its hindquarters."

Le Marche's face went hard.

"So, it was the horse which jolted him."

"Yes and Eustace, Woodville's squire, must be the culprit. Just before the trumpet blast for the second charge, the squire would have held Woodville's horse by its bridle. The trumpet rang out, the horse gathered itself for the charge, Eustace stepped back and with a dagger concealed in his other hand, cut the horse as it burst forward."

The Master Herald paused.

"The rest you know." He nodded at the tent entrance behind him. "We have the squire outside. He claims he knows nothing of this."

I could see from Cranston's close face and hooded eyes, the way he cocked his head slightly to one side that he did not fully accept the Master Herald's story.

"Bring Eustace in!" the coroner snapped.

The Master Herald went back to the doorway of the tent and shouted. Two men-at-arms entered, the hapless Eustace struggling and squirming between them. His face was grey and drawn, his mouth sagging open in disbelief at the accusations which had been levelled against him. Cranston, without a word, refilled his wine cup and offered it to the squire.

"Drink, man," he murmured. "Gather your wits for God's sake! All that has happened is an allegation laid against you, no real proof."

"There is proof," the Master Herald interrupted. "Come outside!"

Cranston followed Lyons out. I trailed behind, quite bemused. (When Sir John exercises his authority, he is like a hunting dog; he seeks out his prey, not letting go, not giving up the scent, not even for a bucket of wine or a flagon of beer.) The unfortunate war horse, still coated in a white, sweaty foam but now unsaddled, stood waiting patiently; two pages either side of its head, held it quiet and docile. Sir Michael took Sir John to the left side of the horse where Eustace would have stood, one hand on his master's bridle. True enough, Sir Michael was right; along the sweat soaked hindquarters there was a long ugly cut; no casualty of the tournament; the horse had been deliberately gashed. Sir John studied this carefully, licked his lips, shook his head and went back inside.

"Sir Oliver," he said. "You knew Woodville?"

"Of course. I have admitted as much."

"He was a good jouster?"

Le Marche pursed his lips.

"Yes," he replied slowly. "Probably one of the best in the king-dom."

"So, did you expect to win today?" Sir John added.

Le Marche looked away.

"Sir Oliver," Cranston repeated, "I asked you an honest question! As one knight to another, did you expect to win today?"

Le Marche shook his head.

"No," he replied softly. "I expected to lose. Woodville was an excellent jouster and horseman."

"Do you think," Cranston persisted, "that if his horse was hurt as he gathered to charge, it would have alarmed him?"

Le Marche laughed drily.

"I doubt it. Sir Robert was an excellent horseman. Any knight has to face such a danger in battle whether it be an arrow, flaming torch or a man-at-arms springing up suddenly in ambuscade. Remember, Sir John, a knight does not control his horse with his hands but with his knees. If there had been such an accident or an attempt to damage the horse, I believe Sir Robert would have controlled it."

"But not," the Master Herald interrupted, "if he was not expecting it. Remember, Woodville was at full charge, lance lowered, shield up, suddenly his horse shies. I still believe," he pointed to where Eustace stood gibbering with fright, his moans peppered with pleas for mercy, "that he could have damaged the horse and for those few seconds Sir Robert lost his concentration."

Cranston pursed his lips and nodded. He turned to me.

"What do you think, Brother?"

I thought of Benedicta and Cranston's wife still being entertained by the ever so courteous gallant.

"I think, Sir John, we cannot stay here all day. There is a tavern nearby, 'The Swooping Eagle'. Perhaps, Sir Michael, you could have it cleared and we can use it to continue our questioning there. Sir John, if you would come with me?"

We walked out of the tent. Across the field the gallant was now a little closer to Benedicta. Lady Maude was gazing soulfully over the field as if she realized the young man was not interested in her and she now pined for the return of her corpulent, but ever-loving husband. Benedicta seemed absorbed. The young man was facing her, his hands in his lap only a few inches from hers, his face masked in concentration as he stared into her eyes. I had to control the sense of panic, remind myself that I was a priest, a monk ordained and given to God. I had taken a vow of celibacy and, although I may have a woman as a friend, I cannot lust, I cannot desire or covet any woman whether she be free or not. I steeled myself. I had to because I felt a growing rage at my condition. A deep longing to be with Benedicta. A sense of hurt that she could find someone else so attractive and entertaining. I knew my anger to be unfair and I remembered an old priest once saying how people think priests are different but we are just ordinary men, exercising an extraordinary office. I looked at Sir John, he just stared down at the ground. I knew what he was thinking, he was impatient with me, yet felt sorry.

"Sir John," I began, taking him by the arm and walking him over to the tilt barrier. "What you said back there, was it true, that a knight guides his horse with his legs rather than his hands?"

Sir John shrugged.

"Of course. Any man who has to fight on horseback knows that you cannot guide your horse in battle if your hands are engaged. That is why each knight forms a close relationship with his horse until his destrier senses every move, even the slightest touch of pressure, where to turn, when to stop, when to rear. Even I," he tapped his great stomach, "when younger, and a little slimmer, was an excellent horseman." Cranston coughed. "Le Marche was correct. Sir Robert was a fine jouster, his reputation was well known. I cannot understand how a horse, even if it panicked or reared, should throw him to such an extent that he would lower both lance and shield. Moreover, there is something else."

"What?" I asked.

Cranston closed his eyes.

"Let us put ourselves in Woodville's position. He is on a horse, he is in armour, his visor lowered, he carries shield and lance. He charges. His horse, stung to agony by a dagger prick, swerves and turns."

Cranston opened his eyes and looked at me.

"Yet Woodville could have reasserted himself, turned his horse away and avoided Le Marche's oncoming lance." He shook his head. "There must be something else. But, come, let us go back to our guests."

Inside the tent Sir Michael was issuing orders. Eustace stood with his hands bound behind his back like a convicted felon waiting to be taken to Tyburn. Cranston went up to him.

"Eustace," he barked. "Did you have any grievance against your lord?"

The squire shook his head, his eyes pleading for mercy.

"He was a good master?"

Eustace nodded.

"So why did you goad your master's horse with a dagger?"

"I did not!" the man screamed. "I did nothing of the sort. Yes, I had my hand on the horse but no dagger. I inflicted no injury."

Cranston turned to Giles.

"Do you two know each other?" he asked.

Eustace looked away. Now Giles became agitated, moving from one foot to another, the tent fell silent. The Master Herald who had been on the verge of leaving turned back.

"I asked you a question," Cranston repeated. "You see, it's quite simple. If Woodville was murdered, two people must have been involved. One at Le Marche's end, putting a point on the blunted lance, the other at Woodville's ready to wound the horse. What I am saying, gentlemen, is the only people who had access to both knights were their two squires. Perhaps," Cranston looked at the Master Herald triumphantly, "perhaps it is not one murderer, Sir Michael, but two. And so I ask you squires again, did you meet before the tournament?"

"No," Eustace murmured. "No, no, this is not fair, our words will be twisted."

Cranston ignored him and looked at Giles.

"You did meet, didn't you?"

The squire nodded.

"What about?"

Giles licked his lips.

"I had met Eustace before," he said. "Quite a few times. We know each other well. When great lords assemble in castles their servants are left to wander around, find food and lodgings. They are left to their own devices. When the royal party went to any castle, be it Sheen or Windsor, Eustace was there."

"Don't tell him!" Eustace yelled. "Whatever you say will be twisted!"

Cranston walked across and squeezed the young squire's mouth in his hand.

"You, sir," he said, "will keep quiet until my questions are answered. And you," he looked at Giles, "you will tell us the truth."

Giles chewed his lip, his eyes pleading with Cranston.

"Eustace has lost money," he began, "in many wagers. He is a gambler, be it dice, the toss of a penny, two flies crawling up a castle wall, two cocks fighting in a ring, bears against dogs, a hunt, a falcon swooping for a heron, you will find Eustace laying his wager."

Giles smiled.

"He is not very successful and usually loses. He came to me three days ago. He asked me who I thought would win the great tournament, his master or mine? He made enquiries about Sir Oliver's health, his horse, his armour, whether he had been practising and so on. Of course, I refused to answer even though he pleaded with me, telling me he had wagered on my master winning." Giles shrugged. "I told him nothing, nothing at all."

Cranston took his hand away from Eustace's mouth.

"Is that true, squire?"

Eustace, realizing the futility of further protests, nodded meekly.

"It's true," he muttered. "I owe money to the Lombards, to the merchants, to the bankers, to other squires. I thought Sir Oliver would win. I wagered heavily that he would."

"So," Le Marche interrupted, "you thought your own master would lose?"

"Yes, yes," Eustace mumbled, "he was nervous of you. He was infatuated with the Lady Isabella. His wits were not as keen." His voice rose. "But no bribes were given, no understandings reached. There was no conspiracy to harm Sir Robert!"

Cranston shrugged.

"Well, sir, it looks that way," he replied. He looked back towards Giles. "The King's serjeant-at-law may well argue that both of you put your heads together and plotted mischief. You, Giles, put a point on your master's lance; while you, Eustace, damaged your master's destrier so when the charge came it was faulted and led to an accident and Sir Robert's death. Perhaps you did not intend that, just a slight accident. Yet, if such a charge can be proved, both of you will hang at Tyburn."

Eustace now broke into tears, shaking his head. Giles just stood there as if carved out of wood, his face implacable.

"I am no murderer!" he hissed. "I do not like my master. I do not like the silly games he plays, either here or elsewhere. When my indenture is completed, before God, I will be pleased to go."

"But my accusation still stands," the coroner persisted. "It would have taken two men to plot Woodville's downfall in this tournament one putting a point on Le Marche's lance, the other damaging Sir Robert's horse. Gentlemen, you are both under arrest. When I have finished my questions, Brother Athelstan and I will return. If we find nothing new, we will order your immediate committal to Newgate prison or, if His Grace the Duke of Lancaster agrees, perhaps even to the Tower. As you know, Sir Robert was a member of the royal household: an attack on him will be construed as treason."

Sir John turned and nodded at the Master Herald.

"Sir Michael, we will join you in the tavern."

As we walked across the tournament field I thought about what Sir John had said.

"Do you really believe," I said, "that there was a conspiracy between the two squires to kill Woodville? That Eustace wanted his master to lose and brought Giles into it?"

"Of course," the coroner replied, "it's possible. There is little love lost between Le Marche and his squire and Eustace is heavily in debt. A good lawyer could prove it and send both of those young men to their deaths."

He stopped and, turning round, waved at his now disconsolate wife. I dare not look. I wanted to reassert myself, concentrate on the matter in hand. There was villainy here, mischief, a knight had been killed and two young men were now being accused. If the accusations were true they would die horrible deaths. Benedicta would have to wait and the problems she caused, perhaps resolved in confession or counselling by a brother monk.

"Sir John," I began, "accept my apologies for my mind being elsewhere but let us look at this afresh. Let's start from the beginning. You have seen Sir Robert Woodville's horse. What about the rest? The lances he used, his armour?"

Sir John nodded.

"A good place to start, Brother."

Cranston turned and yelled instructions to one of the serjeants-at-arms. He then took me by the arm and led me over to the tilt barrier. After a while the serjeant, with a few companions, brought across the dead knight's armour, horse harness as well as the remains of Le Marche's shattered lances. We scrutinized these, particularly the saddle, for any deliberate cut but we could find no faults. The same was true of the lances; those Woodville and Le Marche had used in the first course were broken. In the second joust, however, only Le Marche had shattered his lance, the unfortunate Woodville never had the opportunity to engage his enemy. Cranston showed how the pointed metal tip could be slid on as easily as a knife goes into a sheath. Finally, the armour; Sir John donned the dead knight's helmet and, his voice booming out from behind the visor, pronounced everything satisfactory.

"Sir John," I asked, "when a knight charges, how does he hold the lance?"

Cranston doffed the helmet and picked up Woodville's battered breastplate, the great death-dealing gash in its centre.

"Look," he explained, "years ago a knight would hold his lance under his right arm but" – he pointed to the lance rest on the right side of the breastplate – "nowadays the lance is couched in the rest which is fastened by rivets to the breastplate." He tapped the loose lance rest with his hand. "Or at least it should be. Woodville's, of course, must have been wrenched loose during the joust."

I examined this carefully, the lance rest had been riveted to the breastplate by two clasps. One of these must have broken free. I remembered Woodville swaying in the saddle at the beginning of the second charge. I turned and shouted across at the serjeant-at-arms.

"Is there an armourer here?"

"Yes, of course."

"Fetch him!"

The soldier scurried off. Sir John and I put the breastplate to one side and inspected everything else but we could find nothing unsound. At last the armourer came, lank and greasy, his face grimed with dirt and sweat. He was not too sure on his feet. The fellow must have thought that as the tournament was cancelled, he could spend the rest of the day swigging tankard after tankard of ale. Nevertheless, he had nimble fingers and, with the tools he carried in a small leather bag, he soon had the lance rest completely free. I looked at the breastplate carefully and I guessed the identity of the murderer, not by any evidence or proof but, as old Father Anselm would say, by the application of pure logic. Cranston watched me.

"What is it, Brother?" he grated. "You have found something new, haven't you?"

"Yes," I replied. "Yes, I have!"

I asked the armourer to stand well out of earshot and I gave my explanation. Cranston, at first, rejected it so I called over the armourer. He listened to what I said and his face paled. He stopped, reluctant to answer but Sir John took him by the wrist, squeezed it and the man stammered that I was probably correct. Sir John then called over the captain of the royal serjeants and told him to saddle Woodville's horse and bring it over. Once he had done this, I asked the serjeant to stand, holding the reins of the still exhausted horse in one hand, his dagger in the other. He, too, soon caught the drift of my questions and his ready answers faltered till he was reduced to a few stumbled words or phrases. Cranston ordered both to keep quiet and bring Woodville's breastplate and horse to the "Swooping Eagle". They followed us across the field, out through the noisy colourful fair, to the tavern where the Master Herald, together with the royal serjeants, now guarded both Sir Oliver Le Marche and the two squires in the huge taproom.

At my request Sir John cleared the room except for Giles, Eustace, Sir Oliver and, of course, the captain of the royal serjeants and the Master Herald. Cranston went up to Le Marche lounging in his chair, a wine cup in his hands. He still had that air of diffidence though he had distanced himself from his squire.

"Sir Oliver," he asked, "tell me, how did you prepare for this tournament? I mean, today."

The knight shrugged.

"I told you. I and members of my household, together with this creature," he nodded towards the squire, "brought my armour and lances down to the tournament field. My pavilion was set up, the Master Herald scrutinized the lances as they were lying on the ground before they were placed on the rack."

"I see. And your armour?"

"On its rest in my pavilion."

"And people could come in and out of there?"

"Of course. Lord John of Gaunt as well as other members of the court came in to see me."

I looked towards Eustace who had now regained some composure.

"And the same at the other end of the lists?" I asked.

He nodded.

"Of course. The same routine. Sir Robert's baggage was brought down in a cart and unloaded. I supervised the setting up of the pavilion, and the armour rest and placed Sir Robert's armour there. The Master Herald examined the lances, the horse and saddle." He shrugged. "The rest you know."

"And, of course," I said, "no knight wears his armour until he has to?"

Sir Oliver laughed.

"Of course, in this heat, you do not go strutting around in armour. After an hour like that you would be too exhausted to climb on your horse, never mind couch your lance! Why? What are you saying, Brother?"

"Captain," I turned to the serjeant-at-arms, "in the tavern yard, there's a cart with the lances from the tournament field, those not used. Get one out and stand with it!"

The fellow hurried off and, at my insistence, we followed soon after. The serjeant stood, rather embarrassed and ill at ease, the huge tilting lance alongside him; the butt on the cobbles and its tip towering above him, its pennant snapping in the early evening breeze.

"Captain," I asked, "is that lance capped or blunted?"

He shrugged.

"I cannot say, Brother. I pulled it from the cart by the handle."

"Well, look up, man!"

He tried to.

"What can you see?"

"Nothing," he mumbled. "It's too high and the pennant at the top obscures my view."

I turned.

"Sir Oliver? Sir John?"

Both narrowed their eyes, squinting up into the sky but neither could give a definite answer. I smiled and led them back into the taproom.

"Now, Sir John," I began, "had a theory that Woodville's death was caused by a conspiracy between the two squires. That was a logical deduction; someone at one end of the lists replaced the points on the lance and someone else damaged Woodville's horse. But now I put a new theory. I believe that the same person who put the point on the lance injured Woodville's horse and also ensured that the lance rest on his armour was deliberately weakened. When Woodville charged the second time the lance slipped and this caused Woodville's death."

The tent fell silent. I noticed Cranston had gone to block the exit.

"Now who could do this? Someone who had access to both pavilions. The only person who had that access," I turned to Sir Michael Lyons who had now lost his bluster as the blood faded from his rubicund face, "was you, Sir Michael Lyons, the Master Herald. I suggest this happened: Le Marche's lances were laid in a row on the ground. When you went to inspect them, you crouched down and quite simply placed metal points on three of the lances."

"That's preposterous!" the Master Herald interrupted. "Anyone could have seen the lances were pointed!"

"No, they wouldn't," I said. "They would only see the point if they were looking for it, our serjeant-at-arms has just proved that." I paused. "Now," I continued, "at the tournament, the lances were placed in the rack, in the same order as they were on the ground. The first lance was blunted, the next three pointed. However, everybody thought the lances had been examined. Now Giles here comes to take one. The lances are fourteen feet long, over twice a man's height." I looked at the squire. "He picked it up by the handle, and when the lance is in the air, who sees the point? He carries it to the rack and leaves it there. The next time he touches it he's hurrying in a frenetic haste; his master has already run a course and he needs a fresh lance. Giles runs up, takes the lance from its rack and gives it to his master. Sir Oliver also does not examine the top of the lance, towering some eleven feet above him in the air. He charges. Meanwhile, at the other end of the field Woodville is also waiting. His lance has no cutting edge, no pointed steel to break the armour. What he does not know is that the lance rest on his breastplate has been weakened by you, Sir Michael, when you went to inspect his armour."

"No!" Le Marche shouted out. "If the lance rest was broken, it was damaged when I struck him!"

"That's what Sir Michael would have liked us to think," Cranston added. "But the lance rest was untouched: it was not dented or even marked, it just swung loose on Woodville's breastplate."

Sir Michael, his face now wet with sweat, shook his head.

"This is foolishness!" he snapped. "The lance rest could have swung loose during the second charge or even the first."

"No, Sir Michael," Cranston replied. "This is what happened. Sir Robert ran the first course. He returned, took the second spear and couched it in his lance rest. He began his charge: the pressure of the couched lance pushed the rest, weakened in the first tourney, askew. Now, Sir Robert, a professional jouster, could cope with a wayward horse but not with a 14-foot ash pole which suddenly seemed to have a life of its own. For a few seconds Sir Robert panics: he drops his shield, the lance is askew, his horse, though troubled, still gallops forward, taking him on to the spearpoint of the charging Le Marche. Sir Robert falls dead off his horse, his armour dented and mauled, except for that death-dealing lance rest. Anyone else noticing it was loose would have put it down as a casualty of the tournament but, as has been said, the lance rest was unmarked."

Sir Michael just stared at me.

"You see, Sir Michael," I observed, "most murderers are caught because of evidence. They carry the bloody knife or take something from their victim's body or were the last person to hold the poisoned cup but the evidence against you is based on logic. You were the only person who had the right and the authority to visit Le Marche's pavilion and Woodville's. You alone had the right to touch both Le Marche's lances and Woodville's armour."

Sir Michael just shook his head wordlessly.

"Oh, yes," I insisted, "I believe you are guilty, Sir Michael. And who would blame you, the Master Herald, responsible for the laws and customs of the tournament? You would have investigated Woodville's death and placed the blame wherever you wanted, probably on one or both of these hapless squires. But my Lord of Gaunt summoned Sir John, you panicked and made your most dreadful mistake. Captain!" I turned to the serjeant-at-arms; "I understand Sir Robert's horse is here. Bring it over together with the saddle!"

The soldier hurried out. Cranston turned his back on Sir Michael

THE CONFESSION OF BROTHER ATHELSTAN

and hummed a little ditty between clenched teeth. The two squires stood like statues, their eyes unblinking, mouths open, hands dangling by their sides. Poor lads! They could hardly believe what they were hearing – they, who only a few minutes earlier were facing the possibility of a dreadful death. I saw Sir Oliver take a step towards the Master Herald.

"Sir," Cranston grunted, "I would be grateful if you sat down and did not make a bad situation worse!"

The serjeant-at-arms returned, his face red with excitement, eager not to miss anything.

"Sir John!" he announced, "the horse is here!"

Cranston nodded and turned to the assembled company.

"Please," he said, "you will follow us."

Outside, Sir Robert's horse, cleaner and a little more refreshed, was waiting patiently in the cobbled yard, its great high-horned saddle on the ground nearby. Along its hindquarters still ran the red, wicked-looking gash Lyons had reported earlier . . .

"Now," Cranston beamed. "Eustace, stand where you would, if the horse was saddled and your master waiting to charge."

Eustace shambled up like a sleepwalker and listlessly held the reins. The horse whinnied affectionately and turned to nudge his hand. Eustace patted it on the neck, murmuring quietly for it to be still.

"Well, Eustace," Cranston said, "let us pretend that your left hand is now holding the reins of the horse and you wish to cut the horse where the scar now is."

Eustace's right hand went out.

"See!" Sir Michael shouted triumphantly. "He could have done it!"

"Now," Cranston continued smoothly, "please put Sir Robert's saddle on the horse."

The destrier moved excitedly, its iron hooves skittering on the uneven cobbles.

"Whoa, boy! Whoa!" Eustace whispered.

The serjeant-at-arms adjusted the saddle; first the blue caparisoned cloth, then the saddle itself, going gingerly under the horse's belly to tie straps and secure buckles.

"Good!" Cranston murmured. "Now, Eustace, pretend you have a knife. Try and cut the horse where the scar is."

The serjeant-at-arms gasped with astonishment. Eustace raised his hand, but half the scar was now hidden by the saddle and the saddle cloth. Sir Michael's mouth opened and closed as Cranston confronted him, pushing him roughly on the shoulder.

"I never believed the horse was cut before it charged," he said. "To do that Eustace would have had to cut him as he held the reins but the horse would have bucked immediately. Nor could he have cut the horse after he had released the reins and Sir Robert began to charge, that would have been very dangerous. The horse would undoubtedly have lashed back and a kick from an iron-shod hoof can be as lethal as a blow from a mace. Finally, however, Eustace could never have made that gash, as you have seen the hindquarters were covered by the saddle and its cloth, yet both of them are unmarked."

"Logic!" I quipped to the now sullen Sir Michael. "Once again, Master Herald, we have logic! The only time Sir Robert's horse could have been cut was after the joust when the saddle had been removed, and you did that. You panicked when Sir John was sent to investigate Woodville's death. You had to make certain one or both of those squires got the blame." I patted the horse. "You created your own evidence by cutting this poor horse and showing it to us. Only you could have done that: Sir Oliver and his squire had been detained in their pavilion, Eustace stayed by his master's corpse."

"Why?" Cranston rasped.

Sir Michael gazed back, eyes hard, face closed.

"Oh, I think I know," I said. "Sir Michael has a lovely daughter. It was nice to see her fought over by two stalwarts but Sir Michael, as you remarked earlier, Sir Oliver and Sir Robert were poor men. Why should your daughter and her lands go to men such as those?"

Sir Michael drew himself up.

"You have no jurisdiction over me, Sir John!" he snapped; "I keep my counsel to myself. I demand by the law and usages of this realm that I be tried by my peers in parliament!"

Suddenly both Cranston and myself were shoved violently aside. Sir Oliver pushed through, his face a mask of fury; before we could stop him, he spat full into the Master Herald's face and, with one gloved hand, struck him on the cheek before taking the gauntlet off and throwing it at the Master Herald's feet.

"Laws and usages!" Sir Oliver hissed. "I challenge you, Sir Michael Lyons, to a duel *à l'outrance*, to the death! And, if you are innocent of Sir Robert Woodville's death, you can prove it on my body."

Sir Michael moved his lips silently. He stared at Le Marche and, without demur, picked up the fallen gauntlet.

"I accept!" he replied.

Cranston strode across and knocked the gauntlet from his hand.

"You will stand trial!" the coroner declared. "God has already delivered you into the hands of the law. Why test His anger further?" Cranston turned and nodded at Le Marche. "You will arrest him. Have him conveyed to the Tower, let my Lord of Gaunt now decide."

Cranston picked up his belongings, stared around the assembled company who just stood like statues, their faces still full of surprise and shock at Cranston's revelations.

"Well?" Cranston barked.

Le Marche grasped Sir Michael's wrist. The two squires went to assist and Cranston left the taproom whilst I hastened behind.

"Sir John," I gasped, "why the hurry?"

The coroner didn't answer until we were out of the tavern yard.

"Sir John," I repeated. "Not even a pause for a bowl of claret or a jug of ale?"

Cranston stared back at the tavern. "I will not drink within earshot of that murdering bastard! Because of him, one good man was killed, another nearly lost his honour, and those two squires could have died at Tyburn!" Cranston's eyes narrowed as he stared at me. "You did well, monk."

"Friar," I corrected. "And don't thank me, my lord coroner, thank Queen Logic. Le Marche is too full of honour to do anything amiss. Oh, he likes killing people but according to the rules – whilst the squires? One's too feckless; and can a man who is seriously considering being a priest plot murder?"

Cranston grinned. "If you have met some of the priests I have, yes! But come back to Cheapside. The Lady Maude and Benedicta will be waiting for us in the 'Holy Lamb of God'!"

"Lady Maude may be," I muttered, "but Benedicta seemed more interested in that young courtier."

Cranston turned, his face solemn as a judge. "Tut! Tut! Tut!" he clicked. "Lust and envy in a friar?"

I just looked away.

"Brother!" Cranston was now grinning from ear to ear.

"What is it, Sir John?"

"Didn't I tell you? That young courtier is a friend of mine. I told him to look after Benedicta."

"But, Sir John, she seemed so attentive back." I coughed with embarrassment. "Not that I have any objection."

Cranston's smile became even more wicked.

"Oh, yes, and I told her that he was a friend who also was very lonely and would she talk to him during the tournament."

I grasped Sir John by his fat elbow. "What's the penalty for striking a coroner, Sir John?"

"A cup of claret but, if it's a priest, then it's two!"

# THE WITCH'S TALE
## Margaret Frazer

*Margaret Frazer is the pen name of the writing team of Mary Pulver Kuhfeld and Gail Bacon. Mary Pulver has another story in this anthology under her own name. Between them they have created the character of Sister Frevisse, a fifteenth-century nun at the priory of St. Frideswide's in Oxfordshire. She first appeared in* The Novice's Tale *(1992), followed by* The Servant's Tale *(1993) and* The Outlaw's Tale.

*The following story was inspired by a notice that Mary Pulver read years ago which said: "Roger, Reeve of Rattlesden, with the whole township of Rattlesden, took away from the coroner of the liberty of St. Edmund, Beatrice Cobb and Beatrice, daughter of said Beatrice, and Elias Scallard, indicted for and guilty of the death of William Cobbe, husband of said Beatrice, and thus prevented the coroner from doing his duty."*

*"I have always wondered," Mary commented, "what sort of fellow William Cobbe was that the whole town would collaborate in the freeing of his murderers."*

> *The gretteste clerkes been noght wisest men,*
> *As whilom to the wolf thus spak the mare.*
> Geoffrey Chaucer, The Reeve's Tale

The night's rain had given way to a softened sky streaked with thin clouds. The air was bright with spring, and the wind had a kindness that was not there yesterday. In the fields the early corn was a haze of green across the dark soil, and along the sheltered southward side of a hedgerow Margery found a dandelion's first yellow among the early grass. The young nettles and wild parsley were up, and in a few days would be far enough along to gather for salad, something fresh after the long winter's stint of dried peas and beans and not enough porridge.

Margery paused under a tree to smile over a cuckoo-pint, bold and blithe before the cuckoo itself was heard this spring. Farther along the hedge a chaffinch was challenging the world, sparrows were squabbling with more vigor than they had had for months, and a muted flash of red among the bare branches showed where a robin was about his business. As she should be about hers, she reminded herself.

She had set out early to glean sticks along the hedgerows but there was not much deadwood left so near the village by this end of winter; her sling of sacking was barely a quarter full, and all of it was wet and would need drying before it was any use. But she must go home. Jack would be coming for his dinner and then Dame Claire at the priory was expecting her.

Though she and Jack were among the village's several free souls and not villeins, Margery's one pride was that she worked with Dame Claire, St. Frideswide's infirmarian. They had met not long after Margery had married Jack and come to live in Priors Byfield. In the untended garden behind the cottage she had found a plant she could not identify despite the herb lore she had had from her mother and grandmother. With her curiosity stronger than her fear, she had gone hesitantly to ask at the nunnery gates if there were a nun who knew herbs. In a while a small woman neatly dressed and veiled in Benedictine black and white had come out to her and kindly looked at the cutting she had brought.

"Why, that's bastard agrimony," she had said. "In your garden? It must have seeded itself from ours. It's hardly common in this part of England and I've been nursing ours along. It's excellent for strengthening the lungs and to ease the spleen and against dropsy, you see."

"Oh, like marjoram. Wild marjoram, not sweet. Only better, I suppose?" Margery had said; and then had added regretfully, "I suppose you want it back?"

Dame Claire had regarded her with surprise. "I don't think so. We still have our own." She looked at the cutting more closely. "And yours seems to be doing very well. Tell me about your garden."

Margery had told her and then, drawn on by Dame Claire's questions, had told what she knew of herbs and finally, to her astonishment, had been asked if she would like to see the priory's infirmary garden. One thing had led on to another, that day and others; and with nothing in common between them except their love of herbs and using them to help and heal, she and Dame Claire had come to work together, Margery gathering wild-growing herbs for Dame Claire's use as well as her own and growing plants in her garden to share with the infirmarian, as Dame Claire shared her own herbs and the book-knowledge Margery had no way of having. And for both of them there was the pleasure of talking about work they both enjoyed, each with someone as knowledgeable as herself.

Now, this third spring of their friendship, the soil would soon be dry enough, God willing, for this year's planting. Margery and Dame Claire had appointed today to plan their gardens together, so that Dame Claire could ask the priory steward to bring back such cuttings as they needed when he went to Lady Day fair in Oxford.

But Margery had to hurry. Her husband Jack wanted both her and his dinner waiting for him when he came into the house at the end of the morning's work, and his displeasure was ugly when she failed him. She had left herself time enough this morning, she was sure, even allowing for her dawdling along the hedgerow; but as she let herself into her garden by the back gate from the field path she saw with a familiar sick feeling that Jack was standing in the cottage's back doorway, fists on his hips and a mean grin on his fleshy mouth. He was back early from hedging – Margery would have sworn he was early – and neither she nor his food was waiting and no excuse would make any difference to what he would do now.

Wearily, Margery set down her bundle on the bench beside the door and looked up at him. It was better to see it coming.

"Y'know better than to be late," he accused. "Y'know I've told you that."

"I can have your dinner on in hardly a moment." She said it without hope. Nothing would help now; nothing ever did.

"I don't want to wait!" Jack put his hand flat between her breasts and shoved her backward. He always began with shoving. "I shouldn't *have* to wait!"

Margery stumbled back. Jack came after her and she turned sideways, to make a smaller target, for all the good it would do her. He shoved her again, staggering her along the path, then caught her a heavy slap to the back of her head so that she pitched forward, her knees banging into the wooden edging of a garden bed, her hands sinking into the muddy soil. She scrambled to be clear of him long enough to regain her feet. So long as she was on her feet he only hit. Once she was down, he kicked. His fists left bruises, sometimes cuts. His feet were worse. There were places in her that still hurt from last time, three weeks ago. From experience she knew that if she kept on her feet until he tired, he did not kick her so long.

But her fear made her clumsy. He was yelling at her now, calling her things she had never been, never thought of being. A blow alongside of her head sent her stumbling to one side, into her herb bed among the straw and burlap meant to protect her best plants through the winter. She scrambled to be out of it but Jack came in after her, crushing his feet down on anything in his way.

Margery cried out as she had not for her own pain. "Stop

it! Leave my plants be!" Jack laughed and stomped one deliberately.

"Them and you both," he said, enjoying himself. "You'll learn to do what you're told."

Margery fumbled in the pouch under her apron and, still scrambling to keep beyond his reach and get out from among her herbs, snatched out a small packet of folded cloth not so big as the palm of her hand. She brandished it at him and screamed, "You stop! You stop or I'll use this!"

For a wonder Jack did stop, staring at her in plain surprise. Then he scoffed, "You've nothing there, y'daft woman!" and grabbed for her.

Margery ducked from his reach, still holding out the packet. "It's bits of you, Jack Wilkins!" she cried. "From when I cut your hair last month and then when you trimmed your nails. Remember that? It's bits of you in here and I've made a spell, Jack Wilkins, and you're going to die for it if you don't leave me alone and get out of my garden!"

"It's not me that's going to die!" he roared, and lurched for her.

After two days of sun the weather had turned back to low-trailing clouds and rain. But it was a gentle, misting rain that promised spring after winter's raw cold, and Dame Frevisse, leaving the guest hall where everything was readied should the day bring guests to St. Frideswide's, paused at the top of the stairs down into the courtyard to look up and let the rain stroke across her face. Very soon the cloister bell would call her into the church with the other nuns for the afternoon's service of Vespers, and she would be able to let go the necessities of her duties as the priory's hosteler to rise into the pleasure of prayer.

But as she crossed the yard toward the cloister door, Master Naylor overtook her. He was the priory's steward, a long-faced man who kept to his duties and did them well but managed to talk with the nuns he served, as little as possible. Bracing herself for something she probably did not want to hear, Frevisse turned to him. "Master Naylor?"

"I thought you'd best know before you went in to Vespers," he said, with a respectful bow of his head. Master Naylor was ever particular in his manners. "There's a man come in to say Master Montfort and six of his men will be here by supper time."

Frevisse felt her mouth open in protest, then snapped it closed. Among her least favorite people in the realm was Master Morys Montfort, crowner for northern Oxfordshire. It was his duty to find out what lay behind unexpected deaths within his jurisdiction, then to bring the malefactor – if any – to the sheriff's attention, and to see to it that whatever fines or confiscations were due King Henry VI were duly collected.

Frevisse had no quarrel with any of that, but Master Montfort had the regrettable tendency to prefer the least complicated solution to any problem and find his facts accordingly. He and Frevisse had long since struck a level of mutual hostility neither was inclined to abate. She was not happy to hear of his coming, and she said, "I trust he's just passing on his way to somewhere else? There's no one dead hereabouts that I've heard of."

Master Naylor shrugged. "It's Jack Wilkins in the village, the day before yesterday. They tolled the village bell for him but you were likely in church for Sext then."

"But why is Montfort coming? Is there doubt about the way this Wilkins died?"

"No doubt. His wife shook a charm at him and cast a spell, and he fell down dead. At least three of their neighbors saw it. I'd not have thought it of Margery," he added. "She's never been known to put her herbs to aught but good, that I've heard."

"*Margery*? Dame *Claire's* Margery?"

"That's her, the herbwife who visits here sometimes."

"Does Dame Claire know?"

"No more than you, I doubt. It was witchcraft and murder certain enough. Montfort will have it done a half hour after he's seen her and talked to her neighbors. He'll probably be on the road to Banbury with her before noon tomorrow and she'll be in the bishop's hands not long after that. I'd have reported it all to Domina Edith come week's end with the other village business." He seemed to think that was all the dealing there needed to be with the matter; Jack and Margery were not among the priory's villeins, and so not his responsibility. The lethal use of witchcraft wasn't usual; on the other hand, all herbwives used spells in their medicines, and it was but a small step to misuse them. He would not have mentioned it except he knew of Margery's link with Dame Claire.

The bell for Vespers began to ring. Frevisse said impatiently, "Where is she being kept?"

Master Naylor pointed through the gateway toward the outer yard. "She's in one of the sheds there. I've two of our men guarding her. She's gagged so it's all right; they're safe. There's nothing to be done."

"Dame Claire will want to see her after Vespers," Frevisse said.

"Please you, tell the guesthall servants for me that Montfort is coming. I have to go."

The Vespers she had expected to enjoy was instead a prolonged discomfort of impatience; and afterwards she had to wait until supper was finished and the nuns went out into the garden for recreation time – the one hour of the day their Benedictine rule allowed for idle talk – before she could tell Dame Claire what was to hand.

"*Margery*?" Dame Claire exclaimed in her deep voice. Disbelief arched her eyebrows high toward her veil. "Killed her husband with witchcraft? I very much doubt it. In fact I don't believe it at all! I want to see her."

That was easily done. Frevisse waited at the foot of the stairs to the prioress' parlor while Dame Claire went up to ask permission. Then they went together, out of the cloister and across the inner yard – Frevisse noting there were lights in the guesthall window so Montfort and his entourage must have arrived – through the gateway to the outer yard where a stable hand, surprised to see them outside the cloister, pointed to the shed at the end of the stables where the prisoner was being kept.

"I should have thought to bring a cloak for her, and something warm to eat," Dame Claire regretted as they went. "These spring nights are cold, and she must be desperate, poor thing."

As Master Naylor had said, two stolid stable men were keeping guard inside the shed door, and Margery was gagged and her hands bound at her waist. But a clay lamp set in the corner on the bare earth floor gave a comforting yellow glow to the rough boards of her prison, and by its light as they stood in the doorway – Dame Claire explaining to the guards that they were come with permission to talk with Margery – Frevisse saw that Margery had several blankets, a cloak, and a straw-stuffed pillow to make her a bed along the farther wall, and that beside it were a pot of ale and various plates with three different kinds of bread and parts of two cheeses. Frevisse knew that in such cases as Margery the nunnery provided a blanket and an occasional piece of bread. So who had done this much for Margery?

Margery herself had risen to her feet as the nuns entered. Despite her crime, she was much as Frevisse had remembered her, a middling sort of woman – of middling build, middling young, middling tall, with nothing particular about her, except – to judge by her eyes above the gag – that she was frightened. As well she should be.

Dame Claire finished with the men, and crossed the shed to her, Frevisse following. As Margery curtseyed, Dame Claire said, "Let me loose your hands so you can take off the gag. I've told them you won't do anything. We want to talk to you."

Dame Claire freed Margery's hands, and gratefully she unknotted the cloth behind her head. "Thank you, my lady," she said hoarsely.

"Have something to drink." Dame Claire indicated the ale kindly. "Have they let you eat?"

Margery nodded over the rim of the clay pot as she drank thirstily. When she had finished, she said, "They've been as kind as might be. And village folk have brought me things." She gestured at her bed and food and lamp. She was clearly tired as well as frightened, worn out by too many strange things happening to her. "But I hoped you'd come, so I could tell you why I didn't come t'other day when I said I would."

"I wondered what happened to you," Dame Claire answered. "But I never thought this."

Margery hung her head. "Nor did I."

"They say you killed your husband."

Margery nodded. "I did that."

"Margery, no!" Dame Claire protested.

"Jack came at me, the way he's done ever since we married whenever I've not done right. But this time we were in my garden and he was trampling my plants." It plainly mattered very much to her that Dame Claire understand. "I told him to stop but he didn't care, and I – lost my temper."

"You truly did kill him?" Dame Claire asked, still disbelieving it.

"Oh, yes. Sure as sure. I didn't know the spell would work that way but it did. Took him off afore he could hit me again, just like that."

"What – exactly – did you do?" Frevisse asked carefully. Murder, serious enough in itself, was worse for the murderer when done by witchcraft. Charms and spells were simply part of healing; every herbwife knew some. But if they were turned to evil, they became part of the Devil's work and a matter for the Church as well as lay law.

Margery looked at Frevisse with mingled shyness and guilt, and did not answer.

"Tell us, please," Dame Claire urged. "Dame Frevisse and I want to help you."

"There's no help for me!" Margery said in surprise. "I killed him."

"How?" Frevisse persisted.

Margery hung her head. She twisted her hands in her apron and, low-voiced with embarrassment, said, "I'd been saving bits of him this while. Hair, you know, and his nail cuttings."

"Margery! That's wicked!" Dame Claire exclaimed.

"I know it!" Margery said piteously. "But I was only going to make a small charm. When I'd money for the wax to make the figure. Not kill him, like, but weaken his arm so he couldn't hit me so hard. That's all I wanted to do. Just weaken him."

"But you hadn't made the figure yet?" Frevisse asked. Margery shook her head dumbly. Frevisse pressed, "What did you do then, that you think you killed him?"

"I had the – things in a little packet. I held it up and told him what it was and that he'd better stop what he was doing. That I'd made a charm and I'd kill him if he didn't stop."

"But you hadn't made a charm yet. You said so," said Dame Claire.

"That I hadn't. But I meant to. I really did." She looked anxiously from one nun to the other. "If I make confession and do penance before they hang me, I won't have to burn in hell, will I? Not if I'm truly penitent?"

"Surely not," Dame Claire reassured her.

"But if you didn't have the charm, what happened?" Frevisse asked.

Margery shuddered. "Jack kept hitting and shoving. I knew he'd near to kill me, once he had his hands on me, and I'd never have another chance to make a charm against him, not now he knew. I was that frighted, I grabbed the first words that came to me, thinking to scare him off with them. I didn't even think what they were. I just said them at him and shook the packet like I was ill-wishing him. I just wanted to keep him back from me, I swear that's all. Just hold him off as long as might be."

She broke off, closing her eyes at the memory.

"And then?" Dame Claire prompted.

Faintly, tears on her cheeks, Margery said, "He stopped. All rigid like I'd hit him with a board. He stared at me with his mouth open and then grabbed his chest, right in the center, and bent over double. He was gasping like he hurt, or couldn't catch his breath. Then he fell over. In the path, away from my herbs. He curled up and went on gasping and then – he stopped. He just stopped and was dead."

A little silence held them all. Frevisse was aware of the two men at her back, and knew that everything they were hearing would be told later all around the nunnery and village.

"Margery," Dame Claire said, "you can't wish a man dead. Or rather, you can wish it, but it won't happen, not that simply."

"But it did," Margery said.

And there would probably be no convincing anyone otherwise. But for Dame Claire's sake, Frevisse asked, "What was it you said to him? A spell?"

Margery nodded. "The one for – "

Master Naylor interrupted her with a firm rap on the door frame. He inclined his head respectfully to Frevisse and Dame Claire, and said, "The crowner wants to see her now."

"So late?" Dame Claire protested.

"He hopes to finish the matter tonight so he can be on his way at earliest tomorrow. He has other matters to see to," Master Naylor explained.

Matters more important than a village woman who was surely guilty, Frevisse thought. A woman who was the more inconvenient because she would have to be sent for examination before a bishop before she could be duly hanged.

"We'll come with her," said Dame Claire.

Master Montfort had been given the guesthall's best chamber, with its large bed and plain but sufficient furnishings. The shutters had been closed against the rainy dusk, the lamps lighted, and at a table against the farther wall his clerk was hunched over a parchment, quill in hand and inkwell ready.

The crowner himself stood by the brazier in the corner, his hands over its low warmth. He was short in the leg for the length of his body, and had begun to go fat in his middle, but to his own mind any shortcomings he might have – and he was not convinced that he had any – were amply compensated for by the dignity of his office; he no more than glanced over his shoulder as Master Naylor brought Margery in, then sharpened his look on Frevisse and Dame Claire following her. A flush spread up his florid face and over the curve of his balding head.

"You can stay, Naylor," he said. "But the rest of you may go." Belatedly, ungraciously, he added, "My ladies."

With eyes modestly downcast and her hands tucked up either sleeve of her habit, Frevisse said, "Thank you, but we'll stay. It would not be seemly that Margery be here unattended."

She had used that excuse in another matter with Master Montfort. He had lost the argument then, and apparently chose not to renew it now. His flush merely darkened to a deeper red as he said tersely, "Then stand to one side and don't interfere while I question her."

They did so. Master Montfort squared up in front of Margery and announced in his never subtle way, "I've questioned some several of your neighbors already and mean to see more of them before I'm to bed tonight so you may as well tell what you have to tell straight out and no avoiding it. Can you understand that?"

Margery did not lift her humbly bowed head. "Yes, m'lord."

"You killed your husband? Now, mind you, you were heard and seen so there's no avoiding it."

Margery clearly had no thought of avoiding anything. While the clerk's pen scratched busily at his parchment, recording her words, she repeated what she had already told Frevisse and Dame Claire. When she had finished, Master Montfort rocked back on his heels, smiling grimly with great satisfaction. "Very well said, and all agreeing with your neighbors' tales. I think there's no need for more."

"Except," Dame Claire said briskly, knowing Master Montfort would order her to silence if she gave him a chance, "I doubt her husband died of anything more than apoplexy."

The crowner turned on her. In a tone intended to quell, he said, "I beg your pardon, my lady?"

Dame Claire hesitated. Frevisse, more used to the crowner's bullying, said helpfully, "Apoplexy. It's a congestion of the blood – "

Master Montfort's tongue caught up with his indignation. "I know what it is!"

Frevisse turned to Master Naylor. As steward of the priory's properties he had far better knowledge of the villeins than she did. "What sort of humor was this Jack Wilkins? Hot-tempered or not?"

"Hot enough it's a wonder he was in so little trouble as he was," Master Naylor said. "He knocked a tooth out of one of his neighbors last week because he thought the man was laughing at him. The man wasn't, being no fool, but Jack Wilkins in a temper didn't care about particulars. It wasn't the first time he's made trouble with his temper. And he was known to beat his wife."

"Choleric," said Dame Claire. "Easily given to temper. People of that sort are very likely to be struck as Jack Wilkins was, especially in the midst of one of their furies. He was beating his wife – "

"As he had every right to do!" Master Montfort declared.

As if musing on his own, Master Naylor said, "There's a feeling in the village that he did it more often and worse than need be."

But Dame Claire, refusing to leave her point, went on over his words, "– and that's heavy work, no matter how you go about it. Then she defied him, maybe even frightened him when she said her spell – "

"And down he fell dead!" the crowner said, triumphant. "That's what I'm saying. It was her doing and that's the end of it."

"What was the spell she said?" Frevisse interjected. "Has anyone asked her that?"

Master Montfort shot her an angry look; determined to assert himself, he swung back on Margery. "That was my next question, woman. What did you actually say to him? No, don't look at anyone while you say it! And say it slow so my clerk can write it down."

Eyes turned to the floor, voice trembling a little, Margery began to recite, "Come you forth and get you gone . . ."

If Master Montfort was expecting a roaring spell that named devils and summoned demons, he was disappointed. The clerk scratched away busily as Margery went through a short verse that was nevertheless quite apparently meant to call the spirit out of the body and cast it away. Part way through, Dame Claire looked startled.

In the pause after Margery finished speaking, the clerk's pen scritched on. Master Montfort, ever impatient, went to hover at his shoulder and, as soon as he had done, snatched the parchment away. While he read it over, Frevisse leaned toward Dame Claire, who whispered briefly but urgently in her ear. Before Frevisse could respond, Master Montfort demanded at Margery, "That's it? Just that?" Margery nodded. Master Montfort glared at his clerk and recited loudly, "Come you forth . . ."

The man's head jerked up to stare with near-sighted alarm at his master. The crowner went on through the spell unheeding either his clerk's dismay or Master Naylor's movement of protest. Margery opened her mouth to say something, but Frevisse silenced her with a shake of her head, while Dame Claire pressed a hand over her own mouth to keep quiet.

When Master Montfort had finished, a tense waiting held them all still, most especially the clerk. When nothing happened after an impatient minute, Master Montfort rounded on Margery. "How long is this supposed to take?"

Margery fumbled under his glare. "My husband – he – almost on the instant, sir. But – "

"Spare me your excuses. If it worked for you, why didn't it work for me? Because I didn't have clippings of his hair or what?"

Keeping her voice very neutral, Frevisse suggested, "According to Robert Mannying in his *Handling Sin*, a spell has no power if said by someone who doesn't believe in it. Margery uses herbs and spells to help the villagers. She believes in what she does. You don't. Do you believe in your charm, Margery? This one that you said at your husband?"

"Yes, but – "

"She's a witch," Master Montfort interrupted. "And whatever good you claim she's done, she's used a spell to kill a man this time, and her husband at that. Who knows what else she's tried." He rounded on Margery again and said in her face, "There's a question for you, woman. Have you ever used this spell before?"

Margery shrank away from him but answered, "Surely. Often and often. But – "

"God's blood!" Master Montfort exclaimed. "You *admit* you've murdered other men?"

"Margery!" Frevisse interposed, "*What* is the spell *for*?"

Driven by both of them, Margery cried out, "It's for opening the bowels!"

A great quiet deepened in the room. Margery looked anxiously from face to face. Frevisse and Dame Claire looked carefully at the floor. Red darkened and mounted over Master Montfort's countenance again. Master Naylor seemed to struggle against choking. The clerk ducked his head low over his parchment. Nervously Margery tried to explain. "I make a decoction with gill-go-on-the-ground, and say the spell over it while it's brewing, to make it stronger. It provokes urine, too, and . . . and . . ." She stopped, not understanding their reactions, then finished apologetically, "They were the first words that came into my head, that's all. I just wanted to fright Jack off me, and those were the first words that came. I didn't mean for them to kill him."

Master Montfort, trying to recover lost ground, strangled out, "But they did kill him, didn't they? That's the long and short of it, isn't it?"

Margery started to nod, but Frevisse put a stilling hand on her arm; and Dame Claire said, "It's a better judgement that her husband died not from her words but from his own choler, like many another man before him. It wasn't Margery but his temper that did for him at the last."

Master Montfort glared at her. "That's women's logic!" he snapped. "His wife warns him she has bits of him to use against him, and cries a spell in his face, and he drops down dead, and it's *his* fault? Where's the sense of that? No! She's admitted her guilt. She was seen doing it. There's no more questioning needed. Naylor, keep her until morning. Then I'll take her in charge."

The twilight had darkened to deep dusk but the rain had stopped as they came out of the guest hall. Master Naylor steadied Margery by her elbow as they went down the steps to the yard. No matter how much she had expected her fate, she seemed dazed by the crowner's pronouncement, and walked numbly where she was taken. Frevisse and Dame Claire followed with nothing to say, though Frevisse at least seethed with frustration at their helplessness and Montfort's stupidity. Even the acknowledgement of the *possibility* of doubt from him would have been something.

Margery's two guards were waiting at the foot of the steps in the spread of light from the lantern hung by the guest hall door. They stood aside, then followed as the silent group made their way around the rain-puddles among the cobbles to the gateway to the outer yard. Beyond it was the mud and deeper darkness of the outer yard where the lamplight showing around the ill-fitted door of Margery's prison shed was the only brightness. Busy with her feet and anger, Frevisse did not see the knot of people there until one of them swung the shed door open to give them more light, and Master Naylor said in surprise, "Tom, what brings you out? And the rest of you?"

Frevisse could see now that there were seven of them, four women and three men, all from the village. The women curtseyed quickly to her, Dame Claire, and Master Naylor as they came forward to Margery. Crooning to her like mothers over a hurt child, they enveloped her with their kindness; and one of them, with an arm around her waist, soothed, "There now, Margery-girl, we can see it didn't go well. You come in-by. We've something warm for you to eat." Together they drew her into the shed, leaving the men to front the priory-folk.

Tom, the village reeve and apparently their leader in this, ducked his head to her and Dame Claire, and again to Master Naylor before he said, "She's to go then? No help for it?"

"No help for it," Master Naylor agreed. "The crowner means to take her with him when he goes in the morning."

The men nodded as if they had expected no less. But Tom said, "It makes no difference that there's not a body in the village but's glad to have Jack gone? He was a terror and no mistake and she didn't do more than many of us have wanted to."

"I can't argue that, but it changes nothing," Master Naylor said. "Margery goes with the crowner in the morning, and be taken before the bishop for what she's done."

"She didn't do anything!" Dame Claire said with the impatience she had had to curb in Master Montfort's presence.

Frevisse agreed. "This Jack died from his own temper, not from Margery's silly words!"

"It was apoplexy," said Dame Claire. "People who indulge in ill temper the way Jack Wilkins did are like to die the way Jack Wilkins did."

"If you say so, m'lady," Tom said in a respectful voice. "But Margery cried something out at him, and Jack went down better than a poled ox. God keep his soul," he added as an after-thought, and everyone crossed themselves. Jack Wilkins was unburied yet; best to say the right things for he would make a wicked ghost.

"It wasn't even a spell to kill a man. Margery says so herself."

"Well, that's all right then," Tom said agreeably. "And a comfort to Margery to know it wasn't her doing that killed Jack, no matter what the crowner says. But what we've come for is to ask if some of us can stand Margery's guard tonight, for friendship's sake, like, before she goes."

Dim with distance and the mist-heavy dusk, the bell began to call to Compline, the nuns' last prayers before bed. Frevisse laid a hand on Dame Claire's arm, drawing her away. Master Naylor could handle this matter. There was nothing more for the two of them to do here. Better they go to pray for Margery's soul. And Jack Wilkins', she thought belatedly.

Watery sunshine was laying thin shadows across the cloister walk next morning as Frevisse went from chapter meeting toward her duties. She expected Master Montfort and his men and Margery would be gone by now, ridden away at first light; and she regretted there had been nothing that could be done to convince anyone but herself and Dame Claire that Margery had not killed her lout of a husband with her poor little spell and desperation. But even Margery had believed it, and would do penance for it as if her guilt were real, and go to her death for it.

Frevisse was distracted from her anger as she neared the door into the courtyard by the noise of Master Montfort's raised voice, the words unclear but his passion plain. She glanced again at the morning shadows. He was supposed to be miles on his way by this time. She opened the door from the cloister to the courtyard.

Usually empty except for a passing servant and the doves around the well, the yard was half full of villagers crowded to the foot of the guest hall steps. Master Montfort stood above them there, dressed for riding and in a rage.

"You're still saying there's no trace of her?" he ranted. Frevisse stopped where she was with a sudden hopeful lift of her spirits. "You've been searching the wretched place since dawn! My men have scoured the fields for miles! *Someone* has to know where she is! Or if she's truly bolted, we have to set the hounds to her trail!"

Even from where she was, Frevisse could see the sullen set of every villein's shoulders. But it was clear that the main thrust of his words was at Master Naylor, standing straight-backed at the head of the villeins, deliberately between them and the crowner's rage. With a hard-edged patience that told Frevisse he had been over this already more than once, he answered in his strong, carrying voice, "We have no hounds to set to her trail. This is a priory of nuns. They're not monks; they don't ride to hunt here."

Standing close behind the steward, Tom the reeve growled so everyone could hear, "And where she went, you wouldn't care to follow!"

Master Montfort pointed at him, furious. "You! You're one of the fools who slept when you were supposed to be guarding her! Dreaming your way to perdition while she walks off free as you please! What do you mean, 'where she went'? Hai, man, what do you mean?"

"I mean it wasn't a natural sleep we had last night!" Tom answered loudly enough to send his words to the outer yard, to Master Montfort's entourage and a number of priory servants clustered just beyond the gateway. Frevisse saw them stir as he spoke. "Aye, it wasn't a natural sleep and there's not one of us will say it was. We fell to sleep all at once and together, between one word and another. That's not natural! No more than Jack Wilkins falling down dead was natural. We're lucky it was only sleep she did to us! That's what I say! And anybody who tried to follow her is asking for what happens to him!"

Behind and around him the other villeins glanced at each other and nodded. One of the bolder men even spoke up, "Tom has the right of it!"

A woman – Frevisse thought she was one of four who had come to Margery last night – said shrilly, "You can't ask any decent man to follow where she's gone!"

Master Montfort pointed at her. "You know where she's gone? You admit you know?"

"I can make a fair guess!" the woman flung back. "Flown off to her master the devil, very like, and you'll find no hound to go that trail!"

"Flown off?" Master Montfort raged. "*Flown* off? I'm supposed to believe that? Naylor, most of these folk are the priory's villeins! Warn them there's penalties for lying to the king's crowner and hiding murderers. She's around here somewhere!"

"If she is, we haven't found her yet for all our searching," Master Naylor said back. "Twice through the village is enough for one day, and there's no sign where she might have gone across country. As you say, these are our villeins and I can say I've never known them given to such lying as this. Maybe they've the right of it. You said yourself last night she was a witch, and now she seems to have proved it!"

Master Montfort stared at him, speechless with rage.

"What we say," shouted another of the men, "is you're welcome to come search us house to house yourself, you being so much smarter than the rest of us. But if you find her, you'd better hope she doesn't treat you like she did her husband!"

There was general angry laughter among all the villeins at that; and some from beyond the gateway. For just a moment Master Montfort lost the stride of his anger, paused by the man's words. Then he gathered himself together and rounded on Master Naylor. With a scorn that he meant to be withering, he said, "I've greater matters to see to than hunting down some petty village witch. She was in your charge, Naylor, and the loss is to you, not to me. There'll be an amercement to pay for losing the king's prisoner, and be assured I'll see the priory is charged it to the full!"

"I'm assured you will," Master Naylor returned tersely, his scorn stronger than Master Montfort's.

For a balanced moment he and the crowner held each other's eyes. Then Master Naylor gestured sharply for the villeins to move back from the foot of the steps. Crowding among themselves, they gave ground. Master Montfort's mouth opened, then closed, and with great, stiff dignity he descended, passed in front of them to his horse being held for him beyond the gateway, and mounted. He glared around at them one final time and, for good measure, across the courtyard at Frevisse still standing in the doorway, then jerked his horse around and went.

No one moved or spoke until the splash and clatter of his going, and his entourage after him, were well away. And even then the response among them all seemed no more than a long in-drawn breath and a slow release of tension. Heads turned to one another, and Frevisse saw smiles, but no one spoke. There were a few chuckles but no more as they all drifted out of the gateway, some of them nodding to Master Naylor as they passed him. He nodded back, and did not speak either; and when they were gone, he stayed where he was, waiting for Frevisse to come to him.

She did, because there in the open courtyard they could most easily talk without chance of being overheard so long as they kept their voices low. "Master Naylor," she said as she approached him.

He inclined his head to her. "Dame Frevisse."

"I take it from what I heard that Margery Wilkins escaped in the night?"

"It seems her guards and the friends who came to keep her company slept. When they awoke this dawn, she was gone."

"And cannot be found?"

"We've searched the village twice this morning, and Master Montfort's men have hunted the near countryside."

"They think she used her witch-powers to escape?"

"So it would seem. What other explanation is there?"

"I can think of several," Frevisse said dryly.

Master Naylor's expression did not change. "Just as you and Dame Claire could think of some other reason for Jack Wilkins' death besides his wife's words striking him down."

"And the fine to the priory for your carelessness in losing your witch?"

"It was villeins who had the watch of her and lost her. I mean to make an amercement on the village to help meet the fine our crowner will surely bring against the priory."

"Won't there be protest over that?"

"Villeins always protest over paying anything. But in this I think there'll be less arguing than in most. She's their witch. Let them pay for her. Dear-bought is held more dear."

"They still truly believe she killed her husband?" Frevisse asked. "Despite what we told them last night, they still believe she's a witch with that much power?"

"What else can they believe?" the steward asked quietly in return. "They saw her do it."

"What do you believe?" Frevisse asked, unable to tell from his neutral expression and voice.

Instead of an answer to that, Master Naylor said, "I think a straw-filled loft is not an uncomfortable place to be for a week and more this time of year. And that by the time summer comes there'll be a new herb-wife in the village, maybe even with the same first name but someone's widowed sister from somewhere else, freeborn like Margery was and no questions asked."

"And after all, witchcraft in itself is no crime or sin," Frevisse said. "The wrong lies in the use it's put to."

"And all the village knows Margery has ever used her skills for good, except this one time, if you judge what she did was ill. All her neighbors judge it wasn't," Master Naylor said solemnly.

"They mean to keep her even if it costs them?" Frevisse asked.

"They know she's a good woman. And now that they're certain she has power, she's not someone they want to lose."

"Or to cross," Frevisse said.

Master Naylor came as near to a smile as he ever came, but only said, "There'll likely be no trouble with anyone beating her ever again."

# FATHER HUGH AND THE DEADLY SCYTHE
## Mary Monica Pulver

*When not writing with Gail Bacon as Margaret Frazer, Mary Pulver Kuhfeld
has written a number of crime novels and stories under her maiden name. She
is perhaps best known for her series about police sergeant Peter Brichter, a
dashing detective with a Porsche to match. She has written five novels featuring
his adventures, starting with* Knight Fall.

*The following is her first story about Father Hugh of Paddington, a rather
individualistic fifteenth-century priest who is determined to root sin out from his
parishioners, no matter how he does it.*

The man's death was no accident. That was clear from the first
report, given by an ashen-faced Austin, our steward's assistant.
Austin had been on his way to Deerfield Village to remind our reeve
that tomorrow the women were required in the meadow to rake the
hay the men cut today, when he saw the body.

"Still warm he was," gasped Austin, wiping his broad face with
his hand, "but with all the blood drained out of him, his arm off at
the elbow and his throat open to heaven like a mouth screaming for
vengeance."

Austin, for all his low birth, had a taste for a fancy turn of speech,
acquired from our steward, the indispensable John Freemantle.

"Where is John?" I asked.

"Gone to Banbury, to buy that ambling mare Will Frazee has for
sale," said Sister Harley.

"Oh, that's right." In my excitement I had forgotten. "Where does
the body lie?"

"In the ditch along the fallow field."

"Has the hue and cry been raised?"

"Yes, Madame. There's blood all along the edge of the fallow field
where I found him, great smears, like he was a beast of the forest,
chased down – " Austin stopped, goggling at the memory, wiped

again at his sweating face, then staggered and would have fallen if
Sister Harley had not pushed a stool under him as he went down.
We were in my quarters in the cloister, where Austin had come with
the horrible news.

"You're sure it's Frick Cotter lying dead?" I asked.

"Oh, yes, madam," muttered Austin, wiping his wet hand on his
heavy mat of auburn hair. "There's no mistaking that nose."

Frick was a familiar figure in the village. He owned no strips
in the three big fields around it, and his cottage was one of the
humblest. He kept body and soul together by means honest and
less so, hiring himself out for odd jobs, growing peas and beans in
the tiny garden behind his cottage, collecting and selling wood from
the forest, poaching the occasional rabbit or stealing an egg.

But his main occupation was gossip. For all they talk about
women's tongues going on wheels, there was none so quick to sniff
out a tale or spread it to every ear as Frick. And as if to advertise
his failing, he was the owner of the biggest nose in Oxfordshire.

"Still, poor old Frick," sighed Sister Harley, handing Austin a
drink of wine – in my good silver chalice, I noticed, but I said
nothing. Harley had seen Austin's need and taken the first cup at
hand, which was fine; Austin was a good man.

Sister Harley touched a long, slender finger to her long, slender
nose. "I wonder what story he told to bring this on himself?"

"What do you mean?"

"Murder, of course."

"Surely it was a robbery," I objected. "After all, he was out of the
village and on the high road."

"Rob old Frick?" said Harley. "Of what? He's one of the poorest
men for miles around!"

"But a highway robber, a stranger to these parts, might not know
that," I said.

"You had only to look at Frick to know he was very poor," said
Harley. "No, it was someone driven to fury by Frick's tongue."

"I'm not so sure," said Austin, "it wasn't a knife did this, but
something bigger. A sword, maybe."

"Sword?" Sister Harley turned her aristocratic face to Austin. "But
no one in the village has a sword."

"Nor the ordinary robber," added Austin. "By the cut, the blade
was fresh and keen, not some chipped castoff a robber might carry.
This blade would be swung from a noble hand."

An ugly silence fell in the room. England in these unhappy times
needed a strong man to lead her, but our Henry VI was made of
straw. Local bullies rose and everywhere defied the helpless law. Our

local bully was Lord Ranulf Fitzralph. Rich and with friends at court, he took what he wanted and none dared gainsay him. From what we all knew of him, it was not beyond reason that he might amuse himself by killing a villein.

"But this means he's gone too far at last," I said. "Sister Harley, send word that I want to see John Freemantle the instant he returns. We will send him to the Sheriff and then with a letter to the bishop." For Ranulf could defy the Sheriff, defy even the King; but no man would dare defy the Church. And this was Church business; Frick Cotter was, like every villein in Deerfield Village, the property of Deerfield Abbey. By killing him, Lord Ranulf now found himself at the mercy of not just me, as abbess, or even the bishop, but the Church itself, Vicar of Christ on earth.

It was two hours later that the abbey Mass priest, Father Hugh of Paddington, asked to see me. He is a small, brown fellow, rather common, but he knows the ways of the village, and said he had some information about Frick Cotter to impart.

"My lady," he said from his humble kneeling position, "I am most distressed to report that Frick Cotter was murdered by someone in the village."

"Nay, Father Hugh; Austin reports the wounds on the body would indicate a sword killed him. We need to raise our eyes to Sir Ranulf to find the doer of this wickedness."

Father Hugh rose – the floor of my quarters is tile, nearly as hard as stone, so I require no one to remain kneeling long. "Ah, I wish it were that easy. But I have seen men done to death by the sword, and a closer look at Frick's body tells a different tale."

I recalled that he had in truth seen men injured in battle, while Austin had not. I asked, "What weapon do you think did this, if not a sword?"

"A billhook, perhaps. But I think it was more likely a scythe."

The workers in the meadow today had been cutting hay with their scythes. I had heard some of them whistling merrily as they departed along the road home about half an hour before Austin left for the village – to find Frick's body, freshly killed.

"But surely not," I said. "No one of our own villeins could do a murder." Especially when I had my heart so firmly settled on at last ridding the area of Lord Ranulf. "Who among them would do such a thing?"

"I believe, my lady, that old Frick's gossiping ways may have caught up with him."

I stared at him. "Then you know who it was?"

"No, no, not yet. But it appears Frick was not such a gossip as we thought. That is, for a price, he would not tell all that he knew."

"What do you mean?"

"I mean, he would go to someone whose secret he had discovered, and say that for two cabbages, or a loaf of bread, or a chicken, he would not tell anyone that this someone had feigned sickness to get out of his boonwork plowing in the abbey fields."

"Who feigned sickness?" I demanded.

"No one, Madame," replied Hugh, not covering in time the smile tweaking his mouth; "I but used that as an example. But I have learned two secrets Frick knew about, and that the owners of the secrets were angry with him. It's near Vespers now, too late to continue my search. But with your leave, I will go back in the morning and see what more there is to learn about Frick's little enterprise."

"You think it was one of these two who killed Frick, to keep their secret from being told?"

"Perhaps. Or perhaps it was another, whose secret I don't as yet know."

"But if you can't discover all the secrets, how will you know who did this wicked thing?"

"Madame, I shall trust God to show me the truth."

I said very well and dismissed him, thinking Father Hugh an unlikely sort of vehicle for trusting in. He is popular among our villeins, who find him more approachable than their own priest, but that's because he is shabby, clumsy and unlearned, just like them.

The next day Father Hugh came to me about mid-afternoon with a report. I summoned Sister Mildred, in charge of lay labor, and Sister Harley, my chaplain, to hear it with me.

"I feel there are but three men who might have done this deed," said Father Hugh. "One is Jack Strong. He's the fellow who claimed a bit of waste near the forest and fenced it and has been raising parsnips in it this year. And enriching the soil with the bones and other scraps of the deer he and his son Will have been poaching."

"Jack Strong has been poaching deer?" said Sister Harley, surprised.

"Yes, of course he has," I interjected. "Sister Mildred told me about it months ago. He's only taken three in the past two years, and for all the hunting King Henry does, he'll not miss those few. Though if Jack takes another before winter, I'll have to warn him I know about it. Go on, Master Hugh."

"The second is Tiffany Dickins."

Sister Mildred said, "He's father to Christopher, Madame, who ran away right after Michaelmas last year." Villeins may buy their freedom if they can save the money, or they may run away to a city, where, if they manage to survive a year and a day, they gain the status of citizen, making them free.

Christopher had taken this second choice, and was but two months from his year-day, if he had not by now starved to death, or fallen victim to one of the diseases that infest the cities, or gone to another manor and accepted anew the burden of villeinage for a bit of land and something to eat.

"Have you news of Christopher?" asked Harley.

Father Hugh nodded. "Christopher slips home to visit his family every so often. He was here just last Sunday."

"Why the fool!" I said, because should anyone catch him outside the city, he would forfeit the time he spent there, and must begin again. We could have sent men searching after him, but Christopher was a lazy lout and it would be a waste to send good labor to go after bad – and he would just have run again at first chance. "He ran to Oxford, I believe?"

"Yes," nodded Father Hugh. "But he's finding it difficult to make a living. He comes home to be fed and to court Hob's daughter Megan."

"Does he now!" said Sister Mildred. "We'll have to put a stop to that. It's all very well for him to run off, but I'll not have him trying to steal away Megan!"

I agreed; the girl was a talented weaver and a hard worker, a credit to her family. "Besides, she's only thirteen." I frowned. "You don't think it was Christopher who set upon Frick?"

"No, Christopher left Deerfield Sunday evening. But someone saw Frick speaking to Chris' father this morning as he was coming out to the meadow with his scythe, and said Tiffany walked off with a face like a thundercloud. It may be that Frick saw Christopher during his last visit and offered to keep the news from us, for a price."

"That wicked old eavesdropper; I wish God had struck him blind for a Peeping Tom!" said Mildred.

"Yes, a blind snoop is much less dangerous than a sighted one," said Sister Harley. "And if God had struck, perhaps no mortal would have put his soul in danger by killing him. And then Frick, living his allotted days, might have gone to judgement from his bed, with a priest to shrive him, instead of leaping into eternity with his sins hot and smoking on him. God have mercy on us all, though His ways are ever mysterious." And we all crossed ourselves and hoped to die peacefully in our beds, properly shriven.

"I begin to see that my policy of keeping silent about transgressions among our villeins is not a wise practice," I remarked. "Who is your third suspect, Master Hugh?"

"Evan Harmony. He's been . . . er, delving Toby's wife. Or so Frick hinted to someone."

"Oh, my," I said. Toby, the village blacksmith, was typical of the breed, large and strong, but Toby came also equipped with a violent temper. Evan Harmony wasn't small or frail, but he was no match for our blacksmith. Killing Frick Cotter might seem the obvious way to keep him from telling our blacksmith Evan had made a cuckold of him.

"Perhaps we should look at the blacksmith himself," I said. "If Frick went to Toby with his tale, Toby might have killed him to keep the news from spreading. Or, if Toby didn't believe him, he might not take kindly to someone telling such tales about his wife."

But Father Hugh shook his head. "No, Toby is the sort who uses his hands, or, at worst, reaches for his hammer. A scythe is an awkward weapon for someone not used to it. I think, madam, ladies, our murderer is Tiffany, Jack or Evan, one."

"So which is it?" asked Mildred.

Father Hugh lifted his shoulders. "I don't know," he said simply. "They came home separately and no one saw them along the road. Jack has a bloodstained tunic in his house, but he says it's from the deer he poached – and there's almost half a deer hanging from the rafters in that shed behind his house. Tiffany has a brand new haft on his scythe, but he says he cracked it yesterday in the field and came home a little early to replace it. There are three witnesses who say he left the meadow early, but none of them noticed a cracked haft. Evan knocked Frick down after Mass last Sunday and said if he ever caught him alone he'd kill him. Half the village saw and heard it – some cheered. Frick was not a popular person."

"But you don't know who actually did it?" I asked.

"No, my lady. And I can't think of a way of finding out."

There the matter stood, and would stand, we thought. Then, late in the afternoon, Father Hugh sent word he would like me to come to the stables, as he was about to accuse the murderer.

"Did he say who it is?" I said, rising.

"Nay, madame," said Austin. "He's put on his best robe and carrying the good processional cross, and talks as if he's expecting a sign from heaven. And he's sure enough that he'll get one that he's sent for a beadle to detain the guilty party for your judgement."

Concerned because I do not like anyone, most especially a priest, to trifle with miracles – there is such a thing as getting more than you ask for – and angry with my little priest for rousing my concern, I left the cloister and went into the inner courtyard, where I saw Sister Harley just coming out of the guesthouse. I gestured at her to accompany me. We went out the double wooden doors that led to the big outer yard, with its barns, sheds, and smell of animal muck. The sunlight fell slantwise from a still brazen sky, and the air was hot and motionless. Good haying weather, Sister Mildred would have declared.

She was there, part of a small gathering by the stables, which also included our swineherd, a shepherd, a girl from the kitchen with a bowl of scraps for the chickens, a few others. I made note of their faces, for I would scold them later as idlers, if Sister Mildred did not.

The three suspected villeins were standing beside the beadle with an air of being in custody. Jack Strong, the poacher, was a tallish man, with broad shoulders and a lot of shaggy brown hair. Tiffany of the runaway son was also strongly built, if not so tall, and there was a lot of gray in his dark hair and beard. Young Evan, as befits an adulterous lover, was handsome, with fair hair, a red mouth, and eyes as gray as glass.

The beadle turned at our approach and reported gravely, "Father Hugh assures me one of these three is the guilty one. He asked that they bring their scythes, which I made them do, but all three have been carefully cleaned."

"Yes, all scythes are cleaned after use," said Father Hugh from behind, making me start. I hadn't heard him come up. "They are cleaned and sharpened and put away dry against the next use." He was, as reported, in his best new habit, and dwarfed by the height of the processional cross he carried, which ought not to leave the cloister, especially to be dragged in the dirt of a barnyard.

"For a townsman you know a lot about farm tools," remarked Sister Harley.

"The villeins of Deerfield village are my people, too," replied Father Hugh. "I spend a certain amount of time in their company, and naturally I learn something of their ways. Even the wicked ones. Where are the scythes?"

"Over there by the stable door," replied the beadle.

"Father Hugh squinted against the lowering sun, spied the scythes, and went for a closer look, not noticing the puddle of filth he was walking through, nor how the tail of his good habit dragged in it. Then he looked at the three villeins and ordered, "Each one of you will go and stand beside his scythe!"

The villeins looked at the beadle, who nodded curtly, and each walked across the yard to stand beside his tool, facing Father Hugh and the rest of us. The beadle, frowning officiously, moved closer, but I stayed where I was with Sisters Harley and Mildred. As abbess

I would have to punish the guilty one, but this inquest was man's business.

The ungainly weapons – for so the scythes appeared to me now – leaned against the wall in a row, each very like the other.

Father Hugh began pacing up and down the line, throwing each villein a sharp glance. "When God first made the world," he said, in that measured tone he uses when beginning a sermon, "He chose Adam and Eve to be His stewards on earth. They were his creatures, who swore Him fealty. But then!" The little monk whirled and gestured sharply. "Came the *devil* – " he growled the word – "and he tempted Eve, who foreswore her oath! She went to Adam, who wickedly abjured his on her advice. And therefore all the earth came under the devil's dominion, until our Lord Jesu came and bought it back with His blood, alleluia!" If there is one thing Father Hugh can do well, it is preach. His sermons are as racy as any friar's. He raised a small hand in affected horror. "Yet, O yet, there are those who would still break the oath sworn for them at baptism, and take livery and maintenance of – Beelzebub." He drew out the name with a hiss, and a little tremor ran through us all. "There is among you," he said, turning and pointing a small finger at the villeins, "one who serves *not* God but the devil! Who is so puffed up with PRIDE and ANGER he cannot – *even now that I know who he is* – repent and confess his sin!"

This made an uneasy stir among the trio, but none opened his mouth, even in protest.

"Do you know what Beelzebub means?" asked Father Hugh, and even I shook my head. "*Lord of the Flies*. The filthy fly, engendered in filth, drawn to filth all its life, a true blazon for the livery of its filthy lord, Beelzebub." His voice dropped on that last word and we all leaned forward a little to hear what he would say next.

"And here, in worship of their master, and in witness to the devil's human servant, the flies gather . . . on the weapon used to take the life of Frick Cotter!" Father Hugh pointed suddenly at the third scythe, the one belonging to Jack Strong, deer poacher.

Jack stared at his tool, then kicked at it until it fell, sending the flies in all directions. "Nay, see?" he cried. "Them flies gather where they wist, then go off and gather some'eres else. Thee cannot be blamin' me for where the flies land!"

"Perhaps," said Father Hugh, but as one who knows otherwise, "it is as you say. Very well, all of you, wave the flies off, send them a good distance. Then we'll watch where they gather again."

The villeins set to with a will, shouted and kicked at the dusk and muck of the yard, flapping their tunics at the air, clearing a wide space around themselves and the scythes. Jack worked hardest, which is only natural, but even he was satisfied at last, and they came back and stood each in front of his scythe again. Now even I came closer to watch, because it seemed to me Jack Strong was perfectly right; flies gather here, then there, then are gone, all to no purpose or understanding, unless there is a heap of filth to draw them.

But silence had scarce fallen when they were back, thicker than ever, clustering all along the sharp blade of Jack's scythe, especially near where it fastened to the handle. Their numbers were so great they made a buzz as loud as if from bees.

The other two men stared and crossed themselves, backing off to leave Jack by himself in front of the damning blade. Jack swung at the flies again, but half-heartedly, and watched them collect as swiftly as before. He swallowed, then said, as if continuing a statement, "He says he seen me with the deer, and wanted half to keep his mouth shut. Half! He couldn't eat half a deer, not if he sat in his cottage all day and night stuffing himself; it'd spoil before he ate a quarter of it. And anyway there wasn't a half left; I'd only a half to start with, bein' I'd gone shares with – " Jack stopped, wiped his mouth. "With someone else." His angry gaze moved to me. "We be not horses or oxen, Mistress; we can't live on grass and roots, like!" And continued, to Father Hugh, "With all the work of my own strips in the fields to do, and the bidreaps and boon work for yon nuns, and trying to keep up that little patch we claimed from the waste, my family needs meat. Frick don't – *didn't* need it, not the way he lays idle, and I told him so. I offered to share other of my harvest with him. But he laughs and wipes that nose of his and 'e says, 'Jack, bring half of that deer to me after dark tonight, or I tell what I know.' And I was so angry I just swung at him without thinkin', forgettin' like I was carryin' that scythe, and he flings up his arm and the blade takes it off like it was a stem of grass. I couldn't say who was the more surprised, him or me. But I'd started it then, and though he run I had to ketch him, and finish it, and so I did; and went home as if nothing had happened, and cleaned the blade with grass and dirt and washed it best I could and put it away. I meant to take it off the haft and put it in the fire tonight to rid it of the last of the blood – " He did stop then and pointed at Father Hugh.

"You an' your Beelzebub! St. Mary, what a load of old codswallop! It was blood, that's all; it came like a fountain out of his arm, and his leg when I brought him down after I ketched him up, and, and – I'm surprised there was any left to come out of his throat, though it did, like a river in flood. It clings, does blood, and fills into cracks, like. And it draws flies; anyone who's ever been to a butcherin' knows that. So you can take your Beelzebub and hang him – " He drew breath in a ragged sob. "Just like they'll do to me."

# LEONARDO DA VINCI, DETECTIVE
## Theodore Mathieson

*Theodore Mathieson (b. 1913) turned to writing in 1955 after fifteen years as an English teacher in the public high schools of California. After he had started to sell regularly to* Ellery Queen's Mystery Magazine, *he turned to an ambitious project of writing a series of stories each featuring a famous character from history faced with a puzzling crime to solve. The series began with "Captain Cook, Detective" (1958) and ran on through a dozen stories.*

*The remarkable achievement of the series is that the crime and background in each story is directly related to its main character, using their own particular skills and abilities and linked very firmly to the world and beliefs about him. This required a considerable amount of research, for the series spanned the years from Alexander the Great to Florence Nightingale. The following story is one of the most ingenious, with its step-by-step unravelling of a seemingly impossible crime.*

On a fine late-spring afternoon in 1516, Leonardo da Vinci sat peacefully in the rose-embowered garden behind his mansion near Amboise, with a sketching pad upon his lap, drawing a golden oriole which fluttered occasionally within the confines of a large aviary. Although the Italian master was over sixty now, white-bearded and slightly stooped, the hand that had painted *The Last Supper* and *Mona Lisa* had lost none of its deftness, nor his eyes their keen brilliance. All around rose the gentle, sunwarmed hills of central France, and the bees hummed in the chaparral.

His young servant Jacques stepped hesitantly from the terrace to confront him, then spoke softly.

"Maître, a gentleman from Amboise. He demands to see you."

Leonardo nodded kindly, but before the boy could turn to deliver the message, a tall, sturdy black-haired figure with a thick beard strode across the terrace.

"Ah, Monsieur Blanchard," Leonardo said sympathetically. "You shatter the sylvan peace with your distress. Sit down and observe the golden oriole with me. I do not care to take the bird into captivity like this, but the oriole is most difficult to sketch in its natural habitat – "

"You mistake me, Monsieur," the man said. "I am not Monsieur Blanchard."

"Have my eyes lost their skill?" Leonardo said, blinking up at him. "Indeed, they must have, for you are not the King's minister after all!"

"I am Baron de Marigny, at your service. The Queen is most anxious that you come to Amboise at once."

"The Queen!" Leonardo looked surprised. His Majesty, Francis I, of the House of Valois, favored him. He had invited Leonardo to live in France, had given him this house, opened the castle at Amboise to him, and often sought his company. But the Queen! The regal French beauty had never liked him and had not dissembled from the first.

"How can my humble services be of value to the Queen?" Leonardo asked, temporizing.

"She gave me explicit orders to discuss nothing. At the same time – " Marigny's eyes shifted uneasily to the flutterings of the oriole. "His Majesty was not in favor of her calling you at all."

"But he permitted her to do so?"

"Yes. The Queen's whims are not easily discouraged."

"Then I shall come at once," Leonardo said, moving toward the terrace. "Ever to investigate, to *know* – especially when it is a Queen's whim. Jacques, my cloak!"

The coach carrying Leonardo and the Baron jolted along the narrow, poplar-lined road to within a hundred meters of the gray, rounded contours of the castle, and then debouched into a green open field to the west toward gently rising hills, perhaps a kilometer distant.

"We approach the amphitheater?" Leonardo asked.

"That is where it happened," Marigny said absently. Then his lips thinned and tightened. "They are waiting for you there. They will explain everything."

The coach drew up in a cloud of dust at the entrance of the amphitheater, which lay to the south. Here Francis, passionately fond of tournaments, masquerades, and amusements of all kinds, provided outdoor entertainment for himself, his court, and his guests. Colored flags fluttered from tall masts, announcing the afternoon's gala entertainment, already concluded, and nearly everyone had now departed except a small group sitting beneath a striped canopy inside a circle of soldiers. Leonardo recognized the King and Queen and their retinue.

The minister Blanchard approached Leonardo, his arms outstretched, his pale face smudged with perspiration and dust.

"This is terrible, Monsieur da Vinci. Monsieur Laurier has been stabbed in the chest and lies dead within the amphitheater. Her Majesty wishes you investigate this crime and demands to see you at once."

Leonardo nodded and strode like a noble patriarch to the others sitting beneath the awning. Arriving before the royal pair, Leonardo bowed deeply.

The King, handsome in his large-nosed way, acknowledged the greeting wearily, but his eyes were alert and watchful.

"Before the Queen speaks to you, Leonardo, let me say that I did not wish to disturb you. She is upset and may say things that are personal and uncomplimentary, but I ask you to make allowances. A friend of ours, Philip Laurier, lies dead out on that field. Murdered."

"A foul, most flaunting deed!" the Queen broke in, her voice strident with emotion.

The King raised his hand imperiously. "Let me acquaint Leonardo with the facts. Today we had a fine demonstration of marching formations done by special troops from the Netherlands, from Spain, and from Scotland."

"Is it not the Scottish warriors who wear the skirts?" Leonardo asked curiously.

"Kilts, Monsieur," corrected the minister Blanchard, cracking his knuckles.

"Kilts and tartans," said Francis, "a brilliant uniform of red and green and yellow which, I should imagine, would make these barbarians easy to shoot at."

"These and other colors are set in squares and stripes, Monsieur – a distinctive pattern which differs from clan to clan, from terrain to terrain," said Blanchard.

"Blanchard knows more about it than I do," said the King tolerantly. "He went to Scotland to make the arrangements for their coming."

"*Monsieur Laurier is dead*," chanted the Queen.

The King looked annoyed. "What happened," he said, "was that when the exhibition closed with the Scottish clan parading and playing their weird instruments – "

"Bagpipes," said the minister.

"Then the Queen and I and the others here left the field and returned to the castle. We had just descended from the coach when word came that Philip had been killed upon the field, and we returned here at once."

"*Tell him how he died*," said the Queen.

A look passed between Francis and his wife – hers of acute suspicion, his of impenetrable aloofness.

"Come, Leonardo – and all of you," said the King deliberately, rising and leading the way toward the amphitheater. "You must see how it was."

Leonardo saw how Marigny, his former coach companion, walked close beside the Queen, who paid no attention to him; she appeared to be sleepwalking. Then the King gave a quick sign to Marigny, and the latter came at once to his sire's side, like a hound trained to heel.

"Philip is – was – a promising young nobleman from the south," the King continued as they walked. "He went far in the last year, since he came to court. It was his office at these outdoor affairs to represent the King's power at the close, after all the spectators had gone. He would approach the center of the field, blow a trumpet as a signal to the guards mounted along the hills, and remain in possession of the field until the soldiers had closed formation and retired."

The King and Leonardo, followed by the others, passed through a pair of marble portals into a wide corridor cut from the hills, and entered a dell, the floor of which was covered with thick, springy turf. Elliptical in shape, with only the one entrance, the vale was perhaps two hundred feet long, and fifty at the widest point, close to the midsection. From the arena's level floor the sides sloped gently upward, the reddish earth neatly landscaped with low-lying shrubs – cotoneasters, pyracanths – no one of them high enough to conceal a man. Creepers partially covered the ground, and flat round stones were laid here and there so that one might mount to the hilltop without stepping upon the earth.

At a glance Leonardo could see that no one but himself and the royal party were within the amphitheater – they, and the figure lying motionless upon the greensward close to the center of the field. At the sight of the inert body the Queen gave a cry of dismay.

"It was your order, my dear, that he should remain there," the King said.

"Let me speak now – "

"In a moment, my dear! Let us tarry here. Today, after almost everyone had left, Laurier approached the center of the field. The guards all had their backs to the arena, as is a fixed rule, so they did not see anything. The last three people to leave the arena were Count and Countess Angerville and their daughter."

The King turned to a distinguished-looking middle-aged couple and a beautiful blond girl.

"Tell them what you saw, Angerville," the King said.

"I turned first," Angerville said in a firm, resolute tone. "Philip had just started to raise the trumpet to his lips. We walked on for several seconds and were just about *here*, and then when no sound came, I looked back, my wife and daughter looking back too. Philip seemed to stagger forward – away from us – dropping his trumpet. He turned slightly and we caught the glint of the knife-hilt as he fell. The knife could not have been thrown from the hilltop by any of the guardsmen!"

"They are too distant," the King said, "and the angle is too oblique for accuracy. The knife could only have been thrown by someone standing at the level of the arena floor!"

"*But how could that be?*" cried the girl with the blond hair.

Angerville took his daughter's hand in his. "It is impossible – and yet it happened," he said simply. "My wife and I and our daughter looked all about the arena from where we stood. There is no place of concealment. See there? Even the tiers of marble benches are set flush in the hillside and offer no hiding place. I swear it, *there was nobody within the arena but ourselves*!"

"But you did not mind that Laurier was killed, did you, Angerville?" said the Queen bitterly.

Angerville paled and the King raised his hand, but he could hold the Queen in check no longer.

"You knew your daughter was in love with Monsieur Laurier, and you were afraid they might marry!" the Queen went on. "Oh, the entire court knew about it."

"Your Majesty – " Angerville protested.

"Oh, I don't say you did it, Angerville. You wouldn't have dared. But I cannot stand your hypocritical *concern* – "

She turned and faced Leonardo, her dark beauty wild with passion.

"Monsieur da Vinci – "

"Careful now, my dear," Francis said resignedly. "Leonardo might take offense at your words and return to Italy, and we should be the poorer for it."

The Queen's lips curled in scorn. "Always Francis says to me, until I am weary: 'No other man has ever been born who knows as much as Leonardo da Vinci. Artist, inventor, engineer, mathematician, musician, philosopher – all these and more. He sees everything, he knows everything.' Well, Monsieur, I have not been willing to share my husband's views. I spent my girlhood in Valladolid, where Italian accomplishment is not held in too high regard. I cannot help my feelings."

Leonardo tilted his head in quick sympathy, tinged with satire.

"A friend – of ours – lies dead there." The Queen closed her eyes. "So far as we can see, no one was at his side nor anywhere around to kill him – yet he was stabbed. His Majesty and I shall remain outside the arena until the sun sets. That is in perhaps a little over an hour. We shall answer willingly any and all questions you may ask. If in that time 'the greatest mind in all Europe' can discover who killed Monsieur Laurier, I shall be ready to agree with my husband's opinion of da Vinci's skill!"

In the moment of intense silence that followed the Queen's outburst, Leonardo was aware of the long shadows of the late afternoon, of a cloud of midges, and of the lazy flappings of the festive banners. A hysterical woman had flung down a challenge which the others were waiting to see if he would accept. He needn't accept, of course; he could go back to his peaceful garden and sketch golden orioles, but not for long. A frustrated Queen would leave her husband no peace, and Leonardo felt a return to Florence now would be an anticlimax to his life.

"Very well, Your Highness," he said finally. "I prefer death to lassitude. And I never tire of serving others."

He turned then, and with the minister Blanchard at his heels walked toward the silent figure in the center of the field . . .

Before his death, three years later, Leonardo da Vinci told Francis how and why he set out to work as he did that fateful afternoon.

"When I was a boy in Vinci," the Italian master said, "my closest village playmates told me that a mark made upon the trunk of a tree grew higher from the ground with each year's growth of that tree. First I made sure they *believed* what they said; if they were lying, it would be needless to investigate. When I soon found that even the adults of the village believed this true, I went into the woods, notched a healthy young tree with a fleur de lis, and measured it from the ground. I returned each year for three years and measured again, and found that what everyone said was *not* true. A mark upon the trunk of a tree remains at the same height for the life of the tree, because a tree grows vertically from the crown, while its trunk increases only in girth!" . . .

First, then, that afternoon, Leonardo called Countess Angerville and her daughter to him.

"Are you as certain as your husband, Madame, that there was no one within the arena at the time Laurier was killed?"

"Yes, Monsieur," the woman said without hesitation, and her gray eyes were honest and steadfast.

"And you, Mademoiselle?"

The girl nodded, though she seemed under a spell.

"What did you do when you saw Laurier fall to the ground?" he asked the Countess.

"My husband ran forward to look at him, warning us to stay where we were. Then he ran back and told us to follow him, so that we might tell the others what had happened."

"He forgot the soldiers who stood circling the tops of the hills?"

"I suppose he did, Monsieur."

"Then all three of you ran out of the arena leaving Laurier upon the ground?"

"Yes."

Leonardo turned to the girl. "Is it true, Mademoiselle, as the Queen suggests, that you and Monsieur Laurier wished to marry?"

"No, no!" She seemed to come suddenly alive. "I – I loved him, yes, but – he did not wish to marry me. I know this because there was someone else – "

Her mother laid a warning hand upon the girl's arm, and she fell silent. Leonardo did not press the question. He could guess who her rival was.

"Would it be possible," Leonardo addressed both the mother and the girl, "that Laurier might have conceived this as a way of dramatically committing suicide?"

"No, no," the Countess assured him vehemently. "Philip was ambitious, alive to his very fingertips. The whole world was before him."

Leonardo examined the sprawled body before he had it removed from the field, and withdrew the knife from Laurier's chest, where it had been embedded to the dudgeon. It was a plain hunting knife, razor-sharp, with a yellow bone handle.

The Italian then had minister Blanchard order the soldiers to bring a thick plank into the arena and set it upright – in the exact spot Laurier had occupied. The soldiers obeyed with alacrity.

"Now who is proficient in the art of hurling the knife?" Leonardo asked Blanchard.

"I am," the minister announced quietly. Leonardo was surprised: such a skill appeared at odds with the man's self-effacement.

"And anyone else in the party?"

"It is a common skill here in France," the minister said, shrugging. "Baron de Marigny is my equal, and even the barbarian, Bruce Stewart, the leader of the Scottish troops, has vied successfully with us."

"Ask those two to come here at once," Leonardo said.

Marigny arrived with a gloomy countenance and stood sulkily by as they waited for Stewart, who at last marched vigorously into the arena, resplendent in his brilliant tartan.

"Ach, mon, the laddies tell me you want me to throw the knife," Stewart said, smiling. He was a ruddy-faced Scot with heavy jaws and craggy brows, and he looked as if all of life was a laughing matter. "I'd be muckle pleased to know my competitor."

Leonardo stationed Marigny on the floor of the arena, about fifteen paces from the board, Blanchard halfway up the east side, cautioning him to stand only upon the flat stones amid the creepers; he placed Stewart at the top of the hill, between two guards, whose discipline apparently was so stern that not one had turned to look at the proceedings below. And they had been standing there all afternoon.

Leonardo used the bone-handled hunting knife in the test. Marigny threw first and embedded the knife so deeply in the board that it took two soldiers to pull it out. But first Leonardo studied the angle of the penetration. Blanchard threw second and again Leonardo studied the angle. Stewart made four tries, missing the board altogether thrice, and succeeding only on his fourth try.

"The sun was in my eyes," said the Scot, his face almost as red as his tartan.

"But it was not only the sun," Leonardo told Francis. "It was the distance which made it unfeasible, too, and I consoled him. You were right, Your Highness. The murderer had stood on a level with his victim or slightly above – not as high as I placed Blanchard – for the blade had entered Laurier's chest at only a slight angle, and not acute as it would have been if the knife had been thrown from higher up."

So now Leonardo knew that in spite of three witnesses who claimed the arena was empty, *the murderer was there all the time*! But where?

He had a hint of the truth, but only a hint, and his time was now half used up. He had Blanchard order six soldiers to search carefully the west side of the arena for sign of footprints, for he knew the murderer would not handicap his aim by permitting the sun to shine in his eyes. In the meantime, while the soldiers searched, he detained Stewart and spoke with him.

"When you left the field with your detachment, Monsieur Stewart," he said, "you returned at once to the castle?"

"Aye, marching all the way and cutting tricks. The laddies were in fine form."

"And was any man absent from your group?"

"Not a one. All sixteen of them, acting as one man!" he said proudly.

Leonardo sat down upon one of the marble benches and sighed.

Momentarily he wished he were back in his garden making one of his numerous sketches of the golden oriole. Why should the oriole keep coming into his mind? Da Vinci listened a moment to the silence of his unconscious, for which he had a great reverence, and then said:

"Tell me, Monsieur Stewart, have you enjoyed your sojourn in France?"

"I have, aye. But many of the laddies are homesick and will be glad to leave. It's the country here, you know. Most of Scotland is very bleak and rocky, but there are parts of Appin, where we Stewarts roam, which are like this earth here – gentle and wooded and covered with brush. It reminds the laddies of home."

"Footprints, footprints!" one of the soldiers cried from a quarter way up the western side.

Leonardo hastened up to him and saw two fresh imprints of a shoe beside a stepping stone, both of the right foot. Doubtless someone – the murderer? – had missed his footing, perhaps in the excitement of a quick escape.

The soldiers found no other print on the entire western slope.

"At once," Leonardo cried to Blanchard, "get those guards down from the hill – those five!" He pointed to the men who guarded the major portion of the western side. "Monsieur Stewart, would you accompany him, please?"

The Scotsman nodded willingly and set off climbing beside the King's minister. Halfway up, the minister sat down and rested, and instantly Leonardo took a small drawing pad and crayon from his cloak and in a few deft lines portrayed Blanchard seated, clearly indicating his dejection and fatigue.

"Why do you draw only Blanchard?" Baron de Marigny said querulously, looking over Leonardo's shoulder.

"I draw what I see," the artist replied, putting his pad quickly away and swinging around to face the Baron. "Where were you when this tragedy occurred?"

"I was at the castle," said Marigny, scowling. "I was not feeling well, and I stayed the afternoon in my chamber."

"And yet when the Queen reached the castle on her return from the day's event, she sent you to fetch me, knowing you were ill?"

"I was feeling better. I met them as they arrived, and when Her Majesty received the news of Laurier's death – "

"And what was His Majesty's reaction?"

"He didn't want her to send for you. I told you." Marigny's face grew suffused with anger. "But she was insistent."

The five guardsmen from the hill watch arrived now and lined up for Leonardo's interrogation. Time was growing short. The sun had dipped behind the western hill and the arena lay in blue shadow. One by one Leonardo took a guardsman aside and said, conspiratorially:

"You and I know who slipped by you twice over the hill, don't we, Monsieur?"

Out of five poker faces it was Leonardo's good fortune to find one which mirrored every thought process. The guard denied joint knowledge with Leonardo, of course, but at least the Italian now knew that if one was lying, so in all probability were the other four.

Leonardo was now sure of the solution to the mystery – so sure that he walked out of the arena, the minister Blanchard and Stewart trailing behind him. Marigny remained where he was.

At His Majesty's pavilion the Queen called out, "Your time is about up, da Vinci!"

Many in the group eyed him with suspicion and hostility. Leonardo bowed and said, "One moment, Your Highness." He turned to Count Angerville who stood surveying him calmly from beside the King.

"Where were you seated during the performance?" he asked.

Angerville looked taken aback. "Why, beside His Majesty, on his left."

Francis nodded, frowning. "Angerville was on my left, and Blanchard on my right."

"And did His Majesty speak with you during the presentation?"

Angerville appeared to think hard for a moment. "Only once, I believe."

"And what did he say?"

"Come, come, Leonardo," the King said testily. "Where is this leading us?"

"Perhaps to the truth, Your Highness. What did His Majesty say to you, Count Angerville?"

"He said – " Angerville colored, and looked abashed at the women present. "His Majesty asked me if I thought the Scotsmen wore anything *under* their skirts!"

There was a ripple of laughter in the party, and some of the tenseness and hostility relaxed. Only the King glared fiercely at Leonardo.

"Are you trying to make sport of me?" he demanded.

"God forbid, Your Highness," Leonardo said humbly. Out of the corner of his eye he could see the Queen fidgeting, preparing to quell his questions.

"And where, Your Highness," he said, addressing the Queen, "were you sitting?"

"On a bench on the opposite side of the field, where the women always sit!"

And then, to the surprise of the entire party, Leonardo da Vinci sank down on one knee, bowed his head, and said:

"I confess I do not deserve a higher evaluation in Her Majesty's eyes than I already possess. I have failed to discover how Monsieur Laurier was murdered by an invisible assassin. Moreover, were I given a year, or two years, I do not believe I could solve this mystery. In extenuation, I will say that I am an old man and perhaps my powers of observation have waned. I beg now to be excused."

After a moment the Queen nodded. Leonardo rose, and while the King and his party watched in frozen silence, he walked slowly, almost falteringly, to the coach that had brought him.

But Leonardo da Vinci, in addition to his other accomplishments, was also a fine actor.

Next morning he was sitting in his garden as usual, calmly and confidently making another sketch of the golden oriole when Jacques announced the arrival of the King.

Francis waved Leonardo back to his chair, then sat down on a bench beside him.

"Leonardo," he said at once, "I wish to thank you for what you did for me yesterday. I shall not soon forget it. Now do not pretend further with me. You know who murdered Laurier, and how the miracle was accomplished."

Leonardo said nothing, but watched the King steadily, as if he awaited further word.

"There are times," the monarch said, lowering his eyes, "when it is politically expedient to remove a dangerous subject. Your own countryman Machiavelli has said this. Laurier was a traitor, bargaining in secrets with a foreign power."

Leonardo nodded, knowing the real reason why Laurier had died; the Queen had made that plain for all to see. The King's subterfuge was pathetic, but Leonardo's acceptance of it made it possible for the two men to talk freely about the crime.

"Tell me now what you know, Leonardo."

"I know you had him killed, Sire. When I realized the man whom you chose to commit the murder both entered and escaped from the arena with the complicity of the guardsmen, I knew they had their orders *only from you*. If the cause of the murder had been a simple, spontaneous grudge, and committed, say, by one of the Scottish soldiers or by Stewart himself, there could have been no such collusion."

Francis nodded approvingly. "And you know the man whom I picked?"

"The men," Leonardo corrected gravely. "One to commit the deed, the other to replace him by your side. When I learned that you asked Angerville a question about the Scottish dress, I knew the man on the *other* side of you was not Blanchard. Blanchard, who had been to Scotland, was familiar with all these details, and if he'd been at your other side you'd have directed your question to him. Therefore, the man on the other side of you was someone who superficially resembled Blanchard – Baron de Marigny who looks so much like Blanchard that I mistook him for the minister when he came here to fetch me yesterday. It must have been a shock to him when I addressed him thus. He took pains to make himself up to resemble Blanchard even more, in order to deceive Her Majesty, who sat facing you on the other side of the field."

"Ah, yes," the King said quickly. "Her Majesty liked Laurier – I did not wish to hurt her."

"Of course. And now as to how it was done – "

"I thought my plan would amaze and perplex!" cried the King. "And yet you perceived the truth. You must tell me your methods."

Leonardo pointed toward the aviary.

"By the help of the golden oriole, there, who started a train of thought. I mentioned to Marigny yesterday how the oriole was hard to sketch in his natural habitat, which is among the green and yellow of the woods. His plumage blends into the background of sun-shot leaves in a protective coloration, making him virtually invisible. It is the same with the uniforms of soldiers, which are designed in many cases to help throw a cloak of invisibility about the soldier. It is common knowledge. The brilliant tartan of the Scottish warrior does this, paradoxically. The terrain within the arena, with its red earth and green shrubbery is much like the country of Appin, where the Stewarts live and fight. Stewart himself told me this. And when he climbed up the slope on the shadowed side of the arena with Blanchard, and they rested a moment, I was moved to make a quick sketch of Blanchard, partly *because Blanchard was all I saw*. He appeared to be sitting alone, unless one focused one's eyes especially to detect Stewart beside him . . . Curiously, was it not Blanchard who suggested to you this means of achieving invisibility?"

The King nodded.

"As I reconstructed it," Leonardo went on, "Laurier stood in the center of the field, waiting for the last spectator to leave. He must have seen Blanchard come over the hill and wondered at it. Perhaps it delayed his putting the trumpet to his lips. Blanchard threw the knife at the defenseless soldier, and when the Angervilles turned and saw Laurier clutching his throat, Blanchard must have already crouched upon the side of the hill, with a borrowed tartan concealing him. The sun was still up, and his was the shadowed part of the hill, so he must have been virtually invisible. Then when the Angervilles ran from the arena to fetch help, Blanchard completed his escape."

Suddenly Francis seemed to lose interest.

"Thank you, thank you, Leonardo, you have explained it all with wondrous accuracy. And now I must go – I am needed at Amboise. I shall visit you again shortly."

The King was hastening across the sunny garden when Leonardo stopped him with a final question.

"And what about Monsieur Blanchard? He is to be rewarded for his pains?"

The King whirled around, open-mouthed. Then, as a look of faint concern appeared, he shrugged.

"Poor man, Blanchard," he said. "Her Majesty must have learned he did it, too. They found him by the castle pond this morning, with a hunting knife in his chest. A pity, too, for it was a fine reward I promised him!"

And with that the King disappeared behind a hedgerow, and Leonardo da Vinci, citizen of the world, contemporary of Machiavelli, sat peacefully down to sketching the elusive golden oriole, almost invisible in the sun-brilliant foliage.

# A SAD AND
# BLOODY HOUR
## Joe Gores

*Joe Gores (b. 1931) has excellent credentials for writing detective stories. For twelve years he was a private detective in San Francisco. He has written ten novels and over a hundred short stories and has been a three-time winner of the Mystery Writers of America Edgar Award. He has also written for cinema and television. His TV work includes scripts for* Columbo, Kojak, Magnum *and* Remington Steele.

*It may not take you too long to work out who the mystery detective is in the following story, but once you've done that you may discover there is much more of a challenge for you in identifying the sources of the 396 quotes which are turned into dialogue in the story. The events are those which, four centuries on, inspired Anthony Burgess to write* A Dead Man in Deptford *(1993).*

Perhaps it was unscanned self-love, concern for the first heir of my wit's invention, that brought me back to London from the safety of Dover where The Admiral's Men were presenting Marlowe's *Tragical History of Doctor Faustus*. It was a grisly visit, for elevenhundred a week were dying of the plague. This scourge of God had carried away few of my acquaintance save poor Kit, but his loss was heavy: our friendship had been much deeper than mere feigning.

I finished my business with Dick Field and in the afternoon returned to my rented room on Bishopsgate near Crosby Hall. When I ascended the dank ill-lit staircase to my chamber I found a lady waiting me within. As she turned from a window I saw she was not Puritan Agnes come to see her player husband, but a pretty bit of virginity with a small voice as befits a woman.

"Thank God I found you before your return to the provinces!"

Her words, and the depths of her steady blue eyes, made me realize that she was only about five years younger than my twenty-nine. With her bodice laces daringly loosened to display her bright red stomacher beneath, and wearing no hat or gloves, she might have

been a common drab: but never had I seen a bawdy woman with
so much character in her face. As if reading my thought she drew
herself up.

"I am Anne Page, daughter to Master Thomas Page and until
recently maid to Mistress Audry, wife of Squire Thomas Walsingham
of Scadbury Park, Chislehurst."

All things seemed that day conspired to remind me of poor
Marlowe, for Walsingham had been his patron since Cambridge.

"Then you knew Kit?"

"Knew him?" She turned away as if seeking his swarthy face in the
unshuttered window. "With his beard cut short like a Spaniard's, full
of strange oaths and quick to quarrel for his honour! Knew him?" She
turned back to me suddenly. "Were you truly his friend? By all the
gods at once, I need a man to imitate the tiger!"

"I am young and raw, Mistress Page, but believe me: sorrow bites
more lightly those who mock it."

"Say rage, rather! Oh, were I a man my sword should end it!" Her
eyes flashed as if seeing more devils than hell could hold. "Didn't you
know that last May when Tom Kyd was arrested, he deposed that
Kit had done the heretical writings found in his room?"

"The players were scattered by the closing of the theatres."

"On the strength of Kyd's testimony a warrant was issued; Kit
was staying at Scadbury Park to avoid the plague, so Squire Thomas
put up bail. But then a second indictment was brought, this time
before the Privy Council by the informer Richard Baines. On May
twenty-ninth I was listening outside the library door when the Squire
accused Kit of compromising those in high places whose friendship
he had taken."

I shook my head sorrowfully. "And the next day he died!"

"Died!" Her laugh was scornful. "When he left the library, Kit
told me that two of Squire Thomas's creatures, Ingram Frizer and
Nicholas Skeres, would meet him at a Deptford tavern to help him
flee the country. I begged him be careful but ever he sought the
bubble reputation, even in the cannon's mouth; and so he now lies
in St. Nicholas churchyard. And so I wish I were with him, in heaven
or in hell?"

"But why do you say cannon's mouth? His death was – "

"Murder! Murder most foul and unnatural, arranged beneath the
guise of friendship and bought with gold from Walsingham's coffers!
Kit was stabbed to death that afternoon in Eleanor Bull's tavern!"

I shivered, and heard a spy in every creaking floor-board; it is
ever dangerous for baser natures to come between the mighty and
their designs, and Squire Thomas's late cousin Sir Francis, had, as

Secretary of State, crushed the Babington Conspiracy against the Queen.

"But what proof could you have? You were not there to see it."

"Do I need proof that Rob Poley, back from the Hague only that morning, was despatched to the tavern two hours before Kit's end? Proof that Squire Thomas, learning that I had been listening outside the library door, discharged me without reference so I have become . . ." She broke off, pallid cheeks aflame, then plunged on: "Oh, player, had you the motive and cue for passion that I have! I beg you, go to Deptford, ferret out what happened! If it was murder, then I'll do bitterness such as the day will fear to look upon!"

She admitted she was a discharged serving wench with a grievance against Walsingham; yet her form, conjoined with the cause she preached, might have made a stone capable. I heard my own voice saying staunchly: "To-morrow I'll go to Deptford to learn the truth of it."

"Oh, God bless you!" Swift as a stoat she darted to the door; her eyes glowed darkly back at me from the folds of her mantle. "Tomorrow night and each night thereafter until we meet . . . Paul's Walk."

She was gone. I ran after her but St. Mary's Axe was empty. Down Bishopsgate the spires of St. Helen's Church were sheathed in gold.

Kit Marlowe murdered by his patron Thomas Walsingham! It could not be. And yet . . . I determined to seek Dick Quiney and his advice.

The doors wore red plague crosses and the shops were shuttered as I turned into Candlewick towards the imposing bulk of St. Paul's. In Carter Lane the householders were lighting their horn lanterns; beyond Tom Creed's house was The Bell where I hoped to find Dick Quiney. Though he's now a High Bailiff in Warwickshire, his mercer's business often calls him to London. I hoped that I would find him now in the City.

The Bell's front woodwork was grotesquely carved and painted with red and blue gargoyles, and a sign worth £40 creaked over the walk on a wrought-iron bracket: it bore a bell and no other mark besides, but good wine needs no bush to herald it. Through the leaded casement windows came the tapster's cry, "Score at the bar!" When I asked the drawer, a paunchy man with nothing on his crown between him and heaven, if Dick Quiney were staying there, he gestured up the broad oak stairway.

"In the Dolphin Chamber, master."

The room faced the inner court on the second floor. When I thrust

open the door, Dick, with an oath, sprang for the scabbarded rapier
hung over the back of his chair: forcible entry to another's chamber
has been often used for hired murder. But then he laughed.

"Johannus Factotem! I feared my hour had come. How do you,
lad?"

"As an indifferent child of earth."

"What makes the handsome well-shaped player brave the plague
– oho! September twenty-second tomorrow!" He laughed again, a
wee quick wiry man in green hose and brown unpadded doublet.
"The upstart crow, beautified with their feathers, will give them all
a purge."

"'Let base conceited wits admire vile things, fair Phoebus lead me
to the Muses' springs'," I quoted. "You ought to recognize Ovid –
we read him in the grammar long ago. As for the translation, I had
it from Kit last spring."

"Still harping on Marlowe, lad? We all owe God a death."

"What reports have you had of the cause of his?"

"Surely it was the plague. Gabriel Harvey's 'Gorgon' says – "

"That's now disputed." Over meat I recounted all. "I fear
Walsingham, but if I should be fattening the region's kites with
his – "

"Would you number sands and drink oceans dry? In justice – "

"– none of us should see salvation. Not justice, friendship: forgotten, it stings sharper than the winter wind."

"Pah! Marlowe was hasty as fire and deaf as the sea in his rages.
You'd do him no disservice to leave his bones lie." Then he shrugged.
"But as you say, use men as they deserve and who would escape the
whipping? So you'll off to Deptford, seeking truth."

"I will. If you could go to Harrison's White Greyhound – "

"I'll oversee your interests." He clapped me on the back. "Give
tomorrow to gaunt ghosts the grave's inherited, to-night there's excellent *theologicum* and humming ale made with fat standing Thames
water."

I could find no boats at Paul's Pier; and at Queenhithe, the
watermen's gathering place of late years, were boats but no pilots.
As I started for the Red Knight, a boy hailed me from the dock.

"John Taylor, boatman's apprentice, at your service." Barely
thirteen, he had an honest open face, curly brown hair, and sharp
eyes. "Do you travel to escape the plague?"

I sat down on the embroidered cushions in the stern of his boat.
"No, I'm a journeyman to grief. Westward ho – to Deptford, lad."

The ebbing tide carried us towards the stone arches of London
Bridge, sliding us beneath her covered arcade and crowded houses

like an eel from the hand. As we passed the Tower the boy spoke suddenly.

"Weren't you a player in *The True Tragedy of Richard, Duke of York*, at The Theatre last year?"

"You know much of the stage for one so young," I grunted. Yet I was pleased that he had recognized me, for all men seek fame.

The bells of St. Saviour's on the Surrey Side were pealing eight far behind us when Deptford docks came into view around a bend in the river, crowded with the polyglot shipping of all nations. A sailor with one eye directed me to St. Nicholas Church, the mean stone chapel not far from the docks where Anne Page had said Kit was buried.

The rector was a stubby white-haired man, soberly dressed as befits the clergy, with his spectacles on his nose and his hose hanging on shrunken shanks.

"Give you God's blessings, sir." His piping voice would have been drowned in the Sunday coughings of his congregation. "Even as the holy Stephen gave soft words to those heathens who were stoning him."

"Let's talk of graves and worms and epitaphs. I want to see your register of burials for the present year."

"Here are many graved in the hollow ground, as was holy Lawrence after that naughty man Valerian broiled him on a slow grid." He squeaked and gibbered like the Roman dead upon the death of Caesar, but finally laid out the great leather-covered volume I desired. "Seek only that which concerns you: sin not with the eyes. Consider Lucy of Syracuse; when complimented by a noble on her beautiful eyes, she did tear them out and hand them to him so that she might avoid immodest pride."

"I search for only one name – that of Christopher Marlowe."

"Marlowe? Why, a very devil, that man, a player and – "

"Churlish priest! Kit will be singing when you lie howling! And why have you written only: *First June, 1593, Christopher Marlowe slain by Francis Archer*. No word of his monument or epitaph."

The old cleric, ruffled by my words, chirped like a magpie. "His bones lie tombless, with no rememberance over them."

"But he had high friends! Why, after a violent death, was he given such an unworthy burial?"

"Squire Walsingham himself so ordered." Animosity faded from his whizzled walnut face in the hope of vicarious scandal. "Surely his death was a simple tavern brawl? It was so accepted by William Danby, Coroner to the Royal Household, who held the inquest since Her Gracious Highness was lying at Kew."

"The Queen's Coroner would not be corrupt," I said brusquely. But could he be misled? "Now take me to Kit's grave."

In an unmarked oblong of sunken earth in the churchyard, under a plane tree, was Kit, safely stowed with flowers growing from his eyes. I felt the salt tears trickling down my own face.

"Even as St. Nicholas once restored to life through God's grace three boys who had been pickled in a salting-rub for bacon, so may we gather honey from the weed and make a moral of this devil Marlowe. The dead are as but pictures – and only children fear painted devils – but Marlowe was so evil that God struck him down in the midst of sin."

"Pah!" I burst out angrily, dashing away my unmanly tears. "Your preaching leaves an evil taste like easel! Speak only from the pulpit, father – play the fool only in your own house."

"My Father's House! In His House are many mansions, but none – "

I left his querulous anger behind to search for Eleanor Bull's tavern. Walsingham might have ordered just such a hurried obscure funeral if Kit had died of the plague; but then why had the burial record shown him slain by Francis Archer? And why had Anne Page given me Ingram Frizer as Kit's killer? Had her tale been more matter and less art than it had seemed? Perhaps Eleanor Bull would have the answers.

Playbills were tattered on the notice-post beside the door and Dame Eleanor would have made a good comic character upon the stage herself: a round-faced jolly woman with a bawdy tongue and a nose that had been thrust into more than one tankard of stout, by its color. She wore a fine scarlet robe with a white hood.

"Give you good morrow, sir."

"Good morrow, dame. Would you join me in a cup of wine?"

"By your leave, right gladly, sir." She preceded me up the narrow stairs, panting her remarks over her shoulder in beery lack of breath. "I get few ... phew ... other than seafarers here. Rough lot they be, much ... phew ... given to profanity." She opened a door, dug me slyly in the ribs as I passed. "La! If I but lodge a lonely gentlewoman or two who live honestly by their needlework, straightway it's claimed I keep a bawdy house!"

I laughed and ordered a pint of white wine each. It was a pleasant chamber overlooking an enclosed garden; the ceiling was oak and a couch was pushed back against the cheap arras showing Richard Crookback and Catesby on Bosworth Field. A fireplace pierced one wall.

"Tell me, mistress: did a man named Christopher Marlowe meet an untimely end in your house some months ago?"

"You knew Marlowe, in truth?" She regarded me shrewdly. "For all his abusing of God's patience and the King's English with quaint curses, he was a man women'd run through fire for. Lord, Lord, master, he was ever a wanton! I'll never laugh as I did in that man's company."

I kept my voice casual. "A brawl over a wench, wasn't it? And the fellow who killed him – Francis Archer?"

"La!" She jingled the keys on her silver-embroidered sash. "You must have seen the decayed cleric of St. Nicholas Church – he can scarce root the garden with his shaking fingers, let alone write right a stranger's name. Ingram Frizer was the man who shuffled Kit off."

"I would be pleased to hear an account of it."

"Heaven forgive him and all of us, I say; he died in this very room, on that very couch. God's blood, I don't know what he was doing in such company, as Nick Skeres is a cutpurse and Frizer a swindler for all his pious talk; but all three were living at Scadbury Park and once spied together for the Privy Council. Rob Poley, another of the same, arrived on a spent horse in the afternoon, and two hours later the fight started. By the time I had run up here, Kit was already flat upon the couch, stabbed through the skull above the right eye."

"Wasn't Frizer charged when the guard arrived?"

"Right speedily: but the others backed his story that Kit, who was lying drunk upon the couch, had attacked him through an argument over the score. Frizer was watching Skeres and Poley at backgammon, when Kit suddenly leaped up cursing, seized Frizer's own knife from its shoulder sheath, and started stabbing him in the face. Frizer got free, they scuffled, Kit fell on the knife." She shrugged. "The inquest was the first of June; by the twenty-eighth Frizer'd been pardoned by the Queen and was back at Scadbury Park in the Squire's pay."

I sat down on the couch, muscles crawling. Kit had been as strong and agile as myself from the tumbling and fencing at which all players excel; and even in a drunken rage would the creator of haughty Tamburlaine and proud Faustus stab from behind? *The room seemed to darken; four dim figures strained in the dusk, Kit's arms jerked back, feet thrust cunningly between his, a cry – silence –* murder.

I looked up at Eleanor Bull. "Do you believe their story?"

"I'll not put my finger in the fire." But then her gaze faltered; her thumb ring glinted as she clutched the arras. She turned suddenly, face distorted. "La! I'll speak of it though hell itself forbid me! It was I who saw him fumble at his doublet, and smile upon his fingers, and cry out 'God! God! God!' It was I who felt his legs and found them cold as any stone. And it is I who now declare that here was cruel murder done!"

Her words brought me to my feet. "Then I'm for Scadbury Park to pluck this bloody villain's beard and blow it in his face!"

She cast her bulk before me, arms outstretched. "Oh, master, that sword which clanks so bravely against your flank will be poor steel against the viper you seek to rouse. These other swashers – la! Three such antics together don't make a man. Skeres is white-livered and red-faced; Frizer has a killing tongue and a quiet sword; and Poley's few good words match as few good deeds. But Squire Thomas! Cross him to learn that one may smile and smile and be a villain."

"I'm committed to one with true cause for weeping. Go I must."

"Then take one of my horses – and my prayers with you."

After a few miles of gently rolling downs whose nestled farmers' cots reminded me of my own Warwickshire, I came to Chislehurst. Beyond a mile of forest was Manor Park Road curving gently up through open orchards to the moated main house of Scadbury Manor, a sprawling tile-roofed timber building over two-hundred years old.

I was led through the vast unceiled central hall to the library, which was furnished in chestnut panels. His books showed the Squire's deep interest in the arts: Holinshed's *Chronicles*; Halle's *Union*; Plutarch's *Lives*; Sir Philip Sydney's *Arcadia*, chief flower of English letters. These were bound in leather and set on the shelves with their gilt-edged leaves facing out to show the gold clasps and jewelled studs. On the other shelves were rolled and piled manuscripts – *Diana Enamorada*, *Menaechmi* – which I was examining when a low melancholy voice addressed me from the doorway.

"Who asks for Walsingham with Marlowe's name also on his lips?"

He looked the knight that he so ardently sought to be, elegant as a bridegroom and trimly dressed in silken doublet, velvet hose, and scarlet cloak. His voice was like his thrice-gilt rapier in its velvet scabbard: silk with steel beneath. Lengthened by a pointed beard and framed in coiling hair, his face had the cruel features of a Titus or a Caesar: Roman nose, pale appraising eyes, well-shaped disdainful lips. A face to attract and repel in an instant.

"A poor player who begs true detail of Marlowe's quick end."

He advanced leisurely into the room, giving his snuff-box to his nose. "Your clothes make your rude birth and ruder profession obvious. I knew Marlowe slightly and sponsored his serious work

– not the plays, of course. But why ask me about his death when the plague – "

"I had it from An – from a mutual friend that he was slain, not by plague, but in a Deptford tavern brawl by your man Ingram Frizer."

"Did you now? And this gossip – the trollop Anne Page?"

"No," I retorted quickly, "Tom Kyd in Newgate Gaol."

He sneered and rang a small silver bell. "A quick eye and open ear such as yours often make gaol smell of home; and your tongue runs so roundly that it may soon run your head from your irreverent shoulders. But perhaps even the meanly born can honour friendship."

The man who entered was easily recognized as Nicholas Skeres: he was indeed beet-nosed and capon-bellied, and when he learned of my errand he advanced bellowing as if I would melt like suet in the sun.

"Why, you nosey mummer, Kit was a bawcock and a heart of gold! Why, were he among us now, I'd kiss his dirty toe, I would; for well I loved the lovely bully." He laughed coarsely. "Of course now he's at supper with the worms; but here's Frizer to set you right."

Ingram Frizer had a churchwarden's face but the eye of a man who sleeps little at night. His mouth was an O and his eyes were to heaven, and he aped the cleric's true piety as ill as the odious prattler replacing the well-graced actor upon the stage.

"Poor Marlowe," he intoned unctuously. "He left this life as one who had been studied in his death. Here am I, watching backgammon; there is Kit, upon the couch. He leaps up, seizes my knife – " He moved, and the deadly blade whose hilt was visible over his left shoulder darted out like a serpent's tongue to slash the dancing dustmotes. "He strikes me twice in the face, I pull loose, we grapple, he slips . . . sheathed in his brain. I pluck away the steel, kiss the gash yawning so bloodily on his brow. He smiles a last brave time, takes my hand in feeble grip – but his soul is fled to the Eternal Father."

"Satisfied now, Mars of malcontents?"

"Just one more question, Squire." As my profession is counterfeit emotion, my tone matched Frizer's for buttery sorrow. "Then I will take my leave."

"Nothing will I more readily give you."

"Why did Poley, fresh from the Hague as from the seacoasts of Bohemia, come hurriedly that day to Dame Eleanor's tavern?"

"Question my actions, player, and you'll yield the crows a pudding!" Poley advanced from the shadows; huge, silent-moving, dark and sensual of face, his eyes falcon-fierce and his nose bent aside as if seeking the smell of death. His arms were thick and his chest a brine-barrel beneath his stained leather doublet.

Squire Thomas's sad disdainful smile fluttered beneath his new-reaped moustache like a dove about the cote. "He was just come from Holland. Where better than a tavern to wash away the dust of travel?"

"What of Baines's indictment of Kit that was sure to embarrass you and the others of Raleigh's Circle if it came to court? You had learned of it only the night before; this had nothing to do with Poley's despatch to the tavern on that day?"

His face went ashen, his lips bloodless; his pale eyes flashed and his voice shook with suppressed rage. "Divine my downfall, you little better thing than earth, and you may find yourself beneath it!" With an effort he controlled his emotion. "Apes and actors, they say, should have their brains removed and given to the dog for a New Year's gift."

He held up a detaining hand. "Soft, you – a word or two before you go. I have done the state some service and they know it. Beware! You said Tom Kyd gave you the news of Marlowe's death, then prattled details only Anne Page could have told you. No murder have I done – yet she spreads her scandals. Seek her out in secret and you will feel that the very cobbles beneath your feet do prate to me your whereabouts."

Such a man bestrides my narrow world like a Colossus; yet was he more fully man than I?

"You despise me for my birth, Walsingham; yet nature cannot choose its origin. Blood will have blood if blood has been let, and murder will out for all your saying."

But I didn't feel safe until good English oak was between us.

Ten had struck before I arrived, in defiance of Squire Thomas, at St. Paul's Cathedral Church. During the hours of worship the shrill cries of the hawkers and the shouts of the roistering Paul's Men compete among the arches with the chants of the choir; but then only my boots echoed upon the stones of Paul's Walk, the great central nave.

I loosened my sword, for one may as easily have his throat cut in the church as elsewhere. When a slight figure in homespun darted from behind a pillar, I recognized Anne Page's eyes glowing beneath the coarse grey mantle just before my steel cleared the sheath.

"You come most carefully upon your hour, player. Tell me, quickly, what did you learn?" Present fears forgotten, we patrolled the nave in measured steps. When I had finished she cried: "Oh, smiling damned villain! From this time shall my thoughts be only bloody!"

I cautioned: "Squire Thomas said that he had done no murder."

"Then you're a fool, or coward! On May eighteenth Walsingham sent Poley to find Kit a place to hide in Holland from the warrant brought by Kyd's deposition. But Baines's charge of blasphemy was too serious – Walsingham feared he would be compromised by helping Kit defy it. More, he determined on murder to prevent the public disclosures of Kit's trial." Her voice writhed in its own venom like a stricken serpent. "Oh, player, I would lay the dust with showers of that man's blood. But hold – enough! My quarrel is yours no further."

"I'll not leave you, Anne," I declared passionately.

"You must. Had I met you before Kit – " Her fingers brushed my lips in sexless caress, and regret laid its vague wings across her face. "Too late! Hell has breathed contagion on me; I am fit only to drink hot blood."

I shook my head and declared flatly: "I will walk with you, Anne; take you through the dark night to your home."

Outside the Cathedral it was cold and the air bit shrewdly. Rank river fog, driven by the eager nipping wind, obscured all about us. Noxious plague odours assailed us, and from the muffling smoke came the clop-clop of hoofs as a death cart rattled about its grisly business, the cartmen leaping down with iron tongs to drag the sprawled and sightless corpses from the slops and urine of the gutters.

Through the swirling fog of Dowgate Hill I could see the cobbler's house where last year Rob Greene was lost in death's dateless night. Here Anne broke in upon my reverie.

"Now surely twelve has struck – the moon is down, and it goes down at twelve. It's the witching time of night; in my soul shriek owls where mounting larks should sing. And now I must leave you."

"Now? Here? Surely not here, Anne?"

For we had arrived at Cold Harbour, where criminals impudently mock our English courts and the filthy tenements breed every vice.

"Yes, here," she whispered. "Here night cloaks me from my own sight while my body buys me sustenance to nurse revenge; and here I live only in hope of one day taking Walsingham about some act with no salvation in it, so his heels may kick to heaven while his soul is plunged to deepest hell."

She led me down a narrow alley where rats scuttled unseen and my boots slithered in foul mud; suddenly a man was silhouetted before us, naked steel glittering in his right hand.

"Back – this way!" I warned.

Too late! Behind were two more figures. Light glinted off bared swords, a spur chinked stone. I felt so unmanned with terror of my sins that I could not even draw my sword – for thus conscience makes cowards of us all. But then one of the men called out.

"Stand aside – we seek only the woman."

But I recognized the voice; and with recognition came anger.

"Booted and spurred, Rob Poley?" When I cried his name Anne gasped. "You three have ridden hard from Scadbury Park this night."

"You know us, player? Then by these hands you *both* shall die!"

"If hell and Satan hold their promises." My sword hissed out like a basking serpent from beneath its stone, barely in time to turn his darting steel. "Aha, boy!" I cried, "Say you so?"

But as he gave way before me Anne Page flashed by, dagger high.

"Murderer! Your deeds stink above the earth with carrion men!"

His outthrust rapier passed through her body, showed me half its length behind. She fell heavily sideways. Before his weapon was free I might have struck, but I was slow, for never before had I raised my blade in anger. Then it was too late. He put a ruthless foot against her neck, and jerked free.

"Stand on distance!" he bellowed at Skeres and Frizer. "Make him open his guard. He must not live!"

But by then my youthful blood was roused, and like all players I am expert in the fence. I turned Skeres's blade, shouting: "Now, while your purple hands reek and smoke." I lunged, skewered his dancing shadow in the throat so sparks flew from the stone behind his head, and jerked free. "I know these passes . . . these staccadoes . . ."

My dagger turned Frizer's sword, I covered, thrust, parried, thrust again, my arm longer by three feet of tempered steel. ". . . they're common on the stage . . . here . . . here . . . the heart!"

Frizer reeled drunkenly away, arms crossed over his punctured chest; but what of Poley? Fire lanced my arm and my rapier clattered from my nerveless grasp. Fingers like Hanse sausages closed about my windpipe. I felt myself thrust back so his long sword could reach me.

"Say you so now?" His voice was a snarl of triumph. "Are you there, truepenny?"

My head whirled giddily for lack of blood. In an instant his steel would – but then my dagger touched his belly. "How now!" I cried. "Dead for a ducat, dead!"

With my last despairing strength I ripped the two-edged cutter up through his guts, sprawled over his twitching corpse.

Silence. Moisture dripping from overhanging eaves, hot blood staining my fingers. A rat rustling in the gutter. The turning world turning on, aeons passing. Yet I lay silent in the drifting smoke. Then from beyond eternity a weak voice called me back to life.

"Player – my gashes cry for help – " Somehow I crawled to her, cradled her weakly lolling head against my shoulder. Her voice was small, so very small. "The churchyard yawns below me. I'll trade the world for a little grave, a little, little grave, an obscure grave . . ."

My salt tears gave benediction to her death-ravaged face; her body now was lead within the angle of my arm. "Anne!" I cried. "Anne! Oh, God! God forgive us all!"

"Let not this night be the whetstone of your sword." Her heart fluttered briefly within the frail cage of her body; her whispers touched my ear in failing cadence. "Let your heart be blunted. This death is – a joy unmixed with – sorrow."

No more. I lowered her gently to the waiting earth, struggled erect. My breath still rasped and rattled in my throat; dark walls weaved, receded, shifted; lantern bright above Cold Harbour Stairs, stone slimy beneath my vagrant gory fingers, cold Thames below, whispering its litany *she is dead she is dead she is*.

Falling. Nothing else besides.

Movement aroused me. I lay on the cushions of a waterman's boat, river fog upon my face. Peering forward I saw a familiar figure.

"Lad, how did I come here?"

John Taylor turned anxious eyes on me. "I found you at the foot of Cold Harbour Stairs." He indicated my sword at my feet. "Your blood upon the cobbles led to this – and one that was a woman. But rest her soul, she's dead. Two others were there also, one with his wizand slit, the other drawn like a bull in the flesh shambles."

I thrust my arm into the clear Thames water, found the wound only a painful furrow in the flesh. Frizer had escaped. Anne was dead. I needed time – time to think.

"The Falcon, lad. I'll see what physic the tavern accords."

I gave the boy my silver and went through the entrance, narrow and thick-walled from pre-Tudor days, to the tap-room. Here I was met by a blast of light and noise. I kept my arm against my side to mask the blood. A jolly group was gathered by the bar.

> A cup of wine that's brisk and fine
> And drink unto the leman mine:
> And a merry heart lives long-a.

"Before God, an excellent song!"

"An English song," laughed the singer. "Indeed, we English are most potent in our potting. I'll drink your Dane dead drunk; I'll overthrow your German; and I'll give your Hollander a vomit before the next bottle's filled!"

But this was Will Sly, the red-faced jolly comedian I'd left in Dover! At sight of me he threw his arms wide.

"Out upon it, old carrion! You can't have heard: The Admiral's Men have been disbanded! By William the Conqueror who came before Richard III, Will Sly finds himself in the good Falcon with bad companions swilling worse ale." He suited actions to words, then leaned closer and lowered his voice as he wiped the foam from his moustache. "But you look pale, lad; and your tankard's dry. Ho! Drawer!"

"Anon, sir."

I had barely drawn him aside with my story when a blustery voice broke in. "Players in the corner? Then some man's reputation's due for a fall. In faith, it's better to have a bad epitaph than the players' ill report while alive. But let me tell you what I'm about."

"Why, two yards at least, Tom Lucy," laughed Will Sly.

Lucy was from Charlecote, a few miles from my home – a trying man with severe eyes and beard of formal cut, and the brains of a pecking sparrow.

"Perhaps two yards around the waist, Will Sly, but now I'm about thrift, not waste."

He was always full of wise saws and modern instances, so I cut in curtly: "We'll join you at the bar presently, Master Lucy."

After he had turned about I went on; soon Will Sly's face was as long as his cloak. When I told of the meeting with Anne in St. Paul's he burst out bitterly: "Fool! What if you were seen with this Anne Page? If – "

"Anne Page?" said Lucy to me. "I wondered at the name of the doxy you walked beside on Dowgate Hill hard upon mid-night, player."

Will Sly matched his name. "Then you've been seeing double, Tom Lucy; he's matched me pot for pot these four hours past."

"I'm not deceived in her," said Lucy. "In the Bankside Stews her eyes have met mine boldly, like any honest woman's."

"Then the sun shone on a dunghill!" I burst out.

"Now vultures gripe your guts, player!" Lucy clapped hand to sword dramatically. "This'll make you skip like any rat!" When I stiffened he laughed loudly. "What? A tiger wrapped in a player's hide – or merely a kitten crying mew?"

Will Sly drew me away with a hasty hand. "Make nothing of it, lad – bluster must serve him for wit. He lives but for his porridge and fat bull-beef. But never before have I seen you foam up so, like sour beer, at any man. Is this my honest lad, my free and open nature – " He broke off abruptly, eyes wide at the blood upon his fingers.

"They set upon us in Cold Harbour. I left them stiff."

"How many? All? Dead? Why, you hell-kite, you!"

"There were three – Frizer lived, I think. Man, they made love to that employment! They're not near my conscience."

He shook his head. "Until tonight I'd have thought you incapable of taking offence at any man – nothing deeper in you than a smooth and ready wit. But yonder fat fool may yet breed you unnatural troubles."

"Just keep him from me," I said. "My blood is up."

But Lucy stopped me at the door, still not plumbing my mood.

"Hold, puppy! When a man mouths me as you have done, why, I'll fight with him until my eyelids no longer wag!"

Then he winked broadly at the company, waiting for me to turn away as is my wont. But suddenly I found myself with my rapier in hand, and saw, through the red mists, Lucy's mouth working like a netted luce's.

"Softly, master player!" He backed off rapidly. "I only jested. Er – I hold it fit that we should shake hands and part. You as your desires point you and me – why, I'll go pray."

I saw that he would pass it off as a joke, so I thrust away my sword and ignored his hand to stride from the place with Will Sly behind.

"Why so hot to-night, lad? The rightly great stir only with great argument. When honour's at stake find a quarrel in a straw – "

"Before my eyes they killed her!" I burst out. "Killed Anne!"

"No!" His homely face crinkled in honest sympathy; he turned away. "And you had begun to feel something more for her than pity?"

"I know not, but she and Kit cannot lie unavenged. What is a man if all he does is feed and sleep?"

"A beast, nothing more. And yet, lad, two carrion men crying for burial also shout to me of vengeance taken."

"But Walsingham – "

"Leave him to heaven. Look: he said no murder had he done. Are you God, to judge him false? They might have struck for private reasons, or for hire other than his. Can you be sure they didn't?"

We were at the verge of the river. I could smell the mud and osiers. Across the broad reach of gliding water a few firefly lanterns winked on the London side, for the mist had lifted; from downstream came the creak and grumble of the old bridge in the flood-tide.

*Could* I be sure of Walsingham's guilt? If killing is once started, where did it end?

The calm gliding river had begun to calm my own troubled spirit. My nature was not bloody, my trade was not revenge. Kit had died as he had lived, in violence; but his death, perhaps, had shown me the way to even greater things than he had done: plumb man's nature to its depths, transfigure with creative light the pain and sorrow and suffering of the human spirit – yes! White hairs to a quiet grave mean not always failure, nor does a life thrown away upon a gesture mean success. Perhaps in all of this my mettle had been hardened.

Perhaps . . .

Will Sly spoke as if divining my thoughts: "Forget these sad and bloody hours, lad; the night is long indeed which never finds a day. In these bones of mine I know the world yet shall hear of you. Don't toss your life away upon revenge, as the tapster tosses off his pot of ale, for one day the mass of men will come to honour and revere your name – the name of William Shakespeare."

# PART III
# Regency and Gaslight

# THE CHRISTMAS MASQUE
# S. S. Rafferty

*S. S. Rafferty is the pen name of former reporter and advertising executive, Jack J. Hurley (b. 1930). He has been the author of scores of short stories in the mystery magazines but has only published one book, Fatal Flourishes (1979), which features the adventures of Captain Cork in colonial America.*

*The series started in 1974, in the years leading up to the American bicentennial celebrations, when Rafferty determined to write a detective mystery set in each of the original thirteen states. As continuity between these stories he used businessman Captain Cork, who delights in "social puzzles", and who is accompanied everywhere by his associate, Oaks, who serves as his Watson in recording his cases. The series spans forty years from the earliest case, "The Rhode Island Lights", to the grand finale, "The Pennsylvania Thimblerig", set at the outset of the War of Independence. The following tantalizing crime is set in the year 1754.*

As much as I prefer the steady ways of New England, I have to agree with Captain Jeremy Cork that the Puritans certainly know how to avoid a good time. They just ignore it. That's why every 23rd of December we come to the New York colony from our home base in Connecticut to celebrate the midwinter holidays.

I am often critical of my employer's inattention to his many business enterprises and his preoccupation with the solution of crime – but I give him credit for the way he keeps Christmas. That is, as long as I can stop him from keeping it clear into February.

In our travels about these colonies, I have witnessed many merry parties, from the lush gentility of the Carolinas to the roughshod ribaldry of the New Hampshire tree line; but nothing can match the excitement of the Port of New York. The place teems with prosperous men who ply their fortunes in furs, potash, naval timber, and other prime goods. And the populace is drawn from everywhere: Sephardim from Brazil, Huguenots from France, visitors from

London, expatriates from Naples, Irishmen running to or from something. I once counted 18 different languages being spoken here.

And so it was in the Christmas week of 1754 that we took our usual rooms at Marshall's in John Street, a few steps from the Histrionic Academy, and let the yuletide roll over us. Cork's celebrity opens many doors to us, and there was the expected flood of invitations for one frivolity after another.

I was seated at a small work table in our rooms on December 23, attempting to arrange our social obligations into a reasonable program. My primary task was to sort out those invitations which begged our presence on Christmas Eve itself, for that would be our highpoint. Little did I realize that a knock on our door would not only decide the issue, but plunge us into one of the most bizarre of those damnable social puzzles Cork so thoroughly enjoys.

The messenger was a small lad, no more than seven or eight, and he was bundled against the elements from head to toe. Before I could open the envelope to see if an immediate reply was required, the child was gone.

I was opening the message when Cork walked in from the inner bedchamber. Marshall's is one of the few places on earth with doorways high enough to accommodate his six-foot-six frame.

"I take the liberty," I said. "It's addressed to us both."

"On fine French linen paper, I see."

"Well, well," I said, reading the fine handscript. "This is quite an honour."

"From the quality of the paper and the fact that you are 'honoured' just to read the message, I assume the reader is rich, money being the primer for your respect, Oaks."

That is not absolutely true. I find nothing wrong with poverty; however, it is a condition I do not wish to experience. In fact, as Cork's financial yeoman, it is my sworn duty to keep it from our door sill. The invitation was from none other than Dame Ilsa van Schooner, asking us to take part in her famous Christmas Eve Masque at her great house on the Broad Way. Considering that we had already been invited to such questionable activities as a cockfight, a party at a doss house, a drinking duel at Cosgrove's, and an evening of sport at the Gentlemen's Club, I was indeed honoured to hear from a leader of New York quality.

Cork was glancing at the invitation when I discovered a smaller piece of paper still in the envelope.

"This is odd," I said, reading it:

van Schooner Haus
22 December

Dear Sirs:
   I implore you to accept the enclosed, for I need you very much to investigate a situation of some calamity for us. I shall make myself known at the Masque.


It was unsigned. I passed it to the Captain, who studied it for a moment and then picked up the invitation again.

"I'm afraid your being honoured is misplaced, my old son," he said. "The invitation was written by a skilled hand, possibly an Ephrata penman, hired for such work. But our names have been fitted in by a less skilled writer. The author of the note has by some means invited us without the hostess' knowledge. Our *sub rosa* bidder must be in some dire difficulty, for she does not dare risk discovery by signing her name."

"Her?"

"No doubt about it. The hand is feminine and written in haste. I thought it odd that a mere boy should deliver this. It is usually the task of a footman, who would wait for a reply. This is truly intriguing – an impending calamity stalking the wealthy home in which she lives."

"How can you be sure of that, sir?"

"I can only surmise. She had access to the invitations and she says 'calamity for us,' which implies her family. Hello." He looked up suddenly as the door opened and a serving girl entered with a tray, followed by a man in royal red. "Sweet Jerusalem!" Cork got to his feet. "Major Tell in the flesh! Sally, my girl, you had better have Marshall send up extra Apple Knock and oysters. Tell, it is prophetic that you should appear just as a new puzzle emerges."

Prophetic indeed. Major Philip Tell is a King's agent-at-large, and he invariably embroiled us in some case of skulduggery whenever he was in our purlieu. But I bode him no ill this time, for he had nothing to do with the affair. In fact, his vast knowledge of the colonial scene might prove helpful.

"Well, lads," Tell said, taking off his *rogueloure* and tossing his heavy cloak onto a chair. "I knew Christmas would bring you to New York. You look fit, Captain, and I see Oaks is still at his account books."

When Cork told him of our invitation and the curious accompanying note, the officer gave a low whistle. "The van Schooners, no less! Well, we shall share the festivities, for I am also a guest at the affair. The note is a little disturbing, however. Dame Ilsa is the mistress of a large fortune and extensive land holdings, which could be the spark for foul play."

"You think she sent the note?" I asked.

"Nonsense," Cork interjected. "She would not have had to purloin her own invitation. What can you tell us of the household, Major?"

I don't know if Tell's fund of knowledge is part of his duties or his general nosiness, but he certainly keeps his ear to the ground. No gossip-monger could hold a candle to him.

"The family fortune was founded by her grandfather, Nils van der Malin – patroon holdings up the Hudson, pearl potash, naval stores, that sort of old money. Under Charles the Second's Duke of York grant, Nils was rewarded for his support with a baronetcy. The title fell in the distaff side to Dame Ilsa's mother, old Gretchen van der Malin. She was a terror of a woman, who wore men's riding clothes and ran her estates with an iron first and a riding crop. She had a young man of the Orange peerage brought over as consort, and they produced Ilsa. The current Dame is more genteel than her mother was, but just as stern and autocratic. She, in turn, married a van Schooner – Gustave, I believe, a soldier of some distinction in the Lowland campaigns. He died of drink after fathering two daughters, Gretchen and her younger sister, Wilda.

"The line is certainly Amazonite and breeds true," Cork said with a chuckle. "Not a climate I would relish, although strong women have their fascination."

"Breeds true is correct, Captain. The husbands were little more than sire stallions; good blood but ruined by idleness."

This last, about being "ruined by idleness," was ignored by Cork, but I marked it, as well he knew.

"Young Gretchen," Tell went on, "is also true to her namesake. A beauty, but cold as a steel blade, and as well honed. They say she is a dead shot and an adept horsewoman."

"You have obviously been to the van Schooner haus, as our correspondent calls it."

"Oh, yes, on several occasions. It is truly a place to behold."

"No doubt, Major." Cork poured a glass of Apple Knock. "Who else lives there besides the servants?"

"The younger daughter Wilda, of course, and the Dame's spinster sister, Hetta van der Malin, and an ancient older brother of the dead husband – the brother is named Kaarl. I have only seen him once, but I am told he was quite the wastrel in his day, and suffers from the afflictions of such a life."

"Mmm," Cork murmured, offering the glass to Tell. "I change my original Amazonite observation to that of Queen Bee. Well, someone in that house feels in need of help, but we shall have to wait until to-morrow night to find out why."

"Or who," I said.

"That," Cork said, "is the heart of the mystery."

The snow started falling soon after dinner that night and kept falling into the dawn. By noon of the 24th, the wind had drifted nature's white blanket into knee-high banks. When it finally stopped in the late afternoon, New York was well covered under a blotchy sky. The inclemency, however, did not deter attendance at the van Schooner Ball.

I had seen the van Schooner home from the road many times, and always marveled at its striking architecture, which is in the Palladio style. The main section is a three-storey structure, and it is flanked by one-storey wings at both sides.

The lights and music emanating from the north wing clearly marked it a ballroom of immense size. The front entrance to the main house had a large raised enclosure which people in these parts call a stoop. The interior was as rich and well appointed as any manse I have ever seen. The main hall was a gallery of statuary of the Greek and Roman cast, collected, I assumed, when the family took the mandatory Grand Tour.

Our outer clothes were taken at the main door, and we were escorted through a sculptured archway across a large salon towards the ballroom proper. We had purposely come late to avoid the reception line and any possible discovery by Dame van Schooner. We need not have bothered. There were more than 200 people there, making individual acquaintance impossible. Not that some of the guests were without celebrity. The Royal Governor was in attendance, and I saw General Seaton and Solomon deSilva, the fur king, talking with Reeves, the shipping giant.

It was difficult to determine the identity of the majority of the people, for most wore masks, although not all, including Cork and myself. Tell fluttered off on his social duties, and Cork fell to conversation with a man named Downs, who had recently returned from Spanish America and shared common friends there with the Captain.

I helped myself to some hot punch and leaned back to take in the spectacle. It would be hard to say whether the men or the women were the more lushly bedizened. The males were adorned in the latest fashion with those large, and, to my mind, cumbersome rolled coat cuffs. The materials of their plumage were a dazzling mixture of gold and silver stuffs, bold brocades, and gaudy flowered velvets. The women, not to be outdone by their peacocks, were visions in fan-hooped gowns of silks and satins and fine damask. Each woman's *tête-de-moutin* back curls swung gaily as her partner spun her around the dance floor to madcap tunes such as "Roger de Coverly," played with spirit by a seven-piece ensemble. To the right of the ballroom entrance was a long table with three different punch bowls dispensing cheer.

The table was laden with all manner of great hams, glistening roast goose, assorted tidbit meats and sweets of unimaginable variety. Frothy syllabub was cupped up for the ladies by liveried footmen, while the gentlemen had their choice of Madeira, rum, champagne, or Holland gin, the last served in small crystal thimbles which were embedded and cooled in a silver bowl mounded with snow.

"This is most lavish," I said to Cork when he disengaged himself from conversation with Downs. "It's a good example of what diligent attention to industry can produce."

"Whose industry, Oaks? Wealth has nothing more to do with industry than privilege has with merit. Our hostess over there does not appear to have ever perspired in her life."

He was true to the mark in his observation, for Dame van Schooner, who stood chatting with the Governor near the buffet, was indeed as cold as fine-cut crystal. Her well-formed face was sternly beautiful, almost arrogantly defying anyone to marvel at its handsomeness and still maintain normal breathing.

"She *is* a fine figure of a woman, Captain, and, I might add, a widow."

He gave me a bored look and said, "A man would die of frostbite in her bedchamber. Ah, Major Tell, congratulations! You are a master at the jig!"

"It's a fantastical do, but good for the liver, I'm told. Has the mysterious sender of your invitation made herself known to you?"

"Not as yet. Is that young lady now talking with the Dame one of her daughters?"

"Both of them are daughters. The one lifting her mask is Gretchen, and, I might add, the catch of the year. I am told she has been elected Queen of the Bal, and will be crowned this evening."

The girl was the image of her mother. Her sister, however, must have followed the paternal line.

"The younger one is Wilda," Tell went on, "a dark pigeon in her own right, but Gretchen is the catch."

"Catch, you say." I winked at Cork. "Perhaps *her* bedchamber would be warmer?"

"You'll find no purchase there, gentlemen," Tell told us. "Along with being crowned Queen, her betrothal to Brock van Loon will probably be announced this evening."

"Hand-picked by her mother, no doubt?" Cork asked.

"Everything is hand-picked by the Dame. Van Loon is a stout fellow, although a bit of a tailor's dummy. Family is well landed across the river in Brueckelen. Say, they're playing "The Green Cockade," Captain. Let me introduce you to Miss Borden, one of our finest steppers."

I watched them walk over to a comely piece of frippery and then Cork and the young lady stepped onto the dance floor. "The Green Cockade" is one of Cork's favourite tunes, and he dances it with gusto.

I drifted over to the serving table and took another cup of punch, watching all the time for some sign from our mysterious "hostess," whoever she was. I mused that the calamity mentioned in the note might well have been pure hyperbole, for I could not see how any misfortune could befall this wealthy, joyous home.

With Cork off on the dance floor, Tell returned to my side and offered to find a dance partner for me. I declined, not being the most nimble of men, but did accept his bid to introduce me to a lovely young woman named Lydia Daws-Smith. The surname declared her to be the offspring of a very prominent family in the fur trade, and her breeding showed through a delightfully pretty face and pert figure. We were discussing the weather when I noticed four footmen carrying what appeared to be a closed sedan chair into the hall and through a door at the rear.

"My word, is a Sultan among the assemblage?" I asked my companion.

"The sedan chair?" She giggled from behind her fan. "No, Mr. Oaks, no Sultan. It's our Queen's throne. Gretchen will be transported into the hall at the stroke of midnight, and the Governor will proclaim her our New Year's Sovereign." She stopped for a moment, the smile gone. "Then she will step forward to our acclaim and, of course, mandatory idolatry."

"I take it you do not like Gretchen very much, Miss Daws-Smith."

"On the contrary, sir. She is one of my best friends. Now you will have to excuse me, for I see Gretchen is getting ready for the crowning, and I must help her."

I watched the young girl as she followed Gretchen to the rear of the hall where they entered a portal and closed the door behind them. Seconds later, Lydia Daws-Smith came back into the main hall and spoke with the Dame, who then went through the rear door.

Cork had finished his dance and rejoined me. "This exercise may be good for the liver," he said, "but it plays hell with my thirst. Shall we get some refills?"

We walked back to the buffet table to slake his thirst, if that were ever possible. From the corner of my eye I caught sight of the Dame re-entering the hall from the rear door. She crossed over to the Governor and was about to speak to him when the orchestra struck up another tune. She seemed angry at the intrusion into what was obviously to have been the beginning of the coronation. But the Dame was ladylike and self-contained until the dancing was over. She then took a deep breath and nervously adjusted the neckline of her dress, which was shamefully bare from the bodice to the neck.

"Looks like the coronation is about to begin," Major Tell said, coming up to us. "I'll need a cup for the toast."

We were joking at the far end of the table when a tremendous crash sounded. We turned to see a distraught Wilda van Schooner looking down at the punch bowl she had just dropped. The punch had splashed down her beautiful velvet dress, leaving her drenched and mortified.

"Oh-oh," Tell said under his breath. "Now we'll hear some fireworks from Dame van Schooner."

True to his prediction, the Dame sailed across the floor and gave biting instructions to the footmen to bring mops and pails. A woman, who Tell told me in a whisper was Hetta van der Malin, the Dame's sister, came out of the crowd of tittering guests to cover her niece's embarrassment.

"She was only trying to help, Ilsa," the aunt said as she dabbed the girl's dress with a handkerchief.

The Dame glared at them. "You'd better help her change, Hetta, if she is going to attend the coronation."

The aunt and niece quickly left the ballroom and the Dame whirled her skirts and returned to the Governor's side. I overheard her say her apologies to him and then she added, "My children don't seem to know what servants are for. Well, shall we begin?"

At a wave of her hand, the orchestra struck up the "Grenadier's March," and six young stalwarts lined up in two ranks before the Governor. At his command, the lads did a left turn and marched off towards the rear portal in the distinctive long step of the regiment whose music they had borrowed for the occasion.

They disappeared into the room where Gretchen waited for transport, and within seconds they returned, bearing the ornate screened sedan chair. "Aah's" filled the room over the beauty and pageantry of the piece. I shot a glance at Dame van Schooner and noted that she was beaming proudly at the impeccably executed production.

When the sedan chair had been placed before the Governor, he stepped forward, took the curtain drawstrings, and said, "Ladies and gentlemen, I give you our New Year's Queen."

The curtains were pulled open and there she sat in majesty. More "aah's" from the ladies until there was a screech and then another and, suddenly, pandemonium. Gretchen van Schooner sat on her portable throne, still beautiful, but horribly dead with a French bayonet through her chest.

"My Lord!" Major Tell gasped and started forward toward the sedan chair. Cork touched his arm.

"You can do no good there. The rear room, man, that's where the answer lies. Come, Oaks." He moved quickly through the crowd and I followed like a setter's tail on point. When we reached the door, Cork turned to Tell.

"Major, use your authority to guard this door. Let no one enter." He motioned me inside and closed the door behind us.

It was a small room, furnished in a masculine manner. Game trophies and the heads of local beasts protruded from the walls and were surrounded by a symmetrical display of weaponry such as daggers, blunderbusses, and swords.

"Our killer had not far to look for his instrument of death," Cork said, pointing to an empty spot on the wall about three feet from the fireplace and six feet up from the floor. "Move with care, Oaks, lest we disturb some piece of evidence."

I quickly looked around the rest of the chamber. There was a door in the south wall and a small window some ten feet to the left of it.

"The window!" I cried. "The killer must have come in – "

"I'm afraid not, Oaks," Cork said, after examining it. "The snow on the sill and panes is undisturbed. Besides, the floor in here is dry. Come, let's open the other door."

He drew it open to reveal a short narrow passage that was dimly lit with one sconced candle and had another door at its end. I started toward it and found my way blocked by Cork's outthrust arm.

"Have a care, Oaks," he said. "Don't confound a trail with your own spore. Fetch a candelabrum from the table for more light."

I did so, and to my amazement he got down on his hands and knees and inched forward along the passageway. I, too, assumed this stance and we crept along like a brace of hounds.

The polished planked floor proved dry and bare of dust until we were in front of the outer door. There, just inside the portal, was a pool of liquid.

"My Lord, it is blood!" I said.

"Mostly water from melted snow."

"But, Captain, there is a red stain to it."

"Yes," he said. "Bloody snow and yet the bayonet in that woman's breast was driven with such force that no blood escaped from her body."

Cork got to his feet and lifted the door latch, opening the passage-way to pale white moonlight which reflected off the granules of snow. He carefully looked at the doorstoop and then out into the yard.

"Damnation," he muttered, "it looks as if an army tramped through here."

Before us, the snow was a mass of furrows and upheavals with no one set of footprints discernible.

"Probably the servants coming and going from the wood yard down by the gate," I said, as we stepped out into the cold. At the opposite end of the house, in the left wing, was another door, obviously leading to the kitchen, for a clatter of plates and pots could be heard within the snug and frosty windowpanes. I turned to Cork and found myself alone. He was at the end of the yard opening a slatted gate in the rear garden wall.

"What ho, Captain," I called ahead, as I went to meet him.

"The place abounds in footprints," he snarled in frustration.

"Then the killer has escaped us," I muttered. "Now we have the whole population of this teeming port to consider."

He turned slowly, the moonlight glistening off his barba, his eyes taking on a sardonic glint. "For the moment, Oaks, for the moment. Besides, footprints are like empty boots. In the long run we would have had to fill them."

I started to answer when a voice called from our backs, at the passage doorway. It was Major Tell.

"Hello, is that you there, Cork? Have you caught the dastard?"

"Some gall," I said to the Captain. "As if we could pull the murderer out of our sleeves like a magician."

"Not yet, Major," Cork shouted and then turned to me. "Your powers of simile are improving, Oaks."

"Well," I said, with a bit of a splutter. "Do you think magic is involved?"

"No, you ass. Sleight of hand! The quick flick that the eye does not see nor the mind inscribe. We'll have to use our instincts on this one."

He strode off towards the house and I followed. I have seen him rely on instinct over hard evidence only two times in our years together, and in both cases, although he was successful, the things he uncovered were too gruesome to imagine.

The shock that had descended on the van Schooner manse at midnight still lingered three hours later when the fires in the great fireplaces were reduced to embers, the shocked guests had been questioned, and all but the key witnesses had been sent homeward. Cork, after consultation with the Royal Governor, had been given a free hand in the investigation, with Major Tell stirred in to keep the manner of things official.

Much to my surprise, the Captain didn't embark on a flurry of questions of all concerned, but rather drew up a large baronial chair to the ballroom hearth and brooded into its sinking glow.

"Two squads of cavalry are in the neighbourhood," Major Tell said. "If any stranger were in the vicinity, he must have been seen."

"You can discount a stranger, Major," Cork said, still gazing into the embers.

"How so?"

"Merely a surmise, but with stout legs to it. If a stranger came to kill, he would have brought a weapon with him. No, the murderer knew the contents of the den's walls. He also seems to have known the coronation schedule."

"The window," I interjected. "He could have spied the bayonet, and when the coast was clear, entered and struck."

"Except for the singular fact that the snow on the ground in front of the window is undisturbed."

"Well, obviously someone entered by the back passage," Tell said. "We have the pool of water and the blood."

"Then where are the wet footprints into the den, Major?"

"Boots!" I shouted louder than I meant to. "He took off his boots and then donned them again on leaving."

"Good thinking, Oaks," Tell complimented me. "And in the process, his bloody hands left a trace in the puddle."

"And what, pray, was the motive?" Cork asked. "Nothing of value was taken that we can determine. No, we will look within this house for an answer."

Tell was appalled. "Captain Cork, I must remind you that this is the home of a powerful woman, and she was hostess to-night to the cream of New York society. Have a care how you cast aspersions."

"The killer had best have a care, Major. For a moment, let us consider some *facts*. Mistress Gretchen went into the den to prepare for her coronation with the aid of – ah – "

"Lydia Daws-Smith," I supplied.

"So we have one person who saw her before she died. Then these six society bucks who were to transport her entered, and among their company was Brock van Loon, her affianced. Seven people involved between the time we all saw her enter the den and the time she was carried out dead."

"Eight," I said, and then could have bit my tongue.

"Who else?" Cork demanded.

"The Dame herself. I saw her enter after Miss Daws-Smith came out."

"That is highly irresponsible, Oaks," Tell admonished.

"And interesting," Cork said. "Thank you, Oaks, you have put some yeast into it with your observation."

"You're not suggesting that the Dame killed her own daughter!"

"Major," Cork said, "she-animals have been known to eat their young when they are endangered. But enough of this conjecture. Let us get down to rocks and hard places. We will have to take it step by step. First, let us have a go at the footmen who carried the chair into the den before Gretchen entered."

They were summoned, and the senior man, a portly fellow named Trask, spoke for the lot.

"No, sir," he answered Cork's question. "I am sure no one was lurking in the room when we entered. There is no place to hide."

"And the passage to the back door?"

"Empty, sir. You see, the door leading to the passage was open and I went over to close it against any draughts coming into the den. There was no one in the den, sir, I can swear to it."

"Is the outside door normally kept locked?"

"Oh, yes, sir. Leastways, it's supposed to be. It was locked earlier this afternoon when I made my rounds, preparing for the festivities."

"Tell me, Trask," Cork asked, "do you consider yourself a good servant, loyal to your mistress' household?"

The man's chubby face looked almost silly with its beaming pride. "Twenty-two years in this house, sir, from kitchen boy to head footman, and every day of it in the Dame's service."

"Very commendable, Trask, but you are most extravagant with tapers."

"Sir?" Trask looked surprised.

"If the backyard door was locked, why did you leave a candle burning in the passageway? Since no one could come in from the outside, no light would be needed as a guide. Certainly anyone entering from the den would carry his own."

"But, Captain," the footman protested, "I left no light in the passageway. When I was closing the inner door, I held a candelabrum in my hand, and could see clear to the other end. There was no candle lit."

"My apologies, Trask. Thank you, that will be all."

When the footmen had left, I said, "Yet we found a lit candle out there right after the murder. The killer must have left it in his haste."

Cork merely shrugged. Then he said, "So we go a little further. Major, I would like to see Miss Daws-Smith next."

Despite the circumstances, I was looking forward to seeing the comely Miss Daws-Smith once more. However, she was not alone when she entered, and her escort made it clear by his protective manner that her beauty was his property alone. She sat down in a straight-backed chair opposite Cork, nervously fingering the fan in her lap. Brock van Loon took a stance behind her.

"I prefer to speak to this young lady alone," Cork said.

"I am aware of your reputation, Captain Cork," van Loon said defensively, "and I do not intend to have Lydia drawn into this."

"Young man, she *is* in it, and from your obvious concern for her, I'd say you are, too."

"It is more than concern, sir. I love Lydia and she loves me."

"Brock," the girl said, turning to him.

"I don't care, Lydia. I don't care what my father says and I don't care what the Dame thinks."

"That's a rather anti-climactic statement, young man. Since your betrothed is dead, you are free of that commitment."

"You see, Brock? Now he suspects that we had something to do with Gretchen's death. I swear, Captain, we had no hand in it."

"Possibly not as cohorts. Was Gretchen in love with this fellow?"

"No. I doubt Gretchen could love any man. She was like her mother, and was doing her bidding as far as a marriage went. The van Schooner women devour males. Brock knows what would have become of him. He saw what happened to Gretchen's father."

"Gustave van Schooner," Brock said, "died a worthless drunkard locked away on one of the family estates up the Hudson. He had been a valiant soldier, I am told, and yet, once married to the Dame, he was reduced to a captured stallion."

"Quite poetic," Cork said. "Now, my dear, can you tell me what happened when you and Gretchen entered the den this evening?"

The girl stopped toying with the fan and sent her left hand to her shoulder where Brock had placed his. "There's nothing to tell, really. We went into the den together and I asked her if she wanted a cup of syllabub. She said no."

"What was her demeanour? Was she excited?"

"About being the Queen? Mercy, no. She saw that as her due. Gretchen was not one to show emotion." She stopped suddenly in thought and then said, "But now that I think back, she was fidgety. She walked over to the fireplace and tapped on the mantel with her fingers. Then she turned and said, 'Tell the Dame I'm ready,' which was strange, because she never called her mother that."

"Was she being sarcastic?"

"No, Captain, more a poutiness, I went and gave Dame van Schooner the message. That was the last I saw of Gretchen." Her eyes started to moisten. "The shock is just wearing off, I suppose. She was spoiled and autocratic, but Gretchen was a good friend."

"Hardly, Miss Daws-Smith. She had appropriated your lover."

"No. She knew nothing of how I felt towards Brock. We were all children together, you see – Gretchen, Wilda, Brock, and I. When you grow up that way, you don't always know childish affection from romantic love. I admit that when plans were being made for the betrothal, love for Brock burned in me, but I hid it, Captain, I hid it well. Then, earlier this evening, Brock told me how he felt, and I was both elated and miserable. I decided that both Brock and I would go to the Dame tomorrow. Gretchen knew nothing of our love."

"And you, sir," Cork said to Brock, "you made no mention of your change of heart to Gretchen?"

The fellow bowed his head. "Not in so many words. This has been coming on me for weeks, this feeling I have for Lydia. Just now as you were talking to her, I wondered – God, how terrible! – if Gretchen could have committed suicide out of despair."

"Oh, Brock!" Lydia was aghast at his words.

"Come," Cork commanded sharply, "this affair is burdensome enough without the added baggage of melodrama. Use your obvious good sense, Miss Daws-Smith. Is it likely that this spoiled and haughty woman would take her own life? Over a man?"

Lydia raised her head and looked straight at Cork. "No. No, of course not. It's ridiculous."

"Now, Mr. van Loon, when you entered the den with the others in the escort party to bring in the sedan chair, were the curtains pulled shut?"

"Yes, they were."

"And no one spoke to its occupant?"

"No, we didn't."

"Strange, isn't it? Such a festive occasion, and yet no one spoke?"

"We were in a hurry to get her out to where the Governor was waiting. Wait, someone did say, 'Hang on, Gretchen' when we lifted the chair. I don't remember who said it, though."

"You heard no sound from inside the chair? No groan or murmur?"

"No, sir, not a sound."

"Well thank you for your candour. Oh, yes, Miss Daws-Smith, when you left Gretchen, was she still standing by the fire?"

"Yes, Captain."

"Was her mask on or off?"

She frowned. "Why, she had it on. What a queer question!"

"It's a queer case, young lady."

The great clock in the center hall had just tolled three when Cork finished talking with the other five young men who had carried the murdered girl in the sedan chair. They all corroborated Brock's version. All were ignorant of any expression of love between Brock and Lydia, and they were unanimous in their relief that Brock, and not one of them, had been Gretchen's intended. As one young man named Langley put it, "At least Brock has an inheritance of his own, and would not have been dependent on his wife and mother-in-law."

"Dependent?" Cork queried. "Would he not assume her estate under law?"

"No, sir, not in this house," Langley explained. "I am told it's a kind of morganatic arrangement and a tradition with the old van der Malin line. I have little income, so Gretchen would have been no bargain for me. Not that I am up to the Dame's standards."

When Langley had left, Trask the footman entered to tell us that rooms had been prepared for us at the Major's request. Cork thanked him and said, "I know the hour is late, but is your mistress available?"

He told us he would see, and showed us to a small sitting-room off the main upstairs hall. It was a tight and cosy chamber with a newly-stirred hearth and the accoutrements of womankind – a small velvet couch with tiny pillows, a secretaire in the corner, buckbaskets of knitting and mending.

Unusual, however, was the portrait of the Dame herself that hung on a wall over the secretaire. It was certainly not the work of a local limner, for the controlled hand of a master painter showed through. Each line was carefully laid down, each colour blended one with the other, to produce a perfect likeness of the Dame. She was dressed in a gown almost as beautiful as the one she had worn this evening. At her throat was a remarkable diamond necklace which, despite the two dimensions of the portrait, was lifelike in its cool, blue-white lustre.

Cork was drawn to the portrait and even lifted a candle to study it more closely. I joined him and was about to tell him to be careful of the flame when a voice from behind startled me.

"There are additional candles if you need more light."

We both turned to find Wilda van Schooner standing in the doorway. She looked twice her seventeen years with the obvious woe she carried inside her. Her puffed eyes betrayed the tears of grief that had recently welled there.

"Forgive my curiosity, Miss van Schooner," Cork said, turning back to the portrait. "Inquisitiveness and a passion for details are my afflictions. This work was done in Europe, of course?"

"No, sir, here in New York; although Jan der Trogue is from the continent. He is – was – to have painted all of us eventually." She broke off into thought and then rejoined us. "My mother is with my sister, gentlemen, and is not available. She insists on seeing to Gretchen herself."

"That is most admirable." Cork bid her to seat herself, and she did so. She did not have her sister's or her mother's colouring, nor their chiselled beauty, but there was something strangely attractive about this tall dark-haired girl.

"I understand, Captain, that you are here to help us discover the fiend who did this thing, but you will have to bear with my mother's grief."

"To be sure. And what can you tell me, Miss Wilda?"

"I wish I could offer some clew, but my sister and I were not close – we did not exchange confidences."

"Was she in love with Brock van Loon?"

"Love!" she cried, and then did a strange thing. She giggled almost uncontrollably for a few seconds. "That's no word to use in this house, Captain."

"Wilda, my dear," a female voice said from the open door. "I think you are too upset to make much sense to-night. Perhaps in the morning, gentlemen?"

The speaker was the girls' aunt, Hetta van der Malin, and we rose as she entered.

"Forgive our intrusion into your sitting room, Ma'am," Cork said with a bow. "Perhaps you are right. Miss Wilda looks exhausted."

"I agree, Captain Cork," the aunt said, and she put her arm around the girl and ushered her out the door.

"Pray," Cork interrupted, "could *you* spare us some time in your niece's stead?"

Her smile went faint, but it was a smile all the same. "How did you know this was *my* room, Captain? Oh, of course, Trask must have – "

"On the contrary, my eyes told me. Your older sister does not fit the image of a woman surrounded by knitting and mending and pert pillowcases."

"No, she doesn't. The den is Ilsa's sitting room. Our mother raised her that way. She is quite a capable person, you know."

"So it would seem. Miss Hetta, may I ask why you invited us here this evening?"

I was as caught off guard as she was.

"Whatever put that notion into your head? My sister dispatched the invitations herself."

"Precisely! That's why you had to purloin one and fill in our names yourself. Come, dear woman, the sample of your hand on the letters on your secretaire matches the hand that penned the unsigned note I received."

"You have looked through my things!"

"I snoop when forced to. Pretence will fail you, Ma'am, for the young lad who delivered this invitation will undoubtedly be found and will identify you. Come now, you wrote to invite me here and now you deny it. I will have an answer."

"Captain Cork," I cautioned him, for the woman was quivering.

"Yes, I sent it." Her voice was tiny and hollow. "But it had nothing to do with this horrible murder. It was trivial compared to it, and it is senseless to bring it up now. Please believe me, Captain. It was foolish of me."

"You said 'calamity' in your note, and now we have a murder done. Is that not the extreme of calamity?"

"Yes, of course it is. I used too strong a word in my note. I would gladly have told you about it after the coronation. But now it would just muddle things. I can't."

"Then, my dear woman, I must dig it out. Must I play the ferret while you play the mute?" His voice was getting sterner. I know how good an actor he is, but was he acting?

"Do you know what a colligation is, Madam?"

She shook her head.

"It is the orderly bringing together of isolated facts. Yet you blunt my efforts; half facts can lead to half truths. Do you want a half truth?" He paused and then spat it out. "Your sister may have killed her older daughter!"

"That is unbearable!" she cried.

"A surmise based on a half truth. She was the last person to see Gretchen alive, if the Daws-Smith girl is to be believed. And why not believe her? If Lydia had killed Gretchen, would she then send the mother into the room to her corpse? Take the honour guard who were to carry the sedan chair: if Gretchen were alive when her mother left her, could one of those young men have killed her in the presence of five witnesses?"

"Anyone could have come in from the outside." Miss Hetta's voice was frantic.

"Nonsense. The evidence is against it."

"Why would Ilsa want to kill her own flesh and blood? It is unthinkable!"

"And yet people will think it, rest assured. The whole ugly affair can be whitewashed and pinned to some mysterious assailant who stalked in the night season, but people will think it just the same, Madam."

She remained silent now, and I could feel Cork's mind turn from one tactic to another, searching for leverage. He got to his feet and walked over to the portrait.

"So in the face of silence, I must turn the ferret loose in my mind. Take, for example, the question of this necklace."

"The van der Malin Chain," she said, looking up at the portrait. "What about it?"

"If the painter was accurate, it seems of great worth, both in pounds sterling and family prestige. Its very name proclaims it an heirloom."

"It is. It has been in our family for generations."

"Do you wear it at times?"

"No, of course not. It is my sister's property."

"Your estates are not commingled?"

"Our family holds with primogeniture."

"I do not. Exclusive rights to a first born make a fetish of nature's caprice. But that is philosophy, and beyond a ferret. Where is the necklace, Madam?"

"Why, in my sister's strong box, I assume. This is most confusing, Captain Cork."

I could have added my vote to that. I have seen Cork search for answers with hopscratch questions, but this display seemed futile.

"It is I who am confused, Madam. I am muddled by many things in this case. Why, for instance, didn't your sister wear this necklace to the year's most important social function? She thought enough of it to have it painted in a portrait for posterity."

"Our minds sometimes work that way, Captain. Perhaps it didn't suit her costume."

Cork turned from the picture as if he had had enough of it. "I am told there is an Uncle Kaarl in this household, yet he was not in attendance at the Bal to-night. Did he not suit the occasion?"

"You are most rude, sir. Kaarl is an ill man, confined to his bed for several years." She got to her feet. "I am very tired, gentlemen."

"I, too, grow weary, Madam. One last question. Your late niece was irritable this evening, I am told. Did something particular happen recently to cause that demeanour?"

"No. What would she have to sulk about? She was the centre of attraction. I really must retire now. Good night."

When the rustle of her skirts had faded down the silent hallway, I said, "Well, Captain, we've certainly had a turn around the mulberry bush."

He gave me that smirk-a-mouth of his. "Some day, Oaks, you will learn to read between the lines where women are concerned. I am sure you thought me a bully for mistreating her, but it was necessary, and it worked."

"Worked?"

"To a fair degree. I started on her with several assumptions. Some have more weight now, others are discounted. Don't look so perplexed. I am sure that Hetta's note to us did not concern Gretchen directly. She did not fear for the girl's life in this calamity she now chooses to keep secret."

"How is that?"

"Use your common sense, man. If she had suspected an attempt on her niece's life, would she stand mute? No, she would screech her accusations to the sky. Her seeking outside aid from us must have been for another problem. Yes, Trask?"

I hadn't seen the footman in the shadows, nor had I any idea how long he had been there.

"Beg pard, Captain Cork, but Major Tell has retired to his room and would like to see you when you have a moment."

"Thank you, Trask. Is your mistress available to us now?"

"Her maid tells me she is abed, sir."

"A shame. Maybe you can help me, Trask. My friend and I were wondering why the Dame's picture hangs in this small room. I say it was executed in such a large size to hang in a larger room. Mr. Oaks, however, says it was meant for Miss Hetta's room as an expression of love between the two sisters."

"Well, there is an affection between them, sirs, but the fact is that the portrait hung in the Grand Salon until the Dame ordered it destroyed."

"When was this, Trask?"

"Two days ago. 'Trask,' she said to me, 'take that abomination out and burn it.' Strange, she did like it originally, then, just like that, she hated it. Of course, Miss Hetta wouldn't let me burn it, so we spirited it in here, where the Dame never comes."

"Ha, you see I was right, Oaks. Thanks for settling the argument, Trask. Where is Major Tell's room?"

"Right next to yours, if you'll follow me, gentlemen."

Tell's chamber was at the back of the house where we found him sitting in the unlighted room, looking out at the moonlit yard.

"Nothing yet, Major?" Cork asked, walking to the window to join him.

"Not a sign or a shadow. I have men hiding at the front and down there near the garden gate and over to the left by the stable. Do you really expect him to make a move?"

"Conjecture costs us nothing, although I have more information now."

Although the room was bathed in moonlight, as usual I was in the dark. "Would either of you gentlemen mind telling me what this is all about? *Who* is coming?"

"Going would be more like it," the Major said.

"Going – ah, I see! The killer hid himself in the house somewhere and you expect him to make a break for it when everyone is bedded down. But where could he have hidden? Your men searched the den and passageway for secret panels, did they not?"

"Ask your employer," Tell said. "I am only following his orders – hold on, Cork, look down by the passage door."

I looked over Cork's shoulder to catch a glimpse of a cloaked figure in a cockade, moving among the shadows towards the stable.

"Our mounts are ready, Major?" Tell nodded. "Excellent. Let us be off."

As I followed them downstairs, I remarked on my own puzzlement. "Why are we going to *follow* this scoundrel? Why not stop him and unmask him?"

"Because I know who our mysterious figure is, Oaks. It is the destination that is the heart of the matter," Cork said as we hurried into the ballroom and back to the den door.

Once inside, I saw that Tell had placed our greatcoats in readiness and we bustled into them. Cork walked over to the weapon wall and looked at two empty hooks.

"A brace of pistols are gone. Our shadow is armed, as expected," he said.

"I'll take this one," I said, reaching for a ball-shot handgun.

"No need, Oaks," Cork said. "We are not the targets. Come, fellows, we want to be mounted and ready."

The night was cold as we waited behind a small knoll 20 yards down from the stable yard. Suddenly the doors of the stable burst open and a black stallion charged into the moonlight, bearing its rider to the south. "Now keep a small distance, but do not lose sight for a second," Cork commanded, and spurred his horse forward.

We followed through the drifts for ten minutes and saw our quarry turn into a small alley. When we reached the spot, we found the lathered mount tied to a stairway which went up the side of the building to a door on the second-storey landing. With Cork in the lead, we went up the cold stairs and assembled ourselves in front of the door. "Now!" Cork whispered, and we butted our shoulders against the wood panelling and fell into the room.

Our cloaked figure had a terrified man at gunpoint. The victim was a man in his forties, coiled into a corner. I was about to rush the person with the pistols when the tricornered hat turned to reveal the chiselled face and cold blue eyes of Dame Ilsa van Schooner.

"Drop the pistols, Madam, you are only compounding your problem," Cork said firmly.

"He murdered my child!"

"I swear, Dame Ilsa!" The man grovelled before her. His voice was foreign in inflection. "Please, you must hear me out. Yes, I am scum, but I am not a murderer."

Cork walked forward and put his hands over the pistol barrels. For a split second, the Dame looked up at him and her stern face went soft. "He's going to pay," she said.

"Yes, but not for your daughter's death."

"But only he could have – " She caught herself up in a flash of thought. Her lips quivered and she released the pistol butts into Cork's control. He took her by the arm and guided her to a chair.

The tension was broken, and I took my first look about. It was a large and comfortable bachelor's room. Then I saw the work area at the far end – with an easel, palettes, and paint pots.

"The painter! He's Jan der Trogue, the one who painted the portrait."

"You know about the painting?" the Dame said with surprise.

I started to tell her about seeing it in her sister's sitting-room, but never got it out. Der Trogue had grabbed the pistol that Cork had stupidly left on the table and pointed it at us as he edged towards the open door. "Stay where you are," he warned. "I owe you my life, sir." He bowed to Cork. "But it is not fitting to die at a woman's hands."

"Nor a hangman's," Cork said. "For you will surely go to the gallows for your other crime."

"Not this man, my fine fellow. Now stay where you are and no one will get hurt." He whirled out onto the landing and started to race down the stairs. Cork walked to the door. To my surprise, he had the other pistol in his hand. He stepped out onto the snowy landing.

"Defend yourself!" Cork cried. Then, after a tense moment, Cork took careful aim and fired. I grimaced as I heard der Trogue's body tumbling down the rest of the stairs.

Cork came back into the room with the smoking pistol in his hand. "Be sure your report says 'fleeing arrest,' Major," he said, shutting the door.

"Escape from what? You said he didn't kill the girl! This is most confusing and, to say the least, irregular!"

"Precisely put, Major. Confusing from the start and irregular for a finish. But first to the irregularity. What we say, see, and do here to-night stays with us alone." He turned to the Dame. "We will have to search the room. Will you help, since you have been here before?"

"Yes." She got up and started to open drawers and cupboards. She turned to us and held out a black felt bag which Cork opened.

"Gentlemen, I give you the van der Malin Chain, and quite exquisite it is."

"So he did steal it," I said.

"In a manner of speaking, Oaks, yes. But, Madam, should we not also find what you were so willing to pay a king's ransom for?"

"Perhaps it is on the easel. I only saw the miniature."

Cork took the drape from the easel and revealed a portrait of a nude woman reposing on a couch.

"It's Gretchen!" I gasped. "Was that der Trogue's game? Blackmail?"

"Yes, Mr. Oaks, it was," the Dame said. "I knew it was not an artist's trick of painting one head on another's body. That strawberry mark on the thigh was Gretchen's. How did you know of its existence, Captain? I told no one, not even my sister."

"Your actions helped tell me. You ordered your own portrait burned two days ago, the same day your sister sent me a note and an invitation to the Masque."

"A note?"

"Portending calamity," I added.

"Oh, the fool. She must have learned about my failure to raise enough cash to meet that fiend's demands."

"Your sudden disdain for a fine portrait betrayed your disgust with the artist, not with the art. Then Wilda told us that you had planned to have your daughters painted by the same man and, considering the time elapsed since your portrait was finished, I assumed that Gretchen's had been started."

"It was, and he seduced her. She confessed it to me after I saw the miniature he brought to me."

"Why did you not demand its delivery when you gave him the necklace to-night?"

"I never said I gave it to him to-night."

"But you did. You went into the den, not to see your daughter, but to meet der Trogue at the outside passage door. You lit a taper there, and he examined his booty at the entryway, and then left, probably promising to turn over that scandalous painting when he had verified that the necklace was not an imitation."

"Captain, you sound as if you were there."

The clews were. In the puddle just inside the door, there was a red substance. Oaks believed it was blood. It was a natural assumption, but when the question of your anger with a painter came to light, I considered what my eyes now confirm. Painters are sloppy fellows; look at this floor. Besides, blood is rarely magenta. It was paint, red paint from his boot soles. Then, Madam, your part of the bargain completed, you returned to the den. Your daughter was still by the fire."

"Yes."

"And you returned to the ballroom."

"Yes, leaving my soiled child to be murdered! He came back and killed her!"

"No, Dame van Schooner, he did not, although that is the way it will be recorded officially. The report will show that you entered the den and presented the van der Malin Chain to your daughter to wear on her night of triumph. My observation of the paint in the puddle will stand as the deduction that led us to der Trogue. We will say he gained entry into the house, killed your daughter, and took the necklace. And was later killed resisting capture."

"But he *did* kill her!" the Dame insisted. "He had to be the one! She was alive when I left her. No one else entered the room until the honour guard went for her."

Cork took both her hands.

"Dame van Schooner, I have twisted truth beyond reason for your sake to-night, but now you must face the hard truth. Der Trogue was a scoundrel, but he had no reason to kill Gretchen. What would he gain? And how could he get back in without leaving snow tracks? Gretchen's executioner was in the den all the time – when Lydia was there, when you were. I think in your heart you know the answer – if you have the courage to face it."

To watch her face was to see ice melt. Her eyes, her cold, diamond-blue eyes watered. "I can. But must it be said – here?"

"Yes."

"Wilda. Oh, my God, Wilda."

"Yes, Wilda. You have a great burden to bear, my dear lady."

Her tears came freely now. "The curse of the van Schooners," she cried. "Her father was insane, and his brother Kaarl lives in his lunatic's attic. My mother thought she was infusing quality by our union."

"Thus your stern exterior and addiction to purifying the blood-line with good stock."

"Yes, I have been the man in our family far too long. I have had to be hard. I thank you for your consideration, Captain. Wilda will have to be put away, of course. Poor child, I saw the van Schooner blood curse in her years ago, but I never thought it would come to this." The last was a sob. Then she took a deep breath. "I think I am needed at home." She rose. Thank you again, Captain. Will you destroy that?" She pointed to the portrait.

"Rest assured."

As he opened the door for her, she turned back with the breaking dawn framing her. "I wish it was I who had invited you to the Bal. I saw you dancing and wondered who you were. You are quite tall."

"Not too tall to bow, Madam," Cork said, and all six-foot-six of him bent down and kissed her cheek. She left us with an escort from the detachment of soldiers that had followed our trail.

The room was quiet for a moment before Major Tell exploded. "Confound it, Cork, what the deuce is this? I am to falsify records to show der Trogue was a thief and a murderer and yet you say it was Wilda who killed her sister. What's your proof, man?"

Cork walked over to the painting and smashed it on a chair back. "You deserve particulars, both of you. I said that Wilda was in the den all the time. Your natural query is how did she get there unseen? Well, we all saw her. She was carried in – in the curtained sedan chair. In her twisted mind, she hated her sister, who would inherit everything by her mother's design. One does not put a great fortune into a madwoman's hands."

"Very well," Tell said, "I can see her entry. How the deuce did she get out?"

"Incipient madness sometimes makes the mind clever, Major. She stayed in the sedan chair until her mother had left, then presented herself to Gretchen."

"And killed her," I interjected. "But she was back in the ballroom before the honour guard went in to get her sister."

"There is the nub of it, Oaks. She left the den by the back passage, crossed the yard, and re-entered the house by the kitchen in the far wing. Who would take any notice of a daughter of the house in a room filled with bustling cooks and servants coming and going with vittles for the buffet?"

"But she would have gotten her skirts wet in the snow," I started to object. "Of course! The spilled punch bowl! It drenched her!"

Cork smiled broadly. "Yes, my lad. She entered the kitchen, scooped up the punch bowl, carried it into the ballroom, and then deliberately dropped it."

"Well," Tell grumped, "she may be sprung in the mind, but she understands the theory of tactical diversion."

"Self-preservation is the last instinct to go, Major."

"Yes, I believe you are right, Cork, but how are we to explain all this and still shield the Dame's secret?"

Cork looked dead at me. "You, Oaks, have given us the answer."

"I? Oh, when I said the killer took off his boots to avoid tracks in the den? You rejected that out of hand when I mentioned it."

"I rejected it as a probability, not a possibility. Anything is possible, but not everything is probable. Is it probable that a killer bent on not leaving tracks would take off his boots *inside* the entry where they would leave a puddle? No, I couldn't accept it, but I'm sure the general public will."

The major looked disturbed. "I can appreciate your desire to protect the Dame," he said, "but to *suppress* evidence – "

"Calm yourself, Major, we are just balancing the books of human nature. I have saved the Crown the time and expense of trying and executing an extortionist. God knows how many victims he has fleeced by his artistic trickery over the years. And we have prevented the Dame from the commission of a homicide that any jury, I think, would have found justifiable. Let it stand as it is, Major, it is a neater package. The Dame has had enough tragedy in her life."

The last of his words were soft and low-toned, and I watched as he stared into the flames. By jing, could it possibly be that this gallivanting, sunburnt American had fallen in love? But I quickly dismissed the thought. We are fated to our roles, we two – he, the unbroken stallion frolicking from pasture to pasture, and I, the frantic ostler following with an empty halter, hoping some day to put the beast to work. I persist.

# MURDER LOCK'D IN
# Lillian de la Torre

*Lillian de la Torre (b. 1902) is the grande-dame of American mystery fiction.
A literary scholar of some note, all of her books feature real people and events,
thoroughly researched and brought to life. Her most famous re-creation has been
Dr. Sam: Johnson, the renowned British lexicographer, who had a ready-made
Watson in the shape of his diarist, James Boswell. Starting in 1943, Lillian
de la Torre began a series of stories featuring Johnson, which has run for over
forty years. If anyone is responsible for the shaping of the historical detective
story, it is Miss de la Torre. Two collections of stories have been published,*
Dr. Sam: Johnson, Detector *(1946) and* The Detections of Dr. Sam
Johnson *(1960). The following story did not appear in either collection, and
records the first meeting of the two literary greats in 1763.*

"*M*urder! Murder lock'd in!"
  With these horrifying words began my first experience of
the *detective* genius of the great Dr. Sam: Johnson, him who – but let
us proceed in order.

The '63 was to me a memorable year; for in it I had the happiness
to obtain the acquaintance of that extraordinary man. Though then
but a raw Scotch lad of two-and-twenty, I had already read the
WORKS OF JOHNSON with delight and instruction, and imbibed
therefrom the highest reverence for their author. Coming up to
London in that year, I came with the firm resolution to win my
way into his friendship.

On Monday, the 16th of May, I was sitting in the back-parlour of
Tom Davies, book-seller and sometime actor, when the man I sought
to meet came unexpectedly into the shop. Glimpsing him through
the glass-door, Davies in sepulchral tone announced his approach
as of Hamlet's ghost: "Look, my Lord, it comes!"

I scrambled to my feet as the great man entered, his tall, burly
form clad in mulberry stuff of full-skirted antique cut, a large bushy
greyish wig surmounting his strong-cut features of classical mould.

"I present Mr. Boswell – " began Davies. If he intended to add
"from Scotland," I cut him off.

"Don't tell him where I come from!" I cried, having heard of the great man's prejudice against Scots.

"From Scotland!" cried Davies roguishly.

"Mr. Johnson," said I – for not yet had he become "Doctor" Johnson, though as such I shall always think of him – "Mr. Johnson, I do indeed come from Scotland, but I cannot help it."

"That, sir, I find," quipped Johnson with a smile, "is what a great many of your countrymen cannot help!"

This jest, I knew, was aimed at the hordes of place-seekers who "could not help coming from" Scotland to seek their fortunes in London when Scottish Lord Bute became first minister to the new King; but it put me out of countenance.

"Don't be uneasy," Davies whispered me at parting, "I can see he likes you very well!"

Thus encouraged, I made bold to wait upon the philosopher the very next Sunday, in his chambers in the Temple, where the benchers of the law hold sway. I strode along Fleet Street, clad in my best; my new bloom-coloured coat, so I flattered myself, setting off my neat form and dark, sharp-cut features. As I walked along, I savoured in anticipation this, my first encounter with the lion in his den, surrounded by his learned volumes and the tools of his trade.

But it was not yet to be, for as I turned under the arch into Inner Temple Lane, I encountered the philosopher issuing from his doorway in full Sunday panoply. His mulberry coat was well brushed, his full-bottom wig was new-powdered, he wore a clean linen neckcloth and ruffles to his wrists.

"Welcome, Mr. Boswell," said he cordially, "you are welcome to the Temple. As you see, I am just now going forth. Will you not walk along with me? I go to wait on Mistress Lennon the poetess, who dwells here in the Temple, but a step across the gardens, in Bayfield Court. Come, I will present you at her levee."

"With all my heart, sir," said I, pleased to go among the wits, and in such company.

But as it turned out, I never did present myself at the literary levee, for as we came to Bayfield Court, a knot of people buzzing about the door caught us up in their concerns.

"Well met, Mr. Johnson," called a voice, "we have need of your counsel. We have sent for the watch, but he does not come, the sluggard."

"The watch? What's amiss, ma'am?"

A babble of voices answered him. Every charwoman known to Bayfield Court, it seemed, seethed in a swarm before the entry.

"Old Mrs. Duncom – locked in, and hears no knock – here's Mrs. Taffety come to dine – "

A dozen hands pushed forward an agitated lady in a capuchin.

"Invited, Mr. Johnson, two o'clock the hour, and Mrs. Duncom don't answer. I fear the old maid is ill and the young maid is gone to fetch the surgeon, and Mrs. Duncom you know has not the use of her limbs."

"We must rouse her. Come, Mrs. Taffety, I'll make myself heard, I warrant."

The whole feminine contingent, abandoning hope of the watch, escorted us up the stair. As we mounted, I took stock of our posse. The benchers of the law, their employers, were off on their Sunday occasions, but the servitors were present in force. I saw an Irish wench with red hair and a turned-up nose, flanked close by a couple of lanky, ill-conditioned lads, probably sculls to the benchers and certainly admirers to the wench. A dark wiry little gypsy of a woman with alert black eyes boosted along a sturdy motherly soul addressed by all as Aunt Moll. Sukey and Win and Juggy, twittering to each other, followed after.

Arrived at the attick landing, Dr. Johnson raised his voice and called upon Mrs. Duncom in rolling stentorian tones. Mrs. Taffety seconded him, invoking the maids in a thin screech: "Betty! Annet!" Dead silence answered them.

"Then we must break in the door," said Dr. Johnson.

Indeed he looked abundantly capable of effecting such a feat single-handed; but at that moment a stumble of feet upon the stair proclaimed the arrival of the watch. "Hold!" cried that worthy. "None of your assault and battery, for I'll undertake to spring the lock."

"Will you so?" said Dr. Johnson, eyeing him thoughtfully.

The watch was no Bow Street constable, but one of the Temple guardians, a stubby old man in a seedy fustian coat, girded with a broad leather belt from which depended his short sword and his truncheon of office.

The women regarded him admiringly as he stepped forward, full of self-importance, and made play with a kind of skewer which he thrust into the lock.

Nothing happened.

After considerable probing and coaxing the man was fain to desist.

"'Tis plain, sir," he covered his failure, "that the door is bolted from within."

"Bolted!" cried Mrs. Taffety. "Of course 'tis bolted! Mistress

Duncom ever barred herself in like a fortress, for she kept a fortune in broad pieces under her bed in a silver tankard, and so she went ever in fear of robbers."

"How came you to know of this fortune, ma'am?" demanded Dr. Johnson.

"Why, sir, the whole world knew, 'twas no secret."

"It ought to have been. Well, fortress or no, it appears we must break in."

"Hold, sir!" cried the black-eyed charwoman. "You'll affright the old lady into fits. I know a better way."

"Name it, then, ma'am."

"My master Grisley's chambers, you must know, sir, lie on the other side of the court – "

"Ah, Mr. Grisley!" murmured Aunt Moll. "Pity he's not to the fore, he'd set us right, I warrant, he's that fond of Annet!"

"Mr. Grisley is from home. But I have the key. Now if I get out at his dormer, I'll make my way easily round the parapet, and so get in at Mrs. Duncom's casement and find out what's amiss."

"Well thought on, Mistress Oliver," approved the watch, "for the benchers of the Temple would take it ill, was we to go banging in doors."

"And how if the casement be bolted and barred, as surely it will be?"

"Then, Mrs. Taffety, I must make shift. Wait here. I'll not be long."

Waiting on the landing, we fell silent, listening for we knew not what. When it came, it startled us – a crash, and the tinkle of falling glass.

"Alack, has she fallen?"

"Not so, ma'am, she has made shift. Now she's within, soon she'll shoot the great bolt and admit us."

We waited at the door in suspense. After an interminable minute, the lock turned, and we heard someone wrenching at the bolt. It stuck; then with a shriek it grated grudgingly back, and the heavy door swung slowly in.

On the threshold stood Mrs. Oliver, rigid and staring. Her lips moved, but no sound came.

"In God's name, what is it?" cried Mrs. Taffety in alarm.

Mrs. Oliver found a hoarse whisper:

"Murder!" she gasped. "Murder lock'd in!"

Her eyes rolled up in her head, her knees gave way, and she collapsed in a huddle in the doorway.

"Let me, sirs." The motherly female stepped forward. "When Katty's in her fits, I know how to deal."

Leaving her to deal, the rest of us pressed in, Dr. Johnson, myself, the watch, and the fluttering women. The Irish girl was with us, but her swains, the sculls, I noted, had vanished.

What a sight met our eyes! The young maid's pallet was made up in the passage, by the inner door as if to guard it, and there lay Annet in her blood. She had fought for her life, for blood was everywhere, but repeated blows of an axe or hammer had broke her head and quelled her forever.

In the inner room old Mrs. Duncom lay strangled. The noose was still around her neck. In the other bed old Betty had suffered the same fate. Of the silver tankard there was no trace.

"Murder and robbery! We must send for the Bow Street men!" I cried.

"Not in my bailiwick!" growled the Temple watchman. "*I* am the law in Bayfield Court!"

"So he is, Mr. Boswell," assented Dr. Johnson. "Well, well, if we put our minds to it, we may make shift to unravel this dreadful riddle for ourselves – three women dead in an apartment locked and barred!"

Cold air touched me, and a shudder shook me. The icy air was no ghostly miasma, I soon saw, but a chill spring breeze from the casement, where the small old-fashioned panes nearest the bolt had been shattered when entrance was effected.

"The window was bolted, I told you so!" cried Mrs. Taffety. "Every bolt set! The Devil is in it!"

"The Devil – the Devil!" the charwomen took up the chorus.

"Y'are foolish females!" said the watch stoutly. "Look you, Mr. Johnson, I'll undertake to shew you how 'twas done."

"I thank you, my man – "

"Jonas Mudge, sir, at your service."

"I thank you, honest Mudge, pray instruct me, for I am ever happy to be instructed."

"Then behold, sir! I take this string – " It came out of his capacious pocket with a conjurer's flourish at which the females gaped. "Now pray step this way, sir (leading us to the outer door). Now mark me! I loop my string around the knob of the bolt – I step outside, pray follow – "

On the outside landing Mistress Katty Oliver was sitting propped against the wall with closed eyes, and her friend was assiduously fanning her. They paid us no mind. Lowering his tone, Mudge continued his lecture:

"I bring the two ends of the string with me – I close the door. Now I will pull on both ends of the string, which will shoot the bolt – and so I shall have only to pull away the string by one end, the door is bolted, and I stand outside. As thus – "

As he spoke, he pulled on the two ends of the string. Nothing happened. The unwieldly bolt stuck, and no force applied to the string could budge it.

"An old trick, not always to be relied upon," smiled Dr. Johnson. "I thank you, sir, for demonstrating how this strange feat was *not* accomplished!"

As Mudge stood there looking foolish, there was a clatter on the stair, and three gentlemen arrived on the run. The benchers had come back from Commons. Dr. Johnson knew them all, the red-faced one, the exquisite one, the melancholy one, and greeted each in turn.

"What, Mr. Kerry, Mr. Geegan, Mr. Grisley, you come in an unhappy time."

"Your servant, Mr. Johnson, what's amiss?"

Mistress Oliver was on her feet, her hand on his arm.

"Don't go in, Mr. Grisley, for God's sake don't go in. Come away, I'll fetch you a tot, come away."

"Alack, sirs, murder's amiss!" I blurted.

The two young benchers were through the door in an instant, and the melancholy Grisley shook off his maid's hand and followed. When his eye lit on Annet's bloody brow, he cried aloud.

"Cover her face! For God's sake cover her face!"

Quick hands drew up the crimsoned bed-cloathes, and so we found the hammer. Dr. Johnson's shapely strong fingers handled it gingerly, bringing it close to his near-sighted eyes.

"An ordinary hammer. What can it tell us?"

"Perhaps much, for I perceive there's an initial burned in the wood of the handle," said I, feeling pleased with myself. "A G, sir, if I mistake not."

"A G. Yours, Mr. Geegan?"

The exquisite youth jibbed in alarm.

"Not mine, Divil a whit, no, sir, not mine!"

"Mr. Grisley?"

"I cannot look on it, do not ask me. Kat will know."

The little dark woman took his hand and spoke soothingly to him.

"I think, sir, 'tis the one you lent to Mr. Kerry some days since."

"To me!" cried the ruddy-faced bencher. "You lie, you trull!"

"I don't lie," said the woman angrily. "Don't you remember, you sent your charwoman for it, I gave it to Biddy to knock in some nails?" In a sudden silence, all eyes turned to the red-haired girl.

"No, sir, I never!" she cried in alarm.

"Go off, you trull!" bawled the alarmed Kerry. "I dismiss you! So you may e'en fetch your bundle and be off with you!"

"Nay, sir, not so fast, she must remain!" remonstrated the watch.

"Not in my chambers, the d—d trull! She may take up her bundle outside my door, and be d—d to her!"

I perceived that Mr. Kerry had come from Commons not a little pot-valiant, and thought it good riddance when he stamped off.

Biddy gave us one scared look, and followed him. Young Geegan seemed minded to go along, but was prevented by the arrival of Mudge's mate of the watch. Leather-belted, truncheon in hand, flat and expressionless of face, there he stood, filling the doorway and saying nothing. It gave us a sinister feeling of being under guard in that chamber of death. Mrs. Taffety fell to sobbing, and the women to comforting her. Dr. Johnson was probing the chimneys, neither deterred nor assisted by the blank-faced watchman, when suddenly Mr. Kerry was back again, redder than ever, hauling a reluctant Biddy by the wrist, and in his free hand brandishing a silver tankard.

"'Tis Mrs. Duncom's!" cried Mrs. Taffety.

"Hid in Biddy's bundle! I knew it, the trull!"

The wretched Biddy began to snivel.

"I had it for a gift," she wept. "I did not know murder was in it!"

Dr. Johnson took her in hand: "Who gave it you?"

"My f-friends."

"What friends?"

Biddy was loath to say, but the philosopher prevailed by sheer moral force, and Biddy confessed:

"The Sander brothers. Scouts to the benchers. Them that's gone off."

"They shall be found. And what did you do for them?"

"I — " The girl's resistance was broken. "I kept watch on the stair."

Then it came with a rush: "When Annet went in the evening for some wine to make the old lady's nightly posset, she left the door on the jar as was her wont, that she might come in again without disturbing old Betty; and knowing it would be so, Matt Sander, that's the puny one, he slips in and hides under the bed. When all is still, he lets in his brother, and I keep watch on the stair, and they come out with the tankard of broad pieces – " The wretched girl began to bawl. "They swore to me they had done no murder, only bound and gagged the folk for safety's sake."

"And when they came out," pursued Dr. Johnson, "they shot the bolt from outside. How did they do that?"

"I know not what you mean, sir. They pulled the door to, 'tis a spring lock, I heard it snick shut, and so we came away and shared out in the archway below."

"Which of them carried the hammer?"

"Neither, sir, for what would they need a hammer?"

Then realization flooded her, and she bawled louder, looking wildly about for a refuge. Suddenly, defiantly, Mr. Geegan stepped forward and took her in his arms.

"So, Mr. Johnson," said watchman Mudge smugly, "our problem is solved, we had no need of Bow Street! You come along of me, Mistress Biddy. Nay, let go, sir." Mr. Geegan reluctantly obeyed. "Pray, Mr. Johnson, do you remain here, I'll fetch the crowner to sit on the bodies."

"Do so, good friend. I'll desire all those present – " his eye took in the three benchers and the huddling women "– to bear me company till he comes. Bucket will stand by to keep order. Come, friends, we shall sit more at our ease in the dining room. After you, ma'am. After you, sir."

They went without demur, all save Grisley. In the passage, by Annet's still form on her pallet, he balked. "Shall she lie alone?" he cried piteously. "I'll stay by her while I may."

"And I by you," said Kat Oliver.

Her master sank to the hallway bench, wringing his hands and crying: "O Annet, Annet, why did you not admit me? I might have saved you!"

"Come, sir," soothed his maid, "be easy, you could do nothing."

We left them fallen silent on the bench. Instead of following the others into the dining room, Dr. Johnson led me back into the inner chamber, where two bodies lay coldly blown upon from the broken window panes.

*Johnson* There's more in this, Mr. Boswell, than meets the eye.

*Boswell* Did not the Sanders do it?

*Johnson* And got out through a door locked and barred, and left it so? Biddy saw no hocussing of the lock, and I question whether they knew how to do it.

*Boswell* Mudge knew how. Were they in it together? I ask myself, sir, what is this guardian of the Temple peace, that carries a picklock in his pocket, and knows how to shoot a bolt from without? I smell Newgate on him.

*Johnson* You may be right, sir. They are a queer lot, the Temple watch. But this one is no wizard, he could neither, in the event, pick the lock nor shoot the bolt.

*Boswell* Then how was it done? This seems an impossible crime.

*Johnson* 'Twas all too possible, sir, for it happened.

*Boswell* The women are right, the Devil did it.

*Johnson* A devil did it indeed, but in human form.

*Boswell* One who got in through bolts and bars, and got out again leaving all locked and barred behind him?

*Johnson* There was a way in, for someone got in, and a way out too, that's plain to a demonstration. We must find it.

*Boswell* I am at a loss, sir. Where must we look?

*Johnson* We must look where all answers are found, sir, in our own heads. Perpend, sir. Murder in a locked dwelling, and no murderer there to take – 'tis a pretty mystery, and this one the more complex because it is triple. Let us consider the problem at large. Many answers are possible.

*Boswell* (ruefully) In *my* head, sir, I don't find even one.

*Johnson* Well, sir, here's one: Perhaps there is no murderer there to take, because there is no murder, only accident that looks like murder.

*Boswell* Two old women simultaneously strangle themselves by accident, while the young one accidentally falls afoul of a hammer? Come, sir, this is to stretch coincidence and multiply impossibilities!

*Johnson* Granted, Mr. Boswell. Then is it perhaps double murder and suicide behind bolted doors?

*Boswell* Suicide by the hammer? Unheard of!

*Johnson* And nigh on impossible. Well, then, sir, was the tragedy engineered from without, and no murderer ever entered at all?

*Boswell* The nooses were tightened and the hammer wielded, by someone on the wrong side of the door? This is witchcraft and sorcery, nothing less.

*Johnson* Then suppose there is no murder, the victim is only stunned or stupefied, until the person who breaks in commits it?

*Boswell* Three murders, sir, and the third a noisy one, all in the one minute while we listened at the door? Come, sir, these conjectures are ingenious, but none fits this case.

*Johnson* Then there must be a way in, and a way out. Think, Mr. Boswell: all is not so locked and sealed, but holes exist.

*Boswell* I have it! The keyhole!

*Johnson* A keyhole that not even a picklock could penetrate? Think again, sir. What else?

*Boswell* Nay, I know not, sir. There is no scuttle to the roof.

*Johnson* There is not, sir.

*Boswell* And the chimneys are narrow, and stuffed with soot undisturbed.

*Johnson* So we saw. Not the chimneys. Good. We progress.

*Boswell* How, progress?

*Johnson* When one has eliminated all impossibilities, then what remains, however improbable, must be the truth.

*Boswell* What truth?

*Johnson* Nay, sir, I have yet to test it. Come with me.

In the passage-way Annet lay still under the reddened blankets. Grisley and his maid sat as still on the settle, he with his face in his hands, she at his shoulder regarding him with a countenance full of concern. A blackened old chair with high back stood opposite. Dr. Johnson ensconced himself therein like some judge on the bench, and I took my stand by him like a bailiff.

"Mistress Oliver," he began, "pray assist our deliberations."

"As best I can, sir," she answered readily.

Grisley did not stir.

"Then tell us, in your airy peregrination, in what condition did you find Mrs. Duncom's casement window?"

"Bolted fast, sir, I was forced to break the glass that I might reach in and turn the catch."

"I know, we heard it shatter. You broke the glass and reached in. With both hands?"

"Certainly not, sir, I held on with the other hand."

"Then why did you break two panes?"

"I don't know. For greater assurance – "

"Nonsense! I put it to you, my girl, *you found the window broken*."

"Then why would I break it again?"

"Because you knew at once who had been there before you, and thought only to shield him. So you broke the second pane, that we might hear the crash of glass, and think you had been forced to break in. The broken window would else tell us that the murderer came from Mr. Grisley's casement."

"He never!" cried the woman, on her feet before her master as if to shield him. "Would he kill Annet, that he lusted after?"

"Would he not, if she resisted him? These violent passions have violent ends. No, no. I pity him, but justice must be done. Think, Mistress Oliver, this is the man that slunk around the parapet at dead of night, a hammer in his pocket. With it he breaks a pane, turns the bolt, and enters. The two helpless old women fall victim to his string, lest they hinder his intent. When Annet resists him, in his fury he batters her to death, and so flees as he came. May such a creature live?"

This harangue slowly penetrated the mind of the unhappy Grisley, and he rose to his feet.

"Bucket!" called Dr. Johnson sharply. The watchman appeared. "Take him in!"

"No! No!" cried the woman. "He is innocent!"

"Who will believe it?" countered Johnson. "No, ma'am, he'll hang for it, and justly too. Did you ever see a man hanged, Mr. Boswell? It is a shocking sight to see a man struggling as he strangles in a string, his face suffused, his limbs convulsed, for long horrible minutes. Well, he has earned it. Take him, Bucket."

As Bucket collared the unresisting Grisley, we found we had a fury on our hands. With nails and teeth Kat Oliver fell upon Dr. Johnson. I had her off in a trice; but I could not have held her had not Bucket come to my aid.

"I thank you, Mr. Boswell," said Dr. Johnson, settling his neckcloth and staunching his cheek, "your address has saved me a mauling. A woman's a lioness in defence of what she loves."

"In my belief she's mad," said I angrily, as the wiry little woman wrenched against our pinioning arms.

"That may also be true. A thin line divides great love and madness. Give over, ma'am, let justice take its course. So, that's better – let her go, Mr. Boswell. As to Mr. Grisley, Bucket, to Newgate with him, and lock him in the condemned cell."

"You shan't! You shan't!" sobbed Kat Oliver wildly. "It was I that killed them, it was I, it was I!"

"You, ma'am? A likely story! Why would you do such a thing?"

"Why would I destroy that prim little bitch, that was destroying him? For his sake, gladly. Yet I never meant to use the hammer, that I carried only to break the glass – "

"But," I objected, "Biddy had the hammer!"

"You are deceived, Mr. Boswell. To disclaim the hammer, this woman did not scruple to lie. Well, then, Mrs. Oliver, if not to use the hammer, what was your intent?"

The little woman's eyes looked inward, and she spoke with a kind of horrid relish:

"When I knew the people lay bound and gagged – "

"How did you know?"

"I heard the talk on the landing. I could not sleep for thinking of – I could not sleep, and the boys were drunk and loud. I opened the door and listened. I saw my opportunity. How I entered you know. The old women I finished neatly, with their own curtain cords. The young one – "

"Yes, the young one?"

"The young one I reserved for a more dreadful fate. It was I who shot the front-door bolt, intending to leave her locked in with murder, and see her hanged for it."

"Who could think she did it, when she lay bound?" I demanded.

"Of course I did away with the bonds," said the woman contemptuously.

"Yet you killed her, how was that to your purpose?"

"I meant only to stun her, but she got loose and fought me. I saw red. I killed her. Then I returned as I came."

"And when the people became alarmed and would break in," Dr. Johnson supplied, "you saw it must be you, and no one else, to break the window and effect an entrance there, lest the broken window be observed by others, pointing directly at the folk from Mr. Grisley's."

She made no answer, but turned to her master.

"I did it for you, Edward."

With a blind gesture, Grisley turned away.

"All for nothing, then."

Dining together the next day at the Mitre, we naturally turned our talk to the exciting hours we had spent in Bayfield Court the day before.

*Boswell* Were you not surprised, sir, when Katty Oliver confessed her guilt?

*Johnson* Not at all, sir, I knew it all along. What did she care if the door was battered in? Only the strongest of motives would suffice to set her on that precarious circuit she traversed. She must have known what would be found at the end of it. Nay, more, how did she know it was an easy way around the parapet, if she had not traversed it before?

*Boswell* Yet how eloquently you depicted the unhappy Grisley's crime and his imminent fate.

*Johnson* Thus I put her to the torture, for I could see how much he meant to her; and when I turned the screw with talk of the horrors of hanging, she confessed to save him, as I foresaw she would.

*Boswell* What will become of her? Surely she'll hang?

*Johnson* In the ordinary course, sir, yes. But I had the curiosity to inquire this morning, and by what I learn, she will not hang. It appears that, as Aunt Moll said, she was ever subject to fits, no doubt she committed her terrible crimes in an unnatural phrenzy. Well, sir, when she saw the cells last night she fell into a dead catalepsy and was carried insensible to Bedlam, where 'tis clear she belongs.

*Boswell* And Biddy, what of her?

*Johnson* The Sander brothers, that delivered over the old women bound to be murdered, have made good their escape, leaving Biddy to pay for their crime.

*Boswell* This seems unfair, sir.

*Johnson* Why, sir, receiving of stolen goods is a hanging offence, Miss Biddy cannot complain. But the Temple watchmen are not incorruptible, and the Temple watch-house is not impregnable. Moreover, Mr. Geegan, the son of an Irish Peer, has well-lined pockets. In short, sir, he has spirited away Miss Biddy, who knows whither. And so ends the affair of murder lock'd in.

*Boswell* (boldly) Which I hope I may one day narrate at large when, as I mean to do, I record for posterity the exploits of *Sam: Johnson, detector!*

## AUTHOR'S COMMENT

The hardest thing about writing this story was making it probable. I suppose this is because it actually happened. Real events don't necessarily bother about probability.

It happened, and I tell it as it happened, except of course for the intervention of Dr. Sam: Johnson. The solution is my own. In actual fact the Irish girl was hanged, which seems hard for only keeping watch and accepting a silver tankard; but such was justice in those inhuman days.

In analyzing the "locked-room mystery" and its possible solutions, with singular prescience, Dr. Johnson seems to have anticipated

John Dickson Carr's "locked-room lecture" in THE THREE COFFINS; though the solution that detector Sam: Johnson arrives at is not among those considered by Carr.

The classic "string trick" for bolting a door from outside, here explained by the watchman, was actually demonstrated at the Irish girl's trial, when they brought the door into open court and performed the trick upon it to the amazement of all beholders. You may read all about it in George Borrow's CELEBRATED TRIALS, II, 536–571.

# CAPTAIN NASH AND THE WROTH INHERITANCE
# Raymond Butler

*A trained chef, market researcher and language teacher, Raymond Ragan Butler
has written over a hundred radio plays and further stage and television plays,
including scripts for a soap opera.* Captain Nash and the Wroth Inheritance
*(1975) was his first full-length novel, and a fascinating attempt at establishing
the world's first private detective. There is a sequel,* Captain Nash and the
Honour of England *(1977).*

## AN INTRODUCTION

When I first began to investigate crime in England, the pro-
fession of detection did not exist. The Parish Constable, the
Informer, the Bow Street Runner – these were the only agents of the
Law. Yet England was a lawless place in those days.

It was in 1771 (in my thirtieth year) that I first conceived the idea
of a scientific system of detection and, like all original ideas, it was
received with no great degree of enthusiasm. With the exception of
my cousin Scrope, who was employed in the Commissioners' Office,
I was largely ignored by the Authorities.

As a result, I was forced to work in a private capacity – that is,
outside the protection of the Law. I became a "Private Detective",
the first in modern Europe, I believe.

*An advertisement in* The Daily Courant, *July 5th, 1771*
*A Gentleman of considerable abilities is able to provide a service for
the gathering of information and the detection of crimes. If any have
suffered the attentions of thieves and miscreants and are not happy with
the Law's performance, let them come to me and I shall restore their*

*property and apprehend the villains. My original scientific approach to the art of detection ensures the success of my endeavours. Those who come to me are assured that investigations will be made with all honour and secrecy imaginable.*

*For further particulars inquire of Captain George Nash, late of His Majesty's 5th Regiment of Dragoons, at Mr Trygwell, Bookseller, Greek Court, Soho.*

# I

For my first case, I took the one which looked to be the most intriguing and which promised the most reward financially, for the Wroth family was one of the richest in England.

Accordingly, I presented myself, as requested, at Stukeley Hall upon the following Thursday. I had taken some trouble with my appearance, realizing that since my new profession would seem dubious even to my employers, I would have to make a good impression from the first. I wore a plain green coat, which although no longer in the fashion still had a certain style. My waistcoat, though faded in places, looked bravely enough from the front; and my breeches, though they were as unfashionable as my coat, showed off my legs to great advantage. My buckled shoes were low-at-heel, but I have always worked on the principle that most people look keenest at one's neck, so I wore my best lawn cloth. I left my hair unpowdered, though wig-style, and I buckled on my sword, to let the Dowager Lady Wroth see that she had to deal with a gentleman.

At all events, my appearance seemed to pass muster with the servants. As I rode up to the porte-cochere a lurking groom came forward, touched his forelock civilly enough and led my roan away to the stables. The ancient retainer who admitted me to the house did so without a hint of that insolence he would have used had he been more certain of my true station in life. He merely regarded me with the same hauteur he would have turned upon a Duke. After crossing a cavernous hall, he showed me into a reception room.

"If you will wait in here, Sir, her ladyship will be free directly."

The door gently sighed to behind him.

I looked about me with interest. Considering the legend of their wealth, I was somewhat disappointed with their display of it. This room was ponderously magnificent in its weighty "Roman" way, with a tastelessly painted ceiling and a tiled floor. It was furnished in the style of the Second George, opulent but demodé. The woodwork was profusely carved and ornamented, looking absurd yet brave against the dank austerity of the gloomy walls.

Stukeley itself was a dilapidated relic of the Thirteenth Century, a moated grange built upon the ruins of an old castle. To my eye, it seemed almost unfit for civilized living. Most of the building was well on the way to ruin again and I could see from the exterior that only a few rooms remained habitable. Apparently this was one of them. I found it odd that the family refused to spend their vast wealth on the property. Their neglect seemed almost wilful.

I was drawn to the window by the clash of steel upon steel and the shrill cries of what I, at first, took to be a peacock. I looked through the window.

A fine lawn ran down to the river; green, smooth, and quite deserted. Somewhere behind a mossy wall sword rang on sword and the peacock's cries became almost intolerable.

Then the duellists came into sight and my mouth fell open in blank astonishment. Two young women danced onto the lawn, fencing furiously. They were dressed in the height of French fashion, that is, with too much rigging and wearing monstrous hooped skirts, with ruching and pleating much in evidence. Their hair was greased, powdered, curled and dressed high over enormous cushions and surmounted by imitation fruits, flowers and ships. The size of fashionable heads in those days was notoriously vast, but these were grotesquely so.

They moved like ships in full sail. It was hard to imagine they were made in God's image, for He that made them would never have recognized them with their plumes, their silken vizards, their ruffs like sails, and the feathers in their hats like two flags in their tops to tell which way the wind blew. They looked almost deformed, capering about upon the green lawn.

When the initial shock had faded, I found myself admiring the dexterity with which they handled the foils. Despite their towering plumes and the stiff, unmanageable brocade of their gowns, they moved like professional duellists.

They danced upon the lawn like two creatures in some fable and all the while they fenced, the smaller of the two kept up an amazing clamour. It was as if she had some raucous and frightful bird locked up in her rib-cage. It was she I had mistaken for a peacock!

I looked on in amazement.

Although I have seen many professional women fight (including the great Mary Brindle of New England), I had never seen action to equal this. The smaller woman lunged and thrust at the taller with dangerously bold strokes, which her opponent parried with ease. But it was no formal display of technique – their blades clashed and slithered and threw out sparks in grim earnest.

Suddenly the tall girl slipped as her foot caught in the hem of her gown. She lurched, and made a frantic effort to recover her balance, but failed and fell to the ground in a wild flurry of petticoats. As she fell, the sword flew out of her hand in a great flashing arc. The smaller woman now towered over her, her sword drawn back so that it pointed downwards towards the unprotected breast. Laughing, she seemed to be considering whether or no to plunge her sword into the inert body beneath her. She pricked the bodice maliciously, looking for the softest spot.

I held my breath.

With a quick twist of her body, the fallen girl jerked aside – and the other, startled, lunged. The point of the sword passed within an inch of her side, tearing the fabric of her gown. It penetrated the smooth grass and remained quivering there.

Shrieking with hysterical laughter, the small girl threw herself upon the other, grasped her with both hands by the throat and strove to throttle her!

The other girl, laughing almost as hysterically, seized her wrists and endeavoured to tear them apart. But her tormentor clung to her neck, forcing her nails into the flesh until even I could see the blood begin to fleck her hands. Although the battle seemed to be in largely high-spirits, I thought there must be some danger of their doing each other an injury. I wondered why nobody ran out to call this strange affair to a halt.

Then I noticed that I was not the only observer. Close by the corner of the wall, a young man stood watching this display. He watched them with an intolerant eye, but seemed little inclined to interfere. I received a strong impression that this was no new sight to him.

Squirming, kicking, and striking at her attacker's face, the fallen girl fought desperately to wrench herself free. But she seemed quite helpless beneath the power of the diminutive tornado that bestraddled her. Until, suddenly, this tornado appeared to blow itself out. With a long, agonized cry, she shuddered down the entire length of her body, her grip relaxed, and she collapsed inert upon the other girl's body.

Nobody moved. The girl pinned beneath her fought for her breath. She seemed almost too exhausted to push the still, small form aside.

With slow, deliberate strides, the young man walked over to the prostrate pair and casually, even a little disdainfully, he shoved the girls apart with one delicately arched foot. He then gave the taller girl his hand and hauled her unceremoniously to her feet.

Upright and stationary, she presented a curiously awkward figure. With bad grace, she thanked the young man and, kneeling by the inert figure on the grass, turned her over to face the light. As she did so, she raised a hand to her own head and pulled off her hat.

To my utter astonishment, the architectural wig came away with it, revealing the features of a singularly handsome young man. My amazement grew even greater as he stood up and proceeded to undress upon the lawn.

I gaped as he undid the pointed bodice of his gown and stripped off plumes, brocade and lace. Three petticoats were removed and thrown aside and I saw that he was, in truth, a lean and sinewy young stripling wearing only his breeches beneath the finery. He must have been mortifyingly hot under it all!

Stripped of his encumbrances, he turned his attention to his partner. He took a phial from the phlegmatic on-looker and waved it under her nose. She stirred indolently and sat up suddenly.

She was helped to her feet and she, too, began to disrobe. Off came the wig and the plumes, the gown was torn impatiently from her body, and the tout ensemble dropped to the feet of a cherubic young fellow dressed, like his friend, in nothing but his breeches.

I found myself staring curiously at the ladies' brocade shoes which still adorned their feet. In some odd way I had found this last metamorphosis less unnerving than the first – not simply because I was the less astonished, but because the soft young figure in masculine dress and feminine shoes, though unmistakably a man, had a body that more approached the feminine in its roundness and softness. He was a very young man, no more than seventeen years, I should have said.

All memory of their maniacal duel seemed forgotten between them. Laughing, they threw their arms around each other and teetered away across the lawn in their absurd shoes. They disappeared behind the same wall from which they had so sensationally appeared.

The third young man drifted away in another direction. Even at this distance I could see there had been no love lost between them.

So engrossed had I been in this curious performance, that I had failed to hear the door open behind me. The manservant now coughed discreetly. I turned, feeling strangely as though I had been caught rattling the family skeletons. The servant regarded me with a bright and noncommittal eye. I presumed he had seen the two upon the lawn, but he stared at me impassively.

"Her ladyship is ready to receive you, Sir," he said.

## II

I followed the manservant through the roof-high hall. It was stone-flagged and draughty, with a faintly medieval smell to it. Although the air outside was breathless, a faint wind murmured in the baronial fireplace and the sun had abandoned the attempt to penetrate the mullioned windows. The ceiling and walls were lost in a gloom of shadows, and history lay thick upon the air. I could almost see the ghostly generations of tenants assembled before the high table.

As we climbed the staircase, I examined the family portraits lining the walls. They were a more direct link with the ghostly past. It gave me an odd feeling to think that once, on this same ground, they had walked, but now all were gone like shadows at midday, one generation following another.

Another strange thought occurred to me as we passed the portraits. They were arranged in chronological order, but reaching backwards in time. They ended with the first Lord Wroth (circa 1489) and I could not but fail to notice that, as the family history rolled back into obscurity, the distinctive features of the Wroth clan faded into obliteration. But for the last four generations, at least, the painted faces had betrayed considerable inbreeding. The grandfather of the present Lord Wroth, for example, had a very mad look – a look of almost fatal softness – which no amount of painterly skill had been able to conceal. He was, I recollected suddenly, the husband of the Dowager Lady Wroth, to whom I was now about to be introduced.

The servant knocked briskly on a massive door and a high, querulous voice bade us enter. I was shown into a room the servant called the "solar".

After the gloom of the hall, this room seemed vibrant with light. It gleamed in the burnished woodwork, it sparkled warmly on the brass fireirons, it flashed out from the many mirrors in the room, and it coruscated among the facets of the chandeliers and lustres. The sunlight gave to the room a feeling of splendid unruliness. There was something pleasurably sluttish about it, as though it were unable to control its behaviour after the rigours of the hall. Among the sober furnishings, the sun was *gay*.

And all this gaiety seemed gathered into the person of the mistress of the house. The Dowager Lady Wroth was the most splendidly illuminated creature that I had ever seen. At first glance she seemed to be composed almost entirely of diamonds – they glittered from her ears, her throat, her wrists and her fingers. Her white hair shone with a bluish sheen, her skin had the gleam of coral, and her tabby[1] gown was the colour of daffodils.

With a shock, I realized that this exuberantly youthful figure must be touching her eightieth year. My second thought was that she was monstrous overdressed for a simple country morning. It seemed that fifty years of living among the gentry had not dampened the essentially theatrical spirit of the one-time actress, Sarah Laverstitch.

I, too, had been the object of as close a scrutiny. Her brilliantly undimmed eyes had been evaluating me point by point. She approved of what she saw, apparently, for she smiled and invited me to sit on a sofa of truly regal proportions. Her teeth were startlingly grey in her rosy face, and I now saw that her cheeks were very finely enamelled. I had a strong suspicion that beneath the flattering wig she was as bald as a magistrate.

She came directly to business. If I could satisfy her as to my credentials, she would be interested in using my services.

I presented her with my references and, after a careful reading of them, she asked how soon I would be free to act for her.

"I am at your service now, my lady," I said.

She looked surprised. "You are at liberty?"

I laughed and said frankly: "Business is not yet brisk, Lady Wroth. I have been advertising my services since April, but the public have not, so far, responded as I could have wished. There is still some suspicion of my calling among folk generally."

She nodded sympathetically. "It is understandable, Captain. The public are suspicious both of advertisements and thief-takers. Advertisements are largely unfulfilled promises, and thief-takers are often as rascally as the rogues they take!"

Having shot this barb, she looked slyly at me to see if it had struck home.

"I don't describe myself as a thief-taker, Lady Wroth," I said. "I am more interested in the gathering of information and the detection of crimes. I call myself a detective."

The word was unknown to her, as, indeed, it was still unknown to many.

"A detective?" she asked.

"From the Latin, Ma'am. *Detegere*, to uncover," I explained, and outlined my scientific methods.

"A detective," she said, seemingly impressed with my summary. "Well, that is an original calling."

[1]Watered silk.

"Not entirely original," I said, smiling. "There were detectives of a kind in ancient Egypt. Is not the story of Rhampsinitus, as told by Herodotus, a sort of detective-story?" She returned my smile uncomprehendingly. "But I think it safe to say that I am the only one in existence today."

"You are not attached to the Bow Street Police?" she asked.

"No, my lady. I prefer to work independently. I am a private gentleman. A Private Detective, if you wish."

"Good!" she said, and I noticed a distinct note of relief in her voice. "My commission calls for a man of independent spirit."

"You prefer not to use the Bow Street Police?" I asked, emphasizing the word "police" deliberately, and looking to see how she received it. Even at this early stage in my career, I knew that my employers would be largely comprised of those who would be too embarrassed to use the regular channels of the law.

She looked briefly away and replied shortly: "I think this is not a suitable business for them."

"You think they are not competent?"

"I think they are not *suitable*," she said briskly. "For one thing, I doubt if they would even consider the matter. I am not, as yet, certain that any crime has been committed. Unless you count sheer human folly to be a crime."

I waited for her to explain the matter further. She tapped the arm of her chair with her tortoise-shell fan, and said decisively: "I had better start from the beginning."

"I'd be obliged to your ladyship."

She paused, then shook herself, flashing fire from every facet. She reached for a small brocade bag, and extracted from it a sheaf of papers tied with a frivolous looking ribbon. She held them out to me.

"Read them!" she commanded.

I walked over to her chair and took them from her. The diamonds on her wrists and fingers shivered slightly, and I saw that she was trying valiantly to control a fit of trembling.

The papers were addressed to the Dowager Lady Wroth at Stukeley, Hertfordshire. The writing was neat and clerkly. The first paper was headed "At the Sign of the Anodyne Necklace" and was signed "Asclepius (Doctor)" followed by a string of meaningless and, I suspected, largely fictitious medical degrees. It read, simply, "For Services Rendered".

The other papers, seven in all, were signed receipts. The signature at the foot of each one was large, ill-formed and boorish. With difficulty, I deciphered the name "Wroth".

Lord Wroth had promised to pay the sum of 480 guineas for "Value Received".

My eyebrows rose slightly at the nature of the "Value Received".

| | |
|---|---|
| *Imprimis*, for use of the Royall Chymicall Washball, and for Ridding the Skin of all Deformities | 28 gns |
| *Item*, to use of application to Cure a Stammer | 28 gns |
| *Item*, to preserving Eyes | 28 gns |
| *Item*, to clearing away Phlegm, Rheum and Foul Humours from Breast, Stomach and Lungs | 28 gns |
| *Item*, to Removal of a Ringworm | 10 gns |
| *Item*, to Removal of Pimples | 10 gns |
| *Item*, to enticing of a Lengthy, Hairy and Voracious Worm, conjured from His Lordship's gut | 28 gns |

And more amazing than this:

| | |
|---|---|
| *Item*, to stimulation of His Lordship's Growth in various parts of His Person | 120 gns |

And even more amazing still:

| | |
|---|---|
| *Item*, to curing His Lordship of the Hideous Crime of Self-Pollution | 200 gns |
| | 480 gns |

I looked up. Lady Wroth stared at me with her hard, gemlike eyes. I could scarcely keep the amazement out of my own.

"Well, Sir? What do you think?"

"It seems your grandson suffers from singular ill-health, Ma'am," I said.

Her Ladyship snorted with disgust.

"Tcha! My grandson is in the most blatant good health. This is a brazen humbug! He has got into the hands of this quack. We live in an age of magnificent quacks, Captain Nash. They have cut short more lives with their pills and elixirs than were ever killed off by the plague!"

I waited for her to recover her temper. I was also waiting for her to come more to the point. There was more to it, I was sure, than these bizarre but basically harmless receipts.

"Do you know this 'Asclepius' fellow?" she asked tentatively. She toyed with her fan – a veritable weapon in her hands. It weaved, twisted, snapped shut and opened again. Her fan was the real sign-manual to her emotions, for her face told me nothing.

"I have heard tell of him, Ma'am," I replied. "I think he is far removed from the 'blameless Physician' of Greek legend."

"He is a magnificent quack, Sir!" she exploded. "A self-created doctor. These so-called medical receipts are not worth the paper they are written on."

"But the signature is genuine?"

She paused, then admitted scornfully: "There's not a doubt of it. Only my grandson could manage so illiterate a flourish!"

"Yet you wish to fight this claim on you?"

She positively winced.

"How can I, Sir? There's nothing here I can fight. Wroth could have used such services."

"But a court might question their legality, Lady Wroth," I said quietly.

"Yes, but . . ." She faltered. ". . . There's more."

She proffered me a further sheet of paper.

I read it thoughtfully. It was a cleverly constructed letter. Every word had been carefully chosen to mean precisely nothing if challenged in a court of law. Yet the overall tone was threatening.

These present receipts were the lesser part of his lordship's debt to the Doctor, the writer said. As his lordship was still not yet in possession of his fortune, the writer hoped that her ladyship would honour the debt. There were, however, three more receipts still in the Doctor's possession, for services of a rather more serious nature. These services were highly intimate and in view of the Doctor's sacred oath, would remain *arcanum*. Her ladyship could be assured that the Doctor had no wish to embarrass such an eminent family as the Wroths by publishing indelicate details, and the Doctor remained confident that her ladyship would oblige . . . etc. . . . etc. The value of these receipts amounted to . . . 3000 guineas!

"Well, Sir?" Lady Wroth asked, as I looked up from the paper.

"What does his lordship say about them?"

She snorted again. "He refuses to discuss it, though he admits to receiving some services. What do you suggest I do?"

"I would buy the receipts," I said without hesitation.

She looked surprised and ruffled. Clearly, that was not the answer she expected to hear from me. Her diamonds glittered angrily as she slapped her fan against the arm of her chair.

"You would advise that?" she said sharply.

"Unless you wish to be embarrassed publicly," I said. "It's possible that this is merely some kind of gammon, my lady, but it's possible that these receipts are for genuine services."

"Genuine! I tell you my grandson is in perfect health!"

I said reasonably: "There are many ailments a healthy young man can fall prey to, Lady Wroth; some of a most embarrassing nature."

"To a hair, Sir!" she snorted. "Onanism, for example! The Hideous Crime of Self-Pollution!"

The fan fluttered like an outraged dove.

". . . Or worse," I said carefully.

She considered the possibilities.

"I can think of nothing worse than the pox, Sir. And a young man getting cured of the pox is hardly a matter for blackguarding me."

The truth was out.

"Why should you think these receipts blackguard you, my lady?" I asked.

She looked away and moved uncomfortably.

"My grandson is a singular fellow, Sir," she said.

I had a quick vision of the two young women on the lawn. Suddenly enlightened, I asked: "Does his lordship often duel *en travesti*?"

She smiled grimly.

"You saw them?"

"I saw two young men fencing on the lawn. I did not know them by sight."

"My grandson was the smaller of the two." She grimaced with distaste. "The other is his friend, Mr d'Urfey. A led captain, I believe.[1] Wroth is very proud of his skill with the members. They delight in creating difficulties for themselves. I have seen them fight in all kinds of fantasticals: masks, sacks, with their arms manacled, their hands tied behind their backs, suits of armour . . . blindfold, even. This female rig-out is a favourite device."

"They are both exceptional duellists," I said with genuine admiration.

She looked away, uncomfortably flushed.

I asked delicately: "*Why* do you think these receipts will blackguard you, Lady Wroth?"

Her hands fretted away at the fan. Her voice, when it came, was a mere croak.

"Because it has happened before, Sir!"

She took a deep breath before she continued.

"Six months ago I paid off a low trollop called Dewfly."

She paused.

"Why, Ma'am?"

---

[1] A professional duellist.

"She said she could incriminate my grandson in . . . in some unsavouriness," she finished lamely.

"And was this true, do you think?"

"It could have been. My grandson is rogue-wild." A look of almost superstitious dread came into her eyes. "Young people of quality are so very vicious in these times."

"So you paid this woman off."

"Yes."

"And what exactly do you want of me, Lady Wroth?"

"I want you to rid me of this new menace."

"How?"

"In any way you can . . . legally, of course."

"I see . . ." I said. But, to be honest, I didn't.

"Do you think you can?" she asked anxiously.

"Without buying these receipts for any price, do you mean?"

"I would prefer not to . . . but if I must! . . . There must be no scandal, you see. I have hopes of my grandson making a brilliant match. A girl of good family with £20,000 a year. Nothing must interfere with my plans."

"Then don't you think it would be wiser to settle this man's debt?"

She stood up, shivering with anger. The patina of the great lady cracked slightly, and she swore juicily – an oath from her playhouse days.

"I will not be rooked, Sir! I paid this Dewfly creature because once paid she had no further claim on me. But with a rogue of this sort – " she tapped the papers violently – "there will be no end to it! He'd suck me dry!"

She moved to a porcelain desk and opened a drawer. Taking a money bag from the drawer, she turned to me again.

"What are your charges, Captain Nash?"

I quoted a figure which she promptly reduced by a sixth.

I repeated my figure and for a few moments we argued busily. But eventually she agreed on my price and seemed the better pleased that I had stuck to my word.

She counted out a number of coins and put them in my hand.

"I'll leave the matter entirely to you. Find out what you can about this Asclepius. When you have some ammunition I can use against this – this *Paphlagonian*, come to me and I shall settle with you completely."

I bowed my acceptance. She rang a handbell and almost immediately the door opened and the old manservant looked into the room.

"Captain Nash is ready to leave now, Chives," she said. She inclined her head towards me graciously and bid me good-day. I bowed to her and the interview was over. We left the room.

Chives, it seemed, now had my social measure. Instead of conducting me back through the great hall to the front door, he turned down a mean looking stairway and led me along a grimy passage, past several pantries and a buttery.

We came into the stable yard. My roan waited patiently by the mounting-block. The forelock-touching groom was nowhere to be seen. He too, it seemed, had quickly learned of the "gentleman's" true status.

I unhitched the reins from the post and prepared to mount.

A lordly voice hailed me from the stables.

## III

The voice was crisp and arrogant. It matched the man's profile perfectly. A haughty nose, sculptured cheeks, and a strong, pugnacious chin, which suggested stubbornness rather than strength of character. The eyes, when he turned them upon me, were of a curious fawn colour.

It was the indolent young observer of the fencing match. There was nothing indolent about him now. He marched purposefully towards my horse and took a firm hold of the bridle.

"I want to speak to you," he said curtly.

"I am at your service, Sir," I replied civilly.

The young man bowed in a stiff, unamiable way.

"My name is Wroth, Sir," he said. "Oliver Wroth. I am his lordship's cousin."

"My name is Nash," I began.

"Yes! Yes!" Wroth said abruptly. I know who you are. Moreover, I know *what* you are. You are a Bow Street Man, though you describe yourself in some new-fangled way."

"I work privately, Mr Wroth," I said. "I am a private gentleman." I stressed the last word slightly. Young Wroth's eyebrows rose superciliously.

"You are a Bow Street Man," he said stubbornly. "Or else you are one of Flowery's men.[1] If you are one of Flowery's rogues, you have no place here."

"I am a private individual," I explained patiently. "It is true

[1]Flowery: a notorious thief-taker, subsequently hanged for perverting the course of justice.

that I am licensed as an auxiliary to the Bow Street Police, but I am responsible only to the Mansion House. My occupation is somewhat in the nature of an experiment, Mr Wroth. I am hoping to prove to the authorities that there is scope for a detective force in England. My cousin Scrope Bentham is the Principal Secretary to the Commissioners' Office."

My explanation, and the mention of my well-placed relation, did nothing to mollify young Wroth. If anything, he grew sharper. Plainly, he regarded me as a meddling eccentric. The structure of society was very clearly defined in his mind. Judges, he knew, were gentlemen; lawyers less so. The Bar was a road to wealth and nobility, but any man lower than an attorney was beneath contempt, a battener on the misfortunes of others. That a man who called himself a gentleman should occupy himself with crime was clearly unthinkable to Lord Wroth's cousin.

These thoughts showed plainly enough on his face, but behind this outright hostility, I felt the suggestion of a separate unease.

I soon learned of it. Wroth seemed a man incapable of masking his thoughts.

"What did my grandmother want with you?" he asked bluntly.

"That, Sir, is your grandmother's business," I replied as bluntly.

"On the contrary, I think it is very much my business," he exploded, adding bitterly: "She is my cousin, the damned whore, and we will not have her back."

I said nothing. His light-coloured eyes searched my face for a sign of confirmation. I stared back at him noncommittally.

His face worked furiously.

"Lady Wroth wants you to find and bring her back?" he asked. "Is that it?"

"I can't discuss her ladyship's business with any man, Sir," I said.

"I've just told you, fellow, that it *is* my business," Wroth cried.

I spoke very courteously.

"No, Mr Wroth, you're quite wrong on that point. Her ladyship told me nothing of your cousin. Or of yourself even."

Wroth's brows drew together in a bitter black line.

"Then what?"

I swung myself up into the saddle.

"Is it my cousin Lord Wroth?"

Without answering, I took a firm hold of the reins.

"Is he in trouble again?"

I settled my feet into the stirrups.

"Is my cousin in disgrace?"

"I have told you, Mr Wroth, that I cannot betray her ladyship's confidence." I tipped my hat, clamped it upon my head, and bade him good-day.

I trotted out of the stable yard. I could feel that bright gaze following me until I turned the corner by the coachyard gate.

Once beyond the porter's lodge and out onto the open road, I spurred my horse into a gallop.

Wishing to travel at all speed back to London, I kept to the main road. But straight lines were not a prominent feature of the Wroth landscape; the main road was little more than a bridle path winding through the rich cornfields and meadows, and today was market day. Sheep and cattle, geese and turkeys, were all being driven to town, as they went, and I was reduced to moving at a snail's pace, fuming and cursing.

I was practically at a standstill, trying to extricate from a seethe of greasy sheep, when I heard the brisk tattoo of hooves coming up fast behind me. The furious pace never faltered for an instant, livestock notwithstanding. Blood-curdling shouts rent the air. I turned to see who could be so careless of the beasts. Two whooping riders charged through scattering all before them.

The sheep parted miraculously, like the waves of a fleecy sea, and the young Lord Wroth rode heavily to my side, his horse steaming. A moment later he was joined by d'Urfey.

His lordship spat out a particularly nasty oath and grabbed hold of my reins to halt my horse – an unnecessary move, as it happened, for we were once more trapped by a flowing tide of sheep.

I sat quietly, looking into his lordship's blazing grey eyes. The pale, delicate face was suffused with rage, the head thrown back, his dishevelled hair streaming out behind him. He sat astride his big bay stallion with the sinister grace of an Arabian tribesman.

"My cousin tells me you're here to spy on me," he cried, his voice cutting through the demented bleating of the sheep.

"Then your cousin tells you wrong, my lord," I said evenly, trying to retrieve possession of my reins.

Wroth refused to surrender them and slapped at my hands with the stock of his whip.

"He tells me that you're some sort of Runner. A constable, or an informer. Well, I'm here to tell you, Sir, that I won't tolerate your kind on my land. We are quite feudal here. We have our own methods of dealing with trespassers."

After a short struggle I managed to recapture the reins from him.

"It seems that you have been misinformed on all counts, my lord," I said. "I'm neither an informer nor a trespasser. I came here at your grandmother's invitation, and she has entrusted me with certain business."

He looked at me for a moment with uncertainty, and exchanged a brief, puzzled, questioning glance with d'Urfey. That handsome youth observed me moodily, a restless hand gripping the hilt of his sheathed sword.

"What business?" Wroth asked at last.

"That is your grandmother's affair, Sir," I replied.

Wroth flushed and jerked his head back. His smooth, pretty face turned amazingly ugly of a second.

"Wroth family business is *my* business, Sir. I am the *head* of my family, by God!"

The hand resting lightly on his sword tightened. The knuckles showed whitely. D'Urfey's hand also gripped his sword more purposefully.

The swarming sheep had thinned out slightly. With a gentle pressure of my knees, I urged my roan forward. A gaggle of geese waddled around Wroth's horse, causing it to rear a little, its ears flattening. His master was forced to fall back a yard or so and I took advantage of the incident to move off.

"Is it concerning me that she called you in?" Wroth shouted after me.

I rode on in silence, but I eased my sword out of its scabbard. I thought it very possible that I might have to defend myself, his lordship looked mad enough for any mischief. In his mind there was rather more sail than ballast!

With a rush, he came up behind me, forcing my roan into the hedgerow and cutting off the road before me.

"I asked you – is it me?" he hissed.

"And I have told you, my lord, that I am not at liberty to say."

For a moment we stared each other out. Then Wroth's eyes tilted crazily. D'Urfey had silently manoeuvred himself into position behind my roan. They were about to do me some injury. A furtive signal passed between them, which I rightly interpreted before they could move against me.

With a stabbing flash, I had my sword in my hand, at the ready. It described an undeviating arc in the air and hovered – the point vibrating – a half an inch from his lordship's throat.

Wroth stared at it, bemused.

D'Urfey had drawn his own sword. Now he looked at it foolishly.

"If you will tell your friend to return his sword to its scabbard, my lord," I said easily, "I shall continue on my way."

Wroth frowned, but did as he was asked.

"And now, if you will fall back, Sir, I shall be free to go," I said, my sword held steadily before me.

Wroth paused.

"One moment," he said.

I waited. The young lord regarded me coldly. He sat astride his horse, as rigid as death.

"I think I know why you visited my grandmother," he said huskily, his voice scarcely more than a thread in the clear air. "If you're so inclined, you can do her a great service."

He smiled. A rather crooked, nasty smile. I waited in silence.

"Tell her not to interfere," he said, with sudden passion. "Advise her to pay the man without delay. Otherwise . . ."

He paused. For so fragile a youth, he possessed an amazing quality of menace.

"Otherwise it will be the worse for . . . us."

## IV

I lay upon the splendiferously unplatonic breasts of my mistress, who was known to her world as Clarety-faced Jane. This lady, a trollop by nature, was perhaps my greatest asset in my new-found trade, for Clarety is impeccably informed about London life at all levels. It is understandable enough, perhaps. When a woman spends most of her working life with both feet planted firmly in the air, it is easy enough to keep an ear to the ground. Clarety is adept at her work. She is a complete treasury of secrets, though it is not impossible to unlock her breast if one knows the trick of it.

"Tell me about Asclepius," I asked her, as we rested between the pleasing motion.

"Who, sweet?" she murmured drowsily.

"Doctor Asclepius."

"Oh, him."

I stroked her soft round belly with a hard round coin. She palmed it from me in a nonchalant manner and it disappeared beneath her pillow.

"Cunning Murrell, you mean," she said, with some distaste. "That elevated rogue."

"Cunning Murrell?" I asked. "Why do you call that?"

"Because that's his name. He's just a common or garden 'cunning' man," she said contemptuously. "He travelled the road for years in Wessex. He was famous there as a wise man."

"A wise man?"

"It's not difficult to gain a reputation for wisdom in Wessex," she said scornfully. "Anyway, he prospered there, and grew ambitious seemingly. He moved to town."

"And has he prospered here?"

She laughed shortly.

"The rich and fashionable often find it dull to listen to doctor's advice," she said. "And deadly, indeed, to act upon it. Particularly when they're advised to fast or give up their pleasures. They prefer to go to a man like Murrell with his pills and his potions. But he began in a very low fashion, entertaining the mob with his magic tools."

"Oh? What tools?"

"Well, he has a magic glass that he claims can see through a brick wall!"

"Amazing!"

"Oh, truly!" she scoffed. "A truly amazing instrument. It gained the rogue much fame among the simple country folk."

"But it hasn't impressed the sophisticated London folk?"

She laughed.

"Oh, he don't use tricks like that here," she said. "A man I know got to look at this wonder. He soon robbed it of its mystery."

"What was it?"

"Nothing but a simple arrangement of mirrors in a wooden case. He said a schoolboy could have made it with a little patience and the ruins of a straining-glass. But he does have another instrument, which is far more strange."

"And what's that?"

"It's nothing more than a piece of round dull copper. But he says that by its aid he can tell a true man from a liar. For the liar might stare at it till his eyes are sore, yet he'll never see anything in it but his own self. But if you're a virtuous man, an honest man, then you can see something in it. Something of which Murrell has the secret, something which you must declare to him as proof and test of his truth. But of what that something is, nobody can tell a word, for it seems that nobody has ever seen it!" She laughed uproariously. "But belief in it is as wide as Wessex, and it's served its turn well for him, for it laid the ground-work for his fortune."

She laughed again, causing her breasts to bobble against my arm.

"It's a great time for quackery," she said. "But he has the vantage on most Empirics for sheer effrontery."

She dismissed Murrell and his nonsense by adopting a most indecent posture, and for fully twenty minutes no more was said of a sensible nature.

Despite her opprobrious nickname, my mistress is a greatly desirable woman, tall and graceful in her person, more of a fine woman than a pretty one, but with good teeth, soft lips, sweet breath and an expressive eye. She has a bosom, full, firm and white, a good understanding without being a wit, but cheerful and lively. She is humane and tender, and feels delight where she most wishes to give it. I am a well and strong-backed man, and the time passed agreeably.

After an hour or so of playful toying, cajolery and bribery, I had learned rather more about the former wise man of Wessex.

Asclepius was, indeed, the reincarnation of that Paphlagonian impostor, Alexander, of the Second Century A.D.. Like that ancient charlatan, he had adopted the name of the Greek God of Health, and also many of his practices. By means of the most childish tricks, he had managed to convince an incredible number of credulous people that the God had been reborn in the form of a serpent, with the name of Glycon. Rumour had it that he carried out his treatments whilst draped with this large, tame serpent, which wore a human head. He had a number of other strange practices and, apparently, an answer to all life's ills. His establishment was equipped with almost everything that is necessary for life. If a man had pains in his head, colic in his bowels, or spots on his clothes, the Doctor had the proper cure or remedy. If he wanted anything for his body or his mind, the Doctor's house was the place to look for it. The Doctor could recover a strayed wife, a stolen horse, or a lost memory. He had cured the consumption, the dropsy, gout, scurvy, the King's Evil, and hypochondriac winds. All was done, it seems, by the use of one miraculous cure – no bleeding, no physic. He had, he said, been taught his trade by an Eastern Magus.

"And when he runs out of real sicknesses to cure, he invents his own," Clarety said. "He's invented Moonpall, the Marthambles, Hockogrockle and the Strong Fives."

"Very wise," I said. "If you invent an illness, it is easy enough to invent a cure for it."

She grew serious.

"There is something about him, though. The girls here swear by his 'telling'."

"Oh? Does he deal in the supernatural also?"

Like most women of her type, my mistress is careless of life but terrorized by the thought of "the Beyond". She would not jest about this aspect of the Doctor's activities. It took a great deal of by-play, a small stream of honeyed phrases, and five more coins, before she told me of the Doctor's acquaintance with the occult sciences. He had a familiar, it seems, an oracle who would answer questions put to him. And in illustration of his necromantic skill, he would erect pyramids of numbers, Solomon's key – what the vulgar call the Cabbala – by which he could extract answers at will; either clear, ambiguous or unfathomably mysterious.

I began to see the true nature of the Doctor's practice. When gullible folk seek such answers to their problems, they as often as not give away far more than they receive. The three outstanding receipts on sale to Lady Wroth would contain a great deal more poison than had ever been taken from his lordship's body.

Thus, armed with a little knowledge, I went to confront the Doctor. By dint of gentle bullying, I could, I felt sure, persuade him to part with the embarrassing records of Lord Wroth's follies or vices or worse.

## V

It proved easy enough to find the Doctor's establishment, for the route was well advertised. The posts of houses and the corners of streets were plastered over with his bills and papers urging the public to go to him for remedies. The advertisements had a fine flourish to them, and he had a gallimaufry of cures.

> INFALLIBLE Preventative Pills against The Plague.
> NEVER-FAILING Preservatives against The Infection.
> SOVEREIGN Cordials against the Corruption of the Air.
> EXACT Regulations for the Conduct of the Body in the Case
>    of Infection.
> UNFAILING Anti-Pestilential Pills.
> The ONLY True Plague-Water.
> The ROYAL Antidote against all Kinds of Infection, and such
>    a MIRACULOUS beautifying Liquid that it will Restore
>    the Bloom of 15 to a Lady of 50.

They were such a number that I lost count. He even offered to advise the poor for nothing. Which advice, I had no doubt, would be to buy the Doctor's physic.

All of them were to be had only at the Sign of the "Anodyne Necklace", at the East End of Barnard's Row by the School.

Barnard's Row was a grey-faced, respectable looking street, behind the tall, rambling façade of the Bars. The sign of the "Anodyne Necklace" hung before the most solidly built house in that solidly built street. Plainly, business was thriving, which scarcely surprised me in view of Clarety's information. The public are always ready to throw their money away on physics, charms, philtres, exorcisms, incantations and amulets. It is indeed a golden age of quackery and one remedy is as fatal as another!

I opened the door and entered beneath the swinging sign. A bell jangled, but the room was empty.

To walk into this unusual, strange looking shop, was to be transported to another world entirely. Here in profusion were all the varied ingredients of the cure-pedlar. It was a dark, magical cavern rather than a shop.

There were big pails of pickled entrails and buckets of what I took to be black, salted eggs; they could as easily have been a beast's parts marinading in a preservative. Counters and shelves were laden with jars of brightly coloured powders and packets of black and forbidding dried stuffs. Some of the jars were labelled with such exotic information as that they contained: "Snail's Water", "Oil of Earthworms", "Roast Slugs", "Viper's Fat", and even "Live Lice" – for swallowing, Clarety had informed me.

It was like a witch-woman's pantry. There were dried cuttlefish, dried mushrooms, dried shoots, dried nuts, dried stalks, and from the ceiling there hung the stomachs of dried fish. In one corner there were some curious live reptiles in a glass-box, so ugly-looking that they would have frightened Old Nick himself. From the walls there hung the implements of his trade: a bristling armoury of fierce looking knives, scissors and choppers. The shop could have armed an uprising. It was a place of potent atmosphere and it stank dreadfully.

I stood in the midst of all this strangeness for a moment or two before I called out "Shop!" The eyes of dead fish and live reptiles stared at me unwinkingly. I had an eerie feeling that, somewhere out of sight, more nightmarish eyes were watching me.

I thumped with my cane on the floor. At the rear of the shop a door opened and a bizarre figure emerged from the shadows.

He was a singularly unattractive young fellow of about middle height, thick-set and muscular, with a truculent expression and an aggressive jaw. His hair was of a bright and forbidding red, his eyebrows drawn like a portcullis over small and bloodshot eyes. But his most distinguishing feature was the pair of white buck-teeth which protruded from his upper lip and gleamed with absolute savagery when he smiled. There hung about him an odd, perverse aroma, and he was clad in what seemed to be an archaic livery.

"Can I help you, Sir?"

The voice was low and silky, surprisingly beautiful. A voice well-used to putting the prospective customer at his ease.

I decided straightway to use the brash approach.

"I wish to see Mr. Murrell," I said.

The young man's smile stayed fixed, but gleamed obscenely.

"Mr. Murrell, Sir? You must have the wrong address."

"No, this is the right address. I refer to the old wise man of Wessex, 'Cunning' Murrell."

The smile had faded now, only the red eyes gleamed.

"We have no Mr. Murrell here, Sir," he said bleakly.

"The Doctor, then," I said impatiently. "Asclepius. The 'Blameless Physician'."

The red eyes peered at me ferociously beneath the rufous brows, but his voice remained as smooth as silk tabby.

"Asclepius sees nobody without an appointment, Sir. Is there anything that I can do for you?"

"I doubt it. My business is with your master. Tell him I am come to settle a debt."

The young man's fears were now thoroughly aroused. He examined me closely, computing to make up his mind concerning me. He almost sniffed at me, scenting trouble. At length he said:

"I am empowered to settle accounts, Sir."

"It is not in your power to settle this account," I said. "My business is with your master."

He hesitated. He was now appraising me quite frankly, measuring my physical strength against his own. He decided that I might prove too much for his weight.

"My master is not here," he said stubbornly.

"Then I shall wait."

"He won't be here until very late, if at all today."

"Then I shall make myself comfortable." I settled myself upon a small gilt gesso chair, tipping it back against the low wooden counter.

The red-eyed man observed me sourly for a moment. Then he turned on his heel and faded back into the shadows, the bright red hair doused like a candle in the general murk. I waited for the next pass. Once more, I felt the numerous eyes fixed upon me.

The servant reappeared a moment later. His eyes held my own, his chin was thrust out pugnaciously. He had obviously received instructions. I tensed myself, expecting him to try to hustle me from the shop.

But he said patiently: "If you will state your business, Sir, I'll settle it for you."

"My business is with your master," I repeated.

"My master is not here," he said, as stolidly.

"Then I shall wait."

"He will not be here today."

I crossed my legs, balancing my back against the counter carefully.

"Then tell me where I may find him," I said.

"My master never receives outside of here."

His small red eyes were on my sword, swinging negligently at my side. His foot was placed so that, should the opportunity arise, one quick flip of his leg would send my chair spinning. I eased myself out of the chair, yawning.

It seemed final. If the old impostor refused to see me, I had no means at my disposal of forcing him to do so, short of tackling this brutish young servant physically. I had decided beforehand that the best way to deal with Murrell was to approach him directly and try to browbeat him into relinquishing the receipts. But I could see no purpose in forcing myself on him bodily, thus raising his defences immediately. The situation required some subtlety. Besides, for all I knew, there was a back way out of the premises, and it is impossible for one man to lay siege to a house with several exits. And, in the main, it might not be a bad thing to leave the Doctor sweating a little.

I smiled at the young man affably enough.

"I'll call tomorrow," I said. "At what time will the Doctor receive me?"

The servant hesitated. He said truculently: "He'll be busy tomorrow. Why can't you state your business plainly, and be done?"

"I'll call tomorrow," I said, trying to mix pleasantry and menace in my manner.

His troubled eyes never left me until I myself had left the shop.

I was convinced that the Doctor was still in the shop and so I decided to lay in wait for him.

I quickly spied-out the area. First of all, I made sure that Murrell could not escape me by way of a rear exit. With businesses like Murrell's, there has always to be a backdoor.

The only rear access to the house seemed to be a narrow passage between the houses. I walked quickly down it and found myself in a broad court, surrounded by a high wall.

Satisfied that the Doctor could only leave by one of two exits, I returned to the street, keeping well out of sight of the shop-window.

Like Murrell, I had a trick or two of my own. I, too, possessed a glass, that if it could not see through a brick wall, at least it could look round corners. It was my own invention, a small, round mirror, smoked in order not to reflect the sun's rays, and angled on a telescopic stick. A primitive device, yet with it I could stand out of sight of my suspects and still keep them under observation.

I took my place behind a mews' wall and focused my mirror on the shop.

For two hours I remained stationed there and nothing of any importance happened at all. A few callers came to the "Anodyne Necklace", but not a great press of people, by any means. They almost all entered self-consciously, if not furtively, and they all left carrying small parcels. The Doctor's customers seemed to consist largely of middle-aged women and decrepit old men.

But nobody came out who had not gone in and I began to feel that I was, perhaps, playing a wrong hand.

Within the space of this two hours, the weather had changed dramatically. Warring thunder clouds came up out of the west, and by mid-afternoon the sky was as cold and lowering as a moorland bog.

I thought of abandoning the siege.

Then, at five o'clock, there was a sudden flurry of activity outside the shop. A sedan chair carried by two scrawny looking chairmen came to a stop before the door. The door opened, the red-haired man peeked out, looking left and right. His head disappeared, and a moment later a man and a woman came down the steps.

They were an eccentric pair. The man was an old, dun-coloured man, as dry and precise as arithmetic, hollow-faced, scant of hair, long-nosed, short of chin, and possessed of a most uncivil leer. He climbed into the chair and the chairmen closed the door on him.

The woman who followed him out was a most extraordinary creature. I had never seen her like. She was a strong-looking black woman, as ugly and misshapen as her master, wall-eyed and bandy-legged. It was impossible to tell her age, so marked was her face with the pox and the Evil. She walked with a curious sideways roll, for all the world like a sailor on shore-leave, but this may have been due to the way she was encumbered. On her head towered an enormous turban, topped with a package, which she held secure with one hand. She was saddled like a mule, with a harness of parcels, two small baskets like donkey panniers at her hips, and a bag slung from her shoulders.

The men heaved the chair from the ground and set off at a steady pace, the black woman following like some fantastic pack-horse.

I trailed behind at a discreet distance.

They plunged into a maze of twisting streets and stinking alleys that led towards Cripplegate. The road was pitted with holes filled with last week's rain-water, and everyday's filth. The kennels were running with sweepings and dung.

I walked along, keeping one eye on the chair and one eye out for the natural hazards of the street, and I held a scented sachet to my nostrils, for the stink grew appalling. I kept as close to the walls as I could, as a protection from any slops thrown from the windows, though this grew increasingly more difficult as we penetrated deeper into the slums, for even the walls themselves were plastered with excrescences.

Stepping out from a particularly gruesome protuberance, I was almost bowled over by two horsemen who came careening around the corner. Stepping back into the safety of the wall, I was accosted by a huge young savage who stopped me from proceeding further. We almost came to blows over who would "take the wall".

In the end, I half-drew my sword and the hulking lad stepped aside with a mouthful of coarse abuse.

By the time I reached the end of the street, the sedan chair had vanished into the thick air.

# VI

I searched the surrounding streets rapidly, but without success. I felt vastly discouraged. They had vanished like water down a drain, though leaving less trace. I spent over an hour trying to track down the sedan chair, asking questions of a quantity of people.

But people in this part of the world had little inclination to impart information, even for money. Indeed, people in this part of the world hardly seemed to be of the human race. Every creature I spoke to was as surly as a butcher's dog.

My temper was fairly kindled at my folly. All my walking about in the clammy heat had been totally unnecessary. I should have played the game with more finesse, smoothed my way into Murrell's presence and only then turned upon him. I had made a tactical error in alerting him to his danger. I saw that now. There seemed nothing else for it but to give up for the day.

Two horses dashed out of a side street, showering me with small stones and dry mud. I looked up angrily and then stood staring after them, gawping.

Lord Wroth and d'Urfey sped down the street, endangering the lives of several unwary pedestrians.

I turned my attention eagerly to the street from which they had so precipitously emerged. It proved to be a blind alley of even more sinister an appearance than the rest of the neighbourhood. The buildings to either side had derelict, windowless walls of blackened brick, so tall they cast a permanent shadow across the street.

I walked to the end of the alley. The structure facing me was as featureless as the others. A wall, bare of doors or windows. The only gate was boarded up and had not been opened for months or even years.

I stood there, feeling baffled. I was as sure as certain that the horses had turned out of this street and, indeed, my nose told me pungently that horses had used the area. Physical proof of it lay on the cobblestones. But it seemed impossible that Wroth and his comrade had been visiting in this street. Perhaps the house they had visited stood near by? Perhaps they had only stabled their horses here temporarily?

I walked down the alley once more, and stood looking at the gate. It had a monstrously derelict air about it. I lowered my eyes to stare at the cobbles immediately before it. Stooping, I picked up between my thumb and forefinger a small amount of grey ash. Somebody, only moments before, had emptied the bowl of his pipe here. I then noticed faint silvery scratches on the cobbles. A horse – or two horses – had stood before this gate, their shoes striking restlessly upon the ground.

Why had they been waiting by this particular gate? I looked at it again. It was about a foot and a half above my height. I reached up and grasping the rim of it raised myself to peer over it.

I found myself looking into a narrow yard and at the back part of a tall and crooked house. It leaned perilously towards me, grim and menacing, its windows blank with dust. There appeared, at first, to be no entrance to the building, and then I saw that steps led down to a deep-cut area in which was set a narrow door.

The yard was strewn with rubbish and thick with dirt. Even from my place above the gate I could see the faint trace of footsteps leading across it. They began about a yard away with a deep scuffed mark where a body had landed after jumping, and the returning footsteps stopped by a large box set immediately below the gate.

Almost without stopping to think, I climbed over the gate. I dropped into the grey dust of the yard. There was a narrow, dismal passage at the side of the house which led into what appeared to be a tunnel. I entered it cautiously and was at once plunged into a sable gloom, lit only by the faint light forcing its way through the dingy fanlight of a door at its far end. Dust swirled in my nostrils, and I could feel them beginning to swell. It was a damp, dispiriting place, with a curiously threatening air to it. I walked slowly and carefully, half expecting to be ambushed at every step. With my sword drawn, I opened the door cautiously. It groaned like a soul in purgatory . . .

I was amazed to find myself in a pleasant and expansive courtyard, elegantly paved and set about with vines and jessamine. A screen wall surrounded the courtyard, broken in the centre by an impressive iron-grille gate. The gate was guarded by two stone lions, fiercely rampant, yet with expressions of unshakeable piety. I stepped into the court and turned to look at the house.

It was a middling sort of house, a square rose-bricked edifice. The contrast between its frontage and its rear was remarkable. The façade was charming, strong and placid, with no frippery. The shutters were painted a gay yellow and the large front door had both a canopy and a fanlight.

For a moment, I believed that I had made another mistake. But no, the sedan chair rested in a corner of the courtyard, cooled by the shade of a fragrant tree.

This, I saw, was the house I was looking for. But how had Murrell got here from that warren of dirty lanes behind me? No doubt I could find that out when I faced him. I walked up the broad steps and pulled at the bell-rope.

The bell pealed deep inside the house and I waited for the echoes to die away before I pulled the rope again.

I waited two minutes more and then set the bell a-jangling. There was no response.

After twenty minutes of futile bell-pulling and frustrating door-knocking, it seemed obvious that either the house was deserted, the occupants were deaf or I was going to be ignored. Once again, I had a strange feeling of being watched. I felt that even the lions had their pious gaze upon me.

I tried to peer into the ground floor windows, but I could see nothing; the heavy curtains were drawn tightly against the evening light.

I turned away from the house and decided to leave by the front gate. It was, of course, locked.

For a moment, I was lost for action. It must, I knew, be obvious to whoever was inside (if anybody was) that I, too, had entered through the back-premises, and this must have greatly alarmed them.

And forewarned them. For I would have to return by that direction. I felt a proper annoyance at my lack of thought. Indeed, I seemed to have taken no thought in this matter so far! It was apparent to me now, from the assistant's unusual behaviour in the shop, that the Doctor was the type of man to have any number of enemies of a greater or a lesser sort. It was also apparent from the Doctor's subsequent behaviour that he was a sly and nasty individual who would deal with his enemies in a sly and nasty manner. No doubt, at this very moment, some thoroughbred bruiser lurked below, waiting for my hesitant steps. The criminality is audacious and brutal, I am a brave enough man, but I don't believe in courting ill-fortune. I had no intention of returning through that treacherous black tunnel.

Without further ado, I set one foot on a lion's backside, put the other foot on its kingly head and, making sure that the street was empty, heaved myself over the wall. I dropped down on the other side to find myself in a broad street.

"What street is this?" I foolishly asked a passer-by.

"Why, Paradise Close, to be sure," the surprised man replied.

I pointed at the house I had just left.

"What house is that?" I asked.

He looked affronted.

"Why that, Sir, is the notorious Temple of Health!" and chuntering furiously, he hurried away.

Dr. Godbold's notorious Temple of Health. What had "Cunning" Murrell, alias Dr. Asclepius, to do with that hot-bed of quacksalvery?

And how had the wise man managed to transport himself from the squalid streets of St. Giles' to this ample and respectable close? By magic? More likely by sleight of mind. He certainly hadn't entered by the back-gate through the mucky yard. I had followed the track of only one man through it; and, besides, the sedan chair would never have passed through the narrow confines of the tunnel.

How, then? Was there a third entrance to the house? I decided to try to trace one, should it be so. I would have to accost the slippery fellow in the street if he continued to refuse to meet me. And if the man made use of secret entrances and exits, as seemed likely, it would be as well to know.

The Doctor, I could see, was going to be the devil to catch.

## VII

I had walked around the house three times and had come to the conclusion that the chair had travelled from the street where I had lost it by way of an intricate maze of stinking alleys and ill-lit wynds. It was the only possible way that I could trace, and not very satisfactory, but I was now convinced that there were no secret entrances or exits.

I returned to Paradise Close and settled down to waiting. It was growing dark and a faint gleam of candle-light showed between the curtains. I tried the gate once again and found it locked. I saw no point in vaulting over the wall to hammer on the door. In this uncertain light, I couldn't be sure of the welcome I'd receive.

I found a convenient waiting-place, about five houses away from the Temple, sharing an alcove with a battered Venus. She was a most formidable lady with a monstrously ostentatious bosom, and I felt rather relieved that she was cast in bronze.

The rainclouds swelled and the watery night gathered in, the sun bidding a tearful farewell to the West.

An hour passed and the broad street became deserted. An hour more and it was dark, hot and heavy – the prelude to a storm.

A light showed at the door of the Temple. There were coarse voices raised in anger, and the scrape of steel on a wall. The Doctor, it appeared, was about to take to the streets once more. And this time, his servants were to be armed.

The gate opened and the chairmen jogged into view. A link-boy preceded them, the flame of his torch smoking steadily in the still air. The chair was followed by the Negress, saddled as before with numerous parcels. The chairmen each carried a short sword.

The small procession disappeared into the murky streets. I followed from close enough behind, the link-boy's torch leading me steadily onwards.

They had travelled for about half an hour when the storm broke. What happened then was too confusing for me to understand from a distance. The rain fell in a sudden sheet, and it was either the rain that quenched the light, or else the boy deliberately plunged it into the mud. With a terrified cry, he fled.

Cursing heartily, the chairmen dropped the sedan, and scrabbled in the mud for the torch. One man struck his tinder in an attempt to make some light for the search. A peal of thunder shook the sky and lightning streaked above the black houses.

What happened next occurred with inexpressible speed.

A group of men came running from behind the houses. They were armed with cudgels and cutlasses, and they were yelling like savages. They encircled the sedan and tried to wrench open the door. The chairmen turned and ran, without waiting to defend their master. Only the Negress tried valiantly to ward off the swarm of men, but she was sadly hampered by her harness. She fought like a demon, straddled between the bars of the chair, but a well-placed blow from a cudgel knocked her roughly to one side and she fell over, rolling about the street like a tortoise turned upon its back, trying desperately to rise. Even whilst lying helpless on the ground, she managed to take hold of a stout leg to try to throw a man on his back.

Inside the sedan, the terrified old man kept a desperate hold on the door, but his efforts were futile. With a crack of splintering glass, a sword broke through the window and, plunging into his breast, pinned him firmly against the back of the cabinet. Then the sword was drawn smartly out again and the old man slumped against the window, the shattered glass tinkling to the ground.

The men ran off into the darkness.

I ran to the sedan chair. The Negress had managed to pull herself to her knees, moaning and chattering to herself in some outlandish tongue.

I pulled open the door and reached inside. Blood ran over my hand and the old man groaned horribly. For a moment, I thought that he still lived, but blood gurgled throatily from his lips and he died with a dreadful rattle even as I pressed against his chest. I quickly searched his pockets, only to find them empty.

The Negress came up behind me, hissing fiercely. I turned in time to catch the arm that plunged towards me wielding a wicked looking dagger. I deflected the blow, pushing her heavily to one side. She fell against the sedan chair, which toppled over and fell with an ear-splitting crash to the ground, the momentum of the fall taking her with it. High above the street a few shutters were opened and lights showed at the windows. The citizenry were beginning to take a tentative interest in the affair.

I wasted no more time, but ran off in the same direction that the ruffians had taken. I stopped at the corner of the street, faced with three different directions. Of the murderers, there was no sign.

## VIII

I walked quickly away from the area. When the Negress revived, she would no doubt rouse the neighbourhood and the night-watch would take care of the corpse. I saw no point in implicating myself in Murrell's death.

As I walked through the mean streets, my mind was busy with various conjectures. Who had killed the old man? Was it a purely fortuitous incident? Violence and death were only too common in these streets at night, the Great Unwashed are infinitely more dangerous than any savage tribe. Murrell was, quite possibly, simply an ordinary casualty.

Or was it deliberately designed? Had he been the victim of a plot? The old charlatan must have made many enemies in his career. No doubt Lady Wroth was not the only wealthy aristocrat to be challenged with such a demand. Ours is a licentious age. The possibilities of evildoing are limitless, and Murrell was a man to profit by them. It seemed more than likely that some poor catspaw, harassed beyond endurance, had decided to rid himself of a money-sucking leech. It is an easy enough business to hire an assassin, some men would do the task for the price of a gin, and this matter had a designed look to it. The way the link-boy had doused the light and fled at the precise spot where the bravoes had lain in wait suggested a collusion. Unless the butchers had been following? Then again, the chairmen had put up no fight at all, the Negress had shown more spirit. It could be that they had thought the battle too unequal, but the fact that they had fled in silence with no cries of help, or for the watch, seemed to point to their implication in a plot. It would be interesting to know if they were in the Doctor's service or whether they were casually employed. If they were professional chairmen, then it was the more likely that they had been procured by assassins. It is easy enough to bribe a chairman, they are frequently in the pay of thieves and cut-throats and they will often lead their hirers into a trap, only to run and leave them to be murdered, raped or robbed. Yet Murrell must have trusted them to have had them carry him through the streets at night? He must have known of his danger, or else why arm his men?

The more I thought on it, the more obvious it became that the affair had been managed in some way. The clearest evidence of this was that Murrell alone had been slain by the assassins. And they had not stopped to plunder him. That surely pointed to a planned attempt to silence him. Well, there would be many a timorous soul glad to have him silenced.

How was Wroth involved in tonight's doings? He knew of Murrell's second house and the obscure ways to reach it. He had preferred to call upon the old charlatan in secret. Why had he gone there? To threaten the old man? To warn him? He seemed wondrously concerned to let his grandmother squander his own inheritance to stop the wise man's mouth. What was the secret of Murrell's hold over him? It must be grave to bring him rushing up to town in such a funk. Had he gone to Murrell to take the receipts by main force? And had he failed in his first attempt?

The thought pulled me up short. Had Wroth been implicated in the murder? Having failed to secure the papers at that afternoon's interview, had he arranged to take them by violence tonight?

I shrugged the thought away. Even the foolhardy Lord Wroth would know that Murrell was unlikely to carry such valuables on his person. They would be safely locked away in some chest.

Locked away! The implication struck me like a blow. Whoever had killed the old man had lifted the lid of a Pandora's Box. The nasty contents would scandalize London to its very core!

Once Murrell's death was known, his house would be investigated by the Bow Street Police. Whatever evidence he had against Wroth would become public property. God knows what others would suffer also. Rather than silencing Murrell, they had done the reverse. If a dead man could talk, the old Cunning-man would shout from the rooftops.

Confronted with this fact, I saw that I had two alternatives, both of them equally obnoxious to me. My commission had been to secure the papers by any means legally possible. To fail to do so would part me from a very powerful patroness. It might even put an end to my career at its outset. Yet in order to secure them I would have to place myself in an even more invidious position. Breaking and entering, however justifiable the reason, would not do me any good service with the authorities, should I be discovered.

It was a fine point of morality. Yet, somehow, I must get hold of those receipts.

Two hours later, I had raided the shop in Barnard's Row. I had searched the place from cellar to attic, to no avail. What papers I found were straightforward accounts and bills of lading, quite innocent of double meaning. Either others had forestalled me, or else Murrell kept his secret papers in a less accessible locality. The latter seemed more likely. He was far too wily a rogue to leave such a treasure unburied.

I decided to investigate the house in Paradise Close.

I raised my head above the rim of the gate. The back of the house leaned towards me, as forbidding as God and as silent.

Carefully I eased myself over the gate and dropped softly into the dust of the yard. I moved cautiously towards the house.

I looked at the lower windows and at once ruled them out as a means of entry. Beyond the grimy glass they were either boarded up or covered by an iron grille. I turned my attention to the basement. It was pitch-black at the bottom of the steps, but covered. I risked a light, and struck my tinder. It was a strong looking door and had not been used for an age or more. Cobwebs glittered from the corners and the disturbed dust gleamed all around me. After a brief examination, I realized that nothing short of a battering ram wielded by a dozen men would have any effect on it.

I walked back into the yard and looked up at the house. The overhanging eaves loomed above me. My eye was caught by a protruding object, a water-spout in the form of a gargoyle. If I could climb on to it, it would give me a foot-hold from which I could reach the upper windows.

I looked about the yard and came upon the box that Wroth had used to climb the gate. I heaved it on to my shoulders and carried it back to the house. Placing it beneath the window, I mounted it and stretching my arms upwards towards the gargoyle, I grabbed the spout with ease. Slowly I pulled myself up.

Five strenuous minutes later, I was precariously balanced upon the ugly stone head and my eyes were on a level with the window. I saw with relief that it was a simple affair of plain glass set in a flimsy wooden frame, fastened by an iron catch. I took out my jack knife and inserted it beneath the fastening. Rust flaked from it beneath my pressure and, with a faint squeal, I forced the clasp upwards.

I opened the window and pulled myself over the sill. In a moment I was standing in a room bare of furniture, save for a deal table and three rickety chairs. It was a mournful place, the whitewashed walls were peeling and yellow, the ceiling blackened with decades of dirt.

I creaked across the floorboards and stood behind the shabby door. There was no sound beyond it. My entrance had gone unremarked. I opened the door as quietly as I could, but the hinges still screeched slightly. I looked into a long and narrow corridor, as bare as the room behind me. Pools of water gleamed on the boards in the light of a dusty dormer window. Obviously, the back of the house was little used.

Slowly and carefully I edged my way along the corridor feeling my way with every tread. My steps seemed to creak with devastating effect in the eerie stillness of an empty house.

I came to the end door which was more solidly built. I waited a moment, listening hard for a sign of life beyond it. There was an absolute silence. I turned the handle and pulled the door back inch by careful inch.

A weird blue light filled my eyes. It blazed from a brazier, intense and fierce, and yet soft and lambent. I had never seen a light to equal it. It was a strange mixture of radiance and mystery.

Lesser lights shone in odd corners of the room. One in particular attracted my attention. It was a monstrous lamp that stood on what appeared to be a black marble altar. It was lewdly designed in the shape of a bat, with an erect member.

The lamps illuminated the strangest room that I had ever seen. It can only be described as "Dionysiac" – an orgiastic display of a wild and dissolute character. Over the entire length of the gaudily painted ceiling, naked men ravished naked women in a bewildering variety of postures. Seen from below, it was an outlandish sight; these couples seemed to be copulating in mid-air, and their freedom of movement enabled them to indulge in the most amazing amatory acrobatics.

The murals on the walls were more prosaic, not to say more basic, though the models here, too, were supple in the extreme. The murals were poor copies of the indecent paintings from ancient Roman frescoes. All the known positions of sexual gratification were illustrated, and when human partners were exhausted, the animal kingdom took over, along with creatures from the ancient world: sileni, pans, satyrs and centaurs. But the females were always female, if not more than female.

Along the sides of the room were arranged richly upholstered couches, and several statues stood about the room, all of them highly indecent. There were a number of Egyptian gods, including the god Min, with his proudly displayed phallus. Among the Greek entries were several metamorphoses of Zeus and a bronze Hermes holding a staff carved with a phallic symbol with the tip painted red. Rome was represented by a squatting Cloacina, the Goddess of the Sewer, befouling her own shrine.

An oriental odour perfumed the air, and by the brazier a number of jars were placed. They were filled with "magical" herbs, waiting to be burned: belladonna, hemlock, henbane, verbena, mandrake. All of them powerful narcotics.

In a large glass case were the prostitute's stock-in-trade for the relief of carnal desire – whips, ropes, high boots and oddly constructed instruments whose exact purpose escaped me, but whose meaning was plain enough.

The room was a shrine of sexual abnormality. Apart from curing his patients of their ills, and foretelling their futures, it seemed that Murell also catered for their lusts. That is, if he had any connection with the Temple. Clarety had told me nothing of it and if he had an interest here, she would surely know of it.

Against one wall stood the centrepiece of the whole ensemble. A great bed, an extravagance of crimson silks and glass pillars, perfumed with essences; a bed designed for pleasure, a bed dedicated to the cult of Aphrodite. It was large enough to accommodate at least ten people and, no doubt, often had. Beneath the gleaming canopy hung a mirror, contrived to reflect the transports on the mattress below. I never saw such a bed in my life before. It could have come from the Grand Turk's Seraglio.

I realized that I was looking at the most famous bed in London. Dr. Godbold's Celestial Bed, designed for "the Propagation of Beings Rational and Far Stronger and More Beautiful in Mental as well as Bodily Endowments than the Present Puny, Feeble and Nonsensical Race of Christians. No One exists Frigid enough to Resist the Influence of the Pleasure of Those Transports which this Enchanting Place inspires."

This was the notorious bed, guaranteed to restore the impaired constitutions of emaciated youths and debilitated old men, warranted to revive any constitutions that were not absolutely mouldered away. I had heard that some jaded voluptuaries had paid upwards of £500 for the privilege of fornicating on this bed. Two great lords swore that their heirs had been sired in it when all other means had failed. I tested its resilience; it seemed filled with the most springy hair, but behaved much as any ordinary mattress would.

. . . Dr. Nathaniel Godbold. What was his connection with Murrell? Or was it yet another alias? Was this Temple the real core of his blackguarding activities? This room would prove more fertile when it came to extracting secrets from his customers than the shop in Barnard's Row. Men are at their most vulnerable when taken either in drink or in lust, and under the influence of this sense-saturating room what would they not reveal?

Yes, I felt sure that this house was the centre of the web. I moved to the door and opened it cautiously. With a shock, I started back.

In the hall a figure stood with one finger to his lips, as if bidding me to be silent. Both frozen, we outstared each other.

Then I laughed softly to myself. The figure was a statue. Hippocrates himself. The lamplight flickering on his face had made him seem lifelike.

I walked down a broad corridor, frugally lit by candles in sconces. I opened five doors leading into various rooms, all comfortably furnished, but eerie in the unsteady light of the candles.

In one room, resplendently furnished in marble, another statue of the Goddess Cloacina squatted on a marble pedestal. This, I realized, was the famed Temple of Ease, devoted to those suppliants who suffered from digestive ailments. Again the variously ambiguous instruments were in evidence.

I left the room, and walked down the corridor. A wide staircase descended to the ground floor which was shrouded in darkness. By the head of the stairs stood a heavy, mahogany door. I tried the handle gently. The door remained solidly barred against me.

A few minutes with the blade of my knife, and the door swung open smoothly. The shuttered room was stiflingly dark; a dim assembly of shapes. I struck my tinder.

My eye was caught immediately by the iron strong-box. It stood upon a solid desk.

Naturally, it was locked. It took five minutes of concentrated effort to force the lock, and my heart sank with disappointment at the result. The box contained nothing but a leather-bound book with a faulty clasp. The same neat and clerkly hand that had addressed the letter to Lady Wroth had written a jumble of meaningless phrases and figures in this book. I saw that the book was an elaborate code in the Cant Language, the thieves' dialect. The first thing I could make sense of was a name, "Charles Winstanley" coupled with the date of 18th March 1769 and a place, "Caper's Gardens".[1] My mind turned this information over, and I was suddenly alerted. Had there not been a notorious scandal at Caper's Gardens concerning a certain young rakehell by that name?

I put the notebook in my pocket, thinking that I could probably break this code since I am fairly conversant with the Cant. I searched the rest of the room to no purpose, and descending the stairs, turned my attention to the lower floor.

The hall of this Temple was a testament to Godbold's (or Murrell's) cures. It was ornamented with crutches, walking sticks, ear-trumpets, eye-glasses, trusses and so on, all discarded by grateful patients. Had he been of the Catholic persuasion, the good doctor might have qualified for sainthood.

A bare half hour later, I let myself out by the way I had entered. The rooms below had proved to be conventional reception rooms that gave up no secrets, for they had no secrets to keep.

## IX

I was taking my morning chocolate at the "Black Cat" Coffee-House in Greek Court, and searching diligently through the *Gazette* to see

[1] A pleasure-garden after the fashion of Vauxhall.

what news there was of last night's doings. There was none, which scarcely surprised me, since murder and violent theft are rife in those streets. The people of St. Giles' have a rat's eye view of life, are more fearsome than any brute beast, and nearly as ignorant. The crime would have to be of a very sensational quality for it to be registered in print.

In this instance, I would do better with my ears than with my eyes. I set myself to listen in the neighbouring taverns and coffee-houses.

But not a murmur reached me of Murrell's death. Not even my mistress mentioned it, though her working day is spiced with news of vice and crime. If Clarety-faced Jane has no knowledge of an event, then it has not usually taken place. But no detail of Murrell's death had come to her, nobody had breathed a word of it. This silence intrigued me almost as much as the mystery of his death. It was as if all the world had compacted to treat his murder with the greatest possible secrecy.

Not wishing to display my own association with the affair, I made my enquiries indirectly. It is always best to question Clarety when she is lost in heat, for then her mind is only triflingly occupied with the questions and her answers fall from her lips involuntarily. Accordingly, I set myself to thoroughly arouse her that morning. When she threw her arms around me warmly, I embraced her as warmly. As she wound her arms around my neck with passion, I took her legs with equal force and passed them round my waist. I met her kisses and murmurs of pleasure with just as strong an amorous toying and sucked her tongue as readily as she sucked mine. By the time I loosed her drawstrings and got into her, she was purring with delight and in a good frame of mind to pass on any information to hand. But she knew nothing of Murrell, though I pumped her mind as thoroughly as her body.

I left her scratching herself erotically with a silver piece.

On reflection, I decided to walk back into the filthy maze of St. Giles'. I might, I thought, be better rewarded in the low drinking dens of that quarter. Information, of a sort, is always to be bought in such places, if one can cut through their barbarous jargon.

Turning into the stinking alley of Jay Row, I saw a crowd gathered by an open well. The shrill sound of their conversation rattled against the walls of the houses, making the street hum like a gigantic beehive. A woman howled fanatically, another screamed, men's voices were raised in a righteous anger. I almost hesitated to linger there long enough to find out what disturbed their peace. For the London mob is a thing to be avoided at all times, even the king dare not stand in its way once it is aroused. And this seething mass of dirty humanity was thoroughly aroused. I began to skirt around it gingerly, feeling my way among the mud and filth of the street. The crowd stank so badly that it was all I could do not to raise my wipe[1] to my nose in plain self-defence. Had I done so, they would have set about me at once. Delicacy, in that area, is a red rag to a bull. And they were in a very ugly turn of mind.

Two enormous men appeared to be pulling some object from the well. As I passed by, the crowd fell back slightly and the men dumped their burden on the ground.

It was a dead man. The mob howled with fury.

"Christ a'mighty," said a voice close-by. " 'Tis bad enough with mice, rats and tabbies in the warter – but this dirty, buttocking bastard!"

"'ow the 'ell did 'e get in the supply?" asked another.

"This was the best warter in St. Giles'," wailed a woman. "Now we gotta drink it an' 'e's warshed 'is scabby feet in it."

The mob roared agreement. A woman kicked the sodden body.

I found myself staring at the dead man. His eyes stared back into mine, without light or sense. The head was bent at a peculiar angle to his body as if it had been struck a heavy blow. He looked like some large, pathetic doll thrown casually away by a thoughtless child. The eyes gleamed dully, and a trickle of water ran from the gaping mouth. A knife protruded from the base of his neck. There was no blood, that had been washed away; the water of the well was crimsoned, as I could see in a bucket that had been drawn up. The corpse's skin was a bluish white from some hours' immersion in the well.

A few hours before, he had been young, lithe, very handsome, and *dangerous*.

I was looking at the mortal remains of Lord Wroth's duelling partner. Tom d'Urfey had lost his last fight. His body was already stiffening obscenely in the morning air.

"What happened?" I asked my vociferous neighbour.

A dozen outraged voices clamoured to enlighten me.

"He fell in the well!"

"Dirty maggot!"

"Pushed more like!"

"'e's broke 'is neck, I'd say!"

"Been down there for 'ours, the block, cloggin' the warter."

"We couldn't understand it. Warter just dried up."

"Like a drought it was."

---

[1]Handkerchief.

"A visitation more like!"

"Garn! Got his dessarts, I'd say."

A lively argument ensued as to how the dead man had found his way into the well. Under cover of it, I leaned forward to get a closer look at the body.

I could see at once that he had not bruised himself by falling. The blow had been delivered by a sharp, clean rap from a heavy instrument. It had been performed by somebody who knew what they were doing. A skull-cracking cudgel wielder. Also, he had not drowned. There was not enough water in him for that.

For whatever reason, young d'Urfey had been killed with cold deliberation rather than in a hot-blooded brawl. Concussed and then knifed. And by a dabster in the art.

# X

The following morning, I again read the *Gazette* from the first to the last page, hoping to find some reference to Murrell's death, but there was no mention of it. On the other hand, young d'Urfey's untimely end had been immortalized in five well-turned paragraphs, no less – no doubt because of his eccentric burial place. When murder is a daily commonplace, it is only the unusual detail that will titillate the public's jaded palate.

But, apart from the natural sense of outrage (only a thoroughly unsociable murderer would poison the water supply in this manner), the journal was parlously short of any real information. There was nothing to identify the body, he had neither money nor papers upon him when finally he was handed over to the Bow Street Office and, as a pauper, he was to be thrown into the common grave.

His murder was simply one more unanswerable crime in the calendar of daily violence.

I decided to pay another visit to Murrell's shop, and an hour later I faced his uncivil assistant. The red eyes gleamed more ferociously than ever, and his hair stood up as though brushed backwards by some unseen hand. His smile, though resolute, was skeletal.

"Is your master ready to meet me now?" I asked.

He looked over my shoulder towards the door, almost as if he expected the ghost of his master to waft into the room. His manner, though uncouth, was distinctly more polite than it had been yesterday.

"No, Sir. He is not here. If you will tell me your business, he has empowered me to act for him."

"And I have been instructed to deal only with your master."

"He is not here," he repeated, much subdued.

"Then where may I find him, man?" I snapped impatiently. "This business could have been settled twenty-four hours ago. Twenty-four hours would have made all the difference."

A look of blind panic swept over his foxy face. His Adam's-apple ran up and down his skinny throat until I thought it must surely pop out of his flapping mouth. With a great effort, he set himself to answer me. His voice was like that of a broken bell.

"He is not here. He is not in London . . . You must come again."

"Tomorrow?" I asked ironically.

"Tomorrow," he repeated vacantly.

I stared at him severely. "Where," I wondered, "will you be tomorrow?"

Tipping my hat to him, I turned and left the shop.

It was time to take up my position behind the wall again. I did so, and adjusted my spy-glass.

My patience was soon rewarded on this occasion. From the back access to the shop emerged the strapping Negress, garlanded much as she had been upon the previous night. But today she was pulling a small handcart which was packed tight with boxes. Behind her walked the red-haired assistant, wearing a small-sword and, I suspected from the bulge in his pocket, sporting a loaded pistol.

I allowed them to gain the full length of the street before I emerged from my hiding place. For the rest of our journey together, I kept a street length respectably between us, for I had no desire to confront the Negress again. And as for her fiery attendant, he looked too jittery altogether to be entrusted with fire-arms.

Following them through the rank warrens of St. Giles' proved to be more difficult than one would expect. Apart from the natural hazards of walking through such streets in the darkling light, there was always the possibility of running blindly into them round each crazy twist and bend. Indeed, this almost happened on at least two occasions, the nervous assistant having loitered behind the Negress, obviously fearful of being followed.

I felt relieved when they had left the hideous tangle of St. Giles' and Soho behind them, and we turned into the more spacious quarters of Mayfair, though shadowing them here presented a new hazard, for in the long wide walks I was the more exposed. Trying valiantly to keep them in sight, I began to hang back, hugging the walls. And in the shady reaches of Newick Square, I lost sight of them entirely. I walked along all four sides of the leafy square, looking into the great mews on each side of it, but with no success at first. Then, on the southern side, towards Green Park, I looked into a mews and saw the handcart leaning against a hitching post. I walked under the archway, keeping a watchful eye on the windows. Fortunately, the walls to either side were largely blank-faced.

The yard was empty, as was the handcart. A few wisps of straw stirred limply on the bottom planks. A few wisps of the same straw led me directly to the back door of No. 12, Newick Square. The door was closed, the studs of which looked at the world dead-eyed.

I retraced my steps into the street and stood looking at the even more imposing front door of No. 12, Newick Square, wondering moodily what sort of house it was and what manner of people lived there. Nobody at all respectable, I eventually decided. But somebody with an imposing income – or remarkable wits.

# XI

As I reached the door to my chambers, a familiar voice hailed me. It was as crisp, cool and arrogant in my quarters as it had been in his own stable yard. The eyes were as hard and bright above the proud nose, but his manner was a touch more conciliatory. He bowed almost politely.

"I should like to talk to you, if you are at liberty," he said.

I bowed in reply and waited. Mr. Oliver Wroth was obviously experiencing the greatest embarrassment in seeking me out. Wroth was the sort of man who can define a gentleman as dispassionately as one can define a kipper. He could claim coat-armour, I could claim nothing – not even a decent trade. I watched him writhe for a moment or two. He had no clear idea of how to treat me.

I unlocked my door at last, and allowed him to precede me into my rooms. He seemed impressed by my spartan taste in furnishings (the pure result of my impecunious state). He looked about with interest at my spoils and trophies, the mementos of my travels and adventures, that lay dotted about the room.

"You aren't, I take it, a man of any great property," he said bluntly.

I waved a hand about the room and said airily: "You see before you the full extent of my fortune."

He was amazed at my candour and at my raillery.

"Do you hope to make money from your trade?" he asked at length.

"If there is any to be made."

He looked at me carefully, as if weighing up my chances.

"I should think you could make opportunities," he said guardedly.

He waited for me to make a reply. I disobliged him. After a moment he went on uneasily: "I've been trying to reach you for the last six hours. You're a hard man to track down."

"I have that talent," I said drily and waited again.

He seemed to have fallen into a profound mood.

"Has something happened?" I asked eventually.

"Happened?"

"I gather your cousin's friend is now your cousin's late friend," I said bluntly.

He looked up, startled.

"D'Urfey?"

"Yes."

"He's dead?"

"Yes."

He gnawed at his nether lip for a while and he then seemed to shrug the matter away.

"Well, he's no great loss to the world," he said. "No doubt he met a just end."

"A poetic end, at least. Face down in a public well."

He gazed at me in blank astonishment, but he seemed to be startled rather than shocked.

"A public sewer would have been more fitting," he said savagely, and sat down. "But, no matter for that. I came to see you on other business."

I waited again. At last he said, putting his hand against his wallet suggestively: "Is it quite impossible for you to tell me why my grandmother sent for you?"

"Quite impossible."

"Was it about my cousin Wroth?" he persisted. He appeared not to have heard my reply, but all the same his hand moved the wallet until it showed above his pocket.

"I am not at liberty to say, Mr. Wroth," I said, somewhat severely. ". . . For any price."

He looked at me closely, read my face aright, and his hand fell away from his pocket. He seemed obscurely pleased at my attitude.

After a moment's thought, he reached into his greatcoat pocket and pulled out a bulky envelope. As he handed it to me, I discerned a slight tremor in his hand.

"Read that," he said. "Then tell me if it is why you were hired by my grandmother."

I opened the envelope. It was addressed to Mr. Oliver Wroth in the same neat hand that had written to his grandmother. I drew out a sheet of paper which was unsigned. It proved to be a copy only of another receipt for "services rendered" to Lord Wroth. They proved to be highly original services, and prodigiously obscene. The original of this receipt had been signed by Lord Wroth, an enclosed note explained.

I raised my eyes from the paper and looked into the impassive face of young Wroth. The light eyes glittered faintly, otherwise the handsome face was immaculately composed.

"How much do they demand?" I asked.

"There's more, apparently," he said between his teeth.

"But how much do they ask?"

"£20,000. For all the receipts together. We have to pay them by Saturday or they will publish the details. Once they do, my cousin is finished in society. His chances of making a tolerable match are nil."

"The demand came with this letter?"

Wroth smiled unpleasantly. "Yes."

"You have the letter?"

His smile grew even more unpleasant.

"No. The messenger allowed me to read it, then took it back with him."

"What kind of a man was this messenger?"

"A heavily armed man," he answered wryly.

"Did he have bright red hair and eyes like poker-ends?"

"No. He was a grey-faced man."

"What did he say exactly?"

"Very little. He just delivered the letter. I rather think he knew nothing of the matter himself."

"So there's no proof of demand," I said.

"None at all. Deuced clever, really."

"And there's nothing more to it than this?" I asked sharply.

The question took him by surprise. A look almost of alarm flashed through his eyes and his mouth tightened perceptibly.

"Is this not sufficient?" he asked bitterly. "You know English society. Let a thing be rumoured and it can be passed over. A man can even acquire a kind of clandestine fame. But let it once become public property and a man is as good as dead. My cousin Wroth, at the moment, passes for a brainless young eccentric like a good many of his kind. Many young men of today lack the resources which can lead to a cure imposed by self-discipline – " He gestured towards the paper with distaste. "But once that nastiness becomes common knowledge, there's not a good family in England will be on nodding terms with us, let alone marry into us."

"Where is his lordship now?"

"At home."

"Where was he last night?"

"Last night? Why, at home."

"All the night?"

"To my knowledge. I was myself in London."

"In London?"

"At the Italian Opera House. I went to hear Catiani sing. She has a damned fine voice," he added appreciatively.

"She keeps it in a damned fine chest," I said.

He looked complacent. "It's not too difficult to open, either, if you have the right key," he said modestly. I gathered that he had already tampered with the lock.

"And d'Urfey?" I asked.

"What of him?"

"Isn't he generally inseparable from your cousin?"

I let the implication stand, letting it brew a little. He scarcely seemed to notice.

"Generally," he said. "But not last night, it seems." I tapped the paper.

"Do you intend paying this?"

"If I can lay my hands upon the money."

"Is that possible?"

"Not impossible."

"Your grandmother will no doubt – "

"No!" he said sharply. "She's not to be bothered by it. I can raise the colour elsewhere."

"Oh?"

"I can borrow it. From the Jews, perhaps. From friends."

"Why not go to the Bow Street Police?" I asked reasonably.

"I can't," he said simply. "I have to protect grandmama," and added, as an afterthought: "and my cousin."

I gestured towards the paper again. "But if this is all there is to it – in a matter of this sort, they would say neither muff nor mum – "

"No!"

There was a strained pause. When he spoke, it was with difficulty.

"I can't. Word would get about in the way it does. The scandal would kill grandmama, and ruin us all."

He raised his head arrogantly, his pride mastering his conscience.

I could not shake off a belief that there was something more behind his refusal. Nauseating as this receipt was, I felt there was a worse matter on his mind.

I said as much.

He flushed hotly.

"There's nothing worse. What could there be that's worse than . . . that!" He flicked the paper from my hand and ground his foot upon it angrily.

Suddenly he looked at me in an almost beseeching manner. Strain and anxiety showed plainly in his face. Only pride kept him from complete supplication.

"Can you help me? It's what I came for."

"I might be able to," I said cautiously.


# XII


The Temple of Health stood aloof from the activity of the Close, like a ship pulled high on a beach, away from the invading waves. The windows looked as empty as the house behind it.

The house *was* empty, I knew that well enough, for I had kept it under observation for the last twenty-four hours. Like the shop in Barnard's Row, it had been abandoned with scant ceremony, its occupants fled God knew whither.

Having kept such a close watch on it without a sign of life, I had almost decided to abandon it. But an odd demon of obstinacy kept me at my post. Although I felt that the house had revealed all the secrets it held, I believed that patience would still reward me. For one thing, I was sure that the book I had taken from the strong-box was a key to the mystery. When this key was found to be missing, others would come seeking it. They would naturally come here to this house. So I continued my vigil.

I wondered if they would have understood the book better than I did. So far, my own attempts to break the code had been lamentably unsuccessful. Apart from one or two unimportant details, the book was all Greek to me – except, of course, that I speak a passable Greek.

Daylight was fading and I was on the point of turning away, when a slight movement in an attic window caught my eye. For a moment I wondered if I had imagined it but, as I looked more closely at the window, I saw that a shutter was, indeed, a trifle ajar. At my last inspection it had been fast tight.

Within five minutes I was over the wall, through the passage, and climbing through the back upstairs window. It had been conveniently opened for me by a visitor who had left his tracks clear away from the alley wall.

Padding soft as a cat through the upper rooms, I gained the front stairs. I stood, listening hard, straining for a sound from above or below.

An almost imperceptible creak from the landing above alerted me. I edged back into a recess, my hand easing my sword from its scabbard.

A leg appeared on the bend of the stairs, feeling for the tread. It was an elegant, well-turned, almost delicate leg. A second after, the torso appeared and a moment later I was looking into the smooth face of the young Lord Wroth. In the obscure light, it was truly amazing how much menace was packed into that slight frame. The face, with its fresh, translucent skin, looked at the same time to be old and drawn. The eyes were drained of feeling. He had, I felt, undergone some great emotional crisis in these past few hours.

Like myself, his hand was on the hilt of his sword, yet for some reason he neglected to draw it as I stepped out of the alcove, my sword at the ready.

I gave him a slight bow.

He stared at me with a curious, blind stare. I could swear that he hardly saw me and certainly did not know me.

"What are you doing here, my lord?"

He continued to stare at me, apparently trying to fix me into his scheme of things.

"Do you remember me, my lord?"

He swallowed, frowned, and then nodded. The eyes began to come alive. He flushed painfully and the mad glitter swept through his eyes, and was gone as quickly. His eyes were then as blank as before.

"What are you doing here, my lord?" I asked again, patiently.

"What are you doing here?" he countered vacantly. His fingers began to fret at the hilt of his sword, yet he made no move to withdraw it . . . for the moment.

He was obviously never going to answer me. He behaved like a man whose mainspring had broken. I felt it time to administer a shock.

"Who killed him, my lord?"

"Killed?" he echoed. The word hung like dust in the air.

"Who killed Tom d'Urfey?"

The eyes tilted suddenly and his whole body twitched convulsively. The sword rattled from its scabbard and then scraped along the wall as it dropped to his side. His body sagged dejectedly.

"I don't know," he said dully and sighed deeply.

It was time to administer a second shock.

"Perhaps it was the magician?"

His head reared back and his eyes rolled wildly. For a moment it looked as if he was going to jump over my head and flee. He shrank back against the wall.

"Asclepius," I said. "Alias 'Cunning' Murrell."

He looked over my shoulder fearfully. I half wondered if he expected to see Murrell's mutilated body materialize before him. Then his eyes seemed to clear, the superstitious awe faded, and he looked at me contemptuously, but with a greater awareness in his eyes, almost an interest.

"But then," I said gently, "the good Doctor could hardly have come back from the dead to avenge himself, could he? Despite his powers."

He was regarding me with a definite interest now.

"So it must have been somebody else who murdered your friend," I said.

He breathed out slowly.

"Yes," he whispered. ". . . Yes."

"Why did you come here, my lord?" I asked again.

The interest in his eyes faded. Once more he repeated my own question. This time, however, I got a distinct impression that he was addressing himself.

With a shock I realized that he *was* addressing himself. He had no clear idea of his purpose there.

"Were you looking for something?"

He frowned.

"What did you hope to find here?"

The frown deepened.

I nodded towards the upper regions. "You didn't find it there?"

". . . Not there," he said slowly.

"Down below, perhaps?"

He looked at the lower stairs as though he had never seen them before. Since quite a lot of his pleasuring must have been done between these walls, his lack of comprehension now was highly disconcerting, almost unnerving.

Like a sleepwalker, he began to descend the stairs, a foundling strayed, the sword trailing behind him like a discarded plaything. He seemed to have forgotten my presence. I followed a few paces behind, to see where his steps would lead him, to discover what part of the house would revive his memory.

The trailing sword looked harmless enough in his loose grasp but, remembering his dexterity on the lawn, I kept a tight grip on my own weapon.

It was an eerie experience to walk through those lewd rooms behind this once favoured customer, who responded in no way to what he saw. With his fair, almost angelic face, he looked like a scrubbed, country innocent, a Christian choirboy who had wandered, by chance, into some heathen temple.

Walking thuswise, we reached the reception hall. By this time, the last of the daylight had drained from the sky. The hall was a gloomy cavern of marble and porphyry.

Wroth stood in the hall, at a total loss. He looked around him in a dazed sort of way. Nothing stirred in his eyes.

Then he stiffened suddenly and I stiffened with him. He had heard the faint whine of the iron gate as it swung open. Feet paused before the steps, then climbed them steadily. A key turning in the lock and a streak of dirty twilight swept along the floor as the door fell open.

But long before the door was fully wide, I had pushed Wroth into the safety of a small alcove. I leaned forward slightly, trying to see who had entered. Young Wroth leaned limply against my arm. I could feel him trembling, and his breath was short and shallow. It must, I felt, quickly betray us. I put a hand over his mouth. He struggled for a while, the whites of his eyes alarmingly prominent. Then he seemed to relax, his breathing loosened and I myself breathed more freely. He was not, I realized, in any way afraid. He was, rather, monstrously excited.

Not that my fears for our position were immediately justified. Whoever had entered showed no interest in our hiding place. He had walked purposefully in the direction of the back premises where he struck a tinder and lit a candle. His head disappeared below stairs and a moment later I heard a succession of doors open and shut in the cellars.

There were a few minutes of strained and agonizing silence. Then from below came a muffled oath and a heavy object crashed to the ground. At once, the man came running up the stairs as if the Devil and all his fiends were in pursuit of him. The front door swung open and crashed thunderously behind him.

The reverberations echoed for a few seconds, to be followed by an uncanny silence. Young Wroth gasped like a man surfacing from deep water. He shook himself like a dog. For the first time I saw a real sign of intelligence in his eyes.

"Pelham," he said hoarsely. The name shot out of him like a cork from a bottle.

Pelham? *The* Pelham? The notorious Sir Harry Pelham?

"Pelham?" I asked.

"'Gambling' Pelham."

*The* Pelham. Sir Harry Pelham. What was his connection with this house? I knew he owned a gambling-hell and was reputed to own shares in Mother Wells' brothel, but what was his relationship to Godbold (or Murrell)? A very close one, by what I could judge. He had moved around this house with great familiarity.

I turned to Wroth to question him further, but his eyes were glazed over once again and he had retreated into his own private world.

I decided to investigate below stairs. But what to do with Wroth? I thought it best not to leave his lordship to his own devices. I would be safer with him under my eye. If he came to his "senses", I might well be his next duelling partner. Taking him by his sword arm, I led him to the head of the cellar steps. He came along as docile as a child. In my own sword hand I carried the candlestick, hastily thrown down by Sir Harry in his flight.

We began to descend the stairs . . .

The first room that we came to was the kitchen, a vast place cluttered with the paraphernalia of a well-run establishment. My candle reflected a forest of gleaming copper and dull pewter. There was nothing untoward in its appearance, all was exactly as I had last seen it.

Passing along a short corridor, we came to another door and behind this, I remembered, lay a small office. This, too, was as I had last seen it, save in one particular.

Beyond the office lay yet another room – a room that had not been in evidence at my last visit.

A panel was drawn back in the wall, giving access to a sort of priest-hole. It looked to be no larger than a handsome tomb. Which is what it now was. Sepulchral candles glimmered beyond the wainscot. A rank, stale smell mingled with the headier scent of incense.

I felt Wroth's arm tense beneath my hand and his knuckles whitened on his sword-hilt. My own hand circled his arm in a tight grip as I waited for his next move.

Nothing happened, save that he went limp again. Like a man in a dream he moved forward, under the gentle pressure of my hand. The candlelight flickered as we bent to pass into the secret chamber, then it steadied, and the light magnified with a startling brilliance as the rays were reflected from the innumerable silver and copper ornaments that decked the room. For a moment we were dazzled, then our astonished eyes took in the full, garish horror of the scene.

Gaudy coloured idols stood upon pedestals, surrounded by flowers of a monstrous vulgarity. Strings of glass beads, winking baubles and cheap rosaries were hung from a number of gold crucifixes. A Virgin, with a face as black as midnight, exposed her breasts to an infant Jesus of equal darkness. In one corner stood an enormous wooden cross, surmounted by a black tricorn hat. A skull with brilliants in its eye-sockets grinned at us from beneath it.

It was a foul, obscene, and heathen funeral chamber, and it produced a strong impression on my mind. What effect it had on young Wroth's less regulated senses can only be imagined. His arm trembled like an aspen beneath my fingers.

The centrepiece of these gaudy trappings sat enthroned in a chair. "Cunning" Murrell, his ghastly, lifeless eyes staring beneath his magician's hat, sat waxen-faced, dressed in a robe covered in strange hieroglyphics, his body in a state of rapid decomposition.

The heat of the candles and the rancid odour of the corpse filled the room to turn your stomach.

It was clear now why Murrell's murder had not been reported. In the eyes of his servant, the poor, half-savage Negress, her master had not died. He sat here, among her baubles, awaiting resurrection!

The same thought must instantly have occurred to Lord Wroth. With a weird, echoing howl he tore himself from my grasp and fled up the stairs.


# XIII


It was time to pay a call upon the house in Newick Square, which I now knew belonged to Sir Harry Pelham.

I stood before the imposing door and pulled the bell-rope. A proud and saucy-looking footman opened it to me.

"Sir?" he asked insolently.

"I wish to see Sir Harry Pelham."

"Many do, Sir," he said squarely. "What name shall I give?"

"My name is Nash. Captain Nash."

"And what business may I state, Captain?"

"My business."

"Sir?" The impudent eyes rose superciliously. He sneered at me openly. He was a good man at a door. It began to close imperceptibly. I recognized that he had all the qualifications necessary for a footman.

He had, no doubt, turned away twelve duns that morning. He knew his duty to his master – to lie for him, pimp for him, and allow nobody to cheat him but himself.

"Sir Harry is not receiving today," he said, gazing unseeingly somewhere above my head.

Casually I scratched my nose with a small shiner. His eyes travelled slowly down my face. The movement of the door was halted fractionally.

"My master is not receiving today," he repeated, his gaze fixed upon the coin.

"Will he be at home all day?" I asked.

"He'll be walking out to his club within the hour," he said. With a startling rapidity, the coin disappeared beneath the lace cuff of his sleeve and the door was shut firmly in my face.

I set myself to wait.

Surely enough, the door opened some forty minutes later and the tall, bull-headed figure of Sir Harry Pelham walked down the steps. He strode purposefully in the direction of St. James' and I marched after him as resolutely.

Sir Harry Pelham was a most notorious rake with a scandalous past. He had always sported a reputation. As a student at Cambridge he had drunk the most beer, sworn the deepest oaths, sang the noisiest songs, and fought the most duels. He had honoured all his friends by the most liberal levies on their purses. After expulsion from his college he came to London, where he speedily got rid of the remnants of a small fortune. A sad scamp as a youth, he had grown into a full-blown rogue in manhood. In order to raise supplies, he had to betake himself to such resources as a nimble wit presented to a not over-scrupulous conscience. Detected in false play, kicked out of one gambling-hell after another, until finding them all too hot to hold him, he had taken to arranging card-parties which, despite (or because of) his extreme reputation, were doing very well. He was the perfect rake; he would die of fast women, slow horses, crooked cards and straight drink – but he would die in his own good time.

I caught up with him as he turned into Green Park.

"Sir Harry!"

He looked at me enquiringly. A man with a mortal aversion to bailiffs and constables, he regarded me for a moment as if I had crept from beneath a stone. Then realizing that I was not an agent of the law, the heavy brown eyes regarded me with a sort of dull impassivity. All the same, his hand tightened on his walking-stick, his "oaken towel", his "knocking-down argument", as he called it.

"Sir?"

I bowed.

"What is your business with me, Sir?"

"Murrell's business," I replied.

There was not a flicker of light in that turgid brown stare.

"Murrell?" he drawled. His voice had the easy, insolent quality that can make the most commonplace statement sound like an epigram and this was largely the basis for his reputation as a wit.

"'Cunning' Murrell," I said. "Or Dr. Asclepius, if you prefer that name."

"The 'Paphlagonian'?" he asked lazily, a slight interest stirring in his eyes and his hand encircling his stick with a tighter grip. "What have I to do with his business?"

I smiled at him confidingly.

"You have his business stacked away in your cellars, Sir," I said. "Unfortunately, as you must know by now, you lack the key to it. I have the code-book."

A gleam like a small cinder began to glow in the treacly eyes. A slow and dangerous anger.

"Shall we take a turn about the park, Sir Harry?"

His mind was made up on the instant. Perhaps I was too great a challenge to his gambling instinct. With a slight ironic bow, he indicated a path leading towards a leafy arbour.

We paced together slowly down the path. Not a word was exchanged until we reached the comparative seclusion of the trees.

"Well, Sir?" he drawled.

I waited whilst a nursemaid and her charges passed beyond our hearing. He grew restive.

"Patience is not one of my virtues, Sir," he said.

"Neither is caution, Sir," I replied coolly.

His eyebrows rose.

"The little cavalcade that brought the goods to your back door, Sir Harry," I explained reproachfully. "A veritable circus. I'm surprised that half the children in London weren't on their backs."

Sir Harry sighed dolefully.

"Time would not allow for a more finished performance," he said heavily. "What do you want? You said that you possessed the code-book."

"And you have the provisions," I said. "The patents and the medicines."

My ploy was to confuse him as to my motives. He would not, I felt, do business if he thought it honest.

"The patents! The medicines!" he snapped. "Quackery. Sugar and water! That is what I have invested in."

"Is it all quite useless?" I asked.

The cinders in his eyes now glowed like coals.

"Water cannot be turned into wine, Sir, without a worker of miracles!" he said shortly.

"But there's money to be made from his gulls – once you can read the code."

A dull flush crept into his face.

"There are famous names in that book, Sir Harry," I went on, gently insistent. "The whole world would be interested in the disclosure of their vices."

The stick shook slightly in his hand.

"There is a treasure house between its covers," I said.

A look of the purest anguish showed in his dark eyes.

"Of course," I told him, almost affectionately, "such an enterprise would require a considerable power of organization behind it, if it is to run smoothly. It needs a man confident of his position in society to guide it properly. A man well-used to catering for the whims and fancies of the great and noble."

"True," he agreed, and spat contemptuously. "Murrell was an incompetent, a man without style." His eyes ran over me like a horse-coper sizing up the season's stock. "Do you fancy your chances in this line of work, Mr. er . . .?"

"Nash," I said. "Captain Nash."

"Well, Captain? Do you?"

I shrugged nonchalantly. "I could hardly do less justice to the trade than Murrell did," I replied. "And I'd know where the danger lies."

"The danger?"

"I'd know who my enemies were, Sir Harry."

"And Murrell didn't?"

"He was singularly careless. He should never have entrusted himself to a sedan chair so late at night and in such an area."

Genuine surprise showed in Pelham's eyes. For a brief moment I exacted a look of wary admiration from him.

"How did you know that?" he asked.

"I was there, Sir. I saw it all."

He was puzzled by me. He mused silently for a moment, his large hand massaging the head of his broad-stick.

"He must have received an urgent summons to bring him into those streets at that hour," I said suggestively.

A strange smile played about his lips, but it did not linger.

"Are you saying that I was responsible for his death, Sir?" he asked.

"I am saying that you could be made to seem so."

He raised the stick and struck the ground with a snapping blow.

"You take risks, Sir," he said softly.

"I am merely saying that the charge could be laid at your door, Sir Harry. You would have a hard time proving that you aren't connected with him."

He shrugged wearily.

"Why should I want to rid myself of a partner in a lucrative venture?" he said.

"In order to make the venture more lucrative – for yourself, perhaps?" I suggested.

"Pah! As I said before, miracles need a miraculous hand. Murrell was the magician."

"Murrell was a box of tricks, Sir Harry. No more than that. A sham is what Murrell was, Sir. Such tricks can be taught to any avid learner."

He considered it.

"What do you want from me?" he asked at last.

"Little enough," I said. "I want the Wroth papers."

"The Wroth papers?"

"The receipts signed by Lord Wroth. In return for which you may have the code-book and my silence."

He frowned. "And if I don't have the papers?"

"I think you have them, Sir."

He smiled wryly.

"And if I were to assure you, Sir, that I don't?"

He laughed without amusement, then answered my unspoken question.

"The old rapscallion! I fear our magician may have had more partners than we bargained for."

He laughed aloud – an alarming sound. If a tiger could laugh, he would make a sound like that.

We walked into a clearing and Pelham's laughter turned to a choked gurgle. He fell heavily against a tree, his stout walking-stick breaking beneath him.

A knife had whistled through the green air, catching him in the shoulder a little below his neck.

# XIV

He was not greatly injured, but he was bleeding profusely and swearing like a duchess in labour. The knife lay on the ground where he had flung it. He was trying to stem the flow of blood with a silk handkerchief. He looked up, his face working savagely.

"After him!" he spat. "I'm not dead – nor even dying. After him! Get after him, man!"

He spoke to me much as he would to a hound. I ran across the clearing without another thought, in full cry.

There was no sign of his assailant but a few broken twigs and some leaves swept aside by a cloak. And a small leather pouch. I picked it up and put it in my pocket, then pressed through the trees to where the park spread out in the afternoon sun.

It was a calm enough scene, a typical English park, with the greensward and the red deer grazing. Towards the lake a few people sauntered along the walks.

I skirted the clump of trees in which the would-be assassin had lurked. There was no sign of him. Nothing disturbed the utter stillness of the leafy thicket but the twittering of birds. I made my way cautiously back to Pelham.

He had struggled to his feet and was leaning languidly against the tree which had broken his fall. His hands clutching the material to his wound were soaked with blood.

I took off my neckcloth and attended to his wound as efficiently as I could. He looked at me, his eyes as dull as molasses.

"Did you see him?"

"Him?" I asked.

"Wroth." he answered thickly.

"Wroth!"

His mouth twitched bitterly. "Did you not see him?"

I shook my head.

"Naturally not," he said sarcastically. "You are their man."

I looked at him closely.

"Did *you* see him, Sir Harry?" I asked. ". . . Truly."

His eyes flickered sideways.

"I thought I did. It seemed like."

"Did he wear a bandana?" I asked abruptly.

He looked up from examining the still welling blood, his eyes puzzled.

"A bandana?"

"Yes."

"What do you mean, man?"

"I found this in the wood opposite," I said, and showed him the leather pouch.

"So?"

I turned it over. On the reverse side was an embossed design. A strange device, a barbaric device. I picked up the knife; emblazoned on the cheap gilt hilt was the same design.

His eyelids twitched nervously, for a moment the whites of his eyes gleamed fiercely then, once again, they dulled over. I knew that he had recognized the symbol, it had been prominently displayed in Murrell's funeral chamber.

"So?" he asked again.

"You've never seen this device before?"

He shook his head slowly.

"And yet Murrell was your partner?"

"Is it his?"

"Did you never remark his cabbalistic designs?" I asked. "You must have seen it on the cloth that covered his corpse."

This time I had struck home. The breath whistled out of his body.

"His corpse?"

"You saw it laid out in the Temple of Health."

His eyes met my own. A look of superstitious awe passed over his face.

"Are you ubiquitous?" he asked, at length.

"I was there."

He gestured towards the pouch.

"And this?"

"This held that knife."

His lips twisted ferociously.

"Has Murrell returned from the dead then? To cut down a man who never harmed him?"

"Not Murrell, no. But his slave, possibly."

"His slave?"

"Servant, then."

"The black woman?"

"Yes."

He looked incredulous.

"She thinks I killed her master?"

"It would seem so," I said.

He staggered and shivered violently. I thought he was about to fall and reached out a hand to steady him.

"You'd better get me home," he said.

The impudent footman let us into the house, his face an amusing mixture of concern at his master's condition and surprise at seeing me in attendance. I sent out for a surgeon at once, and saw Pelham stripped and put to his bed. The wound was in his flesh only, but it could have been dangerous had it gone a bare half an inch deeper or higher.

Pelham lay on his crimson damask bed. So far not a murmur of complaint had passed his lips, though he swore roundly and often at the covey of servants who crowded in and out of the vast room. He had forbidden them to send for the Bow Street Men, insisting that it was no more than a common street brawl he had been involved in and not worth the inconvenience of calling in the Law. His servants, who knew their master, were willing enough to give way to him in this.

I stood by a classical fireplace in the elegant Adam room, musing deeply whilst all this activity surged around me. I was trying to create some pattern from the events that had occurred. But nothing emerged with any clarity.

I was mostly concerned with the most recent incident. Why did Pelham think he had seen Wroth in the clearing? Had he seen him truly? If so, why was Wroth there? Had he thrown the knife? The possibility had to be admitted. It was even possible that the knife was his, a gift from Murrell; it was the sort of toy that he'd appreciate. Perhaps Murrell had breathed some magic incantation over it, rendering it as accurate as Achilles' immortal weapon? That was the sort of preposterous flummery to impress his lordship.

I looked at the knife, which lay upon a Pembroke table, its blade encrusted with dried blood. Yes, it was more than possible that Wroth had hurled it; remembering his murderous skill with the foils, this deadly toy seemed a likely weapon for him to use.

But then again, remembering his skill, it seemed more like that he would directly have challenged Pelham to a mad, fanatical duel if he had any quarrel with him. This method of despatch seemed altogether too sinister, too stealthy, for such an impetuous person.

An image of Lord Wroth as he had stood beside me in the Temple came into my mind. He had been curiously reluctant to take his sword from its scabbard, though it had been halfdragged from there. All the mad, murderous rage in him seemed to have died. Could it be that without d'Urfey to jack him up, he had no taste for the game? Lady Wroth had called d'Urfey a "led captain" – could it be that he had allowed young Wroth to seem a better man with a sword than he was in truth? It would have been in his favour to flatter his lordship. And Wroth was not perhaps too mad to realize that he was no match for a stronger man without his friend's support. No match for a man of Pelham's talents, anyway.

In which case, he might well resort to stealthier tricks. But his shot had gone wide of the mark and that fact bothered me if I had to consider him as a suspect. For Wroth had shown he had a good eye for a mark and this knife had been intended for Pelham's exposed neck.

Pelham's neck! The knife that had killed d'Urfey had protruded from the base of his neck, though he had been an unresisting victim when the blow was struck. Was it possible that whoever had killed d'Urfey had killed him in an identical way to Wroth's plans for Pelham? Could it have been a purely fortuitous coincidence? But no, it seemed too close.

Pelham had been mistaken when he thought he saw young Wroth. Unless, of course, the boy believed Pelham responsible for d'Urfey's death and had planned an identical end for the baronet? It had the right, gory, poetical touch to it.

But . . . I turned the pouch over in my hand. The device glittered in the sunlight . . . What of the Negress? This pouch seemed to link her with the crime more fittingly than Wroth. To kill a man by a knife thrown in stealth seemed a more primitive method of despatch than an Englishman would use in a London park. And the knife was obviously connected with Murrell. It had a barbaric feeling about it. It looked to be a ceremonial sort of knife. Such a killing, to a woman like that, would be more in the nature of a ceremony than a plain act of revenge.

But why should she seek to murder Pelham who was her master's friend? And if she had dealt in this way with Pelham, then she must have dealt with d'Urfey in a like manner? Save that one had been unsuccessful, the two means of despatch were the same, and two unconnected murders in the same manner would be stretching coincidence beyond the bounds of probability.

But surely there could be no connection between the murdered youth and the luckily escaped Pelham?

Which brought my thoughts back to Wroth.

Wroth! A sudden thrill passed down my spine. Why had such an important fact escaped my notice before?

Pelham had made no mention of *Lord* Wroth. Or even *young* Wroth. He had simply said "Wroth". Could he have meant the cousin? Could it have been Oliver Wroth that he had thought he saw?

There was a commotion from the servants as the surgeon prepared to leave. I went forward and stood by the footpost of the bed, waiting to put my question to Sir Harry. As the surgeon turned away, he laid an admonishing finger to his lips, as if to say: "No more excitation today, please."

"I have given Sir Harry a draught," he said, self-importantly. "He should sleep quite soundly now."

Pelham already slept extremely soundly.

## XV

I spent the rest of the day in deep thought, equally divided between the pros and cons of the business and the wrongs and the rights of it.

My mood was an uneasy one, for it was growing increasingly apparent to me that I could not continue to act contrary to the Law in this affair for much longer. I ought, at the very least, to report my finding to the Bow Street Office. Two men, both closely connected with this case, had been done to death, and one more had come near to death. That was a matter for the official authorities of the Law, and could I, at this stage of my new career, afford to ignore it?

On the other hand, I had an employer to protect and a living to earn. How could I go to the police with my story, relevant in all its details, without involving her? I had been granted a licence to act as an auxiliary to the police, but how could I count upon future patronage if I were to deliver my employers into the hands of those they most sought to avoid?

No, before I approached the police, or even my cousin Scrope in the Commissioners' Office, I must be able to present them with sufficient evidence to enable them to carry out their duties, yet without involving my employer. (The extortionary aspect had to be suppressed, at least as far as the names of the parties were concerned.)

My spirits sank beneath the weight of this legal incubus. How could I disassociate the Wroth family from these crimes? They were too deeply implicated, if not at the very centre of the matter. How could I possibly keep the two killings separate, and Lady Wroth's name out of both of them, without sacrificing myself in the process?

At five o'clock in the afternoon with the shadows creeping over my worn carpet, I was not exactly in an optimistic frame of mind.

But at six thirty that same evening, I felt slightly improved in my condition.

The door bell rang and I answered it to find Pelham's saucy footman standing on the step. He regarded me with considerably less contempt than he had shown at his own door.

"Yes?" I asked.

He had a message for me from Sir Harry. Could I return with him at once?

"On what business?" I asked tersely.

"Sir Harry's business," he answered jauntily.

"Touché," I said. "One moment."

I left him on the step whilst I returned to my rooms to dress for the street. When I set out with him ten minutes later, my sword hung at my side and I carried the extra protection of a light pistol.

Sir Harry was, apparently, fully conscious and in a hurry to see me. He had very considerately sent his carriage. I took my seat in its elegant interior and the footman hoisted himself aloft beside the coachman. Fifteen minutes later I was being ushered into Pelham's bedroom. Sir Harry eyed me sourly. He was in full possession of his faculties and, but for the bandage showing at his throat, seemed in remarkably good health.

He held out a massive hand.

"I have to thank 'ee, Captain Nash," he said.

"I did nothing, Sir," I replied.

A glimmer of sardonic amusement showed deep in his glutinous eyes. "I have to be assured yet on that point," he said with a wry twist to his mouth.

"Sir?"

"How do I know that I don't have you to thank for leading me into an ambush?" he asked. "I don't know 'ee from Adam, man."

"You know my name, Sir," I said. "And it was you that chose the path we took."

"And it was you that suggested a walk in the park."

There was a nasty pause. He regarded me keenly. If eyes can boil, then Pelham's did.

"You have only my word for it, Sir Harry," I said. "But if I had sought your death, why should I have brought you back to safety? It is not in my interest to do away with such an important connection as yourself."

A look of baffled impatience came into his face.

"Who are you, man? And what's your interest in this business?"

I thought hard for a moment. Would it be best, at this stage, to declare my real interest, or should I continue with my deception? If Pelham had been in league with Murrell then he would know about the Wroth papers and if there was money to be made out of the situation, I could scarcely expect him to ally himself to my cause. On the other hand, I held the code-book, without which he could not act further. If he would not vouchsafe me their return, I had the means to cut him off from a much larger fortune. He was not the man to lose a mackerel for the sake of a sprat.

Perhaps I could bargain with him?

I decided on candour.

"It's as I told you in the park, Sir. I'm interested only in the Wroth receipts."

His eyebrows rose superciliously.

"I am employed by Lady Wroth to obtain certain embarrassing papers concerning her grandson — "

"Which grandson?" he asked sharply.

"The young Lord Wroth."

He frowned. The brown, syrupy eyes looked cunning.

"Oh?"

"These papers were held by Murrell," I said. "Once I am able to place them in her ladyship's hands, my interest in this business is at an end."

He mused on this for a while.

"If Murrell died on account of these papers, they were undoubtedly worth a fortune," he said, at length, flashing a calculating look at me. "And you presumably want them for nothing?"

"No. I am prepared to pay a price."

"How much?"

"I don't know the exact amount . . . yet."

He looked at me in astonishment.

"What do you mean, Sir?"

"I am prepared to exchange the code-book for the papers."

He laughed into his pillows, seemingly diverted by some thought. He recovered himself eventually and said:

"Well, Sir! We shall see about that!" He reached for the bell. I stopped his hand as it touched.

"One moment, Sir Harry."

He looked up at me.

"Yes?"

"You said this afternoon that your assailant was Wroth."

"Yes."

"Did you see him?"

His hand stroked the bell thoughtfully.

"Or did you only imagine that you had?" I asked.

The heavy eyes looked up at me from beneath weary lids.

"Why should I imagine it?"

"If you expected an attack from that quarter," I said with meaning.

A startled gleam showed in his eyes. He looked at me with respect.

"And why should I expect an attack from that quarter?" he asked softly.

"You would know the answer to that, Sir Harry. If you were truly Murrell's partner . . ."

He snuffled into his pillows again, convulsed with silent laughter.

"Ah!" he said. "You thought I meant *that* Wroth."

His shoulders shaking, he rang the bell before I could question him further.

A manservant opened the door.

"Captain Nash is ready to leave now, Griddle," Pelham said.

"And my offer, Sir Harry?" I asked.

He laughed shortly. "Well, Captain, if I had the papers in question, I'd undoubtedly trade them with you," he said. "But, unfortunately, I don't have them, you see."

He bowed from the bed, his shoulders still shaking weakly. I wondered at the nature of the joke. It must be an uncommonly strong one.

Pelham had no intention of enlightening me, it seemed. He dismissed me with an airy wave of the hand. I turned and left the room, his unconfined laughter following me clear out into the hall.

I had to forgo the luxury of the carriage on my return journey, since the offer was denied me. As I walked back to my rooms, I pondered this new development. Why should Pelham think that Oliver Wroth was his assailant? What reason could he have to revenge himself upon Sir Harry? Did Wroth believe that Pelham owned the receipts? Or was there yet another reason? Prior to calling on me at my rooms, young Wroth's main preoccupation appeared to have been the disappearance of his female cousin.

I stopped with my hand upon the door-knob of my room.

His female cousin. The cousin who had so mysteriously disappeared. Was Pelham in some way involved in her disappearance. Was her disappearance in any way connected with the receipts? It might pay looking into. In the meantime, a sound night's sleep would do me no great harm.

I opened the door and stood astonished on the threshold. My rooms looked as though a horde of ruffians had passed through them. Drawers were opened, cupboards unlocked, curtains torn from their rods, upholstery slashed. Even the stuffing in my mattress oozed upon the bed.

I now knew why Sir Harry had found the joke so amusing. The interview with him had been a meaningless rigmarole, empty talk merely. His sole purpose in sending for me had been to make sure that I was out of my rooms when his men came to ransack them.

But the jest was on him. The code-book was not even on the premises. It was safely tucked away elsewhere.

## XVI

Clarety shifted comfortably and spread her legs. She took the coin I gave her and idly stroked herself with it between her breasts, over her smooth white belly and between her thighs. Clarety has a lewd way with hard cash.

"Catherine Wroth?" she said. "Why, her disappearance was no secret. All the world knew of it at the time."

"I never heard of it."

"You could not have been in England then. It was a great scandal in its day. Every coffee-house in London hummed with it."

"What happened?"

"God Himself can tell you, I can't. It remains a mystery."

"But what did folk say had happened?"

"A multitude of things. Most of them the wildest fancies, I've no doubt on it! – facts being in such short supply. But there's one element they all did suppose that's remained evergreen."

"What?"

"They were all of the opinion that she's Pelham's mistress, though her manner of becoming so is open to doubt and rumour ran its full gamut. Some said she ran away of her own free will, some that she had been forced into joining him, and others that she had been coarsely abducted. But all agree that she's now kept by him – in close seclusion, somewhere deep in the heart of the country."

"How do they think she was forced?"

"He blackguarded her."

"How?"

Clarety shrugged.

"Nobody knows," she said.

"But they think she is his mistress now?"

"Oh yes. Why else should she live with him – in the depths of the country? Miles away from civilized folk!"

She shuddered at this doleful prospect, her glorious breasts quivering.

Her performance with the coin had had its usual effect upon me. I was once again ready for the sport. My questions ceased while we kissed and toyed. Her hair, which she had let down about her body, crackled beneath her as we rode upon the bed. It was a very paradise of pleasure and in a short while I got into her and abated my passion.

Then, pleasantly sated, all my questions answered (and all my small change taken), I left the house and walked home, pondering on all she had told me.

Pelham was intimately connected with the Wroth family by two separate scandals, it appeared. I wondered if they could be in any way connected? What could he know of their family history that could both force Miss Wroth into compromising her honour and also feed Murrell's demands? And, if either of the Wroths had attempted to kill him in Green Park yesterday, were they trying to settle two separate scores, or were the two situations dependent on each other?

I kept my mind busy with these conjectures whilst I waited for Pelham to contact me again with regard to the codebook. One thing puzzled me especially. If Pelham had seduced Miss Wroth, why had he not gone on to wed her? She was in every way a prospect – young, beautiful, well-born, and tolerably wealthy in her own right. For a man in Pelham's position it seemed strange that he should neglect such an opportunity to increase his fortune. Nothing stood in his way, as far as one could see. He was a bachelor of equal station in life, and even owned his own parson! Yet he had not tied her to him in a legal way.

Another puzzling aspect of the case was the business of Miss Wroth's horse. For Miss Wroth, like any other redblooded English girl, was passionately fond of her horse Zubaydah. Yet on the day that she had disappeared, she had ridden off from the Hall on her beloved mare and Zubaydah had been found grazing peacefully some ten miles distant to the west of Stukeley. There had been no signs of foul play, or of an accident. The saddle was intact, the horse was calm, unsweated and unmarked. Why she had left this valuable and well-loved animal behind was another mystery. The mare had years of good riding in her still.

Another fact, which I had discovered, was perhaps less surprising. Miss Wroth had taken her jewel-box with her, an heirloom inherited from her mother. At least, it was never seen after her strange departure. The value of the jewellery was not inconsiderable but, oddly enough, she had made no further claim on her fortune. So, whatever Pelham's reasons for seducing the girl away from her family, money had been no great object.

There was, I found, no absolute proof in the rumour that Miss Wroth lived with Pelham, either in captivity or at liberty. Her name had been linked with his during a London season and that was the only basis for it. With a reputation such as Pelham sported, it was natural to suppose that he had, in some way, enticed her away from respectability. But she could, in truth, simply have disappeared of her own free will.

Another disturbing certainty was that the Wroth family had made no *official* enquiry into her disappearance, which suggested, to my mind, that they knew where she was at least, and even tolerated her situation. That is, in public. For whatever reason, and I largely suspected pride, the Wroths had decided to ignore her disaffection. And Oliver Wroth had feared (or pretended to fear?) that I was hired to bring her home!

All this led to one very important point – a point that was becoming increasingly apparent to me. There was considerably more behind this business of the receipts than I had been told. The receipts were only a lure. Had Lady Wroth met Murrell's demands, she would have found herself faced with a larger demand for his suppression of a more criminal exposure – more incriminating even than the nastiness I had read in the paper brought to me by Oliver Wroth. And she, too, I was convinced knew of this, or else why take such trouble?

If there was an unspeakable skeleton in the Wroth closet, who better to rattle it than a man like Pelham? If it was true that the grand-daughter was his mistress, then he could undoubtedly have learned of this secret.

Miss Wroth might well repay investigation. If she was alive, she must have left a trace of her existence somewhere. If she was living with Pelham however remotely, she could be flushed out. If she was alone and independent, then she must have left a trail from Stukeley to wherever she now resided – a bed slept in, a meal taken, a jewel sold or pawned.

The Wroth affair was at a standstill. To search in another direction might reawaken those tell-tale echoes which, returning to one's ears, guide one like a bat to the light of reality.

It seemed logical to begin my search at Stukeley. Besides, I owed my employer a report on my progress.


## XVII


I followed Chives' magisterial back up the oaken staircase, examining the family portraits more carefully than before.

I paused before the portraits of Lord Wroth and Mr. Oliver. To the left of the latter, a faint discoloration on the wall showed where another picture might possibly have hung. The remaining two pictures had been slightly rearranged to cover the omission. Miss Wroth, I surmised, had been banished from the gallery.

Chives, aware that I was no longer immediately behind him, had turned at the door of the "solar".

"Did the lady carry away her own portrait, Chives?" I asked.

He stared at me with his Olympian eyes.

"Her ladyship is waiting, Sir," he said reprovingly, and opened the door. I passed through into that sparkling room. Her ladyship waited for me in her great chair, more resplendent than ever, a veritable sunburst of diamonds. A large cap worn over monstrous high hair, crossed beneath her chin and was tied at the back of her neck. She wore a morning gown of dazzling hue.

I bowed and she replied with a gracious inclination of her extraordinary head.

The door closed softly behind us and she asked impatiently: "Well, Captain Nash? Do you have the receipts?"

"No, my lady," I said. "Nor do I know who has."

She snapped her fan viciously on the side of her chair, her eyes glittering frostily.

"Sir?"

I explained the situation carefully. She listened with a growing rancour.

"Well, Sir," she said, as I finished the tale, "stinking fish don't grow any fresher for lying idle."

She glared at me, seeming almost to accuse me of negligence in the matter; suggesting almost that I was in some way to blame for what had happened.

"I was not asked to protect Murrell's life, Ma'am," I admonished her gently. "Nor d'Urfey's."

She laughed abruptly, without merriment, showing her startlingly grey teeth.

"And what do you deduce from all this, Sir? What do you 'detect'?" she asked sharply.

I regarded her steadily. "I deduce, Ma'am, that Murrell was murdered by someone with an interest in his demise. There are innumerable people interested in that condition. At a guess, I'd say about half London society."

"And what of d'Urfey's death?" she asked less severely. "Is it connected, do you think?"

"There seems to be a tenuous sort of link, Lady Wroth. It seems likely."

"Likely, Sir!" she spluttered. "No more than that?"

"Very likely, if you wish."

"No, Sir," she exclaimed passionately. "I do *not* wish it!"

She sat very still for a while, then busied herself with her hand-kerchief, snuff-box, patch-box, perfume-bottle and headscratcher in turn. She returned to fretting away with her fan, and at length said wearily: "If d'Urfey was involved, then my rascal of a grandson must be involved also."

"Not necessarily, Ma'am," I said evenly. "D'Urfey could have been about his own business."

"His own business?"

Her diamonds sparkled as her hand shook, and I had a sudden flash of inspiration. His own business, indeed. I had a vision of d'Urfey, the dear friend, the boon companion, the sharer of boyish confidences. Could he have been the prime mover in all this? If there were any skeletons to be rattled in the Wroth cupboard, he would be privy to them all. He, d'Urfey, the privileged guest. He could well have been the link with Murrell – and, if his purpose had been served, then, like Murrell, he could have been disposed of.

But in the same way as Pelham? With a knife through his throat? There was a break in my vision, the divine afflatus reascended.

"What are you thinking, Captain Nash?" Lady Wroth asked, looking at me curiously.

Without taking thought, I answered: "If only you would be honest with me, Ma'am!"

She bridled. "Sir?"

"Your ladyship may not be aware that I have twice suppressed information regarding two crimes . . . temporarily. I did it to serve *your* interests. If only you could have more confidence in me."

Her manner relented somewhat. But, all the same, her eyes pierced through me sharply, as she said: "I have told you all I know."

"Not entirely, Ma'am," I answered.

She blinked at my impertinence, but controlled herself. She made the picture of a perfect great lady dealing with an insolent menial.

"For example, Sir?" she asked.

"Where is your grand-daughter, Miss Catherine Wroth?"

An astonished pause. She lost control of herself – her acting days were far behind her. She gaped and spluttered.

"What has that to do with anything, Sir?"

I came to the point.

"Lady Wroth, your grand-daughter disappeared, turning her back on a grand fortune and her place in society. She went in haste and there must have been a reason for it. Rumour has it that she lives with Sir Harry Pelham, and we know that he has some unsavoury connection with Murrell's business. I think there is more to the receipts than is written on them. Murrell had some knowledge of a secret and scandalous nature concerning your family, which he was willing to sell. Somebody must have provided Murrell with that information and I think it may well have been – "

I was going to say Pelham, but she interrupted me with a cry.

"No, Sir! That is a monstrous suggestion. She could no more have passed such information to that – "

She caught herself short, with a furious look for me.

"So she is with Pelham?" I said.

"That, Sir, is none of your business. She has done what she has done, and that is between herself and her Creator. But I know that she is not in any way connected with this business."

"She lives with Pelham and he is connected to it," I said stubbornly.

"Enough, Sir!" she cried, and rose. I was about to be dismissed both from the room and probably from the enquiry.

She hesitated. The façade of the grande dame crumbled and a troubled old lady peered anxiously out at me from behind the elaborate framework.

I spoke gently. "I apologize if I have offended you, Lady Wroth," I said. "But you must admit that you have been less than frank with me."

"I have told you all you need to know, Captain Nash," she replied. "You were commissioned to deal with the receipts only, Sir," adding viciously: "Which you have failed so to do!"

She rang her bell imperiously.

"Not quite yet, Ma'am," I said distinctly.

She looked up in surprise, the bell tinkled to a foolish halt. Her mouth twisted with contempt.

"Are you saying that you can still get them for me?"

"Yes."

She frowned at me.

"How, Sir?"

"I still have an important piece to bargain with, my lady," I said. "The code-book. Pelham will need it soon. He wants it badly enough now – so much so that he is willing to storm my rooms to get it."

She caught her breath.

"Do you think Pelham has the receipts?" She looked almost fearful.

"If he hasn't, I think he knows where he can lay a hold to them," I smiled. "Do you still wish me to act for you?"

"Providing that you can do so without involving innocent people," she said grimly.

The door opened. Chives awaited his instructions. Lady Wroth looked from me to him and back again.

She made up her mind.

"Bring a dish of tea, Chives," she ordered. "Captain Nash is staying for a while longer."

She sat down and beckoned me to resume my seat.

Chives closed the door. Lady Wroth began to tell me about her grand-daughter, Miss Catherine.

And an hour later I rode away from Stukeley, not much the wiser for her confidences. Her ladyship had spoken quite freely, but without imparting the least information. She knew where the girl was, she was in no peril, either physical or moral, and she was not in the least entangled in this sad business.

She would say no more than that. But what she said was highly emphatic. Her grand-daughter was an honest, decent girl that the world traduced. She had her own reasons for behaving as she had and, however wrong-headed she might be, she had behaved with all possible honour. But, in any case, it was none of society's business. It was none of my business.

And with regard to my business, she asked, how soon did I think I should be able to procure the receipts and have finished with the whole squalid affair?

Ah, when indeed? I wondered, as I turned into my street. It depended entirely upon how the action fell from this point on.

But some new development was about to commence, it seemed. For the past four miles, I had been aware of being followed. Obviously I had been tracked all the way from the Hall.

A grey man on a grey mare was trying his best to merge into the grey day, but not altogether succeeding.

And not entirely wishing to succeed, perhaps.


# XVIII

I sat in my rooms waiting for the knocker to rattle or for the bell to jangle, but both objects refused to oblige me. Pelham seemed in no hurry to contact me again. Either he had lost interest in the code-book or else he was experiencing some difficulty in unearthing the receipts.

It seemed scarcely possible that he had lost interest, so the latter solution seemed the more likely. If this was so, I realized that I myself would experience some difficulty in obtaining the receipts. Both Murrell's rufous-haired assistant and the uncomely Negress appeared to have vanished into the limbo of the netherworld and, although I had set my Seven Dials contacts on to trying to discover their lair, I had, so far, received no encouraging news from that quarter.

My best chance remained with Pelham. I had put a man to watch his house in Newick Square. This fellow, Droop by name, was an old and experienced hand at keeping watch. He was to send for me at the slightest sign of any activity and report on all Sir Harry's visitors. To date, he had reported nothing of note, only the comings and goings of tradesmen, nothing at all suspicious, though with a man of Pelham's stamp, nothing could ever seem wholly innocent. But I kept him at his post because I felt sure that if I was to be led in a new direction, Pelham would lay the scent for me.

As I finished my supper, the bell rang. I opened the door to find a ragged-arsed urchin grinning up at me.

"Capting Nash?" he piped.

"Yes, boy."

"Droop says yo're to come, yore 'onour."

He held out a grimy hand into which I fed a coin. With a nod and a wink, he ran off into the night.

Five minutes later I followed him.

At some point I became aware of the man in grey, drifting like a moth from shadow to shadow behind me. He looked to be the greyest man I ever saw, in the uncertain light, grey from head to boots. Even his face seemed to be a subtle shade of grey.

I kept to the main thoroughfares and as much in the light as possible. At that time of the evening, the streets were reasonably crowded with folk taking the air. People flowed and eddied around me. As I walked purposefully towards Newick Square, my pursuer kept up an even pace behind me. When, for the space of a few minutes, I passed through a patch of darkness empty of people, I speeded my steps slightly, expecting the man to make some move, tensing myself for a sudden lethal rush from behind.

But nothing happened. The man kept a discreet distance and I arrived in Newick Square without incident. Droop was waiting for me. He emerged from behind the plinth of a statue, where he had been lurking.

"What is it?" I asked.

"Copper-top," he replied. "He went into the house by the back way about a half an hour ago."

I looked at Pelham's house. Almost all the rooms were ablaze with light, a prodigious waste. One would have thought he was at home to the world instead of being confined to his room.

Had Murrell's apprentice brought the receipts at last? If so, Pelham would soon be in contact with me to arrange for their delivery.

We stood half-hidden behind the plinth and waited. A terrace away, my pursuer waited in his turn. I was dimly aware of his grey shape hovering behind a house corner.

"Don't look around," said Droop hoarsely, "but we're a-being hobserved."

I chuckled. Very little escaped Droop's baleful eye.

"He followed me here," I said.

"Shall I run 'im orf?"

"No. When we leave, I may want you to follow him."

"Foller him follerin' you, d'you mean?"

"Yes."

Droop laughed softly. The notion of a mouser[1] following a mouser amused him greatly.

We waited ten minutes more. Nothing happened to disturb our solitude. The street emptied of people. A carriage passed along the cobbles, its wheels rattling quietly over the straw. A sedan stopped before a neighbouring house and a rouged, patched and powdered old nobleman was carried off to his evening's entertainments.

Presumably all the inhabitants of Newick Square were away for the evening, for their houses were lighted modestly. Only Pelham's house was lit up, as for a ball. The lights streamed from every window, except one. This room I judged to be his bedroom: it was a black oblong and a curious, almost sinister, contrast to the rest of the house.

At one point, I thought I heard a cry wrung from behind the unlighted window.

"Did you hear anything, Droop"? I asked.

"Wot?"

"A cry of some kind."

"Naw."

Droop's ears were foxy-sharp. I must have imagined it, I thought.

The minutes crawled past.

But at last there was a sudden stir of activity from the house. The saucy footman poked his head from behind the great door, looking up and down the street. Droop and I ducked quickly behind our refuge. The door closed.

Five minutes later, a clumsy carriage trundled from Pelham's mews. Creaking heavily, it passed us, turning in the direction of Piccadilly.

I made up my mind in an instant. "Follow that fellow yonder,"

[1]Tracker.

I ordered Droop, and I nodded back towards the grey man, still skulking behind his corner.

I ran swiftly and silently after the carriage. As it paused for a moment before plunging into the busy traffic of Piccadilly, I jumped lightly onto the back axle-tree and settled myself on the perch between the wheels. The carriage dipped a trifle beneath my weight, but as it jolted forward at the instant of my stepping upon it, I trusted my presence to go unnoticed.

Once beyond the Knightsbridge toll-gate and out onto the open road, the carriage covered ground quickly. Indeed, for such an ungainly vehicle, I was amazed at the turn of speed whipped up by the coachman.

An hour or more passed. We were in the country now, somewhere close to the village of Hammersmith. The coach turned towards the river. A breeze sprang up and the leather braces that I clung to grew clammy in the damp night air.

The coach turned off the high road onto a grassy track. I was bumped mightily as we rattled along without decreasing speed. The coachman was in a mortal hurry.

We came to rest at the entrance to a field. There was neither a house nor a hovel in sight. The winking lights of Hammersmith shone a mile beyond. A dismal miasma rose from the river, gleaming ghostly a few yards away. I huddled deeper below the body of the carriage.

The coachman climbed down and opened the gate into the field. He was a hulking fellow, even when he stripped off his greatcoat. He opened the carriage door and reached inside. Breathing stertorously, he dragged some object along the floor and, with a grunting heave, slung it over his shoulder. From my vantage point beneath the carriage, I saw him stride away across the field towards the river, a white, shrouded shape draped across his back.

The horses whickered gently as I slipped from my hiding place. I walked through the gate and, slipping through a gap in the hedge, I followed the staggering coachman down the length of the field. As he dropped the bundle on the marshy ground by the river's edge, I sought shelter behind a leafy tree.

The man did not trouble to look around. He was confident that he was unobserved. Without ceremony, he stripped the white cloth away from the black shape and, taking a deep breath, lifted it up high above his shoulders and hurled it with great force into the river.

It fell with a dull splash and a small wavelet washed up the reedy bank. The coachman waited only long enough to make sure that his burden was far enough out to catch the current of the tide when it

drained away towards the sea. Satisfied, he picked up the white cloth
and turned away from the river. In a moment he was halfway across
the field, the cloth glimmering in the weird light.

I looked towards the river. A dim shape floated just beneath the
surface of the water some four yards out. The current had already
caught it and was tugging it downstream, a hump-backed object like
some obscene fish.

Suddenly the dark mass changed direction. It began to drift
in towards the bank. Greatly excited, I walked along the river's
edge, keeping myself parallel to the floating hump. A tooth of land
projected some five yards distant and I saw that the black mass would
be washed ashore upon it. I ran forward snatching at a broken branch
with which to haul it in.

Two minutes later I was looking at the Thames-soaked body of
Murrell's singular assistant. His hands and feet were lightly bound
with twine, his eyes gazed up at me with lightless horror, the strange
teeth protruding in a grim rictus – a parody of a grimace.

I struck a light and leaned over the body. His wet shirt had been
torn on a floating spar and where the flesh showed I could see faint
blue markings. He had obviously been tortured. My ears had not
deceived me.

Had he been tortured to death? He appeared to have met his death
by some blunt instrument. A dark bruise stood out against the pallor
of his skin. I fingered his head, peering closely at the bruise, moved
the head around with both hands and felt at his ribs. I lifted the lax
hand and examined the fingernails. I let the hand fall. He had died
of a broken neck. Already the body was beginning to stiffen in the
chill night air.


# XIX

The bell jangled through my sleep, cutting into a soft and pleasant
dream. I descended the stairs, more asleep than awake. It had been
three o'clock in the morning before I had trudged wearily up my
stairs to bed.

I opened the door and snapped suddenly into full awareness. I
could not have been more abruptly awakened had somebody dowsed
me with freezing water.

The grey man stood upon my steps, greyer than ever in the bright
morning light.

"Captain Nash?" he enquired in a grey voice, a wraith of a voice,
as solid as a river mist.

"I think you know me, Sir," I said half-severely, half-amused.

He blushed, if that is the word to describe it, for a darkish hue crept under his grey cheeks.

"I should like to speak to you privately, Captain," he said quite meekly.

I examined him keenly. He looked harmless enough in the daylight. Out of the shadows, shorn of all mystery, he presented a rather nondescript, even a pathetic figure.

He carried no arms about him, of that I was sure. I thought it safe enough to admit him.

He sat in my room like a shrivelled elephant. His skin sagged about him like a hide, grey and leathery, with all the lines running downwards in the most depressing way.

"My name is Smith," he said in his whispery voice. "'Coffin' Smith," he emphasized. The epithet conveyed distinction.

I bowed. He flushed again, as if common politeness were in some obscure way an insult to him. He was, I could see, a man well-used to snubs.

He licked his lips nervously and looked about the room. Thinking to put him at his ease, for I feared that he would never get started until I had reassured him, I offered him a pinch of snuff. A man generally gains confidence from the use of trifling properties, such little actions give a release from tension.

He flushed, or "greyed", even deeper and took the snuffbox from me awkwardly. He took the snuff between his fingers with a very gauche air and, with a most unfashionable sniff-sniff, inhaled the powder. After a prodigious sneeze, he said, "God amercy!" and then sat looking as awkward, miserable and grey as ever.

"I'm a mate o' Betty's," he said, and waited. I was obviously expected to know who Betty was, and as I was in ignorance, I thought it best to hold to an enigmatic silence. I could see it greatly impressed him.

"Betty is a good woman," he said and paused again.

"I don't doubt that," I answered evenly.

He darkened again. He seemed to find some critical note in my innocent comment.

"That old bastard used her ill," he said.

I waited a full minute for him to continue, but he only said: "She's a good woman", and flashed me a swift, pugnacious look, as though he expected me to challenge him on this occasion.

"And what does Betty want with me?" I asked, feeling that I must get his story launched before he ran out of confidence altogether.

He hawed and hemmed and sneezed fiercely again.

"She wants to do business with you," he said at last.

"Oh?" I said carefully.

He wiped his nose with a greasy clout.[1]

"Is that why you have been haunting me for the last twenty-four hours?" I asked.

He looked away unhappily, for all the world as if I had caught him with his hand in my purse.

"She wants to do business," he said again.

"What kind of business?" I barked, suddenly losing my patience. He blinked.

"You can trust her," he then said maddeningly. "For all that she's black outside."

Light dawned in a great blinding flash. Murrell's packhorse. The uncomely Negress. Here was her emissary.

"She has the receipts?" I asked.

"She knows where they are," he said.

"Can she get them for me?"

He shook his head.

"No, Captain. But you can."

"I can? How?"

"She'll tell you that. For one hundred guineas."

There was something wrong with this proposition. I pondered it for a moment, then I saw what it was. The price they asked was far too low. One hundred guineas for receipts valued in thousands. Why was she prepared to sell so cheap?

He looked towards me anxiously.

"Are you interested?"

"Is it only the information I shall buy?"

He nodded. "Aye. But it's the only way you'll get them back. You'd never find them in a hundred years without Betty's help."

"Are you sure?"

He looked puzzled by my question.

"What do you mean, Sir?"

"Is she the only one who knows their whereabouts?"

"There's nobody else," he replied stoutly.

I thought of the bruised and tortured body of the redhaired assistant. If he had had knowledge of the receipts, it seemed unlikely that the secret had died with him. I could not imagine that fiercely grinning mouth had remained silent under the pressure of such pain. Pelham must also know by now. In which case, the code-book was still my best lever. And cheaper, too.

[1]Handkerchief.

"There's more to these receipts than you think," Smith said sharply. His grey face looked suddenly deeply cunning.

"Oh?"

"You'll be paying for that, too."

"You must need the money badly to think of selling so cheap," I said.

He moved against the chair-back uncomfortably.

"We need to move away," he said.

Pelham. They were afraid of Pelham.

"The climate here won't suit your mort,"[1] I said, pleasantly.

"Will you buy?" he asked.

"I'd need to know more before I do."

"It's Betty's business," he said. "I'm just her Mercury."

"And when can we strike hands?" I asked.

"Come down to my flash[2] tonight," he said. "Roach's Landings, that's where I hang out."

"No," I said. "You must come here."

I had a vision of my reception at Roach's Landings. A quick blow behind the ear and eternal darkness for George Nash. Did they take me for a gawney?[3]

He shifted from buttock to buttock.

"She won't stir out," he said. "Not 'til we're ready to ship away."

"She must be greatly feared," I said. "Doesn't she trust to her own magic?"

A look of baffled resentment crept into his face, a closed expression to his eye. I decided not to probe any further into his extraordinary relationship with the black savage. I wondered briefly whether Murrell had received a decent interment yet. Presumably the poor creature had now abandoned hope of his return from the dead, for she obviously no longer felt herself protected by his magic.

"Will you come?" Smith asked.

I weighed up the alternatives. Until Pelham made a move, this ill-assorted couple were my chief lead to the receipts. It would be better to trust them – up to a point.

"I'll go to Roach's Landings for the information," I said. "But you must come here for the money."

He paused for only a moment and then nodded his agreement. If I had expected an angry reaction to my proposal, I was to be

[1] Woman. A near-harlot.
[2] Flash-crib: lodging house.
[3] A fool.

disappointed. He accepted my terms stoically. "Coffin" Smith was well-used to toeing other people's lines. He had danced all his life to other people's tunes.

"We'd better go now," he said.

Roach's Landings was arrived at through a snake of stinking streets. It was a place of ruined houses and collapsing walls. Most of the buildings seemed to have foundered in the mud and the rest looked as though a cough would bring them down. The only reassuring constituents of this dismal scene were the sun shining on the waters of the Thames and the boats, those alluring symbols of escape, their masts springing like a bizarre forest behind the chimney stacks. It was a most sinister area, amid warehouses and workshops, surrounded by the huge ramps of the dock walls. Strident voices shattered the air around us and soot stuck to my skin in the oppressive heat. Smith threaded his way through the twisting, dirty alleys with the sureness of long acquaintance. In this part of the world he was entirely confident.

I was far from feeling confident myself. We had passed at least half a dozen gallows, the corpses polishing the King's irons.[1] But there seemed little likelihood that the people we saw were much moved by such grisly warnings. They eyed one with speculative glances and I walked with half my mind to my exposed back. The inhabitants of Roach's Landings were scarcely human. They were treated by their superiors as hardly more than wild beasts, and with good reason. Officers of the Law paraded here in groups of five and then only in daylight. I almost wished that I had dressed with less care that morning.

I kept a ready hand to my sword and felt a mixture of relief and anxiety as we turned in to an alarmingly dark hallway, stinking of cats and piss. A dozen eyes followed us as we mounted the broken stairs. The walls were sweating and peeling, and the air was redolent of damp and despair.

As we reached the head of the stairs, Smith struck a tinder. The air had grown fouler the higher we rose and the only light came from the cracks in the roof, through which the winter rains had seeped.

He knocked on a door in a secret signal. There was no answer. He waited a moment, then repeated the signal.

Again, a still, uncanny silence. Smith caught his breath in a muffled gasp. Something soft and furry brushed against my ankles. There was

---

[1]Hanging in chains inside iron cages. To preserve them for as long as possible, as a warning to evil-doers.

no sound but a faint whisper from behind the wainscot and a dull murmur from far below in the street.

Smith called out her name.

There was no reply. Before I could stop him, Smith had put a shoulder to the door and burst into the room.

He stopped abruptly, aghast at the sight that met his eyes. A cry broke from him, hoarse, pathetic, broken. I would never have supposed such an explicit sound could issue from that grey mouth.

The hot little room was a shambles. The rickety chairs and cheap wooden table lay splintered and broken, shards of crockery lay where they had been hurled. The greasy walls were splattered with blood and bloodied skin curled in the dust of the floor. The most fearful battle had taken place here and the loser lay where she had fallen upon the filthy bed. The Negress, almost naked, lolled across the bloodsoaked pallet. Her eyes had rolled wildly back into her head, her enormous shining legs were cut in notches and other terrible wounds flowered like obscene roses on her breasts and stomach.

It was a cruel and diabolic scene, a mad scene out of Bedlam. She had been put to the sword with a vengeance and must have suffered beyond agony.

Smith stood by the bed. After a deathly pause, he covered the grotesque body with a sheet. In the midst of this reeling, drunken nastiness he looked, of a sudden, immensely composed, almost sedate. When he turned to look at me, his eyes were dry and as lifeless as the corpse.

He began to swear quietly. A string of the most trenchant obscenities dropped from his mouth in his hoarse, grey voice.

## XX

I passed a day in immeasurable gloom, only relieved by a deadly sleepiness, which passed leaving me with the naked prospect of absolute failure. Betty was dead and with her death all my chances of receiving the correct information may well have died also. The outlines of the case seemed like the outlines of a lost boat slowly being buried by the tide.

Betty had known where the receipts were to be got. Pelham may or may not know. If he hadn't known, had he been responsible for the frightful butchery in that squalid room? In which case, had he learned of their whereabouts?

I thought it hardly likely. Looking at that grim body on the bed, looking at the condition of the room, I could scarcely believe that any woman who could fight so hard would disclose her knowledge easily.

I could not shake off the feeling that her secret had died with her.

Pelham must be still as ignorant as I myself.

But more prepared to help himself! Three men had died, and one woman. I knew that he had killed the assistant. If one death could be laid at his door, why not all? It was possible, even logical. And if he was prepared to go to such lengths to secure the receipts, what lengths would he not go to in order to take the code-book?

And yet, so far, I had remained unmolested.

Another thought nagged at my mind. For all Pelham's debauched and tarnished reputation, he had never been noted for savagery. Whenever I thought of the scene in that dismal room, it was the maniacal quality of it that disturbed me most. It accorded ill, somehow, with what I knew of Pelham's methods. It didn't have his grain.

On the other hand, I remembered the body of the redhaired man, the lacerations, the engraved terror on the ghastly, grinning face. Pelham was either losing his finesse, or else he was beginning to employ some vicious skips.[1]

My own situation had become extremely vulnerable. I would have to keep a sharp eye out for danger. The codebook was still my greatest asset, but Pelham, it now appeared, was not the man to sit and bargain when he could obtain his will by shorter means.

In the midst of suchlike cogitations, the bell rang and I opened the door to Pelham's saucy footman. Sir Harry desired to see me urgently, the man said. I was to go at once, the coach stood at my door.

"You may tell your master," I said, "that nothing will induce me to walk into his house. If he has anything whatever to discuss with me, he must come to do it here."

The footman looked very surprised. Then he turned on his heel and went to confer with the coachman, the same hulking fellow who had carried me unknowingly to Hammersmith. I stood watching.

Then the footman hoisted himself aboard, and the coach rattled away into the night.

An hour later the bell jangled again. I lay aside my book and went to answer the door. I opened it to find Pelham standing on the step. He leaned heavily upon his walking-stick. Behind him loomed the enormous figure of the coachman.

[1]Skip-kennel: footmen.

Pelham bowed in his negligent, ironical way and produced a small and elegant snuff-box from his pocket. He took a pinch with a delicate air and raised it to his nostrils.

"Well, Sir, here I am," he said pleasantly enough.

I bowed and, stepping slightly aside, opened the door a trifle wider.

With a swift, upward motion, Pelham flung the contents of the snuff-box in my face. A stinging powder flew into my eyes, which began to swell immediately, smarting most horribly. I started back, half-blinded, the edge of the door still in my hand.

I tried to close the door, but Pelham's foot was against it, blocking its movement.

Out of the stinging cloud of darkness, I was dimly aware of the huge bulk of the coachman lunging forward. The door cracked back against the wall as he thrust it out of my hand. I felt two enormous arms encircle me and I was lifted bodily from the doorway and carried, coughing and sneezing, to the coach.

He bundled me without ceremony into its dressed leather interior.

Pelham was back in his elegant bed, looking as if he had never left it. The footman fussed about him, settling his pillows and straightening his counterpane. He left a full glass of light-coloured liquid on the night table by his master's side and left the room. The gigantic coachman stood behind me.

I was sitting in a mahogany Chippendale chair, my arms securely tied. My eyes still itched abominably from the powder. It burned in my nostrils and my mouth was very dry.

Pelham took a deep swig of the amber liquid. He smiled at me as I ran my tongue involuntarily over my stinging lips. It was a slow, wide smile, quite without malice.

"I'm sorry you felt you had to refuse my invitation, Captain," he said conversationally, for all the world as if we were seated at some evening party. "But I'm glad you saw fit to come along in the end."

"How could I refuse such a gracious request?" I replied, mustering as much ease as I could in the circumstances. I did not feel at all at ease. The silent bear of a man loomed behind me, smelling of leather and horse sweat.

"Why did you refuse?" Pelham asked curiously.

I nodded my head towards my bound hands. It seemed answer enough.

Pelham took another draught from the glass. I watched the liquid tilt into his mouth and my own seemed drier than summer dust. He caught me licking my lips again and raised his glass in a mocking salute.

"My cure-all," he said smiling.

"One of Murrell's prescriptions, I've no doubt," I murmured. He laughed obligingly.

"Good God, man, I'd no more have drunk one of his remedies than I would drink piss," he said. "Murrell was a cheap rogue."

I raised an eyebrow. He looked up at that moment and saw the disbelieving expression on my face. He laughed again.

"A cheap rogue," he repeated. "And a fool."

He lay back on his pillows, gazing ruminatively into the yellow fluid in the glass. His treacle-brown eyes looked fathomless as he asked:

"Where is the code-book?"

I took a deep breath.

"Where are the receipts?" I countered.

Pelham nodded almost imperceptibly. The greasy giant behind me leaned forward slightly and I felt a slight pressure on my shoulder.

Sir Harry yawned.

"I hope you will be reasonable about this, Nash," he said. "I detest unnecessary violence and I despise unnecessary heroics."

The giant's huge hands massaged my shoulders gently.

"We made a bargain, Sir Harry," I said.

"Unfortunately, it's a bargain I can't keep," he drawled, adding insolently: "I give you my word on it."

"And if I insist on your keeping to our agreement?"

The coachman must have been the bastard son of Sally Mapp,[1] only his profession was to throw a man's bones out of joint, not to set them. The fingers digging into my neck seemed to separate each muscle. The pain, though brief, was excruciating. For a minute or two the world went black.

"You are not in a position to insist," Pelham said reasonably. "I must point out that an injury to one's neck is more serious than to any other part of the body. A fracture may cause paralysis, or if Jemmy here should tear your spinal cord . . ." He left the rest to my imagination.

The fingers went to work in earnest now. A light danced before my eyes like a malevolent firefly. Pain shot from my neck in every direction, only to be gathered up again in a tight knot under the giant's probing fingers. I gritted my teeth and began to sweat.

[1] A famous bone-setter of the period.

The torture ceased as Pelham spoke once more.

"Would you believe me, Nash, if I told you that these receipts you are so anxious to find, don't – and never did – exist?"

The fingers relaxed their hold and the red mist in front of my eyes cleared slightly. I looked over towards the bed, which seemed to be floating in a slight haze.

Pelham smiled his slow smile. Again, there seemed to be no harm in it.

"Do you tell me this out of real knowledge, Sir Harry?" I asked. "Or have you exhausted all the possibilities of finding them?"

He frowned, not following my drift for a moment. The implications of what I had said appeared to strike him unexpectedly. His eyes glowed hot as coals. He nodded towards the coachman, with an altogether different expression on his face.

The coachman stepped forward, but this time I was ready for him. I rolled from beneath the plaguily teasing fingers, flexed my knees and sprang upright, carrying the chair with me like some absurd extension of my backside. As I turned in a tight circle, I aimed the chair legs at the man's crotch in a vicious, stabbing motion. With a howl of rage and pain he clutched at his culls and as he did so, I whirled the body of the chair towards his lowered head. I felt like a terrier baiting a bull. But, caught off balance, the bull fell heavily, striking his head against a heavy mahogany dresser. He grunted and then lay still. My wrists felt as if they were clean broken in two and I was still vexatiously imprisoned in the chair.

I turned my attention to the bed. Pelham lay half-stupefied, half-amused at my performance. Suddenly aroused to his vulnerability, be made a belated move towards the bellrope hanging by his bed. With a clumsy stride, I fell against his outstretched hand and pushed him back upon his pillows aiming for his wounded neck. He grimaced with pain as I caught his shoulder, but the effort caused me almost as much agony. I stood panting from my exertions, looking down at him. I must have cut a weird figure, bruised and dishevelled, the chair sticking out behind me.

Pelham lay pale and exhausted on his pillows. He looked almost as if he expected a blow of some kind and had my hands been free, I no doubt would have obliged him.

As it was, my efforts, painful though they had been, had made some effect. The bonds that secured my hands to the chair had loosened, tearing the skin sorely. Now, after a few painful twists of my wrists I had one hand free. I worked upon the other hand, keeping an eye always on Pelham, and very shortly the chair dropped to the floor with a thud.

All this time Pelham lay with his eyes closed, as white as wax. I picked up his drink and took a deep draught of it. The pale liquid ran smoothly enough down my throat, though it hardly slaked the itching dust in my mouth. Then, a small fire was lit in my bowels.

Pelham opened one eye and regarded me speculatively. I looked across the room and found what I most needed at that moment. A brace of duelling pistols lay in their inlaid case upon a tallboy. I lifted a pistol from its nest and, weighing it carefully, walked over to the recumbent body of the coachman, lying like a small mountain of clothes where he had fallen. A pool of blood had formed about a deep cut on his head. He lay as stiff as death in a curiously twisted position, one hand still curving protectively about his parts. I hoped that by now his culls had swollen to an inconvenient size. For a moment I thought I had killed the man. Then he snored suddenly.

I walked back to the bed. Pelham eyed the pistol quizzically.

"Well Sir?" he asked.

"I thank you for your invitation, Sir Harry, but I find that I cannot stay after all."

"A pity," he said wryly. "And how do you plan to leave?"

"Oh, I have a safe-conduct," I answered, and waved the pistol at him encouragingly.

He laughed his pleasant laugh.

"Fortune favours the reckless," he said. "If you have luck on your side you have no need of brains."

On the night table by his side lay a pair of scissors.

I reached up and cut off the silk of the bell-rope, leaving a portion well out of Pelham's reach.

He looked up at me, lazily amused.

"Are you still in the market for the code-book?" he drawled.

"Are the receipts for sale after all?" I asked, binding the silk sash around his arms.

I moved towards the door.

"There are no receipts that I know of," Pelham said quietly. "But if they do exist I'm prepared to pay hard for them. How much do you hope to earn from serving Lady Wroth?"

I told him.

"I will pay you a dozen times more."

I paused on my way to the door. Something in his tone stopped me – a new and unaccountable note of honesty.

He saw my hesitation and said more urgently: "And you may be assured that any such receipts will never be used against his lordship."

I turned towards him. The syrup-coloured eyes were amazingly alert. He looked almost sincere.

"You seem very certain of it," I said.

He smiled a weary smile that barely moved the muscles of his mouth.

"As you said, I've exhausted the possibilities. I'm now convinced that they don't exist."

I looked at him more closely. His expression seemed stripped of all pretences. He gazed at me with an appearance of infinite weariness.

Was what he said true? How could it be? Had three men and one woman died for something that had never existed? A lethal chimera? It seemed impossible.

"You don't believe me?" he asked.

I shrugged. A doubt still lingered.

"If I were to believe you now," I said, "what a fool I shall look when I have delivered the code-book and you go back to blackguarding the Wroth family."

He gestured impatiently.

"I've already told you they won't be troubled," he said.

"My business is to protect my patroness," I answered.

"And mine is to protect my children," he replied to that. "My children," he emphasized tartly and, looking at me with the most intense expression in his eyes, he added slowly and clearly:

"Your protection of Lady Wroth and my protection of my own children amounts to the same thing."

I gazed back at him in blank astonishment.

"As a father, I suffer from a belated sense of duty," he said meditatively. "But I have a sense of duty, nevertheless. My wish to protect Lady Wroth's grandchildren is as great as her own. The only difference in our situation is that they are *not* her grandchildren – and they *are* my flesh and blood."

I continued to gape at him, deprived of speech.

"You may know that Kitty Wroth is reputed to live with me. Well, it's true enough – she does. In some style at my estate in Shropshire. She is the mistress of my house. But not *my* mistress." He smiled wryly as my jaw continued to hang in frank disbelief. "Kitty is my natural daughter. I had her by Lavinia Wroth, as I did young Charlie."

I blinked.

"Kitty was told of this by her mother before she died last year. Being a creature of honour and some spirit, she found she couldn't endure to live on as a Wroth. She said she was my responsibility and that I would have to answer for my actions. She came to me

with nothing but her mother's jewellery and the clothes she stood
up in," he added with some pride. "She wouldn't even condescend
to bring her adored mare."

"But Lady Wroth?" I stammered stupidly.

"She refuses to acknowledge the truth. Always has, and will till she
dies. Call it what you wish, an old woman's pride comes closest to it,
I suppose. A demned curious sort of pride that refuses to believe that
the son she bore was as sterile as a harem-eunuch. Perhaps it's not
so hard to understand, though. She prided herself on bringing fresh,
healthy blood into the Wroth stock. I don't know what miracle she
performed on her husband, but she managed to sire two sons. And
old Thomas Wroth was as incapable of breeding as the last Spanish
Hapsburg. Stukeley has been 'Fumbler's Hall' these two generations
past . . ."

I thought of the lost, silly face of Lord Wroth's grandfather and
conceded that Pelham might have a point at that.

"I can't imagine what humiliations the old woman endured in
trying to breed from old Thomas, but she managed to foal twice.
It explains why she refuses to believe that her own sons weren't
breeders, though. She won't let her eyes tell her the truth. You've only
to see my Kitty to know the truth of it. She has the Pelham eyes."

His own brown, turgid eyes stared resolutely into mine.

"And his lordship?" I asked. Pelham frowned.

"He favours his mother. In every way but his nature."

"And does Lord Wroth know of his true parentage?"

A strange, brooding, crafty look came into Pelham's face.

"Who knows what his lordship knows?" he said.

Who indeed, I wondered. What man in his right senses would
forfeit the Wroth fortune and a title of great quality to acknowledge
himself the bastard son of a worthless rake like Pelham?

I looked up to find Sir Harry watching me with a theorizing look
in his eye. He lowered his gaze.

"What kind of father would I be to ask my son to give up a great
position in life?" he asked with a wry smile. A look of almost benign
amusement crept into his face. "But you can see, Nash, that I have
no great wish to harm him."

"None at all, Sir Harry . . . If what you say is true," I answered.

A flicker of annoyance showed in his eyes.

"If you need further confirmation, Nash, my daughter can supply it."

"But you said she was in Shropshire," I said.

"God's ballock, man! Shropshire is not the end of the world. She
can be reached."

There was a brief and nasty silence. I tried to sort out a number of conflicting questions. Pelham looked at me keenly. I wondered what ideas were running through his head. He said softly:

"You must be assured that I have done all I can to trace the receipts. You must take my word for it that they don't exist. And I will pay you well for the code-book."

A sudden vision entered my mind. I had a picture of two young men dressed in absurd female finery, dancing upon a mint-green lawn, sword clashing upon sword. At the corner of the wall stood a silent observer. A young man with a cool profile, looking on in contempt.

"Tell me, Sir Harry," I asked. "Does young Mr. Oliver know about your part in his cousin's conception?"

He was momentarily startled.

"What?"

"Does he also know the true story, Sir?"

"It is possible that he knows about my daughter, yes."

"And Lord Wroth? Is he aware of *his* true parentage?"

He looked reluctant. "I suppose so, yes."

"And tell me, Sir Harry," I asked carefully. "Is Mr. Oliver also a love-child?"

"Why, Sir," Pelham replied levelly, "from what I hear, Mr. Oliver is the result of a triumvirate. At least three.gentlemen share the honour of his begetting."

There was a long pause while we out-stared each other. I was trying to discover whether he had lied to me and he was trying to ascertain whether I had believed him. It was a deadlock.

In the corner the felled coachman groaned and stirred. Pelham looked towards him expectantly, but the hope faded from his eyes when he saw that the man could be of no service to him yet awhile.

It was time for me to go. I moved to the door.

"Where are you going?" Pelham called after me.

"Why, Sir Harry, to corroborate your extraordinary story, to be sure," I answered.

I walked through the door and pulled it fast behind me, locking it and pocketing the key. There was nobody on the landing or in the hall. With the pistol cocked I walked quickly down the stairs and out into the street.

## XXI

Riding out to Stukeley, I fitted the pieces of the puzzle together as well as I was able. By the time I had reached the great gates to the avenue, I had made some sense of it all despite conflicting evidence. That is, if I were to give credence to Pelham's version of the truth. If I could believe him, the story would run this way:

Sir Harry had fathered both Lord Wroth and his sister Kitty. Young Charles had inherited not the Wroth family inbreeding, but the Pelham wildness. As a natural result of his follies, he had fallen into the manipulative hands of Murrell, who had accidentally discovered the secret of his birth. Knowing that the Dowager Lady Wroth had ambitious plans for her grandson's future, he had decided to capitalize on his discovery. But, being the devious rogue that he was, he had first sounded out his prospective victim. Hence the bogus approach, hinting at unspeakable secrets. The receipts, obnoxious as they were, were not in themselves to be feared. A young man's extravagances, however bad they may seem, would be overlooked by any ambitious family wishing to marry into the landed aristocracy. But if there was a possible doubt of the heir's legitimate right to the title and property, that would be another matter. It would be a secret worth paying out good money to keep undisclosed. If there was a smattering of truth in such a rumour, Lady Wroth would pay to cover the artificial scandal in order to protect her family from the larger threat of the real one.

But Lady Wroth was an obstinate woman and no fool. She had seen the receipts as a test and realized that if she played Murrell's game, she would be playing it to the death. So she had hired me, not to retrieve the receipts but to supply her with enough information to silence Murrell by a counterthreat to his liberty.

Murrell's brutish end had changed the situation only in that a single threat had sprouted a hydra-head. If he had been killed in order to silence him, his murderers had overlooked one important fact – Murrell had accomplices. Others were willing enough to carry on his work.

Yet I could only think that Murrell *had* been silenced. And who had undertaken the task? The list of possible assassins was an impressive one, to judge by the names that featured in the code-book. But out of all his numerous gulls and catspaws, I must concentrate my attention on those most closely connected to my end of this business.

Which led me to another point. If Murrell had not died simply to stop his tongue, then he must have been eliminated for other reasons. If this was so, then there was only one possible suspect – Pelham. I could not see either the red-topped youth nor black Betty with her grey-faced gallant engineering his death in order to inherit his business. Such an enterprise required style and Pelham was the only man for the game. The apprentice had definitely died at his instigation, if not by his own hand. And the poor black woman also?

It seemed possible. They both stood between Pelham and the realization of his plans, if they knew of the whereabouts of the receipts. For Pelham must hold the receipts in order to gain the code-book. And by his own admission, Pelham had exhausted the possibilities of retrieving the papers.

But d'Urfey? How had d'Urfey died?

I could not fit d'Urfey's death into the general scheme. If he had died because he, too, was an accomplice, whose accomplice had he been? I thought it very likely that the young Adonis had played some vital part in the affair, for he seemed the type of man to profit by being well-placed. I thought it likely that he had revealed Wroth's true parentage to Murrell, I thought it more than probable that he had gone to the old charlatan with the proposition to blackguard the dowager in the first instance. And had Pelham, whilst ridding himself of a superfluous partner, also rid himself of the originator?

But that required that Pelham knew of Murrell's discovery and was a party to the plot. Yet I was fairly convinced that, until I had enlightened him, he had had no knowledge of Murrell's involvement with young Wroth. There could be no doubting the concern in his eyes when I had informed him of it.

Unless, of course, he was an actor of genius and his tale had been a fantastication from beginning to end.

I jogged along, trying to slot together the pieces of such information as I had. It seemed to me that I had two separate strands which, taken singly, made some vague kind of pattern, but which, when I tried to weave them together, refused to create a satisfactory whole.

My first theory was that Murrell had been removed by Pelham, the intention being to rid himself of an encumbrance. When I had confounded Sir Harry by appropriating the all-important code-book, he had put the miserable assistants to death in his efforts to find the missing papers. This was my favourite theory, for the last two murders, I felt sure, could be linked directly to Pelham.

But this also left d'Urfey's death unaccounted for; likewise the fact that the attempt on Pelham's own life had some similarity to d'Urfey's.

My second theory was that Lord Wroth and d'Urfey had engineered Murrell's death between them, if they had not actually taken part in the bloody brawl. It seemed the uncomplicated way that a lad like his lordship would deal with a threat to his "honour". The black savage had murdered d'Urfey in revenge, after her own fashion. Then, still being uncertain of the true identity of her master's executioner, she had made a similar attempt on Pelham's life. If she had planned further retribution on Lord Wroth, she had been baulked of her satisfaction by her own violent end.

All this, as I say, made some kind of pattern in my mind, but there were too many inexplicable knots in the weave, too many rough ends. The single strands would not thread together.

That is, if I took Pelham at his word.

If I ignored his tale, of course, the pattern was quite different and made more appeal. Pelham himself was the black, villainous thread throughout. Everything that had happened could be laid to his hand. He had murdered Murrell, the apprentice, the Negress, and possibly d'Urfey. The attack on his own life had been carried out by the black woman and he had tried to confound me by implicating Oliver Wroth.

Which made me think of Oliver Wroth. What, if anything, had he to do with the business? His sole concern, he had suggested, was the protection of his grandmother.

Why had he tried to make me abandon the search for his cousin Kitty? If Pelham's story was true and Lord Wroth was not the legitimate heir, Oliver had more right to the succession. And if Oliver knew this extraordinary story, he would be a rare man indeed not to seek to profit by it. And yet he had tried to dissuade me from finding Miss Kitty, and she was the one who might settle the title on his shoulders.

If only I could disentangle the facts from the fiction in Pelham's story! If only I could ask for the Wroth version of his extraordinary tale.

But how could I approach Lady Wroth on such an indelicate mission? She had hired me to return the receipts, not to uncover a potential cesspit. Was it not enough that I had to go to her saying that no such receipts existed, without insulting her family into the bargain?

I had not worked out the answer to this by the time I was admitted to the house.

## XXII

In the event, my anxiety proved unnecessary, for I was not allowed to see her ladyship. Instead, I was left to brood downstairs for above half an hour. When the door opened, it was Mr. Oliver who came into the room.

He inclined his head by a bare fraction. The unamiable stiffness had returned to his bearing. He advanced towards a table and taking a purse from his pocket he counted out a number of coins.

"This was the price agreed upon for your services, Captain Nash. If you will give me an account of your expenses, we shall conclude this business."

"*We* shall, Sir?" I said, taken with some surprise.

"My grandmother is indisposed. This affair has caused her considerable hardship. She asks me to thank you on her behalf and to settle your account."

"But, Sir," I protested. "My business is not yet at an end."

The curious light-coloured eyes were, of a sudden, as dull as stones.

"I assure you that it is, Captain. We have no further need of you."

"I have not yet – "

"This business is finished!" he said violently. "The receipts were delivered here last night."

"Delivered?" I was stunned. I had come to report the possibility that no such papers existed.

"How?" I asked.

"They were simply delivered," he repeated grimly. "That is all you need to know, I think."

"Indeed, Mr. Wroth," I said sharply. "I think not, Sir."

His eyebrows rose superciliously.

"Really?"

"No, Sir. I have some rights in this matter. It may not have occurred to you, Mr. Wroth, but I have compromised my reputation to some extent in trying to secure the receipts. I feel I have a right to know how they were returned to you and by whom."

He looked down at the purse on the table, his fawn-coloured eyes veiled. When he spoke, it was politely, almost gently.

"I acknowledge that you may feel you have some rights, Captain Nash, and if you have compromised your reputation on our behalf, I thank you." The veil lifted slightly and his eyes flashed like the tips of arrows. "Though the less said about 'compromise' the better, for all our sakes."

He looked at me directly. The expression in his eyes was plain enough. By protecting their name, I would be protecting my own.

"On the contrary, Mr. Wroth," I answered, meeting the challenge. "It is my duty to make a report, of sorts, to the Mansion House."

He blinked.

"Concerning our business?"

"Concerning four deaths, Mr. Wroth. All of which *could* be connected with the receipts."

"You have no proof of that!" he said harshly.

"Do you think not?" I said, and paused. His eyes met mine searchingly, then they shifted away.

"I have not been entirely idle," I went on. "But since I must protect my reputation and as I have obviously forfeited your family's confidence . . ."

He picked up the purse and extracted more coins. He regarded me steadily as he laid out six pieces on the tabletop.

"Captain Nash, if I were to give you my word that none of these deaths are the responsibility of my family, would you . . . could you consider making your report to the Mansion House without involving our name?"

He moved the coins towards me suggestively.

"I don't see how I can, Mr. Wroth, in all conscience."

The hand moving the coins fell abruptly away.

"Do you connect the deaths with my family?" he asked coldly.

"Murrell was blackguarding you, Sir. He died. His assistants died too. Very violent deaths. As for d'Urfey, he was your cousin's closest companion."

"But we are not involved, except fortuitously."

I remained silent. He regarded me bitterly. Then the arrogant façade crumbled and the beseeching, almost supplicating look that I had seen on his face before came into it again.

"My grandmother is dying," he said quietly. "I would like her to die in peace."

"And ignorance?" I asked.

His head jerked back.

"Ignorance?"

I stood the bluff.

"Mr. Wroth, how much do you know of your antecedents?"

He flushed. I saw that I had struck home. Suddenly I was convinced that Pelham had told me the truth.

I had a brief and wild revelation. Oliver Wroth *knew* that he was the rightful heir (if one disregarded Pelham's malicious insinuations about his own conception). Knowing this, one could only guess at the disorder of his feelings. His grandmother's wilful refusal to recognize his true status must goad him beyond endurance. The realization that he could never prove his claim and the thought of losing both title and fortune to a worthless bastard must be almost more than he could bear. He was a young man with a cool head and a strong stomach, that was plain to see. Had he sought a desperate remedy for his wrongs? Knowing that he had no legal means of coming at his inheritance, had he sought to gain something of his own fortune by stealth?

Without fully grasping the extent of his motives, I felt strongly that he *had* been a prime mover in all this. The idea was fantastic, but no less possible for all that.

I observed him very closely as I said: "Sir Harry Pelham says that there are no receipts, Mr. Wroth. He also says that Lord Wroth is his natural son and Miss Kitty his natural daughter. If that is so, I am addressing the real Lord Wroth."

He flushed again and when he replied his voice seemed curiously sealed-off.

"Pelham lies in both cases, Sir. My cousin is who the world thinks he is and the receipts were delivered into our hands last night. This affair is over."

He scooped up the money. All at once he seemed to have regained his composure. He regarded me with the old, crisp arrogance.

"If you will state your expenses, Captain Nash, we shall draw a line under your account. As for your dealings with the Mansion House, you may tell them what you will. If you incriminate my family unnecessarily in the deaths you mentioned we shall, of course, take measures."

The fawny eyes glared at me. Generations of privileged and haughty ancestors looked out from behind them.

"I shall do all I can to protect my grandmother while she lives," he said quietly. "When she is gone, I shall come into my own."

My revelation turned slightly arsy-varsey. I had misjudged him. He was not the man to blackguard his own kin. I now saw why he wished to protect his cousin Kitty. She would be his most valuable witness when he came to claim his rights by Law. And she would undoubtedly be safer under Pelham's protection.

Under the bright pressure of those eyes, I glanced away.

There came an urgent knocking on the door and almost before Wroth could call out the door opened and Chives entered with undignified haste. He was oddly flustered for so impassive a man. I would not have imagined that his careful face could betray so much passion.

"What is it, Chives?"

It took some time before Chives could make himself understood, so great was the extent of his outrage.

"It's the master, Mr. Oliver! His lordship! He's been tak-en!"

"Taken? Taken where? By whom?"

With shaking hands, the old servant proffered a letter sealed with a rusty pin.

"We found this on Knottersmole Common, Sir. His Lordship was out there all morning shooting pigeon. I sent to remind him that dinner would be early today – and Grimes came back with this. It had been nailed to a tree by the lake. His lordship's gone, Sir. There's no doubt of it. We've searched everywhere."

Wroth looked up from the sheet of paper. I saw that on the outside in roughly printed red block-capitals were the words: "LADY WROTH. IN ALL HAIST." The paper looked to have been handled by a number of none too cleanly fingers.

"My cousin has been kidnapped," Wroth said. He handed the paper to me.

The letter read: "IF YOO WONT TO SEE LORD WROTH ALIV AGEN, FOLOW OUR COMANDS TO THE LETER. GETT HOLDE OF 5000 GNS. LD WROTH WILL SEE HIS MANI AFFTER YOO GIV UP THE RIJE. DO NOT TRY AND BAMBOOZ UZ OR CAKLE TO THE RUNNERS. NEETHER RAMP UZ ELS HIS LDSHIP WILL DYE AND THE OLDE LADIE WILL MAK A NEWE WILL.

"WEE WIL GIV YOO 2 DAYS TO GET THE RIJE. PLAIS THE GNS IN A BOKS AND WAYT FOR MOR TIDINGS."

"I don't understand half that jargon," Wroth said, his eyes bleak.

"Just thieves' cant, Mr. Wroth," I answered and could not forbear adding: "The writer seems anxious that you should not offend her ladyship."

His eyebrows rose in the familiar way. "Sir?"

"The letter seems to be directed more towards you, Sir, than her ladyship. Despite the fact that it's addressed to her. It is as though they feared that you might neglect to pay out, Mr. Wroth, unless you are reminded that her ladyship ultimately holds the purse-strings."

The tawny eyes glittered. He snatched the paper from my hand and snapped: "I will remind you, Sir, that our business is at an end. Chives, show the Captain to his horse."

He bowed and walked stiffly from the room.

Chives coughed discreetly from behind a diplomatic hand.

"Her ladyship wishes to see you, Captain," he said.

As we climbed the gloomy stairs, I had an inner conviction that I was about to be replaced in my former capacity; and a nagging conviction, also, that I already knew the answer to the case.

The clue, I felt sure, lay in the composition of the kidnapper's message. The thieves' vocabulary struck a false note somewhere. It was too literary in tone, while the spelling and the grammar were altogether too much contrived!

There was no lack of eyewitnesses to the kidnapping, though their versions of what had happened left more holes in the evidence than otherwise.

A stolid farmhand, working in a field adjoining the common, said he had seen a man who resembled his lordship in build and colouring, enter a black phaeton in company with an older man. He described this man as wearing a grey coat and kneebreeches. His lordship had not seemed to object to being carried off.

A drayman passing the east entrance to Stukeley (the nearest gate to the common) had seen a black and silver *chaise* standing beneath a clump of trees. But he had not seen his lordship or his kidnapper enter the carriage. Another witness (a milkmaid) said a *gig* had been driven away by a fellow wearing a beaver hat and a grey coat.

It would seem that Lord Wroth, who in my estimation was not by nature a quiet lad, had gone quite docilely with his kidnappers. Although he carried a fowling-piece, he had yet been constrained to leave the woods without a struggle. The elderly gamekeeper who had accompanied him to flush the birds had gone for half a mile before becoming aware that the birds that took to the sky at his coming were returning, unshot at, to the trees. Needless to say, he had seen nothing of his master's disappearance.

The crime appeared to have been planned in advance. The black and silver carriage had been seen in the vicinity on many days prior to the abduction, and for a number of nights, dogs in neighbouring kennels had been disturbed by prowlers. Or so willing witnesses hastened to tell me.

Among the eyewitness accounts that I collected, two completely contradictory ones stood out.

A servant at a house in the village said that at three o'clock on the day of the kidnapping, she had seen the black carriage pass by with two men in the back who appeared to be struggling with each other.

Against this was the story of the toll-keeper who, at the same time, had seen a black phaeton going in the *opposite* direction – that is, towards London. There were two men inside, one at the reins and the other partially concealed by a blanket. The driver had flung a handful of coppers in the toll-keeper's face and had cried out that his passenger was "taken sick with the buboes". The carriage had sped with uncommon speed towards London, which had scarcely surprised the toll-keeper, considering the patient's alarming disorder.

In all these conflicting statements only two facts remained constant. Firstly, the carriage, though variously described as a phaeton, a chaise, or a gig, was always black. Secondly, and a detail that I found more rewarding, in all the descriptions the kidnapper was described as being dressed in grey.

When the toll-keeper added the information that the driver's voice was curiously hoarse – as "thick as cheesecloth" was the way he put it – I felt that I was a long way on to retrieving his lordship and my reputation.

I knew only one grey man with a very hoarse voice who could have an interest in abducting Lord Wroth. Yet I feared that he might have little interest in returning the boy to his "mani" alive!

## XXIII

Roach's Landings stank as menacingly as ever in the glaring noonday heat. Wizened brats sailed their boats and fished in the foul gutter as I made my way through a herd of swine snuffling at the piled refuse in the unpaved street.

I climbed the greasy stairs, leaving behind the stench of rotting vegetables corrupting the air and exchanged it for the equally foul stuff that passed for ventilation in the grey man's lodgings.

Just as I placed my foot upon the last flight, I hesitated. The dull murmur of voices drifted down the stairs. I could detect the hoarse tones of the grey man and another strong, harsh voice.

As daintily as a dancing master, I passed up the remaining stairs and tripped like a peewit across the dusty boards to an alcove set at an angle to the grey man's attic. A filthy cloth hung from a rod, giving some protection. Swiftly I eased myself into the narrow confine of the alcove and arranged the frowzy cloth to hide me from any who should mount the stair.

I set my ear to the wall.

The harsh voice seemed to explode in my ear. He could not have been a foot away beyond the wall.

"You ain't very bright, 'Coffin'," he said. "Not at the best of times! I reckon the blackie bedevilled your wits. You should never have got caught up in the likes of this."

The grey man swore hoarsely. "Pike off."

"Where are the papers?" the harsh voice demanded.

Smith's bravery was only temporary. A note of pleading crept into the grey tones as he said patiently: "I've told yer – over and over. They're where they always was – with Himself."

The harsh man spat.

"It's true," Smith whined.

"My master wants them receipts. And I'm to take them back with me. Remember what overtook Betty."

The crude menace in the voice brought an image into my mind. The mad carnage made of that poor black woman with her flowering wounds.

The warning must have affected Smith likewise. I had to strain to hear his cringing reply.

"That game's finished. We been fleeced. We all been fleeced. *He's* made gawneys of us all."

"Stow that tale, Smith, or I'll tap your claret."

A note of desperate sincerity crept into the grey man's tone, so urgent that his wraith-like voice almost acquired substance.

"Hang me, if it's not true."

The other man laughed coarsely. "Hanging's too quick a death!"

Countless cracks of light showed through the diseased plaster. I applied my eye to the largest one and squinted through it.

The grey man, stared back at me disconsolately. For a moment it threw me into a confusion. He seemed so close and his scrutiny was so intent upon me that I imagined he must have seen the glimmer of my eye between the crack. Then I saw more clearly that his gaze was fixed upon a spot a little to my left, which meant that his interrogator stood behind the door.

The grey man's face seemed greyer than ever. His grey shape seemed to reject the light. His eyes, as I could see, stared with desperate hatred at a point some four feet above the ground. I wondered whether the object of his loathing was a knife, a pistol, or a sword.

Whatever it was, I resolved to come to his aid and for that purpose edged towards the door. A hearty shove would easily burst the flimsy wood and the force of my entry would throw the man off balance – if he remained behind the door. Smith and I could settle the resulting argument between us. At all events, I must save the grey man. He was my only hope of finding young Wroth.

What happened next occurred with such dazzling speed that I was taken completely off-guard. The fact that it took place out of sight confused me further. In shifting my position I must have disclosed my presence in some way, though I thought I had moved as lightly as a Ratcliffe fog.

Smith's unwelcome guest must have turned slightly, momentarily distracted by the sound and, quick as a cat, the grey man had attacked. I heard his breath whistle with the effort of it and I felt the wall shake as a weighty body fell against it. Immediately after, there was the deafening roar of a pistol shot reverberating among the rafters, followed by an uncanny silence.

A muffled oath, a groan. Somebody stirred. Sword in hand, I kicked at the door. It flew open and struck against an object lying behind it.

The gargantuan body of Pelham's coachman lay humped against the wall with the life fast ebbing out of him. His hands clutched weakly at his neck from which hung a knife like a bright red barb. My face was the last thing he saw on earth. He snarled feebly, the blood bubbling from his mouth as he died.

The grey man, too, was sinking to his knees, his hands slipping loosely over the bed on which the Negress had met such a terrifying end. I caught him as he dropped face forwards and turned him to the light. Blood soaked my hand.

Unaccountably he was not mortally wounded. The bullet had torn through his right arm only, leaving it a shattered mass of blood, flesh and bone-splinters. He would never again throw a knife with such devastating effect, but he would live to mount the scaffold.

His eyes were beginning to glaze. They seemed suddenly to shrink and to retreat inwards. His skin was the colour of congealed gravy. He fainted in my arms, spotting my linen liberally with his blood.

I patched him up, inexpertly using the bed linen to stem the flowing blood. I am no surgeon, but I did my best for him. For all his grey exterior he was as sound as a horse, and like a horse could have been bled of two quarts. He had survived enough in his lifetime – the pox at least to judge by the condition of his skin – and he would live to contract gaol fever. When I had finished with his arm, I filled his mouth with brandy; he choked slightly, his eyes opened resentfully and were filled with a dull sort of recognition.

"Where's Lord Wroth, 'Coffin'?" I asked.

His lips twisted with a weak defiance. "Pike off," he whispered.

I poked gently at his arm. A wave of nausea flushed the grey face. He swore again, though not so bravely. I reached for his broken arm. He whimpered in anticipation of the pain. My outstretched finger menaced his well-being as I asked again: "Where is Lord Wroth?"

There was no more fight left in him, but he still strove to make a profit from his situation. There is truly no honour among thieves! The informer is the principal support of the law. If one does one's crime with a confederate, and if one has little faith in him, it is always soothing to know that one can run off to the Justice, save one's own neck by telling the whole tale, and perhaps receive a substantial reward in addition.

In his half-fevered state, Smith strove to make such a bargain. My hovering finger brought him up against the reality of his situation. I was in no position – and no mood – to strike a bargain. He howled like a dog before fainting away.

"Where is Lord Wroth, and who is 'Himself'?" I asked, as he recovered consciousness.

He told me then. He told me all. A madder tale I never heard in my life before.

## XXIV

I skirted the edge of the common, making my way towards a coppice. As I reached the first line of trees, I saw a familiar figure ahead of me, flitting noiselessly from tree to tree, intent upon God knows what game.

The figure disappeared into the wood.

There was a dazzle of wings as a covey of birds rose, startled by the report of a gun. The shot had sounded away to my left and I turned in that direction. Silently I plunged between the saplings and forged ahead in the direction of the shot.

A cry rang out through the woods. The cry of some strange demented bird.

I broke into a run, crashing through the trees like a wild boar. Branches flailed at my arms and whipped my back as I pushed through the dense thickets. With a gasp, I braked short at the edge of the trees. A thin branch caught my cheek as I fell into the clearing. I stared, amazed.

"My lord!"

Lord Wroth stood drooping against a tree, his pale face contorted. The fowling-piece he had carried lay where it had fallen in the bracken.

His lordship twisted towards me, his face a livid white.

"Help me!"

Half fainting with pain, he pointed down to where one elegant ankle lay caught in the fierce embrace of a fearsome looking mantrap. He had run into it unsuspecting.

It was an odd mistake for a man to make on his own land, but then Lord Wroth was not on familiar ground. Slope Manor was a good many miles from Stukeley, a remote and unconsidered possession, little used by his family, and a perfect place from which to manage a kidnapping!

Despite her condition, her ladyship had sent for me, demanding to be told all. She lay back upon her pillows, her face the colour of cheap tallow.

I lay the receipts upon the bedcover, Oliver Wroth having allowed me this privilege. She plucked at them merely, regarding them with icy eyes. The Dowager Lady Wroth looked her great age. I gave her, at best, five more months of life.

"Well, Sir," she said gruffly. "I suppose you are to be congratulated on a successful *detection*."

I bowed my thanks for the reluctant compliment.

A sound escaped her. I could not tell whether she sobbed or spat.

"Tell me what you know, Captain Nash."

I glanced at Oliver Wroth, who stood by the bed's canopy. He frowned slightly and shook his head. Her ladyship, looking up, caught the gesture.

"I will be told!" she snapped. "And I will have the truth. It was I who paid for your services, was it not? I want the truth."

Oliver shrugged, and gave his unwilling assent.

So I began from the beginning. I first explained about my attempts to break the code of Murrell's book and what my efforts had revealed.

"You learned something from the book?" she asked.

"Yes, my lady. I subsequently learned something very important. I learned that neither your name nor his lordship's figured among the many distinguished names in it."

"And what did that tell you, Sir?"

"It told me that Murrell was double-dealing his partner Pelham. For you may be sure that Sir Harry would not have countenanced exposing his lordship to scandal."

That brought a muddy flush to her worn cheeks.

"Sir?"

"Rightly or wrongly, Pelham believes himself to be the father of Miss Kitty and Lord Wroth."

She waved away the suggestion with the ghost of a theatrical gesture. But it was a theatrical gesture, empty as air.

"Though, of course," I continued as she lay back, "Murrell *was* double-dealing Sir Harry, and no doubt Sir Harry knew it in some fashion. But he didn't murder the old man. I know this to be true, for Pelham knew nothing of Lord Wroth's involvement and he was genuinely shocked by the old charlatan's death. Moreover, he was dependent upon him. I ruled him out quite early on with regard to that death. Murrell was murdered by his other partner."

"Pelham's other partner?" Lady Wroth asked with a sharp drawn breath. Her old eyes flashed fearfully towards her grandson. That young man was staring gloomily out of the window, as if he would penetrate the depths of the clouds with his naked eye.

"No Ma'am, Murrell's. Murrell was not the man to manage such a business on his own," I said. "He had not the style. Nor, in this particular case, the required knowledge. That knowledge could only have come from a peculiarly placed confidant."

"D'Urfey?"

"Yes, young d'Urfey, though even he was not acting on his own account. He was also in partnership."

Her diamond eyes widened in a chilling gleam, and again she looked towards Oliver Wroth.

". . . Who, Sir?"

But she did not need to ask. She knew the answer in her heart.

"Lord Wroth, Madam."

She half rose in a feeble attempt at protest, but the effort was too great for her and the gesture again too empty. She fell back, her fingers plucking at the counterpane.

"What makes you suppose that?"

"It is no supposition, Lady Wroth. It is a deducible fact. I can give you evidence of it. And as you yourself said, his lordship is rogue-wild. He is heavily in debt and still years away from his inheritance. He needed money and you denied him. So, he was offered a way out of his difficulties."

"Offered a way?"

She seemed to be grasping at this straw of comfort.

"It was d'Urfey's idea originally, Ma'am. It was he who put his lordship up to it."

"But he was killed, and the demands still came!"

"That is why I had to rule him out as being the sole candidate. He simply set the scheme in motion. And afterwards with Murrell dead and both his servants murdered and the receipts still not found, I had to admit that there was yet another partner."

"Pelham," she said stubbornly. "Why could it not be Pelham?"

"Pelham was still looking for the receipts as late as three days ago," I said gently. "He sent his man for them. So, with all the obvious suspects removed, there remained only the one."

She would not allow me to name the one.

"When Mr. Oliver told me the receipts had been mysteriously

returned, but would not say by whom, my suspicions were confirmed. I knew it could only be – "

Again, a gesture stopped me from speaking the name aloud.

From his place by the window, Oliver spoke.

"I discovered them in Charlie's room," he said harshly.

With a dazzle of diamonds, the old lady swept the offensive papers from the bed.

"So you see," I said reasonably, "I could scarcely return property which was already beneath your roof."

She turned away, her expression hidden by the lace edge of her pillow.

"When you hired me to retrieve the receipts," I went on, "I think Lord Wroth took fright. He was afraid that you would discover his complicity in the matter. Accordingly, he tried to warn me off. When I refused to be intimidated, he made a mad dash up to town and tried to put a stop to the whole affair. But Murrell was a greedy fellow and he, in turn, I think, refused to be dissuaded. So d'Urfey arranged for his . . . removal."

"D'Urfey?" she asked dully, her face still hidden.

I spared her what I thought to be the absolute truth, and detected a grateful look in her grandson's eye.

"Your grandson was here at Stukeley on that night."

She didn't move. I had no idea from the unyielding way in which she lay, whether I had been believed or not.

"The black woman, Betty, must have recognized d'Urfey in some manner. In her primitive fashion, she saw her duty to her master. D'Urfey was left to poison a well. Similarly, she felt an obligation to try to eliminate Pelham, since he also could easily have had a motive for assassinating Murrell."

"And my grandson? Why was he not murdered if she knew him to be in partnership with d'Urfey?"

"It is a miracle that he was not, Ma'am. The black woman had a protector of sorts. A man called Smith. For a time I thought he believed that Lord Wroth had revenged himself upon the Negress."

Her head reared sharply from the pillow. She could not frame the question on her lips.

"It was Pelham's coachman, my lady," I reassured her happily. "He was seeking information."

She sank back upon her pillows, sucking what comfort she could from my words.

"And the kidnapping?"

"That was partly Smith's notion . . . but largely your grandson's."

She huddled deeper beneath the bedclothes, shivering slightly.

"Why?" Her voice cracked. She sounded infinitely old, tired, and broken.

"The business with the receipts had failed and Lord Wroth's debts were still unpaid. He grew desperate, and he had only one acquaintance left in St. Giles': the grey man, Smith. *He* was equally desperate. He had every encouragement to leave the country, but lacked the wherewithal. Your grandson sought him out to try to raise the rhino, and between them they concocted the scheme."

There was a silence. Oliver continued to stare out of the window, and her ladyship lay like an effigy in her ponderous bed.

"And are you happy with your piece of detection?" she asked at last.

I bowed for lack of an answer.

The old fingers scrabbled angrily at the counterpane. Her yellowish face appeared suddenly to disintegrate into a hundred ugly lines. Pain and humiliation were stamped funereally behind her eyes. She raised herself upon an elbow and stared accusingly, her voice flailed me like a thin, worn lash.

"Why, Sir! I don't believe a word of it!" she cried. "I think you are completely wrong! You are a rash amateur, Sir, and have no business to meddle! You are nothing but a *raw beginner*!"

She sank back upon her pillows and dismissed me with a limp wave of her hand. She was spent. Dulled forever.

I bowed slightly, having no words. Oliver came and took me gently by the arm. Quietly, politely even, he led me from the room.

"I thank you, Captain Nash," he said gravely.

"*You* thank me, Sir?"

"For not seeking to defend yourself to my grandmother."

"I saw no point, Sir."

"No," he mused sadly, "she is not open to reason and is in no condition to judge."

"To judge what, Sir?"

"Your performance, Captain."

I smiled at his oblique compliment, knowing I would receive no other kind.

"Why, Sir," I replied, "as to that, I must agree with your grandmother. I *am* a raw beginner and what else can I be but a sort of amateur? Mine is scarcely yet a profession!"

## EPILOGUE

So ended my first investigation. Jogging back to town, I contemplated my future. Although I had brought the Wroth affair to an end, I had not done so without damage to myself, having made two very powerful enemies in Sir Harry Pelham and Lord Wroth. True, I had gained the respect of young Oliver, but I did not yet know whether he would gain the Wroth inheritance. (It so turned out that he did not after all try to claim his rights, possibly because to level a charge of bastardy at his cousin would raise doubts about his own birth and bring the whole family into disrepute. A family in the elevated social position of the Wroths would avoid an open scandal at all costs, as I had seen. Lord Wroth grew from a wild youth to a wilder man, married his heiress and sired fourteen children on her before dying in 1835 of gout and old age.)

But to return to the present affair: I was much concerned as to how I was to explain my involvement in the deaths of five people. I would have to take this problem to my cousin Scrope in the Commissioner's Office.

Scrope relieved my fears by putting the situation into some perspective: a young rake had murdered an old charlatan and been slain in turn by a half-savage. She had been done to death by Sir Harry's sadistic coachman, who had come to a bad end himself. His slayer, "Coffin" Smith, had died of gaol fever two days after his committal. Thus the various assailants were all conveniently dead, and death being beyond the Law, the Law would therefore remain silent on the subject.

"But what of the Cunning-man's assistant?" I asked. "He was murdered in Pelham's house."

"Aye, in Pelham's *house*," my cousin answered. "But what proof have you that it was at Pelham's hand? Pelham was confined to his sick-bed at the time."

I remembered my own ordeal whilst Pelham lay in his sick-bed.

"But he may have ordered his death."

"Aye, he *may* have. But it would be his word against yours. And should you lose the suit . . ."

He had no need to elaborate further. Pelham was a potent enough enemy under the present circumstances and there would be little purpose in provoking him further. Though the thought of an unproved murder rankled.

"I seem not to have come out of this too well," I said.

My cousin clapped me on the shoulder encouragingly.

"Not so! Not so, George! You have done middling-well. Fielding's

Runners could not have done better given the strange nature of the Wroth affair."

"But *I* feel that I should have done better. Fielding's men lack science."

"Why, man!" he cried. "What chance have you under the present system? We live in a state of legal anarchy. Would you try to overturn the Constitution at one blow? It has taken Fielding twenty years to show that crime can be suppressed without serious damage to that mythological entity. He has rid us of street gangs and cleared the roads of highwaymen, but is his work fully appreciated? Bones-a-me, if it is! Yet change is coming, cousin! Change is coming! There will be a place for your scientific detection yet. Take heart, George."

He clapped me on the back once more, and misquoted the Bard at me:

> "Thus far thy fortune keeps an upward course,
> And thou art graced with wreaths of victory."

"Well," thought I wryly. "Not a wreath perhaps, on this proceeding, but a chaplet certainly."

My cousin Scrope, caught in the poetic vein, poured out a bumper of Canary and, with further recourse to the Bard, offered this health.

> "All the gods go with you! Upon your sword
> sit laurel victory! And smooth success
> be strew'd before your feet!"

# THE DOOMDORF MYSTERY
## Melville Davisson Post

*Post (1871–1930), was an American attorney in the final years of the last century before turning to writing full-time. His first book,* The Strange Schemes of Randolph Mason *(1896), featured a rather unorthodox lawyer who often bent the law in the defence of his clients. The character later reformed, and the collection,* The Corrector of Destinies *(1908), is regarded as one of the cornerstones of American crime fiction. In creating Uncle Abner, though, Post made a bold move forward. It was the first fictional character to be set in an historical period and who used detective methods. Abner was a country squire in Virginia, in the early days of the nineteenth century. He was an intensely righteous, God-fearing man and a keen observer of human nature, and brought the skills of detection to a peak rivalled only by Sherlock Holmes. Surprisingly the stories never really caught on in Britain, but in America they remain highly respected. Ellery Queen regarded them as "second only to Poe's* Tales *among all the books of detective short stories written by American authors", calling them the "crème du crime". The story reprinted here originally appeared in the* Saturday Evening Post *for 18 July 1914, and is one of the most intriguing of the whole series.*

The pioneer was not the only man in the great mountains behind Virginia. Strange aliens drifted in after the Colonial wars. All foreign armies are sprinkled with a cockle of adventurers that take root and remain. They were with Braddock and La Salle, and they rode north out of Mexico after her many empires went to pieces.

I think Doomdorf crossed the seas with Iturbide when that ill-starred adventurer returned to be shot against a wall; but there was no Southern blood in him. He came from some European race remote and barbaric. The evidences were all about him. He was a huge figure of a man, with a black spade beard, broad, thick hands, and square, flat fingers.

He had found a wedge of land between the Crown's grant to Daniel

Davisson and a Washington survey. It was an uncovered triangle not worth the running of the lines; and so, no doubt, was left out, a sheer rock standing up out of the river for a base, and a peak of the mountain rising northward behind it for an apex.

Doomdorf squatted on the rock. He must have brought a belt of gold pieces when he took to his horse, for he hired old Robert Steuart's slaves and built a stone house on the rock, and he brought the furnishings overland from a frigate in the Chesapeake; and then in the handfuls of earth, wherever a root would hold, he planted the mountain behind his house with peach trees. The gold gave out; but the devil is fertile in resources. Doomdorf built a log still and turned the first fruits of the garden into a hell-brew. The idle and the vicious came with their stone jugs, and violence and riot flowed out.

The government of Virginia was remote and its arm short and feeble; but the men who held the lands west of the mountains against the savages under grants from George, and after that held them against George himself, were efficient and expeditious. They had long patience, but when that failed they went up from their fields and drove the thing before them out of the land, like a scourge of God.

There came a day, then, when my Uncle Abner and Squire Randolph rode through the gap of the mountains to have the thing out with Doomdorf. The work of this brew, which had the odors of Eden and the impulses of the devil in it, could be borne no longer. The drunken Negroes had shot old Duncan's cattle and burned his haystacks, and the land was on its feet.

They rode alone, but they were worth an army of little men. Randolph was vain and pompous and given over to extravagance of words, but he was a gentleman beneath it, and fear was an alien and a stranger to him. And Abner was the right hand of the land.

It was a day in early summer and the sun lay hot. They crossed through the broken spine of the mountains and trailed along the river in the shade of the great chestnut trees. The road was only a path and the horses went one before the other. It left the river when the rock began to rise and, making a detour through the grove of peach trees, reached the house on the mountain side. Randolph and Abner got down, unsaddled their horses and turned them out to graze, for their business with Doomdorf would not be over in an hour. Then they took a steep path that brought them out on the mountain side of the house.

A man sat on a big red-roan horse in the paved court before the door. He was a gaunt old man. He sat bare-headed, the palms of his hands resting on the pommel of his saddle, his chin sunk in his black stock, his face in retrospection, the wind moving gently his great shock of voluminous white hair. Under him the huge red horse stood with his legs spread out like a horse of stone.

There was no sound. The door to the house was closed; insects moved in the sun; a shadow crept out from the motionless figure, and swarms of yellow butterflies maneuvered like an army.

Abner and Randolph stopped. They knew the tragic figure – a circuit rider of the hills who preached the invective of Isaiah as though he were the mouthpiece of a militant and avenging overlord; as though the government of Virginia were the awful theocracy of the Book of Kings. The horse was dripping with sweat and the man bore the dust and the evidences of a journey on him.

"Bronson," said Abner, "where is Doomdorf?"

The old man lifted his head and looked down at Abner over the pommel of the saddle.

"'Surely,'" he said, "'he covereth his feet in his summer chamber.'"

Abner went over and knocked on the closed door, and presently the white, frightened face of a woman looked out at him. She was a little, faded woman, with fair hair, a broad foreign face, but with the delicate evidences of gentle blood.

Abner repeated his question.

"Where is Doomdorf?"

"Oh, sir," she answered with a queer lisping accent, "he went to lie down in his south room after his midday meal, as his custom is; and I went to the orchard to gather any fruit that might be ripened." She hesitated and her voice lisped into a whisper: "He is not come out and I cannot wake him."

The two men followed her through the hall and up the stairway to the door.

"It is always bolted," she said, "when he goes to lie down." And she knocked feebly with the tips of her fingers.

There was no answer and Randolph rattled the doorknob.

"Come out, Doomdorf!" he called in his big, bellowing voice.

There was only silence and the echoes of the words among the rafters. Then Randolph set his shoulder to the door and burst it open.

They went in. The room was flooded with sun from the tall south windows. Doomdorf lay on a couch in a little offset of the room, a great scarlet patch on his bosom and a pool of scarlet on the floor.

The woman stood for a moment staring; then she cried out:

"At last I have killed him!" And she ran like a frightened hare.

The two men closed the door and went over to the couch.

Doomdorf had been shot to death. There was a great ragged hole in his waistcoat. They began to look about for the weapon with which the deed had been accomplished, and in a moment found it – a fowling piece lying in two dogwood forks against the wall. The gun had just been fired; there was a freshly exploded paper cap under the hammer.

There was little else in the room – a loom-woven rag carpet on the floor; wooden shutters flung back from the windows; a great oak table, and on it a big, round, glass water bottle, filled to its glass stopper with raw liquor from the still. The stuff was limpid and clear as spring water; and, but for its pungent odor, one would have taken it for God's brew instead of Doomdorf's. The sun lay on it and against the wall where hung the weapon that had ejected the dead man out of life.

"Abner," said Randolf, "this is murder! The woman took that gun down from the wall and shot Doomdorf while he slept."

Abner was standing by the table, his fingers round his chin.

"Randolph," he replied, "what brought Bronson here?"

"The same outrages that brought us," said Randolph. "The mad old circuit rider has been preaching a crusade against Doomdorf far and wide in the hills."

Abner answered, without taking his fingers from about his chin:

"You think this woman killed Doomdorf? Well, let us go and ask Bronson who killed him."

They closed the door, leaving the dead man on his couch, and went down into the court.

The old circuit rider had put away his horse and got an ax. He had taken off his coat and pushed his shirtsleeves up over his long elbows. He was on his way to the still to destroy the barrels of liquor. He stopped when the two men came out, and Abner called to him.

"Bronson," he said, "who killed Doomdorf?"

"I killed him," replied the old man, and went on toward the still.

Randolph swore under his breath. "By the Almighty," he said, "everybody couldn't kill him!"

"Who can tell how many had a hand in it?" replied Abner.

"Two have confessed!" cried Randolph. "Was there perhaps a third? Did you kill him, Abner? And I too? Man, the thing is impossible!"

"The impossible," replied Abner, "looks here like the truth. Come with me, Randolph, and I will show you a thing more impossible than this."

They returned through the house and up the stairs to the room. Abner closed the door behind them.

"Look at this bolt," he said; "it is on the inside and not connected with the lock. How did the one who killed Doomdorf get into this room, since the door was bolted?"

"Through the windows," replied Randolph.

There were but two windows, facing the south, through which the sun entered. Abner led Randolph to them.

"Look!" he said. "The wall of the house is plumb with the sheer face of the rock. It is a hundred feet to the river and the rock is as smooth as a sheet of glass. But that is not all. Look at these window frames; they are cemented into their casement with dust and they are bound along their edges with cobwebs. These windows have not been opened. How did the assassin enter?"

"The answer is evident," said Randolph: "The one who killed Doomdorf hid in the room until he was asleep; then he shot him and went out."

"The explanation is excellent but for one thing," replied Abner: "How did the assassin bolt the door behind him on the inside of this room after he had gone out?"

Randolph flung out his arms with a hopeless gesture.

"Who knows?" he cried. "Maybe Doomdorf killed himself."

Abner laughed.

"And after firing a handful of shot into his heart he got up and put the gun back carefully into the forks against the wall!"

"Well," cried Randolph, "there is one open road out of this mystery. Bronson and this woman say they killed Doomdorf, and if they killed him they surely know how they did it. Let us go down and ask them."

"In the law court," replied Abner, "that procedure would be considered sound sense; but we are in God's court and things are managed there in a somewhat stranger way. Before we go let us find out, if we can, at what hour it was that Doomdorf died."

He went over and took a big silver watch out of the dead man's pocket. It was broken by a shot and the hands lay at one hour after noon. He stood for a moment fingering his chin.

"At one o'clock," he said. "Bronson, I think, was on the road to this place, and the woman was on the mountain among the peach trees."

Randolph threw back his shoulders.

"Why waste time in a speculation about it, Abner?" he said. "We know who did this thing. Let us go and get the story of it out of their own mouths. Doomdorf died by the hands of either Bronson or this woman."

"I could better believe it," replied Abner, "but for the running of a certain awful law."

"What law?" said Randolph. "Is it a statute of Virginia?"

"It is a statute," replied Abner, "of an authority somewhat higher. Mark the language of it: 'He that killeth with the sword must be killed with the sword.'"

He came over and took Randolph by the arm.

"Must! Randolph, did you mark particularly the word 'must'? It is a mandatory law. There is no room in it for the vicissitudes of chance or fortune. There is no way round that word. Thus, we reap what we sow and nothing else; thus, we receive what we give and nothing else. It is the weapon in our own hands that finally destroys us. You are looking at it now." And he turned him about so that the table and the weapon and the dead man were before him. "'He that killeth with the sword must be killed with the sword.' And now," he said, "let us go and try the method of the law courts. Your faith is in the wisdom of their ways."

They found the old circuit rider at work in the still, staving in Doomdorf's liquor casks, splitting the oak heads with his ax.

"Bronson," said Randolph, "how did you kill Doomdorf?"

The old man stopped and stood leaning on his ax.

"I killed him," replied the old man, "as Elijah killed the captains of Ahaziah and their fifties. But not by the hand of any man did I pray the Lord God to destroy Doomdorf, but with fire from heaven to destroy him."

He stood up and extended his arms.

"His hands were full of blood," he said. "With his abomination from these groves of Baal he stirred up the people to contention, to strife and murder. The widow and the orphan cried to heaven against him. 'I will surely hear their cry,' is the promise written in the Book. The land was weary of him; and I prayed the Lord God to destroy him with fire from heaven, as he destroyed the Princes of Gomorrah in their palaces!"

Randolph made a gesture as of one who dismisses the impossible, but Abner's face took on a deep, strange look.

"With fire from heaven!" he repeated slowly to himself. Then he asked a question. "A little while ago," he said, "when we came, I asked you where Doomdorf was, and you answered me in the language of the third chapter of the Book of Judges. Why did you answer me like that, Bronson? – 'Surely he covereth his feet in his summer chamber.'"

"The woman told me that he had not come down from the room where he had gone up to sleep," replied the old man, "and that the door was locked. And then I knew that he was dead in his summer chamber like Eglon, King of Moab."

He extended his arm toward the south.

"I came here from the Great Valley," he said, "to cut down these groves of Baal and to empty out this abomination; but I did not know that the Lord had heard my prayer and visited His wrath on Doomdorf until I was come up into these mountains to his door. When the woman spoke I knew it." And he went away to his horse, leaving the ax among the ruined barrels.

Randolph interrupted.

"Come, Abner," he said; "this is wasted time. Bronson did not kill Doomdorf."

Abner answered slowly in his deep, level voice:

"Do you realize, Randolph, how Doomdorf died?"

"Not by fire from heaven, at any rate," said Randolph.

"Randolph," replied Abner, "are you sure?"

"Abner," cried Randolph, "you are pleased to jest, but I am in deadly earnest. A crime has been done here against the state. I am an officer of justice and I propose to discover the assassin if I can."

He walked away toward the house and Abner followed, his hands behind him and his great shoulders thrown loosely forward, with a grim smile about his mouth.

"It is no use to talk with the mad old preacher," Randolph went on. "Let him empty out the liquor and ride away. I won't issue a warrant against him. Prayer may be a handy implement to do a murder with, Abner, but it is not a deadly weapon under the statutes of Virginia. Doomdorf was dead when old Bronson got here with his Scriptural jargon. This woman killed Doomdorf. I shall put her to an inquisition."

"As you like," replied Abner. "Your faith remains in the methods of the law courts."

"Do you know of any better methods?" said Randolph.

"Perhaps," replied Abner, "when you have finished."

Night had entered the valley. The two men went into the house and set about preparing the corpse for burial. They got candles, and made a coffin, and put Doomdorf in it, and straightened out his limbs, and folded his arms across his shot-out heart. Then they set the coffin on benches in the hall.

They kindled a fire in the dining room and sat down before it, with the door open and the red firelight shining through on the dead man's narrow, everlasting house. The woman had put some cold meat, a golden cheese and a loaf on the table. They did not see her, but they heard her moving about the house; and finally, on the gravel court outside, her step and the whinny of a horse. Then she came in, dressed as for a journey. Randolph sprang up.

"Where are you going?" he said.

"To the sea and a ship," replied the woman. Then she indicated the hall with a gesture. "He is dead and I am free."

There was a sudden illumination in her face. Randolph took a step toward her. His voice was big and harsh.

"Who killed Doomdorf?" he cried.

"I killed him," replied the woman. "It was fair!"

"Fair!" echoed the justice. "What do you mean by that?"

The woman shrugged her shoulders and put out her hands with a foreign gesture.

"I remember an old, old man sitting against a sunny wall, and a little girl, and one who came and talked a long time with the old man, while the little girl plucked yellow flowers out of the grass and put them into her hair. Then finally the stranger gave the old man a gold chain and took the little girl away." She flung out her hands. "Oh, it was fair to kill him!" She looked up with a queer, pathetic smile.

"The old man will be gone by now," she said; "but I shall perhaps find the wall there, with the sun on it, and the yellow flowers in the grass. And now, may I go?"

It is a law of the story-teller's art that he does not tell a story. It is the listener who tells it. The story-teller does but provide him with the stimuli.

Randolph got up and walked about the floor. He was a justice of the peace in a day when that office was filled only by the landed gentry, after the English fashion; and the obligations of the law were strong on him. If he should take liberties with the letter of it, how could the weak and the evil be made to hold it in respect? Here was this woman before him a confessed assassin. Could he let her go?

Abner sat unmoving by the hearth, his elbow on the arm of his chair, his palm propping up his jaw, his face clouded in deep lines. Randolph was consumed with vanity and the weakness of ostentation, but he shouldered his duties for himself. Presently he stopped and looked at the woman, wan, faded like some prisoner of legend escaped out of fabled dungeons into the sun.

The firelight flickered past her to the box on the benches in the hall, and the vast, inscrutable justice of heaven entered and overcame him.

"Yes," he said. "Go! There is no jury in Virginia that would hold a woman for shooting a beast like that." And he thrust out his arm, with the fingers extended toward the dead man.

The woman made a little awkward curtsy.

"I thank you, sir." Then she hesitated and lisped, "But I have not shoot him."

"Not shoot him!" cried Randolph. "Why, the man's heart is riddled!"

"Yes, sir," she said simply, like a child. "I kill him, but have not shoot him."

Randolph took two long strides toward the woman.

"Not shoot him!" he repeated. "How then, in the name of heaven, did you kill Doomdorf?" And his big voice filled the empty places of the room.

"I will show you, sir," she said.

She turned and went away into the house. Presently she returned with something folded up in a linen towel. She put it on the table between the loaf of bread and the yellow cheese.

Randolph stood over the table, and the woman's deft fingers undid the towel from round its deadly contents; and presently the thing lay there uncovered.

It was a little crude model of a human figure done in wax with a needle thrust through the bosom.

Randolph stood up with a great intake of the breath.

"Magic! By the eternal!"

"Yes, sir," the woman explained, in her voice and manner of a child. "I have try to kill him many times – oh, very many times! – with witch words which I have remember; but always they fail. Then, at last, I make him in wax, and I put a needle through his heart; and I kill him very quickly."

It was as clear as daylight, even to Randolph, that the woman was innocent. Her little harmless magic was the pathetic effort of a child to kill a dragon. He hesitated a moment before he spoke, and then he decided like the gentleman he was. If it helped the child to believe that her enchanted straw had slain the monster – well, he would let her believe it.

"And now, sir, may I go?"

Randolph looked at the woman in a sort of wonder.

"Are you not afraid," he said, "of the night and the mountains, and the long road?"

"Oh no, sir," she replied simply. "The good God will be everywhere now."

It was an awful commentary on the dead man – that this strange half-child believed that all the evil in the world had gone out with him; that now that he was dead, the sunlight of heaven would fill every nook and corner.

It was not a faith that either of the two men wished to shatter, and they let her go. It would be daylight presently and the road through the mountains to the Chesapeake was open.

Randolph came back to the fireside after he had helped her into the saddle, and sat down. He tapped on the hearth for some time idly with the iron poker; and then finally he spoke.

"This is the strangest thing that ever happened," he said. "Here's a mad old preacher who thinks that he killed Doomdorf with fire from Heaven, like Elijah the Tishbite; and here is a simple child of a woman who thinks she killed him with a piece of magic of the Middle Ages – each as innocent of his death as I am. And, yet, by the eternal, the beast is dead!"

He drummed on the hearth with the poker, lifting it up and letting it drop through the hollow of his fingers.

"Somebody shot Doomdorf. But who? And how did he get into and out of that shut-up room? The assassin that killed Doomdorf must have gotten into the room to kill him. Now, how did he get in?" He spoke as to himself; but my uncle sitting across the hearth replied:

"Through the window."

"Through the window!" echoed Randolph. "Why, man, you yourself showed me that the window had not been opened, and the precipice below it a fly could hardly climb. Do you tell me now that the window was opened?"

"No," said Abner, "it was never opened."

Randolph got on his feet.

"Abner," he cried, "are you saying that the one who killed Doomdorf climbed the sheer wall and got in through a closed window, without disturbing the dust or the cobwebs on the window frame?"

My uncle looked Randolph in the face.

"The murderer of Doomdorf did even more," he said. "That assassin not only climbed the face of that precipice and got in through the closed window, but he shot Doomdorf to death and got out again through the closed window without leaving a single track or trace behind, and without disturbing a grain of dust or a thread of a cobweb."

Randolph swore a great oath.

"The thing is impossible!" he cried. "Men are not killed today in Virginia by black art or a curse of God."

"By black art, no," replied Abner; "but by the curse of God, yes. I think they are."

Randolph drove his clenched right hand into the palm of his left.

"By the eternal!" he cried. "I would like to see the assassin who could do a murder like this, whether he be an imp from the pit or an angel out of Heaven."

"Very well," replied Abner, undisturbed. "When he comes back tomorrow I will show you the assassin who killed Doomdorf."

When day broke they dug a grave and buried the dead man against the mountain among his peach trees. It was noon when that work was ended. Abner threw down his spade and looked up at the sun.

"Randolph," he said, "let us go and lay an ambush for this assassin. He is on the way here."

And it was a strange ambush that he laid. When they were come again into the chamber where Doomdorf died he bolted the door; then he loaded the fowling piece and put it carefully back on its rack against the wall. After that he did another curious thing: He took the blood-stained coat, which they had stripped off the dead man when they had prepared his body for the earth, put a pillow in it and laid it on the couch precisely where Doomdorf had slept. And while he did these things Randolph stood in wonder and Abner talked:

"Look you, Randolph . . . We will trick the murderer . . . We will catch him in the act."

Then he went over and took the puzzled justice by the arm.

"Watch!" he said. "The assassin is coming along the wall!"

But Randolph heard nothing, saw nothing. Only the sun entered. Abner's hand tightened on his arm.

"It is here! Look!" And he pointed to the wall.

Randolph, following the extended finger, saw a tiny brilliant disk of light moving slowly up the wall toward the lock of the fowling piece. Abner's hand became a vise and his voice rang as over metal.

"'He that killeth with the sword must be killed with the sword.' It is the water bottle, full of Doomdorf's liquid, focusing the sun . . . And look, Randolph, how Bronson's prayer was answered!"

The tiny disk of light traveled on the plate of the lock.

"It is fire from heaven!"

The words rang above the roar of the fowling piece, and Randolph saw the dead man's coat leap up on the couch, riddled by the shot. The gun, in its natural position on the rack, pointed to the couch standing at the end of the chamber, beyond the offset of the wall, and the focused sun had exploded the percussion cap.

Randolph made a great gesture, with his arm extended.

"It is a world," he said, "filled with the mysterious joinder of accident!"

"It is a world," replied Abner, "filled with the mysterious justice of God!"

# MURDER IN THE RUE ROYALE
# Michael Harrison

*Michael Harrison (1907–1991) was a writer in a variety of fields, but his passion was for mystery fiction, and particularly the world of Sherlock Holmes. He was regarded as one of the foremost Holmesian scholars.*

*The son of a lawyer and nephew of an architect, Michael sought to follow in his uncle's footsteps and studied architecture, but turned to writing and journalism when his first novel,* Weep for Lycidas *(1934), proved a success. Over the next fifty years he wrote over fifty books under his own name and several pseudonyms. Perhaps his most popular was his attempt at an autobiography by Holmes, called* I, Sherlock Holmes *(1977).*

*Harrison did not confine his research to the world of Holmes, but also explored Holmes's fictional predecessor, August Dupin, created by Edgar Allan Poe. He wrote a series of stories in the late 1960s for* Ellery Queen's Mystery Magazine. *A selection were published in America as* The Exploits of Chevalier Dupin *(1968), and then expanded for British publication as* Murder in the Rue Royale *(1972), and it is the title story which is reprinted here.*

*Harrison's Dupin reflects perhaps rather more of Holmes than the Poe original, but the stories are fascinating in themselves and provide us with an opportunity to revisit the world of the first ever fictional detective.*

The murder of Monsieur Cuvillier-Millot, the eminent banker, in his bedroom in the Rue Royale, caused what the newspapers are always pleased to call "a profound sensation." Even in a capital city which, as our friend G— would assure you, has the oldest and most efficient police in the world, crimes are still numerous, and murders not unknown.

Yet the *bizarre* character of this particular crime gave it, as it were, a *permanence* in the public consciousness which prevented its passing out of the public memory within the traditional period of nine days. All murder is, to a greater or lesser degree, a problem for those who are not killed; but this murder of Monsieur Cuvillier-Millot posed problems over and above those customarily inseparable from the violent taking of another's life.

For instance, how, in this case, did the murderer make his escape, from a window on the second floor, literally within seconds of his having fired the one shot which killed the well-known banker? Moreover, how had the assassin made his escape with such miraculous speed that those who forced open the door of the bedroom never caught a glimpse of him?

There were other puzzling features, of course, but these two questions were universally held to be the crucial ones compared with which all others were trifling. One might almost have dismissed the idea that there had been a murderer at all, save that there was a very real corpse in evidence, lying in Monsieur Cuvillier-Millot's four-poster bed, and that the bullet-wound in the back of the corpse's neck could hardly have been self-inflicted. (Were it even possible to suppose that, where then was the pistol which the deceased must have fired in the act of *felo-de-se?*)

The more one reflected upon the many puzzling features of this extraordinary crime, the more puzzling it appeared. The police, though promising a "speedy arrest," within twenty-four hours, as is usual in all cases where the murderer – or, at least, a promising suspect – is not safely lodged in the *Dépôt de la Préfecture de Police*, were obviously baffled. They could scarcely hunt for a suspect among the known burglars of Paris – nothing had been taken from the bedroom of Monsieur Cuvillier-Millot; and though it might have been argued that the thief (supposing the assassin to have been a thief) had been scared off before he had time to rob the banker, surely he had time to snatch up the valuables in plain sight – diamond ring, Bréguet watch and guard, diamond scarf-pin, and a liberally-stuffed pocketbook – which were lying on a dressing-table near the bed.

Then, as to motive, the only person – apart from a hypothetical burglar – who could conceivably have had an interest in the death of the banker was his nephew and presumed heir, who lived with Monsieur Cuvillier-Millot and who, indeed, had played a leading part in the events immediately preceding the discovery of his uncle's dead body. The deceased banker, a widower whose only son had been killed in the Algerian fighting, had sent to London for his sole nephew, the son of a Cuvillier-Millot who had fled to England during the Terror of '93, and, save for fleeting visits to his far wealthier brother in Paris, had never returned to the land of his birth. Gaspard Cuvillier-Millot, heir to the immense fortune of his murdered uncle, had attended one of those English schools which, removing to France after the Reformation, had returned to England more than two centuries later because of the troubles into which the Revolution of 1789 had plunged France.

Following a few terms at Oxford, young Monsieur Gaspard accepted a clerkship in the renowned banking-house of Herries, Farquhar & Co., of St. James's Street, London – a move not uncalculated, one felt, to bring him to the sympathetic notice of his prosperous Parisian uncle. In the London banking-house, whose circular and transferable exchange-notes have made it famous and influential throughout Europe, Monsieur Gaspard served with diligence, until the death of his cousin in a skirmish at Tlemcen brought him to Paris, to take the place of that son whom the banker had lost in military action.

So much of the history of this fortunate young man we owed to G—, the Prefect of the Parisian Police, who called on us just after breakfast two days after the murder which had set all Paris by the ears. Now, on this sunless Spring morning of the year 183–, G— sat in our little back library, or book-closet, *au troisième*, No. 33, Rue Dunôt, Faubourg St. Germain, sipped at his hot chocolate, and gave, generally, the impression of a man at his wits' end.

"When a banker is murdered," said G—, harshly peremptory in tone, as he always was when baffled and filled with anxiety for his reputation and his lucrative appointment under Government, "it involves a good deal more than merely his family. The repercussions on the Bourses of all the capitals of Europe – well, you understand me perfectly, I am sure, my dear Chevalier?"

"Yes, yes, I understand well," replied Dupin, stifling a yawn, for we had sat up late the night before. "Monsieur Cuvillier-Millot had just floated a loan for Brazil of eight million gold francs, another for New Granada of two million, another for Turkey of twenty million, and was about to raise one for Spain of thirty millions, to provide the Iberian Peninsula with a railroad system. Yes, I read the newspapers, too."

"You will know, then," said G—, in no wise abashed by my friend's curt manner, "that we are also too near to the social unrest of 1830 and 1832 not to feel alarmed when something – anything – casts doubt upon the stability of the *régime* under which we live. Two French Revolutions in less than fifty years are enough – but there are always Radical newspapers and irresponsible demagogues to raise the cry of corruption whenever something happens in the world of banking."

"I am well aware of this," said Dupin, reaching out for the heavy pewter tobacco-jar in which he kept his favorite Latakia. "As I am well aware," he added, beginning to fill his meerschaum pipe, "that you have come to ask my assistance in this matter because your own methods have not produced the hoped-for results. Very well, then: tell me what your own methods have yielded thus far."

"Very little, I am afraid," said G— candidly. "We have ascertained the cause of death – that goes without saying – "

"Indeed!" observed Dupin, though with a strong hint of sarcasm in his intonation. He puffed furiously at his pipe, so that it was almost as if from within a cloud that we heard his voice ask, with a deceptive mildness, "And what, pray, was the cause of Monsieur Cuvillier-Millot's death?"

"Why, it was in all the newspapers – "

"I am not concerned with what the newspapers print, or with what I read in their columns. I am asking *you*. What was the cause of the banker's death?"

"Why, a pistol-shot fired into the base of the skull."

"You have recovered the ball?"

"No."

"Why not?"

"Well now, Dupin, why should we have probed for the ball? It was evident beyond doubt what had killed the banker."

"You mean, by that remark, that the usual *sequelæ* of a pistol-shot were present – powder-burns around the wound, blackening of the skin around the point of entry of the ball, and so on?"

"Precisely," replied G—, with a little grimace of self-satisfaction and self-congratulation.

"There has been no *post-mortem* examination of the cadaver?"

"*Que diable*, Dupin! Of course not. Where the cause of death is so self-evident, why on earth should we offend both the living and the dead by anatomizing the corpse? I tell you, the man died of a bullet-wound in the top of his spinal column, immediately under the cerebellum – *here*!" And suiting the action to the word, G— bent his head forward and placed the index finger of his right hand on the spot indicated, a half-inch or so above the upper edge of his tall, starched neckcloth. "In such a place, a bullet-wound is, as you well know, inevitably fatal."

"In such a confoundedly difficult place against which to place the muzzle of a pistol, common justice would hardly deny the assassin the reward of a fatal assault. But tell me, my dear G—, what was the eminent victim doing all this time that the assassin was getting behind him? Was the shot in the back of the neck accidentally aimed there? Was the wound the result of a *ricochet*? Or – stay!! – was the victim perhaps asleep at the time?"

"No," said G—, with a vigorous shake of his head, "that is

impossible. It was the noise of voices raised in some altercation which brought the members of the household – I should say, rather, the *other* members of the household – hurrying toward the door of Monsieur Cuvillier-Millot's bedroom – only, of course, to find it locked, so that the door had to be forced. It was while they were standing outside, debating what to do, that the fatal shot was heard. The door was then attacked vigorously by a couple of footmen – well-built farmer lads from Normandy – and broken open. Their master was lying on his bed – a corpse – and the assassin was nowhere to be seen."

"And the window, you say, was open?"

"With the dimity curtains blowing in – the heavy drapes had been pulled back. On entering the room of death, some hurried to see what might be done for the victim, others ran to the window. But, scan the surrounding courtyards and streets as they would, they saw no sign of anyone who might have escaped from the bedroom, after having murdered their master. And that, Dupin, is what makes the whole affair so very mysterious."

"What, precisely, makes this affair so very mysterious? Are you referring to the fact that, on looking through an open window, no one was seen? I find that possibly the least mysterious fact of all. Now," as he saw that G— was about to protest, "let us consider this matter of the fatal shot, as you call it – "

"As *I* call it!"

"As you call it. Whatever you and your colleagues may have surmised, it is still to be proven that the fatal shot was heard – or, rather that what was heard was the fatal shot."

"But a shot *was* heard. We have a dozen witnesses to depose to that fact."

"Possibly. Possibly not. A dozen witnesses may be as wrong as one. Suppose now that *you* tell *me* what it was these twelve witnesses claim to have heard?"

"Well, let us begin somewhat farther back. I shall briefly mention that it is Monsieur Gaspard's custom to rise earlier than the time at which his uncle stirs, so that he may be downstairs at his desk a few minutes before the bank opens for business at 8:30 A.M. He does not – at least customarily – look in on his uncle, who is called by his valet at half-past seven, with a tray of chocolate and rolls and a morning newspaper.

"However, as Monsieur Gaspard walked along the corridor on his way to the bathroom – yes, there is a modern bathroom, fitted with all the latest conveniences, even to a patent English contrivance for heating water by gas – on his way to this bathroom, I say, of which he takes good advantage judging by his fastidious appearance, Monsieur

Gaspard passed the door of his uncle's bedroom. The door, though of solid mahogany, is not particularly thick, and sounds within the room may be heard by anyone in the corridor. Monsieur Gaspard tells me that he has often heard his uncle's snores as he passed the door.

"Now – to-day is Thursday, so that all this would have happened on Tuesday last – on Tuesday, then, something much out of the ordinary occurred. Monsieur Gaspard rose – I forgot to tell you that no servant calls him; he is awakened by a small alarum-clock which stands on his bed-side table – Monsieur Gaspard rose as usual, donned his *robe de chambre*, went out into the corridor, and walked along in the direction of the bathroom."

"All precisely as usual?"

"All precisely as usual. But – certainly not as usual – were the sounds coming through the door of his uncle's bedroom – sounds of angry voices, of reproaches, of threats, of I don't-know-what. Monsieur Gaspard stopped at once; he has a natural delicacy in such matters, and hardly relished the thought of listening at his uncle's door – "

"Or of being detected in the act of doing so? No matter. Pray proceed with your narrative, which I find most interesting."

"At any rate, as Monsieur Gaspard listened, he became aware that the altercation sounded as though it were approaching a climax. He could distinguish no words, but it was clear that two men were angry, and one was menacing the other.

"Monsieur Gaspard became alarmed, and ran rather to get advice than to get help. He hurried down stairs, and poured out his story to the old *suisse*, who has been with the household since before the first Revolution."

"You have taken this man's evidence, of course?"

"Yes – and the evidence of all who were in a position to be witnesses. Well, to proceed: the *suisse* expressed the view that all should repair, with the utmost despatch, to the bed-room, and there call out – in case Monsieur Cuvillier-Millot required assistance in repelling anyone who was threatening him."

"One moment, please! Why did not Monsieur Gaspard open the door of his uncle's bedroom, and just walk in?"

"He says that he had a nervousness as regards his uncle. The banker was rather a martinet, a domestic tyrant. I can well believe that the nephew may have hesitated to expose himself to the shame of an embarrassing situation. In any case, as was proved later, the door was locked."

"Yes, but he cannot say whether or not the bedroom-door was

locked when he passed it – or, say, when he halted to listen to the stranger menacing his uncle."

"No, he cannot say. I put the question to him, but he could not answer it, one way or the other."

"Hem! So, merely observing that this precious Monsieur Gaspard strikes me as rather a poltroon, let us go on. The *suisse* had no sooner been asked his advice by this far too fastidious nephew than the domestic called for the footmen, and, probably accompanied now by the other servants, led the party to the door of their master's bedroom. Or – stay! – did Monsieur Gaspard, shamed into at least the affectation of resolution, lead the way? Ah, he did lead! Good! And what did the *suisse* and all the domestics have to tell you of the quality of the voices heard through the strong but thin door?"

"Well now, here we strike a formidable difficulty. I had hoped that we might have some evidence which would help us to trace the assassin through someone's recognition of his voice."

"But now there was only silence? The voices had ceased?"

"Just so."

"The banker was dead – and the assassin had fled through the window?"

"Impossible! Just as Monsieur Gaspard and the footmen were readying themselves to break open the door – I mentioned, did I not, that Monsieur Gaspard tried the handle and found the door locked? – just as they had come to the decision to break down the door – "

"One moment, please! *Why* had they come to this serious decision? Did they not first call out and ask Monsieur Cuvillier-Millot if aught were wrong? Ah, you forgot to mention that? Pray continue."

"You were right to remind me of what I had overlooked. It is true that when the group arrived outside the door, Monsieur Gaspard called out, several times, 'Uncle, is anything the matter?' – or words to that effect. But there was no answer; and, at a sign from Monsieur Gaspard, the footmen then advanced to throw themselves against the door. At that moment the shot was heard – just one shot; very clear, though not, as the witnesses say, very loud."

"But unmistakably a shot? On which, with commendable courage – for the man with the firearm might have been waiting inside the bedroom for *them* – the footmen hurled themselves against the door, the lock broke, the door opened, and they fell headlong into the room, to see what you have already described to me – nothing. Now, a most important point. After the shot had been fired, did anyone hear the footsteps of the assassin as he ran across the room to the window? Did anyone hear the window opened?"

"No. The reason is easy to comprehend. On hearing the shot, the female domestics, led by the cook, set up such a cry of shock and terror that an army might have tramped across the room and gone unheard."

"So! And though but one person – Monsieur Gaspard – can testify that voices were raised in quarrel, many can testify that a shot was fired immediately before the door was broken down?"

"All, in fact, who were present. Not only did they hear the report of the firearm, they entered a room full of smoke, to say nothing of the characteristic odor of gunpowder."

"We must recover the ball – if it still be in the dead man's head. Is it?"

"Is it still in the dead man's head? Yes, there is but one wound – that of entry. Evidently the ball did not penetrate with sufficient force to pass through the skull."

"Do you not find that fact remarkable?" Dupin asked.

"How so? It merely means that the charge was a light one; the muscles at the back of the head are very thick and tough – I have known many cases where they have stopped a ball."

"Perhaps. But have you known them to stop a ball fired against the skin? No matter, all these points will be resolved later. What I should like you first to do is to cause a police surgeon to probe for the bullet, and – having found it – to remove it without damaging it in any way. Can this be done?"

G— looked dubious. "The family's friends will not approve. The dead banker is even now lying in state in his drawing-room. But – yes, of course, Dupin, you shall have the bullet. Why do you wish it?"

"I desire to know the type of firearm from which it came."

Dupin and I were present when the two surgeons attached to the Prefecture of Police carried out the *post-mortem* examination of the deceased banker. The formal permission of the dead man's nearest relative – in this case, Monsieur Gaspard – had to be obtained; but, though the young man began to voice objections, G— soon silenced them by representing the necessity of the autopsy in the interests of justice.

The cadaver was decently carried into a small room adjoining the drawing-room, and here the surgeons prepared to extract the ball in whose nature Dupin had evinced so keen an interest.

The corpse had, of course, been washed, and made presentable by those cosmetic arts in which our modern morticians excel.

Having expressed a wish to examine the body – but more particularly the head – before the surgeons cut into it with their scalpels and bistouries, Dupin went carefully over the entire anatomy with a strong magnifying glass. Rising from the most minute inspection of the wound in the neck, Dupin asked G— if the witnesses who had first discovered the body had noticed the characteristic blackening of a gunshot wound.

"Yes, without doubt. It is not present now, I see, but the undertaker's woman would have washed the burnt powder off."

"So thoroughly? The skin, too, does not appear to have been scorched at all. *Diable*, this is a most singular wound to have been caused by a pistol-ball! Monsieur le Préfet, a word with you, please."

Dupin led the Prefect to the far corner of the room, out of hearing of the surgeons, and said, "Unless this household is very different from other households, the washing will be done on a Monday. Today is Thursday. Let an *agent* be instructed to impound all the dirty linen at present awaiting the week's wash. What shall he look for? Well, in the first place, a particularly dirty handkerchief."

No more would Dupin say on this point; and when G—, after having issued the requisite instructions, came back to the room, Dupin took him by the arm and called his attention to the wound, handing over his powerful magnifying glass so that G— might see what my friend had already noticed.

"Observe," said Dupin, "the curious reddening, in perfectly circular form, which rims the wound. This is *not* the customary scorching which occurs with gunshot wounds, but something altogether different. Another point: has either of you gentlemen" – addressing himself to the surgeons – "ever known of a case where, the weapon being brought sufficiently close to the body to cause scorching, there was not some serious derangement of the skin, caused by the escape of gases into the wound opened by the ball? No, gentlemen, and neither have I. Monsieur G— suggested that the curious nature of this wound might be due to the assassin's having used only a small charge of powder – for what reason, I cannot suggest. It may be so. But now, let us proceed."

"To open the cranium, sir?" the elder of the two surgeons asked, a scalpel in his hand.

"Not yet, sir. First, I should like the stomach evacuated. We have with us, I take it, a stomach-pump?"

A stomach-pump having been produced the contents of the dead man's stomach were soon transferred to a covered dish, and to this disagreeable material, Dupin, to whom, in the interests of justice, nothing proved an obstacle, gave his minute attention. Indeed, it was with an air of noticeable triumph that he turned to us, and said, "I am astonished that we did not smell it on the man's breath! What, Monsieur G— ! You, with your sharp scent! Yes, gentlemen – laudanum, and in a very copious draught. Of one thing we may be sure, our dead banker was not very coherent at half-past seven on Tuesday morning, no matter what Monsieur Gaspard heard through the closed door.

"Did the dead man's physician prescribe laudanum? No matter, we shall find out. And now, before you cut, gentlemen, may I beg of you *very carefully* to probe the wound, and tell me exactly how far beneath the surface the ball is lying?"

Watched by a puzzled G— and (I confess it) by a no more enlightened me, the senior surgeon introduced a fine but strong wire probe into the wound, and pushed it gently forward until, encountering an unyielding surface, he assumed that the ball had been reached. Noting the length of wire which had entered the wound before reaching the ball, Dupin quickly translated this length, by means of a pocket rule, into terms of centimetres.

"Just over seven-and-a-half centimetres – three inches" – for, in those days, the old measurements were more commonly employed than the new. "Now, gentlemen, cut, if you please – and I beg of you not to damage the ball in any way."

After a few minutes of the surgeons' grisly labors a leaden ball was placed in Dupin's hand. He examined it with his powerful glass, and uttered a small cry of satisfaction before proffering both ball and glass to G—.

"What do you see, Monsieur le Préfet?"

"How very – how *excessively* – odd!" said G—, staring at the ball resting on his thick palm. "It is – how *very* curious! I see what appears to be a set of teeth-marks in a small circle. Dupin, how do you explain this? Could the firing of the pistol have marked the lead of the ball in this most unusual way?"

Dupin did not answer. Taking back the ball from G—, he dropped it into a pocket of his waistcoat, and said briskly. "The body can now be restored to a seemly appearance, and taken back for its lying-in-state. Monsieur G—, I should be infinitely obliged by a sight of the dead man's sleeping chamber, and, in particular, of the cupboard in which he kept his medicines."

"We walked up stairs, having dismissed the servants who, out of well-trained habit, sought to accompany us. Dupin carefully surveyed the room in which Monsieur Cuvillier-Millot had died.

One had the impression, in watching my friend at work, that those eyes of his observed everything – what was of importance, and what was not – and took away a complete record of visual, auditory, and tactile impressions (not forgetting, of course, the olfactory), to be analyzed and indexed at leisure, over his favorite pipe, in the peace of our little book-closet in the Rue Dunôt.

As we walked across the room to the small dressing-room adjoining, in which it was to be presumed that Monsieur Cuvillier-Millot had kept his medicines, Dupin said idly, "You will already have made some inquiries relative to the character and standing of Monsieur Gaspard? I venture to suggest that you have uncovered some scandalous information?"

"Indeed. I can hardly believe he would have continued in his uncle's favor had the news of his extravagances and debts come to the ears of the worthy banker. What is more, he was – is, I suppose one should say – being strongly pressed for settlement. There is an expensive young person with whom he has contracted one of those alliances generally as costly as they are irregular. However, he may now whistle at his creditors, with all the banker's millions in his pocket. A happy accident – for him, I mean – that the assassin should have put a fortune in his way."

"I see," said Dupin, opening the medicine-chest, which stood on a side-table, "that the late Monsieur Cuvillier-Millot was obviously not a valetudinarian. There is no medicine here that one would not find in most if not all households. Indeed, there is much absent that one might expect to find. Flowers of sulphur. I take this blood-purifier myself. So, I imagine, do most people. Chlorate of potash. Excellent as a throat-gargle. But did Monsieur Cuvillier-Millot suffer from sore throats?

"I can find out. But I suggest that, as he sang in the choir of La Madeleine – yes, he did; does that surprise you? – he had a constant use for chlorate of potash. What else? No laudanum. Well, I hardly expected it. But we shall find it somewhere in the house."

We walked to the window through which the assassin had made his miraculous escape. We opened the casements and leaned out. It was difficult indeed to see how the man could have escaped at all, let alone so quickly that no one had even seen him. I expressed my opinion, and G— concurred.

"When I shall have explained that to you," Dupin said, with a smile, "you will be in possession of all the facts in this extraordinary case. Now I have seen what I need to see. With your permission, Monsieur le Préfet, I shall borrow this iron door-stop."

"Door-stop? But why should you wish to borrow that?"

"When you call at our house this afternoon at five o'clock, precisely, you shall find out why. May I call your attention to this splendid clock on the mantel-shelf? Yes, by Bréguet, of course.

I wonder if, with all this upset, the servant entrusted with the duty has remembered to wind it? Now, where is the key? Ah, yes, here it is – in its proper place behind the clock."

Dupin held it up for the attention of our perfectly mystified eyes. It was an ordinary steel clock-key, of the fashion of some fifty years or more earlier, but of a type which is still favored by the horologists of Paris. A short tube, which fitted into a hole in the clock's face, was attached to a little crank-handle, with a polished wooden knob.

Dupin took out his pocket-glass and most minutely examined this commonplace article of domestic use. "Indeed, someone is to be felicitated on the care with which even the clock-key has been wiped. Still, I have a use for this, and I shall also borrow it, if I may."

"You may borrow what you like, Dupin," said G— in a surly tone. "Your whimsicalities are quite beyond my poor powers of comprehension. But I'm not so sure the servants haven't been upset by all this to-do – in spite of what you say. For instance, that door-stop that you propose to borrow: I take it that you didn't notice that it was not standing by the door, but had been moved to the fire-place – within the steel-fender?"

"Ah!" said Dupin, with a pleased expression, "so you *did* notice that! Bravo! Did you also notice another trivial proof of the servants' unusual neglect – this?"

"What is it?" said G—, coming closer, to peer at the object which my friend was holding between two fingers. "Ah, yes. What is it? A short length of black pack-thread? Is it important? Where did you find it?"

"It may be important. And I found it caught in the handle of the bell-pull just to the side of the fire-place."

At Dupin's request I did not accompany him back to our house, but made my way idly in the direction of the river. I walked down the Rue Royale, crossed the Rue St. Honoré, and, finding myself in the Place de la Concorde, obeyed a whim and paid my ten sous to enter the Navalorama, a spectacle I had never seen before.

This ingenious naval panorama, at the entrance of the Champs Elysées, exhibits a truly convincing representation of some of the most famous battles of history, from Salamis to Navarino, with the vessels and the water in motion, and the guns firing most realistically. So full of interest did I find this panorama – one of the many in Paris – that the time passed quickly, and I had to hail a *fiacre* in order to keep my appointment with Dupin and G— in the Faubourg St. Germain.

The clock in the belfry of St. Germain-des-Prés was just striking five as I entered the vestibule of our house, where I was greeted by Hyacinthe with the intelligence that G— had already arrived – a supererogatory piece of news, since I had seen G—'s spanking English tilbury in our courtyard; and that Monsieur le Chevalier awaited me in the drawing room.

"Bravo!" said Dupin sarcastically, as I entered the drawingroom. "You are learning the English idea of punctuality – which is to be so punctiliously on time as to give the impression of being late! However, since we are now all present, let us go upstairs to our little back library. I am sorry, Monsieur G—, to put you under the necessity of climbing another pair of stairs, but I have something above well worth your seeing. Pray follow me, please."

Obviously in obedience to some instructions given to him while I was absent, Hyacinthe did not accompany us; and, with Dupin leading the way, we came at last to our favorite room on the third floor. The door, as usual, was closed.

Dupin placed his hand on the door-knob, but, no sooner had he done so than a loud report, as of a pistol's discharge, sounded from within the room.

Dupin flung wide the door, and shouted, "The assassin! After him!!"

The window was open – the muslin curtains billowing in the breeze from without and the draught of the opened door from within. Dupin literally hurled himself across the room, to lean half out of the casement, pointing his finger downward, and gesticulating wildly. We crowded after him, thrust ourselves to each side of him, to catch a glance of – what?

"He has vanished!" said Dupin, with a comical expression of disgust. "He must have – no, he cannot have hooked his finger nails into the cracks in the brickwork – yes, I have it! – he must have escaped in one of Mr. Green's balloons. Quick, G—, look up, to see if you can catch a sight of the miscreant disappearing into the clouds!"

G— threw himself into a *fauteuil* with an angry exclamation.

"*Peste!*" he said. "Is this another of your jokes, Dupin? It *is* a joke, of course?"

"If so," replied my friend, with a severe expression, "it is a joke which has cost Monsieur Cuvillier-Millot his life. It was upon certain evidence of eyes, ears, and noses that a theory has been built up of an assassin, striking when Monsieur Gaspard – the man who stood most to gain by the dead banker's decease – was in full sight of a dozen trustworthy witnesses. *He* did not fire the shot. Oh, no! How could he have done so, when the shot was fired on the other side of a locked door?

"But tell me, Monsieur le Préfet, did *you* not hear a shot? Do *you* not smell the burnt gunpowder? Did you not see an open window, and jump instantly to the conclusion – placed so cunningly by *me* into *your* head – that there *must* have been someone who had fired the shot, and that someone *must* have escaped through the window, since he was not visible within the room?

"However, now it is different, is it not? A moment's reflection showed you the impossibility of someone's having escaped through a window so far above the ground, and with no tree or other means by which a man, however agile, could have got away so rapidly. You asked me if this were a joke? It is not a joke. Had you asked me, was this a trick, I should have answered – yes."

"You imply," said G— thoughtfully, "that Monsieur Gaspard is the murderer whom we seek?"

"Monsieur Gaspard," said Dupin decisively, "is without doubt the murderer. He had the motive, the means, and the opportunity, as I propose to demonstrate – though you will have to trick him, as he has tricked you, to extract from him the admission of guilt that you need. Did you find, in the dirty linen, a very dirty handkerchief?"

"Yes. I have it here." G— took a packet from the tails of his coat and handed it to Dupin, who opened it eagerly, examined it, and then put his nose to it.

"Excellent! This is mere lamp-black, since it smells of burnt spermaceti, such as is consumed in lamps, and not of burnt gunpowder. Monsieur Gaspard almost deserved to succeed in his diabolical plan, he was so clever. He used, for the planned killing of his uncle, only such things as were to be found in the house. No traceable purchases of arsenic for him! Lamp-black from an ordinary lamp, to smear around the wound! No, not a single substance or object which was not readily to hand in the mansion."

"But how in heaven's name did he shoot his uncle!" G— cried. Dupin smiled.

"He did not shoot his uncle. *Monsieur Cuvillier-Millot was not shot*. Look at this small piece of plaster-of-Paris: it is a cast of the ball extracted from the dead man's skull."

G— took it, and examined it.

"Why, yes, here are the indentations – the ring of indentations – that I noticed on the ball when it was first extracted by the surgeons. Now this cast shows the indentations as small teeth, sticking up. *Peste!* what does that ring of teeth remind me of?"

"Of *this*, I suggest," said Dupin, producing the clock-key, and indicating the ratchet at the end of the small tube.

"Dupin, what are you suggesting?"

"You will find," said Dupin calmly, "that Monsieur Gaspard, though he did not enter his uncle's room in the morning, did take in his evening cup of spiced wine. On the evening before the discovery of the murder the wine was even more heavily spiced – with laudanum. If the dead man did not use laudanum, you will find it somewhere in the house.

"Then, at some time in the early morning – but not too early – Monsieur Gaspard entered his uncle's bedroom, took a ball, turned the drugged man until he was face downward, and tapped the ball, using a hammer doubtless muffled in cloth, into the unconscious uncle's brain, with the end of the clock-key. This end is about three inches long – and only to that extent was the ball driven into the head; though that was enough to cause death. He wiped the key – there will be blood as well as lamp-black on the handkerchief – and replaced the key behind the clock. He then set up an ingenious device to trick the domestics a few hours later; then, after opening the window, he left the room and locked the door.

"At his customary time of rising he ran downstairs to report the angry voices within his uncle's room – though, of course, poor Monsieur Cuvillier-Millot had then been dead some two hours or so.

"Monsieur Gaspard, having collected all the servants as witnesses, then approached the door. The witnesses will testify that a shot was heard, and the door was then forced open.

"In strict truth, the shot was heard *as* Monsieur Gaspard put his hand on the door-knob; for all he did was to put his finger under the black pack-thread which had been passed *through* the key-hole and *over* the handle of the bell-pull to the side of the fire-place, and which held – by a quick-release hitch such as sailors or horsemen use – this iron door-stop I borrowed, and that you may now return to the house in the Rue Royale.

"The door-stop, released by the quick-release hitch, fell straight down into the steel-fender which surrounds the fireplace. But – and take careful note of this – it fell on to a mixture of two very ordinary substances, to be found in the medicine-chests in most homes: chlorate of potash and flowers of sulphur, a mixture so highly explosive that it takes but a light blow to detonate it."

"*Diable*! Of course!"

"The bang – the smell of sulphur – the open window – who would not have sworn, on twenty Bibles, that he had heard a shot fired, and been just too late to spy the assassin, detected almost – but not quite – *in flagrante delicto*?

"By the way, with his commendable proclivity for using only

the tools to hand, Monsieur Gaspard will have cast himself a ball with the bullet-mould to be found in the case of pistols kept in the library, or gunroom if there is one. Examination under a microscope will establish the origin of the ball taken from the dead banker's head."

G— coughed.

"Dupin . . . excuse me, but since you have helped me thus far, tell me: how shall I bring the fact of his guilt home to this most ingenious ruffian?"

Dupin smiled, and reached for the tobacco-jar.

"Well, my dear G—, you might begin by re-staging the charade with which I startled and annoyed you a few minutes ago. Even Monsieur Gaspard's aplomb might be so shaken to hear *another* pistol-shot in his dead uncle's bedroom that you might well obtain his confession . . ."

It was so. Three months later, despite the advocacy of those Solons of the French Bar whom Monsieur Gaspard retained to defend him, a melancholy procession set out one morning for a certain space within the Barrière de St. Jacques, and here a dastardly assassin paid the ultimate penalty.

# THE GENTLEMAN FROM PARIS
## John Dickson Carr

*This story is another tribute to Edgar Allan Poe and is written by the world's master of the impossible crime. Whether writing under his own name or as Carter Dickson, Carr (1906–1977) produced time and again a masterful series of locked-room mysteries, of which the following is a fine example. Carr was one of the pioneers of the historical detective novel, the best being* The Bride of Newgate *(1950) and* The Devil in Velvet *(1955), though he remains best known for his series of novels about Dr. Gideon Fell, a rather overweight and pompous detective who nevertheless had a talent for solving the impossible. The* Hollow Man *(1935) contains a chapter where Carr provides the definitive lecture on locked-room mysteries, a study which has yet to be bettered.*

Carlton House Hotel
Broadway, New York
14 April 1849

M y dear brother:
    Were my hand more steady, Maurice, or my soul less agitated, I should have written to you before this. *All is safe*: so much I tell you at once. For the rest, I seek sleep in vain; and this is not merely because I find myself a stranger and a foreigner in New York. Listen and judge.

We discussed, I think, the humiliation that a Frenchman must go to England ere he could take passage in a reliable ship for America. The *Britannia* steam-packet departed from Liverpool on the second of the month, and arrived here on the seventeenth. Do not smile, I implore you, when I tell you that my first visit on American soil was to Platt's Saloon, under Wallack's Theater.

Great God, that voyage!

On my stomach I could hold not even champagne. For one of my height and breadth I was as weak as a child.

"Be good enough," I said to a fur-capped coachman, when I had struggled through the horde of Irish immigrants, "to drive me to some fashionable place of refreshment."

The coachman had no difficulty in understanding my English, which pleased me. And how extraordinary are these "saloons"!

The saloon of M. Platt was loud with the thump of hammers cracking ice, which is delivered in large blocks. Though the hand-colored gas globes, and the rose paintings on the front of the bar-counter, were as fine as we could see at the Three Provincial Brothers in Paris, yet I confess that the place did not smell so agreeably. A number of gentlemen, wearing hats perhaps a trifle taller than is fashionable at home, lounged at the bar-counter and shouted. I attracted no attention until I called for a sherry cobbler.

One of the "bartenders," as they are called in New York, gave me a sharp glance as he prepared the glass.

"Just arrived from the Old Country, I bet?" he said in no unfriendly tone.

Though it seemed strange to hear France mentioned in this way, I smiled and bowed assent.

"Italian, maybe?" said he.

This bartender, of course, could not know how deadly was the insult.

"Sir," I replied, "I am a Frenchman."

And now in truth he was pleased! His fat face opened and smiled like a distorted, gold-toothed flower.

"Is that so, now!" he exclaimed. "And what might your name be? Unless" – and here his face darkened with that sudden defensiveness and suspicion which, for no reason I can discern, will often strike into American hearts – "unless," said he, "you don't want to give it?"

"Not at all," I assured him earnestly. "I am Armand de Lafayette, at your service."

My dear brother, what an extraordinary effect!

It was silence. All sounds, even the faint whistling of the gas jets, seemed to die away in that stone-flagged room. Every man along the line of the bar was looking at me. I was conscious only of faces, mostly with whiskers under the chin instead of down the cheekbones, turned on me in basilisk stare.

"Well, well, well!" almost sneered the bartender. "You wouldn't be no relation of the *Marquis* de Lafayette, would you?"

It was my turn to be astonished. Though our father has always forbidden us to mention the name of our late uncle, due to his republican sympathies, yet I knew he occupied small place in the history of France and it puzzled me to comprehend how these people had heard of him.

"The late Marquis de Lafayette," I was obliged to admit, "was my uncle."

"You better be careful, young feller," suddenly yelled a grimy little man with a pistol buckled under his long coat. "We don't like being diddled, we don't."

"Sir," I replied, taking my bundle of papers from my pocket and whacking them down on the bar-counter, "have the goodness to examine my credentials. Should you still doubt my identity, we can then debate the matter in any way which pleases you."

"This is furrin writing," shouted the bartender. "*I* can't read it!"

And then – how sweet was the musical sound on my ear! – I heard a voice addressing me in my own language.

"Perhaps, sir," said the voice, in excellent French and with great stateliness, "I may be able to render you some small service."

The newcomer, a slight man of dark complexion, drawn up under an old shabby cloak of military cut, stood a little way behind me. If I had met him on the boulevards, I might not have found him very prepossessing. He had a wild and wandering eye, with an even wilder shimmer of brandy. He was not very steady on his feet. And yet, Maurice, his manner! It was such that I instinctively raised my hat, and the stranger very gravely did the same.

"And to whom," said I, "have I the honor . . .?"

"I am Thaddeus Perley, sir, at your service."

"Another furriner!" said the grimy little man, in disgust.

"I am indeed a foreigner!" said M. Perley in English, with an accent like a knife. "A foreigner to this dram shop. A foreigner to this neighborhood. A foreigner to – " Here he paused, and his eyes acquired an almost frightening blaze of loathing. "Yet I never heard that the reading of French was so very singular an accomplishment."

Imperiously – and yet, it seemed to me, with a certain shrinking nervousness – M. Perley came closer and lifted the bundle of papers.

"Doubtless," he said loftily, "I should not be credited were I to translate these. But here," and he scanned several of the papers, "is a letter of introduction in English. It is addressed to President Zachary Taylor from the American minister at Paris."

Again, my brother, what an enormous silence! It was interrupted by a cry from the bartender, who had snatched the documents from M. Perley.

"Boys, this is no diddle," said he. "This gent is the real thing!"

"He ain't!" thundered the little grimy man, with incredulity.

"He is!" said the bartender. "I'll be a son of a roe *(i.e., biche)* if he ain't!"

Well, Maurice, you and I have seen how Paris mobs can change. Americans are even more emotional. In the wink of an eye hostility became frantic affection. My back was slapped, my hand wrung, my person jammed against the bar by a crowd fighting to order me more refreshment.

The name of Lafayette, again and again, rose like a holy diapason. In vain I asked why this should be so. They appeared to think I was joking, and roared with laughter. I thought of M. Thaddeus Perley, as one who could supply an explanation.

But in the first rush toward me M. Perley had been flung backward. He fell sprawling in some wet stains of tobacco juice on the floor, and now I could not see him at all. For myself, I was weak from lack of food. A full beaker of whisky, which I was obliged to drink because all eyes were on me, made my head reel. Yet I felt compelled to raise my voice above the clamor.

"Gentlemen," I implored them, "will you hear me?"

"Silence for Lafayette!" said a big but very old man, with faded red whiskers. He had tears in his eyes, and he had been humming a catch called "Yankee Doodle." "Silence for Lafayette!"

"Believe me," said I, "I am full of gratitude for your hospitality. But I have business in New York, business of immediate and desperate urgency. If you will allow me to pay my reckoning . . ."

"Your money's no good here, monseer," said the bartender. "You're going to get liquored-up good and proper."

"But I have no wish, believe me, to become liquored up! It might well endanger my mission! In effect, I wish to go!"

"Wait a minute," said the little grimy man, with a cunning look. "What *is* this here business?"

You, Maurice, have called me quixotic. I deny this. You have also called me imprudent. Perhaps you are right; but what choice was left to me?

"Has any gentleman here," I asked, "heard of Mme Thevenet? Mme Thevenet, who lives at Number 23 Thomas Street, near Hudson Street?"

I had not, of course, expected an affirmative reply. Yet, in addition to one or two sniggers at mention of the street, several nodded their heads.

"Old miser woman?" asked a sportif character, who wore checkered trousers.

"I regret, sir, that you correctly describe her. Mme Thevenet is very rich. And I have come here," cried I, "to put right a damnable injustice!"

Struggle as I might, I could not free myself.

"How's that?" asked half a dozen.

"Mme Thevenet's daughter, Mlle Claudine, lives in the worst of poverty at Paris. Madame herself has been brought here, under some spell, by a devil of a woman calling herself . . . Gentlemen, I implore you!"

"And I bet you," cried the little grimy man with the pistol, "you're sweet on this daughter what's-her-name?" He seemed delighted. "Ain't you, now?"

How, I ask of all Providence, could these people have surprised my secret? Yet I felt obliged to tell the truth.

"I will not conceal from you," I said, "that I have in truth a high regard for Mlle Claudine. But this lady, believe me, is engaged to a friend of mine, an officer of artillery."

"Then what do you get out of it? Eh?" asked the grimy little man, with another cunning look.

The question puzzled me. I could not reply. But the bartender with the gold teeth leaned over.

"If you want to see the old Frenchie alive, monseer," said he, "you'd better git." *(Sic,* Maurice.) "I hearn tell she had a stroke this morning."

But a dozen voices clamored to keep me there, though this last intelligence sent me into despair. Then up rose the big and very old man with the faded whiskers: indeed, I had never realized how old, because he seemed so hale.

"Which of you was with Washington?" said he, suddenly taking hold of the fierce little man's neckcloth, and speaking with contempt. "Make way for the nephew of Lafayette!"

They cheered me then, Maurice. They hurried me to the door, they begged me to return, they promised they would await me. One glance I sought – nor can I say why – for M. Thaddeus Perley. He was sitting at a table by a pillar, under an open gas jet; his face whiter than ever, still wiping stains of tobacco juice from his cloak.

Never have I seen a more mournful prospect than Thomas Street, when my cab set me down there. Perhaps it was my state of mind; for if Mme Thevenet had died without a sou left to her daughter: you conceive it?

The houses of Thomas Street were faced with dingy yellow brick, and a muddy sky hung over the chimney pots. It had been warm all day, yet I found my spirit intolerably oppressed. Though heaven knows our Parisian streets are dirty enough, we do not allow pigs in them. Except for these, nothing moved in the forsaken street save a blind street musician, with his dog and an instrument called a banjo; but even he was silent too.

For some minutes, it seemed to me, I plied the knocker at Number 23, with hideous noise. Nothing stirred. Finally, one part of the door swung open a little, as for an eye. Whereupon I heard the shifting of a floor bolt, and both doors were swung open.

Need I say that facing me stood the woman whom we have agreed to call Mlle Jezebel?

She said to me: "And then, M. Armand?"

"Mme Thevenet!" cried I. "She is still alive?"

"She is alive," replied my companion, looking up at me from under the lids of her greenish eyes. "But she is completely paralyzed."

I have never denied, Maurice, that Mlle Jezebel has a certain attractiveness. She is not old or even middle aged. Were it not that her complexion is as muddy as was the sky above us then, she would have been pretty.

"And as for Claudine," I said to her, "the daughter of madame — "

"You have come too late, M. Armand."

And well I remember that at this moment there rose up, in the mournful street outside, the tinkle of the banjo played by the street musician. It moved closer, playing a popular catch whose words run something thus:

> Oh, I come from Alabama
>     With my banjo on my knee;
> I depart for Louisiana
>     My Susannah for to see.

Across the lips of mademoiselle flashed a smile of peculiar quality, like a razor cut before the blood comes.

"Gold," she whispered. "Ninety thousand persons, one hears, have gone to seek it. Go to California, M. Armand. It is the only place you will find gold."

This tune, they say, is a merry tune. It did not seem so, as the dreary twanging faded away. Mlle Jezebel, with her muddy blonde hair parted in the middle and drawn over her ears after the best fashion, faced me implacably. Her greenish eyes were wide open. Her old brown taffeta dress, full at the bust, narrow at the waist, rustled its wide skirts as she glided a step forward.

"Have the kindness," I said, "to stand aside. I wish to enter."

Hitherto in my life I had seen her docile and meek.

"You are no relative," she said. "I will not allow you to enter."

"In that case, I regret, I must."

"If you had ever spoken one kind word to *me*," whispered mademoiselle, looking up from under her eyelids, and with her breast heaving, "one gesture of love – that is to say, of affection – you might have shared five million francs."

"Stand aside, I say!"

"As it is, you prefer a doll-faced consumptive at Paris. So be it!"

I was raging, Maurice; I confess it; yet I drew myself up with coldness.

"You refer, perhaps, to Claudine Thevenet?"

"And to whom else?"

"I might remind you, mademoiselle, that the lady is pledged to my good friend Lieutenant Delage. I have forgotten her."

"Have you?" asked our Jezebel, with her eyes on my face and a strange hungry look in them. Mlle Jezebel added, with more pleasure: "Well, she will die. Unless you can solve a mystery."

"A mystery?"

"I should not have said mystery, M. Armand. Because it is impossible of all solution. It is an Act of God!"

Up to this time the glass-fronted doors of the vestibule had stood open behind her, against a darkness of closed shutters in the house. There breathed out of it an odor of unswept carpets, a sourness of stale living. Someone was approaching, carrying a lighted candle.

"Who speaks?" called a man's voice; shaky, but as French as Mlle Jezebel's. "Who speaks concerning an Act of God?"

I stepped across the threshold. Mademoiselle, who never left my side, immediately closed and locked the front doors. As the candle glimmer moved still closer in gloom, I could have shouted for joy to see the man whom (as I correctly guessed) I had come to meet.

"You are M. Duroc, the lawyer!" I said. "You are my brother's friend!"

M. Duroc held the candle higher, to inspect me.

He was a big, heavy man who seemed to sag in all his flesh. In compensation for his bald head, the grayish-brown mustache flowed down and parted into two hairy fans of beard on either side of his chin. He looked at me through oval gold-rimmed spectacles; in a friendly way, but yet frightened. His voice was deep and gruff, clipping the syllables, despite his fright.

"And you" – *clip-clip*; the candle holder trembled – "you are Armand de Lafayette. I had expected you by the steam packet today. Well! You are here. On a fool's errand, I regret."

"But why?" (And I shouted at him, Maurice.)

I looked at mademoiselle, who was faintly smiling.

"M. Duroc!" I protested. "You wrote to my brother. You said you had persuaded madame to repent of her harshness toward her daughter!"

"Was that your duty?" asked the Jezebel, looking full at M. Duroc with her greenish eyes. "Was that your right?"

"I am a man of law," said M. Duroc. The deep monosyllables rapped, in ghostly bursts, through his parted beard. He was perspiring. "I am correct. Very correct! And yet – "

"Who nursed her?" asked the Jezebel. "Who soothed her, fed her, wore her filthy clothes, calmed her tempers and endured her interminable abuse? *I* did!"

And yet, all the time she was speaking, this woman kept sidling and sidling against me, brushing my side, as though she would make sure of my presence there.

"Well!" said the lawyer. "It matters little now! This mystery . . ."

You may well believe that all these cryptic remarks, as well as reference to a mystery or an Act of God, had driven me almost frantic. I demanded to know what he meant.

"Last night," said M. Duroc, "a certain article disappeared."

"Well, well?"

"It disappeared," said M. Duroc, drawn up like a grenadier. "But it could not conceivably have disappeared. I myself swear this! Our only suggestions as to how it might have disappeared are a toy rabbit and a barometer."

"Sir," I said, "I do not wish to be discourteous. But – "

"Am I mad, you ask?"

I bowed. If any man can manage at once to look sagging and uncertain, yet stately and dignified, M. Duroc managed it then. And dignity won, I think.

"Sir," he replied, gesturing the candle toward the rear of the house, "Mme Thevenet lies there in her bed. She is paralyzed. She can move only her eyes or partially the lips, without speech. Do you wish to see her?"

"If I am permitted."

"Yes. That would be correct. Accompany me."

And I saw the poor old woman, Maurice. Call her harridan if you like. It was a square room of good size, whose shutters had remained closed and locked for years. Can one smell rust? In that room, with faded green wallpaper, I felt I could.

One solitary candle did little more than dispel shadow. It burned atop the mantelpiece well opposite the foot of the bed; and a shaggy man, whom I afterward learned to be a police officer, sat in a green-upholstered armchair by an unlighted coal fire in the fireplace grate, picking his teeth with a knife.

"If you please, Dr. Harding!" M. Duroc called softly in English.

The long and lean American doctor, who had been bending over the bed so as to conceal from our sight the head and shoulders of Madame Thevenet, turned round. But his cadaverous body – in such fashion were madame's head and shoulders propped up against pillows – his cadaverous body, I say, still concealed her face.

"Has there been any change?" persisted M. Duroc in English.

"There has been no change," replied the dark-complexioned Dr. Harding, "except for the worse."

"Do you want her to be moved?"

"There has never been any necessity," said the physician, picking up his beaver hat from the bed. He spoke dryly. "However, if you want to learn anything more about the toy rabbit or the barometer, I should hurry. The lady will die in a matter of hours, probably less."

And he stood to one side.

It was a heavy bed with four posts and a canopy. The bed curtains, of some dullish-green material, were closely drawn on every side except the long side by which we saw Madame Thevenet in profile. Lean as a post, rigid, the strings of her cotton nightcap tightly tied under her chin, Madame Thevenet lay propped up there. But one eye rolled towards us, and it rolled horribly.

Up to this time the woman we call the Jezebel had said little. She chose this moment again to come brushing against my side. Her greenish eyes, lids half-closed, shone in the light of M. Duroc's candle. What she whispered was: "You don't really hate me, do you?"

Maurice, I make a pause here.

Since I wrote the sentence, I put down my pen, and pressed my hands over my eyes, and once more I thought. But let me try again.

I spent just two hours in the bedroom of Madame Thevenet. At the end of the time – oh, you shall hear why! – I rushed out of that bedroom, and out of Number 23 Thomas Street, like the maniac I was.

The streets were full of people, of carriages, of omnibuses, at early evening. Knowing no place of refuge save the saloon from which I had come, I gave its address to a cabdriver. Since still I had swallowed no food, I may have been lightheaded. Yet I wished to pour out my heart to the friends who had bidden me return there. And where were they now?

A new group, all new, lounged against the bar-counter under brighter gaslight and brighter paint. Of all those who smote me on the back and cheered, none remained save the ancient giant who had implied friendship with General Washington. *He*, alas, lay helplessly drunk with his head near a sawdust spitting box. Nevertheless I was so moved that I took the liberty of thrusting a handful of bank notes into his pocket. He alone remained.

Wait, there was another!

I do not believe he had remained there because of me. Yet M. Thaddeus Perley, still sitting alone at the little table by the pillar, with the open gas jet above, stared vacantly at the empty glass in his hand.

He had named himself a foreigner; he was probably French. That was as well. For, as I lurched against the table, I was befuddled and all English had fled my wits.

"Sir," said I, "will you permit a madman to share your table?"

M. Perley gave a great start, as though roused out of thought. He was now sober: this I saw. Indeed, his shiver and haggard face were due to lack of stimulant rather than too much of it.

"Sir," he stammered, getting to his feet, "I shall be – I shall be honored by your company." Automatically he opened his mouth to call for a waiter; his hand went to his pocket; he stopped.

"No, no, no!" said I. "If you insist, M. Perley, you may pay for the second bottle. The first is mine. I am sick at heart, and I would speak with a gentleman."

At these last words M. Perley's whole expression changed. He sat down, and gave me a grave courtly nod. His eyes, which were his most expressive feature, studied my face and my disarray.

"You are ill, M. de Lafayette," he said. "Have you so soon come to grief in this – this *civilized* country?"

"I have come to grief, yes. But not through civilization or the lack of it." And I banged my fist on the table. "I have come to grief, M. Perley, through miracles or magic. I have come to grief with a problem which no man's ingenuity can solve!"

M. Perley looked at me in a strange way. But someone had brought a bottle of brandy, with its accessories. M. Perley's trembling hand slopped a generous allowance into my glass, and an even more generous one into his own.

"That is very curious," he remarked, eying the glass. "A murder, was it?"

"No. But a valuable document has disappeared. The most thorough search by the police cannot find it."

Touch him anywhere, and he flinched. M. Perley, for some extraordinary reason, appeared to think I was mocking him.

"A document, you say?" His laugh was a trifle unearthly. "Come, now. Was it by any chance – a letter?"

"No, no! It was a will. Three large sheets of parchment, of the size you call foolscap. Listen!"

And as M. Perley added water to his brandy and gulped down about a third of it, I leaned across the table.

"Mme Thevenet, of whom you may have heard me speak in this café, was an invalid. But (until the early hours of this morning) she was not bedridden. She could move, and walk about her room, and so on. She had been lured away from Paris and her family by a green-eyed woman named the Jezebel.

"But a kindly lawyer of this city, M. Duroc, believed that madame suffered and had a bad conscience about her own daughter. Last night, despite the Jezebel, he persuaded madame at last to sign a will leaving all her money to this daughter.

"And the daughter, Claudine, is in mortal need of it! From my brother and myself, who have more than enough, she will not accept a sou. Her affianced, Lieutenant Delage, is as poor as she. But, unless she leaves France for Switzerland, she will die. I will not conceal from you that Claudine suffers from that dread disease we politely call consumption."

M. Perley stopped with his glass again halfway to his mouth.

He believed me now; I sensed it. Yet under the dark hair, tumbled on his forehead, his face had gone as white as his neat, mended shirt frill.

"So very little a thing is money!" he whispered. "So very little a thing!"

And he lifted the glass and drained it.

"You do not think I am mocking you, sir?"

"No, no!" says M. Perley, shading his eyes with one hand. "I knew myself of one such case. She is dead. Pray continue."

"Last night, I repeat, Mme Thevenet changed her mind. When M. Duroc paid his weekly evening visit with the news that I should arrive today, madame fairly chattered with eagerness and a kind of terror. Death was approaching, she said; she had a presentiment."

As I spoke, Maurice, there returned to me the image of that shadowy, arsenic-green bedroom in the shuttered house; and what M. Duroc had told me.

"Madame," I continued, "cried out to M. Duroc that he must bolt the bedroom door. She feared the Jezebel, who lurked but said nothing. M. Duroc drew up to her bedside a portable writing desk,

with two good candles. For a long time madame spoke, pouring
out contrition, self-abasement, the story of an unhappy marriage,
all of which M. Duroc (sweating with embarrassment) was obliged
to write down until it covered three large parchment sheets.

"But it was done, M. Perley!

"The will, in effect, left everything to her daughter, Claudine. It
revoked a previous will by which all had been left (and this can be
done in French law, as we both know) to Jezebel of the muddy
complexion and the muddy yellow hair.

"Well, then! . . ."

"M. Duroc sallies out into the street, where he finds two sober
fellows who come in. Madame signs the will, M. Duroc sands it,
and the two men from the street affix their signatures as witnesses.
Then *they* are gone. M. Duroc folds the will lengthways, and prepares
to put it into his carpetbag. Now, M. Perley, mark what follows!

"'No, no, no!' cries madame, with the shadow of her peaked
nightcap wagging on the locked shutters beyond. 'I wish to keep
it – for this one night!'

"'For this one night, madame?' asks M. Duroc.

"'I wish to press it against my heart,' says Mme Thevenet. 'I
wish to read it once, twice, a thousand times! M. Duroc, what
time is it?'

"Whereupon he takes out his gold repeater, and opens it. To his
astonishment it is one o'clock in the morning. Yet he touches the
spring of the repeater, and its pulse beat rings one.

"'M. Duroc,' pleads Mme Thevenet, 'remain here with me for the
rest of the night!'

"'Madame!' cried M. Duroc, shocked to the very fans of his beard.
'That would not be correct.'

"'Yes, you are right,' says madame. And never, swears the lawyer,
has he seen her less bleary of eye, more alive with wit and cunning,
more the great lady of ruin, than there in that green and shadowy
and foul-smelling room.

"Yet this very fact puts her in more and more terror of the Jezebel,
who is never seen. She points to M. Duroc's carpetbag.

"'I think you have much work to do, dear sir?'

"M. Duroc groaned. 'The Good Lord knows that I have!'

"'Outside the only door of this room,' says madame, 'there is a
small dressing room. Set up your writing desk beside the door there,
so that no one may enter without your knowledge. Do your work
there; you shall have a lamp or many candles. Do it,' shrieks madame,
'for the sake of Claudine and for the sake of an old friendship!'

"Very naturally, M. Duroc hesitated.

"'*She* will be hovering,' pleads Mme Thevenet, pressing the will against her breast. '*This* I shall read and read and read, and sanctify with my tears. If I find I am falling asleep,' and here the old lady looked cunning, 'I shall hide it. But no matter! Even *she* cannot penetrate through locked shutters and a guarded door.'

"Well, in fine, the lawyer at length yielded.

"He set up his writing desk against the very doorpost outside that door. When he last saw madame, before closing the door, he saw her in profile with the green bed curtains drawn except on that side, propped up with a tall candle burning on a table at her right hand.

"Ah, that night! I think I see M. Duroc at his writing desk, as he has told me, in an airless dressing room where no clock ticked. I see him, at times, removing his oval spectacles to press his smarting eyes. I see him returning to his legal papers, while his pen scratched through the wicked hours of the night.

"He heard nothing, or virtually nothing, until five o'clock in the morning. Then, which turned him cold and flabby, he heard a cry which he describes as being like that of a deaf-mute.

"The communicating door had not been bolted on Mme Thevenet's side, in case she needed help. M. Duroc rushed into the other room.

"On the table, at madame's right hand, the tall candle had burned down to a flattish mass of wax over which still hovered a faint bluish flame. Madame herself lay rigid in her peaked nightcap. That revival of spirit last night, or remorse in her bitter heart, had brought on the last paralysis. Though M. Duroc tried to question her, she could move only her eyes.

"Then M. Duroc noticed that the will, which she had clutched as a doomed religious might clutch a crucifix, was not in her hand or on the bed.

"'Where is the will?' he shouted at her, as though she were deaf too. 'Where is the will?'

"Mme Thevenet's eyes fixed on him. Then they moved down, and looked steadily at a trumpery toy – a rabbit, perhaps four inches high, made of pink velours or the like – which lay on the bed. Again she looked at M. Duroc, as though to emphasize this. Then her eyes rolled, this time with dreadful effort, toward a large barometer, shaped like a warming pan, which hung on the wall beside the door. Three times she did this before the bluish candle flame flickered and went out."

And I, Armand de Lafayette, paused here in my recital to M. Perley.

Again I became aware that I was seated in a garish saloon, swilling brandy, amid loud talk that beat the air. There was a thumping noise from the theater above our heads, and faint strains of music.

"The will," I said, "was not stolen. Not even the Jezebel could have melted through locked shutters or a guarded door. The will was not hidden, because no inch of the room remains unsearched. *Yet the will is gone!*"

I threw a glance across the table at M. Perley.

To me, I am sure, the brandy had given strength and steadied my nerves. With M. Perley I was not so sure. He was a little flushed. That slightly wild look, which I had observed before, had crept up especially into one eye, giving his whole face a somewhat lopsided appearance. Yet all his self-confidence had returned. He gave me a little crooked smile.

I struck the table.

"Do you honor me with your attention, M. Perley?"

"What song the Syrens sang," he said to me, "or what name Achilles assumed when he hid himself among women, although puzzling questions, are not beyond *all* conjecture."

"They are beyond *my* conjecture!" I cried. "And so is this!"

M. Perley extended his hand, spread the fingers, and examined them as one who owns the universe.

"It is some little time," he remarked, "since I have concerned myself with these trifles." His eyes retreated into a dream. "Yet I have given some trifling aid, in the past, to the Prefect of the Parisian police."

"You are a Frenchman! I knew it! And the police!" Seeing his lofty look, I added: "As an amateur, understood?"

"Understood!" Then his delicate hand – it would be unjust to call it clawlike – shot across the table and fastened on my arm. The strange eyes burned toward my face. "A little more detail!" he pleaded humbly. "A little more, I beg of you! This woman, for instance, you call the Jezebel?"

"It was she who met me at the house."

"And then?"

I described for him my meeting with the Jezebel, with M. Duroc, and our entrance to the sickroom, where the shaggy police officer sat in the armchair and the saturnine doctor faced us from beside the bed.

"This woman," I exclaimed, with the room vividly before my eyes as I described it, "seems to have conceived for me (forgive me) a kind of passion. No doubt it was due to some idle compliments I once paid her at Paris.

"As I have explained, the Jezebel is *not* unattractive, even if she would only (again forgive me) wash her hair. Nevertheless, when once more she brushed my side and whispered, 'You don't really hate me, do you?' I felt little less than horror. It seemed to me that in some fashion I was responsible for the whole tragedy.

"While we stood beside the bed, M. Duroc the lawyer poured out the story I have recounted. There lay the poor paralytic, and confirmed it with her eyes. The toy rabbit, a detestable pink color, lay in its same position on the bed. Behind me, hung against the wall by the door, was the large barometer.

"Apparently for my benefit, Mme Thevenet again went through her dumb show with imploring eyes. She would look at the rabbit; next (as M. Duroc had not mentioned), she would roll her eyes all round her, for some desperate yet impenetrable reason, before fixing her gaze on the barometer.

"It meant . . . what?

"The lawyer spoke then. 'More light!' gulped out M. Duroc. 'If you must have closed shutters and windows, then let us at least have more light!'

"The Jezebel glided out to fetch candles. During M. Duroc's explanation he had several times mentioned my name. At first mention of it the shaggy police officer jumped and put away his clasp knife. He beckoned to the physician, Dr. Harding, who went over for a whispered conference.

"Whereupon the police officer sprang up.

"'Mr. Lafayette!' And he swung my hand pompously. 'If I'd known it was you, Mr. Lafayette, I wouldn't 'a' sat there like a bump on a log.'

"'You are an officer of police, sir,' said I. 'Can *you* think of no explanation?'

"He shook his head.

"'These people are Frenchies, Mr. Lafayette, and you're an American,' he said, with *somewhat* conspicuous lack of logic. '*If* they're telling the truth – '

"'Let us assume that!'

"'I can't tell you where the old lady's will is,' he stated positively. 'But I can tell you where it ain't. It ain't hidden in this room!'

"'But surely . . .!' I began in despair.

"At this moment the Jezebel, her brown taffeta dress rustling, glided back into the room with a handful of candles and a tin box of the new-style lucifer matches. She lighted several candles, sticking them on any surface in their own grease.

"There were one or two fine pieces of furniture; but the mottled-marble tops were chipped and stained, the gilt sides cracked. There were a few mirrors, creating mimic spectral life. I saw a little more clearly the faded green paper of the walls, and what I perceived to be the partly open door of a cupboard. The floor was of bare boards.

"All this while I was conscious of two pairs of eyes: the imploring gaze of Mme Thevenet, and the amorous gaze of the Jezebel. One or the other I could have endured, but both together seemed to suffocate me.

"'Mr. Duroc here,' said the shaggy police officer, clapping the distressed advocate on the shoulder, 'sent a messenger in a cab at half-past five this morning. And what time did we get here? I ask you and I tell you! Six o'clock!'

"Then he shook his finger at me, in a kind of pride and fury of efficiency.

"'Why, Mr. Lafayette, there's been fourteen men at this room from six this morning until just before you got here!'

"'To search for Mme Thevenet's will, you mean?'

"The shaggy man nodded portentously, and folded his arms.

"'Floor's solid.' He stamped on the bare boards. 'Walls and ceiling? Nary a inch missed. We reckon we're remarkable smart; and we are.'

"'But Mme Thevenet,' I persisted, 'was not a complete invalid until this morning. She could move about. If she became afraid of – the name of the Jezebel choked me – 'if she became afraid, and *did* hide the will . . .'

"'Where'd she hide it? Tell me!'

"'In the furniture, then?'

"'Cabinetmakers in, Mr. Lafayette. No secret compartments.'

"'In one of the mirrors?'

"'Took the backs of 'em off. No will hid there.'

"'Up the chimney!' I cried.

"'Sent a chimney-sweep up there,' replied my companion in a ruminating way. Each time I guessed, he would leer at me in friendly and complacent challenge. 'Ye-es, I reckon we're pretty smart. But we didn't find no will.'

"The pink rabbit also seemed to leer from the bed. I saw madame's eyes. Once again, as a desperate mind will fasten on trifles, I observed the strings of the nightcap beneath her scrawny chin. But I looked again at the toy rabbit.

"'Has it occurred to you,' I said triumphantly, 'to examine the bed and bedstead of Mme Thevenet herself?'

"My shaggy friend went to her bedside.

"'Poor old woman,' he said. He spoke as though she were already a corpse. Then he turned round. 'We lifted her out, just as gentle as a newborn babe (didn't we, ma'am?). No hollow bedposts! Nothing in the canopy! Nothing in the frame or the feather beds or the curtains or the bedclothes!'

"Suddenly the shaggy police officer became angry, as though he wished to be rid of the whole matter.

"'And it ain't in the toy rabbit,' he said, 'because you can see we slit it up, if you look close. And it ain't in that barometer there. It just – ain't here.'

"There was a silence as heavy as the dusty, hot air of this room.

"'It is here,' murmured M. Duroc in his gruff voice. 'It must be here!'

"The Jezebel stood there meekly, with downcast eyes.

"And I, in my turn, confess that *I* lost my head. I stalked over to the barometer, and tapped it. Its needle, which already indicated, 'Rain; cold,' moved still further toward that point.

"I was not insane enough to hit it with my fist. But I crawled on the floor, in search of a secret hiding place. I felt along the wall. The police officer – who kept repeating that nobody must touch anything and he would take no responsibility until he went off duty at something o'clock – the police officer I ignored.

"What at length gave me pause was the cupboard, already thoroughly searched. In the cupboard hung a few withered dresses and gowns, as though they had shriveled with Mme Thevenet's body. But on the shelf of the cupboard . . .

"On the shelf stood a great number of perfume bottles: even today, I fear, many of our countrymen think perfume a substitute for water and soap; and the state of madame's hands would have confirmed this. *But*, on the shelf, were a few dusty novels. There was a crumpled and begrimed copy of yesterday's New York *Sun*. This newspaper did not contain a will; but it did contain a black beetle, which ran out across my hand.

"In a disgust past describing, I flung down the beetle and stamped on it. I closed the cupboard door, acknowledging defeat. Mme Thevenet's will was gone. And at the same second, in that dim green room – still badly lighted, with only a few more candles – two voices cried out.

"One was my own voice:

"'*In God's name, where is it?*'

"The other was the deep voice of M. Duroc:

"'*Look at that woman! She knows!*'

"And he meant the Jezebel.

"M. Duroc, with his beard fans atremble, was pointing to a mirror; a little blurred, as these mirrors were. Our Jezebel had been looking into the mirror, her back turned to us. Now she dodged, as at a stone thrown.

"With good poise our Jezebel writhed this movement into a curtsy, turning to face us. But not before I also had seen that smile – like a razor cut before the blood comes – as well as full knowledge, mocking knowledge, shining out of wide-open eyes in the mirror.

"'You spoke to me, M. Duroc?' She murmured the reply, also in French.

"'Listen to me!' the lawyer said formally. 'This will is *not* missing. It is in this room. You were not here last night. Something has made you guess. You know where it is.'

"'Are you unable to find it?' asked the Jezebel in surprise.

"'Stand back, young man!' M. Duroc said to me. 'I ask you something, mademoiselle, in the name of justice.'

"'Ask!' said the Jezebel.

"'If Claudine Thevenet inherits the money to which she is entitled, you will be well paid; yes, overpaid! You know Claudine. You know that!'

"'I know it.'

"'But if the new will be *not* found,' said M. Duroc, again waving me back, 'then you inherit everything. And Claudine will die. For it will be assumed – '

"'Yes!' said the Jezebel, with one hand pressed against her breast. 'You yourself, M. Duroc, testify that all night a candle was burning at madame's bedside. Well! The poor woman, whom *I* loved and cherished, repented of her ingratitude toward me. She burned this new will at the candle flame; she crushed its ashes to powder and blew them away!'

"'Is that true?' cried M. Duroc.

"'They will assume it,' smiled the Jezebel, 'as you say.' She looked at me. 'And for you, M. Armand!'

"She glided closer. I can only say that I saw her eyes uncovered; or, if you wish to put it so, her soul and flesh together.

"'I would give you everything on earth,' she said. 'I will not give you the doll face in Paris.'

"'Listen to me!' I said to her, so agitated that I seized her shoulders. 'You are out of your senses! You cannot give Claudine to me! She will marry another man!'

"'And do you think that matters to me,' asked the Jezebel, with her green eyes full on mine, 'as long as you still love her?'

"There was a small crash as someone dropped a knife on the floor.

"We three, I think, had completely forgotten that we were not alone. There were two spectators, although they did not comprehend our speech.

"The saturnine Dr. Harding now occupied the green armchair. His long thin legs, in tight black trousers with strap under the boot instep, were crossed and looked spidery; his high beaver hat glimmered on his head. The police officer, who was picking his teeth with a knife when I first saw him, had now dropped the knife when he tried to trim his nails.

"But both men sensed the atmosphere. Both were alert, feeling out with the tentacles of their nerves. The police officer shouted at me.

"'What's this gabble?' he said. 'What's a-gitting into your head?'

"Grotesquely, it was that word 'head' which gave me my inspiration.

"'The nightcap!' I exclaimed in English.

"'What nightcap?'

"For the nightcap of Mme Thevenet had a peak; it was large; it was tightly tied under the chin; it might well conceal a flat-pressed document which – but you understand. The police officer, dull-witted as he appeared, grasped the meaning in a flash. And how I wished I had never spoken! For the fellow meant well, but he was not gentle.

"As I raced round the curtained sides of the bed, the police officer was holding a candle in one hand and tearing off madame's nightcap with the other. He found no will there, no document at all; only straggly wisps of hair on a skull grown old before its time.

"Mme Thevenet had been a great lady, once. It must have been the last humiliation. Two tears overflowed her eyes and ran down her cheeks. She lay propped up there in a nearly sitting position; but something seemed to wrench inside her.

"And she closed her eyes forever. And the Jezebel laughed.

"That is the end of my story. That is why I rushed out of the house like a madman. The will has vanished as though by magic; or is it still there by magic? In any case, you find me at this table: grubby and disheveled and much ashamed."

For a little time after I had finished my narrative to M. Perley in the saloon it seemed to me that the bar-counter was a trifle quieter. But a faint stamping continued from the theater above our heads. Then all was hushed, until a chorus rose to a tinkle of many banjos.

> Oh, I come from Alabama
>   With my banjo on my knee;
> I depart for Louisiana . . .

Enough! The song soon died away, and M. Thaddeus Perley did not even hear it.

M. Perley sat looking downward into an empty glass, so that I could not see his face.

"Sir," he remarked almost bitterly, "you are a man of good heart. I am glad to be of service in a problem so trifling as this."

"*Trifling!*"

His voice was a little husky, but not slurred. His hand slowly turned the glass round and round.

"Will you permit two questions?" asked M. Perley.

"Two questions? Ten thousand!"

"More than two will be unnecessary." Still M. Perley did not look up. "This toy rabbit, of which so much was made: I would know its exact position on the bed?"

"It was almost at the foot of the bed, and about the middle in a crossways direction."

"Ah, so I had imagined. Were the three sheets of parchment, forming the will, written upon two sides or upon only one?"

"I had not told you, M. Perley. But M. Duroc said: upon one side only."

M. Perley raised his head.

His face was now flushed and distorted with drink, his eye grown wild. In his cups he was as proud as Satan, and as disdainful of others' intelligence; yet he spoke with dignity, and with careful clearness.

"It is ironic, M. de Lafayette, that I should tell you how to lay your hand on the missing will and the elusive money; since, upon my word, I have never been able to perform a like service for myself." And he smiled, as at some secret joke. "Perhaps," he added, "it is the very simplicity of the thing which puts you at fault."

I could only look at him in bewilderment.

"Perhaps the mystery is a little *too* plain! A little *too* self-evident!"

"You mock me, sir! I will not . . ."

"Take me as I am," said M. Perley, whacking the foot of the glass on the table, "or leave me. Besides," here his wandering eye encountered a list of steam sailings pasted against the wall, "I – I leave tomorrow by the *Parnassus* for England, and then for France."

"I meant no offence, M. Perley! If you have knowledge, speak!"

"Mme Thevenet," he said, carefully pouring himself some more brandy, "hid the will in the middle of the night. Does it puzzle you that she took such precautions to hide the will? But the element of the outré must always betray itself. The Jezebel *must not* find that will! Yet Mme Thevenet trusted nobody – not even the worthy physician who attended her. If madame were to die of a stroke, the police would be there and must soon, she was sure, discover her simple device. Even if she were paralyzed, it would ensure the presence of other persons in the room to act as unwitting guards.

"Your cardinal error," M. Perley continued dispassionately, "was one of ratiocination. You tell me that Mme Thevenet, to give you a hint, looked fixedly at some point near the foot of the bed. Why do you assume that she was looking at the toy rabbit?"

"Because," I replied hotly, "the toy rabbit was the only object she could have looked at!"

"Pardon me; but it was *not*. You several times informed me that the bed curtains were closely drawn together on three sides. They were drawn on all but the 'long' side toward the door. Therefore the ideal reasoner, without having seen the room, may safely say that the curtains were drawn together at the foot of the bed?"

"Yes, true!"

"After looking fixedly at this point represented by the toy, Mme Thevenet then 'rolls her eyes all round her' – in your phrase. May we assume that she wishes the curtains to be drawn back, so that she may see something *beyond* the bed?"

"It is – possible, yes!"

"It is more than possible, as I shall demonstrate. Let us direct our attention, briefly, to the incongruous phenomenon of the barometer on another wall. The barometer indicates, 'Rain; cold.'"

Here M. Perley's thin shoulders drew together under the old military cloak.

"Well," he said, "the cold is on its way. Yet this day, for April, has been warm outside and indoors, oppressively hot?"

"Yes! Of course!"

"You yourself," continued M. Perley, inspecting his fingernails, "told me what was directly opposite the foot of the bed. Let us suppose that the bed curtains are drawn open. Mme Thevenet, in her nearly seated position, is looking *downward*. What would she have seen?"

"The fireplace!" I cried. "The grate of the fireplace!"

"Already we have a link with the weather. And what, as you have specifically informed me, was in the grate of the fireplace?"

"An unlighted coal fire!"

"Exactly. And what is essential for the composition of such a fire? We need coal; we need wood; but primarily and above all, we need . . ."

"*Paper*!" I cried.

"In the cupboard of that room," said M. Perley, with his disdainful little smile, "was a very crumpled and begrimed (mark that; not dusty) copy of *yesterday's* New York Sun. To light fires is the most common, and indeed the best, use for our daily press. That copy had been used to build yesterday's fire. But something else, during the night, was substituted for it. You yourself remarked the extraordinarily dirty state of Mme Thevenet's hands."

M. Perley swallowed the brandy, and his flush deepened.

"Sir," he said loudly, "you will find the will crumpled up, with ends most obviously protruding, under the coal and wood in the fireplace grate. Even had anyone taken the fire to pieces, he would have found only what appeared to be dirty blank paper, written side undermost, which could never be a valuable will. It was too self-evident to be seen. – Now go!"

"Go?" I echoed stupidly.

M. Perley rose from his chair.

"Go, I say!" he shouted, with an even wilder eye. "The Jezebel could not light that fire. It was too warm, for one thing; and all day there were police officers with instructions that an outsider must touch nothing. But now? *Mme Thevenet kept warning you that the fire must not be lighted, or the will would be destroyed!*"

"Will you await me here?" I called over my shoulder.

"Yes, yes! And perhaps there will be peace for the wretched girl with – with the lung trouble."

Even as I ran out of the door I saw him, grotesque and pitiful, slump across the table. Hope, rising and surging, seemed to sweep me along like the crack of the cabman's whip. But when I reached my destination, hope receded.

The shaggy police officer was just descending the front steps.

"None of us coming back here, Mr. Lafayette!" he called cheerily. "Old Mrs. What's-her-name went and burned that will at a candle last night. – Here, what's o'clock?"

The front door was unlocked. I raced through that dark house, and burst into the rear bedroom.

The corpse still lay in the big, gloomy bed. Every candle had flickered almost down to its socket. The police officer's clasp knife, forgotten since he had dropped it, still lay on bare boards. But the Jezebel was there.

She knelt on the hearth, with the tin box of lucifer matches she had brought there earlier. The match spurted, a bluish fire; I saw her eagerness; she held the match to the grate.

"A lucifer," I said, "in the hand of a Jezebel!"

And I struck her away from the grate, so that she reeled against a chair and fell. Large coals, small coals rattled down in puffs of dust as I plunged my hands into the unlighted fire. Little sticks, sawed sticks; and I found it there: crumpled parchment sheets, but incontestably madame's will.

"M. Duroc!" I called. "M. Duroc!"

You and I, my brother Maurice, have fought the Citizen-King with bayonets as we now fight the upstart Bonapartist; we need not be ashamed of tears. I confess, then, that the tears overran my eyes and blinded me. I scarcely saw M. Duroc as he hurried into the room.

Certainly I did not see the Jezebel stealthily pick up the police officer's knife. I noticed nothing at all until she flew at me, and stabbed me in the back.

Peace, my brother: I have assured you all is well. At that time, faith, I was not much conscious of any hurt. I bade M. Duroc, who was trembling, to wrench out the knife; I borrowed his roomy greatcoat to hide the blood; I must hurry, hurry, hurry back to that little table under the gas jet.

I planned it all on my way back. M. Perley, apparently a stranger in this country, disliked it and was evidently very poor even in France. But *we* are not precisely paupers. Even with his intense pride, he could not refuse (for such a service) a sum which would comfort him for the rest of his life.

Back I plunged into the saloon, and hurried down it. Then I stopped. The little round table by the pillar, under the flaring gas jet, was empty.

How long I stood there I cannot tell. The back of my shirt, which at first had seemed full of blood, now stuck to the borrowed greatcoat. All of a sudden I caught sight of the fat-faced bartender with the gold teeth, who had been on service that afternoon and had returned now. As a mark of respect, he came out from behind the bar-counter to greet me.

"Where is the gentleman who was sitting at that table?"

I pointed to it. My voice, in truth, must have sounded so hoarse and strange that he mistook it for anger.

"Don't you worry about that, monseer!" said he reassuringly. "*That's* been tended to! We threw the drunken tramp out of here!"

"You threw . . ."

"Right bang in the gutter. Had to crawl along in it before he could stand up." My bartender's face was pleased and vicious. "Ordered a bottle of best brandy, and couldn't pay for it." The face changed again. "Goddelmighty, monseer, what's wrong?"

"*I* ordered that brandy."

"*He* didn't say so, when the waiter brought me over. Just looked me up and down, crazy-like, and said a gentleman would give his I.O.U. Gentleman!"

"M. Perley," I said, restraining an impulse to kill that bartender, "is a friend of mine. He departs for France early tomorrow morning. Where is his hotel? Where can I find him?"

"Perley!" sneered my companion. "That ain't even his real name, I hearn tell. Gits high-and-mighty ideas from upper Broadway. But his real name's on the I.O.U."

A surge of hope, once more, almost blinded me. "Did you keep that I.O.U.?"

"Yes, I kepp it," growled the bartender, fishing in his pocket. "God knows why, but I kepp it."

And at last, Maurice, I triumphed!

True, I collapsed from my wound; and the fever would not let me remember that I must be at the dock when the *Parnassus* steam packet departed from New York next morning. I must remain here, shut up in a hotel room and unable to sleep at night, until I can take ship for home. But where I failed, you can succeed. He was to leave on the morrow by the *Parnassus* for England, and then for France – so he told me. You can find him – in six months at the most. In six months, I give you my word, he will be out of misery for ever!

"*I.O.U.*," reads the little slip, "*for one bottle of your best brandy, forty-five cents. Signed: Edgar A. Poe.*"

I remain, Maurice,<br>
Your affectionate brother,<br>
Armand

# THE GOLDEN NUGGET POKER GAME
## Edward D. Hoch

*Edward Hoch (b. 1930), has written a few novels, but is best known as a short-story writer and must be one of the most prolific writers of crime and mystery short fiction of all time, with over seven hundred stories published since his first in 1955. Despite this prodigious output Hoch can still bring a verve and originality to each new story. Hoch's diversity is maintained by the many series characters he has created, amongst them Simon Ark, Captain Leopold, Nick Velvet and Jeffrey Rand. His stories related by Dr. Sam Hawthorne are technically historical mysteries, as Hawthorne, a New England country doctor, recounts cases from his youth in the 1920s and 30s. But more appropriate for this volume are the stories featuring western gunman Ben Snow. The series spans the years 1881 to 1905 and ranges throughout the wild west and as far north as the Yukon, in western Canada, the setting for the following story.*

B en Snow reached for the freshly dealt cards and picked them up carefully. It wasn't the sort of game where one made quick moves that could be misconstrued. Glancing around at the other five players, he decided he had never seen a more unsavory group of men in one place, and that included Dodge City at its worst.

The poker game in the back room at the Golden Nugget had been going on, some said, since the saloon opened the previous summer in one of the wooden shacks that had gone up almost overnight along the main street in Dawson. The saloon was well named because in that summer of '98 gold nuggets were as acceptable a currency as silver dollars in the bars and sporting houses of the Yukon Territory. Most places had small scales for weighing and evaluating nuggets on the spot.

Ben Snow hadn't traveled north to prospect for gold. He'd come as something of a paid bodyguard to a prospector named Race Johnson, who knew a great deal about panning for gold but very little about gunfighting. Even at the age of 38, Ben's reputation with a six-shooter was as firm as ever. People rarely mistook him for Billy the Kid as they had in his younger days, but they still came to him when there was need of a keen mind and a fast gun.

The journey north with Race Johnson had begun in the early spring, a full year after the first wave of the gold rush started. They'd sailed from San Francisco on a tramp steamer jammed to the gunwales with gold-seekers, following the inside channel through the Alaska islands to Skagaway. From there it was a back-breaking journey north to Dawson, starting with a rocky portage over the Chilkoot Pass for which they hired Indians to assist them.

Already some of their fellow passengers were turning back, their meager funds exhausted. After the portage of twenty-five miles, Johnson and Ben had to hire a boat for the journey across Lake Linderman to the headwaters of the Yukon River. Dawson was still more than two hundred miles downriver and it wasn't a pleasant voyage. Ben would have preferred a bucking horse to the rapids they encountered.

It was June when they finally reached Dawson, steering the boat between the occasional ice floes that were a reminder of the hard winter too recently departed. They had camped along the way in abandoned cabins or on the boat itself, seeing fewer and fewer people the farther north they went. That was why the first sight of Dawson itself came as something of a shock. It was a city of tents and shacks, its population mushroomed in a year's time to nearly fifty thousand people. Its muddy main street was lined with saloons like the Golden Nugget, in which the prospectors ate and drank, bought their provisions, and spent a few hours with hard-eyed sporting ladies. Most saloons even rented rooms by the week or month.

A gold nugget – and more often gold dust – was the common currency, and there were professional gamblers like those at the Golden Nugget to grab as much of it as they could. What was left in the prospectors' pockets usually went for supplies, in an economy where a plate of ham and eggs could cost $3.50.

Although dance-hall girls frequented the saloons, the Northwest Mounted Police did their best to keep the prostitutes across the river in an area variously called Louse Town or Paradise Alley. It was reached by a rope bridge not far from the point where the Klondike River branched off from the Yukon. A better bridge for wagons and horses was a mile upriver.

Race and Ben quickly learned of two important events which had occurred during their eight-week journey. On April 25th the United States Congress had declared war on Spain. And of more immediate importance, on June 13th the Yukon Territory had joined the Canadian Confederation.

It was Sam Wellman, owner of the Golden Nugget, who explained the importance of this action to them. "This place is like the end of the world, and until now we were our own law. With this Confederation business, the Mounted Police have more power. They're corralling prostitutes and even arresting some of the gamblers. Dawson will never be the same."

"Even a town at the end of the world has to have laws," Ben pointed out.

Sam Wellman was a big man who liked to make his own laws. He pointed angrily.

"I've had a poker game going in the back room ever since I opened a year ago. They gonna tell me to close it down?"

Race Johnson had his own rules as well. "Look here, Sam – if these Mounties are anything like the cops back home, a few dollars or some gold dust will have them looking the other way."

Wellman was inclined to agree. "But you get all sorts. There's a Sergeant Baxter in charge here and I haven't quite figured him out. If I offered him a little money he might take it. Or he might lock me up for attempted bribery. When I figure out which, I'll know what to do."

Sam Wellman rarely sat in on his never-ending poker game. Ben didn't, either, at first. But it soon became obvious that there was little point in accompanying Johnson to the creek every day. Dawson's diversions were limited to women, booze, and cards, and after considering those possibilities Ben started sitting in on the game.

The prospectors who gambled were mostly the newcomers, those who hadn't yet made the acquaintance of the professional cardsharps like Yancy Booth who made their living off them. Of the five men grouped around the table with Ben the first evening in early July, he had to admit Yancy was the most respectable in appearance, with a string tie and black coat that would have made a banker proud. Still, after a few days of poker with him, Ben knew him to be totally ruthless. After he wiped out a tough-looking prospector named Grogan, winning everything the man possessed and reducing him to actual tears, Ben decided he'd had enough for the night.

As he left the table, a bar girl named Tess approached him. "Want to try your luck at my place, Mister?"

"Where would that be?" Ben sat down on a bar stool.

"Across the river in Paradise Alley."

"I don't trust that bridge."

She laughed and slapped his knee. "I'll carry you across."

"Have a drink with me and I'll think about it."

"Fair enough. Give me a whiskey, Pete."

The bartender's name was Pete Waters and Ben knew he kept a shotgun behind the bar. He wondered if it had ever been used.

"Here you are," Pete said, sliding the whiskey down to Tess.

"How long you been here?" Ben asked the girl. She was prettier than some of the others, with dark hair that framed a soft, inquisitive face.

"I came up last August. It's been almost a year."

"How are the winters here?"

"Cold, but not as snowy as you'd expect. We only had about fifty inches of snow all this winter. I'm used to more than that back in the States. But you can get a frost here in late August, and they last till early June. Summer's nice – usually in the sixties like today – but it's too short."

"You like it here at the Nugget?"

She shrugged. "Sam's good to me. All the bars got their own girls and most don't like outsiders floating around. I been watching you. How come you're not out panning for gold with the rest of them?" she asked.

"I'm here with Race Johnson. You might say I'm his traveling companion," Ben explained.

That brought a short, sharp laugh from Tess. "Bodyguard, you mean. Or hired gunfighter. How's he doing?"

"He brought in a small nugget yesterday."

"He should go farther up the Klondike, toward Bonanza Creek. That's where the first gold was found two summers ago. There are lots of little cabins up there he could use."

"He might do that, but then I'd have to go with him. I prefer staying in Dawson if I can, at least for now."

She took that as an opening to renew her invitation. "Sure you don't want to come over to Paradise Alley with me? If you're gonna stay in Dawson for the winter you'll need a warm place when the temperature hits twenty below."

"That's all the persuasion I needed," Ben said.

She grinned, happy with her conquest. "You can buy a bottle of whiskey from Pete to bring along if you want."

"Sounds like a fine idea."

There was still plenty of daylight left in the long northern summer and Ben followed her across the rope bridge without difficulty. Paradise Alley was composed of a number of wooden shacks built close together.

Several young women called out to Tess as they arrived and one came to meet them.

"Tess, we're having a whiskey party for the boys on Sunday afternoon. You gonna be in on it?"

"Sure, why not? Mary, this here's Ben Snow. He's only been in Dawson a few weeks."

Mary was a plain young woman in her early twenties, running a bit to fat. "Hi, Ben. Welcome to Dawson. Is this your first visit to Paradise?"

"The first time I could face the trip across that bridge."

"Now that you know the way, come to the party on Sunday."

"I will," Ben promised.

He brought Race Johnson with him on Sunday afternoon, and they discovered that a whiskey party in Paradise Alley was something like a tea party back home. The sporting ladies were dressed in their finest duds, complete with straw hats, sailor caps, and a variety of other headgear. Tables had been arranged outside the shacks, and glasses and whiskey bottles were much in evidence. A few of the ladies held pets, little puppies or a cat, and one had a half grown Eskimo husky.

The past few days had been good ones for Johnson. He'd ended the week with a handful of gold nuggets that would bring several thousand dollars. Ben decided he'd have to stick closer to him if he meant to earn his pay. This was especially true at the Sunday whiskey party, which attracted the sort of motley crowd usually found around the poker table at the Golden Nugget. When Ben came upon Yancy Booth sipping whiskey with Tess's friend Mary he even felt compelled to ask, "Who's at the poker game this afternoon?"

Yancy gave an unamused laugh. "When I left, Pete Waters was sittin' in with that crybaby Grogan and a couple of strangers."

"Where'd Grogan get the money? I thought you wiped him out the other night."

"Who knows? He probably panned some gold dust out of the river."

Toward evening, the party started growing boisterous. Race Johnson had gone into a shack with one of the girls and Ben figured he had to stay to see him safely back to their room at the Golden Nugget.

Unfortunately, the noise attracted a pair of Mounted Police, who rode up on horseback. The older of the two wore sergeant's stripes and Ben guessed correctly that he was the Sergeant Baxter he'd been hearing about.

"You there!" the Mountie shouted, getting down from his horse and motioning to Ben. "I don't think I've seen you before – what's your name?"

"Ben Snow."

"I'm Sergeant Baxter. Where are you from?"

"The States. San Francisco, most recently."

"When did you arrive?"

"Third week in June."

The sergeant took out a notebook. "Let me have your gun."

"I – "

"Let me have it – I'm not in the habit of asking twice!"

Baxter's weathered face was one that meant business, and he had another Mountie backing him up. Ben shrugged and handed over his revolver.

The sergeant checked to see that it was fully loaded, then made a note of the serial number and Ben's name. "What's that for?" Ben asked.

"My own private gun-registration system. With this many people around, all carrying weapons, I need some way to keep the peace. This helps a little." He handed the six-shooter back. "Carrying anything else? A boot Derringer, maybe?"

"No."

"All right. Keep your nose clean, Mr. Snow, and you won't have any trouble from me."

Baxter walked away, leading his horse, no doubt seeking other unfamiliar faces.

Ben found Race Johnson just coming out of the shack. "Good party," Race commented with a grin. "A nice way to relax on a Sunday."

"I got stopped by that Mountie – Baxter."

"I heard he's been around. They patrol up the river, too. I guess no one can complain. It's a pretty open town."

Ben sometimes thought it was the lure of adventure, of open gambling and sex, that brought Johnson north as much as the promise of gold. He'd told Ben once that he came from a wealthy family. It was Ben's mention of the endless poker game at the Golden Nugget that finally drew Race in as a participant. His gold-hunting luck continued good by day, and perhaps he thought some of it would rub off on the evening game. Ben sat in with him on Tuesday and Wednesday of that week, watching him draw reasonably good cards and win a few nuggets and some cash from the other players.

On Thursday, the stakes went up with the appearance of Yancy Booth for the first time that week. No one knew exactly where he'd been since Sunday's party. Some said he'd fallen in love with one of the girls in Paradise Alley, but no one took that too seriously. In any event he was back, and his presence was immediately reflected in the amount of money riding on each pot. Race and Ben were in the game that night, along with Grogan and the bartender, Pete Waters. Tess wasn't around, but her friend Mary perched on a bar stool to watch. And even Sam Wellman came out of his office a couple of times when the table became especially noisy – or quiet – with excitement.

Race started out in a bad mood, having himself had a run-in with Sergeant Baxter. But he got over it when he was dealt three aces and won a fair-sized pot. The action continued like that for a couple of hours. Ben noticed that Yancy was losing heavily, but didn't think much of it until the man's mood started turning sour. He began slamming his hand on the table and tossing his cards haphazardly. Ben hadn't seen this side of him before, and it hardly seemed in keeping with his reputation as a professional gambler.

Once at the end of a hand, he came close to accusing Race of having cheated and Ben tensed for possible trouble. But Wellman was standing nearby and managed to quiet him.

"If one of you goes for a gun, you're both outa here – and I mean it. I'm not gonna have the Mounties close me up at the peak of the summer business."

Yancy calmed down until Grogan made the mistake of laughing gleefully when he bluffed him out with a pair of fives. The gambler's eyes hardened to slits and his hand twitched toward his coat, but then he seemed to relax and gain control of himself. That was why Ben was taken off guard a few hands later when Yancy suddenly sprang to his feet.

"That's the last time you deal yourself an ace from the bottom of the deck!" he shouted at Race, and in a flash he pulled a small Derringer from beneath his coat.

Ben moved fast, but Race was faster. His six-shooter was in his hand and firing before Ben could draw. Yancy Booth spun to one side like a dancer and went down. Mary started screaming from her bar stool and Sam Wellman ran out of his office, gun drawn.

Ben sat there feeling like a fool. He'd traveled to the end of the world as the bodyguard for a man who was a faster draw than he was.

Sam Wellman and Pete Waters quickly carried the body away, but Sergeant Baxter and another Mountie arrived on the scene and took Race into custody. Grogan and Ben were told they'd be needed as witnesses.

"That means don't try to leave town," Baxter explained. "There's noplace you can run to around here."

Wellman told Ben that Race would be held in the local jail until a traveling judge – a circuit rider – arrived the following week for the arraignment. The trial would follow soon after, and if he was found guilty Race would be sent down to the larger jail at Whitehorse to serve his sentence.

Ben visited his employer in jail the following morning. "I should have shot him, not you. That's what you were paying me for."

"Hell, don't let it worry you," Race said. "It's a clear case of self-defense. Once the judge hears the testimony, he'll toss it out of court."

"I hope so," Ben said, but he didn't feel half as confident as Race. This was a strange part of the world, and the people up here were no friends of theirs.

The day was cloudy, with a chill in the air to add to his depression. He left the jail and decided a visit to Tess might cheer him up. Crossing the rope bridge to Paradise Alley, he could see little activity among the shacks. The men had gone out to pan for gold and the women were sleeping late.

Tess heard his knocking and came to the door, wrapping a fuzzy pink robe around her. "Come on in," she said.

"Sorry to wake you up."

She yawned. "I had a late night. Want some breakfast?"

"What are you making?"

"Bacon and eggs."

"Sounds good to me."

He watched her start a fire in the wood stove. They talked about the weather, and then Tess said, "I hear Yancy got himself killed again last night."

"Again?"

Her back was to him as she started to fry the bacon and eggs in a large iron pan. "I don't know. Forget it."

"Tell me. You must have meant something by it."

"No, it's just that the same thing happened last fall, about a month after I got here. Yancy got into a fight with a guy at Sam's poker game and the guy shot him. Killed him, so the story went at the time. But it was all hushed up and the fellow who did it got spirited out of town. A couple of weeks later Yancy reappeared, good as new. He told me it had only been a flesh wound and he'd just been hiding out till things blew over."

"I never heard of a *victim* hiding out. Did you see the shooting?"

"No."

"Who did?"

"Most of them have moved on, I think. No, one's still here – that fellow Grogan. I'm pretty sure he was in on the game."

"How about Sam Wellman and Pete Waters?"

"Well, sure. I think Pete was working that night."

"Thanks," he said, getting to his feet.

"Don't you want your bacon and eggs?"

"Another time. Thanks, Tess."

He found Grogan down along a shallow part of the river, panning for gold dust in an area that must have been tried by every miner in Dawson. "How's your luck?" Ben called to the shaggy-haired man.

"Found myself a little dust. Not worth mentioning. Guess I'll have to move upriver."

"If you've got a minute, I'd like to ask you about Yancy Booth."

Grogan was immediately on guard. "What about him? He's dead. That's all I know."

"I hear tell something like this happened before. Everyone thought he was dead and he staged an amazing resurrection."

"I wouldn't know about that."

"You were there when it happened, Grogan. You saw the whole thing."

"I don't know. I got a bad memory."

"What do you owe to any of them? I saw Yancy beat you out of every cent you had in the world last week."

"That was last week."

Ben took a small nugget of gold from his pocket. It was one that Race Johnson had given him as his pay so far. "How about if I break off half of this for you? It'll get you started again and you can tell everyone you panned it out of the river."

Grogan glanced around to make sure no one was watching them. "Yeah. I could tell you about it," he agreed in a voice that was almost a whisper.

Ben picked up Grogan's small hammer and carefully placed the nugget against a rock before hitting it. The split was irregular and he gave Grogan the smaller half. The shaggy man didn't complain. "Now start talking."

"They set it up to fleece this guy who was new to Dawson. Yancy pretended to be shot and they carried him out."

"Sam Wellman was in on it?"

"I don't know. But Pete Waters was. He helped carry the body out. They got some money out of the mark and sent him on his way. Then when it was safe, Yancy turned up alive."

"If the mark shot him, how come he lived?"

Grogan shrugged.

"It was a trick of some sort. I don't know how they worked it."

"All right. Thanks."

"You won't say I told you?"

"Don't worry, Grogan."

He hadn't told Ben much more than Tess had, except for his implication of the bartender. Still, the confirmation of her story was worth the portion of the nugget he'd paid Grogan. His next stop was the jail, where he found Sergeant Baxter laboriously filling out a stack of government forms.

"The job is getting to be all paperwork," he grumbled. "What can I do for you today, Mr. Snow?"

"You have a good memory for names."

Baxter smiled. "It's my business."

"I came about the shooting of Yancy Booth."

"Yes, Race Johnson is a friend of yours, isn't he? You've been here to see him."

"I'm trying to free him."

"Don't try too hard or I'll have you in the next cell."

"I understand Yancy was shot last fall, same as this, only he didn't really die. I was thinking maybe he didn't die this time, either."

Baxter got to his feet and buttoned the collar of his red uniform jacket. "Let's go see. He's over in the icehouse."

He led Ben out the back door of the jail and across a narrow street, adjusting his hat as they went. "I've never been here," Ben said.

Sergeant Baxter unlocked the door of a building on the river bank. "They cut up ice from the river during the winter and store it here for use in the summer, just like in the big cities. I find it makes a good morgue for unclaimed bodies."

"Booth had no family?"

"None that I know of." Baxter led the way past piles of ice blocks covered with a light coating of sawdust. The temperature must have been twenty degrees cooler than outside. "If no one claims him by next week, we'll bury him in potter's field."

They stopped before a rough wooden coffin and the sergeant lifted the lid.

"Look for yourself."

It was Yancy Booth and he'd never be any deader. The naked body was partly wrapped in a winding sheet, but Ben could see the twin wounds near the heart from Race's bullets. "He's dead, all right," Ben agreed. "Are those powder burns around the wounds?"

"Not really. More a powder residue. Black powder leaves a slight residue up to about six feet away. I'd guess these shots were fired from a distance of around four feet."

"That's about right," Ben agreed. "It was a clear case of self-defense."

"The courts will rule on that."

"And Race stays in jail till they do?"

"That's right," the Mountie told him, stepping aside to let Ben precede him out of the icehouse. "I'm not in the habit of turning gunmen loose to do more shooting."

Ben left the jail without seeing Race again. His hope of discovering Yancy was still alive had been dashed. There seemed to be no hope left unless Grogan was right about the bartender's involvement. It wasn't much of a lead, but it was the only one Ben had.

He searched all afternoon for Pete Waters without finding him. Mary said she thought he'd gone prospecting with some of the others up along the Klondike River. That could mean anything. They might decide to camp out overnight or for a month.

Back at the Golden Nugget, the poker game was still in progress. It would take more than a shooting to end it. Sam Wellman was sitting in, dealing a hand of stud to three strangers. "Is Pete working tonight?" Ben asked him.

"He's supposed to, but I haven't seen him. If he doesn't show up soon, I'll have to take over myself."

It was getting dark when Ben decided to call on Tess over in Paradise Alley. There was nothing to be gained by waiting any longer for Waters.

He'd started across the rope bridge in the dusk when a voice called out behind him.

"Snow! Ben Snow!"

Ben turned and saw a shadowy figure barely visible at the end of the bridge.

"Who is it?" he called back.

"Pete Waters – I hear you been lookin' for me!"

"That's right, I have!" Ben started back toward shore, the bridge swaying a bit underfoot.

"Well, you found me – or I found you!"

There was the sudden flare and boom of a shotgun. Ben felt the rope railing come loose in his hand as the spray of buckshot parted its strands. He was drawing his gun when the second barrel discharged and he went off the bridge, still clutching the loose rope railing.

By some miracle, the rope swung him back toward shore, and when his feet hit the water he was almost to dry land. He fell forward onto the river bank, trying not to reveal his location in the darkness. Some twenty feet above him, he heard Waters break open the shotgun to reload it.

Suddenly there was a shout from the opposite shore. "Ben! Ben, are you hurt?"

He recognized Tess's voice calling out of the darkness, but he dared not reveal his position by answering her. She had seen him crossing in the dusk, seen him falling, and now she was hoping he was alive. The bridge above him hung at an awkward angle without one of its rope supports, and outlined against the night sky he saw her venture out a few feet, still calling his name.

Ben heard the shotgun snapped shut and cocked. He scrambled up on the river bank, shouting, "Go back, Tess! It's Waters and he has a shotgun!"

The bartender fired down at his voice and Ben heard the chatter of buckshot striking the rocks around him. He realized suddenly that his arm was bleeding, either from the first shot or the fall.

"Ben!" Tess yelled again.

The bartender's shotgun boomed, but this time there was the crack of a pistol at almost the same instant. Ben saw Waters stagger onto the bridge and fall, his body caught by the rope support as the shotgun slipped from his grip to splash into the river below.

"You can come up now!" Sergeant Baxter shouted down to Ben. "It's all over!"

An hour later, when Ben's flesh wounds had been tended to by Tess and Mary, he sat in Sam Wellman's office at the Golden Nugget and tried to explain what had happened. Wellman and the girls were there, along with Sergeant Baxter, who'd promised to free Race Johnson if Ben convinced him of his innocence. Ben called Grogan in from the poker game to bolster his case, and the man repeated what he'd told Ben.

"Why didn't you come forward with this before?" Sergeant Baxter wanted to know.

"Because I was afraid of Waters and Yancy. If they're both dead, they can't hurt me now."

"You claim the two of them were extorting money from prospectors by pretending Yancy was dead?"

"That's right. Yancy wore a metal pan full of sawdust under his shirt. Pete Waters doctored the bullets somehow, removing some of their powder, so when they were fired at Yancy's chest they just thudded into the sawdust. Yancy pretended to be dead and the mark got arrested. Then, when he paid Waters enough money, Yancy staged an amazing recovery."

"That's what happened last fall," Wellman admitted. "But I never connected it with this week's shooting."

"I hear they pulled the same trick in Whitehorse before they came here," Grogan said.

But Baxter shook his head.

"That doesn't change the fact that this time Yancy was really killed, and by two bullets fired into his chest by Race Johnson. You saw the body yourself, Snow."

"Yes, I did," Ben admitted. "But what I saw convinced me of Race's innocence."

"How come?"

"Remember the residue of black powder around the wounds? It was consistent with the distance between Race and Yancy at the time of the shooting, but it was all wrong for another reason. The powder residue would have been on Yancy's shirt or coat, not on his bare skin. He was shot later, after he'd removed both his shirt and the metal pan that protected him. And that means Race didn't do it."

"Wait a minute," Sergeant Baxter said, holding up his hand as everyone started talking at once. "You're saying Yancy was alive, only pretending to be shot, when Sam here and Waters carried him out?"

"Exactly. He was killed later."

"But why?"

"A falling-out among thieves, I suppose. What safer time to kill Yancy than when everyone thought he was already dead?"

"All right," Baxter agreed. "You've convinced me. If Pete Waters killed Yancy, your friend should go free. Yancy obviously incited Johnson to shoot him as part of the plot."

"Exactly," Ben said. "But I didn't say Waters killed Yancy."

"What? Then who did?"

"Someone had to tamper with the bullets in Race's gun so they wouldn't fire a full charge. Not only that, but whoever it was had to do the same with my gun. I was Race's bodyguard. When Yancy drew his gun, this person couldn't know whether Race or I would shoot first."

"You're saying Waters couldn't have tampered with your gun?"

"Yes. Only you could have done that, Sergeant, when you checked the serial number. You pretended to check the cartridges, too, but with a little sleight of hand you were actually substituting half loaded bullets that wouldn't penetrate the metal pan under Yancy's shirt. You were there when he took it off, and you're the one who killed him, just as you killed Pete Waters later so he wouldn't talk."

Baxter was smiling as he drew his pistol. "I've heard enough from you. Want to try drawing against me?"

"Not with these bullets," Ben said.

The rest were frozen in position, watching the gun in the Mountie's hand. It was Tess who moved first. She picked up a whiskey bottle and brought it down on Baxter's head.

The next day, when Race Johnson had been released from jail, Ben suggested it was time for them to move on. "We've given our sworn statement and that should be enough. But if you stay around Dawson, someone's going to decide you should testify at Baxter's trial."

"What about the gold? There's lots more around."

"Maybe we should head over to the Alaska Territory," Ben said. "I'd just as soon stay clear of Baxter's Mountie friends. They might not like our giving them a bad name."

Race still had some questions about the set-up. "But with Yancy really dead, how could Baxter hope to shake me down for my gold?"

"Probably by offering you a chance to escape. He'd have shot you, of course, after he got your gold. I guess he figured he couldn't resurrect Yancy twice in the same town, but by killing him and then shooting Pete Waters he figured he'd removed all the potential evidence against himself. I should have suspected him sooner than I did. Naturally, he would have examined the body and seen the metal pan under Yancy's shirt. He had to be part of the scheme."

Race glanced sadly down the main street of Dawson. "I was getting to like this place. How soon do we have to leave?"

"Maybe we can stay over a day or two," Ben decided. "I did promise the girls I'd try to help them repair their bridge."

# PART IV
## Holmes and Beyond

# THE CASE OF THE DEPTFORD HORROR
## Adrian Conan Doyle

*It wasn't possible to put together a volume such as this and exclude the most famous fictional detective of all time, Sherlock Holmes. The Holmes stories by Arthur Conan Doyle are not historical detective stories in their own right, even though some of them are set several decades before their date of publication. But since Doyle's death scores of writers have turned their hand to keeping the great detective alive.*

*For this volume, I wanted to include something special, and also saw the appeal of keeping it in the family. Despite the world-wide popularity of the Holmes stories, many fans seem to have forgotten that Conan Doyle's son, Adrian, turned his hand to several sequels. Adrian Conan Doyle (1910–1970) was Doyle's youngest son. He frequently travelled with his father and became dedicated to his memory. After the Second World War Adrian arranged for John Dickson Carr to work on his father's biography. Carr and Adrian became friends and in 1952 the two determined to write up some of the missing cases, those that Watson refers to in his narratives but never published. Although they began plotting the stories together Carr fell ill and Adrian completed the series. The twelve stories were published as* The Exploits of Sherlock Holmes *(1954).*

*The following story "The Adventure of the Deptford Horror," picks up the tantalizing reference in "The Adventure of Black Peter" (1904) to the case of "Wilson the notorious canary-trainer". I also feel the story owes a little to one of the most famous Holmes adventures, "The Speckled Band".*

I have remarked elsewhere that my friend, Sherlock Holmes, like all great artists, lived for his art's sake and, save in the case of the Duke of Holderness, I have seldom known him claim any substantial reward.

However powerful or wealthy the client, he would refuse to undertake any problem that lacked appeal to his sympathies, while he would devote his most intense energies to the affairs of some humble person whose case contained those singular and remarkable qualities which struck a responsive chord in his imagination.

On glancing through my notes for that memorable year '95, I find recorded the details of a case which may be taken as a typical instance of this disinterested and even altruistic attitude of mind which placed the rendering of a kindly service above that of material reward. I refer, of course, to the dreadful affair of the canaries and the soot-marks on the ceiling.

It was early June that my friend completed his investigations into the sudden death of Cardinal Tosca, an inquiry which he had undertaken at the special request of the Pope. The case had demanded the most exacting work on Holmes's part and, as I had feared at the time, the aftermath had left him in a highly nervous and restless state that caused me some concern both as his friend and his medical adviser.

One rainy night towards the end of the same month I persuaded him to dine with me at Frascatti's, and thereafter we had gone on to the Café Royal for our coffee and liqueurs. As I had hoped, the bustle of the great room with its red plush seats and stately palms bathed in the glow of numerous crystal chandeliers drew him out of his introspective mood, and as he leaned back on our sofa, his fingers playing with the stem of his glass, I noted with satisfaction a gleam of interest in those keen grey eyes as he studied the somewhat bohemian clientele that thronged the tables and alcoves.

I was in the act of replying to some remark when Holmes nodded suddenly in the direction of the door.

"Lestrade," said he. "What can he be doing here?"

Glancing over my shoulder, I saw the lean, rat-faced figure of the Scotland Yard man standing in the entrance, his dark eyes roving slowly around the room.

"He may be seeking you," I remarked. "Probably on some urgent case."

"Hardly, Watson. His wet boots show that he has walked. If there was urgency he would have taken a cab. But here he comes."

The police agent had caught sight of us and, at Holmes's gesture, he pushed his way through the throng and drew up a chair to the table.

"Only a routine check," said he, in reply to my friend's query. "But duty's duty, Mr. Holmes, and I can tell you that I've netted some strange fish before now in these respectable places. While you are comfortably dreaming up your theories in Baker Street, we poor devils at Scotland Yard are doing the practical work. No thanks to us from popes and kings but a bad hour on the Superintendent's carpet if we fail."

"Tut," smiled Holmes good-humouredly. "Your superiors must surely hold you in some esteem since I solved the Ronald Adair murder, the Bruce-Partington theft, the – "

"Quite so, quite so," interrupted Lestrade hurriedly. "And now," he added, with a heavy wink at me, "I have something for you."

"Of course, a young woman who starts at shadows may be more in Dr. Watson's line."

"Really, Lestrade," I protested warmly, "I cannot approve your – "

"One moment, Watson. Let us hear the facts."

"Well, Mr. Holmes, they are absurd enough," continued Lestrade, "and I would not waste your time were it not that I have known you to do a kindness or two before now and your word of advice may in this instance prevent a young woman from acting foolishly. Now, here's the position.

"Down Deptford way, along the edge of the river, there are some of the worst slums in the East End of London but, right in the middle of them, you can still find some fine old houses which were once the homes of wealthy merchants centuries ago. One of these tumbledown mansions has been occupied by a family named Wilson for the past hundred years and more. I understand that they were originally in the china trade and when that went to the dogs a generation back, they got out in time and remained on in the old home. The recent household consisted of Horatio Wilson and his wife, with one son and a daughter, and Horatio's younger brother Theobold who had gone to live with them on his return from foreign parts.

"Some three years ago, the body of Horatio Wilson was hooked out of the river. He had been drowned and, as he was known to have been a hard-drinking man, it was generally accepted that he had missed his step in the fog and fallen into the water. A year later his wife, who suffered from a weak heart, died from a heart attack. We know this to be the case, because the doctor made a very careful examination following the statements of a police constable and a night watchman employed on a Thames barge."

"Statements to what effect?" interposed Holmes.

"Well, there was talk of some noise rising apparently from the old Wilson house. But the nights are often foggy along Thames-side and the men were probably misled. The constable described the sound as a dreadful yell that froze the blood in his veins. If I had him in my division, I'd teach him that such words should never pass the lips of an officer of the law."

"What time was this?"

"Ten o'clock at night, the hour of the old lady's death. It's merely a coincidence, for there is no doubt that she died of heart."

"Go on."

Lestrade consulted his notebook for a moment. "I've been digging up the facts," he continued. "On the night of May 17 last the daughter went to a magic-lantern entertainment accompanied by a woman servant. On her return she found her brother, Phineas Wilson, dead in his arm-chair. He had inherited a bad heart and insomnia from his mother. This time there were no rumours of shrieks and yells, but owing to the expression on the dead man's face the local doctor called in the police surgeon to assist in the examination. It was heart all right, and our man confirmed that this can sometimes cause a distortion of the features that will convey an impression of stark terror."

"That is perfectly true," I remarked.

"Now, it seems that the daughter Janet has become so over-wrought that, according to her uncle, she proposes to sell up the property and go abroad," went on Lestrade. "Her feelings are, I suppose, natural. Death has been busy with the Wilson family."

"And what of this uncle? Theobold, I think you said his name was."

"Well, I fancy that you will find him on your doorstep to-morrow morning. He came to me at the Yard in the hope that the official police could put his niece's fears at rest and persuade her to take a more reasonable view. As we are engaged on more important affairs than calming hysterical young women I advised him to call on you."

"Indeed! Well, it is natural enough that he should resent the unnecessary loss of what is probably a snug corner."

"There is no resentment, Mr. Holmes. Wilson seems to be genuinely attached to his niece and concerned only for her future." Lestrade paused, while a grin spread over his foxy face. "He is not a very worldly person, is Mr. Theobold, and though I've met some queer trades in my time his beats the band. The man trains canaries."

"It is an established profession."

"Is it?" There was an irrating smugness in Lestrade's manner as he rose to his feet and reached for his hat. "It is quite evident that you do not suffer from insomnia, Mr. Holmes," said he, "or you would know that birds trained by Theobold Wilson are different from other canaries. Good night, gentlemen."

"What on earth does the fellow mean?" I asked, as the police agent threaded his way towards the door.

"Merely that he knows something that we do not," replied Holmes drily. "But, as conjecture is as profitless as it is misleading to the analytical mind, let us wait until to-morrow. I can say, however, that I do not propose to waste my time over a matter that appears to fall more properly within the province of the local vicar."

To my friend's relief, the morning brought no visitor. But when, on my return from an urgent case to which I had been summoned shortly after lunch, I entered our sitting-room, I found that our spare chair was occupied by a bespectacled middle-aged man. As he rose to his feet, I observed that he was of an exceeding thinness and that his face, which was scholarly and even austere in expression, was seamed with countless wrinkles and of that dull parchment-yellow that comes from years under a tropic sun.

"Ah, Watson, you have arrived just in time," said Holmes. "This is Mr. Theobold Wilson about whom Lestrade spoke to us last night."

Our visitor wrung my hand warmly. "Your name is, of course, well known to me, Dr. Watson," he cried. "Indeed, if Mr. Sherlock Holmes will pardon me for saying so, it is largely thanks to you that we are aware of his genius. As a medical man doubtless well versed in the handling of nervous cases, your presence should have a most beneficial effect upon my unhappy niece."

Holmes caught my eye resignedly. "I have promised Mr. Wilson to accompany him to Deptford, Watson," said he, "for it would seem that the young lady is determined to leave her home to-morrow. But I must repeat again, Mr. Wilson, that I fail to see in what way my presence can affect the matter."

"You are over-modest, Mr. Holmes. When I appealed to the official police, I had hoped that they might convince Janet that, terrible though our family losses have been in the past three years, nevertheless they lay in natural causes and that there is no reason why she should flee from her home. I had the impression," he added, with a chuckle, "that the inspector was somewhat chagrined at my ready acceptance of his own suggestion that I should invoke your assistance."

"I shall certainly remember my small debt to Lestrade," replied Holmes drily as he rose to his feet. "Perhaps, Watson, you would ask Mrs. Hudson to whistle a four-wheeler and Mr. Wilson can clarify certain points to my mind as we drive to Deptford."

It was one of those grey brooding summer days when London is at its worst and, as we rattled over Blackfriars Bridge, I noted that wreaths of mist were rising from the river like the poisonous vapours of some hot jungle swamp. The more spacious streets of the

West End had given place to the great commercial thoroughfares, resounding with the stamp and clatter of the drayhorses, and these in turn merged at last into a maze of dingy streets that, following the curve of the river, grew more and more wretched in their squalor the nearer we approached to that labyrinth of tidal basins and dark evil-smelling lanes that were once the ancient cradle of England's sea-trade and of an empire's wealth. I could see that Holmes was listless and bored to a point of irritation and I did my best, therefore, to engage our companion in conversation.

"I understand that you are an expert on canaries," I remarked.

Theobold Wilson's eyes, behind their powerful spectacles, lit with the glow of the enthusiast. "A mere student, sir, but with thirty years of practical research," he cried. "Can it be that you too? No? A pity! The study, breeding and training of the Fringilla Canaria is a task worthy of a man's lifetime. You would not credit the ignorance, Dr. Watson, that prevails on this subject even in the most enlightened circles. When I read my paper on the crossing of the Madeira and the Canary Island strains to the British Ornithological Society I was appalled at the puerility of the ensuing questions."

"Inspector Lestrade hinted at some special characteristic in your training of these little songsters."

"Songsters, sir! A thrush is a songster. The Fringilla is the supreme ear of nature, possessing a unique power of imitation which can be trained for the benefit and edification of the human race. But the inspector was correct," he went on more calmly, "in that I have put my birds to a special effect. They are trained to sing by night in artificial light."

"Surely a somewhat singular pursuit."

"I like to think that it is a kindly one. My birds are trained for the benefit of those who suffer from insomnia and I have clients in all parts of the country. Their tuneful song helps to while away the long night hours and the dowsing of the lamplight terminates the concert."

"It seems to me that Lestrade was right," I observed. "Yours is indeed an unique profession."

During our conversation Holmes, who had idly picked up our companion's heavy stick, had been examining it with some attention.

"I understand that you returned to England some three years ago," he observed.

"I did."

"From Cuba, I perceive."

Theobold Wilson started and for an instant I seemed to catch a gleam of something like wariness in the swift glance that he shot at Holmes.

"That is so," he said. "But how did you know?"

"Your stick is cut from Cuban ebony. There is no mistaking that greenish tint and the exceptionally high polish."

"It might have been bought in London since my return from, say, Africa."

"No, it has been yours for some years." Holmes lifted the stick to the carriage window and tilted it so that the daylight shone upon the handle. "You will perceive," he went on, "that there is a slight but regular scraping that has worn through the polish along the left side of the handle, just where the ring finger of a left-handed man would close upon the grip. Ebony is among the toughest of woods and it would require considerable time to cause such wear and a ring of some harder metal than gold. You are left-handed, Mr. Wilson, and wear a silver ring on your middle-finger."

"Dear me, how simple. I thought for the moment that you had done something clever. As it happens, I was in the sugar trade in Cuba and brought my old stick back with me. But here we are at the house and, if you can put my silly niece's fears at rest as quickly as you can deduce my past, I shall be your debtor, Mr. Sherlock Holmes."

On descending from our four-wheeler, we found ourselves in a lane of mean slatternly houses sloping, so far as I could judge from the yellow mist that was already creeping up the lower end, to the river's edge. At one side was a high wall of crumbling brickwork pierced by an iron gate through which we caught a glimpse of a substantial mansion lying in its own garden.

"The old house has known better days," said our companion, as we followed him through the gate and up the path. "It was built in the year that Peter the Great came to live in Scales Court, whose ruined park can be seen from the upper windows."

Usually I am not unduly affected by my surroundings, but I must confess that I was aware of a feeling of depression at the melancholy spectacle that lay before us. The house, though of dignified and even imposing proportions, was faced with blotched, weather-stained plaster which had fallen away in places to disclose the ancient brickwork that lay beneath, while a tangled mass of ivy covering one wall had sent its long tendrils across the high-peaked roof to wreathe itself around the chimney stacks.

The garden was an overgrown wilderness, and the air of the whole place reeked with the damp musty smell of the river.

Theobold Wilson led us through a small hall into a comfortably furnished drawing-room. A young woman with auburn hair and a freckled face, who was sorting through some papers at a writing-desk, sprang to her feet at our entrance.

"Here are Mr. Sherlock Holmes and Dr. Watson," announced our companion. "This is my niece, Janet, whose interests you are here to protect against her own unreasonable conduct."

The young lady faced us bravely enough, though I noted a twitch and tremor of the lips that spoke of a high nervous tension. "I am leaving to-morrow, uncle," she cried, "and nothing that these gentlemen can say will alter my decision. Here, there is only sorrow and fear – above all, fear!"

"Fear of what?"

The girl passed her hand over her eyes. "I – I cannot explain. I hate the shadows and the funny little noises."

"You have inherited both money and property, Janet," said Mr. Wilson earnestly. "Will you, because of shadows, desert the roof of your fathers? Be reasonable."

"We are here only to serve you, young lady," said Holmes with some gentleness, "and to try to put your fears at rest. It is often so in life that we injure our own best interests by precipitate action."

"You will laugh at a woman's intuitions, sir."

"By no means. They are often the signposts of Providence. Understand clearly that you will go or stay as you see fit. But perhaps, as I am here, it might relieve your mind to show me over the house."

"An admirable suggestion!" cried Theobold Wilson cheerily. "Come, Janet, we will soon dispose of your shadows and noises."

In a little procession we trooped from one over-furnished room to another on the ground floor.

"I will take you to the bedrooms," said Miss Wilson as we paused at last before the staircase.

"Are there no cellars in a house of this antiquity?"

"There is one cellar, Mr. Holmes, but it is little used save for the storage of wood and some of uncle's old nest-boxes. This way, please."

It was a gloomy, stone-built chamber in which we found ourselves. A stack of wood was piled against one wall and a pot-bellied Dutch stove, its iron pipe running through the ceiling, filled the far corner. Through a glazed door reached by a line of steps and opening into the garden, a dim light filtered down upon the flagstones. Holmes sniffed the air keenly, and I was myself aware of an increased mustiness from the nearby river.

"Like most Thames-side houses, you must be plagued by rats," he remarked.

"We used to be. But, since uncle came here, he has got rid of them."

"Quite so. Dear me," he continued, peering down at the floor. "What busy little fellows!"

Following his gaze, I saw that his attention had been drawn by a few garden ants scurrying across the floor from beneath the edge of the stove and up the steps leading to the garden door. "It is as well for us, Watson," he chuckled, pointing with his stick at the tiny particles with which they were encumbered, "that we are not under the necessity of lugging along our dinners thrice our own size. It is a lesson in patience." He lapsed into silence, staring thoughtfully at the floor. "A lesson," he repeated slowly.

Mr. Wilson's thin lips tightened. "What foolery is this," he exclaimed. "The ants are there because the servants would throw garbage in the stove to save themselves the trouble of going to the dustbin."

"And so you put a lock on the lid."

"We did. If you wish, I can fetch the key. No? Then, if you are finished, let me take you to the bedrooms."

"Perhaps I may see the room where your brother died," requested Holmes as we reached the top floor.

"It is here," replied Miss Wilson, throwing open the door.

It was a large chamber furnished with some taste and even luxury and lit by two deeply recessed windows flanking another pot-bellied stove decorated with yellow tiles to harmonize with the tone of the room. A pair of birdcages hung from the stove pipe.

"Where does that side-door lead?" asked my friend.

"It communicates with my room, which was formerly used by my mother," she answered.

For a few minutes, Holmes prowled around listlessly.

"I perceive that your brother was addicted to night-reading," he remarked.

"Yes. He suffered from sleeplessness. But how – "

"Tut, the pile of the carpet on the right of the armchair is thick with traces of candlewax. But, hullo! What have we here?"

Holmes had halted near the window and was staring intently at the upper wall. Then, mounting the sill, he stretched out an arm and, touching the plaster lightly here and there, sniffed at his finger-tips. There was a puzzled frown on his face as he clambered down and commenced to circle slowly around the room, his eyes fixed upon the ceiling.

"Most singular," he muttered.

"Is anything wrong, Mr. Holmes?" faltered Miss Wilson.

"I am merely interested to account for these odd whorls and lines across the upper wall and plaster."

"It must be those dratted cockroaches dragging the dust all over the place," exclaimed Wilson apologetically. "I've told you before, Janet, that you would be better employed in supervising the servants' work. But what now, Mr. Holmes?"

My friend, who had crossed to the side-door and glanced within, now closed it again and strolled across to the window.

"My visit has been a useless one," said he, "and, as I see that the fog is rising, I fear that we must take our leave. These are, I suppose, your famous canaries?" he added, pointing to the cages above the stove.

"A mere sample. But come this way."

Wilson led us along the passage and threw open a door.

"There!" said he.

Obviously it was his own bedroom and yet unlike any bedroom that I had entered in all my professional career. From floor to ceiling it was festooned with scores of cages and the little golden-coated singers within filled the air with their sweet warbling and trilling.

"Daylight or lamplight, it's all the same to them. Here, Carrie, Carrie!" He whistled a few liquid notes which I seemed to recognize. The bird took them up into a lovely cadency of song.

"A skylark!" I cried.

"Precisely. As I said before, the Fringilla if properly trained are the supreme imitators."

"I confess that I do not recognize that song," I remarked, as one of the birds broke into a low rising whistle ending in a curious tremolo.

Mr. Wilson threw a towel over the cage. "It is the song of a tropic night-bird," he said shortly, "and, as I have the foolish pride to prefer my birds to sing the songs of the day while it is day, we will punish Peperino by putting him in darkness."

"I am surprised that you prefer an open fireplace here to a stove," observed Holmes. "There must be a considerable draught."

"I have not noticed one. Dear me, the fog is indeed increasing. I am afraid, Mr. Holmes, that you have a bad journey before you."

"Then we must be on our way."

As we descended the stairs and paused in the hall, while Theobold Wilson fetched our hats, Sherlock Holmes leaned over towards our young companion.

"I would remind you, Miss Wilson, of what I said earlier about a woman's intuition," he said quietly. "There are occasions when the truth can be sensed more easily than it can be seen. Good night."

A moment later we were feeling our way down the garden path to where the lights of our waiting four-wheeler shone dimly through the rising fog.

My companion was sunk in thought as we rumbled westward through the mean streets whose squalor was the more aggressive under the garish light of the gas-lamps that flared and whistled outside the numerous public houses. The night promised to be a bad one, and already through the yellow vapour thickening and writhing above the pavements the occasional wayfarer was nothing more than a vague hurrying shadow.

"I could have wished, my dear fellow," I remarked, "that you had been spared the need to uselessly waste your energies, which are already sufficiently depleted."

"Well, well, Watson. I fancied that the affairs of the Wilson family would prove no concern of ours. And yet – " he sank back, absorbed for a moment in his own thoughts – "and yet it is wrong, wrong, all wrong!" I heard him mutter under his breath.

"I observed nothing of a sinister nature."

"Nor I. But every danger bell in my head is jangling its warning. Why a fireplace, Watson, why a fire-place? I take it that you noticed that the pipe from the cellar connected with the stoves in the other bedrooms?"

"In one bedroom."

"No. There was the same arrangement in the adjoining room, where the mother died."

"I see nothing in this save an old-fashioned system of heating flues."

"And what of the marks on the ceiling?"

"You mean the whorls of dust."

"I mean the whorls of soot."

"Soot! Surely you are mistaken, Holmes."

"I touched them, smelt them, examined them. They were speckles and lines of wood-soot."

"Well, there is probably some perfectly natural explanation."

For a time we sat in silence. Our cab had reached the beginnings of the City and I was gazing out of the window, my fingers drumming idly on the half-lowered pane, which was already befogged with moisture, when my thoughts were recalled by a sharp ejaculation from my companion. He was staring fixedly over my shoulder.

"The glass," he muttered.

Over the clouded surface there now lay an intricate tracery of whorls and lines where my fingers had wandered aimlessly.

Holmes clapped his hand to his brow and, throwing open the other window, he shouted an order to the cabby. The vehicle turned in its tracks and, with the driver lashing at his horse, we clattered away into the thickening gloom.

"Ah, Watson, Watson, true it is that none are so blind as those who will not see!" quoted Holmes bitterly, sinking back into his corner. "All the facts were there, staring me in the face, and yet logic failed to respond."

"What facts?"

"There are nine. Four alone should have sufficed. Here is a man from Cuba, who not only trains canaries in a singular manner but knows the calls of tropical nightbirds and keeps a fireplace in his bedroom. There is devilry here, Watson. Stop, cabby, stop!"

We were passing a junction of two busy thoroughfares, with the golden balls of a pawnshop glimmering above a street lamp. Holmes sprang out. But after a few minutes he was back again and we recommenced our journey.

"It is fortunate that we are still in the City," he chuckled, "for I fancy that the East End pawnshops are unlikely to run to golf-clubs."

"Good heavens –!" I began, only to lapse into silence while I stared down at the heavy niblick which he had thrust into my hand. The first shadows of some vague and monstrous horror seemed to rise up and creep over my mind.

"We are too early," exclaimed Holmes, consulting his watch. "A sandwich and a glass of whisky at the first public house will not come amiss."

The clock on St. Nicholas Church was striking ten when we found ourselves once again in that evil-smelling garden. Through the mist, the dark gloom of the house was broken by a single feeble light in an upper window. "It is Miss Wilson's room," said Holmes. "Let us hope that this handful of gravel will rouse her without alarming the household."

An instant later, there came the sound of an opening window.

"Who is there?" demanded a tremulous voice.

"It is Sherlock Holmes," my friend called back softly. "I must speak with you at once, Miss Wilson. Is there a side-door?"

"There is one in the wall to your left. But what has happened?"

"Pray descend immediately. Not a word to your uncle."

We felt our way along the wall and reached the door just as it opened to disclose Miss Wilson. She was in her dressing-gown, her hair tumbled about her shoulders and, as her startled eyes peered at us across the light of the candle in her hand, the shadows danced and trembled on the wall behind her.

"What is it, Mr. Holmes?" she gasped.

"All will be well, if you carry out my instructions," my friend replied quietly. "Where is your uncle?"

"He is in his room."

"Good. While Dr. Watson and I occupy your room, you will move into your late brother's bedchamber. If you value your life," he added solemnly, "you will not attempt to leave it."

"You frighten me!" she whimpered.

"Rest assured that we will take care of you. And now, two final questions before you retire. Has your uncle visited you this evening?"

"Yes. He brought Peperino and put him with the other birds in the cage in my room. He said that as it was my last night at home I should have the best entertainment that he had the power to give me."

"Ha! Quite so. Your last night. Tell me, Miss Wilson, do you suffer at all from the same malady as your mother and brother?"

"A weak heart? I must confess it, yes."

"Well, we will accompany you quietly upstairs where you will retire to the adjoining room. Come, Watson."

Guided by the light of Janet Wilson's candle, we mounted silently to the floor above and thence into the bedchamber which Holmes had previously examined. While we waited for our companion to collect her things from the adjoining room, Holmes strolled across and, lifting the edge of the cloths which now covered the two birdcages, peered in at the tiny sleeping occupants.

"The evil of man is as inventive as it is immeasurable," said he, and I noticed that his face was very stern.

On Miss Wilson's return, having seen that she was safely ensconced for the night, I followed Holmes into the room which she had lately occupied. It was a small chamber but comfortably furnished and lit by a heavy silver oil-lamp. Immediately above a tiled Dutch stove there hung a cage containing three canaries which, momentarily ceasing their song, cocked their little golden heads at our approach.

"I think, Watson, that it would be as well to relax for half an hour," whispered Holmes as we sank into our chairs. "So kindly put out the light."

"But, my dear fellow, if there is any danger it would be an act of madness!" I protested.

"There is no danger in the darkness."

"Would it not be better," I said severely, "that you were frank with me? You have made it obvious that the birds are being put to some evil purpose, but what is this danger that exists only in the lamplight?"

"I have my own ideas on that matter, Watson, but it is better that we should wait and see. I would draw your attention, however, to the hinged lid of the stokehole on the top of the stove."

"It appears to be a perfectly normal fitting."

"Just so. But is there not some significance in the fact that the stokehole of an iron stove should be fitted with a tin lid?"

"Great heavens, Holmes!" I cried, as the light of understanding burst upon me. "You mean that this man Wilson has used the interconnecting pipes from the stove in the cellar to those in the bedrooms to disseminate some deadly poison to wipe out his own kith and kin and thus obtain the property. It is for that reason that he has a fireplace in his own bedroom. I see it all."

"Well, you are not far wrong, Watson, though I fancy that Master Theobold is rather more subtle than you suppose. He possesses the two qualities vital to the successful murderer – ruthlessness and imagination. But now, dowse the light like a good fellow and for a while let us relax. If my reading of the problem is correct, our nerves may be tested to their limit before we see to-morrow's dawn."

I lay back in the darkness and, drawing some comfort from the thought that ever since the affair with Colonel Sebastian Moran I had carried my revolver in my pocket, I sought in my mind for some explanation that would account for the warning contained in Holmes's words. But I must have been wearier than I had imagined. My thoughts grew more and more confused and finally I dozed off.

It was a touch upon my arm that awoke me. The lamp had been relit and my friend was bending over me, his long black shadow thrown upon the ceiling.

"Sorry to disturb you, Watson," he whispered. "But duty calls."

"What do you wish me to do?"

"Sit still and listen. Peperino is singing."

It was a vigil that I shall long remember. Holmes had tilted the lampshade, so that the light fell on the opposite wall broken by the window and the great tiled stove with its hanging birdcage. The fog had thickened and the rays from the lamp, filtering through the window glass, lost themselves in luminous clouds that swirled and boiled against the panes.

My mind darkened by a premonition of evil, I would have found our surroundings melancholy enough without that eerie sound that was rising and falling from the canary cage. It was a kind of whistling beginning with a low throaty warble and slowly ascending to a single chord that rang through the room like the note of a great wineglass, a sound so mesmeric in its repetition that almost imperceptibly the present seemed to melt away and my imagination to reach out beyond those fog-bound windows into the dark lush depth of some exotic jungle.

I had lost all count of time, and it was only the stillness following the sudden cessation of the bird's song that brought me back to reality. I glanced across the room and, in an instant, my heart gave one great throb and then seemed to stop beating altogether.

The lid of the stove was slowly rising.

My friends will agree that I am neither a nervous nor an impressionable man, but I must confess that, as I sat there gripping the sides of my chair and glaring at the dreadful thing that was gradually clambering into view, my limbs momentarily refused their functions.

The lid had tilted back an inch or more, and through the gap thus created a writhing mass of yellow stick-like objects was clawing and scrabbling for a hold. And then, in a flash, it was out and standing motionless upon the surface of the stove.

Though I have always viewed with horror the bird-eating tarantulas of South America, they shrank into insignificance when compared with the loathsome creature that faced us now across that lamplit room. It was bigger in its spread than a large dinner-plate, with a hard, smooth, yellow body surrounded by legs that, rising high above it, conveyed a fearful impression that the thing was crouching for its spring. It was absolutely hairless save for tufts of stiff bristles around the leg-joints, and above the glint of its great poison mandibles clusters of beady eyes shone in the light with a baleful red iridescence.

"Don't move, Watson," whispered Holmes, and there was a note of horror in his voice that I had never heard before.

The sound roused the creature for, in a single lightning bound, it sprang from the stove to the top of the birdcage and, reaching the wall, whizzed round the room and over the ceiling with a dreadful febrile swiftness that the eye could scarcely follow.

Holmes flung himself forward like a man possessed.

"Kill it! Smash it!" he yelled hoarsely, raining blow after blow with his golf-club at the blurred shape racing across the walls.

Dust from broken plaster choked the air, and a table crashed over as I flung myself to the ground when the great spider cleared the room in a single leap and turned at bay. Holmes bounded across me, swinging his club. "Keep where you are!" he shouted, and even as his voice rang through the room the thud . . . thud . . . thud of the blows was broken by a horrible squelching sound. For an instant the creature hung there, and then, slipping slowly down, it lay like a mess of smashed eggs with three thin bony legs still twitching and plucking at the floor.

"Thank God that it missed you when it sprang!" I gasped, scrambling to my feet.

He made no reply, and glancing up I caught a glimpse of his face reflected in a wall mirror. He looked pale and strained, and there was a curious rigidity in his expression.

"I am afraid it's up to you, Watson," he said quietly. "It has a mate."

I spun round to be greeted by a spectacle that I shall remember for the rest of my days. Sherlock Holmes was standing perfectly still within two feet of the stove and on top of it, reared up on its back legs, its loathsome body shuddering for the spring, stood another monstrous spider.

I knew instinctively that any sudden movement would merely precipitate the creature's leap and so, carefully drawing my revolver from my pocket, I fired point-blank.

Through the powder-smoke, I saw the thing shrink into itself and then, toppling slowly backward, it fell through the open lid of the stove. There was a rasping, slithering sound rapidly fading away into silence.

"It's fallen down the pipe," I cried, conscious that my hands were now shaking under a strong reaction. "Are you all right, Holmes?"

He looked at me and there was a singular light in his eye.

"Thanks to you, my dear fellow!" he said soberly. "If I had moved, then – but what is that?"

A door had slammed below and, in an instant later, we caught the swift patter of feet upon the gravel path.

"After him!" cried Holmes, springing for the door. "Your shot warned him that the game was up. He must not escape!"

But fate decreed otherwise. Though we rushed down the stairs and out into the fog, Theobold Wilson had too much start on us and the advantage of knowing the terrain. For a while, we followed the faint sound of his running footsteps down the empty lanes towards the river, but at length these died away in the distance.

"It is no good, Watson. We have lost our man," panted Holmes. "This is where the official police may be of use. But listen! Surely that was a cry?"

"I thought I heard something."

"Well, it is hopeless to look further in the fog. Let us return and comfort this poor girl with the assurance that her troubles are now at an end."

"They were nightmare creatures, Holmes," I exclaimed, as we retraced our steps towards the house, "and of some unknown species."

"I think not, Watson," said he. "It was the Galeodes spider, the horror of the Cuban forests. It is perhaps fortunate for the rest of the world that it is found nowhere else. The creature is nocturnal in its habits and, unless my memory belies me, it possesses the power to actually break the spine of smaller creatures with a single blow of its mandibles. You will recall that Miss Janet mentioned that the rats had vanished since her uncle's return. Doubtless Wilson brought the brutes back with him," he went on, "and then conceived the idea of training certain of his canaries to imitate the song of some Cuban night-bird upon which the Galeodes fed. The marks on the ceiling were caused, of course, by the soot adhering to the spiders' legs after they had scrambled up the flues. It is fortunate, perhaps, for the consulting detective that the duster of the average housemaid seldom strays beyond the height of a mantelpiece.

"Indeed, I can discover no excuse for my lamentable slowness in solving this case, for the facts were before me from the first and the whole affair was elementary in its construction.

"And yet, to give Theobold Wilson his dues, one must recognize his almost diabolical cleverness. Once these horrors were installed in the stove in the cellar, what more simple than to arrange two ordinary flues communicating with the bedrooms above. By hanging the cages over the stoves, the flues would themselves act as a magnifier to the bird's song and guided by their predatory instinct the creatures would invariably ascend whichever pipe led to it. Having devised some means of luring them back again to their nest, they represented a comparatively safe way of getting rid of those who stood between himself and the property."

"Then its bite is deadly?" I interposed.

"To a person in weak health, probably so. But there lies the devilish cunning of the scheme, Watson. It was the sight of the thing rather than its bite, poisonous though it may be, on which he relied to kill his victim. Can you imagine the effect upon an elderly woman, and later upon her son, both suffering from insomnia and heart disease, when in the midst of a bird's seemingly innocent song this appalling spectacle arose from the top of the stove? We have sampled it ourselves, though we are healthy men. It killed them as surely as a bullet through their hearts."

"There is one thing I cannot understand, Holmes. Why did he appeal to Scotland Yard?"

"Because he is a man of iron nerve. His niece was instinctively frightened and, finding that she was adamant in her intention of leaving, he planned to kill her at once and by the same method.

"Once done, who should dare to point the finger of suspicion at Master Theobold? Had he not appealed to Scotland Yard, and even invoked the aid of Mr. Sherlock Holmes himself to satisfy one and all? The girl had died of a heart attack like the others, and her uncle would have been the reciprocant of general condolences.

"Remember the padlocked cover of the stove in the cellar and admire the cold nerve that offered to fetch the key. It was bluff, of course, for he would have discovered that he had 'lost' it. Had we persisted and forced that lock, I prefer not to think of what we would have found clinging around our collars."

Theobold Wilson was never heard of again. But it is perhaps suggestive that, some two days later, a man's body was fished out of the Thames. The corpse was mutilated beyond recognition, probably by a ship's propeller, and the police searched his pockets in vain for means of identification. They contained nothing, however, save for a small notebook filled with jottings on the brooding period of the Fringilla Canaria.

"It is the wise man who keeps bees," remarked Sherlock Holmes when he read the report. "You know where you are with them and at least they do not attempt to represent themselves as something that they are not."

From *"Black Peter"* (THE RETURN OF SHERLOCK HOLMES).

*"In the memorable year '95, a curious and incongruous succession of cases had engaged his attention ranging from ... the sudden death of Cardinal Tosca down to the arrest of Wilson the notorious canary-trainer,\* which removed a plague-spot from the East End of London."*

* *In the Wilson case, Holmes did not actually arrest Wilson, as Wilson was drowned. This was a typical Watson error in his hurried reference to the case.*

# FIVE RINGS IN RENO
## R. L. Stevens

*Stevens is one of the pen names of the prolific Edward D. Hoch whom we have
already encountered in this anthology. I could think of no better way to close
this volume than to include a story in which Conan Doyle himself features as a
detective. For that reason I made the one exception to my rule of stories being
set in the nineteenth century or earlier. The following is set in 1910, and brings
our historical detectives into the modern era.*

*In his excellent biography,* The Life of Sir Arthur Conan Doyle, *John
Dickson Carr tells us that Doyle was invited to act as referee for the
heavyweight championship fight between Jack Johnson and Jim Jeffries in
Reno, Nevada, on July 4, 1910. Doyle tentatively accepted, with great pleasure,
but changed his mind a week later and sent his regrets.*

*Now what if Doyle had gone to Reno . . .?*

Arthur Conan Doyle stepped off the train at the Reno depot looking
a bit bewildered. After traveling across an ocean and a continent to
reach the small city near the foot of the Sierra Nevada mountains,
he had at least expected someone would be there to meet him and
take his bags.

"Sir Arthur!" a voice called suddenly, and he turned to see a slim
blond young man striding toward him. "Didn't expect the train to
be on time. They never are!"

"These are my bags," Doyle said, indicating two well-traveled
Gladstones. "You would be Mr. Summons?"

"Charlie Summons, at your service, Sir Arthur."

"The title I value most is that of 'Doctor,' if you don't mind."

"Oh – certainly, Dr. Doyle! This way, please."

"Somehow I expected Reno would be larger."

Charlie Summons turned with a trace of apology. "Well, it's not
London, Sir – Dr. Doyle – but we like to think of ourselves as the
biggest little city in the west. And this fight is really goin' to put us
on the map!"

"It's certainly a lengthy journey by train," Doyle remarked. "I've written occasionally about the American west, but this is my first personal view of it. When I visited the States in '94 I never came further west than Chicago and Milwaukee."

"I read what you wrote about the Mormons of Utah in *A Study in Scarlet*. Could have sworn you'd actually been there!"

Doyle smiled at the compliment. "I read a great deal about your country before coming here."

They had reached the street outside the depot, and Summons was loading the bags into the back seat of an elegant black motorcar with polished brass trim. "This is a 1908 Packard," Summons explained. "You don't see many cars out west yet, but we have a few of 'em available for special visitors like yourself."

"It is quite a handsome vehicle," Doyle conceded, climbing up into the passenger's seat. "I suppose the motorcar is the coming thing in London too, though I do hate to see them replacing the hansom cabs."

Charlie Summons cranked the engine and then jumped in as the car coughed into life. "Times are changing, Dr. Doyle. Last month a biplane took off from a street in Washington right next to the White House."

"I'll remain on the ground, thank you," Doyle said with a smile.

"We've got you a fine room at the Reno Hotel. Everyone important is staying there. There's another writer too – Jack London. He's covering the fight for the San Francisco *Chronicle* and the New York *Herald*."

Doyle's face lit up. "I'll be interested in meeting Jack London. Some people have detected minor evidences of us in each other's stories. When I toured America last time I met Rudyard Kipling in Vermont and we became good friends."

Summons pulled the car up in front of the hotel. "Oh, oh! There's Monica Malone – that means trouble!"

Doyle found himself mildly amused by the man. "And what trouble might such a comely young woman offer?"

"She read how you helped solve that mystery in England a few years back, and she imagines you're Sherlock Holmes himself. She'll be wanting your help."

"Holmes! Is that name going to haunt me here too?"

But he climbed down from the car and went to meet the young lady. "Dr. Conan Doyle?" she asked. "I must speak with you on a most urgent matter."

"Nothing is so urgent right now as the fight that will take place in two days. I am not here in my capacity as an author – or as a doctor – but as a referee." Though he was 51 years old and only recently married to his charming second wife, Doyle still had an eye for a beautiful woman. Miss Malone's cameo face reminded him of a girl he had known long ago, during his university days.

"I realize I'm intruding on your time," she said apologetically, "but if you could only listen to my story – "

"My dear young lady, I have only just arrived in your city. I have important meetings with the principals in this prizefight, and you understand I must attend to that business first. But should you chance to be in the neighborhood early this evening, I will try to find time to speak with you."

"That's most kind," she said.

Then, before Doyle could say more, he was whisked away by Charlie Summons. "We're running a bit late, Dr. Doyle. They're waiting for us."

Summons settled him into a front room with windows overlooking South Virginia Street. The hotel was crowded with guests, and even in the halls Doyle was aware of money changing hands. Obviously the fight was attracting a great deal of betting interest.

After a half hour in which Doyle unpacked and washed up, Summons escorted him to a first-floor meeting room where a number of men were awaiting him. Doyle's first impression was that the sporting classes were much the same in America as in England. Colonel Raff Grayson, who seemed to be one of the fight's promoters, could easily have acted a role in Doyle's prizefighting drama, *The House of Temperley*, which was playing at London's Adelphi Theatre.

"So good of you to make the journey, Dr. Doyle," he said, rising to shake hands. "The problems of selecting a referee acceptable to both sides in this fight has been immense. The color question – black versus white – has raised needless tensions on all sides. Frankly, you were the only person acceptable to both managers."

Doyle bowed slightly. "I consider that a sincere compliment, especially since I know so little of American boxing."

"The rules are much the same as in your British sport," Colonel Grayson assured him. "The Marquis of Queensberry is well known here. But our main problem was finding a referee whom both sides trusted. As you know, Jeffries has come out of retirement to win back his heavyweight title from this black man, Jack Johnson. Feelings are running high, and there is even talk of race riots in some American cities."

"All seems peaceful here," Doyle observed.

"Don't be deceived. A man was knifed to death near the depot two nights ago – a reporter out here to cover the fight. His killer has not yet been found."

"I know enough about the American west," Doyle said, "to realize that the price of human life is not high out here. A wrong word spoken during a poker game, I understand, can lead to a stabbing or shooting."

Grayson exchanged glances with the other men, whom he had not yet introduced. "Come, Dr. Doyle, we feel ourselves far more civilized than that! The west of 1910 is far removed from the west of 1890."

"Perhaps," Doyle admitted. "Even passing through New York I read of a recent diamond robbery and killing. Crime is certainly not confined to the western states."

"In any event, precautions have been taken for Monday's fight. As one of the promoters I can assure you the crowd will be under complete control."

A large man of indeterminate middle age spoke up. "I was a fighter myself, Dr. Doyle. I know what it's like to stand in the center of a ring and hear the crowd shouting for blood after an unpopular decision."

The Colonel made the belated introductions. "This is Nevada Wade, Dr. Conan Doyle."

Doyle smiled. "Sounds like a cowboy's name."

"Cowboys and boxers aren't much different," Wade agreed. "I was a heavyweight contender in my fighting days, but I never had a crack at the championship."

He looked like a man who could still hold his own in the prize ring, and Doyle wondered why he had retired. From the looks of the large diamond ring on his little finger he might well have come into money. "When will I see the site of Monday's battle?" Doyle asked, shifting his attention back to the Colonel.

"We'll go out to the fairgrounds tomorrow morning. The ring and the seating are already in place, but the workmen are still adding the finishing touches." He looked up at the ornate wall clock. "Only forty-eight hours to fight time, Dr. Doyle. Less than that, really."

He made an effort to introduce the others in the room – backers and managers and promoters – but Doyle found himself quickly engaged in more conversation with Nevada Wade. "I understand there's a new Sherlock Holmes play in the Strand this summer."

Doyle nodded. "*The Speckled Band* opened last month, and it's been quite successful."

"One of my favorite stories – the one with the snake."

Americans never failed to amaze him. This man with a cowboy's name and callused fists had actually read his stories! "That is the one. We tried using a real snake on stage – nonpoisonous, of course – but it didn't work out. Now we have an ingeniously jointed dummy manipulated with black thread like a puppet. It is most effective."

"I should like to see the play sometime," Wade said.

"Perhaps we will have an American production."

Charlie Summons appeared at Doyle's side and whispered, "If you want to scram out of here, I'll help you."

"Scram – ?"

"On the weekend of a big fight this crowd'll be drinking all night. I already told the Colonel you needed to rest after your long trip out here."

"Thank you," Doyle said, and he was genuinely grateful.

He ate with Summons in the hotel restaurant, listening to the slim young man's tales of Reno's sporting life. At one point he asked, "Just what is your connection with Colonel Grayson?"

"Oh, the Colonel pays me. I run errands for him – things like that."

Doyle had earlier noticed the bulge under the other man's coat, and now he commented upon it. "Are you his bodyguard too?"

"What? Oh, you mean the gun? This is still the west, Dr. Doyle. You'll find a good many men carrying weapons."

"Interesting."

"I guess they don't carry guns in London."

"No, not in London. Not even our police-officers."

Charlie Summons took a sip of the wine Doyle had ordered with the meal. "Say, this isn't bad."

"My tastes run more to French than to California wines, I'm afraid. But as you say, it isn't bad." He was beginning to like the young man for some reason, perhaps because he was so typically American.

"You going to see Monica Malone?" Summons asked suddenly.

"Who?"

"The girl outside the hotel when you arrived."

"I'd completely forgotten about her."

"She'll prob'ly come around tonight to see you."

As Doyle was to discover within the hour, the young man's prediction proved accurate. He had barely left Summons and started up to his room when Monica Malone intercepted him. She clutched a folded newspaper in one hand, and as she spoke there were tears in her eyes. "I must see you, Dr. Doyle. You said you would talk with me."

"And I will. But I can hardly invite you up to my room.

Let us sit in that corner of the lobby where we won't be disturbed."

She followed him to a red plush sofa partly hidden by a tall fern in an ornate jardinière. "Thank you so much, Dr. Doyle. These last days have been a nightmare for me."

He sat down beside her. "I assume you are referring to the brutal murder of your fiancé near the railway station two nights ago."

"Someone has told you who I am!"

"No, not really, Miss Malone. But I noticed your agitated state, and the fact that you are carrying a copy of yesterday's newspaper folded so that an account of the killing is visible. You also wear an engagement ring, which you twist nervously with your fingers, as if you were considering removing it. The conclusion seems a likely one."

"You sound like Sherlock Holmes himself!"

"Please!" He held up a hand to silence her. "I pretend no special powers to solve this mystery. But tell me what happened."

"Tom – my fiancé, Tom Andrews – came out here last month to cover preparations for the fight. He was a reporter for *Ring & Turf*, an eastern sporting weekly. I arrived yesterday to join him and discovered he'd been murdered."

"I understand the fight has touched off some scattered violence because of the racial aspects."

"No one would have killed Tom for that reason – he was completely fair to both men! They'd more likely have stabbed Jack London – he's been wondering aloud about the Negro having a yellow streak."

"What about one of the other reporters? Had your fiancé been on bad terms with any of them?"

She shook her head, fighting back the tears, and he wanted to comfort her somehow. To give her a few moments to compose herself, he took the folded newspaper from her hand and read the brief account of the murder. There had been no witnesses, and the young reporter's wallet was found intact. So robbery could not have been the motive. The fatal stabbing near the railroad station must have had another cause.

"Could he have gone there to meet someone arriving by train?" Doyle asked.

"But who? I wasn't due until yesterday and he knew that."

"Still, a great many persons are arriving daily for the fight. He might have gone to meet one of them."

"I think he knew he might be killed, Dr. Doyle."

"Why do you say that?"

"He left a message for me at his hotel. Just a brief note – I have it here." She opened her purse and produced an envelope with a folded piece of paper inside.

Doyle read it aloud. "'*Dearest Monica*: *If anything should happen to me before you arrive, remember the fifth day of Christmas. All my love, Tom.*'" He studied the note with a deepening frown. "The fifth day of Christmas? What could that mean?"

"That's why I want your help, Dr. Doyle – I don't know! I tried to talk with the police about it, but they paid no attention. They're too busy keeping things calm before Monday's fight."

He continued to study the note, the only message from a man he'd never known, a man now dead. "Did you know Tom last Christmas?"

"Certainly. He gave me this ring then."

Doyle was instantly alert. "Just one ring?"

"Of course. Why do you ask?"

"In the old carol, *The Twelve Days of Christmas*, there is a line that goes, '*The fifth day of Christmas, my true love sent to me five gold rings.*'"

"Of course! We always sang that at Christmas-time! Tom was sending me a message about five gold rings. But what rings?"

"I don't know," Doyle admitted.

"Engagement rings?"

"One other possibility presents itself. This weekend in Reno the word *ring* has another meaning."

"A prizefighting ring!"

"Perhaps." He folded the note and returned it to its envelope. "He left this at the hotel for you?"

"Yes, at the desk."

"Let me keep it for a time. Something might occur to me."

"Thank you, Dr. Doyle. If you can find the person who killed Tom – "

"We won't go quite that far yet." He rose. "Please excuse me now. I have had a tiring train trip, and I am anxious to get some sleep."

"I'll look for you tomorrow."

He smiled at her. "Tomorrow I must go to the fairgrounds to inspect the scene of the action and meet the participants. But I will try to help you in any way that I can."

"Thank you, Mr. Holmes – I mean, Dr. Doyle."

He watched as she crossed the lobby to the street, and then went up to his room. Once more that confounded Sherlock Holmes had intruded on his life.

On Sunday morning he walked down to the Reno railway station using the newspaper account of the tragedy to seek out the scene of the crime. He thought that he had found it, and was bending to examine a stain on the sidewalk, when a familiar voice hailed him.

"Dr. Conan Doyle! What brings you out this early?"

It was Colonel Raff Grayson, just alighting from his motorcar. He seemed to be alone. "Good morning, Colonel. I'm just exploring a bit of your city."

"Nothing to see down at the depot. But if you'll wait while I pick up some freight I'll drive you out to the fairgrounds."

His freight proved to be a wooden cage of pheasants, which Doyle helped him carry to the back seat of the motorcar. "Will you be having a pheasant shoot after the fight?" he asked the Colonel.

"No, just a pheasant roast. These birds are only two to three pounds each, but at two servings a bird I have enough here for ten of us. I figure my wife and me, Nevada Wade and his lady, both fighters and their women, yourself, and Mr. Jack London. I hope you'll be able to join us."

"I'd be pleased," Doyle said, "though I don't know whether Mr. Johnson and Mr. Jeffries will feel up to roast pheasant after fighting fifteen rounds."

Colonel Grayson smiled. "Oh, I think Jeffries will finish the black boy much quicker than that. Just off the record, of course."

Doyle was silent, avoiding any hint of favoritism on the day before he was to referee the event. He waited until they were on the road, heading for the fairgrounds, before he spoke. "Did you know the reporter who was murdered the other night?"

Colonel Grayson turned to smile at him. "The old detective instinct getting you, Dr. Doyle? I didn't know him, but Charlie Summons had played cards with him a few times these past weeks. Charlie says he was a nice fellow."

"Who do you think stabbed him?"

"The fight is attracting a certain criminal element to Reno, Dr. Doyle. It's unfortunate but true."

The Reno fairgrounds was at the northeast edge of the city. Today, under a warm July sun, it was a beehive of activity. Motorcars and wagons were parked everywhere in a haphazard fashion, while workers climbed over the grandstand putting the finishing touches on the seats and refreshment stands.

As they approached after parking the automobile, Charlie Summons hurried forward to meet them. "You'd better come quick, Colonel! Johnson and Jeffries are both here, and I'm afraid they'll start fighting a day early!"

They found the two heavyweights at the center of a growing circle of partisan supporters. Jack Johnson, his gleaming black head catching the noonday sun, was taunting the grizzly Jim Jeffries. Johnson never lost his smile, not even when one of the crowd called out, "What about the yellow streak, Johnson?"

"I will show you tomorrow who has the yellow streak." And still smiling he turned his back on Jeffries.

Colonel Grayson quickly interrupted to introduce the fighters to Conan Doyle. Jim Jeffries shook his hand vigorously. "I been reading those Sherlock Holmes stories – he's a great one, he is!"

And Johnson was no less enthusiastic. Doyle was amazed they would welcome an Englishman so warmly to referee their fight. He was really beginning to enjoy himself for the first time since his arrival when Nevada Wade approached with a short, light-haired man in his mid-thirties. At the sight of them Jack Johnson stalked away.

"Dr. Arthur Conan Doyle, this here's a great admirer of yours – Mr. Jack London."

London shook Doyle's hand with as much vigor as Jeffries had. "A pleasure to meet you, Dr. Doyle – or Sir Arthur."

"Dr. Doyle suits me fine. I read your book *The People of the Abyss* with a great deal of interest, Mr. London."

"I wrote it while living in London for some months in 1901. My funds had run out and I actually lived with those poor East End people." London smiled. "Later I rented a room in the home of a London detective. It wasn't 221B Baker Street, though."

"I should hope not," Doyle replied with a chuckle. Summons and the Colonel went off to unload the pheasants, while Nevada Wade continued to stroll with the two authors. Doyle was anxious to see the ring itself, and to get the feel of the place. When they reached it he went up the steps and climbed between the ropes, closely followed by London.

"There is nothing quite so invigorating as the prize ring," the American said. "I've been here ten days writing up the training camps and the fight preliminaries."

Doyle bent to examine London's eye. "As a physician skilled in such matters, I could not help noticing the fading after-effects of a black eye. Have you been engaging in some fisticuffs yourself, Mr. London?"

"That happened two weeks ago, in an Oakland bar. It was in all the papers, I'm afraid. A drunken brawl, they called it."

"Was it?"

London sighed, gazing out at the empty rows of seats, and changed the subject. "My wife gave birth to a daughter on June 19th. The baby only lived three days."

"I am sorry," Doyle said.

Nevada Wade joined them in the ring, "Which of you chaps has published the most?" he asked, flashing his diamond ring.

Doyle laughed. "Oh, Mr. London is far ahead of me. How many books is it now?"

"Twenty-four," London answered almost mechanically. "Though I hardly have your fame."

"Tell me something," Doyle pursued. "In *The People of the Abyss* you showed a real compassion for the poor and downtrodden of London's East End. Yet your writings thus far about the fight have shown a decided racist slant. How do you explain this seeming contradiction?"

Jack London shrugged. "I am what I am, Dr. Doyle. And we will see tomorrow who the better fighter is."

"Jeffries can't come back," Nevada Wade said. "Once they've retired they never come back."

"We'll see." London gave a slight bow in Doyle's direction. "Until tomorrow."

Doyle watched the younger writer climb out of the ring, then turned to Wade. "An odd sort of chap – a real contradiction."

"He's had some hard times, Dr. Doyle."

"He mentioned his daughter's death."

"That's only part of it."

Doyle was reminded of the other death in recent days, and of the message Tom Andrews had left for Monica. "Tell me, Mr. Wade, is this the only prize ring brought in for the fight?"

"Brought in?" Wade didn't grasp the question.

"I mean, are there any other boxing rings in Reno?"

"Well, sure." He removed his western hat and scratched at his balding head. "The Athletic Club has one, and the Boxing Club. And right now each of the two training camps has a ring."

"Counting this one, that would make five in all."

"Well, I guess so," Nevada Wade conceded. "What about it?"

Doyle shrugged. "Now, tell me about yourself. You say you boxed professionally?"

"That was a good many years ago, but the sport was my life then."

"Why did you give it up?"

"In the west a man has to live the best way he can. Some gamblers wanted me to take a dive and when I won instead, they broke my hands. I decided it was better to be a gambler than a fighter."

"Are you betting on tomorrow's fight?"

"Sure thing."

"Which way?"

"Like I said, Jeffries can't come back. If there's to be a Great White Hope, it isn't Jim Jeffries."

"Which side is the Colonel on?"

"The other side," Wade answered with a dry chuckle. "He's always on the other side."

Doyle stood for a moment in the center of the ring, turning first one way, then the other, imagining himself as he would be the following day. He touched his mustache, smoothing the ends with their long waxed points. "They say Johnson is something of a clown in the ring, constantly taunting his opponent."

"He play-acts a lot, it's true," Wade agreed. "But it'll be a Jeffries crowd here tomorrow."

"It should be an interesting fight."

Doyle dined again that evening with Charlie Summons, finding himself increasingly taken with the little man. But before they'd had time to relax over coffee and cigars, Monica Malone rushed up to the table. "Dr. Doyle, I must see you! Will you be long?" I've been looking everywhere for you."

Doyle excused himself and followed her out to the hotel lobby. "What agitates you so, my dear girl?"

"I didn't want to speak in front of that man."

"Summons? He was a friend of your fiancé."

"I doubt that," she said. "But what I have to tell you is that I recognized someone Tom did know – a man named Draco. He's connected with the rackets back east. Tom wrote an exposé about him – how he doped a race horse."

"Giving him a motive for wanting to kill your fiancé. Where can I find this man?"

"I just saw him entering a bar down the block."

"Did he recognize you?"

"I don't think so. He wouldn't remember me."

Doyle made his regrets to Charlie Summons and set off down the block to the bar Monica had indicated. She pointed out a tall, dark-haired man lounging against a corner of the bar, and Doyle approached him.

"Mr. Draco, I presume?"

The face that turned to him was scarred and ugly. It was plain to see how Monica had recognized him so easily. Doyle remembered Jack London's black eye from the barroom brawl, and prayed the writer would never end up like this. "What do you want?" Draco asked.

"Just to talk. My name is Arthur Conan Doyle."

The name obviously meant nothing to the man. "You a Limey?"

"I'm from England, yes. I am over here to referee the fight tomorrow."

"Yeah?" This interested him.

"I believe you know a man named Tom Andrews."

Draco muttered an obscenity.

"He was murdered here in Reno three nights ago. Did you know that?"

"If I'd been in town I'd of done the job myself."

"But you weren't in town?"

"Just got in today. Come for the fight."

Doyle was inclined to believe the man. Besides, his statement could be easily checked. "I have been told you drug race horses. Wouldn't think of trying your skill on a prizefighter, would you?"

"Not a chance! Listen, I'll tell you about your friend Tom Andrews, in case you still think he's some sorta saint." The man stepped a bit closer, and Doyle could smell gin on his breath. "Sure, I doped a horse or two in my day. Andrews found out about it and wrote his story. But he didn't turn it in to his editor right away. Oh, no. He came to me first and showed it to me. Said he'd tear it up if I'd give him five thousand dollars."

"Interesting. What did you do?"

"Told him I wouldn't be blackmailed and kicked his butt outa my office." He smiled at the memory. "I didn't have no five grand anyhow."

"So he printed the article?"

"Damned right! Ruined my racing career."

"What are you doing now?"

"Picking up a buck any way I can."

"Do five rings mean anything to you? Five rings in Reno?"

Draco looked blank. "Not a thing."

Doyle put down money for another gin and left the man there. In the street, fighting to keep her place on the crowded sidewalk, Monica was waiting. "What did you find out?" she demanded.

"Nothing. Draco only just arrived in Reno."

"So he says!"

"Let me escort you back to your hotel, Miss Malone. The city is growing more crowded by the hour, and the streets may not be safe for a young woman."

"I can take care of myself."

"I am sure you can. But the person who killed Tom might find it very easy to knife you in a crowd. Your inquiries could be worrying him."

She paled at his words. "Perhaps you're right."

"Come along."

"I was foolish to think of you as Sherlock Holmes. There's nothing you can do for me or Tom."

"I never pretended to be Holmes," he insisted. But was it true? Five gold rings . . .

He started humming it to himself as they walked. *Seven swans a-swimming, six geese a-laying, five gold rings, four colly birds, three French hens, two turtle doves, and a partridge in a pear tree.*

Ahead of them a boy set off a string of firecrackers in the gutter. It was the eve of America's Independence Day, an odd time to be humming Christmas carols to oneself.

Five gold rings . . .

"You're right," he told her at the door of the hotel. "I'm not Holmes."

She turned to gaze into his eyes. "I only wish that you were."

The morning dawned warm and sunny. There would be a shirtsleeve crowd at the fight in a few hours. Doyle hoped the decision would be clean-cut. Any uncertainty as to the outcome could only carry over into the streets of Reno.

Charlie Summons called for him promptly at nine, escorting him out to the motorcar. "Beautiful day for it, Dr. Doyle."

"That it is, Charlie."

"The Colonel has a tent up on the fairgrounds, for his celebration dinner afterwards."

"Too bad you're not included on the guest list."

Charlie snickered. "Colonel Grayson said he might include me, if one of the fighters doesn't feel up to eating."

Though the fight was still some hours off, people were already streaming into the grandstand. Many carried picnic lunches and bottles of beverage. And the crackle of fireworks had become almost constant. "Is this how they celebrate your Fourth of July?" Doyle asked.

"You'll get used to the noise," Summons assured him.

In the striped tent set off beyond the parking lot they found Colonel Raff Grayson making last-minute preparations. "I will have chefs to prepare dinner after the main event," he told Doyle. "By that time I'm sure you'll have worked up an appetite."

Doyle nodded.

Nevada Wade came in with a young woman clinging to his arm. "The press is searching for you, Dr. Doyle. They want an interview with Sherlock Holmes!"

"I'm not – " Doyle began, then fell silent. What difference did it make? He could be Sherlock Holmes if they wanted him to be.

Outside, heading toward the press tent, he came upon Monica Malone. "Here for the fight?" he asked.

"I'm here to settle with Tom's killer."

"What?"

"One of the reporters told me Tom was on Draco's trail. He was sure Draco was heading for Reno to close some sort of crooked deal. I have a gun in this handbag, Dr. Doyle, and when I see Draco – "

"My dear, don't even talk such foolishness!" He grasped at the purse, feeling the metallic weight of it. "I'd better take that."

He slipped the small weapon out of the purse and dropped it in his pocket.

"That won't stop me," she insisted. "If you can't do anything, I will!"

The crowd was thickening around them. Spectators mingled with souvenir vendors, and at that moment Doyle's eyes were caught by a gold American eagle on the cover of an Independence Day program. "Birds," he muttered to himself.

"What did you say?" Monica asked.

"Of course! They were all birds! I remember now!"

"What are you talking about?"

The excitement welled within him. "Hurry, woman! Find some police-officers and bring them to Colonel Grayson's tent!"

Then he was on his way. The first person he saw as he burst into the tent was Draco. The ugly man turned from his task, surprised at the sudden intrusion. "You again!"

And then Colonel Grayson came forward. "Can I be of service, Dr. Doyle?"

"On the contrary, Colonel. I came to assist you in dressing those birds for dinner."

Grayson shot a glance at the table behind him. "You needn't concern yourself – "

Doyle felt the hardness of Monica Malone's gun in his pocket, and he drew it out. "Just stand there, both of you. Police-officers will be here soon enough."

"Police? For what?"

"To arrest you for murder, Colonel. You killed Tom Andrews when he tried to blackmail you."

"That's insane!"

"Is it? Andrews was killed near the railway station, because that is where he found you awaiting your delivery. Just as I found you yesterday morning. He left a message for Monica Malone, telling her to remember the fifth day of Christmas. In the old carol the fifth day's gift was five gold rings. Not wedding rings, or prize rings. I finally remembered something I read long ago. In the carol the gifts of the first seven days are all birds. The five gold rings referred to five ring-necked pheasants – like those on the table behind you. I didn't count the birds at the station yesterday, but I remembered you had enough to feed ten guests, at two servings per bird. Therefore, five birds – five ring-necked pheasants."

Grayson started to move then, but Monica lifted the tent flap and entered with the police. "What's all this?" one detective asked. "Aren't you Arthur Conan Doyle?"

Doyle handed over his weapon and picked up a carving knife instead. "If you'll cover the Colonel, we'll see what's in these five birds."

He slit them open, one after another, and carefully extracted a number of small hard objects. "Wash them off and you will find they are diamonds – no doubt from that New York robbery a few weeks back. Colonel Grayson was acting as a fence for the loot, and probably planning to resell it to Draco here. Somehow Andrews found out about Draco's involvement and tried to blackmail the Colonel. That's when he was killed. I should have known those birds were valuable. Grayson sent Charlie Summons to meet me at the station, but he went himself – and alone – to pick up a heavy cage of pheasants."

But how did you know there were jewels in the birds?" Monica asked.

Arthur Conan Doyle smiled. "The diamonds? Well, you see Sherlock Holmes once solved a case in which a carbuncle was hidden inside a Christmas goose. But come, it is almost fight time and I must be in the ring."

*Jack Johnson stopped Jim Jeffries in the fifteenth round, thus retaining the heavyweight championship of the world. And Jack London wrote, "Jeff today disposed of one question. He could not come back. Johnson, in turn, answered another question. He has not the yellow streak."*

*His article made no mention of Sir Arthur Conan Doyle.*

# AFTERWORD: OLD-TIME DETECTION
# Arthur Griffiths

*The following article appeared in the April 1902 issue of* Cassell's Magazine, *and I thought it might be of interest to readers in showing the historical development of the real-life detective. Arthur Griffiths (1838–1908), was a renowned army officer who rose to the rank of major. Noted for his discipline he entered the prison service in 1870, first as deputy-governor at Chatham and later as one of Her Majesty's Inspectors of Prisons, a post he held until 1896. He retired from the army in 1875 and turned to writing and editing in his spare time. His early novels, starting with* The Queen's Shilling *(1873) drew upon his experiences in the Crimean War, but he later turned to a series of popular detective thrillers, and a number of sensational tales of prison life, including the very popular* Criminals I Have Known *(1895). He was one of the noted experts of his day on the history and development of the police service.*

The modern detective, whether of fact or fiction, had no exact prototype in the past. The constable was an officer of the law attached to a particular locality, but except to raise the hue-and-cry, take up the criminal when he was caught, he exercised few of the functions of the police officer. A century ago there were a round dozen of Bow Street runners whose services might be engaged by private parties, but they cannot be said to have been remarkable for astuteness. The ingenious piecing together of clues, and the following up of light and baffling scent, was the work, generally, of the lawyers engaged by the parties aggrieved.

One of the earliest cases on record of this clever detection of a great fraud was the upsetting of the claim made in 1684 by a certain Lady Ivy to a large property in Shadwell. The contention was over seven acres which her ladyship, who was the widow of Sir Thomas Ivy, claimed on the strength of deeds drawn, or purporting to be drawn, in the 2 and 3 Philip and Mary, or 1555–6, and which gave her ancestors the land. The case was tried before the "famous," or rather infamous, Judge Jeffreys, and it was proved to the satisfaction of the jury that the deeds were forged. It had been discovered that the style and titles of the king and queen as they appeared in the deed were not those used by them at that date. In the preambles of Acts of Parliament in 1555–6, Philip and Mary were styled "King and Queen of Naples, princes of Spain and Sicily," not as in the deed, "King and Queen of Spain and both the Sicilies." Again, in the deed Burgundy was put before Milan as a dukedom; in the Acts of Parliament it was just the reverse. The style did in effect come in later, but the person drawing the deeds could not prophesy that, and as a fair inference it was urged that the deeds were a forgery. Other evidence was adduced to show that Lady Ivy had forged other deeds, and it was so held by Judge Jeffreys. "If you produce deeds in such a time when, say you, such titles were used, and they were not so used, that sheweth your deeds are counterfeit and forged and not true deeds. And there is *Digitus Dei*, the finger of God, in it, that though the design be deep laid and the contrivance sculk, yet truth and justice will appear at one time or other."

Accordingly, my Lady Ivy lost her verdict, and an information for forgery was laid against her, but with what result does not appear.

Fifty years later, a painstaking lawyer in Berkshire was able to unravel another case of fraud which must have eluded the imperfect police of the day. It was an artful attempt to claim restitution from a certain locality for a highway robbery which had never occurred.

Upon the 24th March, 1847, one Thomas Chandler, an attorney's clerk, was travelling on foot along the high road between London and Reading. Having passed through Maidenhead thicket and in the neighbourhood of Hare Hatch, some thirty miles out, he was set upon by three men, bargees, who robbed him of all he possessed – his watch and cash, the latter amounting to £960, all in bank-notes. After the robbery, they bound him and threw him into a pit by the side of the road. He lay there some three hours, till long after dark, being unable to obtain release from his miserable situation – although the road was much frequented, and he heard many carriages and people passing along. At length he got out of the pit unaided and, still bound hand and foot, jumped rather than walked for half a mile up hill, calling out lustily for anyone to set him loose. The first passer-by was a gentleman who gave him a wide berth; then a shepherd came and cut his bonds, and at his entreaty guided him to the constable or tything man of the Hundred of Sunning, in the County of Berks.

Here he set forth in writing the evil that had happened him, with a full and minute description of the thieves, and at the same time gave notice that he would in due course sue the Hundred for the amount under the statutes. All the formalities being observed, process was duly served on the High Constable of Sunning, and the people of the Hundred, alarmed at the demand which, if insisted upon, would be the "utter ruin of many poor families," engaged a certain attorney, Edward Wise, of Wokingham, to defend them.

Mr. Wise had all the qualities of a good detective; he was ingenious, yet patient; cleverly piecing together the facts he soon picked up about Chandler. Some of these seemed at the very outset much against him. That a man should tramp along the road with nearly £1,000 in his pocket was quite extraordinary; again, that he should not escape from the pit till after dark, and that his bonds should have been no better than tape, a length of which was found on the spot where he was untied. He seemed, moreover, to be very little concerned by his great loss after he had given the written notices to the constable, concerning which he was strangely well informed, with all the statutes at his fingers' ends as though studied beforehand, and he ordered a hot supper and a bowl at the Hare and Hounds in Hare Hatch, where he kept it up till late in the night. Nor was he in any hurry to return to town and stop payment of the notes at the banks, but started late and rode leisurely to London.

It was easy enough to trace him there. He had given his address in the notices, and was found to be the clerk of Mr. Hill, an attorney in Clifford's Inn. It now appeared that Chandler had negotiated a mortgage for a client of his master's upon certain lands in the neighbourhood of Devizes for £500, much more, as it was proved, than their value. An old mortgage was to be paid off in favour of the new, and Chandler had set off on the day stated to complete the transaction, carrying with him the £500 and the balance of £460, supposed to be his own property, but how obtained was never known. His movements on the days previous were also verified. He had dined with the mortgagee, when the deed was executed and the money handed over in notes. These notes were mostly for small sums, making up too bulky a parcel to be comfortably carried under his garters (the safest place for them, as he thought), and he had twice changed a portion – £440 at the Bank of England for two notes, and again at "Sir Richard Hoare's shop" for three notes, two of £100 and one of £200. With the whole of his money he then started to walk ninety miles in twenty-four hours, for he was expected next day at Devizes to release the mortgage.

Mr. Hill had kept a list of the notes made out in Chandler's handwriting, which Chandler got back, in order, as he said, to stop payment of them at the banks. His real object was to alter the numbers of three notes from Hoares', which he wished to cash and use, and he effected this by having a fresh list made out in which these notes were given new and false numbers. Thus the notes with the real numbers would not be stopped on presentation. He did it cleverly, changing 102 to 112, 195 to 159, 196 to 190, variations so slight as to pass unnoticed by Mr. Hill when the list (as copied) was returned to him. These three notes were cashed and eventually traced back to Chandler. Further, it was clearly proved that he had got those notes at Hoares' in exchange for the £400 note, for that note presently came back to Hoares' through a gentleman who had received it in part payment for a captain's commission of Dragoons, and it was then seen that it had been originally received from Chandler.

While Mr. Wise was engaged in these inquiries, the trial of Chandler's case against the Hundred came on at Abingdon assizes in June, and a verdict was given in his favour for £975, chiefly because Mr. Hill was associated with the mortgage, and he was held a person of good repute. But a point of law was reserved, for Chandler had omitted to give a full description of the notes as required by statute when advertising his loss.

But now Chandler disappeared. He thought the point of law would go against him, that the mortgagee would press for the return of the £500 which he had recovered from the Hundred, that his master Mr. Hill had now strong doubts of his good faith. The first proved to be the case; on argument of the point of law, the Abingdon verdict was set aside. There was good cause for his other fears. News now came of the great bulk of the other notes, which reached the Bank from Amsterdam through brokers named Solomons, who had bought them from one "John Smith," a person answering to the description of Chandler, who, in signing the receipt, "wrote his name as if it had been wrote with a skewer." The indefatigable Mr. Wise presently found that Chandler had been in Holland with a trader named Casson, and then found Casson himself.

Mr. Hill was in indirect communication with Chandler, writing letters to him by name "at Easton, in Suffolk, to be left for him at the 'Crown' at Ardley, near Colchester, in Essex." Thither Mr. Wise followed him accompanied by the mortgagee, Mr. Winter, and the "Holland trader," Mr. Casson, who was ready to identify Chandler. They reached the "Crown" at Ardley, and actually saw a letter "stuck behind the plates of the dresser" awaiting Chandler, who rode in once a fortnight from a distance, for "his mare seemed always to be very hard rid." There was nothing known of a place called Easton, but Aston and Assington were both suggested to the eastward, and in search of them Mr. Wise with his friends rode through Ipswich as far as Southwold, and there found Easton, a place washed by the sea, and "being thus pretty sure of going no further eastward." But the scent was false, and although a young man was run into, whom they proposed to arrest with the assistance of "three fellows from the Keys who appeared to be smugglers, for they were pretty much maimed and scarred," the person was clearly not Chandler. So finding "we had been running the wrong hare, we trailed very coolly all the way back to Ipswich."

Travelling homeward, they halted a night at Colchester, and called at an inn – the "Three Crowns" or the "Three Cups" – where Chandler had been seen a few months before. Here, as a fact, after over-running their game near four-score miles, "they got to the very form – yet even there lost their hare." This inn was kept at that very time by Chandler in partnership with his brother-in-law Smart, who naturally would not betray him, although he was in the house when asked for.

For this, Chandler thought Colchester "a very improper place for him to continue long in"; there were writs out against him in Essex, Suffolk, and Norfolk; so he sold off his goods and moved to another inn at Coventry, where he set up at the "Sign of the Golden Dragon" under the name of John Smith. Now still fearing arrest, he thought to buy off Winter, the mortgagee, by repaying him something, and sent him £130. But Winter was bitter against him, and writs were taken out for Warwickshire. Chandler had in some way secured the protection of Lord Willoughby de Broke; he had also made friends with the constables of Coventry, and it was not easy to compass his arrest. But at last he was taken, and lodged in the town gaol. Two years had been occupied in this pertinacious pursuit, and Mr. Wise was greatly complimented upon his zeal and presented with a handsome testimonial.

Chandler, who was supposed to have planned the whole affair with the idea of becoming possessed of a considerable sum in ready money, was found guilty of perjury, and was sentenced to be put in the pillory next market-day at Reading from twelve to one and afterwards to be transported for seven years.

A curious feature in the trial was the identification of Chandler as John Smith by Casson, who told how at Amsterdam he (Chandler) had received payment for his bills partly in silver, £150 worth of ducats and Spanish pistoles, which broke down both his pockets so that the witness had to get a rice sack and hire a wheel-barrow to convey the coin to the Delft "scout," where it was deposited in a chest and so conveyed to England.

As the years ran on, it was claimed for the officers of Bow Street that they effected many captures, and the names of such men as

Vickery, Lavender, Sayer, Donaldson, and Townshend are still remembered for their skill. None of them did better, however, than a certain Mr. Denovan, a Scotch officer of great intelligence and unwearied patience who was employed by the Paisley Union Bank to defend it against the extraordinary pretensions of a man who had robbed it and yet sued it for the restoration of property which was clearly the Bank's and not his. For the first and probably only time known in this country, an acknowledged thief was seen contending with people in open court for property he had stolen from them.

The hero of this strange episode was one Mackcoull, a hardened criminal who had entered the Royal Navy to escape arrest, had served with credit but on discharge in 1785 had relapsed, returning to evil courses, and he is said to have eclipsed all his former companions in iniquity. He was proficient in every line, had been "pugilist, horse-racer, cockfighter, gambler, swindler, and pickpocket, choosing churches as his favourite hunting-ground." His self-possession was so great that he was commonly called the "Heathen Philosopher" by his associates. Bank burglary now promised to be a more profitable business than any, and he started in it well equipped with the best implements and well-chosen confederates.

His robbery of the Paisley Union Bank in Glasgow was cleverly planned and boldly executed. He was assisted by two men, French and Huffey White – the latter a convict at the hulks whose escape Mackcoull had compassed on purpose. They broke in one Sunday night, July 14th, 1811, with keys carefully fitted long in advance, and soon ransacked the safe and drawers, securing in gold and notes something like £20,000. Of course they left Glasgow, travelling full speed in a post-chaise and four first to Edinburgh, and then *via* Edinburgh, Haddington, Newcastle, southward to London. In the division of the spoil, which now took place, Mackcoull contrived to keep the lion's share. White was apprehended, and to save his life a certain sum was surrendered to the Bank, but some of the money seems to have stuck to the fingers of a Bow Street officer, Sayer, who had negotiated between Mackcoull and the Bank. Mackcoull himself had retained about £8,000.

In 1812, after a supposed visit to the West Indies, he reappeared in London, where he was arrested for breach of faith with the Bank and sent to Glasgow for trial. He got off by a promise of further restitution, and because the Bank was unable at that time to prove his complicity in the burglary. An agent, who had handed over £1,000 on his account, was then sued by Mackcoull for acting without proper authority, and was obliged to refund a great part of the money. Nothing could exceed his effrontery. He traded openly as a bill broker for Scotland under the names of James Martin, buying the bills with the stolen notes and having sometimes as much as £2,000 on deposit in another bank. At last he was arrested, and a quantity of notes and drafts were seized with him. He was presently discharged, but they were impounded, and by-and-by he began a suit to recover "his property," the proceeds really of his theft from the Bank. His demeanour in court was most impudent. Crowds filled the court when he gave his evidence, which he did with great effrontery, posing always as an innocent and much injured man.

It was incumbent upon the Bank to end this disgraceful parody of legal proceedings; either they must prove Mackcoull's guilt or lose their action – an action brought, it must be remembered, by a public depredator against a respectable banking company for trying to keep back part of the property of which he had robbed them. In this difficulty they appealed to Mr. Denovan, and sent him to collect evidence showing that Mackcoull was implicated in the original robbery in 1811.

Denovan left Edinburgh on the 8th January, 1820, meaning to follow the exact route of the fugitives to the south. All along the road he came upon traces of them in the "post-books" or in the memory of inn-keepers, waiters, and ostlers. He passed through Dunbar, Berwick, and Belford, pausing at the latter place to hunt up a certain George Johnson, who was said to be able to identify Mackcoull. Johnson had been a waiter at the "Talbot" Inn, Darlington, in 1811, but was now gone, where, his parents (who lived in Belford) could not say. "Observing, however, that there was a church behind the inn," writes Mr. Denovan, "a thought struck me I might hear something in the churchyard on Sunday morning," and he was rewarded with the address of Thomas Johnson, a brother of George's, "a pedlar or travelling merchant." "I immediately set forth in a post-chaise and found Thomas Johnson, who gave me news of George." He was still alive, and was a waiter either at the "Bay Horse" in Leeds or somewhere in Tadcaster, or at a small inn at Spittal-on-the-Moor, in Westmoreland, but his father-in-law, Thomas Cockburn of York, would certainly know.

Pushing on, Denovan heard of his men at Alnwick. A barber there had shaved them. "I was anxious to see the barber, but found he had put an end to his existence some years, ago." At Morpeth, the inn at which they had stopped was shut up. At Newcastle, the posting-book was lost, and, when found in the bar of the "Crown and Thistle," was "so mutilated as to be useless." But at the "Queen's Head," Durham, there was an entry: "Chaise and four to Darlington – Will and Will." The second "Will" was still alive – an ancient postboy who remembered Mackoull as the oldest – a stiff, red-faced man," the usual description given of him. The landlady here, Mrs. Jane Escott, remembered three men arriving in a chaise, who said they were pushing on to London with a quantity of Scotch banknotes. At the "Talbot" Inn, Darlington, where George Johnson lived, the scent failed till Denovan at another inn, the "King's Head," ascertained that the landlord remembered three fugitives coming from Durham, and that he had observed that three such queer-looking chaps should be posting it.

At Northallerton there was evidence; that of Scotch notes changed and at York news of George Johnson, who was found at last at a fish hawker's in Tadcaster. Johnson's evidence was most valuable, and he willingly agreed to give it in court at Edinburgh. He had seen men at Dunbar, the oldest, "a stiff stout man with a red face seemed to take the management and paid the post-boys their hire." He had offered a £20 Scotch note in payment for two pints of sherry and some biscuits, but there was not change enough in the house, and White was asked for smaller money, when he took out his pocket-book stuffed full of bank-notes, all too large, so the first note was changed by Johnson at the Darlington Bank. Johnson ws sure he would know the stiff man again, amongst a hundred others, in any dress.

There was nothing more now till the "White Hart," Welwyn, where the fugitives took the light post coach. At Welwyn, too, they had sent off a portmanteau to an address, and this portmanteau was afterwards recovered with the address in Mackcoull's hand, the other two being unable to write. At Welwyn Mr. Denovan heard of one Cunington who had been a waiter at the inn in 1811, but left in 1813 for London, who was said to know something of the matter. The search for this Cunington was the next task, and Mr. Denovan pushed on to London hoping to find him there. "In company with a private friend, I went up and down Holborn, from house to house, inquiring for him at every baker's, grocer's, or public house," but heard nothing. The same at the coaching offices, until at last a guard who knew Cunington said he was in Brighton. But the man had left Brighton, first for Horsham, then for Margate, and then back to London, where Mr. Denovan ran him down at last as a patient in the Middlesex Hospital.

Cunington was quite as important a witness as Johnson. He declared he would know Mackcoull among a thousand. He had seen the three men counting over notes at the "White Hart";

Mackcoull did not seem to be a proper companion for the two; he took the lead and was the only one who used pen, ink, and paper. Cunington expressed his willingness to go to Edinburgh if his health permitted.

Since Denovan's arrival in London he had received but little assistance at Bow Street. The runners were irritated at the way the case had been managed. One of them, Sayer, who had been concerned in the restitution, flatly refused to have anything to do with the business or to go to Edinburgh to give evidence. This was presently explained by another runner, the famous Townshend, who hinted that Sayer's hands were not clean, and that he was on very friendly terms with Mackcoull's wife, a lady of very questionable character, who was living in comfort on some of her husband's ill-gotten gains. Indeed, Sayer's conduct had caused a serious quarrel between him and his colleagues, Lavender, Vickery, and Harry Adkins, because he had deceived and forestalled them. Denovan was, however, on intimate terms with Lavender, another famous runner, whom he persuaded to assist, and through him he came upon the portmanteau sent from Welwyn, which had been seized at the time of Huffey White's arrest. Huffey had been taken in the house of one Scottock, a blacksmith in the Tottenham Court Road, also the portmanteau, and a box of skeleton keys. The portmanteau contained a great many papers and notes damaging to Mackcoull, and in the box were house-breaking implements, punches, files, and various "dubs" and "skrews," as well as two handkerchiefs of fawn colour with a broad border, such as the three thieves often wore when in their lodgings in Glasgow, immediately before the robbery.

How Mr. Denovan found and won over Mr. Scottock is the chief feather in his cap. His success astonished even the oldest officers in Bow Street. Scottock was the friend and associate of burglars constantly engaged in manufacturing implements for them. He had long been a friend of Mackcoull's, and had made many tools for him, those especially for the robbery of the Paisley Union Bank, a coup prepared long beforehand. The first set of keys supplied had really been tried on the Bank locks and found useless, so that Scottock furnished others and sent them down by mail. These also were ineffective, as the Bank had "simple old-fashioned locks," and Mackcoull came back from Glasgow, bringing with him "a wooden model of the key-hole and pike of the locks," which enabled Scottock to complete the job easily. "I wonder," said Scottock to Mr. Denovan, "that the Bank could have trusted so much money under such very simple things." Scottock would not allow any of this evidence to be set down in writing, but he agreed to go down to Edinburgh and give it in Court, swearing also to receiving the portmanteau addressed in the handwriting of Mackcoull.

Denovan's greatest triumph was with Mrs. Mackcoull. She kept a house furnished in an elegant manner, but was not a very reputable person. "She was extremely shy at first, and as if by chance, but to show me she was prepared for anything, she lifted one of the cushions on her settee, displaying a pair of horse pistols that lay below," on which he produced a down-barrelled pistol and a card bearing the address "at the public office, Bow Street." Then she gave him her hand, and "we understood each other." But still she was very reticent, acting, as Mr. Denovan believed, under the advice of Sayer, her friend, the Bow Street Runner. She was afraid she would be called upon to make restitution of that part of the booty that had gone her way. Denovan strongly suspected that she had received a large sum from her husband, and had refused to give it back to him – "the real cause of their misunderstanding," which was indeed so serious that he had no great difficulty in persuading her also to give evidence at Edinburgh.

Such was the result of an inquiry that scarcely occupied a month. It was so complete that the celebrated Lord Cockburn, who was at that time counsel for the Bank, declared "nothing could exceed Denovan's skill, and that the investigation had the great merit of being amply sustained by evidence in all its important parts." When the trial of the cause came on in February, and Denovan appeared in Court with all the principal witnesses, Johnson, Cunington, Scottock, and Mr. Mackcoull, the defendant – it was only a civil suit – he was unable to conceal his emotion, and fainted away.

Next month Mackcoull was arraigned on the criminal charge, and after trial was found guilty and sentenced to death. But he cheated the gallows. Even before the verdict was given his changed demeanour was noticed in Court; he frequently muttered, ground his teeth, or looked around with a vacant stare. Afterwards he broke down utterly, and although reprieved, his mind gave way.

# Appendix
# THE CHRONICLERS
# OF CRIME
## The forerunners of
## Sherlock Holmes

The following traces the adventures of fictional detectives from 2000 BC to 1870, nearly four thousand years of detection. It's by no means exhaustive but I believe it covers the majority of novels and stories. I'd like to hear from anyone who knows of any significant omissions. I have excluded stories which are more historical crime than detection, particularly those from the Victorian period. I have also drawn the completion date at 1870, as thereafter the "modern" detective/police novel takes over, and the number of Sherlock Holmes stories would fill a book of their own.

### Ancient Egypt

Agatha Christie, *Death Comes as the End* (1941), *c*2000 BC.
As death follows death the survivors in an Egyptian family try to identify the murderer.
Elizabeth Peters, "The Locked Tomb Mystery" (1989), *c*1400 BC.
Amenhotep Sa Hapu, a venerated Egyptian sage and scholar, investigates a robbed tomb. Reprinted in this anthology.
Anton Gill, *City of the Horizon* (1991), 1361 BC.
In the days after the death of the reformist pharaoh Akhenaten, Huy the Scribe, jobless and fearing for his life, finds himself becoming the world's first private investigator. Followed by *City of Dreams* (1993) and *City of the Dead*.

## Ancient Greece

Brèni James, "Socrates Solves a Murder" (1954), *c*400 BC.
  One of two short stories where Socrates uses his powers of
  deduction to solve two murders. The first is reprinted in this
  anthology. The second is "Socrates Solves Another Murder"
  (1955).
Theodore Mathieson, "Alexander the Great, Detective" (1959),
  323 BC.
  One of Mathieson's stories in *The Great Detectives* (1960) featuring
  famous historical characters solving crimes.


## Ancient Rome

John Maddox Roberts, *SPQR* (1990), 70 BC onwards.
  First in a series featuring Decius Caecilius Metellus, a Roman
  official and a member of a noble Roman family, who lived through
  the most turbulent period of Roman history. The series continues
  with *The Catiline Conspiracy* (1991), *The Sacrilege* (1992) *The Temple of
  the Muses* (1992), and *Saturnalia*, plus the new short story, "Mightier
  Than the Sword", in this anthology.
Ron Burns, *Roman Nights* (1991), 43 BC onwards.
  Features the young Roman senator Gaius Livinius Severus who
  finds himself engulfed in danger and intrigue in the turbulent days
  after the death of Julius Caesar. Sequel is *Roman Shadows* (1992).
Edward D. Hoch, "The Three Travelers" (1976), 4 BC.
  In which the Three Wise Men on their way to the birth of the
  Messiah, find they have to investigate the theft of one of their
  precious gifts.
Anthony Price, "The Boudica Killing" (1979), AD 60.
  Features the old and grizzled soldier Gaius Celer whose battle-
  weary knowledge allows him to resolve a murder in ancient
  Britain. An earlier story by Price, "A Green Boy" (1973), also
  features Celer but is set some years later, about AD 77.
Lindsey Davis, *The Silver Pigs* (1989), AD 70.
  Set in the days after the death of Nero, this is the first of the novels
  about Marcus Didius Falco, who finds himself embroiled in a plot
  against the new emperor Vespasian. The investigation takes him
  to ancient Britain. The sequels are *Shadows in Bronze* (1990), *Venus
  in Copper* (1991) *The Iron Hand of Mars* (1992), and *Poseidon's Gold*
  (1993).
Barbara Hambly, *The Quirinal Hill Affair* (1983), AD 116.

What starts with a kidnap, leads young Marcus Silanus deeper and deeper into the Roman underworld. Reprinted in paperback as *Search the Seven Hills* (1987).

Wallace Nichols, "The Case of the Empress's Jewels" (1950), AD *c*174.

The first of sixty-one stories about Sollius, the Slave Detective, which ran in the *London Mystery Magazine*, concluding with "The Two Musicians" (1968). Reprinted in this anthology.

## The Dark Ages

Phyllis Ann Karr, *The Idylls of the Queen* (1982), AD *c*500.

Combines murder and fantasy in the days of King Arthur, as Sir Kay investigates the murder of Sir Patrise.

Peter Tremayne, "Murder in Repose" (1993), AD 664 onward.

The first of the stories about Sister Fidelma of which the second, "The High King's Sword" is included in this anthology.

## The Mystic East

Robert Van Gulik, *The Chinese Gold Murders* (1959), AD 663.

In reading order, the first of the stories about Judge Dee, a real-life Chinese magistrate who lived from 630–700. Van Gulik wrote fifteen other books about Judge Dee. In sequence they run, *The Lacquer Screen* (1964), *The Chinese Lake Murders* (1960), *The Haunted Monastery* (1963), *The Monkey and the Tiger* (1965), *The Chinese Bell Murders* (1958), *The Chinese Nail Murders* (1961), *The Chinese Maze Murders* (1962), *The Emperor's Pearl* (1963), *The Red Pavilion* (1964), *The Willow Pattern* (1965), *Murder in Canton* (1966), *The Phantom of the Temple* (1966), *Necklace and Calabash* (1967) and *Poets and Murder* (1968). The stories in *Judge Dee at Work* (1967) interweave throughout the novels.

Theodore Mathieson, "Omar Khayyam, Detective" (1960), *c*1100.

Another of Mathieson's stories in *The Great Detectives* (1960).

## The Middle Ages

Ellis Peters, "A Light on the Road to Woodstock" (1985), 1120.

The earliest chronological setting of the stories about Brother Cadfael, of which the second, "The Price of Light", is included in this volume. Cadfael's world is an England split by the civil war between King Stephen and Queen Matilda. The novels, starting with *A Morbid Taste for Bones* (1977), begin in the year 1137. The series continues with *One Corpse Too Many* (1979), *Monk's-Head* (1980), *Saint Peter's Fair* (1981), *The Leper of Saint Giles* (1981), *The Virgin in the Ice* (1982), "The Eye Witness" (1981), *The Sanctuary Sparrow* (1983), *The Devil's Novice* (1983), *Dead Man's Ransom* (1984), *The Pilgrim of Hate* (1984), *An Excellent Mystery* (1985), *The Raven in the Foregate* (1986), *The Rose Rent* (1986), *The Hermit of Eyton Forest* (1987), *The Confession of Brother Halvin* (1988), *The Heretic's Apprentice* (1989), *The Potter's Field* (1989), *The Summer of the Danes* (1991) and *The Holy Thief* (1992).

P. C. Doherty, *Satan in St. Mary's* (1986), 1284.

The first of the novels featuring Hugh Corbett, a clerk to the King's Bench in the latter part of the reign of Edward I. After this case, in which he investigates the death of a goldsmith and murderer found hanged inside a locked church, Corbett rises to the position of Edward's master spy. The series continues with *Crown in Darkness* (1988), *Spy in Chancery* (1988), *The Angel of Death* (1989), *The Prince of Darkness* (1992) and *Murder Wears a Cowl* (1992).

Umberto Eco, *The Name of the Rose* (1980), 1323.

A highly atmospheric, gothic novel about the investigations of Brother William into deaths in a remote Italian monastery.

P. C. Doherty, *The Death of a King* (1985), 1344.

Follows the undercover investigations of Edmund Beche, a clerk at the royal chancery, into the death of King Edward II.

Paul Harding, *The Nightingale Gallery* (1991), 1376.

Introduces Brother Athelstan, parish priest of St Erconwald's, in Southwark, and assistant to Sir John Cranston, Coroner of the City of London. The series concentrates on impossible crimes in a disgustingly real London. Later novels are *The House of the Red Slayer* (1992), *Murder Most Holy* (1992) and *The Anger of God* (1993). The first Athelstan short story is included in this anthology.

Margaret Frazer, *The Novice's Tale* (1992), 1431.

Set in the priory of St. Frideswide, in Oxfordshire, during the infancy of King Henry VI. Introduces Sister Frevisse, hosteler of the priory who sets out to solve the bizarre death of the unwelcome Lady Ermentrude. Later novels are *The Servant's Tale* (1993) and *The Outlaw's Tale*. The first Sister Frevisse short story is included in this anthology.

Mary Monica Pulver, "Father Hugh and the Deadly Scythe" (1990), 1450s.

The first of the stories about Father Hugh, priest of Deerfield Village in Oxfordshire. The story is reprinted in this anthology. Sequel is "Father Hugh and the Miller's Devil" (1990).

P. C. Doherty, *The Fate of the Princes* (1990), 1483–1487.

An investigation into the death of the princes in the tower by Francis Lovell, a close ally of Richard III. The death of the princes is one of history's most famous mysteries. A modern-day novel about their disappearance is *The Daughter of Time* (1951) by Josephine Tey. One set a few years after the period, in 1536, is *A Trail of Blood* (1970), by Jeremy Potter, where Brother Thomas of Croyland Abbey is asked to solve the matter once and for all.

Elizabeth Eyre, *Death of a Duchess* (1991), 1490s.

Labelled "an Italian Renaissance whodunnit", it introduces Sigismondo, a man from nowhere, who is employed by the Duke of Rocca to find a kidnapped girl, but soon finds himself investigating a murder. Sequels are *Curtains for the Cardinal* (1992) and *Poison for the Prince* (1993).

Theodore Mathieson, "Leonardo da Vinci, Detective" (1959), 1516.

Another of Mathieson's stories in *The Great Detectives* (1960) featuring famous historical characters. This one is reprinted in this anthology. Set in the same period (1520), with the first detective in the New World, is "Hernando Cortez, Detective" (1959).

## The Tudors and Stuarts

Michael Clynes, *The White Rose Murders* (1991), 1517.

The first novel featuring the memoirs of Sir Roger Shallot, Justice of the Peace, who, following the battle of Flodden, finds himself investigating the death of a physician, poisoned in a locked and guarded chamber in the Tower of London. The second novel is *The Poisoned Chalice* (1992).

J. F. Peirce, "The Double Death of Nell Quigley" (1973), 1585.

The first of a series featuring the investigations of Will Shakespeare, Detective. The stories ran in *Ellery Queen's Mystery Magazine* from 1973–5 and have not been reprinted in book form. Another story with Shakespeare as detective is "A Sad and Bloody Hour" by Joe Gores (1965), reprinted in this anthology.

Edward Marston, *The Queen's Head* (1988), 1588.

The Elizabethan stage is the background for this series about the investigations of Nicholas Bracewell, agent of the troupe of players,

Lord Westfield's Men. The murder of an actor is just the start of a series of investigations following in the wake of the execution of Mary, Queen of Scots. Later novels are *The Merry Devils* (1989), *The Trip to Jerusalem* (1989), *The Nine Giants* (1991) and *The Mad Courtesan* (1992).

Theodore Mathieson, "Galileo, Detective" (1961), 1520.

Another of Mathieson's stories about the Great Detectives, but one not included in the book. In this story Galileo's unpopularity in Italy forces him to undertake his experiment of falling bodies at the Leaning Tower of Pisa. Two more falling bodies force him to turn detective.

Leonard Tourney, *The Players' Boy is Dead* (1982), 1601.

The Elizabethan stage is also the background for the first novel featuring Matthew Stock, clothier and constable in the county of Essex. Stock, a man who hates fuss and attention, soon finds himself having to solve a murder amongst a troupe of travelling players. Later novels are *Low Treason* (1983), *Familiar Spirits* (1984), *The Bartholomew Fair Murders* (1986), *Old Saxon Blood* (1988) and *Knaves Templar* (1991).

Theodore Mathieson, "Don Miguel de Cervantes, Detective" (1959), 1605.

Another of Mathieson's stories in *The Great Detectives* (1960), this one featuring the author of *Don Quixote*.

John Dickson Carr, *Devil's Kinsmere* (1934), 1670.

A narrator in 1815 tells the story of his grandfather, Roderick Kinsmere, and the murder of a man in a tavern against a wider background of court intrigue. This novel was rewritten in 1964 as *Most Secret*.

John Dickson Carr, *The Devil in Velvet* (1951), 1675.

One of Carr's novels where a person from the modern day is whisked back in time and so is able to bring twentieth-century perceptions to the thinking of the day. Despite that mechanism, this is one of Carr's best novels. A Cambridge professor goes back in time to solve a murder that is about to happen.

## The Eighteenth Century

Theodore Mathieson, "Daniel Defoe, Detective" (1959), 1719.

Another of Mathieson's stories in *The Great Detectives* (1960), this one featuring the author of *Robinson Crusoe*.

S.S. Rafferty, *Fatal Flourishes* (1979), 1730s–1770s.

A series of stories which feature Captain Cork, a businessman and entrepreneur in the American colonies who has a fascination for "social puzzles". The stories span a period of forty years and travel around each of the original thirteen states. "The Christmas Masque", from the middle period, is reprinted in this anthology.

Robert Lee Hall, *Benjamin Franklin Takes the Case* (1990), 1757.
Written as the recently discovered chronicles of Nicolas Handy who, in 1795, set down his adventures with Benjamin Franklin during his days in England. The sequel is *Benjamin Franklin and a Case of Christmas Murder* (1991).

Lillian de la Torre, *Dr. Sam: Johnson, Detector* (1946), 1763–1783.
The longest-running series of historical detective stories, written over a period of forty years. The series started with "Dr. Sam Johnson: Detector" in *Ellery Queen's Mystery Magazine* in 1943. More stories are collected in *The Detections of Dr. Sam: Johnson* (1960). The story in which Johnson and Boswell first met, "Murder Lock'd In", is included in this anthology.

Theodore Mathieson, "Captain Cook, Detective" (1958), 1770 and "Dan'l Boone, Detective" (1960), 1777.
Two more stories from Mathieson's *The Great Detectives* (1960).

Ragan Butler, *Captain Nash and the Wroth Inheritance* (1975), 1771–1772.
Novel of Britain's first private detective, reprinted in full in this anthology. Sequel is *Captain Nash and the Honour of England* (1977).

Charles Sheffield, *Erasmus Magister* (1982), 1777 onwards.
A collection of three novellas featuring the fantastic investigations of Erasmus Darwin.

David Donachie, *The Devil's Own Luck* (1991), 1792.
A nautical detective: Harry Ludlow, a privateer, tries to solve a murder aboard ship of which his own brother stands accused. The second novel is *The Dying Trade* (1993).

John Dickson Carr, *Fear is the Same* (1956), 1795.
Another of Carr's novels where a person from the modern day is whisked back in time, this time to the days just after the French revolution.

J. G. Jeffreys, *The Thieftaker* (1972), 1798.
Jeremy Sturrock of the Bow Street Runners (under whose name the books were published in England) finds himself involved with highway robbery in the first novel, but is soon involved in crime on the international scene in the Napoleonic era. The first novel was entitled *The Village of Rogues* for British publication. Later novels are *A Wicked Way to Die* (1973), *The Wilful Lady* (1975), *A Conspiracy of Poisons* (1977), *Suicide Most Foul* (1981), *Captain Bolton's Corpse* (1982) and *The Pangersbourne Murders* (1983).

## The early Nineteenth Century

John Dickson Carr, *Captain Cut-Throat* (1955), 1805.
Set at the time of the Napoleonic wars. British agent Alan Hepburn gets involved in a series of murders of sentries in the French army whose bodies are left with a message signed by Captain Cut-Throat.

Melville Davisson Post, *Uncle Abner, Master of Mysteries* (1918), 1800s.
Seventeen stories, of which the first published was "Angel of the Lord" (1911), featuring the powerful deductive work of a god-fearing country squire in Virginia – the first genuinely historical detective in fiction. This book along with other previously uncollected stories was later published as *The Complete Uncle Abner* (1977). In 1979 John F. Suter began a new series of Uncle Abner stories in *Ellery Queen's Mystery Magazine* starting with "The Oldest Law". One of Post's stories is reprinted in this anthology.

John Dickson Carr, *The Bride of Newgate* (1950), 1815.
Richard Darwent, sentenced to death for a murder he did not commit, is reprieved at the last moment, and begins his hunt for the real murderer.

Richard Falkirk, *Blackstone* (1972), 1820s.
Edmund Blackstone, a Bow Street Runner, finds himself moving in exalted circles. In this first novel he has to protect the infant Princess Victoria from a threat of kidnapping. Later novels are *Blackstone on Broadway* (1972), *Blackstone's Fancy* (1973), *Beau Blackstone* (1973), and *Blackstone and the Scourge of Europe* (1974), in which he is despatched to St. Helena to investigate the security of the island-prison of Napoleon.

John Dickson Carr, *Fire, Burn!* (1957), 1829.
Detective-Inspector John Cheviot suddenly finds himself back in the year 1929 helping Robert Peel establish the police force, only to find himself accused of murder.

Michael Harrison, *The Exploits of the Chevalier Dupin* (1968), 1830s–1840s.
Starting in 1965, Michael Harrison wrote a new series of stories featuring Edgar Allan Poe's trail-breaking detective C. Auguste Dupin. The expanded British edition was published as *Murder in the Rue Royale* (1972). The title story is reprinted in this anthology, as is John Dickson Carr's "The Gentleman from Paris" (1950), which features Poe as one of the main characters.

Theodore Mathieson, "Florence Nightingale, Detective" (1960), 1854 and "Alexander Dumas, Detective" (1961), 1840s.

The first is included in Mathieson's *The Great Detectives* (1960), but the second has only appeared in magazine form.

John Dickson Carr, *The Hungry Goblin* (1972), 1869.

One of Carr's best historical novels featuring Wilkie Collins as the detective. A more recent novel featuring both Wilkie Collins and Charles Dickens as detectives is *The Detective and Mr. Dickens* by William J. Palmer (1990), set in 1851.

And there we conclude our survey. Stories set from the 1870s on become increasingly "modern", featuring either an established police force (as in the novels of Anne Perry, H. R. F. Keating, John Buxton Hilton and Julian Symons), or well-known historical characters (as in the works of Peter Lovesey and Donald Thomas), or Sherlock Holmes and his many associated characters, as in the works of Michael Harding, Glen Petrie, M. J. Trow and many more.